CONTENTS

FOREWORD

I have been involved with education and training for much of
my adult life and take a keen interest in its evolution in the
UK. I have been the chairman of the Adult Literacy and Basic
Skills Unit for the past four years which has made me even
more aware of the frustration and lack of fulfilment of adults
who have failed to learn to read and write during their
formative years. More recently I've been appointed chairman
of the National Advisory Council for Education and
Training Targets, the initiative to ensure that we aim higher
in achieving both educational and training standards. The UK
badly needs to raise its sights and improve its skill base.

I am very conscious that the best way to motivate people is to
help them realise progression in their careers and to provide a
framework whereby they can begin to improve their career
prospects. For all of these reasons I am a strong supporter of
General National Vocational Qualifications which I believe
provide a real opportunity to gain both a broad education and
work skills.

Chairman: NACEATT

ACKNOWLEDGEMENTS

The authors would like to thank the following individuals for their support, encouragement and contributions:

Margaret Berriman, Alex Clark, Roger Parker, Mary Hamley, Sheri Hill, Key Kelly, Tony Newbould, Ian Millard, John Merchant, Sue Friery, Alastair Clelland, Stephanie Swaine, Bryan Oakes, Julie Ashton, Steve Wain, Aubrey Nokes, Kate Johnson, Michael Bushby, John McGrath, Marilyn Elliott, Robert Young, Roger Newman, Liz Robertson, Brian Yeomans, Phil Guy, Sue Woollat, Don Clarke, Justine Lindley, Colin Bunn, Brian Heslop, Martin Coles, Mike Ellis, Martin Turner, John Teesdale, Steve Jones, Maria Green, Claire Montgomery, Nualla Artt, Martin Coles, Jill Matthews, David Morley-Davies and Linda Deaves

In particular, we would like to express our gratitude and appreciation to both the teaching and library staff at Darlington College of Technology and The Nottingham Trent University, the editorial, production, marketing and sales teams at Heinemann Educational, officers at NCVQ who have read and commented on the script and finally our families for their patience and understanding.

The authors and publishers would also like to thank the following for permission to reproduce photographs and other material, and for providing advice and information:

Amalgamated Engineering Union; Apricot Computers Ltd; B & Q PLC; BT; Banking Ombudsman; British Airways; British Bakeries; British Nuclear Fuels PLC; The Burton Group PLC, Business and Technician Education Council; Controller of Her Majesty's Stationery office for HMSO material, Crown copyright; East Midlands Electricity PLC; The Economist Newspaper Ltd; Eden Vale Ltd; Ford Motor Company Ltd; Hanson PLC; Halifax Standard Trust Management Ltd; IBM United Kingdom Ltd; The Independent; Japan Information and Cultural Centre; Jusrol Ltd; Kettle Foods; Marks & Spencer PLC; Midland Bank PLC; Mintel International Group Ltd; Money Management Review; National Westminster Bank PLC; Nissan Motor Manufacturing (UK) Ltd; Procter & Gamble Ltd; Shell Education Service; Tesco PLC; Thorn EMI PLC; Northern Electric PLC; Understanding Industry; Whitbread PLC; Yorkshire Bank PLC.

We would also like to thank the following for permission to reproduce photographs on the pages noted:

Dick Barnatt p165; J Allen Cash p221; Hulton-Deutsch Collection p120; Philip Parkhouse 230; Press Association Ltd p254; Universal Pictorial Press and Agency Ltd pp344, 347.

INTRODUCTION

Studying how organisations plan, mobilise and control their resources in order to achieve their objectives will soon help you to realise that you are engaged in a similar developmental process albeit one on a significantly smaller scale. It is very important, particularly in the early stages of a GNVQ course, that you fully understand in broad terms what you want to achieve. You will have constructed, in your own mind at least, some form of action plan which relates to your ambitions and goals.

The first step you have taken on this route to achievement is to enroll on a GNVQ Level 3 course in Business. By following this course you are:

- developing commercial skills which will help you to prepare for employment in either private or public sector organisations
- providing yourself with a generally accepted qualification with nationwide credibility which can be used as a stepping-stone to other qualifications in the higher education sector
- undertaking a process which will help you prepare yourself for a wide range of professional business areas
- achieving a recognised level of academic attainment.

What is a GNVQ Level 3 in Business?

▪ GENERAL NATIONAL VOCATIONAL ▪ QUALIFICATION ▪

General refers to the fact that the qualification is not specifically for one type of job, industry or vocational area. Because you will learn many transferable skills it is possible to move into other vocational areas or into higher education.

National means that the qualification has widespread acceptability and influence which will help you when you apply for courses and jobs.

Vocational means the qualification focuses on a broad area of employment which, in this case, involves understanding the commercial and business functions and activities of all types of organisations.

Qualification is the successful outcome from having undertaken this course. Level 3 involves A level equivalent work and is designed for those who are capable of undertaking employment which involves supervisory and administrative skills.

▪ THE COURSE ▪

The Business GNVQ 3 comprises eight mandatory units and at least four optional units. Each unit covers a broad vocationally identified body of knowledge and understanding. For example, Unit 1 looks at 'Business in the Economy'. Each GNVQ unit is split into elements. Every element identifies a more specific type of skill or knowledge and understanding. In the first unit there are three elements which are:

1.1 Explain the purposes and products of business
1.2 Explain government influences on business
1.2 Investigate the supply of goods and services by business.

Element 1.1 looks like this:

> **Element 1.1: Explain the purposes and products of business**
>
> **Performance criteria:**
> 1 demand for goods and services is identified and described
> 2 demand in relation to particular product is identified
> 3 industrial sectors are identified and described
> 4 the product of businesses in different industrial sectors is identified and described
> 5 purposes of selected business organisations are explained
>
> **Range:**
> **Demand:** needs, wants and effective demand; consumption and income; demand and price; elastic and inelastic
> **Industrial sectors:** primary, secondary, tertiary
> **Product:** goods; services
> **Purposes:** profit-making; public service; charitable
> **Evidence indicators:**
> An analysis of selected businesses with an explanation of why businesses exist, an explanation of their product and an explanation of demand in general and demand in relation to a particular product. In addition, the candidate should demonstrate an understanding of the implications of the range dimensions and the key principles in respect of them. The unit test will confirm the candidate's coverage of range.

Performance criteria describe the body of knowledge you will ?. The work that you will undertake during the course will be geared to achieving the performance criteria in each element.

Range identifies broadly the areas to be covered by the performance criteria.

Evidence indicators provide a series of suggestions, ideas and actions which can be used to achieve the standards required in each element.

This book is specifically written to reflect the development of the Business GNVQ Level 3 qualification. It therefore covers each of the eight units and twenty-five elements of the Business GNVQ. Some of our chapter titles vary a little from the element titles because they reflect *our interpretation* of the work required by each element.

Assessment

The last sentence in element 1.1 refers to the unit test which will be required 'to confirm the candidate's coverage of range'. In this book we have provided test questions to cover each of the Business GNVQ Level 3 units. These are at the back of the book. The purpose of these questions is to provide you, in a variety of formats,

with experience, practice and help. Each set of questions has:

- 30 short answer questions per element (except for chapters 20, 23, 24 and 25 which have a reduced number)
- 2 practical activities for each element. These are designed to assess the range and, wherever possible, to put you in a realistic vocational context
- 15 objective questions. These questions are designed to differentiate between the skills and abilities of each candidate.

The most important way your performance will be assessed during your GVNQ course is through your portfolio of evidence. Evidence is the work you produce – it may be assignments you have completed, details of work experience, audio or video recordings of a presentation you may have given, a detailed account of the part you played in some group activity – all manner of activities.

You must keep your portfolio up-to-date and you should review your work regularly. Look at the performance criteria of the scheme; make sure you have covered these. If you decide something is not good enough, do it again. This could make the difference between gaining a pass, a merit or a distinction.

To be awarded a GVNQ you must also have demonstrated that you have reached the required standard in the **core skills** of communication, application of number and information technology. Review your skills with your tutor. If they are not good enough, draw up an action plan outlining how you are going to improve them and stick to it. Make sure that the work in your portfolio shows your full abilities in these core areas.

The most important component of your evidence portfolio will probably be your assignment work. An assignment is usually a long piece of work which will involve you in the development of a range of skills. Each assignment will help you to show or provide evidence that you have achieved the standard necessary to gain your GNVQ. In order to help you with this process we have provided an assignment at the end of each chapter in this book. There is one exception in Chapter 9 where, at a suitable point, we provide an extra assignment. Your tutors are very likely to give you other assignments based on business and industry in your own locality. They will also give you tasks to build on your strengths and to strengthen your weaknesses.

Identifying skills with knowledge and understanding is an important part of the vocational education process. The purpose of emphasising skills development during a course is to:

- put you into realistic situations
- help foster a student-centred active-learning approach to work
- re-inforce and expand the impact of assignments.

By linking assignments to skills during evidence collection your tutors are creating situations in which your vocational education can be transferred to other situations at a later stage.

Completed assignments are only one form of evidence that you have produced the outcomes required. Other techniques and activities appear in the evidence indicators section for each element. Your tutors will periodically provide you with information, ideas and opportunities to collect evidence. For example, evidence may be:

- collected from group activities in the classroom. Records of your role in a business game or simulation may be kept in your file as evidence
- obtained from your work placement. Reports from supervisors may be used to claim evidence
- drawn from other activities with which you are involved such as a club treasurer or secretary
- presented in the form of a video, photograph or tape
- collected as newspaper cuttings or other extracts from the media or even personal research which you might have undertaken.

How do you achieve your GNVQ Level 3 in Business?

It would be wrong for us to say that a GNVQ is going to be an easy route to the next stage of your career development. In fact with a GNVQ considerable onus for the success of your learning experience is going to be placed upon your shoulders. In order to cope with this degree of responsibility you must learn to discipline yourself into a pattern of working which enables you to utilise your talents fully. The way to do this is to construct an action plan and then to follow it.

Personal action planning involves identifying the final goal then a series of objectives in order to reach the goal.

As you move from objective to objective you will need to monitor constantly progress and amend actions where necessary. Planning will help you to achieve your ambitions and, at the same time, develop greater awareness both of your ability to learn and also of your strengths and weaknesses.

▪ THE JARGON ▪

At this stage it may be helpful to look at some useful definitions of terms you will come across during your GNVQ Business course.

Business a general term which is used to include any organisation, and its activities, which exist for commercial or public service reasons. For example, a launderette, Marks & Spencer, British Rail etc.

Product the output of an organisation which could be in the form of goods or services. For example, this book would be an example of a good and a haircut would be an example of a service.

Consumers the general public who buy goods and services or who receive goods 'free' of charge. 'Free' goods or services are paid for through taxation. When I eat an apple I am consuming a good. When I travel in a taxi I am consuming a service and when I walk under a street lamp at night I am consuming a 'free' service.

Customers businesses or individuals who pay a supplier for specific goods or services. When you buy clothes from a shop you are a customer. When that shop buys garments from its supplier, it is a customer.

Market a general term used to include all buying, selling and exchange of goods and services for money or credit. The market for computers consists of many large and small-sized sellers and many individual and organisational buyers.

Demand people's wants backed by the ability to pay for a good. Demand occurs at a number of levels: individual demands; market demand and aggregate demand. Individuals demand goods and services such as T-shirts, trainers, stereos etc. If we add up all the demands of individuals for goods we arrive at the market demand. For example, the market demand for T-shirts. Aggregate demand (National Output) is the total demand for all goods in the economy. A general rule is that more will be demanded at lower rather than at higher prices.

Supply the quantities of goods that will be supplied at different prices. More will be supplied at higher rather than at lower prices. Supply occurs at a number of levels; individual supply, market supply and aggregate supply. An example of individual supply would be the contribution of one supplier of T-shirts to the T-shirt market. Market supply would be made up of the supply of all T-shirt suppliers. Aggregate supply (National Output) is the total supply of all goods in the economy.

Industrial sectors the three major classifications of business activity: primary, secondary and tertiary. Primary industry is concerned with extracting natural resources. Secondary industry manufactures and constructs goods. Tertiary industry produces services.

Business sectors all goods and services available through public and private sector business.

Economic relationships all businesses operate in environments in which they are influenced by economic changes and forces. These changes and forces are inter-related. For example, if demand rises then prices will rise – this might encourage some producers to increase supply.

As you will see in this book there are many economic factors which are inter-related that affect individuals and organisations. For example, there are relationships between interest rates and the amounts that people spend. There are relationships between training of workers and the quality of goods produced.

Report an oral, written, visual or computer-aided presentation of the candidate's work. An oral report must be supported with notes and/or visual aids.

▪ POSTSCRIPT ▪

Finally, our aim in writing this book has been to provide you with a useful resource which can be used both in and out of the classroom during each stage of your course. The materials have been widely researched and extensively tested. It is our belief that the dynamic world of business is a fascinating place and we have tried to translate this belief into this product. We hope that the nature of the activities and experiences it contains will, together with your course, provide you with the motivation to learn, develop and achieve.

Dave Needham
Rob Dransfield

chapter **1** # THE PURPOSES AND PRODUCTS OF BUSINESS

This chapter looks at the ways in which businesses produce goods and services to meet the wants and needs of consumers. Business activity sets out to satisfy demand from consumers. Businesses that successfully meet customers' needs can do so at a profit. However, not all organisations set out simply to make a profit – some, like charities, attempt to meet needs that profit-making organisations cannot serve. The chapter describes how business activity can be split up into a number of categories – e.g. primary, secondary and tertiary industries. It also looks at the objectives of different types of business organisations, and at different types of economic system that operate in different countries at different times.

Everybody has **wants** and **needs.** At the moment I would like a new computer with more memory. I need to have food, clothing and shelter to get me through each day. When I have bought my new computer I will probably start to want something else. Before deciding to buy anything I will look around at the alternative models and brands. I will probably carry out some research to see what is the best offer on the market.

Some of the things that I buy are **regular purchases**. For example, I read *The Independent* newspaper every day. I find it interesting and informative. However, if the standard of its stories and articles began to fall I might decide to switch to an alternative newspaper. If the quality of another paper started to improve I might decide to switch to reading that one.

Every day millions of consumers also make decisions to buy '**one-off' items**, like a new car, as well as making regular purchases. Producers decide what products to make and in what quantities. In a market economy these producers will be guided by **consumer demand**.

The demand for a product is a want backed up by money to make the purchase. If everyone starts demanding a particular item of fashion clothing then producers will rush to make that item.

Task

What fashion items are currently in demand? Are there a lot of producers making these items or just a few?

Producers therefore need to be sensitive to the wants and needs of consumers. They need to provide a product – something that provides satisfaction for consumers.

As we shall see, the most successful producers are those that manage to satisfy consumer demands. They are the ones that can get:

The right goods to the right place (the 'market') at the right time and at the right price.

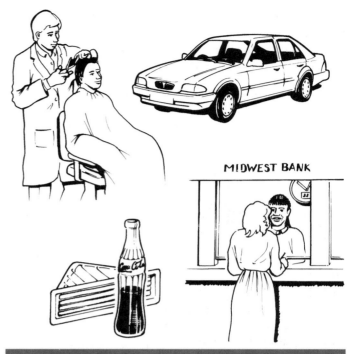

State what might happen to the following producers:

a The fashion house that produces top-quality fashion garments six months after items were at their sales peak.

b The high street baker of fine quality bread that is able to undercut rivals' prices by 5 per cent.

c The motorway service station that charges prices for petrol that are 10 per cent higher than in the nearest town 50 miles away.

d The sports paper that prinst its next day's edition at 4 o'clock the previous evening.

e The cut price supermarket in the exclusive part of town.

· GOODS AND SERVICES ·

It is important at this stage to draw a distinction between **goods** and **services.** A good is something that you can touch and see and that provides satisfaction for consumers. The following are obvious examples of goods: oranges, bread, cars, television sets and, Coca Cola. Goods can be divided into immediate **consumption goods** and consumer **durables** which last for a period of time. A sandwich is an example of an immediate consumption good. An oven is a consumer durable – it is used for cooking over a long period of time.

Services provide satisfaction for consumers but the service itself is not a physical thing. You could not put a service on the table, or drive around in a service. It is something that is done for you or for an organisation and which provides satisfaction: a hair cut, a college course, car insurance, banking etc.

Task

Which of the following provide goods, and which provide services?

- a firefighter ● a lecturer ● a food processing operative ● a steelworker
- a soldier ● a zoo keeper
- an accountant ● an electrician
- a journalist ● a waitress
- a film extra ● a coffee grower ● a building worker
- a picture framer ● an usherette at the cinema ● a roofer.

Clearly it is not easy to draw hard and fast lines between goods and services. Some activities arguably provide both a good and a service.

Case Study

Meeting the needs of students in a market economy

In the middle of February 1993, the Audit Commission (a body that looks at how well public organisations are spending money) reported that a third of 16 to 19 year old students were failing to complete their courses satisfactorily. This was at a time when more and more students were staying on in colleges and schools. It was revealed that low success rates and small teaching groups in schools and colleges were wasting an estimated £330 million a year.

The Commission suggested that funding given to colleges should take account of the number of students who drop out or fail to get the qualifications they are aiming for.

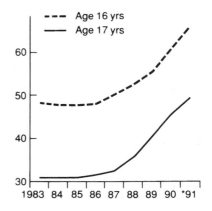

Figure 1.2 *Percentage of 16–17 year olds in full-time education in England*

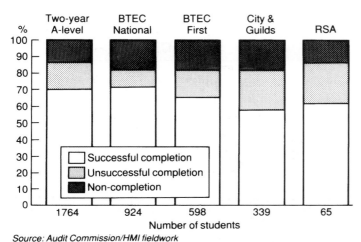

Source: Audit Commission/HMI fieldwork

Figure 1.1 *Failure rate on full-time courses of 16–19 year olds*

The Commission also felt that colleges should give far more attention to the individual needs and wants of applicants for college courses and also look at their abilities. More advice and counselling should be given to make sure that students were going on the best courses for them. One way would be to give students predictive tests before joining that would indicate the likelihood of success in a particular course.

In 1933, 35 per cent of the 600 000 young people who reached 16 remained at school, while 32 per cent transferred to further education or sixth-form colleges.

Educating a student on an A-level or vocational course costs an average £3000 a year. Spending on full-time courses for the age group totals about £2 billion. The Commission's report therefore argued that completion rates should increase to 80 per cent rather than the figures of 30–40 per cent dropping out of some courses.

Some colleges had much higher success rates than the average. Many would argue that this could be attributed to customer care and providing courses to meet the real needs and wants of students. For example, Newcastle College in North Staffordshire was already meeting the 80

per cent target in 1993. The college had 1500 students with average class sizes of 15 people. Completed application forms are carefully scrutinised to check that the courses selected suit the careers that the students want to follow. Students are talked to before starting courses to make sure that they are choosing the right options. The college works closely with local schools and the careers service to look at the aptitudes and abilities of students, their career choices and the courses offered by the college. The aim is to make students aware that the college is concerned with meeting their best interests.

Student attendance is checked by a computer-linked class register. A central unit keeps a record of students' school qualifications and their final destination in employment or higher education. Counsellors advise new entrants, monitor progress and advise on careers and university courses. These procedures offer a way forward for other colleges.

1 Do colleges provide a good or a service? Explain your answer.
2 What factors are likely to determine the sorts of courses offered?
3 What factors should determine the sorts of courses offered?
4 Why is it important for colleges to meet the needs of their students?
5 What do you understand by the term 'customer care'?
6 Why is customer care important?
7 How do the experiences at Newcastle College compare with those at your own school or college?
8 What suggestions would you make to your own school or college in catering for the wants and needs of students?

· INTRODUCING DEMAND ·

Each year millions of students enjoy working at schools and colleges following a range of courses. One of the most popular options is Business. All young people and many adult returners to education are entitled to follow courses which meet their needs. The government is keen to support GNVQ courses in Business because of the important part they play in preparing students for the world of work, and for life in modern society. Colleges receive funds from the government for each student place, up to a certain number. We can therefore say that there is a substantial **demand** for places on GNVQ courses. Wants and needs are backed up by money.

Primary demand

Many goods are demanded for their own sake. This week you may purchase a new T-shirt or a pair of trainers. You are almost certain to buy something to eat, such as a sandwich or a packet of crisps. All these items are demanded for their own sake. When goods are wanted for their own sake we say there is a *primary* demand for them.

Derived demand

Many other goods have a *derived* demand. Derived demand arises when a good is wanted not for itself but for what it goes into making. For example, a printer does not buy paper because he enjoys having reams of paper sitting around in his workshop but because he will use that paper to make newspapers and books which are in prime demand.

Task

Which of the following are examples of a prime demand and which of a derived demand?

- A farmer's demand for pesticides to spray on apples.
- A greengrocer's demand for apples to stock in a shop.
- A child's purchase of apples from the greengrocer.

- The purchase of a restaurant meal.
- A radio station's purchase of a popular compact disc.
- The Post Office's purchase of bicycles for its delivery people.
- A school child's purchase of a football strip.
- A Premier Division football club's purchase of a football strip.

· THE SUPPLY OF GOODS AND SERVICES ·

Businesses are decision-making units that supply goods and services. Some business units supply to the final consumer, whilst others supply to other producers. As you will find out during this course, it is not easy to supply the right goods, at the right time, in the right place and at the right price. Suppliers need to be aware of the demand signals that come from buyers. They need to be able to anticipate likely changes in demand. Suppliers need to increase supply when demand is high and to reduce demand when supply is low. We will follow this up in detail in Chapter 3. There are all sorts of business units concerned with making supply decisions, including:

- the ice-cream van selling cones and choc-ices outside a park or school gate
- the large multinational clothes manufacturer selling its garments throughout the world
- the public service organisation, such as the meals-on-wheels service
- the charity organisation such as Oxfam working to supply famine relief.

Each of the above organisations is concerned with making a supply decision involving scarce **resources.** Production resources are relatively scarce: if we use a particular piece of wood to make a table, we cannot use the same piece to make a chair. Decision-making over a use of scarce resources involves:

- making a *choice* (we can do either this or that)
- making a sacrifice (if we choose to do this with a resource we cannot also do that).

Opportunity cost

The concept of opportunity cost is an important one in all decision-making and particularly in the business world.

Opportunity cost means the next best alternative that is sacrificed when we carry out a particular action. Individuals, groups, communities and nations are continually making decisions. When you make a decision to buy one thing you sacrifice *options*; for example, when you decide to buy a compact disc the real cost to you is the thing that you have to go without (e.g. a new item of clothing). When the government decides to build a new hospital, the real cost may be a new school that might otherwise have been built. When a business decides to invest in new computers the alternative sacrificed might be a wage increase to staff.

Task

Explain how an understanding of opportunity cost would affect the business decision-making of each of the following groups of individuals.

1 Jill works for herself illustrating children's books. She works from home and frequently takes commissions over the phone from clients. Jill has been asked to give a talk at a school 100 miles from home. She will be paid a fee of £150 but no expenses. Jill has worked out that it will cost her £15 for petrol and about £10 for wear and tear on the car. She therefore anticipates making a profit of £125 for the day. She is not sure whether this will be worthwhile.

2 Southampton Boat Builders and Repair Yard is a business that normally does a lot of small repair jobs, and makes small fishing boats. They have recently received an order for three larger fishing boats from a big company. They have decided to refuse all other new work to meet these orders. The job will take them six months and may lead to a larger order. They have calculated that they will make twice as much profit from concentrating on the large order.

3 John normally works a 30-hour week for £5 an hour. He has been offered a rate of £6 an hour if he will agree to work a 35-hour week. John has calculated that he will be better off by £60 a week.

· TYPES OF BUSINESS ACTIVITY ·

Business activity involves turning good ideas into a working business organisation. Effective business organisations have the ability to translate good ideas into practice and to generate substantial profits or other benefits to the community. As we shall see later in this chapter, it is necessary to develop good business systems in order to turn **inputs** into **outputs**. At the end of the day there are millions of outputs in a modern economy based on many more inputs.

Business activity can be conveniently divided into:

- extractive (primary)
- manufacturing and construction (secondary)
- services (tertiary).

Extractive industries – like farming and mining – take out things that are already provided by nature. Farmers grow and harvest crops, while miners take out fuel, minerals, etc. Primary industries sometimes produce raw materials like iron ore (that goes into making steel) and oil (that makes petrol, plastics etc.), as well as producing final products like fish and oranges.

Manufacturing and construction industries make, build and assemble products. Manufacturers use raw materials and parts derived from other industries. A *semi-manufactured good* is one that is only partly made, and most products involve several stages of production. Examples of manufactures are books, furniture, cars, chocolates and oil rigs.

Service industries are particularly important in modern Britain. Services give something of value to people but are not physical goods. Examples of services are banks and public transport. Services are sometimes classified as *direct* (to people – e.g. the police, hairdressing) or *commercial* (to business – e.g. insurance, business post). However, this is not a very good classification because most commercial services like banking and the post are as much used by individuals as by business.

Task

Set out column headings as below and then classify the activities as primary, secondary or tertiary industries.

Primary Secondary Tertiary

Fishing, shoe making, shoe repair,

coal mining, laundry, bottling spring water, market gardening, transport, key cutting, road sweeping, cloth making, mushroom growing, book illustration, road building, signwriting, theatre, window cleaning, oil refining, chocolate manufacture, building, advertising, insurance, retailing, civil service, oil drilling.

Task

The following *Standard Industrial Classification* breaks industry down into divisions and example groupings within divisions. Carry out a class survey in your town to find out the percentage of business enterprises that fit into each of the categories shown. Alternatively, approach your local Job Centre. They should be able to provide you with a breakdown of employment in your area into each of the categories shown. They should also be able to provide you with a national breakdown. How do the two contrast? Find out which Industrial Divisions are expanding and which contracting. Try to explain these trends.

DIVISION 0 – Agriculture, forestry and fishing
Farming and horticulture
Forestry
Commercial sea and inland fishing

DIVISION 1 – Energy and water supply industries
Coal-mining and manufacture of solid fuels
Extraction of mineral oil and natural gas
Production and distribution of electricity, gas and other forms of energy

DIVISION 2 –Extraction of Minerals and ores, manufacture of metals, mineral products and chemicals
Metal manufacture
Extraction of stone, clay, sand and gravel
Manufacture of non-metallic mineral products
Chemical industry (includes paints, varnishes and inks, pharmaceutical products, some perfumes, etc.)

DIVISION 3 – Metal goods, engineering and vehicle industries
Foundries
Mechanical engineering
Electrical and electronic engineering
Manufacture of motor vehicles and parts
Instrument engineering

DIVISION 4 – Other manufacturing industries
Food, drink and tobacco manufacturing industries
Textile industry
Manufacture of leather and leather goods
Timber and wooden furniture industries
Manufacture of paper and paper products, printing and printing products
Processing of rubber and plastics

DIVISION 5 – Construction
Construction and repairs
Demolition work
Civil engineering

DIVISION 6 – Distribution, hotels and catering, repairs
Wholesale distribution
Retail distribution
Hotel and catering (restaurants, cafes and other eating places, public houses and hotel trade)
Repair of consumer goods and vehicles

DIVISION 7 – Transport and communication
Railways and other inland transport
Air and sea transport
Support services to transport
Postal services and telecommunications

DIVISION 8 – Banking, finance, insurance, business services and leasing
Banking and finance
Insurance
Business services
Renting of movables
Owning and dealing in real-estate

DIVISION 9 – Other services
Public administration, national defence and social security
Sanitary services
Education
Medical and other health services, veterinary services
Other services provided to the general public
Recreational services and other cultural services
Personal services (laundries, hairdressing and beauty parlours)
Domestic services
Diplomatic representation, international organisations, allied armed forces

· DE-INDUSTRIALISATION IN · DEVELOPED COUNTRIES ·

There has been a lot of talk about **'de-industrialisation'** in Britain in recent years. The term suggests empty factories and shipyards. The general feeling is that de-industrialisation is a problem and not something to be welcomed.

The common sense meaning of de-industrialisation is a decline in the importance of industry within the economy. But how do we measure this decline?

- Should we look at the numbers employed or the industrial output?
- Are we concerned with *absolute* decline or with *relative* decline compared with other sectors?

The concern with de-industrialisation has *not* been the result of falling industrial production in the advanced industrialised countries. Production has actually continued to increase. Today more products are produced, there is greater variety and new models have replaced older ones. For example, there is no comparison between a computer today and one of twenty years ago, a modern car uses fuel more efficiently, and living standards have risen (see page 16).

However, as manufacturing has become better (not just in improving quality and efficiency but also in responding to environmental concerns and other challenges), it has also become smaller. In every advanced nation, industry employed a smaller proportion of the workforce in 1990 than it did in 1980; in virtually every nation, it also contributed a smaller proportion of the national output. Everywhere, the 'slack' has been taken up by *services*. It was in 1959 in the United States that, for the first time, the service sector of a nation became larger in terms of gross national product (GNP) than the industrial sector; in the 1990s the service sector in every country is much bigger, contributing 70 per cent of the GNP in the United States, Britain and France, 64 per cent in Italy, 60 per cent in Germany and 56 per cent in Japan.

Between the 1960s and 1993 the number of jobs in manufacturing in Britain fell from almost two-fifths (38.4 per cent of the total) to less than a quarter (22 per cent).

Factors causing the decline in manufacturing

The decline of manufacturing is not a uniquely British phenomenon. The same pattern is typical of all major industrial countries. However, the British case stands out as being an early and extreme case of de-industrialisation. The number of people employed in manufacturing has fallen since the early 1960s *at an accelerating rate*. Whether or not this is seen as a problem depends on why such a change has taken place.

There is considerable evidence that, as economies develop over time, gradual shifts take place between the primary, secondary and tertiary sectors. At early stages of development there is a shift away from agriculture towards industrial and service activities, as the relative importance of agricultural products (food in particular) declines in people's consumption and manufactured goods and services become more important. As incomes continue to rise the share of manufacturing in output and employment tends to decline, and that of services tends to increase.

Important causes of de-industrialisation

There are many explanations of de-industrialisation. Here are two important ones. (You can read more about the process in *Industrialisation and Development* by Hewitt, Johnson and Wield, Oxford University Press, 1992.)

1 De-industrialisation can result from a change in the pattern of *international specialisation*. A country that discovers a natural resource is likely to experience some de-industrialisation. Production of this new sector will increase rapidly and the share of other sectors, including manufacturing, is reduced. Can you think of an example?

The obvious one was the discovery of North Sea oil. This changed Britain from being a net importer to being a net exporter of oil and led to a reduction in the share of manufacturing industry in output and employment. This type of de-industrialisation is not necessarily bad. With the development of oil as an export Britain did not need such a large manufacturing base.

2 *Lack of competitiveness in manufacturing* can lead to de-industrialisation. It is this case which is really the major cause of concern. A country that is becoming less competitive in manufacturing will see its share of world exports of manufactures decline and its imports increase. Declining employment in the manufacturing sector will not be sufficiently offset by increased employment of labour in other sectors. The slow growth of domestic manufacturing will lead the country to fall further behind its competitors as productivity increases lag, and a vicious circle of decline is set in motion, with rising unemployment and a deteriorating balance of payments.

Case study

The continued decline of manufacturing in the 1990s

As businesses withdrew from the areas where competition was toughest in the recession of the early 1980s, entrepreneurs started to concentrate on sheltered areas of the economy. A technological gap grew between Britain and the leading exporting countries, particularly Germany and Japan.

The attitude of the government was unhelpful. It seemed to be saying that there was little or no future for manufacturing in Britain. This discouraged investment in manufacturing.

Conditions in the economy encouraged expansion in other areas. But when consumer spending increased in the 1980s there were few home-produced goods, so consumers bought imported manufactures. British businesses meanwhile concentrated on areas where there was little competition (e.g. high street and out-of-town shopping as well as financial services). Instead of investing in manufacturing, the sector was allowed to deteriorate further.

1 *Do you agree that:*
    a there is a technological gap between Germany and Japan and Britain in manufacturing
    b manufacturing has been starved of investment
    c the government has given the impression that there is little future for manufacturing?
2 *What is happening to manufacturing businesses in your locality?*
3 *What views do local manufacturers have about the questions in 1 above?*

■ THE GROWTH OF THE SERVICE ■ SECTOR

There are three main reasons for the growth of the service sector of the economy.

First, as societies become richer, they choose to spend a higher proportion of their incomes on buying services rather than things.

Second, it has so far proved very much harder to wring additional **productivity** out of services than out of manufacturing. Greater productivity in a car plant means more robots on the production line: the product does not suffer, indeed probably the reverse. However, if greater productivity in a school is measured by fewer teachers in the classroom, quality of education suffers immediately.

Third, as countries become richer, they are able to 'export' their profits in the form of investments in other countries. It is evident that a number of countries have invested in manufacturing in developing countries. In turn, the rewards are returned in profits, interest and dividends that can be spent on leisure services.

There is no sign at all that the shift of demand towards services will cease. Indeed, there is a powerful reason to expect it to accelerate – namely the ageing population in industrial societies. The proportion of people over 60 will continue to rise in every developed country for at least a generation. By the year 2020, more than 30 per cent of the population of Germany and Italy will be over 60. Older people are more likely to spend their income on health care, holidays and domestic services. The countries that increase living standards most quickly in the future will be those that can improve the way they run service societies.

Services can be divided into four main groups: **financial service**s and **distribution** tend to be in the private sector, whereas **health** and **education** tend to be in the public sector.

Technology can be used to transform each of these areas. In financial services we will see more than ever before the development of paperless money. Financial services are becoming increasingly tailored to the needs of individual customers. In distribution, the benefits of bulk retailing are likely to be grafted on to much wider swathes of the industry, with resultant cost-cutting. In health, technological advances have led to people living longer. The focus of health care will now shift to raising the quality of care and fitness throughout people's lives. Education, too, will become a continuous process, involving people of all ages. Workers can expect to be retrained to take on completely different skills several times during their careers.

▪ STARTING OUT IN BUSINESS ▪

People start their own business for a variety of reasons. Some have a bright idea that they think will make them rich; others find themselves unemployed and start their own business to survive; some can only be themselves when they are their own bosses; others want to make a particular contribution to their community and can see no other way of doing it except by setting up on their own. Millions of businesses have been started up in this country in the second half of the twentieth century. Some of them are today's household names such as Iceland, Body Shop, and Virgin. Others are small business concerns serving a local market, such as the florists at the city railway station, the plumber or newsagent. Many other businesses have been set up, flourished briefly and then crashed.

A common cause of failure is poor planning. A **business plan** sets out a clear pathway for a business in its first year or two of operation. It should answer questions such as: 'How much cash will I need and when?', 'How am I going to reach my customers?' and 'What equipment and raw materials will I need?'

Another common cause of failure is the unpredictable nature of the **environment** in which businesses operate. For all businesses the environment is constantly changing. Some changes are highly unpredictable and are difficult to plan for. Consider the following headlines:

LONG HOT SUMMER COOLS DEMAND FOR ICE-CREAM!

SHOCK! RESEARCH INDICATES DANGER OF MAD COW DISEASE!

INTEREST RATE RISES FORCE SMALL BUSINESSES TO THE WALL!

RECESSION MAKES BIG COMPANIES DELAY PAYMENTS!

TAXES CURB PURCHASES OF ELECTRICAL EQUIPMENT!

Case Study

The bus tour operator

David Curry set up Jorvik Tour Bus Ltd in York in1984. One day he was reading in his Sunday newspaper about tourist buses in London. He thought it was a good idea, realising that there was a real need to be met taking tourists around the historic city of York. At the time David was in his early twenties and had recently passed his Public Service Vehicle and Heavy Goods Vehicle driving tests.

In order to get the company off the ground he needed a licence from the Department of Transport. At the time there were no other tourist bus companies in York, but the National Bus Company opposed the setting up of the new business. However, David won his case at a public hearing.

He set up in business with one (closed-top) bus and charged tourists £1 each for the tour. The National Bus Company tried to hit back by setting up its own tour service, charging 10p. In 1986 David decided to improve his service and removed the top of his own bus by hand with a metal grinder.

The company went from strength to strength. By 1990 David had eight open-toppers. The company was now offering alternative tours to places like Harrogate, the Dales and Herriot Country.

However, in the early 1990s things started to go wrong. The Gulf crisis dented the number of tourists to York. As the recession began to bite, consumers began to spend

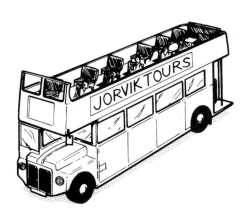

less. Scenic tours became one of the luxuries that consumers were less prepared to spend money on.

David responded by cutting the price of tickets (from £3.50 to £2.50). He sold two buses and scrapped one. By August 1992 he was running buses with very few passengers, and in October 1992 he stopped trading.

1 *Was the Jorvik tour bus idea a good one? Explain your answer.*
2 *What factors led to the rise of the company?*
3 *What factors led to its fall?*
4 *What does the case study tell us about the environment in which businesses operate?*
5 *What lessons can be learnt about business planning?*

DECISION-MAKING IN A CHANGING ENVIRONMENT

A business is a decision-making unit that sets out to produce a product in the form of a good or service. Business studies is concerned with exploring the decision-making process.

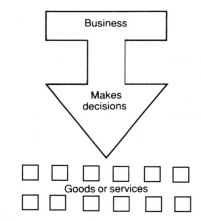

Figure 1.3 *Decisions to products*

Any business that we study operates in an environment of changing forces that are **interdependent.** Some of these changing forces are illustrated in Figure 1.4. We shall be looking in detail at each of these systems later. At this point, however, we can give simple examples of how each can influence a business unit.

In recent years there has been much discussion over whether supermarkets should be able to trade on Sundays.

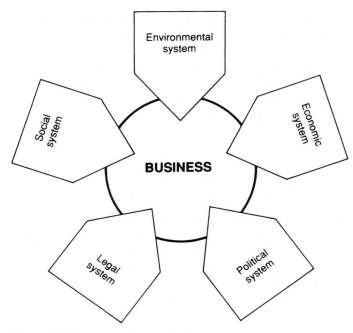

Figure 1.4 *Forces acting on a business*

As time moves on the attitudes of groups that make up societies change. A hundred years ago many people would have been horrified at the thought of Sunday trading. Today social attitudes have changed. Go down to your supermarket on a Sunday and you will find people from all walks of life.

In the early 1990s it is still against the law to sell many goods on Sundays. Some local councils attempt to use the legal system to prosecute traders who break the law. However, many of these prosecutions have been unsuccessful and some traders continue to ignore the law.

Traders are able to get away with this partly because there is a general feeling that the Conservative government supports Sunday trading. New laws are made in Parliament. There is a general feeling, therefore, that the political system is working against the existing legal system and that change will soon take place.

The organisation of buying and selling is a major function of the economic system. Today many buyers find that they have more time to make purchases on a Sunday. Perhaps they are too busy on other days of the week. At the same time there are many people who are prepared to work on a Sunday. Supermarket chains see the possibility of adding to their sales and profits by opening on a seventh day.

Every business operates within an environmental system. Supermarkets are large buildings which can add to or detract from a local environment. Supermarkets can be noisy and busy places. Householders living close to a supermarket may be unhappy about the noise and fumes created in their area – alternatively they may be pleased that they have such an amenity.

· FACTORS OF PRODUCTION ·

Imagine that you are visiting a modern car plant, what would you see? The first and most obvious sight would be large areas of land and building. Inside you would find machinery and employees. In order for the machines to work they need to use energy, raw materials and semi-finished products – glass for the windows, tyres, electrical systems etc.

A business enterprise is therefore a **unit of production** that sets out to bring together and to organise **factors of production** to produce goods and services.

The factors of production are the ingredients that make an enterprise 'work'. They are: labour, capital, energy, materials and information.

- **Labour** is the energy provided by the employees. Work carried out takes a number of forms, such as handling information, sorting out information, communication and control, as well as more obvious manual tasks.
- **Capital** is represented by the machines and tools, without which there would be no production.
- **Energy** comes from the raw materials – the fossil fuels, electricity, gas and steam – that make machines work.
- **Materials** are needed to make any product, finished or semi-finished.
- **Information** is the know-how, and all the accumulated experience of members of an organisation that provides a driving force behind the enterprise.

Another way of looking at factors of production is to divide them into: land, labour, capital and enterprise. *Enterprise* is then regarded to be the factor that brings the other factors together to produce goods in order to make profits. *Land* is considered to be all the gifts of nature (e.g. water, coal, farm land). Using this alternative classification, the **rewards** to the factors of production are said to be:

Land	→	Rent
Labour	→	Wages
Capital	→	Interest
Enterprise	→	Profits

Task

Listed below are some of the things needed to make a box of chocolates. Make four headings of the factors of production (land, labour, capital, enterprise) and list the items under the correct headings.

● *chocolate* ● *factory land* ● *machinery operator* ● *cardboard box* ● *nuts* ● *owner of the business* ● *shop* ● *sugar* ● *accounts clerk* ● *factory* ● *raisins* ● *computer* ● *chocolate icing machine*

What would be needed to make a pair of jeans? Draw a pair of jeans and then list the items you think would be needed under the headings of factors of production.

· ADDING VALUE ·

Here is a list of some of the ingredients that go into making a typical car:

- *Raw materials*: steel, iron work, aluminium, other non-ferrous metals, paint and solvents, textiles and leather, plastics.
- *Finished products*: windows, tyres, engine.
- *Fuels*: gas, electricity, oils.

If the car producer purchases during a year £70 million worth of raw materials and finished products, and makes 30 000 cars which it sells for £10 000 each, the firm receives £300 million for its cars. The **value added** in the process of production is therefore £230 million.

The business will seek to combine its factors of production in the most effective way to add value to its inputs. It will then sell its finished products in the market place.

Distribution of value added by a business

We can show in diagrammatic form how a business distributes the value it adds during production. Figure 1.5 shows the value of sales to customers on the left-hand side, and what is left for distribution among members of the business on the right-hand side. Then Figure 1.6 shows what happens to the added value created by the business (i.e. how it is distributed).

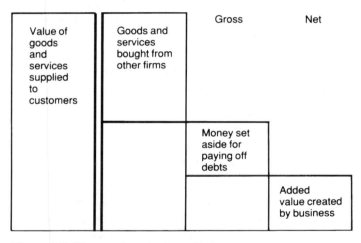

Figure 1.5 *The creation of value added*

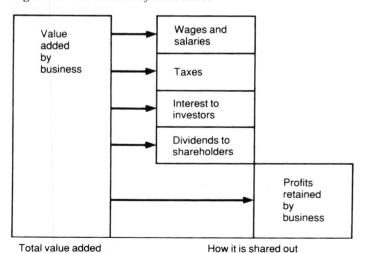

Figure 1.6 *The distribution of value added*

· THE IMPORTANCE OF FINANCIAL · MANAGEMENT

In Figure 1.6 the bottom line shows 'profits retained by business'. However, **profit** will only result if a business carefully manages its finances.

Case Study

The business soufflé

A catering group rose like a soufflé. In little over ten years it grew to more than 60 trading outlets. The owner of the business, however, found it increasingly difficult to manage the organisation. First came complaints about hygiene, followed by a string of prosecutions. Then the main supplier insisted on putting in an accountant to probe the group's finances.

The group concluded a staff pay deal which raised wages by 50p an hour. This resulted in serious financial problems. Despite expert help and advice from the supplier, to whom the group owed over £300 000, matters failed to improve.

Like a soufflé exposed to a blast of cold air, the company collapsed. Debts amounted to several million pounds.

Weak financial management is one of the key reasons for business failures. Many businesses measure their trading success mainly in terms of their profits (the 'bottom line'). However, it is often the case that they should be more concerned about their **cash flow**.

Every business needs to have cash available at the bank to pay its bills. A manufacturing company, for instance, needs money to buy stock or raw materials to make the goods it intends to sell. But the company will not get its money back until it has sold the goods. If debtors (people and companies that owe money) are slow in paying their bills, then the manufacturing company could run into cash flow problems.

A company should try to arrange its affairs so that if debtors are slow in paying, there is still enough cash in the company's current account at the bank to pay important

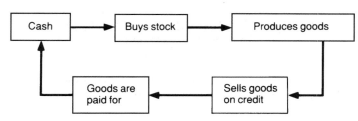

Figure 1.7 *The money cycle*

bills. Better still, the company should devise effective ways of preventing late payments.

· SERVING THE MARKET ·

Any business needs to be able to answer three fundamental questions:

- What should it produce?
- How should it produce?
- Who should it produce for?

Goods are 'good' because they meet consumer needs and wants. What was the last thing you had to eat? What was the last item of clothing you bought? What was the last hobby item or entertainment you spent money on? Of course, these things will have given you a great deal of pleasure, but did you really *need* them? Could you have got by with something a bit simpler?

Task

Look at the diagram below. Which of the things in the ellipse would you say are wants and which are needs?

Now draw two circles, one with just 'wants' in it, the other with just 'needs'.

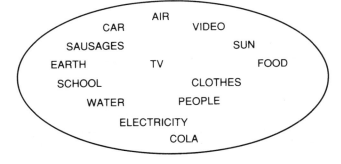

1 Which is the bigger circle?
2 Does everybody in the world have all their needs yet?
3 What evidence can you draw upon to back up your argument?
4 If everybody does not have all their needs met, then why not?
5 Is it possible to change this?
6 Can you do something about this?
7 Who else needs to be involved to make the change?
8 How can changes be made?

One of the first steps in setting up a business is to plan the **marketing** of the product or service. Marketing boils down to creating, producing, promoting and delivering a product or service that meets customers' needs. It is necessary to make sure that people want to buy what is made. An alternative is to find out first what people want to buy in the product category in which you are interested, and then plan to make it.

For any type and size of business, four of the most important marketing questions are:

- Who are you selling to?
- What do they want?
- When and where do they want it?
- What price are they prepared to pay?

The questions are all interlocking. You cannot really answer the first until you have an idea of your answer to the second, and you cannot answer the third and fourth unless you have already answered the first two.

In practice, a company will know that its expertise and experience lie within a certain category of products, and that there is a wide range of different people who are potential customers for different products in that category. It is the matching of a particular product with a particular customer segment that creates a good business.

· CONVERTING INPUTS INTO OUTPUTS ·

One of the prime concerns of any business is to convert inputs into outputs in order to satisfy the wants and needs of its consumers.

Case Study

Making dog biscuits

A company that makes dog biscuits carries out a number of processes within its factory. Look at Figure 1.8 to see how the dog biscuits are made.

1 *What processes (grinding, transporting, etc.) can you identify in the production of dog biscuits?*
2 *What inputs can you identify in the production of dog biscuits?*
3 *Try to illustrate the inputs, processes and outputs involved in dog biscuit production in a simple diagram using a similar outline to the one shown below.*

The company knows that to stay in business it must produce a good quality product. It must keep the costs of making the dog biscuits as low as possible. It must sell the dog biscuits to its customers at a price that they can afford. The money it receives for the biscuits is used to pay its costs, including wages. Any money left over is profit.

The company needs certain things to make the dog biscuits. They are shown in Figure 1.9.

The company produces 11 500 tonnes of dog biscuits every year. The annual costs of the inputs needed to make this quantity are shown in the table.

Ingredients	£1 466 250
Energy	£ 126 500
Labour	£ 28 750
Maintaining buildings and machinery, heating and lighting	£ 11 500
Administration	£ 74 750
Haulage and distribution	£ 202 975
Packaging	£ 718 750

TOTAL COST OF PRODUCING 11 500 TONNES IS £ _____

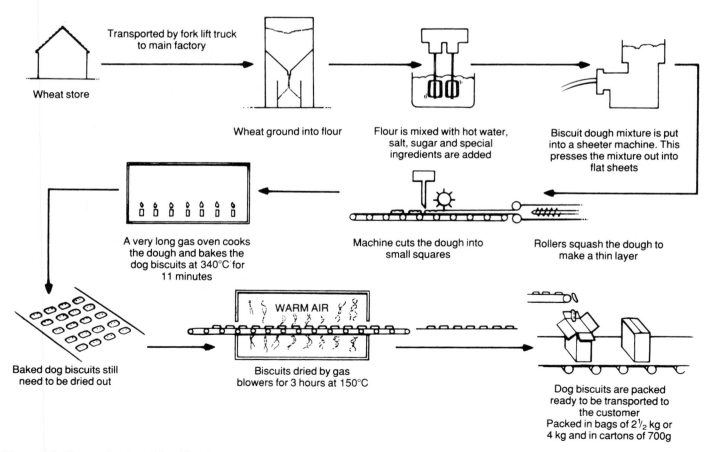

Figure 1.8 *The production of dog biscuits*

Wheat store — Transported by fork lift truck to main factory — Wheat ground into flour — Flour is mixed with hot water, salt, sugar and special ingredients are added — Biscuit dough mixture is put into a sheeter machine. This presses the mixture out into flat sheets

A very long gas oven cooks the dough and bakes the dog biscuits at 340°C for 11 minutes — Machine cuts the dough into small squares — Rollers squash the dough to make a thin layer

Baked dog biscuits still need to be dried out — Biscuits dried by gas blowers for 3 hours at 150°C — Dog biscuits are packed ready to be transported to the customer. Packed in bags of 2½ kg or 4 kg and in cartons of 700g

WARM AIR

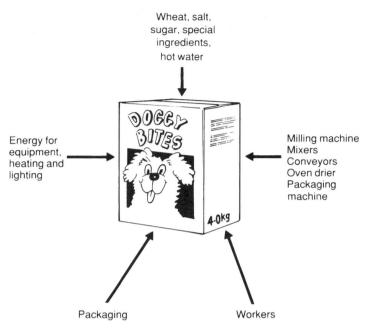

Figure 1.9 *Inputs needed to make dog biscuits*

1 Which input costs the most?
2 Which input costs the least?
3 How much does energy cost the company each year?
4 How could the company cut costs?
5 How much does the company spend on packaging?
6 How much does it cost the company to make one tonne of dog biscuits? (We can call this the average cost per unit.)
7 How many 4 kg boxes of dog biscuits could be produced by the company?
8 If the company sold each 4 kg box of dog biscuits for £1 would it make a profit?
9 Calculate the profit the company would make if it sold the 4 kg boxes of dog biscuits for £1.10, £1.25 and £1.40.
10 Design a packet for dog biscuits. What would, or should, the customer want to know about?

· SYSTEMS THEORY ·

A system **processes** inputs to produce outputs. For example, in the dog biscuit factory the ingredients and other inputs will be processed by the production system to produce outputs.

The production process takes place within defined **boundaries**, which are usually fairly obvious. The inputs flow into this system. Some of the resources used will be **current resources** (e.g. the salt, sugar, wheat and energy). What actually goes into the production process will be **'filtered'**: there will be barriers that select what goes into the production. For example, quality control ensures that no fragments of glass enter the production system. Current resources then combine with elements (or fixed assets) such as machinery and buildings, and flow from one element to another element across **links** between the elements. For example, the dough for dog biscuits flows from the dough mixing element, through the rollers and into the gas ovens. At the end of the production line there will also be output filters: some outputs will be filtered into different lines (e.g. when making different types of biscuits), other outputs may be sub-standard and flow into the waste channel.

The system is **controlled** by a user, who puts in the **primary** inputs and the **secondary** inputs. The primary inputs are the settings (control parameters) which control the operation of the system (e.g. the speed of the line, the temperature, the quality standards, the hours worked and so on). The secondary inputs are the current resources.

Closed and open systems

The systems model we have described above illustrates an **open system**. In an open system the *outputs do not affect the inputs*.

In a **closed system** the outputs do affect the inputs. In a closed system a comparator compares the outputs with a pre-established value, and if the outputs do not meet this value the inputs are adjusted. For example, a thermostat in a room regulates a heating system to a pre-established temperature; when the temperature reaches a given high level the heating is turned off, and when it reaches a low level it is turned on. In the same way, if the contents of a particular product do not meet the specifications established for the comparator, then the comparator instructs the system to alter the inputs appropriately. If the dog biscuits proved to be too brittle the comparator might suggest that more water is added to the mix, or that temperatures need to be reduced.

In setting up a production system it is important to establish goals for that particular system. These goals should be expressed in terms of particular performance indicators. For example, target quantities of output can be established, or targets can be set for minimising waste, breakdowns to machinery and so on.

1 The text has mentioned a number of terms related to systems theory. Try to familiarise yourself with them, and in your notebook or folder define the following:

Open system	Closed system	Input
Output	Process	Boundaries
Filter	Current resources	Elements
Links	Controller	Primary inputs
Secondary inputs		

2 Look at a particular production system in a local business. Try to identify each of the elements outlined above. What are the goals of the particular system that you have studied? What performance indicators are used to check whether these goals are being achieved? What happens when the system falls shorts of its goals?

Sub-systems

In all but the smallest organisations there are usually a number of **sub-systems** operating at the same time, and these interact with each other. For example, in a business there is likely to be an accounting system, a production system, and a marketing system. It would be unrealistic to assume that the boundaries between these systems can be drawn rigidly. A key criterion for measuring the success of any system would be that the outputs measured in money terms will be greater than the inputs.

. THE WIDER ENVIRONMENT IN WHICH . BUSINESSES OPERATE

The only constant factor in the environment in which businesses operate is change, as the next case study demonstrates.

The purchasing power of incomes

Figure 1.10 shows, in hours, the work time needed since 1971 to pay for selected items, for a married couple with the husband the only earner (source: Family Expenditure Survey 1993).

	1971	1981	1986	1990
White sliced loaf	9 min	8 min	6 min	5 min
1 lb rump steak	56 min	60 min	46 min	40 min
500 g butter	19 min	20 min	16 min	13 min
Pint of milk	5 min	4 min	4 min	3 min
Dozen eggs	22 min	17 min	15 min	12 min
100 g coffee	22 min	20 min	21 min	14 min
Pint of beer	14 min	13 min	13 min	11 min
20 cigarettes	22 min	20 min	21 min	17 min
Motor car licence	40h 31m	27h 11m	25h 39m	17h 55m
Colour TV licence	19h 27m	13h 12m	14h 37m	12h 32m
Litre of petrol	8 min	8 min	6 min	5 min

Figure 1.10 *Purchasing power*

1 What does the table show?
2 What impact will the changes shown have on businesses?
3 Will the impact be felt by all businesses in the same way?

The operation of a system is critically influenced by its **total environment,** which is best studied under several headings.

The natural environment

Nature has always exerted a great influence on the way in which businesses operates. For the manufacturer of dog biscuits a good wheat harvest will bring down raw material costs. The **natural environment** provides opportunities and exerts constraints on human activities. Rain and sunshine will make crops grow. Lack of rain will cause famine and starvation. In recent years we have become particularly aware that human activity can also feed back into nature. Chemicals deposited in the atmosphere from power stations return to earth in the form of acid rain, whilst other gases form chemical reactions, depleting the ozone layer.

The social environment

The **social system** is the fabric of ideas, attitudes and behaviour patterns that are involved in human relationships. Within a society, ideas and attitudes develop as to how long people should work, what is 'men's work' and 'women's work', and how new technology should be used. The dog biscuit manufacturer may find that he or she cannot recruit sufficient labour on a Sunday to run a particular shift efficiently.

The legal and political environment

Every society is governed by a set of **laws** and **codes** established by the legal and political framework. Business systems must operate within these opportunities and constraints. For example, food production is governed by laws relating to the handling of foods, types of allowable ingredients, descriptions and labelling of goods and so on. In the wider field the way in which businesses operate is influenced by **political relationships** between countries. For example, in July 1993 British companies were not allowed to sell goods to Serbia. The British government was exerting sanctions on the Serbian government to discourage the expansion of a 'Greater Serbia'.

The technological environment

We live in an age of **technological revolution**. Businesses that take on board new technologies are frequently at considerable advantage. In the 1990s many Eastern European countries are disadvantaged because they still use older technologies.

We can relate the changing technological environment to our dog biscuits example. A *gas oven* has for a number of

years been used to bake dog biscuits. This works in just the same way as a domestic gas oven, so a gas flame warms the inside of the oven and heat energy is transferred to the biscuits to cook them. The biscuits travel through a long oven on a conveyor belt, and they are in the oven for about 11 minutes at a temperature of 340°C. The heat energy travels to the inside of the biscuit and a crust forms on the outside of the biscuit before the inside has completely dried out. The crust traps moisture inside the biscuit.

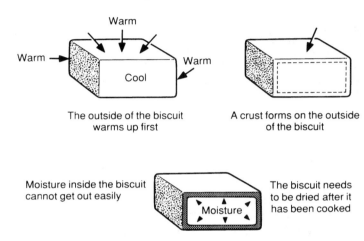

Figure 1.11 *What happens when a biscuit is cooked in a gas oven*

When the biscuits come out of the oven they have to be dried for three hours. A gas burner warms the air for this purpose. After drying, the biscuits must be left for a further 24 hours to settle before they can be packed.

Today a different form of energy can be used to cook the biscuits. Ovens that use *radio-frequency energy* are an

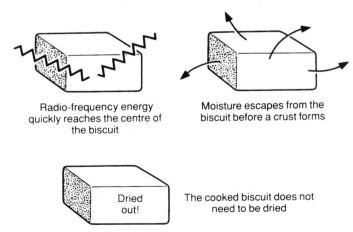

Figure 1.12 *What happens when a biscuit is cooked in a radio-frequency oven*

alternative to gas, oil or electricity fired hot-air ovens. Radio frequency energy is similar to the energy used in domestic microwave ovens, and these energies very quickly reach the inside of the foodstuffs being cooked. Cooking times are shorter, and the biscuits dry out before a crust forms on them. There is no need to dry the biscuits or let them settle, so they can be packed shortly after cooking. Radio-frequency ovens are shorter and so take up less room than ordinary gas, electric or oil-fired ovens.

The industrial relations environment

The most important resource of a company is the **workforce** – the people who work for it. **Industrial relations** is concerned with communication between the representatives of the employer and representatives of the employees. Business performance is keenly influenced by the quality of internal relations within the organisation. An organisation is most likely to be effective when employees feel a sense of responsibility for what they are doing and are concerned to produce a quality product.

Businesses may also be affected by the wider industrial relations environment. When a particular type of labour is in short supply and wages are rising nationally, employees are influenced to seek pay rises for themselves.

Other environments

We shall be exploring the economic background against which firms operate at length throughout the book. Here we can mention that businesses are continually influenced by many other outside factors – such as population changes and changes in tastes.

Conflict or consensus?

Do businesses operate in a society in which people share values, or is there a fundamental **conflict of interests**? There are different schools of thought on this issue.

When we examine a global issue such as the use of nuclear power, there are clear differences of opinion between various groups (Figures 1.13 and 1.14).

The same can be said about acid rain and the greenhouse effect. Isn conflict, then, an *inherent* part of society?

Figure 1.13 *Demonstrating a point of view*

Figure 1.14 *Demonstrating another point of view*

Marxist thinkers (people whose ideas have been influenced by Karl Marx) believe that while central values serve to keep society together, these values represent the interests of the 'ruling classes'. Education and other systems encourage conformity. Marx (1818–1883) argued that history developed in stages, determined by changes in the way humans organise their lives. The move from one stage to another was brought about through the struggle between different social classes, which resulted in revolutions. Marx thought that the French Revolution of 1789 marked the first change in modern Europe. It left behind the 'feudal' stage, in which peasants were exploited by landlords. He believed that after the revolution European society moved into a later, 'capitalist' stage of history; production shifted from the land to the city, from peasants to the urban working class (or 'proletariat'). Landlords were replaced by factory owners and investors ('bourgeoisie') as the leading class in society.

Marx said that, under capitalism, employees are forced to sell their labour cheaply and lose control of their working lives. He thought they would be freed through class struggles, led by a revolutionary party which would defeat the bourgeoisie through revolution and take history into its next, 'socialist' stage in which workers would gain control over the government and production.

This stage would eventually give way to the last historical stage: true communism. A 'communist' society would work according to the principle 'from each according to his ability, to each according to his need'. The state would simply wither away.

Marx felt that the 'working class' is misled into being loyal and hard working in a society where it is exploited. The working class falsely accepts the ideology (ideas, values and justifications) of a society in which it is exploited. Realisation of this position inevitably leads to **conflict.**

In contrast, many other thinkers believe that society is based more on **consensus** – that is, on shared values. For most people the nation, and the local community, are units on which they can focus these shared values, which may include patriotism, loyalty, community spirit and obedience to the law. The American writer Talcott Parsons argued that 'fundamental values underpin the social system and without them it could not function'.

A synthesis (coming together) of these two contrasting theories is presented by the idea of **pluralism.** A plural society is made up of many different groups – ethnic groups, religious groups, age groups, style and fashion groups, interest groups, etc. Members of these share many of the same and similar values, but some of their values are so fundamentally different that consensus is disturbed by periods of conflict.

Case Study

Crisis for democracy?

In November 1992, Anthony Sampson's *The Essential Anatomy of Britain* was published by Hodder and Stoughton. Anthony Sampson is a widely respected analyst of political power in Britain.

Sampson argues that thirty years ago the landscape of British power was much more varied than it is today. In the 1960s there were far more people who could influence decisions, including trade unionists, outspoken professors, indignant scientists and eccentric churchmen. Now all the spotlights are trained centre-stage, where a single party has been in power for 14 years, led by

politicians whose experience is largely limited to politics and finance, and who are removed from grass-roots public opinion. He sets out three major factors that have led to this crisis for democracy.

First, during the 1980s the traditional powers that counterbalanced government power were cut down by Margaret Thatcher. These were, for example, local government, the unions and the universities.

Second, the continuation of a single party in office greatly limits the choice available to voters, and makes civil servants far more dependent on the patronage of one set of people for their jobs. The ideas of civil servants are likely, therefore, to reflect those of their political masters.

Third, and most importantly, far more decisions are being made *in Europe*, by the Commission and the Council of Ministers (see Chapter 2), and by national politicians making decisions **in secret** with their key advisers.

The same process of loss of grass-roots power is also evident in finance and industry. Shareholders have become less able to check what goes on in company boardrooms, and directors have been able to award themselves massive salary increases in some cases.

Task

Study the national news media to find evidence of decisions that are made by politicians and senior business people who have not sought out grass-roots opinions. (An example is the attempt in 1992 and 1993 to close coal mines, leading to a spectacular public backlash!)

Large-scale or small-scale studies of societies

When studying a society we can take an **holistic** view (looking at things as a whole), or alternatively study small-scale interactions. An holistic study might, for example, be concerned with looking at the relationship between unemployment and inflation in the whole economy. A small-scale study might be concerned with looking at how individuals in a small business interact with each other. Both perspectives are valuable in their own ways.

· THE ECONOMY AND BUSINESS ·

Resources are said to be scarce relative to our wants and needs. This assertion is, however, being increasingly challenged today. Questions are being raised as to how we **manage** our resources. For example, the continent of Africa is by no stretch of the imagination overpopulated, yet year after year vast tracts of it are subject to famine. These areas coincide with extensive military activities largely financed by richer countries. In the mid-1990s the world has *record supplies of grain and meat reserves –* indeed a major problem is lack of storage space. A growing number of thinkers argue that a major problem of the twentieth century has been a *mismanagement* of resources.

These issues bring to light the fundamental economic questions:

> WHAT SHOULD BE PRODUCED?
> HOW SHOULD IT BE PRODUCED?
> WHO SHOULD GET IT?

The function of an economic system is to resolve these three questions.

A simple circular flow model illustrates the way in which resources are used by firms to produce goods that are purchased by households. Figure 1.15 shows how rewards to factors of production are distributed.

· DIFFERENT TYPES OF NATIONAL ECONOMY ·

Not all countries operate identical economic systems. Economies can be classified according to the amount of government involvement in decision-making. At one extreme a **free market** system has no government interference. At the other extreme, in a totally **planned** system, the government pays a considerable part in making business decisions.

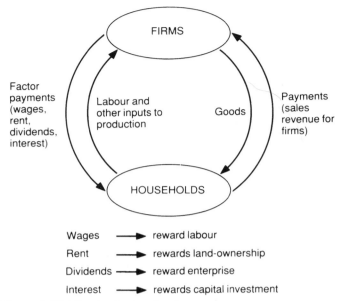

Wages $\longrightarrow$ reward labour
Rent $\longrightarrow$ rewards land-ownership
Dividends $\longrightarrow$ reward enterprise
Interest $\longrightarrow$ rewards capital investment

Figure 1.15 *The simple circular flow system*

Free market systems

A **free market** exists when the government plays no part in controlling markets. Decisions are made freely (without interference) by buyers and sellers. Buyers continue to buy items provided they feel that they are getting value for money. If consumers consider that they would get better value for money by buying one brand of petrol rather than another, they will buy it.

Producers will increase their output of goods in response to **consumer demand**. When prices rise producers will have an incentive to produce more – they may now be able to make more profit (provided the cost of making the increased output does not exceed the revenue from selling the extra bit).

Free market systems do not exist in perfect form in the real world because governments of all countries today insist on at least a small role in controlling economic activity.

Advantages of the free market system

1 Consumers are able to 'vote with their money' for the goods they want to be produced. Popular items are likely to be produced in larger quantities and at relatively low prices.

2 Because demand represents consumer needs and wants, resources are channelled into these lines. Resources will not be channelled (wastefully) into unpopular lines.

3 Because the government does not interfere in the economy, consumers can spend their own money in ways they see fit. The argument is that you will know what purchases will give you most satisfaction. A government official spending money on your behalf is less in tune with your needs and wants.

4 A free market system can respond quickly to changes. In other words it is *dynamic*. In the 1960s and 70s teenagers tended to buy records, but today they are far more likely to buy tapes and compact discs. The music industry helped to bring about the changes, and today music shops supply what the consumer wants.

5 Scarce resources do not have to be wasted on administering the system.

Disadvantages of the free market system

1 There are no checks against monopolist practices by large producers.

2 Large and powerful interests (such as big companies) have far more influence than smaller ones.

3 Although consumers can vote with their money, some will have more money than others.

4 The market system does not guarantee that a minimum standard of needs will be achieved by everyone. Market economies tend to be characterised by great inequalities in wealth and income.

5 Some goods are 'non-excludable'. Supplying these goods to one person means that other people will also benefit. For example, if we improve pavements in the town centre then everyone who goes there will benefit. It would be impossible to make just the users of the pavements pay for this service.

6 A free market only works effectively if we assume that all consumers have perfect knowledge of the features of all goods available in the market and where they can be found. This is clearly unrealistic. Buying decisions are frequently made on the basis of imperfect knowledge: I may buy petrol from a particular service station, not realising that there is another outlet 200 metres up the road selling cheaper petrol.

7 In the real market-place consumers are fed a lot of misinformation, particularly through advertising.

Task

Make a list of ways in which you have imperfect knowledge of products, making it difficult to make consistent buying decisions.

The planned system

In some economies major decisions are made by a **central planning body**. The planning authority collects information about the quantities of resources (e.g. coal, steel, bricks, etc.) that might be available in a given time period (e.g. five years).

The central planners ask local planning bodies to say what quantity of resources they will need and how much they will produce, before deciding on how to allocate (give out) the available resources. They have to give careful thought to this in order to ensure the best value to society in a given period of time. Plans can be adjusted from time to time to deal with any problems that might arise.

In the 1990s the number of planned economies in the world is falling as many countries switch to market systems. Planning is still, however, important in China, Burma, Laos, Cambodia, Vietnam, Mongolia and Cuba.

Task

Study the national media to find examples of countries that are either increasing or decreasing the extent of central planning. Why are the changes being made?

Advantages of the planned system

1 The system allows targets and plans to be established for the whole economy. The central planning body is able to issue instructions to all the enterprises in the economy informing them of their own individual targets. In effect the central plan is the solution to an enormous set of simultaneous equations because all the enterprises in the economy will be interdependent – the output of the coal industry will form part of the input of the energy, steel and many other industries. It follows that the ability of the steel industry to meet its target will depend, to a large extent, on the performance of the coal industry. In the former Soviet Union planners were able to build a systems model of the whole economy. The model was set out on the floor of a huge shed, and planners could move around models of inputs and outputs in order to try to balance the equations for future plans.

2 Revisions can be made by the central authority which has access to a great deal of information, especially on how the total economy is operating.

3 Plans can be made to ensure that basic needs are met for all the people. For example, until recently unemployment was unheard of in the Russian economy, and bread was heavily subsidised.

4 Long-term planning is possible for all resources, and all industries.

5 Wasteful duplication of products can be cut out (e.g. you would not have two postal services in the same area).

6 Goods and services can be distributed evenly.

Disadvantages of the planned system

1 There is no competitive spur. Competition tends to increase the quality of products. If the state produces everything then it does not operate in a competitive environment.

2 A major danger is that local planners might deliberately overestimate the resources they need in order to get projects finished more quickly, so boosting their local output (because this makes local officials look good). Resources can be wasted in this way.

3 The costs of running a planned system are high. Bureaucrats are needed to make the plans, and run enterprises from their offices.

4 Bureaucrats may slow down progress in order to keep their jobs. For example, an official working for a declining industry may have a vested interest in making that industry seem vitally important to the national economy.

5 The absence of the profit motive removes the spur to individual effort and enterprise.

6 Black markets may develop in planned economies where the market fails to deliver the goods that consumers want.

Case Study

Weaknesses of a planned economy

The following letter appeared in *Pravda* (the former Soviet newspaper) in late 1989:

'To obtain your coal coupon is one thing: you are only half way there. Now as for actually getting your coal . . . The night before, you take your place in the square at the gates of the coal depot. You queue all night long only to discover that there isn't enough coal for everyone. The reasons vary: sometimes lorries don't arrive, sometimes people are off sick.

How can it be that in a centralised system, with fixed prices, providing people with adequate supplies of heating fuel is such a complicated procedure? It's been a whole year since our local paper raised the issue and still no results.

Another problem: the allocated maximum amount of coal per family – 1.5 tons – is not enough, particularly during severe winters like last year. What's more all we get is low-grade coal. Only half of it is any good – the rest is dust. As a result, towards the end of the winter, people are compelled to buy coal illegally on the black market and to pay the earth for it.

Something should be done about the whole system: people should be able to buy coal at official coal depots without coupons. Not of course, for 15 to 18 roubles per ton, but twice or even three times as much. And the coal would have to be better quality.

V. Karienko

1 *Does this letter indicate that the planning system provided for the needs of all the people?*
2 *What weaknesses does the article expose in the planning system?*
3 *How were consumers able to combat weaknesses of this system?*

4 *What alternatives to the planning system was the letter writer suggesting?*

5 *What suggestions would you make for improving the distribution of coal in the former Soviet Union?*

6 *What problems have been encountered in changing this system?*

▪ THE MIXED ECONOMY ▪

Mixed economies involve a blend of private enterprise and government involvement in economic activity. In economies such as those of the European Community and Japan, decisions are made by three groups – producers, consumers and the government.

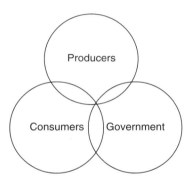

Figure 1.16 Interconnection between decision-makers in a mixed economy

In these countries a large proportion of business capital is privately owned. Private owners are free to decide how their resources ought to be employed. The owners of the enterprises are free to decide their own production targets, to produce whatever quantity and quality of output they choose and to buy whatever amounts of factor inputs they feel are necessary.

Governments in such countries make contributions to the economy in two senses:

- They are owners of resources in their own right because they are responsible for running certain services for the nation – such as defence, public health and welfare.
- They have the power to change and influence private decisions made by producers and consumers when they feel that these decisions may not otherwise fairly reflect the best interests of the community. For example, the

government sets high rates of taxes to discourage cigarette smoking and the widescale drinking of alcohol.

Views as to how the mixed economy should operate change over time. In the United Kingdom the size of the government sector has grown substantially in the twentieth century (up until 1979). Successive governments gradually built up the Welfare State, and nationalised industries increasingly took over the 'commanding heights of the economy', including rail, coal, steel, airways, postal services and telecommunications. Since 1979 the government sector has been reduced. The 'Thatcher years' were characterised by **privatisation.** Government-run industries such as gas and steel were returned to private ownership. The emphasis was very much on industries moving upwards and away from dependence on the government. Since 1990 John Major's government has continued with the policy of privatisation, but the policy has moved towards recognising that government industries have an important part to play still. However, these government industries need to be increasingly accountable to their consumers.

The main *advantages* of mixed economies are that they combine the best elements of planned economies and free markets. The government is able to coordinate major areas of industrial policy, to provide a safety net for weaker members of society, to make sure that markets run smoothly, and to enable effective competition. The main *disadvantages* are that they combine the worst elements of the two systems: government interference stifles initiative and enterprise whilst competition favours the strong at the expense of the weak.

Case Study

Government intervention in industry

In 1987 Michael Heseltine, before he became the government minister responsible for industry, published a book called *Where There's a Will*. In it he argued the following case:

The capitalist economies with which we have to compete do not operate on the theory held in Britain that government is an onlooker in the industrial game or at best a referee. In most of these countries, there are partnerships between the government and the industrial world.

France and Germany share with Japan the sense of national purpose which so many observers note in our competitors but do not find in Britain. This purpose is based on partnership.

In many of the high technology fields, the role of the government is the manifestation of French will . . . We would not have a major civil airframe manufacturing capability in Europe today if it were not for France. We would not have a launcher capability in the space field but for France . . .

It is not intervention that is wrong: in the modern world, it is unavoidable. What was wrong before was the subsidising of losses and the cosiness and lack of professionalism associated with that. Intervention and featherbedding are not the same thing. The trick is to distinguish between them.

The evidence is that there will be continuing development and growth in, for instance, aerospace, robotics, telecommunications and biotechnology. These are all areas which Britain's competitor governments are supporting. Government and industry in Britain must talk together about what markets exist, could be created or are under threat . . .

In his 1989 book *The Challenge of Europe: Can Britain Win?*, Heseltine argued:

Government will have to fund much of the seed-corn exploration which alone can lead to breakthroughs but which is too costly or too risky for the private sector to pay for without assistance. Above all, there is one cardinal rule for intelligent, responsible politicians: they should stop pretending that this sort of industrial support is a doctrinal intrusion into the working of the market place.

1 *What type of economic system is Michael Heseltine in favour of?*
2 *How does he see this type of system operating? What is the role of the government in the system?*
3 *What arguments does he put forward to support his views?*
4 *Do you agree with him? Explain your answer.*

Task

1 Look at the purchasing decisions below. In a mixed economy would a decision be made by a planning official or a private citizen?

a Buying new school books.
b Employing more doctors at a local hospital.
c Buying a word processor.
d Maintaining the local leisure centre.
e Maintaining public parks.
f Expanding the services of a local bank.
g Buying medical syringes.
h Reducing the mileage travelled by police vehicles.
i Increasing holiday expenditure.
j Having a hair cut.
2 Look at the decisions about production which need to be made below. Do you think they would be made by a planning official or a private entrepreneur in a mixed

economy?

a Building a new airport.
b Building a new road.
c Building a new daycare centre for the elderly.
d Building a town hall.
e Cutting back on military services.
f Further restricting opening times at the local library.
g Making a new aircraft engine.
3 Which of the following decisions do you think should be made by private individuals and which by government officials?

a Building of new roads.
b Provision of parking facilities.
c Creating a law that requires drivers to wear seatbelts.
d Programming television.

DISLOCATION OF NEW MARKET ECONOMIES

One of the key issues in international business education today revolves around how Eastern block countries can be supported in transforming their central planning systems to include free market principles. Free market principles include:

- competition
- extensive privatisation
- the use of prices to decide what goods will be produced.

However, a centrally planned system cannot be dismantled overnight to be replaced by a market economy. Within a system organisations and attitudes develop over a period of time. Once these organisations and attitudes are established they are very difficult to change. People in the Eastern bloc countries, for example, have become used to full employment and subsidised food. Inevitably they are resistant to changes that involve huge job losses and soaring prices. The move to market forces has led to a virtual collapse in distribution systems.

The governments of some of the Eastern bloc countries have been reluctant to change to market forces in one step. Instead they have chosen a dilute form of **partial markets**. Being neither one thing nor the other these partial markets have been ineffective. In addition, opponents of change have tried to sabotage the efforts, leading to a worse state of affairs.

Foreign multinationals such as the western car giants have invested in large-scale industry at the expense of the small and medium-sized companies. They have also sought monopoly status (where they are the only firm in the market), which goes against the whole idea of competition. Inevitably Eastern bloc countries will experience a great deal of **dislocation** and hardship before things start to get better. They must also overcome traditional mistrust between the West and the Eastern bloc.

European Community countries have offered to provide technical support to the Commonwealth of Independent States so that it can develop its substantial oil and gas industries. It is, of course, widely recognised that EC countries are currently looking for alternative sources of supply to some of the unstable Middle Eastern countries.

and sausages, as well as some raw materials. However, the privatisation programme was to continue. Mr Chernomydrin argued that the move to a market economy needed to be carried out slowly 'with a human face' rather than a 'big bang' that would lead to hardship.

1 What are the dangers of bringing back price controls?
2 What are the dangers of not bringing back price controls?
3 Should price controls be brought back?
4 Is it better to go for the 'big bang' or for gradual change?
5 What is the latest state of affairs in the Russian economy?

Case Study

Changes in Russia

In January 1992, price controls on many products were lifted in Russia in order to bring in free market reforms. The prime minister responsible for introducing the reforms was Yegor Gaidar. In the first year 40 000 state enterprises were privatised. Government plans included extending regional autonomy, stimulating investment and converting military plants to civilian production. It was recognised that the process of change would take a long time before the beneficial effects of free markets would be seen. Of course, one of the immediate changes was that prices soared and this was not a popular measure.

In December 1992, Mr Gaidar was removed by opponents of the free market reforms. The new prime minister was Viktor Chernomydrin. The first major policy move of the new prime minister was to reimpose price controls on essential goods in an attempt to curb inflation and calm growing public anger over economic hardship. By the end of 1991, inflation was around 25 per cent *per month* with the annual total estimated at more than 2000 per cent. According to the Itar-Tass news agency, Mr Chernomydrin aimed to 'curb inflationary processes and unjustified growth in the prices for certain staple foodstuffs, consumer goods and services'. Goods placed under complete state control included bread, tea, salt, sugar, milk, butter, spirits

ORGANISATIONAL GOALS AND OBJECTIVES

Etzioni (*Modern Organisations*, Prentice Hall) defines organisations as 'social units that pursue specific goals which they are structured to serve under some social circumstances'. Goals can be defined as a future state of affairs which the organisation strives to achieve. Most organisations will set down guidelines for activity which serve as standards by which the success (i.e. the effectiveness and efficiency) of the organisation can be judged.

Task

Choose three organisations with which you are familiar and find out what their prime goals are. What guidelines have the organisations used to measure their success?

Features of an organisation

We can identify certain key features that are possessed by most organisations:

- An organisation must have a name (e.g. The Baptist Church, St John Ambulance Brigade, Barnsley Football Club). Businesses also have names (e.g. The Late Shop, Tie Rack, National Westminster Bank).
- We have already seen that organisations have **objectives**. We look at some of these objectives below.
- Organisations have **rules** and **regulations**. Some of these are written down formally on paper. Other informal codes of practice are not written down but people recognise and respond to them. Some of the rules will be imposed externally by the government in the form of laws.
- Organisations have **patterns** and **structures**. Usually there will be a chain of command. Some organisations are hierarchical with decisions being passed from the top downwards. Other organisations will be more democratic with many decision-makers with equal or similar powers.
- Within an organisation different members will have positions ranging from the managing director to the caretaker. Positions are sometimes referred to as **posts** or **offices**. Each position will have set tasks associated with it.
- Organisations usually have a **chain of authority**. In a hierarchical organisation someone at a lower level may need to get permission from a superior to do something.
- Within an organisation different officers will have the **power** to carry out particular actions. Powers may be written down in a formal contract. Other powers may be informal. Individuals are recognised to have particular powers to carry out a course of action.
- **Records** are an important feature. Nowadays many records are kept in computer files – often in databases. Written records are also important. Most organisations will store records for several years.

Some theorists argue that the behaviour of members of an organisation is mainly governed by the goals which its decision-makers have set for it.

Task

The last task asked you to identify three organisations. Who has the power to determine the goals of these organisations? To what extent are they able to influence the behaviour of members of these organisations? Why does this influence vary between the organisations that you have examined?

Once those with power in an organisation have established its goals, they can then establish the objectives for getting there. (Objectives should be testable – after a certain period of time you should be able to test how far you have moved towards meeting particular objectives.)

There is likely to be some difference between the organisation people think they are operating, the organisation that actually exists, and the organisation that is best suited to the needs of the time. I may think that I am running a first-rate, modern and interesting business studies course, my students might think that it is boring, and the reality may be that I am twenty years behind the times (of course this is not true!). As times change organisations move on.

Classifying organisations by their objectives

Business organisations

We shall see in the next chapter that business organisations take several forms, ranging from small one-owner businesses to multinational corporations. Some businesses are concerned with making goods – we call these **industrial organisations**. Some are concerned with buying and selling – we call these **commercial organisations**. Some are concerned with banking and insurance – these are **financial organisations**.

Government organisations

Government organisations operate at both a local and a national level. They are accountable to representatives elected by citizens. They are concerned with running the country.

Public corporations

Public corporations are owned by the government on behalf of the people. Examples are the British Broadcasting Corporation and British Coal. They set out to produce goods and services to serve all the people of the country.

Quangos (quasi-autonomous non-government organisations)

These are unelected public bodies. They are run by boards of directors to manage a particular initiative. For example, local TECs (Training and Enterprise Councils) are responsible for providing training opportunities and schemes on behalf of local employers.

Economic interest groups

These are organisations representing groups of people with a shared interest. Examples are the Consumers' Association (representing consumers), the Confederation of British Industry (employers) and the Trades Unions Congress (trade unions).

Trade unions

Trade unions are economic interest groups. They are given a special status in law. They represent groups of employees in bargaining situations both nationally and in individual plants.

Legal organisations

There are a number of legal organisations responsible for administering and supervising the legal process. Examples are the courts, the Monopolies Commission, etc.

Political organisations

Many groups of people form themselves into political organisations. Some of these are highly organised (e.g. the Conservative Party). Others are less organised, such as pressure groups campaigning against a particular issue like the destruction of the countryside.

Charities

Charitable organisations have a special status in law. In the past charities were set up to provide for the helpless and needy (the poor, the homeless . . .). Nowadays many organisations have adopted charitable status in order to gain tax and other advantages (e.g. public schools).

Mutual help organisations

Some organisations have been set up so that members can help each other rather than setting out to make a profit. Cooperatives are a good example – any surpluses may be shared among members. Some labour organisations work on this basis: members club together to provide support for the sick and needy.

International and multinational organisations

Many organisations now have a membership in several nations, either at a government or private level. Examples are the European Community and the Red Cross/Crescent. Business organisations may have tentacles in many countries (e.g. Marks & Spencer, Laura Ashley, BP).

Task

Name at least three organisations that would fit into each of the categories outlined above.

SETTING OUT AIMS AND OBJECTIVES

Anyone starting a business must set out goals and objectives clearly. An outsider examining the business at a later date might find that it had moved away radically from these initial aims and objectives, because the company that set out to be the market leader may in fact have changed its goals (possibly simply to survive).

Many organisations try to set out a brief **mission statement**. This statement shows people within the organisation (as well as outsiders) what its core values are. The mission statement provides a clear focus for action.

Case Study

Quality first

The mission statement of Thornton's Confectioners reads as follows:

- At Thornton's it's quality first all the time, right through the business.
- Our aim is to delight our customers with exceptional products and caring service.

Thorntons

- Our goal is to be widely recognised as the best specialist retailer and manufacturer of quality confectionery.
- Our success depends upon all of us – our drive for continuous improvement and the best use of our individual skills, expertise and potential.
- Through our determination and commitment to 'quality first' we shall achieve strong and consistent profit growth, an enjoyable and rewarding working experience and a positive contribution to the community at large.

Most businesses today set out their aims and objectives in some form of **business plan**. We can regard this as representing the formal goals of the organisation.

However, within an organisation's day-to-day running there will be many informal elements. The partners who agree on paper to work from Monday to Friday may informally work on a seven-day week. On paper all grievances may be required to be presented to a senior manager, but informally they may be taken to someone else.

Organisations operate in an ever-changing environment. It is therefore important for the organisation to be flexible. Etzioni talked of an **effectiveness systems model** whereby the organisation explores changes that have occurred and how they affected the ability of the organisation to serve its goals. Organisational change (whether it be modest or fundamental) requires changes to existing processes and patterns of behaviour, and in some cases major changes in attitudes. Earlier in the chapter we saw that if Eastern European countries are going to assimilate change then they need some sort of effectiveness model. The same is true of large companies in a recession, when old and new practices need to be re-evaluated so that effective changes can be made. You can soon see that this model is helpful in many circumstances.

Developing goals

Professor Kotter (*A Force for Change*, Macmillan) argues that:

'The development of good business direction is not an act of magic. It is mostly a tough, sometimes exhausting, information-gathering and analytical process. People who help develop such visions and strategies are not magicians. They tend to be broad-based strategic thinkers who are willing to take risks.'

Strategy involves looking at the larger picture and developing major decisions and directions for an organisation to move in. It is concerned with the 'Generalship of business'.

When Robert Horton became Chairman of BP in 1989 his first task was to spend months on research and discussions with people throughout the company. This resulted in Project 1990, a vision for BP's future. Horton's vision was that BP could become the 'world's most successful oil company in the 1990s and beyond'. It involved a complete rethink of the direction the company was moving in, slimming down on non-essential administrative workers and buying in a lot of services that had previously been carried out by BP employees, as well as moving into some speculative exploration ventures that could pay off handsomely if successful. (However, unfortunately Horton made a lot of enemies within the company and in 1992 he resigned.) In the case of General Electric in America, Jack Welch set out to be best or second best in every field of GE's business. Everything else was ruthlessly cut out.

Today managers and employees sit down to work out mission statements. These statements must then be communicated throughout the organisations. With a clearly established mission everyone involved can work with shared values towards a goal that they understand, have helped to set, and can believe in.

Task

As a group of students working on common assignments together, establish a mission statement for your working syndicate.

Establishing goals

We have seen that every organisation needs to establish its goals, perhaps encapsulating its philosophy in its mission statement. The major route to achieving these goals will depend on strategy. It is important to be clear what is meant by **strategy** and **tactics.** These terms originate from military use. Military strategy before and during a battle is the general policy overview of how to defeat the enemy.

Strategy involves defining the major aims and objectives as well as developing means for achieving them. Having established its general strategy, an organisation can then work out its day-to-day tools and tactics to meet the strategic goals.

Tactical decisions need flexibility. A tennis player might have a match strategy of playing with great power to force opponents into errors. The player may practise his or her game to perfect the skills and power to implement this

strategy (by, for example, practising forceful serving.) During particular games that player may alter tactics (e.g. by serving long or short, to this side or that side of the court).

Task

Describe three situations in which you apply strategies to seek to attain particular goals. What sort of tactics do you apply to back up your strategy? How often do you have to alter your tactics? In what ways? How frequently do you have to modify your underlying strategy? How does this affect your actions?

Business aims

Businesses are set up for many different reasons. Profit may be an important motive but it is certainly not the only one. Many people are prepared to take a cut in earnings because of the satisfaction and freedom of working for themselves. Businesses generally have a wide range of possible aims, including:

- to make as much profit as possible
- to be the number-one product in a given market
- to maximise sales
- to grow quickly
- to operate in a wide range of markets
- to provide owners with a steady income
- to provide the freedom for the owner/s to express themselves in the work they enjoy.

Profit maximisation

Profit maximisation occurs when there is the greatest possible difference between the total cost of production and the revenue gained from selling the goods. If we assume that all goods can be sold at a given market price, revenue can be shown on a diagram by a line which rises from left to right (see Figure 1.17). We shall see later that in fact most businesses have considerable freedom in setting prices so that in the real world the line would not be so simple.

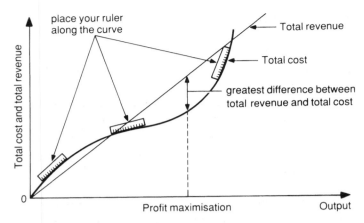

Figure 1.17 *Profit maximisation*

Costs rise as a firm increases its output. Initially as this happens, the total cost of production rises, but the rate of increase falls. Place a ruler on the total cost curve in Figure 1.17 and you will see that as you move it up the curve the ruler begins to tilt downwards to the right. This is because as you increase output you are able to spread fixed costs (such as rent and rates) over a wider area. Then comes a point at which the curve begins to rise again more steeply (check this out with the ruler). Profit maximisation will occur at the point of greatest difference between total cost and total revenue.

Task

Think of a form of production that you may be familiar with – making cakes. Try to reason out why the total cost of producing cakes will increase

- first at a falling rate,
- then at a rising rate,

as you expand production.

For businesses to operate in this way in the real world we need to assume that:

- they want to maximise profits
- they are able to calculate the point of profit maximisation
- the markets do not change.

In the real world, costs continually alter as does consumer demand.

Firms may be reluctant to act as pure profit maximisers because this might involve losing public goodwill, and may encourage the government to investigate their practices. However, all organisations do need to consider carefully the need to be profitable. An organisation that goes out of business can help no-one.

Market leadership

Many firms seek to be **market leaders**. They may want to sell more products than all rival brands combined, or simply to sell more than the next best selling brand. The most reliable indicator of market share is relative – that is, the ratio of a company's market share to that of its largest competitor:

Relative market share = $\dfrac{\text{Market share of the company}}{\text{Market share of nearest competitor}}$

A well-known study (by the Boston Consultancy Group) argued on the basis of statistical evidence that a ratio of 2:1 would give a 20 per cent cost advantage. The implication is that if you dominate a market you are able to produce on a larger scale than your rivals. You can therefore spread your costs over a larger output. You can then produce more cheaply than rivals. You can then plough back your higher profits into research, advertising and expansion in order to protect your market leadership.

Task

Find out who the market leader is in particular markets such as disposable nappies, washing powder and lawn mowers. What advantages do they have over competitors? How do they seek to protect their market leadership?

Sales maximisation

Some business organisations seek to maximise sales. **Turnover** is a term that means the value of sales in a given period of time. Clearly, if you are making sales then you may well be taking revenue away from competitors. The larger the volume of sales the more your fixed costs can be spread.

Business managers have an interest in the sales of their branch or department being high. For one thing, this helps to boost the size of their department and hence their salary.

Task

Consider a firm that has fixed costs of £100 000 and additional costs of 50 pence for each unit produced. What will be the average cost per unit to produce:

a 5000 units
b 20 000 units
c 500 000 units?

How does this example show the benefit of sales maximisation? What problems are caused if the firm is not able to sell a lot of its output?

Growth

Firms can benefit from **growth.** A firm that grows quickly will find it easier to attract investors and will be able to produce on a larger scale. However, one of the biggest mistakes that business people make in the early days is that of over-trading. Running a large business is quite different from running a smaller one. Large businesses are quite different to manage and all sorts of problems arise from over-trading: for example, there might not be enough cash to pay bills in the short term, managing more staff can be difficult, and so on.

Wide range of markets

Operating in a number of markets makes it possible to spread the risk. If one market fails another may support the loss. However, opening into new markets also exposes a business to fresh risks. It may be better to operate in a small number of well-known markets rather than exposing yourself to new risks.

Steady income

Satisficing is an alternative to maximising. A firm may set itself the task of attaining clearly realisable goals rather than stretching itself to the limit. This makes considerable sense when the firm does not want to take unnecessary risks. It may feel that it is better to be able to meet its orders with a margin to spare, to meet financial targets comfortably and to build up a reputation for delivering to its stated goals.

This does not indicate complacency. It may indeed be seen as sound business sense. Successful businesses trade and operate over many generations. (In the longer term a satisficer may make larger profits than a short-term high-flying profit maximiser.) Throughout the 1980s the Polly Peck company was heralded as the high-flying company of the decade, but in the early 90s the company collapsed – it had over-traded and failed to keep proper account of its activities. In 1992 the ambitious Maxwell Corporation collapsed with staggering debts. At the same time organisations with sound long-term strategies such as Marks & Spencer and Shell UK have gone from strength to strength.

Task

Look at the financial pages in some quality newspapers. Which firms can you identify as being:

a sales maximisers
b growth firms
c satisficers?

From the information available, which of these companies would you regard as having the best long-term prospects?

Freedom of expression

Many people set up a small business simply because it provides them with an opportunity to be creative and work for themselves. Why work for someone else when you can work for yourself, make your own decisions and take the profit?

Element assignment

Developing a business idea

This assignment can help you provide evidence for assessment, or claim the following Core Skills:

Communication

Communicate in writing
Participate in oral and non-verbal communication

Personal skills

Transfer skills gained to new and changing situations
Relate to and interact effectively with individuals and groups
Work effectively as a member of a team
Apply a range of skills and techniques to develop a variety of ideas in the creation of new/modified products, services or situations

▪ INVESTING IN THE SANDWICH BOOM ▪

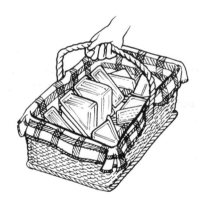

The sandwich business is booming. Supermarkets are increasing their range and many large cities have phone-in sandwich delivery services.

But how do you start a sandwich business?

Sally decided to set up a small sandwich delivery business to earn money and have some fun. First she carried out research in the area where she planned to deliver.

'I thought busy business people in the area where I lived needed better quality lunches. I looked around the local lunchtime places and asked people what was on offer. The choice was very limited, so I thought there would be no difficulty in improving on that.'

Bread research

'I wanted to make unusual sandwiches, and I needed a variety of good quality breads. I visited local supermarkets and bought their range of breads which I tested for taste and texture. Bread has to be the right shape and size, and complement the fillings.

'Since I couldn't find a pitta bread that was the right shape or size, I have invented my own using dried yeast, strong white flour with wheatgerm, water and a little olive oil. The bread is rolled out in stone-ground flour, from a country flour mill, and this gives a nutty flavour.'

Fillings

'I chose fillings using flavours from around the world, such as the Greek sandwich with feta cheese and olives. There is also a vegetarian choice, with avocado, tomato and alfalfa sprouts. All the fillings were tested on friends and their comments were noted before I made my menu choice.'

Costing it out

Banks may lend money to help small businesses to get started, and some banks have special offers such as free printing of menus and business cards.

For this small business it was necessary to buy special catering equipment and a basket with tablecloth, napkins, plates and containers for the delivery round.

The selling price of each sandwich was costed according to the bread used, the price of the filling and the packaging; then this sum was doubled to cover labour and other expenses.

Food hygiene

Where food is on display for sale, the establishment has to be registered with the local Environmental Health Department and will probably be visited by an Environmental Health Officer on a regular basis to ensure that the premises conform with the requirements of the Food Safety Act and Food Hygiene Regulations.

Starting off

Since Sally couldn't afford promotion or advertising, she just set off with a basket full of sandwiches, fruit, cakes, crisps and drinks.

Her efforts were rewarded the next day when a satisfied customer remarked, 'Thank you for making such decent sandwiches.'

What changes had to be made?

'The weather affects what people choose. If it's sunny they prefer salads, but the weather can suddenly change and the salads I have made remain unsold. Shop assistants don't like eating raw onions as it can make their breath smell and that's not good for customers.

'People turned out to be very adventurous in the choice of sandwiches. Club sandwiches and avocado, bacon, lettuce and tomato are the two best-sellers, and I've stopped making plain ham and beef sandwiches.'

The future

'I'd really like to open a shop or get a helper, since the delivery takes up so much time. But that all costs money so we will have to wait and see.'

Tasks

This case study highlights some important details that need to be considered in setting up a small enterprise, namely:

- coming up with an idea
- finding out if there is a market
- looking at the competition
- product research
- costing it out
- pricing
- looking at the legal requirements
- promotion and advertising
- looking to the future.

Task 1

Working in small groups, study a small local business to find out what was done under each of the above headings when it was set up.

Prepare a group presentation for the rest of the class. The presentation should be 20 minutes long. Use visual aids – diagrams and charts, examples of products, illustrations etc.

Task 2

Identify an opportunity for setting up a small business of your own to provide a product or service to be sold in your local area. Carry out some detailed research using each of the headings outlined for the sandwich business. Look at possible competitors, different ways of providing the product or service, etc. Produce your findings in the form of a 2000 word report supported by charts and diagrams.

chapter **2** # EXTERNAL INFLUENCES ON THE ORGANISATION

Business life can be fully understood only when viewed against a background of interdependence and complex interrelationships. All organisations operate with many external influences on their activities, and in this chapter we examine a wide range of such influences.

Furthermore, the environment in which an organisation exists is in a constant state of change. People responsible for running the organisation must be fully aware of changes in the external influences if they are to respond positively with effective measures to meet the organisation's objectives.

The activities of organisations do not take place in books – they take place in the real world. In this world there are many **outside** influences that affect the ways in which an organisation as a whole can act, and which therefore affect the ways in which individ-ual members of the organisation can behave. For example, you may need to make an urgent parcel delivery to the other side of town, but the speed with which you can get it there depends on the speeds of other motorists on the road, the ease with which you can get someone to carry your parcel, the speed limits on the roads, the direction taken – and many other factors.

The activities of any organisation are therefore affected by happenings outside itself, as well as being influenced by activities within the more controlled area of its own environment. The outside influences can be at a local level, a national level, and an international level.

What do these external influences really mean for the operation and running of a business organisation? In the real world some of the key influences of business activity are:

- the customers
- the suppliers of goods and services
- competitors
- people living near the business premises
- central and local government decisions
- European Community legislation
- trade unions.

· TYPES OF EXTERNAL INFLUENCE ·

In studying organisations we usually classify external influences under the following headings:

- economic
- social
- political
- legal
- technological
- environmental.

While this classification is useful in theory it is well worth remembering that in the real world these factors are all intermeshed.

Figure 2.1 *The organisation in its complex intermeshed environment*

Economic influences

These are the effects of decisions made in society as to how to allocate resources (see Chapter 1). Choices are made by individuals, groups, organisations, governments, countries, and international groups. Economic decisions are also made on a global level – for example, to reduce the emission of gases that create the 'greenhouse effect'.

Decisions are made by individual consumers to buy, for example, hamburgers rather than vegiburgers, quiche rather than steak, cheesecake rather than yoghurt and so on. Changing patterns of consumer spending clearly affect the fortunes of individual enterprises.

Decisions made by trade unions to attempt to increase wages influence business costs, and decisions made by businesses to close down an old plant (or open a new one) clearly influence the fortunes of members of a local Job Club.

Economic decisions made by groups of trading countries to reduce import taxes influence all the businesses that previously paid the higher levels of taxes.

Changes in the economy therefore have a major influence on organisations.

Social influences

Society is in a constant state of change, and organisations form just one part of it. Society expands and contracts, as the population changes, and social forces are dynamic. Values and attitudes in society frequently change – for example, we talk of attitudes becoming more or less permissive.

Society is made up of many systems, such as the education system, the health system, law and the justice system, and so on. Each of these systems is in turn made up of many sub-systems which interact with each other.

These social changes affect organisations in many ways. For example, membership of most of the main churches has fallen steadily throughout the twentieth century as people have become less interested in religion.

Political influences

Political pressure comes from both national and local government, and from the work of pressure groups. Governments spending less on defence and the health services has a direct impact on organisations working in these areas. Political decisions are made by groups with large powers vested in them to represent the wishes of the community.

Legal influences

National and international laws affect the running of organisations in many ways. Every organisation, and individuals working for them, must have a clear picture of their rights and responsibilities. Many larger organisations employ legal specialists whose job it is to be familiar with relevant laws and to communicate appropriate information to other members of their organisations.

Technological influences

Technological influences and changes have been with us since the dawn of civilisation. However, today the pace of technological change is very rapid. Innovation and change is the order of the day, and all organisations need to update their approaches continually.

Environmental influences

A major spin-off of economic and technological changes has been the threat to the environment that new developments present. Natural and man-made environments have always affected the ways in which organisations operate. Today, however, there is greater awareness of this influence, and for many organisations there is a fear that environmental deterioration can cause very real problems.

Task

For this task you should work in groups of three or four. You will be considering a specific outside influence on one large company, British Airports Authority plc.

BAA is at present the world's largest international airport group. It owns eight UK airports, handling in total 70 per cent of UK passenger traffic and 85 per cent of air cargo. The airports owned by this group are at:

Aberdeeen	Stanstead
Edinburgh	Heathrow
Glasgow	Gatwick
Prestwick	Southampton

The following are some financial and other results for the company in the 12-month period up to 31 March 1991:

Revenue	£834 million
Profit before tax	£247 million
Earnings per share	37·8 pence
Tangible fixed assets	£2875 million
Capital expenditure	£503 million
Passengers	72 million
of which on international flights	56.9 million
Air transport movements	791 000
Cargo	968 000 tonnes

A very important source of revenue for BAA is **duty free sales**, and nearly half of this revenue comes from customers travelling between countries in the European Community (EC).

However, the European Commission has proposed thatduty free sales in this category are to be abolished. Although to date no final decision has been made by the Council of Ministers on this important issue, BAA accepts that ultimately intra-Community duty free sales will cease, but that a lengthy transition period may be required to make the necessary adjustments.

Task
- You and your group make up a Working Party of senior BAA managers. You are all very busy but have managed to meet for 30 minutes.
- You are aware of the potential loss of revenue to BAA resulting from the European Commission's proposals. You have to produce an outline proposal or series of proposals to be considered by the BAA Board of Directors at their next board meeting.
- Try to agree on five major proposals. The proposals should be headed as follows: 'Suggested proposals to offset any revenue losses from the proposed abolition of intra-community duty and tax free sales'.

· THE ECONOMIC FRAMEWORK ·

We can look at the effect of the **economy** on organisations at a number of levels. Organisations may be as directly affected by local changes as by national or international ones. For example, the closure of the American naval base at Dunoon will hit local people harder than would the effects of a world recession. **Macroeconomics** is the study of large-scale economic changes that tend to affect the whole of a nation's economy. However, we should always remember that 'macro' trends affect different groups and individuals in different ways.

The national economy can be seen as a systems model (see Figure 2.2). Organisations use inputs such as labour and machinery to create goods and services. If the demand for goods is higher than the stock available, then organisations will employ more inputs to increase production. Prices may start to rise (scarcity) and unemployment to fall (more jobs). On the other hand, if supply is greater than demand there will be unsold stocks and companies may begin to discard workers, to invest less in new machinery, and to reduce prices. This is a simple model of the economy.

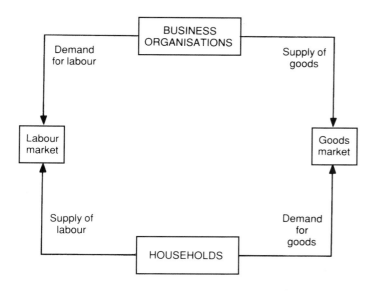

Figure 2.2 *Simple systems model of a national economy*

A more complex model of the economy

The simple model of the economy in Figure 2.2 shows that it is made up of two basic groups – **business organisations** and **households**. Households supply labour and other factors of production to organisations (e.g. funds for investment). In return households receive incomes for their services, which they then spend on the outputs produced by businesses. If the businesses supply products that households wish to purchase, then this system will work very well. Indeed, in a market economy led by market-conscious business units, although some goods will be temporarily unsold, new products will be developed to replace those that are outmoded. Firms employ labour and other factors. Firms supply goods and services to the market. Firms also purchase capital items (e.g. machinery), raw materials and partly finished goods in the market-place.

Task

Using examples of a household and a business organisation with which you are familiar, show that:

a the household (i) provides factor services to the market economy, (ii) earns income from these services, and (iii) purchases goods from producers

b the business organisation (i) buys factor services, (ii) buys raw materials, and (iii) buys capital equipment and semi-finished goods.

In the real world, economies are more complex. We need to add government and international transactions to our model. The government buys and sells goods. For example, the government buys armaments and health care in the market-place, and it sells products and services such as the outputs of its nationalised industries. The government is the major purchaser of goods in the United Kingdom.

Trading between nations is also significant. Finished goods, partly finished goods, raw materials and foodstuffs are imported and exported. The service sector (e.g. financial services) also accounts for a considerable volume of trade.

We therefore need to represent government activities and international trade in a more complex model. This is shown in Figure 2.3.

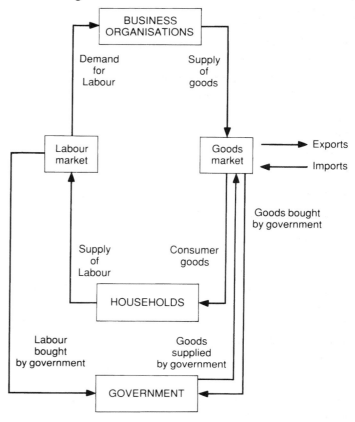

Figure 2.3 *Labour and goods markets in an open economy with government*

Aggregate demand

Aggregate demand is the total level of demand in the whole economy. Aggregate demand is made up of:

- demand by consumers for goods and services (call this C)
- demand by producers for goods that go into further production (call this I, for investment demand)
- government demand for goods and services (call this G).

Furthermore we need to *add* the demand from foreigners for our goods and services (exports, X), and *subtract* the demand (M) by our citizens for foreign goods and services, because money leaves the country. A useful measure of aggregate money demand is therefore:

> **Aggregate money demand** = C + I + G + X – M

We have said that the amount people spend in an economy will be received by the providers of goods and services. If we want to be absolutely accurate, however, we should account for indirect **taxes** and **subsidies**.

If you buy a packet of sandwiches in a bakery the owner of the bakery will not be able to use all this money in his business. Some of the revenue will be paid over to the government in VAT (value-added tax) and other indirect taxes. When measuring aggregate money demand, therefore, we should *subtract* indirect taxes. Furthermore, some sellers will receive more than the sales price of their goods, probably as a result of government subsidies. A subsidy should therefore be seen as an *addition* to consumer demand, provided by the government. A more comprehensive definition of aggregate money demand (AMD) is therefore:

> AMD = C + I + G + X – M – indirect taxes + subsidies

Aggregate demand and aggregate supply

When aggregate money demand in the economy *equals* aggregate money supply (AMS), then the economy is in temporary equilibrium. If this state of equilibrium remains then prices will remain steady, and so too will the level of production (see Figure 2.4).

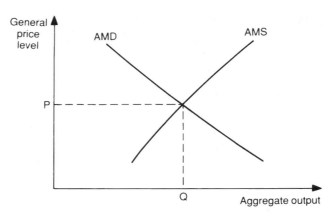

Figure 2.4 *AMD = AMS*

However, in the real world economic forces are continually changing. Conditions of aggregate demand and supply frequently alter, and economies tend to go through a **trade cycle** (see Figure 2.5). For a few years demand increases, prices start to rise, and unem-ployment to fall. This is followed by a period of slump when prices fall and unemployment increases again.

Indicators

During a boom, a number of **economic indicators** related to demand all tend to increase. The main indicators are:

- production
- employment
- sales.
- interest rates
- investment

During a recession these indicators then fall.

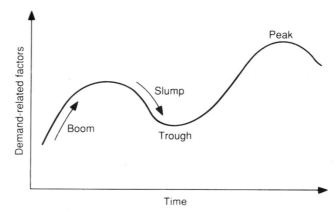

Figure 2.5 *The trade cycle*

Task

Study some economic reports in a national newspaper. Are the commentators talking about a period of boom or recession? Are we near to a peak or a trough? When is the economy expected to slow down or warm up? What problems are caused by the current position in the trade cycle?

Unemployment and inflation

Unemployment and inflation are economic problems which have repercussions for a large number of individuals and organisations. When **unemployment** is at a high level, the population as a whole has less money to spend, and this affects many firms and industries. In a period of **inflation**, rising prices are likely to affect everybody in one way or another.

There is always considerable disagreement over the exact number of unemployed people in the UK at any time, because only those receiving state benefits and registered for work are counted in the **official statistics**. This misses out some married women who, if their husbands are working, cannot receive benefit. People on various training schemes are also not included, nor are men over 60 who have been unemployed for a long time. The unemployment figures therefore depend very much on the way they are collected.

The RPI

Inflation is also measured in several different ways. To the government, inflation means a general increase in the level of prices. Statisticians use the **retail price index** (RPI), which is an average of price changes and shows the general change over a period of time. Some items in the index will rise, some will remain the same, others will fall.

The RPI is calculated in the following way. About 7000 households throughout the UK keep a record of all their spending over a two-week period. This gives a picture of the 'typical items' bought by an 'average household'. The items are recorded in the index. Each month, government officers make a record of about 150 000 prices of some 350 different items up and down the country. The average price of each of these items is calculated.

Using these data the average inflation rate can be calculated. Each individual price change is given a 'weight' which depends on how important it is in the typical household's spending pattern. For example, food makes up about one-fifth of a typical household's spending, so that a 10 per cent rise in the price of food would raise average prices by one-fifth of this – 2 per cent.

Price changes are measured over a definite period of time so that it is possible to compare the changes from one period to another. The matter of choosing a starting (or 'base') date for an index is important, the aim being to choose a time which is 'normal' – that is, when nothing abnormal or unusual is happening.

The base date is given an index of 100. We can then say, for example, that if in 1974 the RPI stood at 100 and today it is 350, prices *on average* have risen three and a half times over that time.

Calculating the RPI

In an imaginary country, Averageland, Mr Average spends half his income on food, a quarter on clothing and the remaining quarter on entertainment. We can thus give these items 'weightings' out of 10: food 5, clothing $2\frac{1}{2}$, entertainment $2\frac{1}{2}$. In 1974 (the base year) food cost on average £1 per unit, clothing £5 per unit, and entertainment £2 per unit. In 1990, food in Averageland cost £2 per unit, clothing £7.50 per unit, and entertainment £3.00 per unit. We can analyse these changes in prices as follows:

	Original index	New index	Expenditure weighting	New index $\times$ weighting
Food	100	200	5	1000
Clothing	100	150	$2\frac{1}{2}$	375
Entertainment	100	150	$2\frac{1}{2}$	375

The total of the last column is 1750. In order to find out the new RPI in Averageland we must divide this total by the total number of weights (10), so:

$$\text{New RPI} = \frac{1750}{10} = 175$$

This shows that, *on average,* prices rose by 75 per cent. Food doubled in price, whereas the other two items increased by one and a half times. Food was the most significant item in the index because Mr Average spends as much on food as on clothing and entertainment combined.

Task

Do Mr or Mrs Average exist in the real world? Is the answer to this question important either to individual families or to the government?

Task

- In Redland, the average consumer spends seven-tenths of his or her income on wine, two-tenths on bread and one-tenth on cheese. In 1993 (the base year) the price of all these items was £1 per unit. In 1989 wine had fallen to 50p per unit, bread had gone up to £2 per unit and cheese had risen to £4 per unit.

a What is the new index for 1993?
b Has it risen, fallen or remained the same?
c Give at least three reasons why the weighting might need to be altered in 1993.

- In Blueland, the public buy four items – eggs, cheese, bread and salt. Four-tenths of their income is spent on cheese, and two-tenths on each of the other three items. Between 1960 (the base year) and 1994, eggs doubled in price, cheese went up by 50 per cent, bread remained the same and salt went down by 10 per cent. Calculate the new index relative to the base year.

WHAT CAUSES ECONOMIC BOOM OR SLUMP?

This is a very complex question, and in any good library there are shelves full of books devoted to the subject. The analysis that we give here presents a very simplified view.

Booms and slumps arise almost inevitably from changes in market **demand** and market **supply** on a grand scale. On the **demand side**, changes in demand are likely to come from:

- consumers
- investment decisions
- governments
- exports.

Consumer demand varies with incomes. When incomes are rising people are likely to spend more. When people have more **disposable income** they will spend more – for example when taxes are lowered. People are also likely to spend more when it is easier to borrow money, and the cost of borrowing (i.e. the interest rate) is low.

Investment demand is likely to be high when the economy appears to be booming. At this time business people will be optimistic – they can expect good returns on their investments. Investment by businesses will also be higher when interest rates fall, because loans are less expensive.

Government demand is likely to be higher when the government is trying to encourage a boom. This may be to reduce unemployment or to make people feel better before an election. A government will also spend more if it believes this to be the right thing to do. For example, a government may feel that it has an important role in securing high standards of health care and education.

Export demand is likely to be high when a country's products are relatively cheap on world markets. The volume of world trade is likely to be highest when there is a general world boom.

Demand will be lower in situations which are the opposite of those outlined above.

On the **supply side**, output is likely to increase when goods can be produced more efficiently. This may be because factors of production become more effective, there are fewer problems in the production process, or when technology improves.

THE GOVERNMENT'S ROLE IN THE ECONOMY

In the nineteenth century the UK government played only a small part in the control of the economy. Today, the most desirable role of the government in this sphere is open to debate, but most people accept that it should at least try to influence economic activity. Why has this change in attitude taken place? We shall look at some of the more important reasons.

Widespread unemployment in the 1920s and 1930s
In some towns in the 1920s, over half of the potential labour force were unemployed. Many people felt in the light of the terrible suffering during this period that the government should play a central role in **creating and sustaining employment**.

Rapid inflation in the 1970s
The 1970s was a period of rapid increases in prices. People felt the effects of inflation in different ways, depending amongst other things on how much power they had to raise their own incomes to cope with price rises.

The general effect of price rises is to distort the working of the price system. Trading ideally needs to take place in settled price conditions. If you expect to be paid £100 in three months' time you will be very disappointed to find that when you receive payment you can only purchase half of the goods that you would have been able to obtain today.

If people become reluctant to trade, then fewer goods will be produced to sell. If fewer goods are made, fewer people are employed in production. Price disturbances can therefore cause the whole economy to stagnate.

The Citizens' Charter
Many industries previously owned by the government – such as telecommunications, fuel and power – have been privatised (sold to shareholders). Other industries, such as rail and coal, may be privatised in the future.

Services such as health and education operate in the 1990s far more on the basis of local management. This means that local managers (such as headteachers and school governing bodies) are responsible for spending their own budgets in the way they see fit to use resources effectively in their own areas. However, the government still continues to play the major role in providing funds from taxes and other sources – government spending still accounts for nearly a half of all spending in the country.

The other side of this story is that there is far more emphasis on public accountibility. Local managers need to be able to show how they are spending their funds. They need to manage their budgets wisely. Citizens are to be given far more right to complain. For example, under the government's **Citizens' Charter** rail-users will be entitled to refunds of their fares if trains fail to run on time, and motorway contractors can be fined for coning off sections of road when no work is taking place.

Task

Look at a copy of the Citizens' Charter at your local library. Outline some of the major changes it sets out to make public servants more accountable for their actions. The Citizens' Charter was drawn up by a Conservative government, but the Labour Party has also published its own charter. How is this similar to and different from the Conservative government's charter?

Today all governments, whether they like it or not, are heavily involved in macro-economic management e.g. the decision of the Conservative Government to withdraw the United Kingdom from the EC's European Exchange Rate Mechanism (ERM) and subsequent pressure to return to it, (See also page 75.)

GOVERNMENT AROUND US

In Britain the government plays a very big part in all our lives. It encourages individuals and organisations to do some things and discourages other activities. As a person grows from childhood to adulthood a multitude of rules and regulations come and go. Here are a few:

5 You become of 'compulsory school age'.
You can see a U or PG category film at a cinema unaccompanied.

You have to pay child's fare on trains, and on buses and tubes in London.
You can drink alcohol in private – for example at home.

7 You can open and draw money from a National Savings Bank account.

10 You can be convicted of a criminal offence if it is proved you knew what you were doing was wrong.
If you are guilty of homicide you could be detained 'during Her Majesty's pleasure' for a specific period – including a life sentence.

12 You can buy a pet.
You can be trained to participate in dangerous public entertainments subject to the grant of a local authority licence.

13 You can get a part-time job, but there are restrictions – for example, you cannot work for more than two hours on a school day or a Sunday.

14 You can go into a pub but you cannot buy or drink alcohol there.
You can possess a shotgun, airgun, air rifle, or ammunition.
A boy can be convicted or rape, assault with intent to commit rape and unlawful sexual intercourse with a girl under 16.
You may be employed on a weekday as a street trader by your parents.

15 If you are a boy you can be sent to prison to await trial.
You can see a category 15 film.
You can open a Post Office Girobank account.

16 You can leave school.
You can marry with parental consent.
A girl can consent to sexual intercourse.
A boy can join the armed forces with parental consent.
You can buy cigarettes and tobacco.
You can have beer, cider or wine with a meal in a restaurant.
You can enter or live in a brothel.

17 Criminal charges against you will be dealt with in the adult courts.
You can hold a driving licence.

18 You are an adult in the eyes of the law.
You can vote in elections.
You can serve on a jury.
You can buy alcohol in a bar.

21 A man may consent to a 'homosexual act' in private with a partner over 21.
You can become an MP.
You can hold a driving licence for a heavy goods vehicle or large passenger vehicle.
You can apply for a licence to sell alcohol.

The above examples illustrate just a few of the ways in which the government limits or allows the activities of young people. In the same way, there are literally thousands of regulations and laws that encourage or constrain the activities of organisations. Throughout this book you will come across relevant laws and regulations in such areas as the protection of consumers, rights in the workplace and government controls over the powers of large firms in the market-place.

The electoral system

In the United Kingdom citizens are able to choose people to represent them at a number of levels.

At a *national* level they can choose Members of Parliament. MPs represent people who live in a particular area (a constituency). Who is your local MP? What is your local constituency? What political party does your local MP belong to?

At a *European Community* level, electors can choose Euro-MPs. The European Parliament is one of the three major Community institutions. It is the only directly elected institution, so it is doubly important that all European citizens exercise their right to vote. The Maastricht Treaty has given the European Parliament more powers, as we shall see later. Who is your Euro-MP? What Party do they belong to? What is your Euro-constituency?

At a *local* level you can vote for local councillors. The local council is concerned with affairs in your locality. What is your local council area? Who is your local councillor? What party does he or she belong to?

The electoral system for national government

In the British electoral system the country is divided into 651 single-member constituencies. Representatives are elected to Parliament by the first-past-the-post (simple majority) method, which awards seats in the House of Commons to the candidates with the largest number of votes in each constituency. The boundaries of the constituencies are reviewed every 10–15 years to take account of population movements or other changes.

Under this system the strongest party in the House of Commons may have an absolute majority of seats with less than an absolute majority of votes. The system is generally considered to favour two-party competition, especially between parties whose support is concentrated geographically, and to discriminate against parties with support spread across constituencies. For example, the Liberal Democrats currently have a lot of support spread across the country, but only in parts of the West Country do they have the majority of voters behind them. The Labour Party is particularly popular in inner London, the North East and North West. The Conservative Party has the bulk of the support in the South of England.

Forming a government

The party which wins most seats at a general election, or which has the support of a majority of members in the House of Commons, is usually invited by the Sovereign to form a govenment. The party with the next largest number of seats is officially recognised as 'Her Majesty's Opposition', which has its own leader (who is paid a salary from public funds) and its own 'shadow cabinet'. Members of both parties, or any independent MPs who have been elected, support or oppose the government according to their party or their own view of the policy being debated at any given time. Because the official Opposition is a minority party, it seldom succeeds in introducing or changing legislation. However, its statements and policies are important, since it is considered to be a potential government – and would become so if successful at the next general election.

The law

Parliament is responsible for creating new laws which affect the economic life of the country in may ways. These new laws therefore affect businesses. If the government raises income tax rates, for example, people have less money to spend, which affects sales. Government actions bring into play a wide range of changes to taxes – these changes then become law through a Finance Bill, which becomes an Act of Parliament (a new law).

Tasks

1 Make a list of three ways in which government regulations influence activities (i) in your school or college, and (ii) on roads and motorways.

2 Write a commentary on a rule change that is currently taking place and which is having an affect on businesses in your community. Perhaps you can interview some local business people to find out what their views are about the proposed changes.

Case Study

A privatisation

This case shows many of the complex steps that had to be carried out in privatising British Gas in 1986.

In 1948, the gas industry had been nationalised by the Labour Party in government. However, the Conservative Party from 1979 onwards was keen to privatise a range of industries. Detailed plans were set out by civil servants to prepare the privatisation process. On 7 May 1985 the plan was announced to a packed House of Commons.

A Bill had then to be presented to the House of Commons for discussion, as well as to smaller committees of Members of Parliament who also raised questions and raised issues. bills need to be presented three times to the House of Commons – with amendments normally being made at each stage. The Bill then has to be presented to the House of Lords for approval. The Lords

British Gas

November 1986: Shares in British Gas launched on the stock market

24 August 1986: The State owned British Gas Corporation ceases to exist, and British Gas PLC established

18 August 1986: The Office of Gas Supply – the regulator of the industry – established

During first half of 1986: Government makes a series of announcements about the brokers who will handle the sale

25 July 1986: Bill receives Royal Assent

1948: Gas is nationalised

1973: The British Gas Corporation is established – a nationalised industry, responsible for finding, distributing and selling gas

21 July 1986: Commons consider, and agree, Lords' amendments to bill

17 July 1986: Third reading of bill in Lords

24 April – 9 July 1986: Bill considered in committee and then on report, over ten days

10 April 1986: Lords second reading

26 March 1986: Bill arrives in the Lords

25 March 1986: Third reading of bill in Chamber

17 March 1986: Report stage of bill

May 1979: Conservative government elected

1981: British Telecom successfully privatised

1982: Ministers begin to think of future privatisation plans

June 1983: Conservative government re-elected

17 December 1985–6 March 1986: Bill considered in standing committee, over 32 sittings

10 December 1985: Commons second reading

28 November 1985: Formal publication of Gas Bill – first reading in the Commons

May–November 1985: The bill is drafted

September 1983: Department of Energy civil servants begin work on plans to privatise gas industry

April 1985: Cabinet agrees that gas should be privatised in the next parliamentary session

7 May 1985: Plans announced publicly by a statement to the House of Commons

are able to suggest further amendments. The Bill is then presented back in the Commons. Once the Bill has been approved it is presented to the Queen for her Royal Assent, when it becomes another Act of Parliament. At the end of this process British Gas plc became a legally recognised body.

Over the years a complex system of laws has developed. Some laws have not come from Parliament but have arisen through common practice. It is often impossible to find out when these laws first came into being (this is called **'common law'**). An example is the right of people to walk on a particular village green. Other laws are new laws that are passed by Parliament this is called **'statute law'**.

The law courts have an important role in protecting the rights of individuals and groups. When the law of the land has been broken cases are taken to the criminal courts, whereas when there is a disagreement between groups or individuals the case may be taken before a civil court.

Task

Which of the following would be taken to a criminal court and which to a civil court?

a A firm catches one of its employees stealing the firm's property.

b A firm is taken to court for making its employees work longer than the national legal limit.

c A newspaper prints an inaccurate and defamatory story about the managing director of a major company.

d A consumer buys a product which fails to meet the standard claimed in advertising.

e A farmer claims that when a neighbour dams a river it is cutting off his water supply.

f An employee who is sacked by his employer claims that he has not received sufficient compensation.

g Two publishers produce books with the same title and with similar covers.

The legal framework

United Kingdom competition law is made up of four principal Acts of Parliament, dealing with separate aspects of competition policy. They are the Fair Trading Act 1973, the Restrictive Trade Practices Act 1976, the Resale Prices Act 1976 and the Competition Act 1980. Each Act gives the Director General of the OFT and the Commission, or the Restrictive Practices Court, different responsibilities.

These laws can be split into two categories:

- In the case of the Restrictive Trade Practices Act and the Resale Prices Act, action is taken in the courts.
- In the case of the Fair Trading Act and the Competition Act, practices are examined by the Director General, the Commission and the Secretary of State.

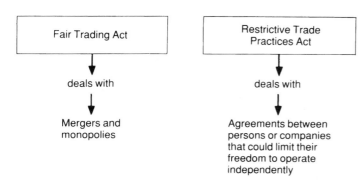

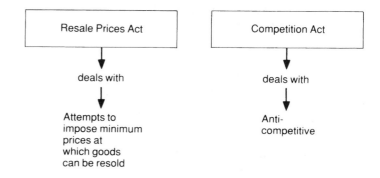

Figure 2.5 *Four competition Acts*

Keep a diary of newspaper cuttings dealing with cases involving the four laws relating to competition. What happens to companies that infringe these laws?

Monopolies

Where a company or group of companies has market power, there is the potential for the market to be harmed in a number of ways. Excessive prices, reductions in the level of service and unfair restrictions on entry into the market are typical examples of what can happen, in the absence of effective competition. This will harm consumers.

Defining a monopoly

Although we normally think of a **monopoly** as the sole supplier to a particular market, United Kingdom law uses a wider definition. Under the Fair Trading Act, a monopoly is defined first as a situation where a company supplies or buys 25 per cent or more of all goods or services of a particular type in the whole country or in a particular area (e.g. the South East).

The Act also defines a complex monopoly as a situation where a group of companies that together have 25 per cent of the market all behave in some way that affects competition.

Task

Think of examples of national or local monopolies. In each
case try to suggest why the monopoly position might help consumers, or be harmful to them. How would you go about testing this?

Figure 2.6 *How monopoly malpractices are handled*

The public interest

There is no assumption that monopolies are wrong in themselves. The invention of a new device, for example, will inevitably make the inventor a monopolist to start with, even if the device provides a benefit to the public. The 1973 Act simply defines situations where it is *possible* that market power could be misused, and recognises that this *may* be against the public interest. It is for the Commission to say what is and what is not in **the public interest.**

Dealing with monopolies

The Director General keeps a constant eye on British industry, looking at how major companies are operating, and at allegations and complaints.

Once he or she feels that there may be evidence of monopoly malpractice in a particular industry, the case is referred to the Commission. However, at this stage no companies are named; it is simply suggested that the Commission should investigate a particular aspect of competition (e.g. prices) in that industry.

The Commission then investigates and makes a report to the Secretary of State, with suggestions for possible action. The Secretary and the Director General then decide what should be done. This might involve asking companies to make promises to change, or asking for promises backed up with measures to make sure that the promises are kept.

Case Study

Newspaper distribution

In October 1991, the Office of Fair Trading decided not to refer the distribution of national newspapers to the Monopolies and Mergers Commission. The decision was described as a gross injustice by the National Federation of Retail Newsagents, which represents about 30 000 small newsagents and which campaigned for the enquiry.

Newspaper and magazine distribution in the UK is dominated by three wholesalers which account for more than 80 per cent of the market between them. WH Smith speaks for a 45 per cent share, followed by John Menzies at about 25 per cent and Surridge Dawson at around 10 per cent. The balance is accounted for by local wholesalers.

Newsagents are worried about changes in the distribution network which have led to major wholesalers obtaining exclusive distribution rights for titles in a particular area. The complaints were about a lack of alternative wholesalers for newspapers and magazines in their area, increases in carriage charges, and being forced to stock publications they did not want. Although the OFT admitted there were restraints on competition in the way newspapers were

distributed, 'it could see no reason for believing that there is any loss to the public sufficient to justify a reference'.

However, the OFT was concerned that there may be restrictive agreements between wholesalers. It was considering court action against one such local agreement in the Blackpool–Preston area. The OFT found that one wholesaler had agreed not to supply certain newspapers and magazines to newsagents in the Preston area in return for another wholesaler agreeing not to supply these newspapers and magazines in the Blackpool area.

1 Why is there considered to be a monopoly situation in newspaper and magazine distribution?
2 Why did retailers want this monopoly position to be investigated?
3 What does your local newsagent think? Perhaps you can also find out what the local wholesale manager thinks.
4 Does the article present any evidence of unfair monopoly practices?
5 Why do you think the OFT decided not to refer this case to the Commission?
6 Do you think the Director General was justified in failing to call for an investigation?

Anti-competitive practices

In a competitive market, companies can be expected to adopt policies intended to give them a competitive edge. This can lead to benefits in terms of efficiency, better

Figure 2.7 *Market power*

quality goods and services, and so on. However, sometimes firms use practices which may be harmful to competition. Practices that may be acceptable in one market where competition is strong may be unacceptable in another where there is less competitive activity.

Under the Competition Act, an **anti-competitive practice** is defined as *any practice that has, or is intended to have, or is likely to have the effect of restricting or preventing competition.*

The ability of a firm to influence the market depends on its **market power**. Market power stems from having a large share of the market, having a leading brand name, or being able in some way to prevent new firms from entering the industry (perhaps as a result of patent rights). Companies are covered by the Act if they have more than 25 per cent of a market or a turnover of more than £5 million.

If an alleged anti-competitive practice is reported to the Director General, he or she can set up an investigative team to look into it. On the basis of the investigation the Director General must decide whether he or she thinks that it is anti-competitive. If it is felt to be so, the practice can be referred to the Commission which must decide whether it is against the public interest. A report is then produced within a period of four to eight weeks. The Secretary of State and the Director General may then insist that the businesses involved abandon the practice if it is felt to be unacceptable.

Resale price maintenance

Attempts by manufacturers or suppliers to enforce a minimum price at which their goods can be resold by dealers or retailers restricts competition and can keep prices higher than they would be otherwise. Resale price maintenance is unlawful under the Resale Prices Act except for goods granted an exemption. Goods exempted at present are books and pharmaceuticals.

Task

Why do you think that books and pharmaceuticals are exempted by the Resale Prices Act? Try to find out by interviewing somebody in the book trade. You may find that different opinions are given by the small and the large bookshops.

Under the 1976 Act it is unlawful to try to establish minimum prices. It is also unlawful to stop supplies or to offer less favourable terms to dealers whom the supplier believes to be responsible for price cutting. A supplier is, however, entitled to withhold goods from a dealer who is pricing them as 'loss leaders' (that is, as goods sold at a loss in order to attract customers towards profitable items).

The Director General has the power to seek a court injunction to force the parties involved to scrap a retail price agreement.

Mergers

Under the Fair Trading Act, a **merger** is said to take place when two or more companies 'cease to be distinct'. The aim of competition policy is not to prejudge mergers but to examine the merits of individual mergers. The advantages in each case must be weighed up against the disadvantages.

The 1973 Act lays down two tests to decide whether a particular merger can be investigated:

- *the assets test* – that the total gross assets of the company to be taken over exceed £30 million in value
- *the market-share test* – that, as a result of the merger, 25 per cent or more of the supply or purchase of goods or services of a particular description in the United Kingdom or a substantial part of it comes under the control of the merging enterprise.

The critical factor in deciding whether a merger should be allowed to take place is again the public interest. Those most likely to cause concern are horizontal mergers, where two companies supplying the same sort of product or service combine. However, vertical and conglomerate mergers may also be investigated.

Companies are expected to notify the Director General if they hope to merge. The Director General will conduct a preliminary investigation before deciding whether to advise the Secretary of State to refer the merger to the Commission. Companies are stopped from acquiring each other's shares while the investigation takes place. If they have already started to merge they will be ordered not to join their operations together. The Commission reports to the Secretary of State who decides, in consultation with the Director General, whether or not the merger is in the public interest.

A merger in the public interest?

Two companies are hoping to merge. At present one company has 32 per cent of the market and the other has 26 per cent. The assets of each company are in excess of £50 million.

These companies both manufacture finished goods for retail sale. Because of the perceived high quality of their product, they will only deal with selected retail outlets, and under the new (merged) company structure these outlets will be allowed to sell the product only if they agree to a mark-up of exactly 35 per cent. In addition there will be a number of regulations as to how the product can be displayed and offered to customers. The companies are confident that the new company will shortly capture all of this exciting and rapidly developing market.

Prices are expected to remain high in this industry, and product performance and quality are likely to improve rapidly with breakthroughs in research and development. The UK is a world leader in this product, and many new jobs will be created. UK prices compare favourably with those of the foreign competition.

1 List the facts making it likely that this proposed merger would be referred to the Commission.
2 What arguments can be put in favour of this merger?
3 What do you think the likely outcome would be?

Restrictive trade practices

All commerce is based on agreements of one form or another. The buying and selling of goods and services would be impossible without them. In such agreements, businesses agree to do certain things. However, some of these commitments may restrict competition.

The Restrictive Trades Practices Act covers agreements affecting goods and services. Companies must **register** certain types of agreement that they make with other companies. These may cover all sorts or areas, including:

- restrictions on prices or charges
- conditions on which business is conducted
- geographical divisions of business
- people with whom business can take place
- the quantity of goods to be produced
- the manufacturing process to be used.

Agreements can be in any form, including the spoken word. All such agreements must be registered.

The Director General of Fair Trading refers suspect agreements to the Restrictive Practices Court, which will strike down any restrictions found to be against the public interest. Parties to an agreement therefore need to be able to prove to the Court that there are real benefits from their restrictive practices.

Describe the roles of the following in the United Kingdom's competition policy:

a the Director General of Fair Trading
b the Secretary of State for Trade and Industry
c the Monopolies and Mergers Commission
d the Restrictive Practices Court.

. EUROPEAN COMMUNITY . COMPETITION LAW

The European Community has its own competition regulations which in a number of cases go above and beyond national laws. Article 85 of the Treaty of Rome forbids agreements which may adversely affect trade between the 12 member states, and in particular which have as their object a limitation of competition within the European market. This includes price fixing, market sharing, restriction of production or technical development, and the imposition of discriminatory terms of supply. Such agreements are automatically not allowed unless given an exemption by the European Commission.

A European Merger Control Regulation allows the European Commission to control mergers which have a 'community dimension'. This is defined as those mergers where the parties have a total worldwide turnover exceeding 5 billion ECU and at least two of the parties have a Community turnover exceeding 250 million ECU unless each of the undertakings achieves more than two-thirds of its turnover in one and the same Member State. Special rules apply for banking, financial, and insurance institutions.

The role of the European Commission

The European Commission is directly responsible for the application of European legislation in the United Kingdom. The Commission may act on the basis of agreements which have been made before them, on complaints or on their own initiative. They may seek information in writing or by inspectors making visits to firms who would always be accompanied by staff from the Director General's Office. Commission inspectors have wide-ranging powers to ask questions and to obtain information. Before deciding that a law has been broken, the Commission issues a statement of objection to the parties concerned, who then have the opportunity to reply to the Commission, both in writing and orally, before representatives of Member States. The European Commission also hears the opinion of an advisory committee of competition experts from Member States, including a representative of the Director General.

Task

The section above looks in detail at UK competition policy. You should sort out the detail and concentrate on:

a understanding the four main areas covered by legislation

b the main officials responsible for putting these laws into effect

c actions which can be taken to create a more competitive environment.

A good way of studying this area is to follow cases reported in the press. This should reinforce the idea of varying interpretations of the 'public interest'.

Case Study

Restrictive practices by Tetra Pak

In October 1991, the European Commission fined Tetra Pak, the Swedish/Swiss company that invented sterilised packaging for liquids, a record £52.5 million for abuse of its dominant market position. The Commission's investigation began as the result of a complaint in 1983 by an Italian competitor, Elopak.

Tetra Pak was accused primarily of adopting restrictive contract clauses. Sir Leon Brittan, the Commissioner responsible for competition policy, said: 'The infringements have involved almost all products manufactured by Tetra Pak and have had a damaging impact on competition in all EC member states.'

By insisting that customers use only Tetra Pak packaging machines and cartons, the company effectively stifled competition. Product guarantees were made dependent on this commitment. The company also controlled delivery and fitting of spare parts for machinery owned or rented, and in many contracts imposed a monthly maintenance charge that was adjusted in line with customer loyalty rather than the actual maintenance required.

Rental agreements ran for a minimum of three years – nine in the case of Italy – and sometimes included punitive discretionary penalties for companies that allowed contracts to lapse. Carton labelling and, in some cases, monthly reports were required of clients, who risked finding themselves host to surprise inspections.

The measures ensured that the company could safely adopt predatory pricing policies. The costs of machines and cartons in different member states varied by factors of 300 per cent and 50 per cent respectively.

Tetra Pak is appealing to the European Court of Justice.

1 Why was the European Commission concerned with this case of abuse?
2 What seem to be the most telling allegations of abuse against Tetra Pak?
3 Give examples of the restrictive practices involved.
4 Which of these practices seem to be in the public interest and which against the public interest?

5 *Why do you think Tetra Pak employed these restrictive practices?*

6 *What do you think will be the verdict of the Court of Justice?*

MAIN OBJECTIVES OF GOVERNMENT ECONOMIC POLICY

In an ideal situation there would be no price increase, no unemployment, a steady growth of national output, a healthy trading position with other countries, and a steady and predictable exchange rate between our currency and those of other nations. However, in the real world prices increase, there are unacceptable levels of unemployment, national output increases in stops and starts, there are frequent balance-of-payments problems, and the exchange rate goes through highs and lows.

These five variables are the central focus for government economic controls. The way in which the government tries to influence these variables is very important. Government economic policies affect organisations in a direct way.

GOVERNMENT CONTROL OF THE ECONOMY

In this section we look at three different ways of dealing with the economy. Each way is supported by people with different views as to how the economy works. The three policies we look at are:

- laissez-faire
- demand-side economics
- supply-side economics.

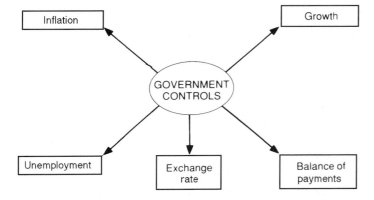

Figure 2.8 *Government controls on economic variables*

Laissez-faire policy

The French expression *laissez-faire* means 'leave it alone'. It therefore signifies government non-interference in the economy.

The theory behind laissez-faire is that free markets will lead to the best use of resources. If people want goods they will choose them by voting (with their money) for them to be produced. They will also make themselves available for work so that they can earn money to buy goods. Employers will employ labour so long as they can make a profit.

This theory was applied throughout the nineteenth century. The economy grew rapidly and many new products were invented and developed. When some goods become old-fashioned they are replaced by new goods. Wages fall in some industries and rise in other industries. Some people will temporarily be unemployed, but they will be taken up in the newer industries. The natural state of affairs for the economy is thus one of full employment.

The mass unemployment of the 1920s could be explained by the fact that trade unions and other groups did not allow wages to fall in a period of recession. If wages and other prices had fallen then employers would have been prepared to employ labour in the new growing industries.

Demand-side economics

Demand-side economics was developed to provide an alternative explanation of the massive unemployment of the twenties and thirties. Much of the early work in this field was carried out by the economist John Maynard Keynes. Keynes argued that full employment was just one possible state for the economy.

Keynes maintained that the factors which create supply do not always lead to a demand for goods. Earners of money do not always spend it. This can lead to a fall in national expenditure, and to a reduction in output as suppliers are not able to sell stocks of goods.

We can illustrate this theory by using a circular flow diagram. In Figure 14.7, all income earned by households is re-spent by them on goods and services.

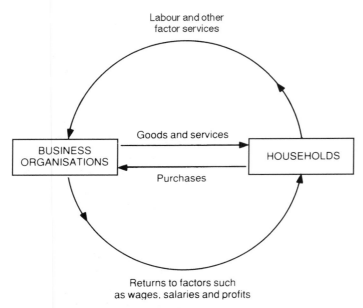

Figure 2.9 *The simple circular flow diagram*

In the real world, however, we do not re-spend all our incomes on domestically produced goods. Some of our money is *saved*, some goes in *taxes*, and some goes on *imports*. In other words, some money is *leaked* from the circular flow.

At the same time, money demand is injected back into the system in the form of *investment* by businesses in new equipment and machinery. Some money demand is injected by *government expenditure* and some money demand is injected by *export* sales (see Figure 2.10).

If we look at the demand side of the picture, we can see that aggregate monetary demand is made up of

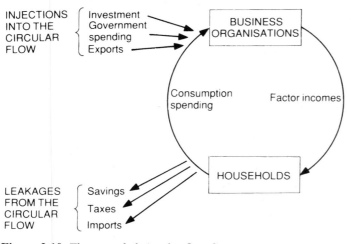

Figure 2.10 *The amended circular flow diagram*

consumers' expenditure, investment expenditure, government expenditure, and exports. In the real world there is no guarantee that the total of this demand will be sufficient to create full employment. Indeed, demand fluctuates from one month to the next.

In particular, investment demand is quite volatile. If business people are confident that the economy will boom for a period of time they will be keen to invest. However, when they are gloomy they will cut back heavily on investment projects. If you watch business news programmes you will frequently hear references to **business confidence**.

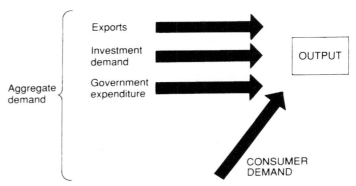

Figure 2.11 *The demand for goods and services*

Task

What is the current state of business confidence in the economy? What are the likely effects for investment?

Changes in demand factors can have a dramatic impact. For example, when a building contractor loses a contract to build a new plant, he or she may have to lay off workers. These workers then forgo their wage packets. They buy less in local shops. The local shops then 'feel the pinch'. They buy in fewer stocks and reduce the overtime of staff. In turn these people have smaller incomes and they spend less.

The multiplier effect

The **multiplier effect** measures the change in total demand in an economy as a result of an initial change in demand. The size of the multiplier depends on the size of the leakages from the circular flow. If leakages are a high proportion of income, then the multiplier will be low, and if leakages are a low proportion of income then the multiplier will be high. The multiplier can be measured mathematically in the following way:

$$\text{Multiplier} = \frac{1}{\text{marginal propensity to leak}}$$

The **marginal propensity to leak** is the fraction of *extra* income earned by the average person which is leaked from the circular flow. It is obtained by adding together the marginal propensity to save, the marginal propensity to be taxed, and the marginal propensity to buy imports.

This sounds complicated but it is not. For example, if the typical citizen saves one-quarter of his or her extra income, is taxed one-eighth of his or her marginal income, and spends one-eighth of marginal income on imports, then the marginal propensity to leak is $\frac{1}{4} + \frac{1}{4} + \frac{1}{8}$, which is $\frac{1}{2}$. If the marginal propensity to leak in the economy is one-half, then the multiplier will be 2.

The multiplier is a useful tool in showing us that a change in aggregate demand will lead to further changes in demand.

The accelerator

The **accelerator** is another simple but useful tool. It shows us that if consumers' demand falls by a little bit, this may have a much bigger consequential effect on the machinery and capital-goods industries.

One way of classifying industry is into companies that produce capital goods and ones that produce consumer

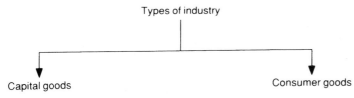

Figure 2.12 *Classification of industry*

goods. Consumer-goods producers buy machinery from the capital-goods industries. Each year they will need to replace machinery that is wearing out. For example, they may replace 10 per cent of their machinery. Now if the economy is in a slump they may not buy any new machinery at all. Just imagine the effect if all consumer-goods producers did the same thing. There would be little demand for capital goods. The capital-goods industry would have a massive downturn in orders. Many capital-goods companies would be crippled. We can therefore say that a relatively small downturn in orders for consumer goods will have a vastly *accelerated* effect on capital-goods companies.

It is not surprising, therefore, that capital-goods producers look carefully at the economic forecasts of booms and slumps. When they are gloomy they will start to make cutbacks, and these cutbacks may be *multiplied* into a slump in consumption which feeds back into an *accelerated* slump in investment. The accelerator and multiplier effects therefore work together.

The impact of demand

Our demand-side analysis so far has shown the tremendous power of demand to influence the fortunes of the economy, and hence of organisations. Falling demand leads to recession, unemployment and wasted resources.

On the other hand, excess demand can lead to rising prices and the effects of inflation. Rising investment can have a multiplied effect on expenditure. The same is true of increases in exports, and government spending or indeed an increase in consumer spending. If demand rises and supply is not able to expand at the same rate, then inflation will result.

The Phillips curve

Most economists recognise that there is a trade-off between unemployment and inflation. If the government is worried about inflation then it will need to dampen down demand. It can do this by, for example, raising interest rates to reduce borrowing and cutting back its own spending. This will lead to a slow-down in the economy and to unemployment. If the government feels that the unemployment level is unacceptably high then it can

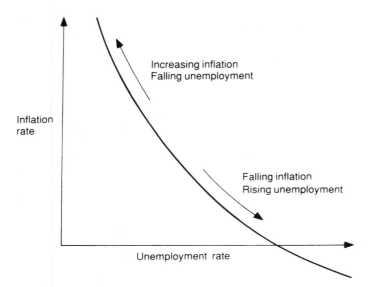

Figure 2.13 *The Phillips curve*

increase demand, perhaps by lowering interest rates and increasing its own spending.

The **Phillips curve** is an attempt to show a statistical relationship between unemployment and inflation. When inflation is rising unemployment is falling, and when unemployment is rising inflation is falling. Today the notion of the Phillips curve is used to describe this trade-off. However, it is clear that the position of the Phillips curve moves from one period to the next.

Task

Upturns and downturns in the economy are frequently referred to in the media. When they occur they have dramatic impact – closures, or the opening of new organisations to meet new demand, the spread of unemployment or inflation etc. Every organisation will feel some of these effects. Find out from your work placement or work experience how these external economic influences are affecting the organisation you are involved with. Try to develop a series of statistics which help to describe the trends that you outline.

Supply-side economics

During the 1980s there was a big switch in economic policy away from demand-side to supply-side theories. Whilst demand management had worked very well after 1945, the policy eventually ran into trouble.

After the war most governments used Keynesian policies (i.e. the ideas of Keynes). To counteract unemployment the government would use its own spending to pump up demand in the economy. However, a major fault of this policy was that outdated industries were artificially supported. Instead of inefficient units being cut out they continued to survive on government subsidies. This meant that the United Kingdom was losing its competitive edge in world markets.

The supply of goods in the economy rose very slowly in the 1960s and 1970s. Because supply was rising slowly, an increase in demand tended to lead to both rising prices and an increased reliance on foreign imports. Too many imports led to an increasing national debt, and the government was then forced to cut back on spending to reduce imports. Britain experienced **stagflation** – a stagnant economy that was not growing, coupled with inflation. Demand management did not seem to be working.

The cure possibly came with new policies that the Conservative government began to introduce in 1979. These policies concentrated on increasing supply rather than increasing demand. A whole host of measures was introduced to get supply going. These included:

- reducing income tax to encourage people to work longer hours
- reducing taxes on profits made by companies
- reducing benefits to those out of work
- reducing subsidies to loss-making industries
- privatising rather than nationalising industries
- reducing the size of the civil service
- reducing government spending
- passing laws to reduce trade union powers
- measures against monopolies and restrictive practices
- encouraging competition amongst groups such as solicitors, opticians, and even in the health service and schools.

The emphasis of this policy was to use supply as the means to drive the economy forward.

Task

How effective do you think supply-side measures have been? Select two or three of the examples of supply-side measures in the text and try to find out what the effects have been of implementing these policies. Why are different groups and individuals likely to have different views as to how effective these policies have been?

Case Study

New plans

The table below outlines the Labour Party's industrial and economic programme was started in 1992 and intended to replace that of the Conservative Party.

1 Which of the proposals seem to you to be demand-side and which supply-side policies?

2 Which of the plans are likely to be effective in your view?

3 What do you think will be the overall effect of the policies on the economy?

4 Explain how the plans are likely to effect one organisation you are familiar with.

Labour's industrial and economic plan

INDUSTRY:
NEW MANUFACTURING INVESTMENT PROGRAMME
■ additional capital allowances for plant and machinery
■ tax allowances for investment in new technology
■ tax incentives for individual investment in smaller businesses

CITY:
NEW RULES GOVERNING TAKEOVERS
■ bidders to prove that merger is in public interest
■ requirement to disclose bid intentions at early stage
■ workers to get statutory right to be consulted
■ wider public interest test for bids

INVESTMENT:
NEW NATIONAL INVESTMENT BANK
■ providing long-term funding for small and medium-sized businesses
■ mobilising private capital for long-term public infrastructure projects
■ British Technology Enterprise (to foster links between academia and industry)

INNOVATION:
■ New tax incentives for R & D
■ Technology Trusts formed by industry/City/academia/government
■ Government to spend 5 per cent of R & D budget with firms employing under 500

REGIONAL POLICY:
■ New regional development agencies for England

■ Strengthened role for Welsh and Scottish Development Agencies
■ Regional agencies to take on some of National Investment Bank's responsibilities

TRAINING:
■ New training schemes for 16–19-year-olds to replace YTS
■ Schemes to be based on qualifications and closer link between educational and vocational training qualifications
■ All school-leavers to receive training before entering employment
■ Legal obligation to firms to spend 0.5 per cent of payroll on training

INDUSTRIAL RELATIONS:
■ Statutory right to join union and take strike action
■ Secondary action allowed in certain circumstances
■ Creation of Industrial Relations Court

TAXATION:
■ Top rate of income tax to be raised to 50 per cent and greater number of bands
■ upper limit on national insurance contributions to be scrapped

PUBLIC OWNERSHIP:
■ National Grid to be taken back into public ownership
■ Return of water industry to public ownership a priority but no timescale
■ British Telecom to be renationalised if public stake still at 49 per cent

SPENDING:
■ Commitment to a 'priority programme' costed independently at £20bn–£35bn
■ Labour's only costed commitment is to raise pensions and restore child benefit to 1987 value

Today the trend seems to be to work with a combination of supply-side and demand-side ideas.

· FISCAL POLICY ·

Fiscal policy is the government's policy with regard to public spending, taxes and borrowing. The government can try to influence the level of demand in the economy through directly altering the amount of its own spending in relation to its total tax revenues.

A **deficit budget** arises when the government spends more than it takes in taxes (see Figure 2.14). The government can then borrow money from banks and other sourcesor sell gilts in order to carry out its own expenditure policies. The difference between government spending and tax revenue is known as the **public sector borrowing requirement** (PSBR). The logic of the deficit budget is simple. If there is not enough spending in the economy to create enough demand for goods to give everyone a job who wants one, then the government can

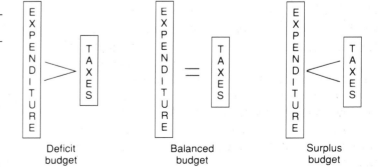

Figure 2.14 *Types of budgets*

boost spending itself. However, as we have seen above this may have inflationary effects.

A **balanced budget** describes a situation whereby the government matches its spending with taxes. The idea behind the balanced budget is that the government should not encourage price increases. There is also a belief that the government itself should spend as little as possible, because private individuals and groups are in a better position to make their own spending decisions.

A **surplus budget** arises when the government takes in more revenue than it spends. This is known as a **deflationary policy** because one outcome is a cut in inflation.

Balancing expenditure and revenue

Any form of government – whether it be at local, national or European level – needs to raise revenue in order to carry out its expenditure policies. Many supply–side economists feel that the smaller the role that the government plays in the economy the more efficient the system is likely to be. The larger the part that government plays in running things, the more employees it will need to carry out purely administrative tasks. For example, in 1993 the Scottish Office – which looks after the interests of 5 million people – employed over 6240 officials. On a wider front we are used to hearing criticisms of the bureaucracy of the European Community at Brussels.

From 1994 the British government will announce its plans for expenditure and revenue-raising both at the same time (in the autumn). Figure 2.15 shows the government's planned expenditure for 1993–4.

The sums in Figure 2.15 should be seen as representing the monies made available to different government departments for their spending. They then need to control their spending to keep in line with what is available. Each year government ministers argue the case for having more money available for their department (or at least to have as few cutbacks as possible). The figures are expressed in 'real terms' (in other words an allowance has been made against inflation).

Note that some of the figures are distorted because of transfers between departments. For example, the amount

Defence	22.0
Foreign Office	1.1
Overseas development	2.1
Agriculture, fisheries, food	2.6
Trade and industry	2.4
Employment	3.5
Transport	6.0
DOE – housing	7.4
DOE – environmen	1.3
DOE – psa	0.1
DOE – local govt.	$27.4
Home Office	5.7
Legal department	2.4
Education	8.9
National Heritage	0.9
Health	27.9
Social security	60.7
Scotland	12.6
Wales	5.9
N. Ireland	6.4
Chancellor's dept.	3.2
Cabinet Office	1.6
Local-authority self-financed spending	10.4
European Communities	1.3
Reserve	3.7
Control total	~~227.5~~

Figure 2.15 *Planned expenditure for 1993–94 (£ billion) at 1992 prices in real terms*

of money spent on education appears small. In fact much of the spending on education is carried out by local government. (Transfers take place between the following sectors: DOE, local government, education, health, social security, Scotland and Wales.)

Task

Find out the most recent figures for government expenditure plans (these are published in national newspapers in the autumn), or look them up in a back number of the *Economist* magazine. How have expenditure plans changed since 1992–93? What have been the main changes? What has caused some departments' expenditure totals to rise while others have fallen?

The pie chart in Figure 2.16 shows where the money to meet government expenditure was expected to come from in 1993–4. Taxes are collected by the Inland Revenue, the Customs and Excise Department and by other collected agencies (e.g. the local council collects council tax).

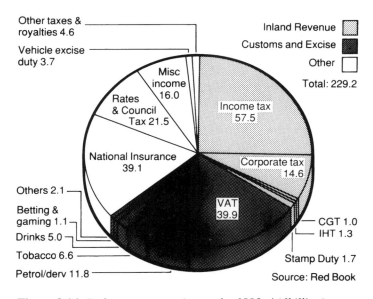

Figure 2.16 *Budget revenue estimates for 1993–4 (£billion)*

Income tax is money levied on incomes earned above a certain amount. Corporation tax is tax paid on business profits. Inheritance tax is paid on large gifts and monies left in wills. Stamp duty is paid on financial transactions that involve large sums of money (i.e. the purchase of a house). Value-added tax has to be paid on the value created at each stage of production. Then there is a range of duties which are paid on such items as drink, tobacco and petrol. National Insurance is paid as a contribution to the state by all employers and employees in order to provide benefits in times of hardship.

· MONETARY POLICY ·

Monetary policy is concerned with controlling:

● the quantity of money in the economy
● the price of money in the economy.

Monetary policy is felt to be important today. Most people now feel that there is a strong link between the amount of money in the economy and inflation. The view is that if people start spending money at a faster rate than new goods come on to the market, then prices will rise. **Monetarists** believe that it is essential to eliminate general price rises because of the way they destabilise industry and the economy. Uncertainty about prices means that industry cannot concentrate on its main task – producing goods. People become dissatisfied and the whole economic order starts to crumble – people fail to pay up on time, businesses are reluctant to invest, there is more industrial unrest, and so on.

Definition of money

There is more than one way to express the quantity of money in the economy.

If all people used only coins and currency notes to make their purchases, calculating the quantity of money would be easy. Instead, people use a variety of forms of money, the most obvious being coins and notes, cheques, credit cards, and other forms of credit payments. Today it is also common practice for people to draw money out of building society and other savings accounts to make purchases. A wide range of new facilities for making payments is developing. So, it is almost impossible for the government to know how much money is available to citizens to spend on goods at a particular moment in time.

In order to control the quantity of money, the government must decide on the definition of money which it thinks most accurately determines people's likely expenditure. It will then seek to control changes in the supply of money according to this chosen definition.

Task

Study recent newspaper articles and other sources to try to discover the commonly used definitions of money. These definitions change fairly frequently. Examples are M0 and M1.

The role of banks

The Bank of England has an important part to play in controlling the lending of high street banks and other financial institutions. The measures available to the Bank for limiting increases in cash and lending include giving advice and instruction to other banks on how much to lend and whom to lend to, and raising interest rates to discourage borrowing.

The lending institutions, such as banks, need to be carefully supervised by the government because of their tremendous powers of lending. They can grant **overdrafts** and **loans** and a wide range of other lending arrangements to customers.

A bank's customers carry out a relatively small number of their transactions using cash. Financial institutions, by creating credit instruments such as cheques and credit cards, make it possible for individuals and organisations to borrow money and make payments by means other than cash. The more these credit instruments are expanded, the more purchasing power there is in the economy. It is essential that the government does not let this spending get out of hand. It therefore sets targets and builds up a framework for controlling the financial system. The Bank of England plays an important part in policing this system – it licenses financial institutions and keeps a watchful eye on their lending practices.

Task

Find out from your local bank manager what limitations are currently placed on the bank's lending by government. How much are banks able to lend in a given period of time? What conditions do they establish for granting loans? Does the amount they can lend vary from time to time? In what circumstances are they likely to lend more money?

As well as controlling the quantity of money in the economy, the government can and does also control the **price of money**. Minimum interest rates can be quickly altered by the Bank of England, and the change will rapidly spread to all financial institutions such as banks and building societies. This is another way of controlling the quantity of money borrowed. If interest rates rise, people are more reluctant to borrow money.

Task

The following role play involves a union wage negotiation in the car industry. For this activity you will need to split into two groups. One group will represent management and the other group trade union officials.

You must negotiate a wage settlement to be operative from November. The two parties involved are the managers of the Foroyta Car Company and the union officials of the blue-collar workers of Foroyta. The negotiations cover 25 000 workers.

In recent years workers in few other companies have achieved the increases enjoyed by workers at Foroyta, but their pay package has set a target for union negotiators in the crucial two months after Christmas when most major settlements are struck. After an 'inflation-plus' increase last year of 13.4 per cent, the aspirations of union leaders should be more modest this time. Last year the deal was settled after a strike, but this year there is a lot of unemployment in the economy and the union is keen to protect its members' jobs. Recently the company has announced the redundancies of 1000 workers at one of its key plants. Car sales are down and the company is going through a difficult financial phase. There is little hope, however, of employees' representatives being happy with anything at or below the inflation rate, which stands at 4.1 per cent and is not likely to rise in the coming year.

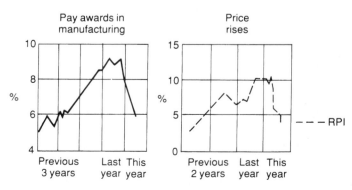

Figure 2.17 *The economic trends*

Although pay settlements have been falling throughout the year, as the charts show, inflation has been falling even more quickly. And except in sectors particularly hard hit by the recession, workers will be expecting – indeed demanding – rises above the RPI. While in the second half of last year they settled for less than inflation rates that were at or near double figures, this year they are likely to achieve basic rate increases in excess of the RPI.

The table below shows percentage settlements for other groups of workers this year.

Already made

August	BBC	5.7 plus £50
	Rolls Royce	pay freeze (9 months)
	Johnson Wax	7.2
September	Police	8.5
	Local authority	6.4
	Vauxhall	5.0
	Kwiksave	7.0

To come (current demands)

November	FOROYTA	?
	Rover	7.5
	Jaguar	7.0
	British Coal	4.2
January	Nissan	7.0
	Michelin	6.0

Once you have carried out your negotiations and arrived at a settlement, discuss how external economic influences have affected members of the blue-collar trade union at Foroyta.

▪ SOCIAL INFLUENCES ▪

The way in which society is organised and the social values the people have both influence the operation of organisations. In some countries people are prepared to work for very long hours, whilst in others they are not. In some countries great emphasis is placed on equal opportunities, but in other countries the idea is largely ignored. In some countries young people expect to have a say in how organisations should be run, in other countries older people have far more influence. These and many other social factors influence organisational behaviour.

Every society has its own **culture**, and culture affects attitudes and behaviour. Culture is a term used in many

varied ways. Two anthropologists once studied 164 definitions of culture and wrote a book about the varying definitions. They concluded that it is not yet possible to find a satisfactory definition that can be used in every circumstance. Talcott Parsons defined culture as 'the complex of values, ideas, attitudes and other meaningful symbols created by man to shape human behaviour and the artifacts of that behaviour as they are passed down from one generation to the next'.

Ingredients of the cultural environment will clearly influence organisations, groups and individuals working within a society or operating in different societies. Some important cultural ingredients are listed in Figure 2.18.

MATERIAL	ABSTRACT
Architecture	Language
Painting	Religion
Music	Law
Sculpture	Folklore and superstition
Jewellery	Attitudes to women
Gestures	Attitudes to family
Hairstyles	Attitudes to work
Cooking	Attitudes to bargaining
Tools	Attitudes to selling
Other products	Role models
Computers	Courtship
Games	Ethics
Dancing	Etiquette
Advertisements	Hygiene

Figure 2.18 *Some cultural ingredients*

When we explore cultural environments it immediately becomes obvious that societies differ in their cultural values. It follows that organisations wishing to operate in a different cultural setting must tread warily. We can bring this home by looking at a few examples:

Language. A literal translation of 'Coke adds life' informed Japanese consumers that Coke could raise their dead relative. GEC–Osram is a long-established lighting division of the British General Electric Corporation, but in Polish the word *osram* means excrement!

Attitudes towards women. In India and the UK, women have become national political leaders, whereas in some states in the Middle East some women wear black and walk behind their husbands.

Aesthetics. White is regarded as the colour of mourning in Japan, and purple is associated with death in many Latin American countries.

Superstition. Most US hotels have eliminated mention of the thirteenth floor.

Religion. Procter & Gamble was attacked in the 'Bible-belt' of the southern United States for spreading Satanism through its registered trademark – a crescent moon and thirteen stars. The rumour started in 1980 and by 1982 the company was receiving 15 000 calls a month to its customer services department. Eventually it had to discontinue use of the logo on packaging.

Personal hygiene. When American firm Helen Curtis introduced its Every Night shampoo line in Sweden, it renamed the product Every Day because Swedes usually wash their hair in the morning.

Population size and make-up

A major social influence on organisations is population. If a population is decreasing then organisations will find it more difficult to retain members, to recruit employees, to attract customers and so on. In times of increasing population the reverse may be true.

It is not just the size of the population that is important, but also the make-up of relevant sections of the population – for example, the ratio of the old to the young, male to female.

As the population structure of the UK changes over the next few decades there will be many major changes facing organisations. Study the shapes in Figure 2.19, which show the age/sex pyramids for the UK for 1970, 1990 and the projected forecast for 2010.

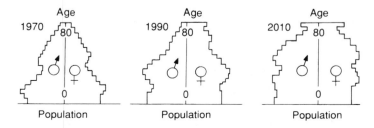

Figure 2.19 *Age/sex pyramids*

Task

What major changes in the population structure are highlighted by the pyramids in Figure 2.19? How might these changes affect:

a hospitals? **c** banks?
b schools? **d** manufacturing companies?

Task

In 1990 a major problem facing many companies was the shortage of young people entering the job market. It is estimated that in the first five years of the decade there will be 20 per cent fewer school-leavers.

1 Explain how this problem has been alleviated by a period of recession.
2 What strategies could companies employ to deal with the problem of fewer school-leavers? Write a report outlining three main strategies. A useful starting point might be to look at strategies employed by companies that you have worked for.

• POLITICAL INFLUENCES •

In politics, those who have power and authority decide on issues and courses of action. They decide whether to spend money on this or that thing; whether to carry out one course of action or another; whether to allow one thing or another. Since many of these decisions affect us and the organisations with which we are involved, it is in our interests to know how decisions are made.

Most modern Western governments are elected by the people. People's government is known as **democracy**.Members of Parliament typically represent about 60 000 people.

However, our democracy involves more than simply choosing people to represent us. We also have the freedom to express opinions that are critical of the government, other bodies and individuals. We also have uncensored media, free from the controlling hand of government, and an independent legal system.

Decision-makers can therefore be influenced by a wide range of individuals and groups, including political groups, the media, pressure groups and others.

Political groups

Political parties are organised groups of people who share similar sets of ideas and beliefs. These political parties publish **manifestos** setting out the sorts of policies they would like to see come into effect.

Task

Write to the head office of a major political party (or several) asking for a manifesto. How would the policies of this party (or parties) affect the activities of an organisation with which you are familiar?

Political parties can have an enormous impact on the decision-making within organisations. New laws are passed through Parliament, and it is the party with a majority vote in Parliament which will be able to see a wide range of its policies become laws. These policies will cover such issues as:

- how large the public sector should be
- who should manage the public sector
- national policy for transport
- how to control pollution
- how much money to spend on various services, such as education and defence.

Opposition parties can also influence the decision-making process by voting against the government, by canvassing support, and by making the public aware of a wide range of concerns.

National government

Government **ministers**, chosen by the **Prime Minister**, have responsibility for running specific departments, covering areas such as health, defence, education and so on. Those ministers responsible for major issues work closely with the Prime Minister – they form the Cabinet and many of the key policies are shaped by this group. Ministers are supported by **civil servants**. These people are not politicians; they are employed by the state to research new proposals and suggest possible courses of action that ministers might like to follow up. They are therefore concerned with collecting and processing information.

Task

Identify from a newspaper, the television news or elsewhere a new Bill going through Parliament. Keep a diary of how the Bill progresses. Is it, for example, opposed by any individuals or groups? Does it have to be altered? How does it fare in the House of Lords? Does it become a new law? How popular is the measure?

Case Study

The Children Act 1989

In October 1989 the Children Act became law. The law is an attempt to reform the rules relating to children's welfare in the light of a number of scandals which had resulted in children suffering from ill-treatment and lack of proper care. The main features of the new law are shown in Figure 2.20.

However, even despite these reforms and the tightening of regulations regarding children's homes, and improved complaints procedures, many experts feel that the changes are inadequate. They question the provisions for children leaving care, who often end up on the streets,

Key elements

- A new concept of 'parental responsibility' (the rights, duties, powers, responsibilities and authority given to parents by law)
- New duties on local authorities to support families with children in need
- A new framework for protecting children from the risk of harm and to ensure a proper education
- New local-authority duties towards children living away from home or with foster parents or being looked after by childminders or nannies
- New unified court system with specially trained judges and magistrates

Key principles

- The welfare of the child is paramount
- Families should bring up children wherever possible, with help where children are in need
- Courts only to make orders where this is better than no order
- Courts must avoid delay
- Children should have a say in decisions about their future and will have certain rights to complain about local authority services
- Parents must participate in decisions about their children even when they are no longer living with them.

Figure 2.20 *Main features of the new Children Act*

sleeping rough, or in prison, with few educational or training opportunities.

The Act makes it much harder to remove children from their families. Taking a child into the care of a local authority becomes the last option and, even then, strictly time-limited.

1 *Study recent reports from the press to judge how well the Children Act is faring.*
2 *Are there fresh calls for reform, or is there generally a favourable press for the Act?*

Local government

Local government is in the hands of **local councils**, who are elected. Over half of the funding for local councils comes from national government funds, in the form of **support grants**. In recent years there has been a lot of **privatisation** of local services, and local government

officials are responsible for handing out contracts for such things as running leisure centres, maintaining parks, refuse collection and keeping the roads clean. Contracted firms that fail to meet quality standards have contracts removed.

On the one hand there has been a greater emphasis placed on giving powers to the local government, whilst at the same time some powers have been taken away (for example, the delegating of budgets to individual schools).

Task

Each year your local council puts a leaflet through your letterbox explaining local services. Make a list of these services and how they are funded. What powers does the local council have in your area?

Local authorities have considerable influence over the ways in which the organisations in their area are run. Taxes are levied on local businesses and individual citizens. The local authority also has considerable powers for granting or refusing permission for new buildings or businesses, and licences for particular activities. For example, if you were going to set up a 'fast food' business or a pub you would need permission from the local council. The council is also responsible for local roads and the supervision and licensing of car parks, as well as many other services.

The media

The media include all forms of written communication to the public, such as newspapers, magazines and books, and all forms of transmitted communication, such as radio, television and cinema. The media play an important part in a number of areas of industrial society:

- in the transmission of information
- in the shaping and reinforcing of opinions
- as large employers, and as parts of larger media groups.

Transmission of information

The **mass media** reach a wide audience. A single edition of a mass-circulation newspaper can reach up to 10 million people, and a popular television programme may be seen by 15 million viewers. It is estimated that 95 per cent of the population became aware of the British Gas share issue through an expensive advertising campaign involving a fictitious character, Sid.

The obvious means of getting messages across to the general public is through television and national newspapers. Important public information can be communicated quickly to large numbers of people, as has been demonstrated by recent campaigns about the disease Aids.

Shaping and reinforcing opinions

There is a continuing debate as to how and to what extent the media influence people's behaviour. Advertisers are prepared to pump millions of pounds into promotions of their products in the media. These campaigns are often highly successful and similar adverts may be used for many years. Recently, even political parties have been prepared to pay huge sums, using advertising agencies, to promote a party image.

The media as employers

Apart from the BBC, which is a large employer in the public sector, most of the other mass media concerns are parts of large groups with a range of media and non-media interests. Many also have interests overseas. Hence the media are major employers.

Pressure groups

Pressure groups put **pressure** on organisations to modify or change their ways. They may be made up of just a few people – such as a group of parents demanding a public enquiry into practices in a hospital where their children appear to have had inadequate treatment. Alternatively they may be large international pressure groups – such as the environmental group Greenpeace.

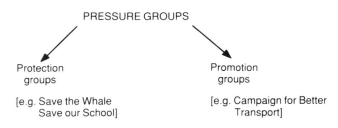

Figure 2.21 *Pressure groups*

Pressure groups do not fall readily into categories. Some are highly organised with paid officials, subscription charges and planned meetings – these groups may last for several years. Others may be 'three day wonders', being set up on the spur of the moment, lacking any real structure and vanishing as quickly as they arose.

Task

List eight pressure groups with which you are familiar. Try to find out more about the organisation of these groups. Are they highly organised or just a loose collection of individuals? What are the common characteristics of the groups that you have described?

Two main types of pressure groups are commonly recognised, protection and promotional.

Protection groups

These are set up to fight on a specific issue, such as danger on a local road threatening the lives of school-children. In other words, these groups seek to protect their interests against an outside threat. Other examples are a parents' protection group set up to oppose the planned closure of a local playgroup or nursery school, or rail commuters objecting to the threatened closure of a train service. A protest meeting will usually be called at which tactics are decided.

Promotional pressure groups

These are more formal groups which are sometimes highly organised and fight campaigns on a wide range of issues. Examples are Greenpeace and Friends of the Earth.

Such groups have clearly defined, long-term objectives. Their sustained pressure on various authorities helps to create radically new perspectives from most organisations, including businesses, trade unions, schools and colleges. They use measures which vary from madcap adventurist stunts to high-profile media advertising campaigns.

Case Study

Library charges

Gotham City College of Arts and Technology has decided to make students pay to use the college library. Clearly this will disadvantage students who are not able to pay the charges. It may also discourage students who have rarely used the library from starting to do so. Moreover, the policy seems to go against the notion of making education accessible to everyone.

The business managers of the college argue that all college services should pay their way. They argue that charging for use of the library will improve the quality of the service offered, and will make it possible to buy many new resources.

1 *Do you think that the students should be made to pay for library facilities?*
2 *Imagine that, as a student at the college, you have decided to set up a pressure group to campaign for free library services. How would you go about organising a pressure group to have maximum impact?*
3 *How would you attract supporters and maintain the interest of these supporters?*

· LEGAL INFLUENCES ·

Laws are a major factor constraining the operations of organisations. This is true of a children's home, a charity, a church or a company. Laws in the United Kingdom come mainly from three sources: common law, statute law and EC law.

Common law is the term used to describe a set of laws that have developed over hundreds of years, through custom and practice. Their exact origin is unknown or uncertain, but they are accepted as true laws despite that. For example, some footpaths have existed since before the first land records were ever kept; today these paths belong to the public and nobody can build on them, plough them up or fence them in – they are 'public footpaths'.

Statute law is concerned with laws that come into being as a result of Acts of the UK Parliament. These can be amended or repealed if circumstances suggest that they no longer serve the intended purpose. As time passes, a number of laws become out of date, others become untidy. Every now and then new laws need to be passed to tidy up an existing law in a particular area – for example, laws about how companies should operate, laws about health and safety in organisations, and so on.

Most statutory laws run to thousands of pages. It is therefore sensible for an organisation to seek expert legal advice, both when it is first set up and when changing its existing practices.

Every new employee should find out about his or her rights and obligations in the context of the organisation. In Chapter 10 we look at a number of rights and obligations that you will have in your workplace.

The third source of laws in the United Kingdom is the European Community. This is the subject of a case study on page 73.

Case Study

The European Court of Justice

The European Court of Justice is run by judges from the 12 countries of the European Community. Sitting in Luxembourg, it settles arguments where community laws are concerned. These laws affect:

● individual people
● companies

- other organisations (e.g. hospitals, schools) in all the countries of the EC.

In July 1991 the Court of Justice made a ruling which overturned part of the UK's Merchant Shipping Act 1988. Lawyers said that Britain had known since 1973 when it signed the Treaty of Rome that it must abide by Community law. The significance of this case was that it showed that the EC can invalidate laws even when dealing with matters which are traditionally associated with sovereignty.

The case stemmed from a conflict that arose in the early 1980s when Spanish vessels decided to re-register as British fishing boats, giving them access to British quotas of catches. In 1988, after widespread protests from British fishermen, the UK government brought in a rule that 75 per cent of the directors and shareholders of companies owning British vessels must be British citizens.

It was this piece of legislation that was challenged as discriminatory in the European court. Lawyers involved in the case said the decision came as no surprise – already in 1990 the court had made an interim judgement that the Merchant Shipping Act should be suspended until a final judgement could be made.

The ruling, which established for the first time that a UK law could be shelved on suspicion that it broke an EC law, proved a clear indication that the House of Commons now plays second fiddle to EC law.

The UK government had argued that it had a right under international law to decide whether vessels could be registered as British. This argument was dismissed by the European court, which decided that the Act discriminated against other EC countries. The judgement said that if a vessel was owned by a British company, and was operated out of the UK, then it was entitled to be registered as British.

1 *Why was this judgement important in setting out who makes laws in the European Community?*
2 *What are the likely knock-on effects of this judgement?*
3 *What are the implications for organisations in the United Kingdom? What should they do about it?*
4 *What are the implications for members of organisations?*

▪ TECHNOLOGICAL INFLUENCES ▪

Throughout history, society has undergone change. The **industrial revolution**, for example, changed people's lives radically. It brought great **wealth** to the mill and factory owners, but it also brought **social upheaval** by throwing thousands out of work from their traditional occupations.

Today the **pace** and the **scope** of change are as fast and as varied as ever. To illustrate the speed and magnitude of technological change, consider the following facts. In 1950 the size of a computer with the same power as a human brain, using the technology of the day, would have been enough to occupy the whole of London. By 1960 a computer with the same capacity would have fitted inside the Albert Hall, and by 1970 inside a double-decker bus. By 1980 it could be carried in a taxi, and in 1990 it would fit inside a TV set.

This example gives some insight into the rate of change that has taken place in just one part of one industry. Change presents great challenges for businesses and other organisations. As we have seen, organisations are part of society and they must change along with that society, or they run the risk of becoming irrelevant and outmoded. Change is therefore not only something that an organisation must learn to cope with, but also something that can be turned to advantage.

Case Study

Technology at Seiko

The commercial contest over the technology and accuracy of timepieces was settled in the 1980s. Seiko, the leading Japanese watchmaker – it makes 131 million watches a year, compared with the 89 million made by the entire Swiss watch industry – rose to international prominence in the late 1960s with its highly accurate quartz technology.

In the early days the competitive edge was gained through accuracy. In more recent years Seiko has concentrated on design and style. Each year a team of 150 designers launches 2000 new products. To succeed, Seiko has to keep up with the relentless pace of change of style in the clothes and jewellery people wear, how they furnish their living rooms and decorate their walls. Seiko watch 'collections' are rolled out twice a year in line with the practice in fashion houses.

Seiko's new design strength is still largely supported by technological strength. Its most recent developments (early 1992) are complex chronometers with several mini-dials set within the main dial. Until now such watches were only available from the most exclusive watchmakers. Seiko has managed to make them with a technology that can be applied to mass production.

It has also been able to develop a wide range of specialist watches of appeal to groups such as divers, swimmers, athletes, joggers and motor-racing enthusiasts.

When watchmakers were selling a technology rather than a style, it was easier to make products which would sell around the world. But with fashion and style becoming increasingly important, so design has to reflect local tastes in different markets. Seiko sets great store in 'area merchandising' to develop watches for regional markets. For example, Seiko employs specialists in France, the UK, the USA and Italy specifically to develop regional products in these areas.

1 List the various ways in which Seiko can be said to have been influenced by change.
2 How did Seiko manage to turn technological change to its advantage? What is the likely outcome of the company's actions?
3 For the staff of the company, what are the likely implications of the changes you have listed?
4 List what you believe to be the major advantages and disadvantages of technological change (do not restrict your answer to the company that creates the change).
5 What other forms of change can you think of that might affect a business?

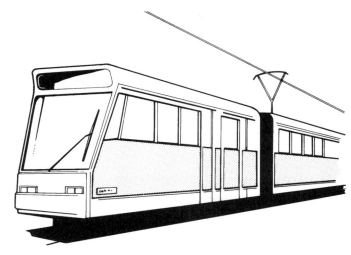

Figure 2.22 *City transport of the future?*

technologies that have created modern low-cost manufacture. Alternative technologies are now needed to deal with the resulting problems.

In some cities the traffic congestion is so bad that local councils have realised the need to reduce the numbers of vehicles on their roads. They know that people will not stop using their cars until there is another suitable way for them to travel.

Nottingham, Manchester and Sheffield intend to introduce rapid-transport (RT) systems. Coaches will run along tracks laid in the road. The RT systems will derive their electrical energy from overhead cables. It is hoped that a clean, reliable and efficient RT service will encourage people to leave their cars and use public transport again.

1 You are the public relations officer with a council that is planning to build an RT system. Your remit is to design posters to tell people about the advantages of the new system. What messages would you try to get across?
2 As the public relations officer you have also been invited to give a talk to local people to tell them about the new RT system. Plan such a talk, which should emphasise the good things about the new way of travelling.
3 Will RT be good for everyone? Write lists of the advantages and disadvantages of the RT system.

· ENVIRONMENTAL INFLUENCES ·

Organisations operate today in a world which increasingly has been forced to become aware of environmental

Case Study

Change not always for the good

When you travel around any large city you cannot fail to notice the noise, the congestion and the pollution caused by road traffic. In this context the products of technology in transport have caused problems. The motor car, from being an expensive luxury enjoyed by the few, has now become a highly affordable item as a result of the concerns. Whether **environmental consciousness** has become a genuine concern by all organisations, or is being manipulated by some as a subtle **marketing tool**, remains to be seen. For example, it would appear that motor vehicle manufacturers are responding to environmental pressures, but the trend is still towards more and more in-car gadgets, which inevitably increase the weight and hence the petrol consumption. The producers would argue that they are responding to consumer demand. At the same time it is clear that the life-cycle of products is shortening in response to increased competition and change. Volkswagen, for instance, has recently reduced the expected life-cycle of its new products from 11 to 8 years.

With a shortening of the life expectancy of products it becomes easier to accommodate the '**green agenda**' if consumers vote with their money for 'greener' cars. Some companies are currently designing vehicles with totally recyclable parts.

As we shall see in Chapter 19, many customers are concerned by 'green' issues. Organisations therefore need to respond positively. This pressure clearly demands that organisations should make their employees more environmentally aware.

Poison in the water

On 6 July 1988, at 4.30 pm, the driver of a tanker from a chemical supply company arrived at the Lowermoor water treatment plant in Cornwall, with a delivery of aluminium sulphate. The gate was locked and the plant deserted. However, the driver, who had never been to Lowermoor before, had been given a key by a colleague and so unlocked the gate and drove in. But where was he to put his delivery of aluminium sulphate?

He had been told that the tank was 'on the left', but he found that there were several tanks on the left. He came to a hatch set in the ground and found that he could open it with the gate key. Concluding that this was the correct tank, he poured in the chemical. The aluminium sulphate *should* have gone into a separate storage tank from which it would have been dispensed at a maximum of 50 parts per million to help cleanse the water supply. Inadvertently

---

the driver had poured it into a tank which allowed the undiluted chemical to join the water supply to be dispensed to consumers in the South West.

When the disastrous error was discovered, the water company blamed the chemical supply company. The water company said that the chemical should have been delivered on 4 July or 5 July, and that in any case it did not accept deliveries after 4 pm. It queried how the driver had obtained the key. The water-workers union suggested that the key was one of a number handed out to contractors to help break the water-workers' strike of 1983.

1 Comment on the seriousness of this incident.
2 What general lessons does the case present for organisational responsibility towards the environment?
3 What are the lessons for employees working for organisations?
4 What experiences have you had of working in situations in which your actions or inactions were a potential threat to the community? How well trained were you to prevent risks?
5 How high on an organisation's list of priorities should be a responsibility towards the external environment?
6 Do you think that environmental concerns provide too much pressure on the way organisations operate today?

ECOLOGICAL AND ENVIRONMENTAL RESPONSIBILITIES

Your environment is everything that surrounds you – where you live, the people you know, the living and non-living things around you:

Environment to each must be,
All that is, that isn't me.

All living things have four vital needs:

SUN	EARTH
AIR	WATER

For millions of years, plants and animals have been on this planet. For 40 000 years they have shared it with us, humankind. In the last few decades, however, we have begun to destroy this world by damaging the balance of our four vital needs.

- We damage the balance of sunlight by making holes in the ozone layer.
- We fill the air with harmful gases.
- We put acid into the rain.
- We poison the earth with chemicals.

Everything we do to our environment affects us and every other thing which shares this world with us.

The surge of **environmental awareness** reinforced by pressure groups and political and media activity has resulted in an important cultural shift – environmental concern has joined other commonly held values. *It is a shift that organisations cannot escape.*

The environmental challenges to industry are now well established. First, there is **regulation.** Regulation can be seen as a relatively quick and visible way of changing industries' behaviour. In Britain, the Environmental Protection Act – and specifically 'integrated pollution control' – has changed the basis of pollution regulation. Membership of the European Community also forces the UK to adopt community standards.

Perhaps more important is **consumer pressure.** More consumers are looking for products that are 'ecologically friendly'. There is also **investor pressure** – those who provide finance for businesses are increasingly questioning the environmental soundness of their investments.

From the inside there is **employee pressure.** People who are concerned citizens at home do not become environmental slobs when they arrive at work. Management pressure is also very important. For example, the Advisory Committee on Business and the Environment, set up to help thrash out environmental issues with the government, is made up of senior managers from major companies.

The Environmental Protection Act 1990

This Act created two new systems for regulating industrial pollution. **Integrated pollution control** (IPC) will apply to more than 5000 existing industrial processes with the largest pollution potential, and will regulate all their releases to land, water and air. It will be enforced by an Inspectorate of Pollution. The second system, to be enforced by local authorities, will cover 27 000 **complex processes**, and will control only their emissions to air. Under both systems, operators will have to employ the 'best available techniques not entailing excessive cost', to minimise releases of the most polluting substances, and to 'render harmless' all releases from their processes.

IPC extends the sorts of control previously applied only to air pollutants to all the wastes – gases, solids and liquids – generated by companies. The new Inspectorate will ensure that the least environmentally damaging solution overall – the 'best practicable environmental option' or **Bpeo** – is chosen to deal with these.

Task

Obtain some petroleum jelly, which you can get in a chemist's shop. Take six stiff white cards and smear them with some of the jelly. Place the cards in a variety of places – some where you would expect the air to be clean (perhaps in a tree) and some where it is dirty (maybe near a busy street). Leave the cards in place for a few days and then collect them. Write down the signs of pollution you found and what they appeared to be from.

Develop a proposal for reducing some of these pollutants. Try to make your proposal one that fits in with the notion of being the best practicable environmental option – Bpeo.

Responsibility for pollution

There can be no doubt that we must all play a responsible part in preventing or reducing pollution. Individuals and organisations can work to control the pollution they cause. An essential starting point is an awareness of pollution and its causes.

Water pollution

Much **water pollution** comes from factories, which take fresh water in from a river, use it in a manufacturing process, and then discharge it back into the river. The discharge often contains chemicals and oils which kill fish and other living things in their food chain. Other causes of water pollution are agricultural waste and chemicals which seep through the soil into rivers and lakes.

Oil is a potent pollutant. In March 1989, the ship the Exxon Valdez poured more than 10 million gallons of oil into Prince William Sound in Alaska, following which millions of fish and birds died. When sea-birds dive through oily waters the oil sticks to their feathers, which then can no longer keep out the cold and wet. The birds die if the oil is not cleaned off.

Air pollution

As yet, we have not been able to harvest the forces of wind, sun or water to meet all our energy needs, and we will probably continue using coal, oil and gas for many more years. These are responsible for a lot of **air pollution**. Power stations burning coal or oil pour dangerous sulphur dioxide into the air. Car and lorry exhausts add nitrogen oxide.

To produce one unit of electricity, a power station sends into the air ten grams of sulphur, three grams of nitrogen oxide and a thousand grams of carbon dioxide. One kilogram will fill 20 balloons.

Task

Check back on your electricity reading chart at home and find out how many units of electricity your family uses in a day. Multiply your units by the amounts of pollution given in the text to discover how much your family adds to air pollution from your use of electrical power alone.

Noise pollution

Noise is experienced when the ear picks up unwanted vibrations, most of which come from machinery of some kind. At its most intense – for example a jet plane taking off – noise can cause actual physical pain.

New roads can bring the nuisance of traffic noise into people's homes, often in areas which previously enjoyed peace and quiet. New road developments to carry freight from the Channel Tunnel are a case in point.

Noise is particularly annoying at night, when it can interrupt sleep. There is nothing new in this. In the times of the Roman Empire the capital's residents complained so vigorously about the disturbance caused by cart traffic that the Emperor Augustus put a ban on all carts leaving or entering Rome at night!

Case Study

Public concern about the environment

The public's attitude towards the environment is a key influence on organisational activity. Opinion polls suggest that most people's concern for the environment is a little fickle and strongly influenced by media coverage.

When times are good and the economy is growing, people worry about the fate of the planet and that of future generations. When recession bites, these concerns tend to be pushed aside by more immediate concerns about personal security. However, polls do indicate that a substantial proportion of the population – about a fifth – have had their environmental consciousness raised permanently.

For example, once a month for a number of years MORI has been asking the public: 'What would you say is the most important issue facing Britain today?' and 'What do you see as other important issues?'. In the late 1980s the environment appeared high on the public's agenda of concerns.

MORI has also been asking people whether they have done any one of 12 'green activities' in the last year or two. These include walking in the countryside, buying 'green' products in supermarkets, joining an environmental group and writing letters on environmental issues to MPs and newspapers. Those who answer 'yes' to five or more of these activities are counted as **environmental activists**. The percentage of these rose from 14 in 1988 to 31 in 1991. (See Figure 2.23.)

1   *What conclusions would you draw from the bar-chart?*
2   *Do you feel that raised environmental awareness is likely to be a short-term or long-term trend?*
3   *What are the implications for organisational activities?*

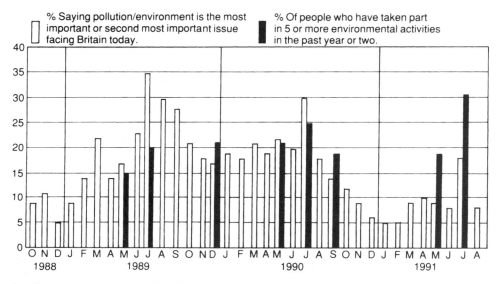

Figure 2.23 *Concern for the environment – results of a MORI poll*

4 *Design an action plan for your organisation to improve its environmental consciousness.*

5 *Carry out a market research survey along the lines set out by the MORI survey. Do your findings coincide with the MORI findings? Explain your results and compare them with the MORI survey.*

Green audits

In 1986 a new environmental law was passed in the United States. It did not require organisations to fix anything, install anything or clean up anything. All it obliged them to do was submit (to the Environmental Protection Agency) an annual list of the quantities of hazardous chemicals they had released into the environment. The Agency would publish the information in a Toxics Release Inventory. The aim was to create a massive shift in power away from government and industrial regulation and towards the public.

Local communities in the USA are now able to knock on companies' doors armed with detailed information about what is being put into their air and water. Environmental groups have found the inventory a valuable campaigning resource. In industry, senior management and other employees have started asking pointed questions about why such large amounts of costly raw materials and

valuable products are being thrown away. Many businesses have been able to set up new strategies for saving waste and cutting down on pollution. In Britain there is growing pressure for **environmental auditing**. The Environmental Protection Act paved the way for further registers on industrial pollution, waste disposal sites, contaminated land and so on.

Some of the 'green' investment funds have joined environmentalists in arguing for compulsory audits which provide information on companies' raw material and energy consumption as well as pollution. The Trades Union Congress (TUC) has urged its members to demand **green audits** in workplace negotiations.

Leading oil and chemical companies have been running auditing programmes since the 1970s. These are generally intended to show up weaknesses in environmental management systems and breaches in internal standards. Companies also like to take an audit of another company's environmental legacy before considering a merger. The findings of such audits are intended for management's eyes, rather than the public's.

In 1990, the European Commission produced a draft idea to enforce environmental audits on companies in a number of leading industrial sectors. However, the Commission is now expected to suggest only a voluntary scheme.

Carry out a rough environmental audit of the place where you work. Are there any obvious areas for environmental improvement? Are there policies which could be changed to improve the environment?

COSTS AND BENEFITS OF ORGANISATIONAL ACTIVITY

When weighing up the effects of any activity it is necessary to assess:

- who are the winners and who are the losers
- the size of their gain or loss.

This is difficult because people have varying views and give different values to things. Whereas one person would not mind the property next door being converted to a fish and chip shop, another would regard this as an absolute disaster. Where one person sees a new road as being a benefit because it reduces the time taken to get to work, another sees it as a danger to children. Where one person sees fast food outlets as being an improvement to the quality of life, another sees them as representing unhealthy eating standards.

Task

List what you consider to be the benefits of fast food outlets. Who benefits? How do they benefit?

Now list the disadvantages. Who suffers? How do they suffer? Is it possible to say whether the disadvantages outweigh the advantages?

Even when it is possible to measure costs and benefits in money terms, it is easy to underestimate the 'real' effects. For example, if a new office development creates 100 jobs paying average salaries of £10 000, it is quite easy to compute the increased earnings in the area. However, it is impossible to attach a value to the excitement felt by somebody who is being taken on to work in the office and who has not worked for the previous five years. Attaching money values to costs and benefits, therefore, can at best be only a very rough measure. Costs and benefits can be **private** or **social**.

Private costs and benefits

When an individual or organisation carries out a project, costs and benefits are calculated from a private point of view. For example, when a business decides to build an extension it will weigh up the extra costs and revenues that will flow from that extension.

Social costs and benefits

Social costs and benefits go beyond the individual or group to consider all the individuals and groups who will be affected by an action or policy. If a business wants to build an extension, the local planning authority takes into consideration all the other groups and individuals who would be affected – the builder of the extension and his employees, the people who would work in the new extension, the implications for neighbours, and so on.

Produce a report seeking planning permission for a proposed service station. Your particular responsibility is to explain the benefits that the new station will bring to local people. In your report, you are expected to explain the various ways in which a service station 'adds value' to the products it sells – fuels and lubricants, tyres and accessories, items for the shop – to the advantage of customers.

There are many possible ways of setting out your report, but you should aim for clarity and ease of reading. The sequence of thoughts must be simple to follow. Here is one possibility:

Title. This tells the reader what the report is about.

Contents list. This reveals in more detail what the report is about.

Terms of reference. This informs the reader what you were asked to do. You could say: 'I have been asked to study the proposed service station and report on the benefits it would provide for the community. The report will be presented to the planning committee.'

Procedure. This explains how you set about collecting the information. Did you write to people to ask for their opinions? Did you carry out face-to-face interviews? Did you visit other service stations in nearby towns?

Findings. This could well be the longest part of the report. It should give all the facts you have collected.

Summing up. This is a brief reminder of your findings.

Recommendations. These are the actions you think should be taken by the planning committee as a result of your findings.

Signature. This tells everyone that it is your work.

others are not. In areas not covered by law, pressure groups often form to put forward their cases.

The media often bring to our attention examples of both successful and questionable business activities – insider trading of shares, the use of animals for testing cosmetic and pharmaceutical products, tobacco sponsorship, trading links with nations such as Iraq, and so on. As a result, consumers have become increasingly aware of the ethical values underlying business decisions.

A new breed of environment-friendly, caring, community-conscious corporate citizen is emerging in British industry. For example, Peterborough-based Thomas Cook is funding the building of a local hospital; Butlins is offering day visits for under-privileged children; and Cadbury raised about £500 000 for young sufferers of cerebral palsy with its 'Strollerthon', which attracted 12 000 walkers. Kentucky Fried Chicken is operating with the Tidy Britain group to remove litter and educate people on how to improve their environment.

Two factors are accelerating the switch to corporate responsibility. First, according to work carried out by both the Henley Centre and MORI, there is a massive swing away from the attitudes of the 1980s. Greed is no longer good – ethics are in.

Secondly, products are becoming increasingly similar, so that one way to differentiate products is emotionally. Companies are trying to prove they have social values, which have an emotional impact on their consumer. There are four main areas in which this can be shown: the environment, the local community, the 'fitness' of a company and its employees, and investments in the community.

• ETHICS •

Ethics are moral principles or rules of conduct which are generally accepted by most members of a society. An ethic is a guide as to what should be done or what should not be done. It involves what one believes to be right and what is considered to be wrong. From an early age, parents, religions and society in general provide us with moral guidelines to help us to learn and form our ethical beliefs. Many ethics are reinforced in our legal system and thus provide a constraint to business activities, while

Produce a list of what you consider to be the ten main ingredients of an 'ethical' company. How can you as an employee contribute to the creation of company ethics?

Decision-making in the European Community

● The EC is an *economic* union – for example, it is a free trade area.
● The EC is a *political* union – for example, it has a parliament.
● The EC is a *social* union – people are able to travel freely between countries and the community has its own social policy.
● The EC is a *legal* union – it has its own community laws.
● The EC is a *technological* union – with policies for the sharing of new technologies.
● The EC is an *environmental* union – with policies for dealing with the very real problems of pollution and other environmental matters.

The European Community is made up of 340 million people living in 12 member states. Those citizens with a vote choose the people they want to represent them in the European Parliament. There are 567 Members of this Parliament (MEPs). The number from each country is shown in Figure 2.14. The European Parliament meets in Strasbourg. The MEPs discuss European matters and any laws that are being suggested or changed – they do not themselves propose new laws. They do not sit in country groups, but in groups of people with similar ideas.

The community laws are made by ministers from the governments of each of the 12 countries. The Council of Ministers meets in Brussels. These ministers draft the new laws which will be discussed by the European Parliament. The Parliament can change the proposals for new laws if it does not like them.

There is also a Commission in Brussels made up of 17 Commissioners. Their job is to monitor the need for changes in the laws and to identify ways of making sure the laws are kept.

Some people want the EC to have more power to make more rules for the whole community. Other people think that countries should have more power to make their own laws without interference from the EC. Others think that things are just about right at the moment.

1 Which do you think has the most power – the Council of Ministers, the European Parliament, or the Commission? Give reasons for your answer.
2 Which body do you think should have the most power? Again, give reasons.
3 What would be the advantages if all 12 countries were governed from the EC bodies? What would be the disadvantages? Would these advantages and disadvantages be the same for everyone?

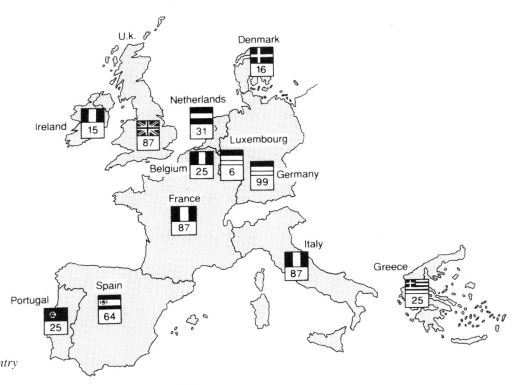

Figure 2.24 *The number of MAPs in each country*

• EUROPEAN COMMUNITY •

How the community is governed

The EC Commission is the controlling body of the European Community. Its headquarters is in Brussels, the capital of Belgium. The Commission is a body of 17 people, two each from the larger nations of Germany, France, Italy, Spain and the United Kingdom and one each from Belgium, Denmark, Greece, Ireland, Luxembourg, the Netherlands and Portugal. The Commissioners (as they are known) serve for four-year renewable periods. On appointment, they cease to act as Germans or Frenchman or Britons and try to act only in the Community interest.

The Commission proposes new policies and laws based on the Treaties and other objectives agreed by member states. It also has the job of ensuring that these laws, when passed, are properly enforced in the member states. However, the laws themselves are made by the Council of Ministers, but only after two other bodies have been consulted.

Consultation

First, an opinion on a proposed law has to be sought from the European Parliament. The Parliament is elected every five years. (The next election is in 1999.) The European Parliament is made up of elected politicians from the many different European political parties and represents the views of the people. Besides its right to be consulted on all Commission proposals, the European Parliament has the final say on the Community's budget and has the power to censure the Commission.

Second, the opinion of the Economic and Social Committee has to be sought. This is a 189- member committee of representatives from such bodies as trade unions, employers' associations and consumer groups throughout the Community.

Law making

Once opinions have been obtained from the representative bodies, the proposal then passes to the Council of Ministers, which decides whether or not it should become Community policy or law.

The Council is composed of 12 ministers, one from each member state, and unlike the Commissioners, these ministers act very much as representatives of their own country. Each one weighs up the proposal and, in the case of the more important matters, they all have to agree before it can become law. In order to strengthen the Community's effectiveness, the number of cases where decisions can be taken on a majority vote has recently been increased. The European Parliament is more closely involved in majority decision-making. The Commission mediates on Council debates which are often animated as ministers defend national viewpoints. Once a proposal becomes law, it must be observed in all the member states. Anyone breaking it may be taken before either their own national courts or the Community's Court of Justice in Luxembourg.

A European Council, which is made up of the Heads of State of government of the 12 and the Commission President, meets at least twice a year in order to set broad guidelines for the Community.

The Maastricht Treaty in a nutshell

The Maastricht Treaty extends the EC's responsibilities into a number of new areas.

It creates a direct link between voters and their elected representatives. It gives the European Parliament the final say on:

● defining the right to live and work across the EC
● ensuring that degrees and other academic and vocational qualifications are accepted across the EC

- services, such as trans-European transport, energy and telecom links
- EC research and development budgets
- environmental action programmes
- new EC members
- working towards co-operation on education, public health, consumer laws and culture such as maintaining identiy of regional languages such as Gaelic, Basque and Catalan
- completing Single Market measures.

EC-wide directives

The Treaty also stipulates that member countries will be free to make their own legislation, except when EC-wide legislation could prove more effective. For example, if you want to protect Britons buying time-shares in Spain or Portugal then it is sensible to have an EC directive which will protect them throughout the Community.

The treaty also aims to build on the success of the 1992 Single Market programme and makes provision for new members to join.

The contentious Social Chapter

The **Social Chapter** has been a source of crisis over the future of the Maastricth Treaty. It provides for the adoption of minimum community-wide requirements for the protection of workers' health and safety.

It would also establish the principle of equal pay for women and men for work of equal value. The agreement, signed by eleven member states, excluding Britain, follows the *Social Charter*. That was adopted by the eleven in 1989, to put flesh on the bones of the Chapter, and led to measures such as the working time directive with a proposal for a 48–hour week, to which Britain objected.

The Chapter sets out broad policy objectives, without details. Britain secured an opt-out from the Social Chapter in negotiations.

The eleven other members said that their objectives under the Chapter were the promotion of employment, improved living and working conditions, proper social protection, dialogue between management and labour, and the

development of human resources with a view to lasting high employment and the combating of social exclusion. The British opposed it on the ground that it would allow working conditions to be decided at Community level and would add unacceptable costs to business.

The Chapter allows that the Community provisions will not apply to ay, rates, the right of association, the right to strike or the right to impose lockouts. One aim of the Chapter was to avoid so-called '**social dumping**' – the move of investment to countries with lower standards. There is concern that it is alredy taking place in Britain, with the transfer of jobs by Hoover from France to Scotland.

Task

Set out in detail six reasons why Britain should adopt the Social Chapter, and six reasons why Britain should reject it. Which side is more convincing?

Study newspaper reports to see if you can find evidence of 'social dumping' in Britain.

The exchange rate mechanism

The exchange rate mechanism (ERM) helps to control the rate of exchange of currencies between EC members. If the rate of exchange stays the same over a period of time, this encourages trade. If I sell a French person a car, expecting to be paid in francs for it in three months time, I will be pleased if when I convert the francs into pounds I receive as many pounds then as I would receive today (i.e. the rate has stayed fixed over the three months). However, if the pound falls against the france I will be disappointed when I convert the French francs into pounds because they will then buy far less of my own currency. The ERM is an attempt to keep exchange rates relatively fixed.

In the ERM, currencies are allowed to move up and down a little against each other but within agreed limits. However, some member countries have found it difficult to keep within these limits, and Britain was forced to leave the ERM when it could not keep within the boundaries set for the pound.

A number of countries that have strong currencies would like to see a single currency at some date in the future. Strong currencies include the Dutch Guilder and the German Mark.

The European Commission and the European Parliament pass legislation which is superior to UK legislation in areas like public sector procurement, freedom to work in member states, product standards etc. The Single Market is, however, an opportunity to sell British goods to far more members.
At the same time European companies are better placed to sell goods to British consumers. Prepare a presentation (including a few overhead images) outlining the opportunities and threats of the Single Market for British businesses.

The Maastrict Treaty sets out the challenge to member states to move gradually towards a common currency by the end of the century. This involves moving steadily towards increasingly fixed rates of exchange.

Arguments against the Maastricht Treaty

There are two main arguments against Maastricht. The first is that national governments will lose the power to make important political decisions. The ability to make your own decisions is called sovereignty. National institutions like the Bank of England and Parliament will have to give up major powers to a European Central Bank and to the European Commission in Brussels and the European Parliament in Strasbourg (see Chapter 15). However, it is important to remember that the principle of subsidiarity enables many decisions to be made at national and regional levels.

Second, with a single currency the British government will no longer control its own monetary policy. It will not be able to set the supply of money or the interest rate. For example, in a period of unemployment it would not be able to increase demand in the economy by lowering interest rates. The interest rate would be set by the European Central Bank and sterling would disappear.

· TRADE WITH THE REST OF WORLD ·

In the 1960s it was commonplace to talk to an international division of labour. There ws an industrial centre (Western Europe and North America) and a primary producing periphery (e.g. cotton from Africa, rubber from South America, etc). Today the picture has changed.

Industry has now been widely dispersed and there are many global companies manufacturing their products in several companies. The reasons for this are manifold. For example, plant has been set up in low-wage countries. With modern technology it is possible to employ expensive capital (e.g. a car plant using relative unskilled local labour). Developments in the fields of transport and communications – such as containerisation, jet transport, international direct dialling, fax, electronic mail etc. – make it possible for dispersed production operations to be coordinated from a single head office. A **multinational company** is one that has plant in many countries.

Firms from advanced industrial countries have sought to increase their profits by setting up at low-cost locations. This export of capital has led to a fall in investment in industry in advanced industrial countries and increasing levels of unemployment. The Third World now produces a greater share of world industrial output, although in recent years this growth has slowed considerably. In the 1930s, two-thirds of Third World manufactured exports went to other Third World countries and only a third to the developed world; today the proportions have been reversed.

However, developed countries still buy in only a very small percentage of their total imports form Less Developed Countries (LDCs). In certain markets such as clothing and footwear LDC's have gained a bigger market share.

Studies have shown that, while the United Kingdom has lost jobs as a result of buying imports from LDCs, in fact this has been more than offset by jobs created from selling British goods to LDCs.

Today the world trading market is very competitive. Major players in international markets are companies from the United States, particularly in high-technology modern manufactured products such as computers, cars, aircraft and military equipment. Japan and South Korea have shown spectacular growth in exports from the 1960s onwards. These countries concentrated on producing goods for export to Western markets, and so now they use 'state-of-the-art' technology in a range of products from cars to electronics. The Japanese have also been major *investors* in other countries. They have bought up industry and plant in European countries in order to get inside the Single Market. For example, there are many large Japanese car plants in the UK today. There is some criticism that Japanese and South East Asian countries export vast quantities of goods to the West and buy little in return.

Now there are a number of powerful new economic areas which are becoming highly significant on the international scene for example, the countries which make up the Pacific rim. At the same time the area of China which borders on Hong Kong is moving towards rapid industrialisation. These countries cannot be considered as 'less developed': they have a high standard of education and vocational training; living standards approach or are better than those in Europe; and they have high rates of investment and growth but low wages. Clearly it will become increasingly difficult for British companies to compete against them in the global market.

In the modern world the success or failure of enterprises in Britain is closely tied up with the success or failure of the whole world economy. We should not forget this. It is easy to think just of ourselves, but if all countries did this then everyone would suffer. British business needs to look outwards to the whole world picture.

. THE GENERAL AGREEMENT ON . TARIFFS AND TRADE (GATT)

Trading can create jobs and income throughout the world. If I buy a car from another country then people in that country will have more money to spend. Some of that money may be spent again in this country. If British workers concentrate on these lines of production at which they are most efficient, then foreign workers can concentrate on those lines at which they are most efficient. A problem arises, however, when countries do not allow trade to take place *freely*. Some countries place **tariffs** (taxes) on imports from other countries, and sometimes they limit the **quantities** (quotas) of imports.

The General Agreement on Tariffs and Trade is an agreement between most of the trading nations in the world to reduce tariffs, quotas and other restrictions..

Case Study

Japanese car manufacturing in the UK

In December 1992, Toyota opened its first European plant at Burnaston near Derby. It is the biggest manufacturing investment ever made by a foreign company in Britain. When it reaches full capacity it will produce 200 000 cars a year and help the UK' trade balance by £400 – 500 million. Its opening follows those of the Honda plant in Swindon in October 1992 and Nissan in Sunderland which has been running since 1986 (the plant produced 180 000 cars in 1992).

It is estimated that UK car production will rise from 1.2 million vehicles in 1992 to 2 million in 1997. This means that the deficit on the automotive trade balance will turn into a surplus by the late 1990s.

The Japanese factories will create additional benefits for the UK economy. They have attracted investment from parts makers and have encouraged other manufacturers to look at Britain as a base. General Motors, which shunned the UK in the 1980s, has boosted its Vauxhall production at Luton and has opened an engine plant on Merseyside. The new car factories create local jobs, which cause a boost to the local economy – for shopkeepers, travel agents, and anyone that has a business to run.

In the long run it is likely that the new factories will send shock waves through the car industry. By 1999 they will be making between 1.2 million and 1.7 million cars. Total European production is expected to be about 14.6 million, so their share will be between 8 and 11 per cent. On top of this there will be direct imports from Japan (perhaps giving the Japanese 20 per cent of the European market).

Some people think that one of the existing six manufacturers – Ford, General Motors, Fiat, Volkswagen, Renault, and Peugeot–Citroen – will be forced out of business. However, this depends on the success of the Japanese at being able to sell their products. The car market is weak in a period of recession. More and more people are looking for high-quality cars and value for money. The Japanese have a reputation for being able to produce superb quality cheaply. By the late 1990s the Japanese factories are expected to be able to produce 6000 000 cars using 10 000 employees. In 1992, Ford produced 447 000 vehicles with 35 000 employees.

In 1992, Ford made a loss of £685 million on its European operations, having been profitable throughout the 1980s.

1 Why are Japanese car manufacturers setting up in Britain?
2 What are the most important effects of the Japanese setting up here?
3 Who benefits and who loses out as a result of these changes?
4 What is the likely effect on the UK balance of payments?
5 Why do the Japanese have such a competitive advantage in car production?
6 What factors are likely to maintain this advantage?
7 What are the threats to Japanese car production in the UK?
8 To what extent are the fortunes of the UK economy dependent on effective partnership with Japanese car producers?

Location of business activity

The **location** of a factory or shop where an organisation intends to operate undoubtedly has a major effect on its performance. Locating an organisation is expected to be a long-term commitment and clearly decisions taken today will have lasting implications. The owner of a small organisation may not want to leave his or her neighbourhood, and the problem then may be not where to locate but rather finding a suitable site. In contrast, large organisations view the world as their market, and numerous factors taken together influence the choice of location.

Whatever the type of organisation, the aim will be to locate where the difference between benefits and costs is maximised. It is important to minimise unit costs and maximise outputs from given quantities of resources.

We now consider the most important factors influencing the choice of location.

Transport

Transport costs are particularly crucial if raw materials or finished goods are bulky. If the output of an industry is more expensive to transport than its inputs, it is a **bulk-increasing** industry, and common sense suggests that it is more likely to locate near to its market. Market orientation is also important when the product is perishable – bread is an example.

On the other hand, if the raw materials are bulky and costly to transport and the industry is a **bulk-decreasing** industry, it is beneficial to save on transport costs by locating close to where the raw materials are available. For example, steel plants tend to be located on or near the coast where they have access to imported iron ore.

In practice, decisions are not quite as clear-cut as the above might suggest – markets tend to be spread out and raw materials come from a number of suppliers. So, the nature of the industry, the spread of the market, the availability of raw materials and their influence upon costs of transport all have to be weighed against each other.

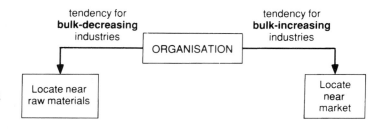

Figure 2.25 *Location of plant*

Case Study

Technical Operations Ltd

Technical Operations Ltd, a manufacturer of specialised computer components, is in the process of reviewing its factory location, at present at site A in Figure 2.27. The company has identified three other possible locations for a factory – at B, C or D.

The management of TOL understands the need to take many factors into consideration when deciding upon the most appropriate new location. These factors include:

- grants from the government
- labour costs
- the cost of transporting raw materials to the plant
- the cost of transporting finished goods to the market.

TOL will relocate its plant where the sum of all these costs is minimised. Production costs are constant wherever the factory is located.

It has been established that national and local government grants will reduce all costs by 25 per cent at locations B and D only. As for the other costs, *for each 10 000 components produced* they are as follows:

- labour: £7300 at A, £7500 at B, £8400 at C and £7900 at D
- transporting *raw materials:* £14 per mile by road, £8 per mile by canal, £9 per mile by rail
- transporting *finished goods* to the market *at C:* £18 per mile by road, £10 per mile by canal, £12 per mile by rail.

You are required to compare the costs involved and then provide a recommendation to the TOL management. You can do this by calculating the total costs of providing specialised computer components at each of the alternative locations and comparing these with the total cost of staying at the existing site. The preferred location will be the one with the lowest total cost.

To help you to keep your figures organised, copy out the table below and fill it in as your calculations proceed.

	A (£)	B (£)	C (£)	D (£)
Labour				
Raw materials transport				
Finished goods transport				
Totals				
Less government grants				
Total cost per 10 000 units				

1 Find the location with the lowest total running cost.
2 How would the cost of removal of existing stocks be taken into account in a real situation?
3 What other information might TOL require before making a relocation decision?
4 How much is the difference in total cost between the lowest and highest cost locations if sales reach 95 000 next year?

Integration with group companies

A large organisation will usually want to locate its plants where work can be easily **integrated** with other plants in the same group.

Labour and housing

Labour and certain skills are more readily available in some areas than in others. House prices and rents vary considerably between areas, and this may limit **labour mobility.**

Services

There are five standard **services** to be considered: gas, electricity, water, waste disposal and drainage. Some

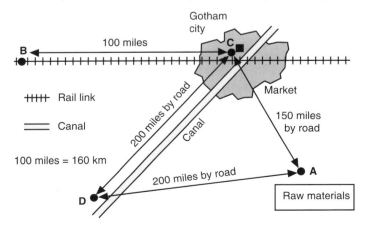

B ◄— 100 miles —► Gotham city / C / Market
Rail link
Canal
100 miles = 160 km
200 miles by road
Canal
150 miles by road
200 miles by road
D
A
Raw materials

industries use considerable quantities of water (e.g. metal-plating, food preparation). Disposal of waste can be expensive, so a careful assessment has to be made of all requirements.

Land

Land costs vary considerably from area to area. Sometimes the geology of land has to be looked at to see whether it can support heavy weights

Regional characteristics

Each region has particular characteristics. For example, **climate** might be an important factor in the manufacture of foodstuffs or perishable goods. **Local regulations** may affect certain types of activity on a site. Finally, some organisations like to locate in an area with a reputation for hosting similar businesses, or where training facilities are available locally.

Safety requirements

Certain types of industry may be considered to be a **danger** or nuisance to their local environment (e.g. nuclear power stations, chemical plant or munitions works). Public concern increased during the 1980s after the Union Carbide disaster in Bhopal, and the catastrophe at Chernobyl.

Communications

The accessibility of sea ports, airports and motorways is an important factor. A good **infra-structure** encourages industries to move to a region. Towns such as Northampton, Peterborough, Telford and Milton Keynes can all credit some of their development to their infrastructure.

Government influences

Disproportionate rates of **unemployment** in various parts of the UK have been a prominent feature of the last 30 years. Government intervention in the location of industry

Good communications are important

is designed to provide more balanced economic growth which distributes wealth and employment more evenly. There are financial incentives for organisations to locate in certain areas. In particular, selective assistance is provided for projects that create or safeguard employment.

Task

List the factors that would be important for locating each of the following:

a a college
b a brewery
c a bank branch
d a car manufacturing plant
e a large supermarket
f a steel plant.

Ranking of factors

There will be certain **limiting factors** to the choice of site. For example, a chemical plant needs to be near a major water supply, manufacturers need to be close to a source of labour, and a bookshop ideally needs to be in the centre of a town or city. Choosing a site means taking all of the relevant factors into consideration and attempting to assess them in relation to each other. One technique of doing this is **ranking.**

Weights are assigned to each of the factors, the most important being given the highest numbers. The choices of site are ranked according to the relative strengths of the factors at those sites – for example, the ranks would be 3, 2 and 1 if there were three choices of site. Finally, for each site the weights are multiplied by the ranks and a total score obtained. This is easier to understand when we look at an example.

In Figure 2.27, the ranks attached to the relative importance of four locational factors for each of two locations appear on the left of each cell, and the ranks multiplied by the weights appear in bold type after the diagonals. Location B is the most desirable location using this method.

| Factor | Weight | Possible locations | |
		A	B
Transport	5	1/**5**	2/**10**
Land	3	2/**6**	1/**3**
Amenities	3	1/**3**	2/**6**
Communications	3	2/**6**	1/**3**
Totals		**20**	**22**

Figure 2.27 *An example of the ranking technique*

Teesside Development Corporation

Teesside was hit heavily by the recession in the early 1980s when many thousands of workers lost their jobs with major employers such as ICI and British Steel. During the 1980s Teesside became an area of extensive industrial dereliction, with continuing high rates of unemployment.

Teesside Development Corporation came into operation on 15 May 1987 with a remit to regenerate 19 square miles of derelict industrial land on both banks of the River Tees and in the town of Hartlepool. It was set up by the government to stimulate the economy and improve the living and working environments of those living on Teesside. The initial development strategy was to achieve this with new jobs and services to enrich the quality of life. Nine initiatives formed the overall strategy for Teesside (see Figure 2.28).

☆ **Industrial development** – New sites and factories, including the Enterprise Zone at Middlesbrough

☆ **Commercial development** – New offices, leisure and shopping facilities

☆ **Land** – Strategic purchases of land to achieve regeneration

☆ **The river** – Rejuvenate its use with developments such as Hartlepool Marina and Tees Offshore Base

☆ **The environment** – Stimulate environmental change

☆ **Marketing** – Create a new and deserved image for Teeside

☆ **Training and retraining** – Meet the needs of new industries in the manufacturing and service sectors

☆ **Housing** – Improve existing housing stock and encourage new house-building

☆ **Transportation** – Improve the road infrastructure

Figure 2.28 *Initiatives for Teesside*

In the Corporation's first three years of development work, it brought in over 100 new companies and created 7500 jobs. One such company was a pipe-trailer manufacturer from Bradford-upon-Avon. Teesside Corporation helped by providing:

● abundant semi-skilled and skilled labour, wages paid for the first three months
● freehold land at £35 000 per acre
● grants to cover 15 per cent of capital costs, including land and building
● low-interest finance for 50 per cent of capital costs
● assistance towards consultancy costs
● direct consultancy from Corporation staff

● a site linked to a motorway.

Such companies have come to recognise the benefits Teesside can provide and have served to provide a wave of confidence about the future of the area.

1 Why did the government set up Teesside Development Corporation?
2 What does the Corporation aim to do?
3 Describe how the Corporation helps:
 a companies
 b the people of Teesside
 c the infrastructure
 d the environment.

Plant size

The **scale of operations** is usually measured by the number of units produced over a period of time. Large organisations are able to produce their goods and services at more competitive prices because they can spread their fixed costs over a larger output. If the amount of production increases, average unit costs over most production ranges are likely to fall because the organisation will benefit from **economies of scale** (the advantages it gains from becoming larger). All organisations aim for the scale of production which suits their line of activities best, and this is achieved when unit costs are at their lowest for the output produced. Beyond this point an organisation starts to find that inefficiencies or **diseconomies of scale** (the disadvantages of being too large) push unit costs up (see Figure 2.29).

If output increases at a faster rate than the inputs, average unit costs will be falling and an organisation is said to be benefiting from **increasing returns to scale.** Beyond the point at which average unit costs are at their lowest, the increase in output will be less than the increase in input, so that average unit costs are pushed up and the organisation is suffering from **decreasing returns to scale.**

Internal economies of scale enable an organisation to manage its operations more efficiently. They result from an organisation being able to use better technology, management and business practices as it gets larger. *External* economies of scale are factors outside the direct control of an organisation from which it benefits as an industry becomes larger or an area prospers.

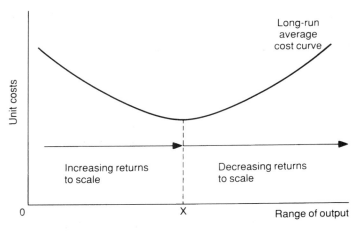

Figure 2.29 *Returns to scale*

Internal economies

Technical economies. Larger organisations have the ability to use techniques and equipment which cannot be adopted by small-scale producers of the same good or service. For example, an organisation might have three machines, each producing 2000 units per week at a unit cost of £1. As the organisation becomes larger it could replace these three machines with one machine producing 10 000 units per week at the lower cost of 75p per unit. If a small organisation tried to use such a machine, costs would be excessive in relation to its output and the machine would probably become obsolete before the end of its physical life.

Labour and managerial economies. In a very small business it is not unusual for one person to be 'jack of all trades', constantly adjusting skills and switching from one job to another. A large organisation, on the other hand, employs a number of specialised staff on its management team – accountants, marketing managers, personnel officers etc. Specialised roles tend to improve the overall quality of work and decision-making processes, and reduce overall unit costs if the output is sufficiently large.

Commercial economies. In the commercial world, larger organisations enjoy considerable benefits. For example:

● They can afford to devote more resources to market research and product research.
● Raw materials can be bought in bulk and larger discounts obtained.
● They can exercise buying power in their markets (i.e. demand extended credit periods).

- They sometimes have a financial stake in suppliers or retail outlets.
- Overheads may be spread over a larger output.
- Centralisation may make the organisation more efficient.

Financial economies. Large organisations are viewed in a different light by the financial world. As they are (usually) a more sound investment, they find it easier to raise finance, often at preferential interest rates. A further financial advantage is that they may be able to raise capital by issuing new shares on the Stock Exchange.

Risk-bearing economies. As well as having a financial stake in both suppliers and outlets, a larger organisation may have the ability to diversify across a range of products and operations to spread risks. By doing so an organisation covers itself against too much dependency on one area.

Task

Explain why a small organisation may be at a disadvantage when attempting to serve the same market as a large organisation. Can you think of any advantages that the small organisation may enjoy?

External economies

Concentration. If similar organisations develop in the same geographical area, a number of benefits arise – for example, a skilled labour pool, a reputation for the area for the quality of its work, local college courses tailored to meet the needs of that particular industry, and better social amenities.

Information. Larger industries have information services and employers' associations designed to benefit the actions of members (e.g. the Motor Industry Research Association).

Disintegration. In areas where certain industries develop, component industries or service industries develop to help with maintenance and support processes.

Case Study

ZX Hardware Ltd

ZX Hardware Ltd has responded to the general growth of interest, amongst young children and teenagers, in both computers for educational purposes and computer games. Over the last few years the organisation has developed through a massive expansion programme and rapidly increasing popularity. The following figures have been drawn from the financial statements of the business:

	1989	1990	1991	1992
Yearly outputs (units)	1350	1670	2940	5000
Number of machines	12	15	18	20
Number of employees	18	20	24	28
Number of products	2	3	5	9
Cost of manufacture per unit (£)	74.50	69.70	62.30	50.10

1. *Examine the figures carefully. What economies of scale have taken place? Describe how they might help ZX Hardware Ltd.*
2. *What other information can you extract from the table (e.g. output per machine, labour productivity)? What do these figures tell you about growth taking place in the company?*
3. *What other benefits not shown by the table will ZX Hardware Ltd obtain as it becomes larger?*

Growth

Organic growth is said to occur when an organisation obtains economies of scale through gradual development, often through re-investing profits, expanding its market share and developing new products. Such growth can take a long time. A quicker and more dynamic type of growth is possible through mergers, takeovers, deals and acquisitions which involve the integration of a number of organisations under a single umbrella organisation.

A **horizontal merger** takes place when two or more organisations with products of a similar nature at the same stage of production join together. A horizontal group will therefore consist of a number of integrated organisations at the same stage of production – for example, a group of motor manufacturers or supermarkets. By bringing organisations 'under the one roof', economies of scale can be achieved. Profitability should be increased and the integrated group will have greater market power and will have reduced competition.

A **vertical merger** takes place when two or more organisations producing products of a similar type but at different stages of production join together. **Backward vertical integration** involves the takeover of a supplier, and **forward vertical integration** involves merging with an organisation at a later stage in production. A vertical integration helps to secure sources of supply or secures outlets in the marketplace. In doing so it helps an organisation to achieve closer control at every stage of production. Breweries tend to be vertically integrated throughout their stages. In Figure 2.30 it can be seen how an organisation may integrate both horizontally and vertically.

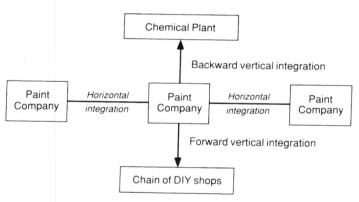

Figure 2.30 *Forms of integration*

Horizontal mergers

All the following mergers took place in 1991:

- Aérospatiale Helicopters (France) and MBB (Germany) joined forces to become Eurocopter International to compete with the powerful American helicopter manufacturers.

- Northern Foods paid £25.9 million for Bodfari Foods of Cheshire to increase its share of the national milk market from 13 to 13.5 per cent.
- Clarke Foods bought Lyons Maid to become the second largest ice-cream manufacturer after Unilever.

1 *Identify economies the above organisations might obtain.*

2 *How might these integrations affect the actions of their competitors?*

Not all integrations are either horizontal or vertical. It is a common practice today for organisations that are only loosely connected to join together in order to maximise risk-bearing economies. This is a feature of **conglomerate integration**. A conglomerate spreads risks by choosing different types of organisations in which to invest. This allows it to balance out variations in return – swings and roundabouts. As a result each of the subsidiaries may be substantially different in nature. For example, Hanson PLC is a conglomerate with widely diversified interests, including tobacco, batteries and building products.

Scan the financial pages of newspapers and professional business magazines. Make a short list of recent mergers, takeovers and acquisitions. Comment on the motivations behind them.

Diseconomies of scale

Large organisations are significantly more difficult to manage, and tend to suffer from certain inefficiencies.

Human relations. Large numbers of employees are more difficult to coordinate and manage. For example, communicating information and instructions may be difficult, especially through many layers of management. Contact between those who make the decisions and those who receive instructions is reduced, and this can lead to a low level of morale, a lack of purpose and industrial relations problems.

Decisions and coordination. The sheer scale of production may limit the ability of management to respond to the market and make good decisions. In a large organisation both the quality of information reaching the decision maker and the quality of instructions passed on can be severely affected by size. Difficulties may also arise because of excessive paperwork, regulations and meetings.

External diseconomies. Large organisations become well known in the community and efficient public relations is essential to overcome unfavourable attitudes of interest groups. For example, public displeasure with the actions of a large organisation may lead to consumer boycotts or necessitate the development of alternative products.

Element assignment

Responding to economic changes

This assignment can help you produce evidence for assessment, or claim the following Core Skills outcomes:

Communicating
Communicate in writing
Participate in oral and non-verbal communication

Personal Sills
Transfer skills gained to new and changing situations
Using information sources
Identify and solve routine and non-routine problems
Use a range of thought processes

You work in the personnel department of a large high street department store. Because of a general economic recession that has lasted for the last two years, the company is considering making redundancies. Profit margins have been squeezed to such an extent that the company has reached the point at which it is paying the minimum acceptable dividend to shareholders and is able to plough back only the barest minimum of capital into the business.

The personnel department is not keen to lay off workers because of the waste it would involve. Management is currently talking about laying off 30 employees (who on average have each worked for the company for five years).

The employees have all been extensively trained (the average expenditure on training per employee is £600 per year). As the number of young people in the population is falling it may in the longer term be difficult to recruit new staff.

The Personnel Manager has brought to your attention the following newspaper articles which show that the government is trying to get the economy going. She wants you to use the articles as the basis for a presentation to be made to senior managers of the store arguing that it would be wasteful to lay off workers.

Article One

. . . GO, GO, GO, BILLIONS FOR BORROWERS, BUILDERS AND DRIVERS

The Chancellor of the Exchequer dramatically put Britain back in the fast lane to prosperity yesterday.

He gave a multi-billion pound boost to drivers, industry and housing and declared: 'this is a strategy for growth'. His mini-budget was haled by small businesses and captains of industry.

The Chancellor's Autumn Statement stunned City cynics and brought cheering members of the government party to their feet in the Commons. He sliced another 1 per cent off interest rates (he has already reduced interest rates by 3%) and mortgages, scrapped car taxes – worth £400 off the average new motor.

The Chancellor also handed more public building work to private industry, and freed town hall cash for 153 000 new homes.

School and hospital spending will rise above the rate of inflation.

Article Two

CHANCELLOR RAISES BORROWING TO FUEL GROWTH

The Chancellor cut interest rates yesterday by a further point to 7 per cent, and launched a £4 billion, three-year package for growth that will contribute to the highest public borrowing for 17 years.

City economists said they were worried that the Government might run into difficulties next year financing such a large increase in borrowing.

The Chancellor's Autumn Statement gave priority to investment – offering 'hope, help and opportunity by switching resources to programmes that support the long-term prosperity of the country'.

Some critics feel that the heavy borrowing that the government needs to carry out to meet the expansionary programme will need to be met by increased taxes next year.

Task
Prepare a presentation for senior managers. The emphasis in your presentation should be on avoiding redundancies because of the waste that will occur. Your presentation will need to cover the following:

1 The likely effects of the Chancellor's Autumn statement for general economic conditions in the country.

2 *The likely consequences for the high street trade of your business, (a) in the short term and (b) in the longer term.*

3 *Other factors which are likely to lead to an increasing demand for your products in the medium to long term.*

4 *The cost of redundancies both in the short term and long term.*

5 *You will also need to prepare some arguments which would counter assertions from managers that the recession is likely to continue. (What might they say? How can you combat these claims?)*

You should present your ideas in a clearly set out word processed text.

You may want to use the following headings:

- Outlook for the economy
- Outlook for our business
- Cost of redundancies
- Benefits of retaining labour
- Conclusion. Why we should not make redundancies.

You may wish to role play this meeting. One group should represent the personnel department and will draw on the arguments in their presentation to form an economic "survival plan" for the company's future. A second group should represent senior management and develop their own positive programme of action for beating the recession. Each side should try to persuade the other of the value of its ideas.

chapter **3** # INVESTIGATING GOODS AND SERVICES

This chapter describes goods and services provided by a range of small and large businesses. It looks at different types of business organisation in the private and public sectors. It starts by looking at the importance of channelling scarce resources into meeting the needs of consumers in the market-place. The chapter progresses to explore ways of building on good ideas in order to provide an organised business proposition. The chapter builds on some of the economic relationships discussed in the previous chapter and introduces concepts such as demand and supply, costs and prices.

Students are encouraged to set up their own business working in teams. The chapter therefore introduces some of the principles of teamwork which are developed later in the book.

▪ THE MARKET-PLACE ▪

The market-place brings together **consumers** and **producers**. Consumers are able to signal their preferences and choices by 'voting' with their money for certain goods and services. This week Brussel sprouts may be highly popular, so they are quickly sold out. The sellers realise that there is a healthy demand, so tomorrow they may bring fresh stocks to the market and sell them at higher prices, and next year farmers may grow more sprouts to meet the expected demand. At the same time a particular type of apple may not be selling well, so shops are left with stocks which go off. Consequently the farmers will next year pick a small quantity of these apples.

Every day millions of individual **buying and selling decisions** are made. When I go to buy a new shirt I am more concerned with my own buying decision than with the state of the market. However, my decision to buy one shirt rather than another has a tremendous impact if there are thousands of other consumers making decisions

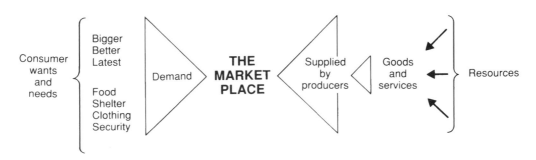

Figure 3.1 *The market-place brings together consumers and producers*

similar to my own. If we all want pink flowery shirts then it will pay manufacturers to switch resources (such as labour, machinery and raw materials) into making them. They may be able to make lots of them in a continuous production run at low cost and for a high profit. If I am the only person who wants a pink flowery shirt then I will struggle to find one, and I can expect it to be priced accordingly.

. IDENTIFYING A BUSINESS . OPPORTUNITY

People choose to set up their own business for a variety of reasons. Most people at some time or another have said things like: 'If only someone sold *x* here they could make a fortune', or 'I have a great idea for a new product'.

- At Christmas someone comes up with a new idea for hanging Christmas cards – a simple idea that would not require much capital. Perhaps it would present a business opportunity
- A group of teenagers notice that cars get stuck in a long queue at traffic lights in a busy area of a city. They decide to offer a car windscreen washing service. All they require are cloths, buckets, water, soap and a considerable amount of cheek!
- A newspaper seller working outside a busy railway station finds that travellers arriving at the station frequently ask the whereabouts of the nearest florist. He therefore has the idea of setting up his own flower stall located on the station forecourt.

There are many ways of coming up with a bright idea. Figure 3.2 shows a few suggestions. Try to add two examples of your own for each suggestion.

Most of the ideas that you come up with will already have been thought of and tried before, but sometimes a

genuinely new idea arises. Examples are the Rubik's cube and the Sony Walkman. However, most claims to 'new ideas' can rarely be attributed to just one person.

Your task is to examine the possible infringement of a **patent.** Imagine that the patent taken out on an invention has been challenged in a court of law by someone claiming to have invented (or patented) it first. In other words the idea may have been stolen.

Andreas Pavel filed a patent for an invention at the London Patent Office in 1977. The diagram shows what he invented.

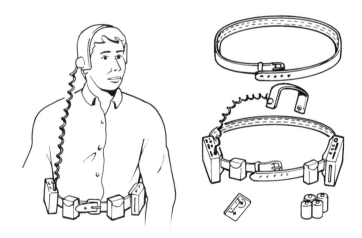

What do you think was the device that Andreas Pavel claimed to have invented?

In 1992, Pavel took a large international company to court, claiming infringement of his patent. The *Sony Walkman* became available in the shops in 1979.

There are two important requirements for a patent to be granted to an inventor of a new thing:

- It must contain a new idea.
- It must also have an inventive step (it should be more than just a development of an older idea).

Does the Sony Walkman infringe the patent taken out by Pavel in 1977? Set down your conclusions by using the following format:

FOR EXAMPLE:	
Developing a hobby	Making wooden toys
Using your skills	Plastering/painting
A chance idea	A musical toothbrush
Spotting a gap in the market	A home hairdresser
Improving a product or service	A better restaurant
Combining two existing ideas	Coffee shop/bookshop
Solving problems for people	Financial adviser
Listening to people	Teenagers want a mobile disco

Figure 3.2 *Some ways of thinking of business opportunities*

Differences	Similarities

Conclusions

Possible business ideas

Here are a number of possible business ideas for student groups to work on:

- Running discos
- Compiling a local guidebook or calendar
- A car-washing and valeting service
- Making cheap jewellery
- Making decorative candles
- Making wooden toys

- Producing a news sheet
- Making badges
- Making stuffed toys
- Bicycle repairs
- Production of a musical
- Screen-printing T-shirts
- Running a coffee shop
- Selling home-made sweets or cakes

Task

1 Which of the business ideas mentioned above are, in your opinion, most likely to succeed?
2 Now brainstorm a list of ideas which you think might be suitable. Write down all suggestions, however frivolous! Then try to eliminate the weakest ideas, so that you are left with just a few.

Assessing a new business idea

Later on we shall be looking at how to develop a detailed **business plan**. Before you can construct such a plan

you will need to know about such things as finance (Chapters 19 and 20) and Marketing (Chapters 7, 8 and 9). However, at this early stage it is helpful to think generally about your new business idea. The following list sets out the main considerations:

- IDEA – what is your idea? Is it a product or service?
- MARKET – who makes up the potential market? Who will you sell it to?
- ADVERTISING – how will you tell people about your product? Where will you advertise?
- EQUIPMENT – what equipment will you need to run your business?
- FINANCE – how much finance will you need? Where will you get it from?
- THE PRODUCT OR SERVICE – give more details about your product or service. How much will you charge? Are you trying to make a profit? How much?
- PREMISES – what sort of premises will you need? Where will the premises be?
- THE LAW – what are the legal requirements? Where can you find out such information?
- ORGANISATION – who will do what in the business? Who makes the decisions? Will there be rules setting out how the business will operate?
- ADVICE – where can advice be obtained?

Working as a team

Teamwork is an essential part of business life. The producer of a good or service relies on the quality of supplies bought in, and workers on a production line rely on the quality of inputs arriving from other workers. Interdependence is ever present in business.

So what is a team? A helpful definition that you might like to use is:

A team is a small group who have developed to the stage where they are able to perform effectively, each member adopting the role necessary to work with others, using complementary skills.

Practice in teamwork and cooperation with others towards a common goal will help you to develop insights into processes such as **conflict** and **consensus**.

Task

1 Working as a team of students, make a list of the skills possessed by each group member (a **skills audit**). Discuss how these skills could complement each other.

2 Brainstorm as a group a list of features that lead to good teamwork (e.g. good time management).

For a group to exist it must identify itself as a group (e.g. The Mountaineering Club, the Gary Glitter Appreciation Society, The Student Motorcycling Society, etc.). In addition there needs to be:

- a set of written or unwritten rules, known to the group members (e.g. an accepted way of dressing)
- some form of sanction for breaking rules (e.g. being ignored by other group members)
- a common aim or purpose (even if it is just to have a good time mixing with each other at college)
- a form of communication (e.g. a set way of greeting each other – Hiya Dude!)
- a way for group members to identify themselves as belonging to the group (e.g. status symbols, patterns of speech, hairstyles, etc.)
- ways by which individuals can achieve their own goals as a part of the group, for them to continue membership (e.g. to enjoy friendship while gaining a useful qualification).

Group task

Imagine that your business studies tutor has asked students to work in groups of three on an assignment that will take six weeks. The assignment is to find out why new companies have located on an industrial estate on the edge of town. For the assignment individual students will need to interview managers at three companies, and share this data with the rest of their group. They will then have to produce a group presentation in which all take part. The assignment must be completed by the deadline date and involves hard work and good group cooperation.

Student A
Karen Greaves

Student B
Winston Roberts

Student C
Saroj Panja

Student D
Mary Reynolds

Which three of the following four group members do you think would make the best team? Working in groups of three or four, read through the materials and then discuss each of the potential team members before making a decision.

Karen Greaves is hard-working and conscientious. She has had experience of working in an office for a small company. She is a Guide Leader and has won several leadership badges. At times she can be a bit overpowering and may dominate other members of the group.

Winston Roberts is a quiet student who produces a good-quality work to tight deadlines. He also has the knack of coming up with bright and imaginative ideas. In his spare time he works as a taxi driver.

Saroj Panja is known to be a big of a joker. At times he has a 'relaxed' attitude to work. His great ability is to pull other members of a team together. He can surprise people with his effort when the chips are down.

Mary Reynolds is an extremely hard-working and serious student. She is a good sharer of ideas and will help others out. When not working on college tasks she tends to keep to herself.

When you have carried out the task compare the results of different groups. How did group members work together? What roles did participants play in the discussions? Did some students tend to dominate discussions?

The team members

How well a team works together depends on the mixture of personalities and abilities of group members. If everyone wants to lead or everyone wants to follow it is unlikely that the group will interact very well together.

Robert Belbin identified eight roles which may be crucial to teamwork. Of course, individuals will take on more than one of these roles at different times. Indeed it is possible that team members may take on all these roles at different times.

- *The chairperson* – Presides over the group, and coordinates team efforts.
- *The shaper* – Is a would-be chair of the group. He or she drives the team on to complete the task successfully.
- *The plant* – This person may be rather shy but is successful at creating ideas and new proposals.
- *The monitor evaluator* – Someone who is able to analyse a situation, to look at what is going on, to suggest ways forward, to check the quality of progress and make pertinent comments.
- *The resource investigator* – Usually an extrovert who mixes well with other group members and can bring new contacts and ideas to the team. The ideas need to be worked on by more methodical members of the group.
- *The company worker* – This person, who is usually a very hard worker who can turn ideas into manageable tasks, tends to be good at administration rather than as a leader.
- *The team worker* – Is very good at supporting the team. He or she helps to encourage others and to support and harmonise the working of the team.
- *The finisher* – Makes sure that tasks are completed and deadlines are met. The finisher does not allow unfinished business to be left waiting.

Clearly a blend of all of these characteristics is important in teamwork.

The components of groupwork

Whenever a group works together there will be three strands involved in moving from the start of the decision-making process to the finish. These strands are illustrated in Figure 3.3.

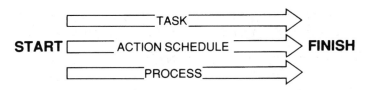

Figure 3.3 *The three strands of decision-making*

The task

The **task** is the content of the work. For example, the task of a student meeting may be to choose a student representative. The task of a piece of groupwork may be to produce an effective assignment. The task is the conversion of information and opinions from members into recommendations, reports or other outcomes. In general terms this covers what has to be done and why. Most groups give a lot of attention to the task.

Action schedule

The **action schedule** is concerned with how a group will be organised to do a given task. The schedule will cover such questions as who will fill the necessary roles, how progress will be checked and monitored, and how it will be ensured that the group finishes the task on time. It will also deal with the procedures of decision-making: how to ensure that everyone has a say, how conflict will be dealt with, etc. In general the action schedule will cover the 'where' and 'how' of decision-making.

An action schedule for a meeting might set down when the meeting will take place, who will attend, who will run the meeting, how decisions will be voted on and other procedural matters.

Process

The **process** is the interaction which takes place between members of a group. It is about how people work together, their relationships and the feelings created by their behaviour within the group. It involves **interpersonal skills** such as listening to others and helping others to join in a discussion. It involves expressions of feelings and the giving and receiving of feedback. In general it covers 'who does what' and 'when'. Many groups, unfortunately, pay little attention to process.

The three threads of group working are all important in group decision-making. It is obvious that a group that concentrates on its action schedule and its process entirely may have a wonderful time, but it may not achieve the task. It will not be long before morale will suffer and the group disintegrates. In contrast, concentration purely on the task is likely to lead to arguments about how things should be organised, and inattention to group members' thoughts and feelings will led to mishandled resources and to misunderstandings.

Because teamwork is an important personal skill you will need to be aware of the three elements outlined above. Do not forget the importance of process. When you carry out tasks involving small groups, some students can act as process observers. The process observer will need to watch how the group works together, and report the results back to the group at the end of a work session. The process observer should look at aspects of groupwork including:

- Who initiated activities?
- Who supported others in the group by helping them when appropriate?
- Who harmonised the group by seeking consensus and common purposes?
- Who listened to others and respected their contributions?
- Who collected and organised information for the group?
- Who made it easier for the group to make progress by involving others?
- Who in the group was reliable?
- Who blocked progress?
- Who interrupted others?
- Did anyone carry out actions which damaged the confidence of others?

The information provided by the process observers can be used to reflect on group dynamics and group interaction. Steps can then be taken to improve the quality of group working.

- Knowing when to shut up
- …

Produce the profile on one sheet of A4 paper. The sheet should be easy to understand, and provide a simple checklist so that you can monitor your progress in developing process skills.

Skill	Good at:	Quite good at:	Poor at:
Starting a discussion			
Helping others to join in			

During the course you should review your process skills profile to see what progress you are making. You could discuss your profile with other students (peer group assessment).

Developing a real team

Jon Katzenbach and Doug Smith in their book *The Wisdom of Teams: Creating the High-Performance Organisation* (Harvard Business School Press, 1993) argue that there is a threshold that a group must cross before it becomes a team. They define a team as:

A small number of people with complementary skills who are committed to a common purpose, performance goals, and an approach for which they hold themselves mutually accountable.

Task

Working in a group of three or four, make a list of important process skills. Here are four to start your list:

- Starting a discussion
- Helping others to join in
- Building bridges between team members

Task

Consider three groups that you belong to. Assess to what extent they meet the definition of a team as defined by Katzenbach and Smith.

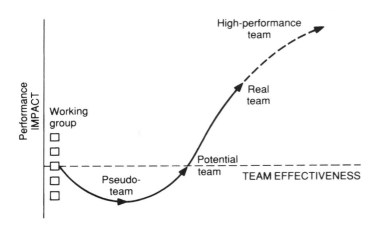

Figure 3.4 *The performance curve*

Katzenbach and Smith argue that managers need to be able to understand the ingredients of a team if they are to run a successful organisation. They set out a simple framework for the development of teams, and show a team performance curve (Figure 3.4).

1. The working group: This is a collection of individuals for whom there is no real opportunity or need to become a team. Each working group member produces something that helps the task to be completed without feeling a real part of a team. Being a part of the working group places no more demand on the individual than if they were working independently.

2. The pseudo-team. In this situation there is no joint benefit of being a part of the team. Indeed, each member's performance is worse than if working alone. This is because there is no focus, no common sense of purpose, and no set of goals. The group members are confused as to what they should be doing or how they should be working together. At some stage in your life you are almost certain to work in a pseudo-team. It is very frustrating. Members are 'feeling their way in the dark'. This may generate antagonism between group members, and the team will quickly crumble.

3. The potential team. This is a collection of individuals with a clear performance need. They are seriously seeking to improve their impact on it. In other words, they are aware that there is a need for something to be done, and they want to do something about it. Unfortunately, however, they lack clarity about their aims as well as the discipline needed for a common working approach. Also they will not have

established the final criterion – mutual accountability. Many organisations are full of potential teams. This provides a real opportunity and a challenge for management.

4. The real team. It is worth repeating that a real team is 'a small number of people with complementary skills who are committed to a common purpose, performance goals, and an approach for which they hold themselves mutually accountable'.

5. The high-performance team. As well as meeting the definition for a real team, this group will also be deeply committed – even beyond the team set-up – to the personal growth and success of its members. It will significantly out-perform other teams.

Task

How would you classify teams that you are familiar with on the team performance curve? Make a study of a 'high-performance team' to show why they are so successful (e.g. the Red Arrows). Alternatively make a study of a pseudo-team: what are they doing wrong?

▪ TYPES OF BUSINESS OPPORTUNITY ▪

Figure 3.5 shows the production of a manufactured product, a hammer made of steel and wood. In the production of a hammer a number of bulky raw materials are used. The iron and steel works will ideally need to be situated close to supplies of coal, limestone and iron ore. If the raw materials are to be imported then the steelworks will need to be near a port. The wood will need to be processed close to the site at which trees are felled. The semi-finished manufactured items can then be transported to the tool factory where the hammers will be assembled. The final stages of **adding value** involve transporting the finished hammers to a shop for sale. Energy is an important input of production at each stage, whether it be to heat the blast furnace or to provide heat and light at the shop.

Manufacturing provides an important source of business opportunities. During the Industrial Revolution Britain was

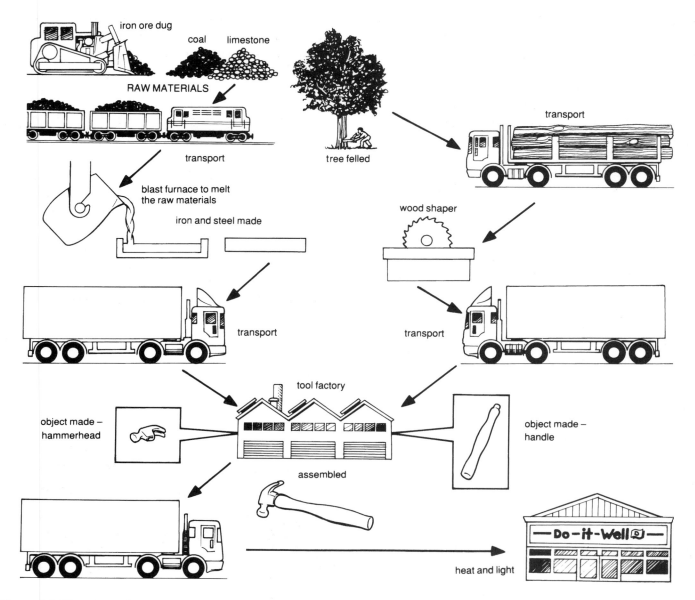

Figure 3.5 *The principal stages in producing a hammer*

the first to develop manufacturing on a large scale. Manufacturing created much of the wealth of the country. The nineteenth century saw massive increases in production in coal mining, steel, textiles, machine tools, engineering and many other industries. These changes were supported by a revolution in transport – canals, navigable rivers, roads and then rail (later to be followed by air transport). The construction of railways in America and other overseas countries, together with the continuous improvements in the technique of shipbuilding, made it profitable, by the 1880s, for large quantities of grain and meat to be exported to Western Europe from overseas. The same continuous reduction in transport costs gave English and other manufacturers a world market.

Continuous improvements in the technique of producing iron and steel gave a great impetus to the growth of railways. The railways and rolling stock in turn demanded very large quantities of iron and steel. The increased demand made possible **economies of scale** in the production of iron and steel, which further cheapened the prices of rails and rolling stock. Cheap transport also increased the demand for iron and steel by the expansion of manufacturing and the consequent growth in the orders for plant and equipment of all kinds. At the same time it enabled iron and steel works to obtain coal or iron ore (or later, scrap) from a distance at a lower cost than before. Thus the development of the iron and steel industry helped the development of railways and shipbuilding. The Industrial Revolution witnessed an upward spiral in demand from manufacturing industry. It is not surprising that today many commentators are worried about the declining importance of manufacturing output in Britain.

· TYPES OF BUSINESS ACTIVITY ·

Businesses are either in the private sector or the public sector of the economy. Private-sector businesses are owned by private individuals and groups. Public-sector businesses are owned by the government (see Figure 3.6).

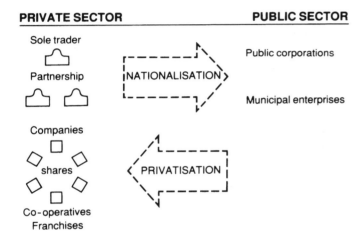

Figure 3.6 *Private-sector and public-sector businesses*

The main types of business organisation in the private sector are shown in Figure 3.7.

A share is a piece of paper showing that you are the part-owner of a business. Shareholders in companies and co-operatives have the legal protection of **limited liability.** Sole traders and ordinary partners cannot have limited liability.

Limited liability means that, if the business goes bankrupt because it is unable to meet its debts, the shareholders/owners will not be liable (responsible by law) to lose their possessions to pay the money that is owed. The maximum amount that they could lose is the amount that they have put into their shares.

Type of enterprise	Who owns the business?	Who controls the business?	Usual sources of finance
Sole trader	One person	One person	Owner's savings, bank loans or overdraft, profits
Partnership	Two or more partners	The partners	Partners' savings, bank loans or overdraft, profits
Company	Two or more shareholders	The directors	Share issues, bank loans or overdraft, venture capital, profits
Co-operative	Two or more members	Managers and other co-operators jointly	Share issues, bank loans or overdraft, profits

Figure 3.7 *Main types of business organisation in the private sector*

The sole trader

The **sole trader** is the most common form of business ownership and is found in a wide range of activities (e.g. window cleaning, plumbing, electrical work, busking). Figure 3.8 shows a breakdown of sole proprietors into industrial groupings in 1991.

Grouping	Percentage
Construction	20.3
Production	5.7
Agriculture	6.9
Other services	8.7
Motor trades	6.0
Business services	5.0
Catering	7.9
Finance	10.2
Retailing	18.6
Wholesaling/dealing	5.2
Transport	5.5

Figure 3.8 *Number of units as a percentage of the total for sole traders*

Task

Give examples of local businesses which could fit into each of the groupings in Figure 3.8. You could carry out a survey of local businesses, and store your information in a computer database.

Present the information given in Figure 3.8 in the form of pie chart using a graphics plotting package.

No complicated paperwork is required to set up a sole trader business. Decisions can be made quickly and close contact can be kept with customers and employees. All profits go to the sole trader, who also has the satisfaction of building up his or her own business.

There are disadvantages. As a sole trader you have to make all the decisions yourself, and you may have to work long hours (what do you do if you are ill or want a holiday?). You do not have limited liability, and you have to provide all the finance yourself. As a sole trader you need to be a jack-of-all-trades, and just because you are a good hairdresser does not necessarily mean you have a head for business!

Task

Write a short case history of a sole trader in your neighbourhood. When did he or she set up? What is the business? What are the advantages and disadvantages to this person of being a sole trader?

The partnership

An ordinary partnership can have between two and twenty partners. Professional partnerships may have more. People in business partnerships can share skills and the workload, and it may be easier to raise needed capital.

A group of vets is able to pool knowledge of different diseases and groups of animals, and two or three vets working together may be able to operate a 24-hour service. When one of the vets is ill or goes on holiday, the business can cope.

Figure 3.9 shows a breakdown of partnerships into industrial groupings.

Grouping	Percentage
Construction	11.2
Production	6.5
Agriculture	16.0
Other services	6.0
Motor trades	5.2
Business services	3.4
Catering	12.5
Finance	7.3
Retailing	24.0
Wholesaling/dealing	4.8
Transport	3.1

Figure 3.9 *Number of units as a percentage of the total for partnerships*

Task

1 Present the information in Figure 3.9 in pie-chart format using a computer graphics plotting package.

2 Compare the pie-chart for partnerships with that for sole traders. What are the key differences

3 Carry out a survey of local partnerships. Try to find examples that would fit into each of the groupings outlined in Figure 3.9.

Partnerships are usually set up by writing out a **deed of partnership** which is witnessed by a solicitor. This sets out important details such as how much each partner should put into the business, how the profits and losses will be shared, and the responsibilities of each partner.

Partnerships are particularly common in professional services (for example, doctors, solicitors, accountants). A small business such as a corner shop may take the form of a husband and wife partnership.

The main disadvantages of partnerships are that people can fall out (she doesn't work as hard as me!), ordinary partnerships do not have limited liability, and partnerships can rarely borrow or raise large amounts of capital. Business decisions may be more difficult to make (and slower) because of the need to consult all the partners. There may be disagreements about how things should be done. A further disadvantage is that profits will be shared.

There is also a special form of partnership called a **limited partnership**. Limited partners (sometimes called 'sleeping partners') can put money into a partnership and have the protection of limited liability. However, they play no part in the running of the business. The business will be run by at least one non-limited partner.

Companies

A **company** is set up to run a business. It has to be registered before it can start to operate, but once all the paperwork is completed and approved the company becomes recognised as a legal body.

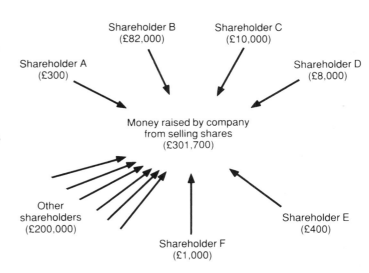

Figure 3.10 *A company raises money from its shareholders*

The owners of a company are its **shareholders.** However, other individuals and businesses do not deal with the shareholders – they deal with 'the company'.

Shareholders put funds into the company by buying **shares.** New shares are often sold in face values of £1 per share, but this is not always the case. Some shareholders will only have a few hundred pounds' worth of shares, whereas others may have thousands of pounds' worth. This is shown in Figure 3.10.

The capital of the company

The promoter or directors of the company can apply to the Registrar of Companies for permission to issue new shares. The amount that the Registrar agrees to is called the **approved capital**.

The **issued capital** is the value of the shares that are actually sold to shareholders. A company may choose not to issue that full value of its authorised capital: it may hold back a certain amount for future issue.

Shares can be issued for payment in stages over a period of time. Each stage is then termed a 'call'. There may be three or four calls before the full price is finally paid. The **paid-up capital** is the money that has been received for these partly-paid shares.

Task

Obtain the prospectus of a new company. This will show details of the offer of shares for sale. What is the value of the authorised capital? How much capital is actually being sought? What arrangements are being made for the payment of the shares?

Task

Study a local private company. Who owns it and who controls it? How much share capital does it have? What are the advantages and disadvantages of this organisational form for this particular company?

Private companies

Private companies tend to be smaller than public ones (discussed below) and are often family businesses. There must be at least two shareholders but there is no maximum number. Shares in private companies cannot be traded on the Stock Exchange, and often shares can only be bought with the permission of the **board of directors**.

The board of directors is a committee set up to protect the interests of shareholders. The members of the board choose the managing director, who is responsible for the day-to-day running of the business. The rules of the business set out when shareholders' meetings will take place and the rights of shareholders.

Private companies may find it possible to raise more cash (by selling shares) than unlimited-liability businesses. The shareholders can also have the protection of limited liability.

The main disadvantages compared with unlimited-liability businesses are that they have to share out profits among shareholders and they cannot make decisions so quickly. They cost more to set up.

Public companies

A **public company** has its shares bought and sold on the Stock Exchange. Companies can go to the expense of having a 'full quotation' on the Stock Exchange so that their share prices appear on the dealers' visual display screens. Alternatively they might choose to enter the 'unlisted securities market', or what is known as the 'third market' – whereby they only trade a small proportion of their shares and prices are not quoted in the financial press.

The main advantage of selling shares through the Stock Exchange is that large amounts of capital can be raised very quickly. One disadvantage is that control of a business can be lost by the original shareholders if large quantities of shares are purchased as part of a 'takeover bid'. It is also costly to have shares quoted on the Stock Exchange.

In order to create a public company the directors must apply to the Stock Exchange Council, which will carefully check the accounts. A business wanting to 'go public' will then arrange for one of the merchant banks to handle the paperwork. Selling new shares is quite a risky business. The Stock Exchange has 'good days' (when a lot of people want to buy shares) and 'bad days' (when a lot people want to sell). If the issue of new shares coincides with a bad day a company can find itself in difficulties. For example, if it hopes to sell a million new shares at £1 each and all goes well, it will raise £1 million; but on a bad day it might only be able to sell half its shares at this price.

One way around this problem is to arrange a 'placing' with a merchant bank. The merchant bank recommends the company's shares to some of the share-buying institutions with which it deals (pension funds and insurance

Figure 3.11 *Choosing the management in a private company*

companies, for example) who may then agree to buy, say, one-tenth of the new shares. In this way the merchant bank makes sure that the shares are placed with large investors before the actual date of issue comes round. Then, even if it is a bad day on the Stock Exchange when the shares are issued, the company's money is secure.

Another common method by which public companies raise share capital is to offer new shares for sale to the general public. Very often the shares will be 'underwritten' by a merchant bank. The company's shares are advertised in leading newspapers and the public invited to apply.

When a company is up and running, a cheaper way of selling is to write to existing shareholders inviting them to buy new shares. This is a **rights issue**.

Task

In the second half of the 1980s, advertisements appeared regularly in the national press from new companies offering shares for sale. In the early 90s this was reduced to a trickle. Fewer companies were starting up and, with a general feeling of pessimism about the recession, there were lots of 'bad days' when investors would be unlikely to buy new shares. As we move into the mid-1990s there are a number of companies hoping to offer shares to the public. Study the quality newspapers. How many companies are offering shares for sale? How successful are they in having their shares bought?

Case Study

The growth of Floral Prints Ltd

In 1920, Mavis Stein set up her own dressmaking business in Norwich. She employed four seamstresses to work on the patterns she produced. The business flourished and was soon producing dresses for a number of wealthy private clients in Norwich.

Mavis then joined up with Jenny Jones, an up-and-coming fashion designer from the London School of Fashion.

The partnership they formed concentrated on high-quality 'up-market' garments. The garments were sold to fashion houses in London and Norwich. The partnership deed set out that each would put £2000 into the business, share the work and the profits. They would be entitled to two weeks' holiday a year.

Mavis was to concentrate on the commercial side of the business (i.e. the buying and selling). She would purchase materials and equipment, and meet buyers. She would also handle the accounts. Jenny was to concentrate on the design and production and manage the workforce, which in the 1950s had risen to two tailor cutters and 16 seamstresses. They also employed a full-time secretary and bookkeeper.

In the 1960s, Mavis suffered a prolonged illness. The deed of partnership was altered. Mavis left her money in the business and became a sleeping partner, with the profits being divided 60:40 in Jenny's favour.

In 1970, Jenny retired and it was decided to form a private company known as Floral Prints Ltd. Initially shareholders were mainly friends and relatives. Mavis and Jenny between then held 55 per cent of the shares. Shares were also sold to employees. A number of employees who had been with the business from the start were given additional shares. The board of directors, which was chaired by Mavis' daughter Rose, appointed Steven White as the managing director.

During the 1980s, Floral Prints established a national chain of boutiques. In order to finance this expansion the company went public. In 1985 the company was taken over by a large German company. It still trades under the original name.

1 Who originally owned and controlled the business?
2 What would be the benefits of becoming a partnership?
3 Would there be any drawbacks?
4 Why do you think the business became a private company?
5 What would be the advantages and disadvantages of becoming a private company?
6 Who owned and controlled the private company?
7 Why do you think the business became a public company?
8 What would be the advantages and disadvantages of becoming a public company?
9 Who owned and who controlled the public company?

Co-operatives

Co-operatives are increasingly popular as a means of business organisation. At one time they were only to be found in agriculture and retailing, but in recent years the biggest growth areas have been in service occupations and in small-scale manufacturing.

The basic idea behind a co-operative is that people join together to make decisions, work and share profits. There are many different types of co-operative; we consider here the three most commonly found in business.

Retail co-operatives

The first successful co-operative in this country was set up in the northern town of Rochdale in the last century. Twenty-eight weavers clubbed together to start their own retail shop, selling a few basic grocery items. The profits were to be shared according to the amount spent, and everyone would have an equal say in how the shop was run.

The basic ideas started in Rochdale continue in today's Co-op. On buying £1 share in the Co-op you are entitled to go along to the annual general meeting to discuss policy.

Consumer co-operatives are usually registered as limited-liability companies.

Task

Find out how your local co-operative retail outlet is organised. How can you become a member? Where are meetings held? How can you have a say in policy? How are profits distributed?

Annual Meetings of Members

GRANTHAM FRIDAY, 29th APRIL
THE LEISURE CENTRE, UNION STREET, at 7 p.m.

Members are warmly invited to join their Members' Council representatives for refreshments from 6.30p.m. until 7p.m.

Admission on production of Members Share Book

Greater Nottingham Co-operative Society Ltd.

Producer co-operatives

Producer co-operatives are usually registered as companies 'limited by guarantee', which means that each member undertakes to fund any losses up to a certain amount. There are many types. A workers' co-operative, for example, is one that employs all or most of its members. In a workers' co-operative members:

- share responsibility for the success or failure of the business
- work together
- take decisions together
- share the profits.

Other examples of producer co-operatives are groups to grow tomatoes, to make furniture or to organise child-minding.

The main problems that such co-operatives face are finance and organisation. Co-operatives sometimes find it difficult to raise capital from banks and other bodies because they are not groups that seek to make profits primarily. A number of co-operatives in recent years have, however, been able to raise finance by selling shares. Some larger co-operatives have also found that it is necessary to set up a management structure in order to get decisions made.

Marketing co-operatives

Marketing co-operatives are most frequently found in farming areas. The farmers set up a marketing board to be responsible for, among other things, grading, packaging, distributing, advertising and selling their produce.

· FRANCHISING ·

In America over one-third of all retail sales are made through firms operating under the **franchise** system. It is a form of business organisation that is becoming increasingly popular in the United Kingdom.

Franchising is really the 'hiring out' or licensing of the use of 'good ideas' to other companies. A franchise grants permission to sell a product and trade under a certain name in a particular area. If I have a good idea, I can sell you a licence to trade and carry out a business using my idea in your area. The person taking out the franchise puts down a sum of money as capital and is issued with equipment by the franchising company. The firm selling the franchise is called the *franchisor* and a person paying for the franchise is called the *franchisee*. The franchisee usually has the sole right of operating in a particular area.

This type of trading is common in the fast-food industry, examples being Spud-U-Like and Pizza Hut. Further examples are Dyno-Rod (in the plumbing business), Tumbletots, Body Shop and Prontaprint.

Where materials are an important part of the business (e.g. hamburgers, confectionery, hair conditioners) the

franchisee must buy an agreed percentage of supplies from the franchisor, who thus makes a profit on these supplies as well as ensuring the quality of the final product. The franchisor also takes a percentage of the profits of the business, without having to risk capital or become involved in the day-to-day management.

The franchisee benefits from trading under a well-known name and enjoys a local monopoly. Training is usually arranged by the franchisor. The franchisee is his or her own boss and takes most of the profits.

Task

Write down two lists to summarise the advantages of franchising to (i) the franchisor and (ii) the franchisee. Can you think of any more examples of firms operating under this system?

· SMALL AND LARGE FIRMS ·

Under the Companies Act, a small firm was defined as one having fewer than 50 employees. The Bolton Committee defined a small company as being one with fewer than 200 employees.

The government does not publish statistics on the size of firms in service industries, but statistics for manufacturing are published in *Business Monitor*. Most manufacturing companies employ fewer than 99 workers (see Figure 3.12). If statistics were provided for services we would find a heavy emphasis on the small scale, although banks and insurance companies are very large employers.

Number of employees	Total units		Total employment		Total net output	
	Number	% of total	Millions	% of total	£ millions	% of total
1–99	134 707	96.4	1.2	24.5	24 954	18.9
100–499	3 966	2.8	0.8	16.3	18 861	14.3
500–1499	721	0.5	0.6	12.2	17 044	12.8
1500+	395	0.3	2.8	57.1	71 536	54.0

Figure 3.12 *Size of firms by employment and output, 1990*

What does Figure 3.12 tell us about the contributions of small and large firms to national output? Why do so many small firms continue to exist? What advantages do large firms have over small ones?

A **small firm** is likely to be a sole trader, a partnership or a private company. It is also likely to operate on one site and to have a limited amount of specialisation of departments.

Small firms often serve a niche in the market. Communications between members are almost invariably good, and the company is able to respond to changing circumstances.

Study two small firms. What are the advantages and disadvantages of this form of organisation? Compare your findings with those of other students. Can you make any general comments?

Large firms are most likely to be public limited companies, although some private companies and even partnerships are large. They may operate from several locations in more than one country. They may employ many people, have extensive specialisation, and use considerable quantities of capital. All this means that large firms can produce larger outputs with lower unit costs.

Study one large company (the company report will give you ample information). Where does it operate? How many people does it employ? What is its turnover? How much profit does it make? What evidence is given in the report that it benefits from being large?

· THE VALUE OF ENTREPRENEURSHIP ·

'Enterprise' was the buzz-word of the 1980s. Enterprise is often associated with starting and running a business. However, every kind of job, every kind of activity, needs enterprising people. Nobody should be put off from starting a business simply by fear of failure, or by fear of losing interest. If you do have to give it up and start working again for somebody else, you will almost certainly find that your particular brand of enterprise and skill can still flourish – to everyone's benefit. You will also be all the wiser for your experience.

Recent emphasis on the power of small businesses as a dynamo for the economy reverses the emphasis in the 1950s and 60s on the importance of size. In 1967, for example, Michael Shanks wrote in *The Innovators* (Pelican):

> 'The trouble is, however, that a large proportion of British Industry consists of small firms and, while there is no necessary relationship between size and efficiency, many of the trends in modern technology do appear to favour large units.'

Nowadays a lot more emphasis is given to small firms. Note, for example, the following quotation from Tim Eggar, Minister of State for Employment, in *Small Firms in Britain* (Employment Department, 1989):

> 'The substantial growth of the small firms sector and its increasing strength and diversity are the results of the determined efforts of many thousands of men and women who have taken the decision to start and run their own business. Small businesses also make an important contribution to the quality of life through the fulfilment they offer to the entrepreneur and the extension of consumer choice and service for the rest of the community.'

New enterprises come up with new ideas. If these enterprises are allowed to flourish these new ideas will soon spread to the rest of the economy as other entrepreneurs copy the ideas. The government therefore has an important role to play in encouraging new enterprises so that the benefits of these ideas can be spied widely in the country.

Working as a group, draw up a list of enterprise opportunities in your area. What factors will help these ideas to be a success? What factors will limit the success of these ideas? How can limitations be reduced? You will need to consider what resources will be required in order to put these ideas into practice.

BUSINESSES IN THE PUBLIC SECTOR

Most people expect **public-sector organisations** to seek to increase the welfare of all citizens. In recent years, the shape and style of management in the national public sector has changed enormously. Today all three major political parties emphasise the role of **accountability** in the public sector. In other words, public-sector organisations are expected to show that they are using money wisely – that they are not wasting scarce resources. In 1993, for example, the new Director General of the BBC, the new Head of the Prison Service, and the new Chief Constable of the Metropolitan Police force were all chosen because of their business expertise.

From 1979 onwards, managers in government were repeatedly told that they were sluggish, inward-looking and even incompetent in comparison with their equivalents in the private sector. Public-sector managers were accused of being wasteful, unresponsive and resistant to new ideas. This is rarely the case today. In schools, hospitals, transport organisations and many other areas of the public sector, business planning takes place in a detailed way. Public-sector managers are explicitly defining tasks, pinning down who is responsible for doing them, measuring whether they have been done and how well, and establishing clearly what they cost, as well as controlling the cost.

The government has a shareholding in some businesses and direct ownership of a number of major enterprises. Local government also has a stake in some business activities.

Local government enterprises

Local councils often run business activities. For example, in municipal car parks attendants may be employed to collect parking charges and to check that no-one is using the car park without paying. Swimming pools, day nurseries, bus services, parks and leisure centres may all be run by the council, although services are increasingly being offered to tender by private firms.

Finance to run municipal enterprises usually comes from **local taxes** and from charges for using the services.

The local council may also sponsor **job creation schemes**. For example, it might set up **enterprise workshops** where people can start up a business in premises with a very low rental charge.

Central government enterprises

In the United Kingdom certain business activities are run by one of the following:

● a government department
● a company in which the government has a shareholding
● a public corporation.

Activities run by a government department

When an activity is run by a government department, a Minister is in overall charge, and the department is staffed and run by **civil servants**. An example of this is the Department of Inland Revenue which deals with the collection of some taxes.

From a business point of view there are a number of criticisms of such an organisation:

● Decisions are made slowly because there are many links in the chain of command.
● The organisation is not forced to be efficient – there is no competitive spur.
● It is difficult to protect the public's interest by checking on how the department is run.

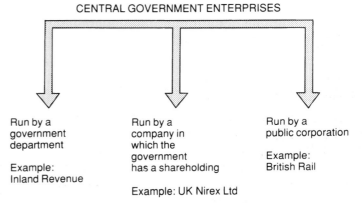

Figure 3.13 *Central government's involvement in business*

Companies in which the government has a shareholding

Over the years the British government has had shareholdings in a number of public companies, including BP and Rolls-Royce. The shareholding has often been a form of **subsidy** to the company to help it carry out research, compete with overseas companies, or avoid **unemployment** of the workforce.

In recent years the government has been selling off these shareholdings in the belief that companies should stand on their own feet.

Activities controlled by public corporations

Public corporations, the main form of direct government involvement in business, are owned by the state on behalf of the people. They are felt to be a suitable form of **public ownership** because, although the state owns the corporations, their controllers are given a lot of freedom to make their own decisions.

Public corporations are set up by Act of Parliament, an example being the Coal Industry Nationalisation Act 1946. They are also called **nationalised industries.**

Although a public corporation provides a marketable good or service, it is different from a normal company in that the managers are not accountable to shareholders – instead they are accountable to the government. Also, although today public corporations are expected to be profitable, in the past they were given wider **social responsibilities**.

Once a public corporation has been set up by Act of Parliament, a government Minister is made responsible for the industry concerned. For example, the Minister of Transport is responsible for British Rail. However, the Minister chooses a chairperson (not a civil servant) to run the industry on a day-to-day basis.

The government sets yearly **targets** for the particular industry to meet, and the chairperson and managers must then decide on the best way to meet these. The government might, for example, set the British Broadcasting Corporation a target of making a 15 per cent return on capital employed in 1997. The corporation must then decide on how to meet this target in conjunction with its commitment to provide a high quality of programmes. In other words, it must decide on how much to spend on programmes, how much to pay in wages and so on. The corporation is supposed to have the freedom to make these day-to-day decisions and there is a lot of heated debate in the press and Parliament if the government tries to interfere.

Case Study

Sweeping modernisation at the BBC

John Birt took over as Director General of the BBC in January 1993. He immediately promised an effective BBC which would clear away red tape, territorialism and confusion.

The BBC's television services had overspent by £38 million in 1992. Mr Birt therefore said that a priority was to appoint a new finance director. Key structural changes would include:

- streamlining the operation to focus on aims and objectives, policy and performance
- the separation of programme production from commissioning and scheduling in television and radio, buying in programmes from a range of sources
- the creation of a separate resources, engineering and services department to run the production side of the BBC.

Public corporation	Public company
Set up by Act of Parliament	Set up by issuing prospectus and offer to buy shares
Owned by government	Owned by shareholders
Run by chairperson and managers appointed by government	Run by management team chosen by directors representing shareholders
Aims to provide a public service as well as having commercial goals	Commercial goals

Figure 3.14 *Contrasting public corporations and public companies*

1 Is it important to be financially accountable?

2 What will be the effects of the restructuring on:

a the number of people working for the BBC

b the efficiency of its organisation

c the quality of programmes?

3 Is it a good idea to buy in programmes rather than to make them?

4 The BBC will become more 'streamlined'. Is this a good thing?

5 Should the BBC have a business person as its Director General?

Up to 1979 many public corporations were given large financial **subsidies** by the government. There were two main reasons for this:

● to try to maintain jobs in declining industries (e.g. coal and steel) because they were major employers.

● to encourage the corporations to continue to run services which, although not profitable (and so of no interest to private firms), were of great social benefit to certain individuals, groups or communities.

Today public corporations are encouraged to concentrate more on meeting financial targets, and to be more profit and client conscious. Members of the public do have some control over the running of the public corporations. They can make a complaint to their local MP who can then raise the matter when the corporation is being discussed in Parliament. In addition, a committee of MPs has the job of keeping an eye on each of the corporations, and each has a consumer council to which complaints can be made.

· PRIVATISATION ·

One of the major policies of the Conservative governments of the 1980s and early 90s was **privatisation** – that is, putting public sector businesses into private hands. Examples of privatisations are British Airways, British Telecom and British Gas. In the mid-1990s the government is hoping to sell off parts of the railway and coal industries. However, there is a considerable feeling that these industries do not lend themselves readily to privatisation. For example, railways require such large units of capital that safe management of the railways can only be effectively carried out by a public corporation. Some parts of British Rail (e.g. commuter lines in the south-east) are run for the public good and can never be profitable.

The usual build-up to privatisation is to remove inefficient parts of an industry, cutting back on employment and redundant equipment. Shares are then offered to the public.

A number of reasons have been given for privatisation. Firstly, it creates wider **share ownership** – the idea is that, by owning shares in public services like the telephones, electricity, water or gas, people will feel more involved. Secondly, privatisation is supposed to make these industries more **competitive.** It is felt that if some of these industries are encouraged to compete more they will produce a better service. In the past losses were made up by taxes; losses today could lead to bankruptcy. Thirdly, money from the sale of the industries should enable the government to **lower taxes**. Fourthly, the industries themselves can raise money more easily for **investment.** And finally, the Conservative government sees its role as deciding on policy and making laws, not running companies.

Task

Study an example of a privatisation (either in the UK or another country). Why was the industry privatised? How is the ownership of the industry changed? What problems were involved in the privatisation? How can you measure the success of the privatisation? Is the privatisation likely to be a success?

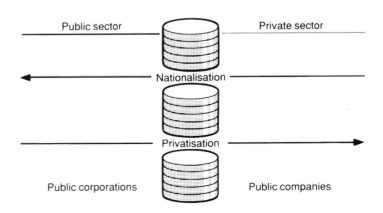

Figure 3.15 *Privatisation and nationalisation*

There are many opponents of the principle of privatisation. They say that the public already owns these industries, so why should they be asked to pay for shares in order to continue to participate in ownership? Some opponents also say that in competing to make profits these industries tend to cut services which are a real benefit to certain individuals, groups and communities, and that money raised from the sale really helps to cut the taxes of the better off.

Case Study

Making railways more competitive

In July 1991, John Major introduced his Citizen's Charter which set out consumer rights as the 'central theme of public life' for the 1990s. The proposed consumer rights would extend throughout the National Health Service, education and transport to the privatised gas, water, electricity and telecommunications utilities.

The White Paper (a document setting out the government's intentions for new laws) indicated that the officials with responsibility for supervising public utilities (the utility regulators) would have new powers, including the option to award compensation for reasonable complaints by consumers. This would mean clearer commitments to quality of service, fixed appointment times and new means of seeing complaints through. There would be a charter standard for public service quality which would entitle those who can prove they meet the high standards to use a new 'chartermark'.

In the rail service, passengers whose trains are 'unreasonably' late or cancelled will be able to call on tough new compensation rules. In addition the government is developing proposals to privatise parts of British Rail.

Passengers who cannot take their normal train because of cancellation can get a refund. Annual season ticket holders are entitled to a renewal of their tickets to compensate them for poor service in the previous year.

It is proposed that British Rail privatisation should include ending BR's monopoly over running trains on some lines, and the appointment of an independent regulator to ensure fair access to the rail network for private train companies, and fair charging for track use. The charter states that: 'Exposing the railways to the discipline of the private sector will be by far the most effective way of making sure the passenger gets a fair deal.' It is likely that some bus companies might run their own trains on some lines. However, they are unlikely to use their own rolling stock at first. They will simply paint up existing BR rolling stock and seek to run services more efficiently than in the past.

1 *What do you understand by the following terms: regulation, privatisation, competition, monopoly, and the 'discipline of the private sector'?*
2 *What benefits might result from the new suggestions for competition? Who would reap these benefits?*
3 *What do you think are the likely costs of the suggestions? Who will feel these costs?*
4 *How will it be possible to determine whether benefits will exceed costs?*
5 *Why is it likely that different groups and individuals will have different views about the changes?*
6 *Do you think that 'the discipline of the private sector' is likely to make British Rail more effective? Explain your reasons.*
7 *What are the main arguments for the government running the railways?*

Database Activity

Carry out research to find details of four public corporations, five recently privatised concerns, and four long-term public companies.

Find out the date when each organisation was set up, nationalised or privatised. Who is the chairperson and/or managing director of each organisation? What lines of business is it involved in? How many people are employed? What is the annual turnover? What is the latest profit figure? What other important data should you include in the database?

1 Load a database package and set up a file to contain the information you have collected. Use the following headings: company name, date, chairperson or MD, activities, employees, turnover, profit.
2 Sort the file into alphabetical order, and print it.
3 Sort the file using various measures such as size or success and reprint it.

4 As you progress with the course, you may want to update information. Perhaps you can also add new organisations to your file.

· BUSINESS ETHICS ·

Business decisions should not take place within the framework 'anything goes'. Every society needs a set of principles and moral codes to work to. A responsible business needs to have a clear idea of 'right and wrong' behaviour. This is the subject of **business ethics**.

Task

Make a list of examples of what you consider to be 'wrong' behaviour for a business. Scour some newspapers in order to add to these examples.

Case Study

British Airways wrongs Virgin

On 12 January 1993, British Airways was ordered by the High Court to pay £610 000 libel damages, and costs put at £3 million, to Richard Branson and the Virgin airline. The chairman of British Airways offered Mr Branson an unreserved apology for a dirty tricks campaign.

The libel case arose out of allegations made in an open letter from Branson to BA's directors in December 1991. The subversive campaign, which split into several parts with codenames such as Mission Atlantic, Operation Barbara, Hunters and Helpliners, included (according to Branson) illegal hacking of computer information on Virgin flights, and approaching Virgin passengers at airports and telephoning them at home They were told by British Airways employees that Virgin flights had been cancelled (when they hadn't) and were asked to rebook on British Airways flights. There was poaching of Virgin passengers by individuals falsely claiming to work for the airline (they really worked for British Airways). Finally, it was said that documents relating to these activities had been shredded by BA employees.

In effect, British Airways was fighting fiercely to keep its share of airline business away from Virgin, mainly on routes to America. British Airways was the much bigger company fighting against a smaller business which operated by offering cut-price flights.

1 Is it acceptable to carry out some of the practices that British Airways was accused of? Explain your answers.
2 Was the court correct to fine British Airways?
3 What are the implications of the case for (i) British Airways, and (ii) business in general?

Insider dealing is another example of questionable business practice. This consists of trading in the stocks of a company on the basis of undisclosed information by people who have privileged access to knowledge about likely share price changes. The possession of this knowledge makes it possible for an employee to buy or sell stock according to whether the news is good or bad and thus have an unfair advantage over the company's owners, the stockholders. In the US the classic example is the Texas Gulf Sulphur case. The company had made a valuable mineral strike in Canada and the management delayed disclosure for several days during which certain officers of the company bought Texas Gulf stock and made handsome profits when the good news was finally announced. In the 1980s there were many examples of insider trading in both the United States and Britain. A number of people who were caught out were given fines and prison sentences.

Another example of unethical behaviour was the use by the late Robert Maxwell of the pension fund of *Daily Mirror* employees (Maxwell owned the *Mirror*) to carry out other financial dealings. Because of the stock market crash he was not able to put the funds back into the pension fund.

Businesses need to have an ethical base – this is sound commercial sense. Today people are the most important resource of a business, and employees want to work for companies they can be proud of.

Consumers nowadays have far more access to details about businesses than ever before. They are concerned about the environmental position of an enterprise, its employment record in the Third World and many other things. Consumers will vote with their money for ethical products from ethical companies.

Today there is an increasing number of ethical investors. Shareholders will ask questions about the practices of businesses at annual meetings. Investors can and frequently do ask questions about a business's equal opportunities record, the countries it trades with, the way it produces its products and so on. In this text you will find numerous references to business ethics.

· SUCCESS OR FAILURE ·

At the beginning of this chapter you were invited to suggest business ideas of your own. Perhaps you will seek to put some of these into practice by setting up your own college or school-based company to provide a product or service. Remember that this will require careful planning and organisation.

At the end of the day, however business success often depends upon factors outside the control of firms. Economic conditions such as interest rates, consumer confidence and demand, legal constraints, the impact of the Single European Market, fashion etc. all affect business success or failure. The following illustrations highlight what can go wrong:

- A young entrepreneur had the bright idea of setting up his own home-delivery pizza business working from his own house. He thought that it would be easy to get planning permission. However, neighbours objected to his application, and it was rejected. He could not afford to set up elsewhere.
- During the 1980s a number of British manufacturers of yoghurts were making good sales. However, in the 1990s a German company called Müller began to see the whole of Europe as being its home market. It introduced its popular 'twin pots' to Britain and quickly captured the lion's share of the market.
- During the second half of the 1980s the British economy was really booming. Many businesses borrowed money to expand. In the early 1990s interest rates soared and then the economy crashed. Many businesses could not

afford to pay back even the interest on money they had borrowed.

Business life is therefore highly unpredictable. There are many factors lying outside the control of the entrepreneur.

· THE GOVERNMENT AND · THE ECONOMY

The government has a major role to play in a mixed economy (see Chapter 2). It is heavily involved in business activity:

- It tries to encourage certain activities such as training and small business growth.
- It tries to discourage other activities such as the creation of pollution or unfair trading practices.
- It taxes businesses.
- It buys and sells goods and services from and to business.
- It sets out the rules under which business activity can take place.

Encouraging business activity

The government can encourage business activity in many ways. For example, it provides subsidies to some loss-making rail lines, and subsidies to help football clubs to create safer all-seater stadiums. It provides Job Centres, and Job Clubs to help employees to find work and employers to recruit labour. In education it has steered the National Curriculum in the direction of providing more relevance to the world of work. It has encouraged vocational qualifications like the GNVQs which provide skills and knowledge of great relevance to the business world.

Discouraging business activity

There are many ways in which the government can discourage certain activities. Certain activities can be declared illegal. The Monopolies and Mergers Commission, for example, can prevent the joining together of large companies if this will lead to them controlling too large a section of the production or market of a commodity. Price fixing is illegal in most markets. The production of harmful substances is against the law. Certain items cannot be sold over the counter to children.

Traders and companies that break the law will frequently be prosecuted. This would apply, for example, to industrialists who dump more than the allowed quantity of waste into rivers and streams. In January 1993, when the tanker Braer spilled vast quantities of crude oil on the shores of the Shetland Isles, the British government was adamant that the principle of 'the polluter shall pay' would be upheld.

Finally, the government can take contracts away from a company. The government has been known to blacklist companies that carry out undesirable activities.

Business taxes

Industry pays a range of taxes. Business rates are paid to the local council and corporation tax is paid to the government on profits over a certain size. National Insurance is collected and paid by firms to the government for all employees. Businesses also collect value-added tax and customs and excise duties for the government.

Task

Find out from a local company whether it is discouraged by the government from carrying out certain activities. Does it get financial support for some activities?

The provision of services

Central and local government provide a range of services that benefit businesses. The government plays a major role in creating the **infrastructure** (i.e. the backbone of services and facilities) to help business run smoothly. This includes the building and maintenance of roads and other forms of communication, and the provision of various sources of energy and power. A wide range of other services are provided, including the collection of refuse, street cleaning and the gritting of roads. In the 1990s, many of the services have been privatised so that government buys in these services from private contractors.

Buying and selling goods and services

The government is the biggest single purchaser of goods and services in the United Kingdom. A wide range of businesses sell their goods and services to the government, including advertising agencies, insurance companies, banks, laundries and munitions manufacturers. The government also sells goods and services through nationalised industries and other enterprises.

Task

Who provides the following services in your local area, and how is the quality of the service monitored?

a Leisure centres **d** parks
b Car parking **e** Public lavatories
c School grounds

Setting out the rules

The government, through Parliament and local councils, sets out the law of the land. Laws frequently change and when the rules change individuals and businesses will feel the effects of these changes in different ways.

A reducing role for the public sector?

Governments throughout the world are questioning the need for extensive government involvement in their economies. This is as true of Western countries as it is of countries emerging from communism in Eastern Europe. Tight control of public spending in the UK reduced the share of government spending as a percentage of all spending to 40 per cent in 1990. However, it is unlikely that the government will be able to continue to reduce spending without causing serious weaknesses in existing services, such as education and health.

Figure 3.16 shows how government spending changed during the 1980s. The Conservative government set out to cut government spending and to lower taxes. During the 1980s the government was able to cut back the growth in its spending (12.6 per cent over the decade). Because the economy was growing quickly this reduced the government's share of all spending.

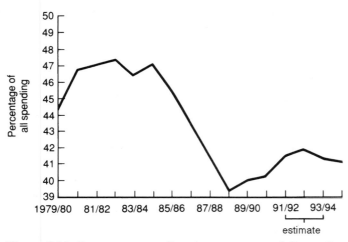

Figure 3.16 *Government spending as a percentage of all spending*

In the early 1990s, government spending is expected to rise as a percentage of all spending. This is partly due to the recession. For example, as unemployment rises the government has to spend moreon social security. Also, with an ageing population (people are living longer) more will need to be spent on pensions and care of the elderly.

There has also been a change of emphasis. The 1980s philosophy was 'the less government the better', but now the government is more in favour of the 'social market'. The government may intervene to make the markets work better. Public spending on training, roads, small businesses etc. can help to improve the working of the market and to make firms more efficient. At the same time education, health and other social services are vital if the quality of life is to be sustained and improved.

Government economic measures

The government can influence the environment in which businesses operate in a number of ways. We shall mention some government economic policies here and return to them later.

Fiscal policy

Businesses do well when a lot of money is spent in the economy. Money can be spent by:

● Consumers (individuals and groups who spend money on goods that give personal satisfaction – fish and chips,

videos, cars etc.).
● Firms – on investment (e.g. firms buying machinery, equipment, investing in buildings).
● The government – on consumer goods (e.g. medicines in NHS hospitals, books in schools) and on capital goods (e.g. new schools, hospitals).
● Foreigners – on consumer goods (e.g. Scotch Whisky) and capital goods (e.g. British machine tools).

The government exerts a big influence on how much is spent in the economy. It can deliberately manipulate the amount of spending in the economy through **fiscal policy**. Fiscal policy is the relationship between government spending and taxes. To increase spending in the economy the government can increase its own spending, lower taxes, or impose a combination of lower taxes and increased spending. To reduce spending in the economy the government can reduce its own spending, raise taxes, or impose a combination of reduced spending and raised taxes.

In 1992 the government raised £177.8 billion in taxes. This total was made up as follows:

Income tax	£59.6 billion
VAT	£40.0 billion
Local taxes (private and business)	£22.1 billion
Corporation tax	£16.8 billion
Petrol duties	£11.8 billion
Spirits, beer, wine, cider and perry duties	£5.3 billion
Tobacco duty	£6.6 billion
Vehicle excise duty	£3.2 billion
Taxes on capital	£2.4 billion
Customs duties	£1.9 billion
Other	£8.1 billion

Task

Set out the table of 1992 tax revenue in the form of a pie-chart using a computer graphics package.

It is apparent from the table of tax revenues that the government can increase demand in the economy in a wide variety of ways. For example, it could reduce income tax so that people have more spending money. If it wanted foreigners to spend more on British goods it might reduce taxes on exported goods.

Monetary policy

The government can also influence demand in the economy through its **monetary policy**. In the United Kingdom the government is responsible for printing money and controlling the banking system through the Bank of England. If it increases the amount of money in the economy then there will be more available for spending in shops, pubs, clubs, cinemas etc. The government can print more money to finance its *own* spending.

However, when spending increases prices are likely to start rising. A general increase in the level of prices is called **inflation.** Inflation is always a problem because it sets up a vicious cycle of further wage and price rises. People on fixed incomes, such as pensioners, lose out because their income will not buy as much. Businesses become reluctant to give credit over long periods.

As well as controlling the quantity of money in circulation, the government also sets the price of obtaining money. The price of borrowing money is known as the **interest rate**. A lender of money will want to have it paid back *with interest*, because he has sacrificed being able to use the money for a certain period of time. When there is plenty of money in the economy it will be cheap to borrow, and vice versa. So if the government wants to encourage borrowing it will lower interest rates, and if it wants to discourage borrowing it will raise interest rates.

Monetary policy can be defined as the *deliberate control of the price and quantity of money in circulation in order to influence the amount of spending in the country*. We shall have a lot more to say about monetary and fiscal policy and the role of the government in the economy in this book.

. THE LOCATION OF BUSINESS . ACTIVITY

When I am trying to find my way out of a town I have not visited before, I will not usually stop for petrol until I have found the right road. I will then stop at the first filling station on the left on the road out. I am not alone in doing this – market research indicates that a high proportion of motorists behave in this way. A good spot to locate a filling station is, therefore, on a major route out of town on the left-hand side. Similarly, when I am looking for a

newsagent I will go to one where I can park my car outside the front door if it is raining, and I avoid the newsagent which is at a busy road junction.

Location is of major importance to all enterprises. In the past many *primary industries* were based in the countryside, whereas *secondary industries* were located outside large towns and cities. This was because they needed a labour force (from the town) while at the same time needing land (on the edge of town slightly away from housing). As towns expanded, houses were built further out of town. The industries which were once on the edge of town became surrounded by other developments. As traffic built up on the roads the old locations became less attractive because it was difficult for transport to get into them. As time moves on factors affecting location change.

Tertiary industries are more flexible. Services industries are located in a variety of locations in city centres (solicitors, estate agents, banks), in suburbs (corner shops, laundrettes, smaller banks, etc.) and in rural areas (village shops, leisure parks, etc.).

We have looked at factors affecting location in greater depth in Chapter 2.

Every firm has some idea of 'the best site'. The best site is the one that maximises advantages and minimises disadvantages. This is not always the site where money costs are lowest – for example, a department store should ideally be on or near the high street, where property costs are highest. The following sections examine some of the characteristics of a good location.

Closeness to point of sale

Many firms find it important to be close to their market. They need to be at a point where they can control the sale of their product. Service industries in particular need to be in amongst their customers. Insurance companies, graphic designers (producing business cards, advertising leaflets, etc.) and banks, for example, need to be located in business centres. Hairdressers, retailers and cafes need to be in shopping areas.

Manufacturers also benefit from being close to their markets when transportation costs are high and when products do not travel well. Some products, for example, become much bulkier when the component parts that make them up have been assembled. For this reason, producers such as furniture manufacturers will often be found close to their market.

When products are non-durable they tend to be produced on a local basis. Examples are fresh baked bread and cakes, and market garden produce.

Task

Make a list of ten local businesses which need to be close to their markets. Find out from their owners exactly why it is so important to be close.

Closeness to raw materials

Some firms and industries use heavy and bulky raw materials. The final product may be a lot smaller and lighter than the ingredients that go into it. Finished steel is lighter than the total quantity of iron ore, limestone and other materials used in its manufacture. Food processing firms are frequently found close to centres of agriculture. In Lincolnshire and Norfolk, for example, there are many large producers of frozen, packeted, canned and bottled foods.

As a general rule, products that *lo*se bulk in their production (e.g. steel, food processing) are more likely to be located near their raw materials. Products that *gain* bulk during their production (e.g. furniture, oil rigs and other heavy mechanical installations) are more likely to be located near to their markets.

The need to be away from centres of population

Some businesses and industries need to be located away from centres of population because of the social consequences of their activities. Firms that cause noise because they use heavy power tools, drills and saws benefit from beingwhere they cause least nuisance – they are likely to have fewer complaints and inspections, and less need for special measures to reduce the nuisance.

Task

Look at a number of firms that are located away from centres of population in your area. Why do they need to be where they are?

Room for expansion

Some firms need a lot of space. Obvious examples are farms, mines and quarries. Production lines can be thousands of metres long in industries such as modern breweries, confectionery plants and car plants. These industries need to be situated where land is plentiful and relatively cheap.

Government help

Money and other incentives are offered to firms by local and national government bodies to set up in certain areas.

Money has been made available for new businesses in certain inner city areas, and to firms setting up in towns where there have been many redundancies caused by the closure of steelworks and mines.

Communications

Distribution expenses may be an important part of a firm's costs. Delays and hold-ups can be a real handicap. Wholesalers and large-scale retailers need to be close to major transport links. For example, a modern newspaper wholesaler needing to get products to the market at breakneck speed needs branches close to major roads, rail links and airports.

Labour force

With the growth of modern technology it is important for firms to have access to a highly skilled labour force. It costs money to train people, and so firms are keen to set up where a skilled labour force already exists.

The living environment

In the 1990s the environment in which we live is a highly important locational factor. There are a wide number of factors involved, including quality of housing, schools, recreation and leisure facilities. If a firm can keep its employees motivated, this helps to keep its training and other costs down – and its output up.

Today, traditional factors influencing location are breaking down. Computer technology enables more people to work at home and to use various communications packages to link their computer terminals with those 'back at the office'. In a real sense, work can be seen to be moving to the workers and the workers can choose where they work.

At the same time certain areas of the country have suffered from dereliction and decline. Although in these areas there are many people who want a job, employers are unwilling to move to areas that have long since lost their advantages. Coal and steel centres, for example, are no longer required if these products can be imported much more cheaply.

A **market** exists when buyers and sellers come into contact. In some markets the buyer and seller may meet

face to face every day. In some markets they may rarely meet – they may simply contact each other by letter, phone, fax or messenger.

The market-place has a number of ingredients. The key players are the **buyers** and the **sellers,** and these two groups interact. The interactions involve:

- **communication**
- an **offer for sale**
- an **exchange** (usually goods or services for money or credit).

INTERACTIONS

Figure 3.17 *The market-place*

POWER RELATIONS IN THE MARKET-PLACE

The distinguishing feature of a **market economy** is that **consumers** are free to spend their money in the ways they think fit. Consumers are free to choose one pair of jeans rather than another, Coke or Pepsi, margarine or butter, and so on. This freedom of choice is supposed by many people to support the argument that 'the consumer is king' in a market economy. The consumer effectively 'votes' (with his or her income) for resources to be channelled into certain goods rather than others. The clothes shop that fails to keep up with fashion trends will rapidly find out that sales fall off. But how much power does the consumer really have? Inevitably, there are a number of important restrictions to consumer power.

Firstly, individual consumers only have limited **incomes.** With the development of new market-based economies in Eastern Europe in the early 1990s, it did not take consumers long to find out that without incomes they had very little power in the market-place. This is true of any market economy – the possession of a sizeable income gives an individual far greater power to claim scarce resources for his or her own use.

Secondly, the power of consumers depends in part on the intensity of **competition** in the market-place. If there are three petrol stations at the end of your street they are far more likely to respond to your wishes than if there is only one petrol station within 20 miles.

Thirdly, consumers have more power **the greater the proportion of a commodity** they purchase. For example, a wholesaler who buys half the output of a potato farm may be able to influence the size, type and quality of potatoes grown on the farm. The wholesaler may also be able to negotiate a bulk discount. A person who turns up at the farm gate to buy one bag of potatoes will have far less influence.

Fourthly, consumers have greater influence if they can organise themselves into **buying groups**. For example, departments within a college may buy stationery in bulk on special terms.

Fifthly, consumers have greater influence the more they know about a product. The greater the **knowledge** the better the opportunity to make an informed purchase from a position of strength. An experienced computer operator is unlikely to be taken in, for example, by 'woolly' sales talk.

Finally, consumers are in a stronger position if they are supported by **consumer rights organisations** and government **legislation.** Consumer and government bodies can help to spread information, and to insist on minimum standards in production and selling.

Task

1 Describe five situations in which consumers have considerable influence in the market-place. Explain why in each case consumers have such influence.
2 Describe five situations in which consumers have little influence in the market place. Explain why in each case the consumer's influence is limited.
3 To what extent do you think the consumer is king in the market place?

To summarise these points, we can say that consumers have more power in markets in which:

- they have considerable buying power
- competition exists
- individual consumers are responsible for significant proportions of all purchases
- they are organised into buying groups
- they are informed
- they are protected.

It follows, then, that *producers* have more power when all or some of these considerations do *not* apply. For example, producers have considerable powers when consumers have little information about what is available, there are few suppliers, or there are many consumers.

At the end of the day, one of the key factors determining power relations is the **urgency** with which a purchase or a sale needs to be made.

Task

1 Can you remember times when you were asked to pay what you considered to be 'extortionate' prices and still made a purchase? Why did you buy the goods?
2 Can you think of situations when a seller is likely to have to make a sale at a price well below what he would have wished? Why might he be forced to make the sale?

▪ DEMAND AND SUPPLY ▪

Relations between buyers and sellers in markets can be better understood when we have explored **price theory.** This involves bringing together two elements – demand and supply.

> DEMAND is the quantity of a good that a consumer will be prepared to buy at a given price.

If the price of a printer for a computer is £500, John will be prepared to buy one printer. If it is more than £500 he will not be able to afford one. If the price fell to £300 he might be prepared to buy two – one for home and one for his office. We can set out John's demand for computer printers in a little table:

Price	Quantity
More than £500	0
£500	1
£250	2

Quite clearly, as the price of printers falls they will become more affordable, and consumers will be prepared to purchase them instead of spending their money on alternatives. One printer will be very useful to John, as will two. However, if the price continues to fall there will come a point at which John has enough printers, and then further price falls will not entice fresh purchases at the same rate.

▪ MARKET DEMAND ▪

In the example above we concentrated on *individual* demand for a product. Some markets may be made up of just a few consumers, some will be made up of a few hundred, whilst others will be made up of thousands or even millions of consumers. We talk of **global markets** where demand for a product is worldwide.

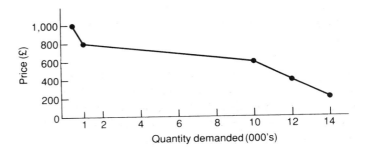

1 Identify four products for which total demand is limited to under ten customers.
2 Identify four products that have a few hundred customers.

3 Identify four products that have a nationwide demand.
4 Identify four products that have a global demand.

Demand schedules can be set out by adding together the individual demand schedules of all consumers in a particular market. For example, the demand schedule below shows the likely national market for a particular type of printer in a six-month period – the figures have been collected from the market research carried out by the manufacturers:

Price of printer (£)	Quantity demanded
1000	500
800	1000
600	10 000
400	12 000
200	14 000

Task

Study the demand schedule given in the text for printers.

1 What do you think would be the best price to charge for printers? Explain your answer.
2 Why would other prices be unsuitable?
3 What further information would you require to be able to select the most appropriate price to charge? (You may want to select a price which is not indicated in the table.)

The information in the demand schedule table can be illustrated in the form of a demand 'curve' (see Figure 3.18). It is convenient for us to think of demand as fitting a

Figure 3.18 *Demand for a company's printer at various prices*

nicely drawn demand curve, but of course in the real world demand patterns are not so simple. The demand for products varies considerably with fresh price changes. Some price rises will have little effect on quantities bought, whilst other quite small price rises may be critical.

Elasticity of demand

Elasticity of demand is a measure of how much the quantity demanded of a good responds to a price change.

- Demand is said to be **elastic** if the proportional change in quantity is greater than the proportional change in price – for example, if the price increases by 5 per cent and the quantity demanded falls by 6 per cent.
- There is **unitary elasticity** of demand when the proportional change in quantity is equal to the proportional change in price – for example, if the price falls by 5 per cent and demand rises by 5 per cent.
- Demand is said to be **inelastic** if the proportional change in quantity is less than the proportional change in price – for example, if the price falls by 5 per cent and demand increases by only 4 per cent.

For all normal goods a rise in price will lead to a fall in demand and a fall in price will lead to a rise in demand.

The responsiveness of consumers to price changes is critical when considering price changes. We can safely conclude that sellers may consider price reductions if demand is *elastic,* and they may consider price rises if demand in *inelastic.*

However, as we have seen, elasticity varies considerably as we alter the price. We can use Figure 3.19 to describe the

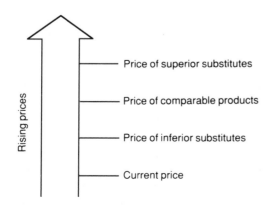

Figure 3.19 *Prices of soft drinks in the market-place*

implications for a soft drinks manufacturer of increasing his price. If he does this, at first sales will not fall off by much, because consumers will remain loyal to his cheaper brand which is better than slightly higher priced (but inferior) substitutes. At first, then, demand will be inelastic as the price rises. However, as his price rises into the bracket of prices charged by comparable and superior products, then demand for his brand will become increasingly elastic. Sellers need to carry out extensive market research to find out what will be the likely effects of raising prices.

Measuring elasticity of demand

Elasticity of demand can be calculated in the following way:

$$\text{Elasticity of demand} = \frac{\text{Change in quantity demanded (\%)}}{\text{Change in price (\%)}}$$

Demand is said to be elastic when the value of such a calculation is greater than 1, and inelastic if less than 1. Unitary elasticity is when the result is equal to 1 (unity).

Task

Calculate the elasticity of demand in the following instances.

a A publisher raises the price of a book from £10.00 to £12.00. Sales fall from 12 000 copies a year to 6000.

b An ice-cream seller raises the price of cones from 50p to 60p and sales drop from 600 a week to 500.

c A clothes shop reduces the average price of garments from £50 to £40 and weekly sales rise from 100 garments to 120 garments.

d Fares on the London underground are reduced by 10 per cent and the number of passengers increases by 25 per cent.

The slope of the demand curve

We can make a useful simplification by showing that when demand is elastic the slope of the demand curve is relatively flat; when demand is inelastic the slope is relatively steep; and when demand is unitary the shape will be what is called a 'rectangular hyperbola' (see Figure 3.20). For unitary elasticity changes in price will be matched by the same proportional change in quantity demanded.

It is important to stress that in setting out these general guides we are, in fact, simplifying mathematical reasoning.

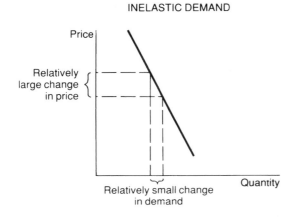

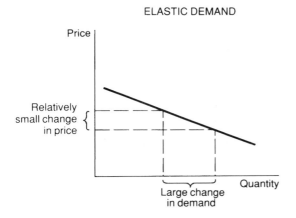

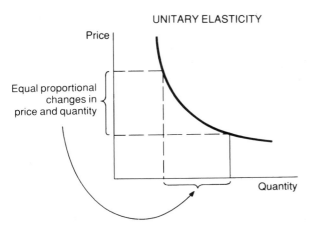

Figure 3.20 *Simplified demand curves*

Factors influencing elasticity of demand

Correct pricing is critical. If prices are judged by consumers to be too high then the lack of sales may ruin a business. If prices are too low it may not be possible to recover costs. We shall consider the important factors influencing demand elasticity.

The price of competitive products. In competitive markets sellers have little choice over what prices they charge. When competitors alter prices firms may have to alter their prices too, particularly when prices fall.

The proportion of income that households spend on a particular commodity. Most households spend a lot on housing, clothes, fuel and food. When the prices of items in these categories rise, households may be forced to cut back spending. However, there are items that are bought rarely and cost relatively little – for example, salt, food seasoning, shoe laces, and so on. When these items rise in price, quantities bought will not be greatly affected.

The price of a good or service. We have already seen that the current price is critical (Figure 3.18). If it is already considered to be high, then a price rise may lead to a greater fall in demand than if the initial price is considered low.

The necessity of making a fresh purchase. When my watch is old I can still use it provided it works well – I do not have to purchase a new one. This is not the case with soup – when I have finished one tin I will want to buy another fairly soon because I like soup. The demand for consumer durables may therefore be more elastic as a result of a price increase than the demand for consumer disposables such as foodstuffs.

Whether a good is a basic necessity or not. Goods which are 'essentials' will have inelastic demands. We cannot easily do without items such as bread and milk, but we can do without many exotic and fancy foods that we only buy on special occasions. The same applies to many other commodities such as clothes and luxury models of cars.

Perhaps the most important factor influencing elasticity of demand is the time period in question. In the short term, consumers may feel it is necessary to buy a particular good or service. Given more time, however, they may better appreciate the benefits of looking around and switching to alternatives. A product which at one time seemed indispensable may lose its sales base as time moves on and new substitutes replace it.

Task

1 Identify a product which you think has an inelastic demand at its current price level. Carry out some research to find out if other consumers agree with your perception.
2 What factors may lead the elasticity of demand for the product you have chosen to become more elastic in the course of time?
3 Identify another product which appears to have an elastic demand at its current market price. What strategies can the seller adopt to try to decrease the elasticity of demand for his product (perhaps so that he can raise its price)?

Group Task

In this activity you will need to work together with two or three others. The object is to find out how a *local firm* makes a pricing decision for a particular product or small range of products. Obviously some product pricing decisions are sensitive areas for some companies. However, for many products this is not the case and local business owners will be pleased to discuss the matter with you.

The aim of the assignment is to find out:

a how the firm arrives at a pricing decision
b the likely effects on sales of charging higher or lower prices.

Choose a group leader who will be responsible for coordinating the work. The duties of the group leader will be to ensure that the group works as a team, to manage the working environment, and to make sure that records are kept. A record sheet (see Figure 3.21) should be set out on a word processor and a suitable number of copies run off.

1 At the beginning of each session the group leader should collect earlier record sheets and take note of any

memos from the lecturer or supervisor. It is a good idea to keep a record of attendance.
2 *The first few minutes of each session should be spent on group discussion, and checking progress on the assignment.*
3 *Ten minutes before the end of each session the group will need to discuss progress, update record sheets and prepare a memo for the lecturer or supervisor.*

To start off the assignment the group will need to think about the sort of questions to ask a local business manager about pricing decisions. **Hints:** Who at the company has this sort of information? When and how are they most likely to be able to supply you with the information? Will it be best to work through contacts that a group member has? Is there someone at the place where you work part-time who may be prepared to talk to your group? Will it be best to look at a range of contacts,

---

LOCAL PRICING ASSIGNMENT:
Group record sheet

The group leader should hand this form to the supervisor or lecturer before the end of each session.

Group name.....................................

Date...

Absentees..

Checklist (tick when completed)

All group members' record sheets completed and returned

Textbooks returned/signed out

Discs returned

Computers switched off or left on main menu

Area tidy

Group task completed

Memo for supervisor or lecturer

Signed

....

Supervisor or lecturer's reply:

....

Figure 3.21 *Group record sheet*

bearing in mind that some companies will not be able to talk to you? Will you need to do some background research so that you know a bit about the company and its products before you start the assignment?

You should then draw up a checklist of key questions about pricing. Set these out in a logical order.

In your group, draft a letter to make the necessary arrangements to visit the company or have someone come to talk to you. Discuss the draft with your lecturer or supervisor, who should countersign the letter before it is sent.

If you decide to make the initial contact by telephone, you will need to follow this up with a letter confirming the arrangements.

Organise the work

When you start to gather information try to organise it in a way that is easy to understand. Put your ideas in the form of a report which you can present to other members of your group – and perhaps to members of the company that you have been working with.

Movements along the demand curve

For convenience we will now draw the demand curve as a straight line in order to simplify the text (see Figure 3.22).

- If the price of a good rises we can refer to 'a move up the demand curve'. What happens to demand as the price rises to P1 in Figure 3.22?
- If the price of a good falls we can refer to 'a move down the demand curve'. What happens to demand as the price falls to P2 in Figure 3.22?

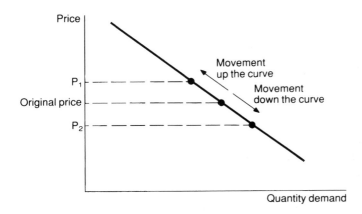

Figure 3.22 *A simplified demand curve drawn as a straight line*

Shifts in the demand curve

Price is not the only factor that alters demand. Other factors include:

- the price of complementary products
- the price of substitute products
- changes in tastes
- changes in incomes
- changes in population.

However, at the time we draw a demand curve we assume that these other influences do not come into play *at that particular time*. As time moves on, however, one or more of these other factors may exert an influence and cause the original demand curve to shift to the left or right. Indeed, in the real world these factors are constantly changing. Some may work in the same direction, or at other times against each other. It will be clearer if we first look at them in isolation before looking at a combination of their influences.

Complementary products

Complementary products are those you use together. For example, my computer keyboard complements my screen and printer; my business studies textbook is complemented by a workbook; and my car radio is complemented by my car. When the price of a desktop computer falls I may be more inclined to buy a printer as well. If the price of ham rises I may be inclined to buy fewer eggs.

Substitute products

Many goods **compete** with one another. When one brand of soap powder becomes more expensive I may switch to a

Figure 3.23 *Complementary products*

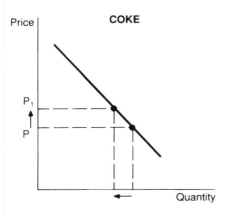

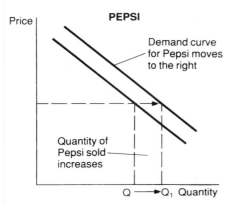

Figure 3.24 *What happens to the demand for Pepsi when the price of Coke increases*

cheaper rival. The same is true for canned drinks such as Coca-Cola and Pepsi-Cola, for brands of petrol such as Shell and BP, and for newspapers such as the *Sun* and the *Daily Mirror*. In Figure 3.24 we can see the effect of a rise in price of Coke on the demand for Pepsi, whose price remains unaltered.

Tastes

Tastes obviously affect demand. Clothing fashions change not only with the seasons but from year to year. Many of this year's garments will end up as cast-offs. This year's car registration will drop in popularity once next year's appears. The life-cycle of a product depends very much on whether it is in a fashionable sector of the market or in a sector that lasts for a long

period of time. When tastes move in favour of a good its sales will boom, and when tastes move against a good its sales will fall. If it is quite difficult to think of products and brand names that are in decline, this is because many of them slip gradually from memory.

Income

Income is an important determinant of expenditure. In a period of recession, high street sales will slump and expenditure on most goods will fall. This is particularly true of luxury items and incidental extras. In the boom years of the late 1980s, **niche marketing** developed. We saw the growth of firms such as Tie Rack, Knicker-box and Sock Shop. In the early 1990s, with a period of recession, the profits of these concerns slumped as consumers had to hold back their expenditure for more essential items.

Population

When the population increases generally, so too will the demand for goods – in a particular country as well as on a global scale. However, population tends not to rise uniformly, and marketeers are more interested in the **distribution of population**. For example, they will be interested to note the current trend towards an ageing population. As we move towards the twenty-first century we have a far higher percentage of people past official retirement age – so that products can be developed for this group, with promotion geared towards the channels that reach them.

Task

Explain what movements are likely to occur in the demand for products in each of the following examples:

1 Reading becomes less popular in a time of recession. What will be the effects on the demand curve for fiction books?

2 The number of young children increases at a time when it is fashionable for children to have 'designer' clothes. What will be the effects on the demand curve for designer clothes for children?

3 The prices of cameras rise at a time when average incomes are increasing. What will be the effect on the demand for camera films?

4 The prices of newspapers rise at a time when people are reading fewer magazines, and people are using teletext as a common substitute for receiving news items. How might this affect the demand for newspapers?

5 The price of ice-cream falls owing to improvements in production methods during a long hot summer. How might these changes affect the demand for ice-cream cornets?

6 Firework parties at home become more popular at a time when incomes are falling and people have fewer children. How might this affect the demand for fireworks?

Need for market research

We can see from the foregoing examples that there are many factors influencing demand and that these frequently work against each other. Demand in the market-place will be in a constant state of change. Market research is therefore essential to predict future changes and to raise awareness of current changes.

Case Study

The changing demand for white bread

In the 1980s, white bread acquired something of a social stigma. As a result, sales fell in volume by 7 per cent while sales of other types of bread jumped by nearly 20 per cent. Since about 1960, consumption of white bread has fallen from close to 40 oz per person per week to just 15 oz. Britain remains bottom of Europe's bread eating league, consuming about 56 loaves per person per year against 100 in Italy and Germany.

But white bread looks to be back in favour. While wholemeal brands account for 22 per cent of the market, brown bread 9 per cent and wheatgerm and ethnic bread 1 per cent, white bread sales can still claim a massive 67 per cent of a market worth £2 billion.

That share seems certain to grow, according to market research. The average white loaf today now costs about 12p less than the equivalent wholemeal loaf (because of cheaper flour, economies of scale and lower profit margins for distributors and retailers).

A recent survey by advertising agency Coley Porter Bell found that more than two in five consumers had not changed their shopping habits in the interests of health. Around 44 per cent said that they had not stopped buying anything because they thought it was unhealthy, and 43 per cent had not added anything to their weekly grocery basket on health grounds. Half of those asked were unable to name a manufacturer they associated with either healthy or unhealthy products.

The report concluded that nutritional value remains at the bottom of the list of reasons consumers give for buying food. Only 17 per cent thought it was the most important factor, against 60 per cent who cited taste and 23 per cent who put cost first.

1 *Identify different segments of the bread market highlighted above.*

2 *Explain how demand has altered in two of these segments in recent years. What factors might have affected these shifts in demand?*

3 *How would you go about finding out about possible future shifts in demand patterns? What sort of questions might you need to ask to elicit information?*

4 *What is your opinion of the interpretation of the figures for changes in demand?*

5 *Carry out your own research into what factors influence the demand for different types of bread. What factors cause changes in demand?*

Movements along the demand curve and shifts in demand

Demand for most products changes fairly frequently. You can check this out by going to your local newsagent each day at about 5 pm. On some days the newspapers will be almost sold out whilst on other days there will be a large stock left over. Demand varies with the weather, the news stories of the day, the day of the week and many other factors. Demand for newspapers falls off in the summer holidays and rises towards Christmas. Perhaps you could carry out an investigation to find out how demand fluctuates for newspapers at your local newsagent.

In the section on demand we have seen that the slope of the demand curve changes. Sometimes it is steep (relatively inelastic) whilst at other times it is flatter (relatively elastic). When the conditions of demand change, the demand curve will shift to the left or right.

In each of the situations below explain what the likely effect on the demand curve will be for a particular newspaper, *The Daily News*.

1 A rival newspaper, *The Daily Planet*, goes out of business.
2 More people switch to newspaper reading and away from journals and magazines. This is because newspapers such as *The Daily News* begin to publish their own magazines and supplements.
3 In a period of recession people cut back on general household expenditures.
4 A new paper with a similar format to *The Daily News* enters the market.
5 The prices of all newspapers increase.
6 The average length of commuter journeys by train decreases.
7 The government bans the use of newspapers for wrapping up fish and chips.

• FOOTNOTE •

Perhaps the easiest way of calculating the *price elasticity of demand* is to look at the change in total revenue as a result of altering price. If a producer wants to maximise revenue, then it makes sense to raise price if demand is inelastic and lower price if demand is elastic.

A useful way of thinking about elasticity is to remember that:

● Demand is *unitary* when, if you raise or lower price, the total revenue earned remains constant.
● Demand is *elastic* when, if you lower price the total revenue increases, and if you raise price the total revenue decreases.
● Demand is *inelastic* when, if you lower price the total revenue decreases, and if you raise price the total revenue increases.

It is essential to remember that revenue is only one side of the profit equation. For example, if British Rail lowers ticket prices and gets a *more than proportional* increase in demand from passengers, its revenue will increase. However, it will probably lose out if it is too costly to use more carriages, or employ more ticket attendants.

• MARKET SUPPLY •

As we saw in Chapter 1, organisations have many different reasons for existing. Some may want to maximise profits or sales, while others will be content to break even or make a modest profit. To simplify our supply analysis we will assume that companies seek to make profits.

The profit from selling a good is the difference between the price at which it is sold and the cost of producing it. The quantities of the good that the company offers will therefore depend on the price it receives for each unit sold relative to the cost of producing each unit.

As price rises (other things remaining the same), the company will at first make a larger profit on each item it sells. This will encourage it to make and sell more. However, the company may face rising costs as it expands production beyond the limit that it had originally planned (for example, the cost of paying employees at overtime rates will increase). For these reasons we should expect that companies will offer more for sale at higher prices, and as they increase their output they will ask for higher prices.

We can either draw a supply curve for an individual company, or a market supply curve from adding together

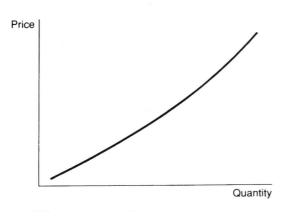

Figure 3.25 *A simple supply curve*

all the individual supply curves. A typical supply curve will slope upwards from left to right (Figure 3.25).

Task

Study the supply curve in Figure 3.26.

1 How much of the commodity would be supplied at:

a 15p   **c** 13p   **e** 11p   **g** 9p
b 14p   **d** 12p   **f** 10p   **h** 7p

2 Draw in the supply curve and explain its shape.

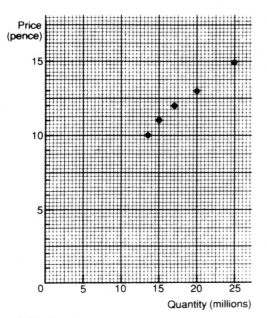

Figure 3.26 *Supply curve*

Elasticity of supply

Elasticity of supply measures the responsiveness of supply to changes in price. It can be measured by:

$$\text{Elasticity of supply} = \frac{\text{Change in quantity supplied (\%)}}{\text{Change in price (\%)}}$$

Supply is said to be elastic when the quantity changes by a greater proportion than the price change. Inelastic supply is when the quantity changes by a smaller proportion than the price change.

The time factor

Time has a great influence on elasticity of supply. We can identify three time periods.

The momentary period. At a moment in time it is impossible to alter supply. In a shoe shop at 3.30 pm on a Saturday afternoon there may be only three pairs of size 7 trainers. In business we define the momentary period as that in which it is impossible to alter both our fixed factors of production (such as the machinery or buildings in a processing plant) and our variable factors (such as labour and energy).

The short period. Between 3.30 pm and 4.00 pm on a Saturday afternoon it may be possible to rush extra training shoes to the shop from a local warehouse. In business we define the short period as the period in which fixed factors remain fixed, but variable factors can vary.

The long period. Because of a general increase in the demand for trainers, a factory producing trainers may expand its plant and equipment. In business we define the long period as the period in which all factors of production can become variable.

We can illustrate elasticity of supply in different time periods as in Figure3.27. Momentary supply is represented by a vertical line, short-period supply by a relatively inelastic supply line, and long-period supply by a relatively elastic supply line.

What constitutes a short or long period varies from company to company and from industry to industry. For example, it takes a lot longer to increase fresh flower

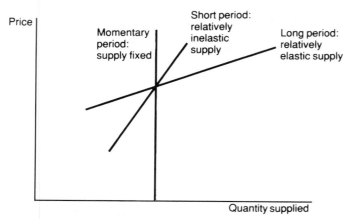

Figure 3.27 *Influence of the time factor on elasticity of supply*

production than it does to expand artificial flower production. Some products have an extended long term (e.g. coffee and rubber production), while others have a shorter long term. If you have ever grown cress on your window sill you will know that it can be grown within days.

Task

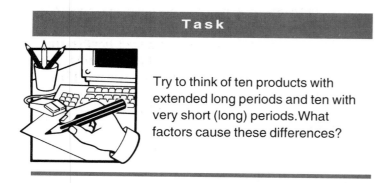

Try to think of ten products with extended long periods and ten with very short (long) periods. What factors cause these differences?

The effect of spare capacity

Elasticity of supply also varies according to how close to **capacity** a company or industry is running. For example, if a factory is using only half its machines, it would be relatively easy to expand production. However, if the factory is already working at full capacity, then the company would have to invest in new plant in order to expand its supply.

The availability of components and raw materials

In order to expand production it is necessary to increase inputs. If **inputs** are readily available, then supply will be far more elastic than if inputs are scarce.

The cost of producing additional outputs

If the **extra cost** of producing additional units is rising sharply, then producers will be reluctant to expand output in response to higher prices.

Shifts in the supply curve

The cost of production of an item is made up of the prices of the various inputs, including raw materials and the machinery used to make it. Rises in the prices of some of these factors will increase production costs, and this results in a reduction in supply at each and every price (see Figure 3.28). The supply curve shifts to the left – at any given price less will be produced and offered for sale than before. For example, 1990 saw a rise in interest rates (i.e. the cost of borrowing money), and this increased the cost of production of many goods. Of course, a fall in production costs has the opposite effect.

Taxation imposed on output or sales has the same effect – producers and sellers are effectively taking less money at each price. On the other hand, improvements in **technique,** which make it possible for any given quantity of a product to be made or sold at a lower cost than before, will have the opposite effect.

The **conditions of supply** may be altered by such things as changes in the weather, fires, floods, dust-storms or earthquakes, although such changes are often only temporary. Weather conditions can lead to large or small harvests, and hence increases or shortages in the supply of wheat and other crops.

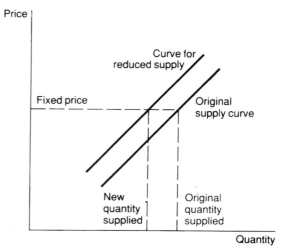

Figure 3.28 *Shift in the supply curve*

Task

State what will be the likely effect on supply in each of the following instances:

a improvements in technology in the car industry

b very high demand for tickets on cup final day

c the development of more effective pesticides for use on cereal crops

d an increase in the cost of the raw materials required for housebuilding

e an increase in demand for small-engined cars.

THE INTERACTION OF DEMAND AND SUPPLY

Figure 3.29 shows the outline demand and supply curves for jars of strawberry jam in a particular week. We can combine these two curves on a single drawing to illustrate how prices are determined in the market-place. The point at which the two curves cut is the point at which the wishes of both consumers and producers are met (Figure 3.30).

We can now see that at a price of 60p for a 350 g jar, 100 000 tonnes of jam would be bought in the market-place each week. At this price consumers are happy to buy 100 000 tonnes and sellers are happy to supply this quantity. This is called the **equilibrium point** because there is nothing forcing a change from it.

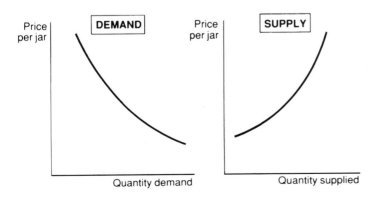

Figure 3.29 *Demand and supply curves for strawberry jam*

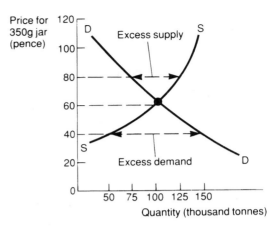

Figure 3.30 *Market equilibrium for strawberry jam*

We can see why this point is an equilibrium one by considering non-equilibrium points. For example, at 80p a jar consumers would be prepared to purchase only 75 000 tonnes while suppliers would be prepared to make 125 000 tonnes available to the market. At this price sellers would be left with unsold stocks and would quickly contract supply to the equilibrium point. If the price was below the equilibrium – at say 40p – demand would be for 150 000 tonnes with producers only willing to supply 50 000 tonnes; in this situation, strawberry jam would be snapped up as soon as it was put on the shelves, and stocks would run out. Prices would soon be raised towards the equilibrium point.

Markets in motion

The simple explanation of demand and supply of strawberry jam provided above gives us an important insight into how markets operate. Producers and consumers respond to **price signals**, and in this way their wishes and plans are coordinated by the **market mechanism**. These wishes and plans change regularly since the factors influencing supply and demand are in a constant state of change.

For example, improvement in standards of living in a country will increase demand generally, but it will also affect costs – the money paid to an employee as wages for his or her work is *income* from the employee's point of view, but to the employer it is a cost. Furthermore, improvements in manufacturing techniques often increase the supply of particular goods without increasing costs. It is obvious that *any* change has knock-on effects throughout the market-place. These changes are not isolated, and they are happening all the time. Consider the case of up-market cook-chill meals sold by outlets such as Marks and Spencer and Sainsbury's.

If an increase in supply is coupled with a decrease in demand, the price of the good will fall. If a decrease in supply is coupled with an increase in demand, the price of the good will rise. However, if an increase in supply is coupled with an increase in demand, or a decrease in supply by a decrease in demand, we know that output is likely to increase in the first case and contract in the second – *but we cannot be sure what will happen to price in these* circumstances.

Changes in the market-place lead to adjustments by consumers and producers. Demand and supply curves change shape and position, and very quickly a new equilibrium position is established. However, this will only be a temporary equilibrium point because markets are characterised by **change.** Indeed, one beauty of the market-place is that it can quickly accommodate changes. However, Eastern European countries that are converting their economies away from central planning (see Chapter 1) are finding that adjustments cannot be made quickly when the price mechanism has been suppressed for a long time.

▪ INCOME ELASTICITY ▪

Another important measure of elasticity is **income elasticity**. This expresses how demand responds to changes in income. In most years the total income of the country rises (i.e. the national income increases). As incomes rise so does the ability of consumers to buy new goods: people move into bigger houses, acquire bigger cars, buy a range of new gadgets, clothes and food. More expensive goods can replace inferior products.

Income elasticity can be measured by:

$$\text{Income elasticity} = \frac{\text{Change in quantity demanded (\%)}}{\text{Change in income (\%)}}$$

Normal goods are ones for which demand increases as income goes up. Inferior goods are ones for which demand falls as income goes up.

▪ CONSUMER AND INDUSTRIAL ▪ MARKETS

Organisations can be classified according to the goods or services they produce. One simple division is into consumer markets and organisational markets. Another name for the latter is industrial markets.

Consumer markets are made up largely of individuals who buy things for personal and home use. Consumers typically buy from retailers and purchases tend to involve fairly low money values. Examples are:

- goods with a short shelf-life, made for immediate use (e.g. foodstuffs)
- durable goods with a longer life and which are bought less often (e.g. cars and televisions).

Industrial or organisational markets are made up of buyers who purchase goods and services to use in making or providing other goods and services. They include:

- industrial consumption goods which have a frequent purchase pattern but a limited life (e.g. chemicals and fuels)
- industrial durable goods which have a longer life (e.g. machinery and equipment).

Some organisations sell products in both consumer and industrial markets. A motor manufacturer like Volkswagen produces private motor cars as well as lorries.

Identifying markets

Manufacturers and sellers need to have a great deal of information about potential customers. Chapter 7 deals extensively with how to obtain this information.

▪ INTERDEPENDENT MARKETS ▪

The links between industrial and consumer markets are just one aspect of the **interdependent market process.**

A large multinational motor vehicle manufacturer, for example, makes a range of moulded metal parts in a factory, usually called a foundry. In the foundry, iron is melted and poured into moulds, which are made of sand. Metal products that are made by pouring molten metal into moulds are known as 'castings'.

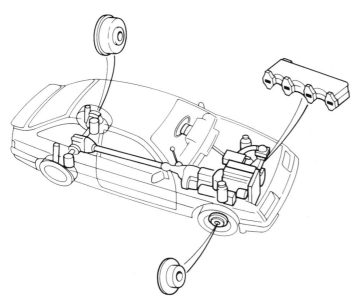

Figure 3.31 *Brake and engine castings*

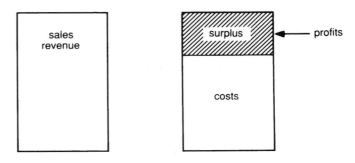

Figure 3.32 *Sales revenue – costs = profit*

The moulded parts produced in the foundry include brake discs, brake drums and engine manifolds. Look at Figure 3.31 to see where they are located in the finished motor car.

If the demand for motor vehicles increases, there will be an increase in demand for brake discs, brake drums, manifolds and many other components. In turn this creates a demand for **intermediate products** such as iron and sand. In addition it creates further demand for more moulds, more capacity at the foundry, and so on. More employees are required, and more managers. As more employment is created incomes begin to rise – people can therefore spend more on cars and many other items. The market economy is thus an interdependent one.

Prices provide **signals** to all sectors of the market economy. Decisions can then be made in response to these signals. No army of people sitting in offices could possibly work as effectively as the price system in signalling changes to the millions of components that make up an economy.

▪ GETTING GOODS TO MARKET ▪

Businesses will only supply goods to the market if it is profitable to do so in the long term. This involves ensuring all the costs of production are covered by the sales revenue as well as there being a small surplus (profit) on top of this. (See figure 3.32.)

As we shall see later in the book, costs are made up of two elements.

- Fixed costs – which stay the same however many goods are made.
- Variable costs – which increase as the number of goods produced increases.

The price of a good is the sum of money charged for it. As a general rule, the more it costs to produce a good, the higher the price will be charged if a profit is to be made.

Getting goods to the national market

The economy is made up of many industries each producing particular outputs e.g. the shoe industry, the insurance industry, the car industry etc.

If we add together the output of all these industries we arrive at the national output – which we refer to as gross domestic product (GDP).

The gross national product (GNP) includes income from overseas investment, e.g. the earnings of companies like BP, Unilever etc., but this is still money which can be spent in the home market. Business economists and planners, who need to interpret economic trends, will use the statistical breakdown within the GDP and GNP tables for forecasting. The greater the national output, the larger the number of products available for consumers in a country to use. If the national output increases people become better off.

For the first quarter of 1993 national output rose by 0.2 per cent. Output had fallen continuously from the third quarter of 1990 to the first quarter of 1991 and was then flat. In April 1993 Norman Lamont, Chancellor of the

Exchequer claimed the rise in output meant the end of the recession and 'recovery was under way'. See figure 3.33.

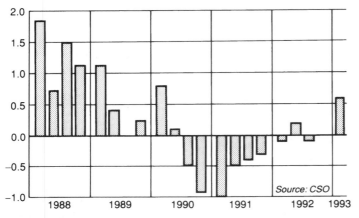

Figure 3.33 *National output: gross domestic product, excluding oil, % change on quarter*

Wealth and welfare

A country becomes more wealthy as the quality and quantity of factors of production in the economy increases, for example by having better machinery, improved hospitals, a more healthy, trained and skilled labour force. However, we must be careful not to confuse wealth with welfare. Welfare involves the well-being of all citizens. A new hospital might increase both the wealth and the welfare of a country. However, could we say the same about a new tobacco factory?

Task

Explain ways in which each of the following might (a) increase, (b) decrease the wealth and the welfare of people in an economy.

- the building of a new school
- the building of a new motorway
- the building of a brewery

As industries and countries become better at producing goods, national output will increase. However, this does not always mean that people are better off. For example, having more lorries on the roads may increase some people's welfare and decrease that of others.

Task

Look at a local development. In what ways does the development lead to

- an increase in the community's welfare
- a decrease in the community's welfare?

Task

Investigate a business sector in your locality. Find out how the business sector

- adds to
- detracts from local wealth and welfare.

Element assignment

Privatisation or nationalisation

This assignment can help you provide evidence for assessment, or claim the following Core Skills outcomes:

Communication
Participate in oral and non-verbal communication

Information Technology
Use a range of technological equipment and systems

Personal Skills
Relate to and interact effectively with individuals and groups
Work effectively as a member of a team
Use information sources

Presentation of the case for privatisation or nationalisation of a particular firm or industry

Work in groups of four or five. Each should prepare a 20-minute presentation to the whole group using three overheads. The presentation should demonstrate your ideas in favour of or against a particular case.

Use the following checklist to prepare your presentation:

To plan and organise the presentation
Plan to
- [ ] Set out your objectives.
- [ ] Set out a main idea and a clear conclusion.
- [ ] Set out your introduction clearly.
- [ ] Think about your audience, their interests and their level.
- [ ] Brainstorm some main ideas.
- [ ] Plan handouts and overheads.
- [ ] Keep a clear thread linking main points.

To prepare for the presentation
Make sure you:
- [ ] Practise.
- [ ] Check the equipment.
- [ ] Order your notes and handouts.

To develop the visual aids
Make sure you:
- [ ] Make them clear and easy to look at.
- [ ] Choose the correct type of chart.
- [ ] Use computer graphics packages.
- [ ] Use 18-point or 24-font sizes on overheads.
- [ ] Have clear titles.
- [ ] Talk to the audience, not to the visual.
- [ ] Place yourself in the centre of the stage.
- [ ] Use a pointer, but not too often.

To stop being nervous
Plan to
- [ ] Take deep breaths.
- [ ] Move during the presentation.
- [ ] Establish eye contact.

Delivering your presentation
Plan to:
- [ ] Be aware of what you say and how you say it.
- [ ] Speak with a strong clear voice, and don't speak too quickly.
- [ ] Be animated, clear and enthusiastic.
- [ ] Use eye contact to make the presentation conversational and personal.

Questions and answers
Plan to:
- [ ] Prepare for questions and practise the answers.
- [ ] Ask for questions by stepping forward with hand raised.
- [ ] Watch the questioner and listen carefully.
- [ ] Repeat the question to make sure everyone has heard it.
- [ ] Keep the same bearing as in your presentation.
- [ ] Use eye contact and look at the whole audience.

chapter 4 ADMINISTRATIVE SYSTEMS

In administering any activity there is a need to organise, control and make decisions. An administrator has to take responsibility not only for his or her own actions, but also for the activities of others. Most administrative tasks require a range of talents in addition to a knowledge of the work, experience and judgement.

As organisations grow, develop and employ more people they have to define roles for each of their employees through a structured framework. Such structures will serve to divide work within the organisation and enable administrators to coordinate, monitor and control their activities.

This chapter looks at the nature of administrative activities and then at how organisations structure their systems in order to meet their administrative needs and the relationships created by such structures. it also examines the need for different levels of authority, responsibility and accountability.

· THEORIES OF MANAGEMENT ·

Over many years, considerable efforts have been made by theorists to develop a clearer understanding of how managers and administrators can spend their time most efficiently. This work has contributed to the development of management theories as a science. For such theories it is possible to identify four broad functions that characterise all **administrative activity**. These are:

- **planning** – deciding what provisions need to be made in the future
- **organising** – making sure that all resources are available at the right moment
- **controlling** – making sure that things happen as they were planned
- **doing** – becoming actively involved in the task at hand.

Having identified these four functions it is possible to relate each to a specific level of management responsibility (see Figure 4.1). **Senior** or **top managers** in an organisation tend to spend a lot of their time planning, some time organising, a lot of their time

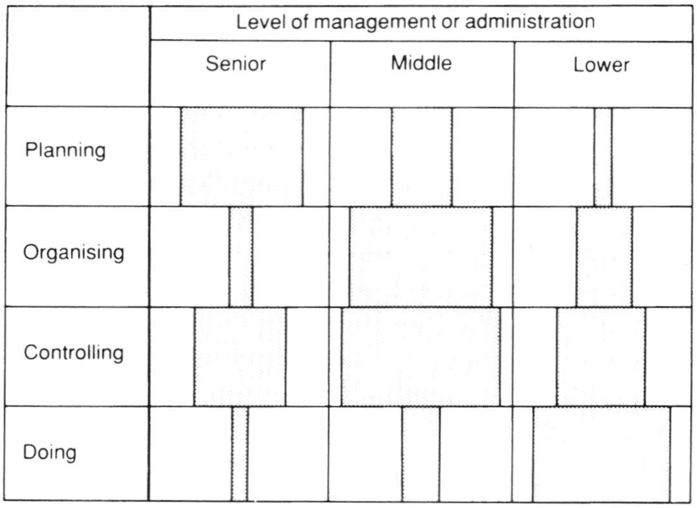

	Level of management or administration		
	Senior	Middle	Lower
Planning			
Organising			
Controlling			
Doing			

Figure 4.1 *The activities of managers at different levels*

controlling but very little time actually involved in the tasks. **Middle managers** spend less time planning, more time organising, more time controlling and more time doing the work. **First-line** or **lower managers** contribute little to planning, are involved in some organisation and some control, but spend most of their time actively involved in the task at hand.

Case Study

Transforming EMI

Jim Fiffield joined EMI Music in May 1988, while in his mid-forties, and became President and Chief Executive Officer a year later. With an impressive career background in one of the largest US consumer product groups, he quickly gave new impetus to the substantial investment already being made in the business. EMI had a worldwide presence, but overall profitability was held back by its relatively small share of the crucial US market. This also limited the availability of US artists with international 'superstar' potential to help develop the strong businesses elsewhere in the world.

Working with his team of executives he set out to instil a 'winning culture' among EMI's 8000 employees worldwide. EMI's regional businesses, covering over 35 countries, were set challenging performance targets. Their ability to respond rapidly to new trends and to develop the all-important artist and repertoire base was aided by strategic acquisitions and partnerships with leading independent record companies. These added powerful new stars to EMI's global galaxy. Compact disc and cassette manufacturing and distribution were consolidated into major regional resources, as a separate, specialised operation. This allowed substantial cost savings. In parallel, a series of acquisitions built EMI's music publishing business into the world leader in its field. This business now contributes a significant share of total profit.

EMI Music ranks as one of the world's 'Top Three' music companies, with annual sales of over £1 billion. But, to Jim Fifield, the continuing goal is to be 'Number One'.

1 *What sort of role should a chief executive like Jim Fifield have in a large organisation like EMI?*
2 *To what extent should the actions of Jim Fifield influence middle and lower managers? How important is it that he should be able to communicate easily with other managers and staff?*

· THE NATURE OF ADMINISTRATION ·

When someone first starts to work for an organisation in a 'junior' position, his or her role is usually limited to a series of clearly defined tasks. As the employee begins to understand more about the functioning of the organisation, his or her duties can develop so as to include a range of simple administrative tasks. The employee's ability to be able to **organise**, **control** and **make decisions** will be crucial to many of these tasks.

Just as you have to organise and control your social activities, the success you have with your work role will depend on how well you can develop your organisational and administrative skills. Imagine you are arranging a party for a group of friends. You might have to

- identify a mutually convenient date
- check that a suitable venue is available
- decide who to invite
- make sure everyone knows when and where the party is taking place
- arrange for the food and refreshments
- borrow some records, tapes and CDs.

Each of these tasks involves you in *organisational* activity. If you had an offer of help from a friend, you might ask that person to sort out the invitations, order some glasses from the off-licence and buy and prepare some food. At the same time you have to oversee all the activities to ensure that the preparations are running smoothly: you are involved in *administration*. You have to monitor the completion of the tasks, providing guidance and help where necessary. You have to make decisions. As the administrator of the event – the party – you set out the plan, work out what needs to be done, work on many of the arrangements yourself, delegate, monitor the preparations;

and finally, on the night you make sure that everything runs smoothly.

Task

Make a list of all your work activities. If you are not working, interview someone who is and then make a list of his or her work activities. In either case, indicate which activities involve *organisational* skills and which involve *administrative* skills (some may involve both). Explain briefly the essential difference between organising something and being an administrator.

Responsibility and skills

There is clearly a difference between carrying out day-to-day routines and identifying tasks which require some administration. Administrative tasks involve someone taking on **responsibility**. This responsibility means that someone has to ensure that whatever is meant to happen does actually happen. Administrators must therefore develop **managerial skills**. Whereas routine jobs can be undertaken by virtually anyone given the right background and training, most administrative tasks require an understanding of people and how they work together, a knowledge of the work of the organisation, experience, good judgement and the ability to make decisions.

Task

State which of the following positions involve managerial skills:

a *nurse*
b *teacher*
c *production-line worker*
d *sales representative*
e *farmer*
f *chief inspector of police*
g *pub landlord*
h *gardener.*

Most people require some form of managerial skill; the type and extent depend on the *degree* of responsibility they

want to accept. For example, someone delivering milk to households has to take responsibility for a milk-float, make decisions about what products to carry on it, collect correct money, try to sell customers new products, cater for all of their dairy requirements and generally keep customers happy. To do this well clearly involves some managerial skills.

THE NEED FOR ADMINISTRATIVE SYSTEMS

Nearly everyone at some time or other thinks about starting a business of their own. You often hear people say, 'Someone could make a fortune out of that' or 'I wish I had thought of that idea first'. So imagine that you decide, having left college and having worked for a large organisation for a few years, to 'go it alone' and set up your own business buying and selling jewellery by mail-order.

Consider your role in this new organisation. If you did not employ anyone else at the start, you would soon find that you needed to become a jack-of-all-trades, able to turn your hand to every aspect of the business. For example, you would be involved in buying the jewellery, designing a catalogue and having it printed, finding out the sort of people who would like to buy the jewellery, putting together a mailing list and sending the catalogues out, taking orders by phone and mail, dealing with all correspondence, sending the orders out, keeping the accounts, getting the money in and banking it, as well as all the other issues needing daily attention.

We can show diagramatically how this business is organised. Your role would be at the centre of a range of functions for which you would be personally responsible (see Figure 4.2).

Operating on your own is rarely easy. There are times when, as owner, you require the help or advice of others

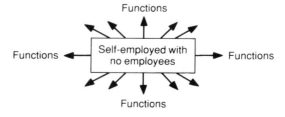

Figure 4.2 *Organisation in a one-person business*

with special skills, such as an accountant, a bank manager or a solicitor.

As the business expanded you would find it necessary to employ some form of help, possibly part-time at first and then full-time. As you began to employ other people you would relinquish some of the work you had been doing, and this would require a reappraisal of your role as well as the creation of roles for others within an organisational structure.

Task

Assume that you start up and run a jewellery mail-order business. In the business's first year you decide you can afford to employ four other people. What roles would you expect for each of these staff? Draw a simple diagram of the organisation strucure.

This simple example shows that, as an organisation develops, it has to consider the roles of everybody within it. It has to be **organised** in the best possible way to meet its objectives efficiently. This involves defining the relationships between departments, as well as between managers and other employees, so that all employees know what they should be doing, where they fit into the organisation, and to whom they are responsible.

· ORGANISATIONS IN HISTORY ·

If we look back in time we can see that there has always been a need to organise people. Probably the first large-scale organisations were Egyptian state monopolies used for building the pyramids. At the head of the organisation was the Pharaoh whose authority was invested by divine right and who delegated authority to a **vizier** who acted as prime minister, chief justice and treasurer over an elaborate bureaucracy, at the bottom of which were the slaves.

Over the medieval period serfs replaced slaves at the bottom of the economic and social order and, for a long time, businesses were viewed as a necessary evil. By about 1750 the ideological and cultural stage was set for the

advent of the **industrial revolution**. Industrialisation resulted in the birth, growth and development of a massive number of organisations. At the same time there was a growing awareness of the need for division of labour and specialisation.

· SPECIALISATION ·

Division of labour involves the breaking down of a production process into a number of clearly defined specialist tasks. It is based upon the fact that the total output of a group can be increased if, instead of each person trying to do everything, each specialises in a particular skill or activity. The most famous early observation of division of labour was that by Adam Smith in a pin factory and quoted in *The Wealth of Nations*. He noted that where operations were divided and where workers specialised, output was far greater than it would otherwise have been.

Task

Consider the organisation you either work in or attend. To what extent do employees in this organisation specialise? Make a list of the advantages and disadvantages of this division of labour.

Specialisation is fundamental to modern societies and, as well as division of labour, includes:

- specialisation of equipment
- specialisation by plant
- specialisation by firms
- specialisation by industry
- specialisation by region or nation.

If we consider the massive number of goods or services consumed weekly by an average household, we can begin to appreciate how so much depends on people and organisations specialising in order to satisfy our needs and wants.

Specialisation is often explained in terms of the theory of **comparative advantage**. This states that resources are used in the most cost-effective way when they are used in areas where they are most **efficient**. For example, a golf professional might be good not only at her sport but also as a solicitor. However, she concentrates on her golf because golf is her best line. By specialising she is concentrating on an area where she is more talented.

4 Narrow specialism may make it difficult for factors of production to respond to change.
5 Generalism is often more useful than specialism. A generalist is often in a better position to look at the various parts of an organisation to devise an overall strategy.

Task

Make a list of ten large organisations (e.g. BP, Glaxo, Marks and Spencer, your local hospital). In what ways do these organisations specialise? How does such specialism contribute to the quality of the goods or services the consumer receives in each instance?

The advantages of specialisation

1 Resources can be concentrated where they are most productive.
2 Factors of production become more efficient if they are directed towards a set task. For example, labour becomes more efficient the more skilled the worker becomes at a particular task.
3 Specialisation allows a larger output to be produced at a lower unit cost.
4 Concentrations of specialists can lead to sharing of skills and experience.
5 Specialisation makes it possible for us to have a higher standard of living. By specialising, people and nations can develop their talents and then trade their goods and services.
6 Specialisation means that one job can be done well rather than a number of jobs done badly.

The disadvantages of specialisation

1 Specialisation can lead to a boring lack of variety. If workers repeat the same task over and over again they may become disillusioned and this will affect their morale.
2 Specialisation can present a problem where one stage of production is dependent upon another stage.
3 Specialisation may lead to workers becoming little more than machine operators and this could lead to a loss of skills.

Case Study

Anglia motorbikes

Anglia motorbikes have captured the attention of nostalgia lovers throughout the world over many generations. The stylish, slow-revving, large-capacity machines built using traditional skills and techniques were products caught up in a time-warp.

Until recently, each of the six available models was custom-built by craftsmen to customer specifications. However, dwindling profits and increasing costs per unit led to the management of Anglia realising that the organisation had come to a crossroads. If the business was to continue to exist, it had to modernise. Out went all of the traditional practices and in came massive investment in technology, the installation of production line working and greater specialisation. The table at the top of page 34 shows some relevant figures.

1 *Study the figures and comment upon how production line working, greater division of labour and specialisation appear to have affected Anglia's:*
   a *employees*   c *shareholders*
   b *management*   d *customers.*
2 *Suggest an alternative business strategy to the one adopted by Anglia.*

• MODERN THEORIES •

Great lessons were learnt from the industrial revolution. As entrepreneurs (people with 'good ideas') directed their efforts to increasing their share of resources and the sizes of their businesses, they realised that it was just not possible for one person to control all aspects of a business's activities and that human inputs were more than just tools of business. Such ideas about business,

Year	Number of models	Output	Profits £(000)	Sales £(000)	Days lost in industrial disputes	Days lost by sickness
1991	6	534	85	1602	18	1245
1992	2	1658	541	4974	1420	3460

administration and bureaucracy have been further developed by theorists.

Henri Fayol was one of the first people to try to work out what managers should do and how they should do it. In 1916, after many years thinking about his job as a manager, he published a small book called *General and Industrial Management*. In this book Fayol identifies five functions of management:

- **Planning** – looking ahead and making provision for the future
- **Organising** – making sure a business has everything it needs and managing its resources
- **Command** – directing and managing people
- **Coordination** – harmonising activities to achieve successful results
- **Control** – making sure things happen the way they were planned.

Look at Fayol's five functions of management. Consider whether it would be possible to do without any of these functions. Give reasons for your answer.

Having outlined five functions of management, Fayol then identified the following principles or guidelines for management:

1 *Division of work* – the need to specialise
2 *Authority and responsibility* – the right to command others

3 *Discipline* – firm but fair
4 *Unity of command* – an employee receives orders from one superior only
5 *Unity of direction* – everyone pulls the same way
6 *Subordination of individual interest to general interest* – the group's needs come first
7 *Remuneration* – the pay must be fair
8 *Centralisation* – the extent to which authority is delegated through departments
9 *Chain of authority* – ranging from ultimate authority to lower levels
10 *Order* – there must be a place for every employee
11 *Equity* – treating employees well fosters loyalty
12 *Stability of tenure of staff* – 'job security'
13 *Initiative* – thinking out a plan and executing actions
14 *Esprit de corps* – teamwork and harmony build up the strength of the organisation.

Definding the job for the Prime Minister

If we want to consider seriously what the Prime Minister is for and what the role of PM entails, there is no easy answer because there is no job description. Asquith's famous one-liner was that the office of Prime Minister is 'what the holder chooses and is able to make of it'. The roles of other Ministers are not a problem because their duties are laid down by law.

Professor Anthony King of the University of Essex has examined the job of the Prime Minister and has concluded that 'outlines of the job remain roughly the same and change only slowly through time, but the way in which the job is done varies enormously'. He does, however,

PRIME MINISTER
JOB DESCRIPTION

point to seven tasks regarded as mandatory for Prime Ministers:

- the appointment and dismissal of Ministers
- the appointment of certain civil servants
- chairing the Cabinet and its committees
- appearing twice a week for PM's question-time
- representing the government at Summit meetings
- acting as Minister for the secret services
- choosing the moment to dissolve Parliament.

1 Comment on the role of the Prime Minister. For example, is the role as limited as that indicated by Professor King?

2 Think about how you would feel in a Prime Minister's role. Look at Fayol's fourteen principles and guidelines for management and consider how you would apply them to the office of PM. For each principle, state how you think it is applicable and how you would apply it.

F. W. Taylor also contributed to organisation theory by pointing out that there is **inefficiency** in nearly all of our daily acts. He showed that the remedy for inefficiency is not solely the appointment of an unusually talented administrator, but rests with scientific (that is, methodical) management. His idea was that management is a true science.

Max Weber considered the growth of large organisations and predicted that this growth would require a formal set of procedures for administrators. He felt that bureaucracy could be used with large and complex organisations and described bureaucracy as having:

- a well-defined *hierarchy* of authority
- a clear *division of work*
- a system of *rules*
- a system of *procedures*.

Each of the theories from the early days of Adam Smith has been designed to improve our understanding of the working of organisations. From such theories we can see that every organisation needs division of work supervised by a hierarchy which has some form of structure.

ORGANISATIONAL STRUCTURE AND DESIGN

As we saw earlier in this chapter, an organisational structure is designed to coordinate and monitor people, activities and resources. A formal structure ensures that everybody can see their role within the organisation.

Consider again the small organisation we mentioned at the start of the chapter. If you as owner of the jewellery mail-order business employed four people you might have given them the roles of buyer, office junior, mail room clerk and accounts clerk. One possible organisation chart is shown in Figure 4.3.

Notice that the business has been organised to reflect the **activities** of each of the members of staff. We can also see that each of these staff is responsible to one manager only, the owner. The chart therefore has a **pyramid structure**, in which the authority for management decisions starts from the top and extends downwards in a hierarchical pattern.

```
          ┌─────────┐
          │  Owner  │
          └────┬────┘
   ┌──────┬────┴────┬──────────┐
┌──┴──┐┌──┴───┐┌────┴────┐┌────┴─────┐
│Buyer││Office││Mail room││ Accounts │
│     ││junior││  clerk  ││  clerk   │
└─────┘└──────┘└─────────┘└──────────┘
```

Figure 4.3 *Organisation chart of small mail-order jewellery business*

Task

Obtain an organisation chart either from your place of work or from the institution you attend. You will be asked to study this later.

What would need to happen if the jewellery business expanded? Perhaps a second warehouse is purchased, professional managers are taken on and more staff are employed. The business might also move into other product lines such as watches and clocks. As the organisation grew the organisational structure would have to change to reflect such developments. At this stage the crucial decision would be *how to divide up the business* so that the various parts could be managed efficiently.

Dividing up an organisation

Dividing up an organisation is often referred to as **departmentation**. For example, because customers are all over the country it might be sensible to divide the business by regions. Or would it be easier to divide by functions, processes etc.? The **design** of the new organisational structure would be crucial to the success of the business. It would have to:

● bring together every part of the organisation
● relate each part of the organisation to every other part
● show where the authority of individuals and departments lies
● enable those within the organisation to assess their roles and status.

Departmentation is the process by which certain activities or sections of an organisation are grouped logically and then assigned to managers. The way in which this is done depends on the aims of the organisation. The five main methods of grouping employees are by:

● function
● product
● process
● geographical area
● type of customer.

As we shall see later, a **matrix structure** can be used to combine grouping methods.

Task

Look at the organisation chart you have obtained. Is the organisation divided up by one of the five methods we have mentioned?

Division by function

This is probably the most common way of grouping employees. **Functional organisation** means that the business is divided into broad sectors, each with its own specialism or function. Examples are 'Production' and 'Sales'. Though every organisation will have its own method of structuring its functions, we shall look at some typical divisions within a large organisation.

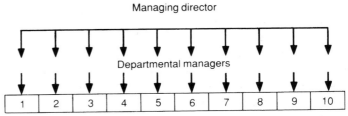

Figure 4.4 *Division by function*

The company secretary

The law requires that every company has a **company secretary**, who is responsible for all legal matters, and often advises other departments. Duties include filling in the Memorandum and Articles of Association when the company is started. He or she also acts as a link between shareholders and directors and handles correspondence to and from shareholders, informing them of company meetings and other important matters. Often a company secretary will have some other responsibilities, such as that of **office manager**.

The administration department

Many large organisations have a central **administration** office which is responsible for controlling paperwork and supporting other departments with facilities such as filing, mail, word processing and data handling. Modern offices use computers and information technology extensively.

It is common practice for an administration department to appoint an office manager with the responsibility for coordinating **office services** and offering expert advice to departmental managers. The work of an office manager might include organising clerical training, advising departments on layout, equipment and practices, coordinating the supply of equipment and stationery, standardising office practices and setting up an effective communications system within the organisation – such as mailing or phone systems.

Case Study

Centralisation of office services

Many organisations prefer to centralise their office services within an administration department. This means that all paperwork is filed together centrally, that a typing pool deals with all word processing requirements and that mail is dealt with by a mail room. It is thought that greater efficiency can be obtained if these and other services are carried out by a specialist department.

Viewpoint 1 – Rob Butcher had been working at Smartco for 20 years in the accounts office. He enjoyed his job and felt that all the amenities and services he required were always at his fingertips. When office services were centralised the departmental secretary was moved to a typing pool, the photocopier was taken away so that all requirements were met by a print room, and all of the correspondence files were now filed centrally. If he required a service he found that he had to fill in a form to request it.

Viewpoint 2 – Jan Smith was responsible for the reorganisation at Smartco. Despite resistance to the changes from some staff, it was her opinion that centralisation of office services led to easier covering for staff absences, a fairer distribution of work amongst clerical staff, and greater uniformity of procedures. She also felt that many of the savings could be spent upon better systems and equipment.

1 *Examine the two viewpoints and explain whether your sympathies lie with Rob or with Jan.*
2 *Why might it be necessary to take into account the special requirements of some departments when centralising services?*

The accounts department

The **chief accountant** supervises the work of the accounts department. The managers of an organisation need to be constantly aware of relevant financial matters. Computers and calculators help to speed up accounting procedures.

The accounts department may be further sub-divided into two sections. Then the *financial accounting section* will be responsible for keeping records of events as they occur. Records need to be kept of both cash and credit transactions. As well as keeping day-to-day records the section will be responsible for producing periodic records such as the annual accounts. The departtment will also have the responsibility of keeping accurate VAT records. The *management accounting section* will influence the direction of the organisation based upon its analysis of figures for the present and predictions for the future. Costings, budgets and targets for achievement are all vital. Wages, pensions, PAYE and national insurance and similar employee details will all be handled by the accounts department.

The marketing department

The **marketing** function is responsible for identifying, anticipating and satisfying consumer requirements profitably. Although sometimes marketing and sales departments are combined, there is an important distinction between the two. Whereas marketing is concerned with ensuring that the organisation produces what the customers want, sales is about selling what the organisation has.

The marketing department will therefore be primarily concerned with investigating consumers' needs and wants. This will involve **market research** to find out who comprises a particular market, what they want, where they want it, how much they will pay for it and the most effective way of promoting it. So that the wishes of consumers can be tied in with new product development, there will be close co-operation between the marketing department and the production planning/research and development departments.

The sales department

The main responsibility of the sales department is to create **orders** for goods and services. The size of the department and the ways of operation vary considerably. For example, some organisations employ a large sales force working on a regional basis. Other organisations depend upon advertising to stimulate sales and employ only a small sales team.

Task

Look at the distinction between marketing and selling. Comment on how the roles differ, and consider which of the two areas you would prefer to work in. Give reasons for your answers.

The information technology department

In a modern organisation, staff may work either directly with or have access to **information technology**. Information technology (IT) refers to the large and developing body of technologies and techniques which are used to obtain, process and disseminate information to employees.

The responsibilities of this department would include computing, telecommunications and office developments. Though these three areas used to be viewed as distinct, they are progressively merging together and playing a greater role in business activity.

The IT manager is there to exploit IT in the organisation and provide the guidance, support and expertise necessary to accomplish this.

The production department

Production involves the performance of activities necessary to produce a good service that satisfies the customer. It is often argued that this part of the business is the most difficult to carry out. It involves getting the quality of the good or service just right, and it usually employs the largest amount of capital, assets, labour and other factors in the organisation.

The personnel department

The **personnel** function has three principal areas of responsibility:

- It is responsible for the recruitment and training of staff within the organisation.
- It is responsible for ensuring that their terms and conditions of employment are appropriate, competitive and properly administered.
- It is responsible for employee relations policy.

Also, see Chapter 10.

Task

In 1992 the economy of the United Kingdom moved towards recession. Jobs were lost across a range of industries. Those in work, more often than not, saved for a jobless day despite the continuing slide in interest rates. Industrial pay awards fell sharply. Working in groups, explain how such events might affect the operation of a *personnel department*.

The community projects department

Larger organisations in the UK are aware that they are more likely to thrive in a successful and receptive community. A **community projects manager** might be appointed with the responsibility of overseeing a range of projects – such as help to local small businesses, an educational service and environmental concern units.

Case Study

The Bank of England

The Bank of England was founded in 1694 because William III was short of money to finance the war against France. Today, if anybody is asked what the Bank does they probably say 'prints money'. However, issuing new money is only a small part of its work.

The Bank now occupies a privileged position at the centre of our financial system. It is administered by a Court of Directors which in many ways is similar to the board of a company. The Court consists of the Governor, Deputy Governor, four executive directors and twelve non-executive directors, all appointed by the Crown on the advice of the Prime Minister.

Though the Bank's main business is carried out at Threadneedle Street in London, it also occupies other offices in the City and has branches in major cities throughout England. For operational purposes the Bank is divided by function as shown in the table.

1 *Explain why the Bank of England divides its activities by function.*
2 *What are the benefits it gains by doing so?*
3 *How important is it for employees in the Bank of England to understand clearly how their organisation is divided?*

The Governor and Deputy Governor The Court of Directors	
Banking department	carries out the banking business – providing services to City institutions, government, overseas banks and other customers
Registrar's department	maintains a register of government and other stocks (much of the work is heavily influenced by the mood of the financial markets)
Corporate services	provides support services for the Bank – such as personnel, administration, finance, business systems etc.
Policy and markets division	responsible for activities in the financial markets
Finance and industry divisions	monitor industry and commerce throughout the UK
Banking supervision	responsible for protecting bank depositors and ensuring the health of the banking system
Printing works	designs, prints and destroys banknotes.

Figure 4.5 *How the Bank of England is organised*

facilities. As the range of products increases it may become more practicable to handle each type of product in a separate division of the company, so structuring the organisation upon **product lines**. For example, some publishers have a newspapers division, a magazine and periodicals division and a book publishing division.

Division by product

As an organisation grows, so too may the range of products it offers. At the beginning it may be straightforward to handle all the products with common

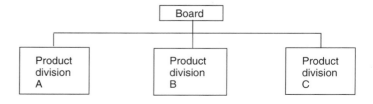

Figure 4.6 *Division by product lines*

Hanson PLC

As a multinational organisation with several types of business interests, Hanson PLC structures its activities in the UK by product. It has the following divisions:

a The *consumer group* includes Imperial Tobacco with names such as Embassy, John Player Special, Lambert & Butler, St Bruno, Henri Wintermans and Castella; Ever Ready with Silver Seal and Gold Seal; and Seven Seas, the world's largest supplier of vitamin and mineral supplements in capsule form.

b *Building products* includes ARC, Greenways, London Brick, Butterley Brick, Crabtree and Marbourn.

c *Industrial products* includes Robinson Willey, Smith Meters. Switchmaster, Berry Magicoal, SLD Pumps and Rollalong.

1 Comment briefly upon how Hanson PLC structures its UK activities.

2 Why might an organisation like Hanson PLC, which is a vast conglomerate, be more likely to structure by product?

The great advantage of dividing by product is that all divisions can concentrate on their own market areas. It also becomes possible to assess the profitability and effectiveness of each sector. For example, some organisations sell off or merge unprofitable divisions if the particular industry or area shows little promise; this allows the company to concentrate on more profitable areas. Division by product can also allow parts of organisations to engage in joint ventures with other companies. CocaCola and Nestlé both have interests in drinks and beverages, and they recently entered into a joint venture to manufacture a fresh range of ready-made beverages under the Nescafé and Nestea brand names. Deals like this are expected to become more common and are viewed as preferable to takeovers.

Division by process

Many manufacturing or service operations consist of a series of sequences or processes. Each of these requires division of labour with separate skills, different types of machinery, and often in a different working environment (e.g. a paint shop, an upholstery workshop, a production line). Where this happens it could be appropriate to set up a department to monitor and manage each **process**. For example, a manufacturer of chicken nuggets could be divided by process as shown in Figure 4.7.

Storage department	Manufacturing department	Freezing department	Packing department	Despatch department
Process 1	**Process 2**	**Process 3**	**Process 4**	**Process 5**

Figure 4.7 *Division by process in a manufacturer of chicken nuggets*

Make up an example of a situation in which an organisation could divide its activities by process. Indicate how you would divide its activities.

Division by process allows an organisation to set up teams of specialists involved with each stage. It also allows points in the production process to be identified if things go either well or badly. Division by process will, however, only work effectively if there is a steady flow from one process to another. If one process department produces too much or too little, problems can occur as stocks build up or run out. This might occur if workers in one process department go on strike or if one department has particularly high absenteeism. Another problem might arise if the departments fail to communicate with each other.

Division by geographical area

A large organisation may have branches and divisions not only throughout the country but also across the world. For example, BP boasts of its operations in more than 70 overseas countries. Such organisations, rather than attempting to control all their activities directly from a head office, may decide to divide up their operations according to regions or countries. A large retailer such as Marks & Spencer, which has shops on every major high street in the UK as well as in cities across the world, will have groups of shops organised into regional and international divisions.

Figure 4.8 illustrates a company with five domestic divisions and three overseas divisions.

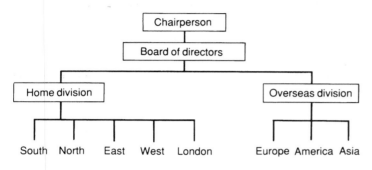

Figure 4.8 *Grouping by geographical area*

Yorkshire Water

Yorkshire Water is the guardian of a water environment which stretches from the industrial conurbations of south and west Yorkshire to the rural and recreational areas of the Yorkshire Dales, Moors and North Sea coast. Every day, around the clock, Yorkshire Water collects, treats and puts into the supply system on average some 302 million gallons of water serving around four and a half million customers and some 160 000 commercial premises. The scale and spread of activities across a large geographical area necessitate dividing the region into distinct areas (see Figure 4.9).

1 Yorkshire Water is 'one of the ten water and sewage businesses of England and Wales'. Why do you think water companies are split according to regions and have then further divided themselves geographically?

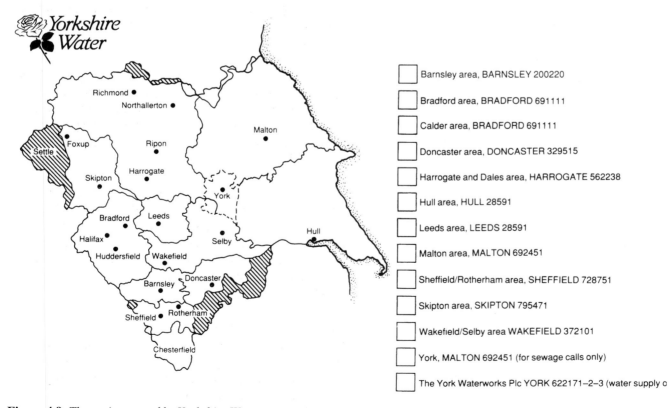

Figure 4.9 *The region served by Yorkshire Water*

2 Make lists of the advantages and disadvantages of organisations being divided geographically.

Being organised geographically makes it easier for a large enterprise to respond quickly to local issues and problems and to tailor its strategies to local conditions (language, laws, customs etc.). At the same time it might be possible to cut through a lot of 'red tape' if regional divisions are allowed to make their own decisions. In addition, governments often look more kindly on divisions of foreign multinationals if there is a local head office and manufacturing facility.

However, having too many regional divisions can lead to duplication of facilities, lack of coordination and communication breakdowns. An extensive regional structure requires a series of management positions, and this might lead to a division taking on a life of its own, pulling against the parent organisation and ending up at loggerheads with the head office.

Division by type of customer

This type of division is particularly common where it is felt that different categories of customers require different treatment. For example, an organisation may treat its industrial customers differently from its retail customers.

Banks, in particular, are divided in order to cater for various customer requirements. They have a foreign currency desk, a mortgage advisor, a separate desk for enquiries, and departments dealing with account services for private and business account holders.

The main advantage of this approach is that each department can concentrate on the special needs of its customers. However, the departments may be costly to set

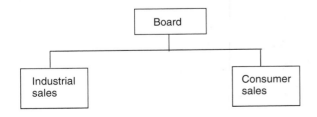

Figure 4.10 *Division by type of customers*

up and run, particularly in terms of staffing, and may only be cost-effective when there is sufficient demand from all types of customers.

Task

Find an organisation that is divided by customer type. Comment on how this has been done and then indicate whether you feel the strategy has been successful.

The matrix structure

A **matrix structure** can be used to combine the grouping methods we have identified. In such a matrix it is probable that each member of the organisation belongs to two or more groups. A matrix is thus a combination of structures which enables employees to contribute to a mix of activities.

For example, in Figure 4.11 employees are organised both by function (personnel, marketing) and by product (product division). In this example some workers from each product division will be accountable to a personnel manager and a marketing manager, as well as to their divisional manager.

The matrix enables the organisation to focus upon a number of aims at the same time, and gives it the flexibility to respond to new markets where there is an increase in demand for its goods and services – for example, servicing different types of customers with different products in different regions. Another great benefit is the cross-fertilisation of ideas between departments.

On the other hand, a matrix may be difficult to understand, so that employees lose sight of operational aims. The system might also involve more than one chain of command, leading to power struggles, contradictory orders and general confusion.

143

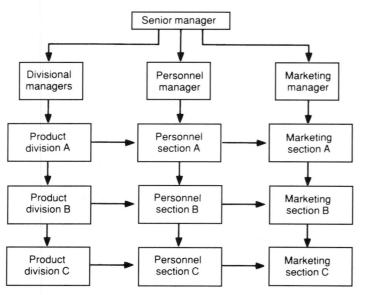

Figure 4.11 *Part of a matrix structure*

· SPAN OF CONTROL ·

Span of control refers to the number of employees who are directly supervised by one person. The manager who tries to supervise too many people may be overworked so that his or her staff are unable to perform their duties effectively. On the other hand, if a manager has too few people to supervise, their time might be wasted.

Task

How many people come under your supervisor's or lecturer's span of control? Does this number appear to be too few or too many? What do you believe to be the optimum span of control in their situation?

The question of how many immediate subordinates one manager can cope with has been debated for a long time. A principle followed in many large organisations is that no manager can deal effectively with more than five or six. In 1921, General Sir Ian Hamilton wrote that between three and six is the ideal number, depending on the level in the organisation. Various surveys show, however, that managing directors deal with anything between one and 24 managers directly. Clearly a lot depends on the level – it is

probably considerably easier for a manager to supervise 20 shop-floor employees undertaking menial tasks than for a managing director to supervise the work of four directors.

Unity of command

Just as one person cannot be expected to supervise too many people, each person should themselves have only one superior to whom they have to report. This is known as **unity of command**. If an employee is accountable to more than one supervisor it can be difficult for him or her to know which of their assignments to do first, or there could be conflicting instructions on the same assignment. This can affect both morale and the way the task is done.

Task

Are you subject to unity of command either at work or at college? How does this affect the way you perform your tasks?

Responsibility, authority and accountability

The number of hierarchical levels and the span of control are two important dimensions in an organisation's structure. The board of directors is **responsible** to the shareholders for the performance of the organisation. In return for this the shareholders give the directors **authority** to make decisions on their behalf. When the directors use their authority they are then **accountable** to the shareholders for what they have done and from time to time might have to justify their actions.

We have looked at two levels of control, but in each part of the organisation there will be different levels of responsibility, authority and accountability. The more senior managers will be concerned with making **strategic decisions** affecting the overall policy of the organisation. As we look down the hierarchy, decision-making will become more **tactical** and designed to meet the short-term, constantly changing circumstances of the organisation.

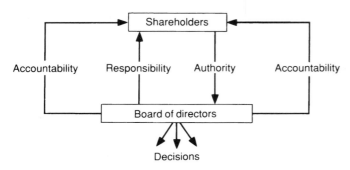

Figure 4.12 *Responsibility, authority and accountability*

Delegation and decentralisation

These are terms associated with authority. **Delegation** is simply the passing down of authority from a superior to a subordinate. **Decentralisation** goes much further – it is a philosophy of management which determines what authority to pass down. It then develops policies to guide the staff who have this authority delegated to them, and implements controls for monitoring their performance.

Case Study

Delegation and decentralisation

Phil works for a small company as a buyer. Though he normally works under close supervision, the Managing Director has asked him to cover while the Purchasing Manager is on holiday.

Sally works for a large company as a buyer. She is given an annual budget and a series of guidelines which determine what she can do and what she cannot do. The particular aspect of her job she likes is the freedom to make decisions. Her activities are constantly monitored in regular meetings with her supervisor, and each year she has an appraisal interview.

1 Explain how the two examples help to emphasise the principles of delegation and decentralisation. Which situation would you prefer to work in?

2 What are the dangers of too much delegation and decentralisation?

· ORGANISATION CHARTS ·

A large enterprise – one with many employees – may have a **flat** or a **tall** organisational structure (see Figures 4.13 and 4.14), depending on the nature of its business.

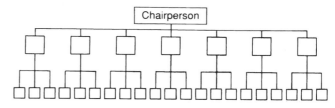

Figure 4.13 *A flat organisational structure*

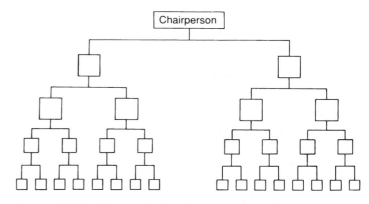

Figure 4.14 *A tall organisational structure*

Task

Consider to what extent the management structure in the organisation you attend or in which you work is either flat or tall. Which type of structure would you feel to be the best for morale? Which type would be best for efficiency?

An organisation chart is a *visual device* which shows the structure of the enterprise and the relationships between workers and divisions of work. Thus the chart:

- shows how the organisation is structured
- indicates each employee's level of responsibility and to whom each reports

- shows lines of communication
- indicates possible lines of promotion.

Many organisations make their charts public, and they may issue a copy as part of their promotional materials, sometimes in a house magazine and often in an annual report. It is not uncommon for names and/or photographs to be put on the chart in order to emphasise the personal aspect of management. This is also a common practice in education to familiarise pupils with names and faces when they start secondary school.

An organisation chart thus provides a clear, simple picture of an organisation's structure. This is also helpful when the roles and performances of individual elements have to be assessed. The chart can also help a manager to decide whether to delegate and decentralise.

Task

Outline the advantages and disadvantages of putting both names and pictures on an organisation chart.

Relationships

Organisation charts depict a series of **formal** relationships and patterns of authority. There is an important distinction between line, functional, staff and lateral relationships.

A **line relationship** is a traditional relationship in a hierarchical body. There are direct communication links between *superiors* and *subordinates*. Each member of the organisation has a clear understanding of the chain of command, to whom they should report and for whom they are responsible.

A **staff relationship** exists where a member of staff has an assistant who supports him or her in day-to-day activities. This assistant will have an advisory role and have no direct line relationship (see Figure 4.17).

A **functional relationship** occurs when a department exists to provide specialist advice and services to other departments across the organisation. Purchasing, personnel, information technology and office

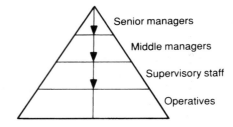

Figure 4.15 *The downward flow in a line relationship*

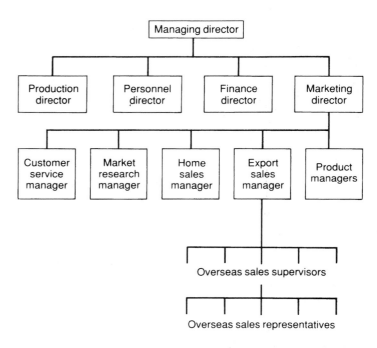

Figure 4.16 *Line relationships in one part of a large marketing department*

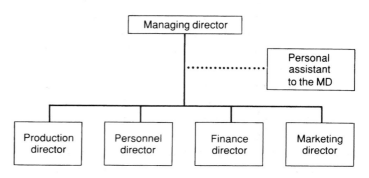

Figure 4.17 *An example of a staff relationship*

administration are all departments which cut across an organisation to provide a series of specialist services.

Medium and large organisations often *combine* elements of line and functional relationships. Whereas a line department (such as marketing) tends to concentrate on achieving the organisation's business objectives, functional relationships complement such activities to improve the way they are carried out. This also means that line departments only need to familiarise themselves with their core activities and can rely on help through their functional relationships.

Task

Is there ever likely to be a situation where a functional relationship might hinder or conflict with a line relationship? Explain your answer.

A **lateral relationship** occurs where managers and other employees at or around the same level of responsibility and from different departments co-operate on projects – particularly in a matrix. For example, a project might involve assistant managers from marketing, production, purchasing, sales and research and development.

Informal relationships

In the real world no organisation can function solely on the basis of a **formal structure** of relationships as depicted in its organisation chart. There are also **informal relationships** in the workplace between employees at all levels and from all backgrounds which help to ensure that things get done. For example, an accountant from the finance department may regularly check details with a particular clerk in the purchasing department before making decisions, because he or she knows that this particular person is 'on the ball' and close to the core activities of the organisation. Other informal relationships arise through social groups, organised outings or sports and recreational activities. Wherever people meet there is some form of social system, and the relationships established from these meetings may become useful in the workplace.

Case Study –

Yorkshire Bank PLC

Over the last 70 years Yorkshire Bank has undergone a phenomenal growth in its activities and is today recognised as one of the foremost banking organisations in the UK, with branches across the country providing a comprehensive range of services. Study the bank's organisation chart (Figure 4.18).

1 Comment on how Yorkshire Bank is divided up.
2 Taking into account the nature of the organisation, does the chart seem to indicate a flat structure or a tall structure?
3 Show examples from the chart of lateral, functional and line relationships.
4 How might such a chart help employees at the bank?
5 Why are organisation charts often shown in landscape form?

Case Study

Splitting up the railways

British Rail is a public corporation with a turnover of nearly £3 billion. It employs well over 100 000 staff, with a passenger volume of over 20 billion passenger-miles in addition to freight activities. The organisation is currently split up into five manageable units (see Figure 4.19 page 148).

For several years British Rail has been directed by the government to prepare itself for privatisation. Many people, however, feel that the organisation is too unwieldy to privatise, and there have been rumours that the privatisation might be dropped altogether.

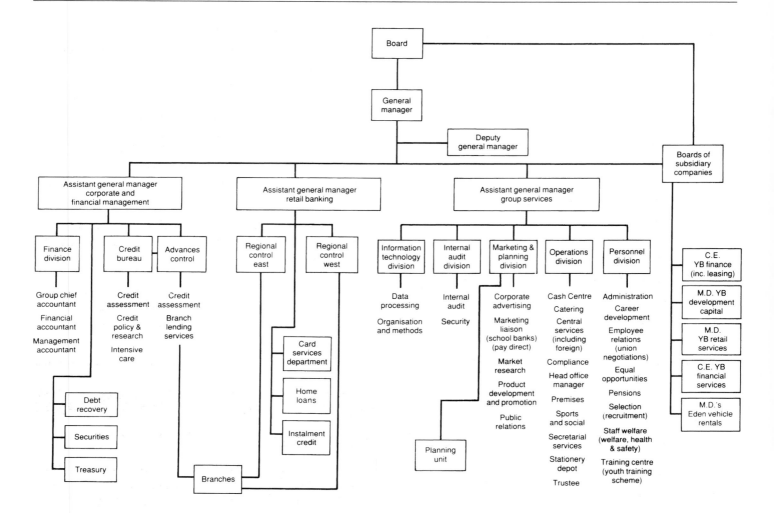

Figure 4.18 *Yorkshire Bank's organisational chart*

The crucial question seems to be, if the enterprise is privatised should it be sold as a lump or as discrete packages? If it is sold as packages, how should these be structured?

The Secretary of State for Transport, against the advice of

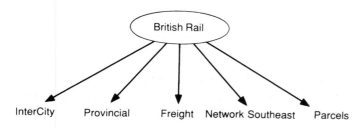

Figure 4.19 *The units of British Rail*

BR senior managers, has decided not to sell BR in a single lump. He fears that this would merely create a private-sector monopoly and would not improve the service. He is also opposed to a scheme of dividing the organisation into seven regional packages, as a romantic way of returning to the situation that existed before the railways were nationalised.

Current thinking is to sell the *freight* division first. This division is profitable, and should boom as road congestion increases and can be helped by the opening of the Channel Tunnel and new technology. Many feel that if this division is privatised it will be able to respond more quickly to business developments and overcome the image of unreliability. *InterCity*, too, will probably be easy to privatise as it is another money-maker. Other areas, however, are supported by large subsidies and will be tougher to sell off.

Another idea is to put each part of the organisation out to tender, perhaps line by line, in the same way that bus services have been deregulated. Bidders would get a subsidy but would have to compete on price and quality. The problem with this is that breaking the organisation up into small units would result in inefficient use of resources.

Whatever ideas are put forward over the next few years, the future of the railways as we know them, and the structure of the organisation, hinge upon many external factors.

1 *Comment on the present structure of British Rail. Can you make a guess at the type of organisation chart it has (flat or tall)?*

2 *How would the conversion of British Rail into small units affect line, functional and lateral relationships?*

3 *What might the break-up of BR do to the morale of the workforce?*

4 *Why would the break-up of the organisation into small units be inefficient?*

5 *Working in groups, suggest how you would (assuming you are given the powers to do so) divide the railways business. Report your ideas back and then compare them with those from other groups.*

Case Study

Eigth-freight Ltd

Eight-freight is a small private company providing courier delivery of envelopes and parcels to guaranteed time schedules. The following staff are employed by Eight-freight:

Managing Director: Sarah Williams
Personal Assistant: Sue Jones
Marketing Director: Ron Atkinson
Marketing Managers: David Platt and Mark Walters
   (each with two assistants)
Personnel Director: Joe Jordan
Personnel Officer (Staffing): Jane Whitehouse
Personnel Officer (Training): Robin Fitzwarren

Finance Director: Sheila Williams
Finance Manager: Adrian Mole (who has four assistants)
Operations Director: Jimmy Saville
Operations Managers: James Schultz and
   Jimmy Edwards (both of whom have responsibility for
   20 couriers) – James takes responsibility for all
   northern work and Jimmy for all southern work
Company Secretary/Administrator: Peter Williams
Administrative Officer: Jane Redmond (who has
   responsibility for two typists, a reprographics operator
and a receptionist).

1 Draw an organisation chart for Eight-freight Ltd. Give one example each of a line, staff, functional and lateral relationship.
2 Comment on how Eight-freight Ltd is divided.
3 Jimmy Saville has suggested that Eight-freight Ltd form a mixed hockey team to play regularly on Sunday mornings. How might this affect relationships in the organisation?

Element assignment

The organisation of a factory

This assignment can help you provide evidence for assessment, or claim the following Core Skills outcomes:

Communication
   Communicate in writing
   Participate in oral and non-verbal communication

Personal Skills
   Transfer skills gained to new and changing situations
   Relate to and interact effectively with individuals and groups
   Work effectively as a member of a team
   Identify and solve routine and non-routine problems

The two organisational charts on page 53 show the functional organisations of a factory making recipe dishes for Marks and Spencer.

Working in groups find out in detail about the tasks performed by employees in each of the functions outlined. For example, in the Personnel Department what would be the roles of the personnel manager, personnel officer, safety and training officer, personnel assistant, and nurse?

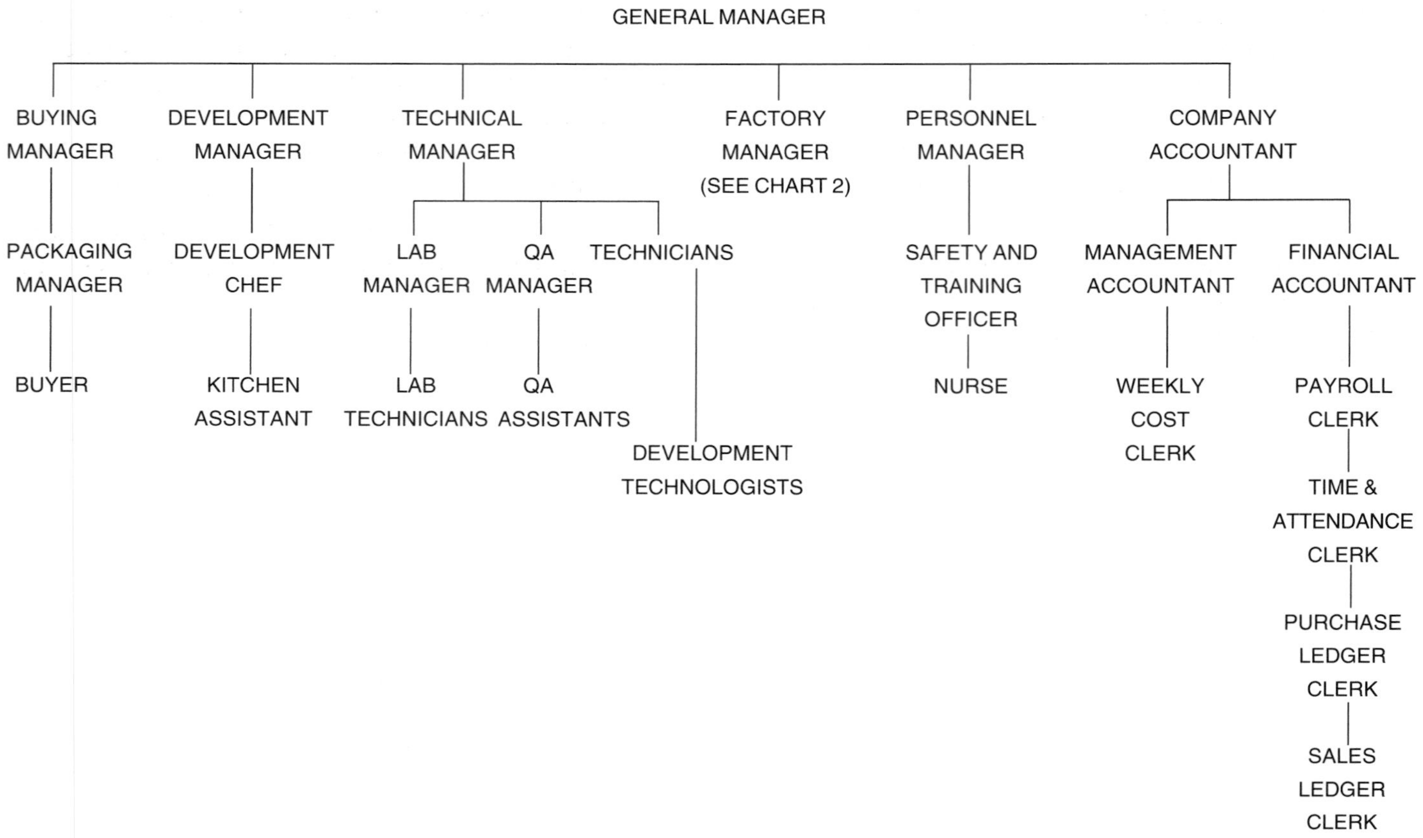

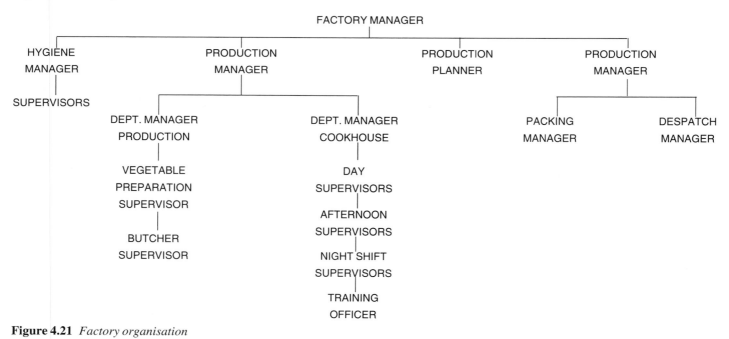

Figure 4.20 *Management structure*

Figure 4.21 *Factory organisation*

Each group should concentrate on two or three functions. Carry out your research by reviewing texts about functional organisation; also refer to and consult real organisations in your locality. Find information from family and friends. You may not have a food processing plant in your locality but most large organisations will have similar organisational structures.

Each group should copy out their section of the organisation chart onto a large sheet of flip chart paper and use it to make their presentation to the rest of the group.

How do the functions you have studied relate to the other functions shown? For example, what is the relationship between accounts and sales? Each group should find out about the lines of communication and working relationship between the function it has studied and other parts of the organisation.

(NB the factory manager has overall responsibility for the factory with a production manager directly below him in the line.)

chapter **5** COMMUNICATION

Central to all administrative functions is the need to be able to communicate both inside and outside the organisation. Communicating effectively with others can be very difficult. For example, how often have you failed to understand an instruction or misinterpreted a statement? In all organisations the purpose of setting up an effective communications system is to create a mechanissm that gets things done. Such systems will ensure that messages are received, understood, accepted and then, as a result, action can take place.

This chapter looks at the nature of communication within the context of administration. Basic communication skills are analysed and then related to internal and external communication systems.

· THE NEED FOR COMMUNICATION ·

At the heart of management at all levels of responsibility lies a fundamental requirement to be able to communicate. A manager must be able to communicate effectively with all people within his or her span of control. In fact, managers and administrators tend to spend by far the majority of their time communicating with others. If communication as a basic business skill takes up so much time, a knowledge of how to communicate well has to be viewed as a vital requirement for all managers and administrators.

Communication is the two-way process of passing on ideas and information. All organisations need good, clear paths of communication. In Chapter 4 we saw how systematic lines of communication help to create a structure which coordinates the activities between different parts of an organisation. Effective communication in an organisation, however, goes further than this. It enables an organisation to make everyone aware of what they can achieve. It also helps employees solve problems through the use of technical language referring to the more scientific aspects of their work. Finally, by providing a uniform way of giving people information and an opportunity to put their ideas across, communication can be used to avoid misunderstandings, save time, resolve conflicts and provide all employees with a tool to express as clearly as possible what they really mean.

We all have to communicate. To communicate well requires the development of the basic skills of speaking, listening, reading and writing. In addition it involves an awareness and an understanding of the subject, the audience and the environment. Successful communication requires not only that information should be transmitted, but also that it should be fully received and understood. Listening and reading skills are therefore just as important as speaking and writing skills.

Form small groups. Each member of the group should prepare a talk lasting for about one minute and then deliver it to the other members of the group. Analyse the problems encountered by both the speakers and the listeners.

Transmitters and receivers

The process of communication involves a **transmitter** (or sender) sending **messages** to **receivers.** A transmitter should put information into a form the receivers can understand, and this might involve oral, written or visual messages. This process is known as **encoding.** The transmitter chooses a particular medium to use to send messages to the receivers – letter, report, fax, phone call etc. The receivers then interpret the messages through a process of **decoding**.

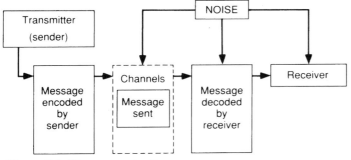

Figure 5.1 *The communication process*

Though a message flows from the sender to the receivers, there is no guarantee that the receivers will either receive the full message or even understand it. This is because the process may be subject to some form of interference or barrier to communication which affects the smooth flow of information. Communication problems of this nature are known as noise and may lead to the downfall of the message. Noise can take the form of any barrier acting as an impediment to the smooth flow of information. Here are a few examples:

- *Language problems* – The language used may not be fully understood, particularly if a receiver comes from a

different background from the sender or has considerably less knowledge, technical or otherwise.

- *Jumping to conclusions* – The receiver might read into the message what he or she expects to see, rather than what is really there.
- *Lack of interest* – The receiver may not be prepared to listen to the message. The message has to be designed to appeal to the listener.
- *Competing environment* – Background sounds (real noise) or interference from other activities in the work environment may influence the message, particularly if it is long or complicated and requires concentration by the receiver.
- *Channels of communication* – Effective communication will be hampered if the means chosen to pass the message is poor.
- *Cultural differences* – We all have different perceptions of the world according to our background and experiences, and this may result in our interpreting a message in different ways.
- *Steps in the message* – If there are too many stages in the message (i.e. if it is too complicated) it may not be properly understood.

Identify at least one situation in which a barrier to communication has affected your interpretation of a message.

· BASIC COMMUNICATION SKILLS ·

Communication skills must cover listening, speaking, reading, writing and information technology (IT).

Listening

We tend to think of **listening** as easy. However, we converse with quite a few people during an average day and 'listen to' so much information that it is very easy to forget what we have heard. Sometimes people try to listen to several conversations (i.e. messages) at the same time and only ever pick up snippets of information and never the full picture of events.

Listening involves:

- the process of physically hearing a message
- interpretation of the message
- evaluation, when decisions are made on how to use the information.

A problem with listening to messages can be that, unless you are making notes at the same time, much of the information received is forgotten and not followed up.

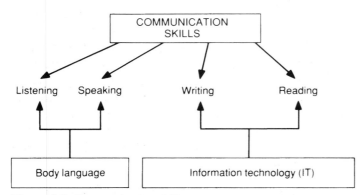

Figure 5.2 *Communication skills*

Task

Form small groups. Starting with the statement 'When Paul went out of the house he met Sarah', each member of the group should in turn add a simple item of new information; for example, 'When Paul went out of the house he met Sarah and John'. Continue to go round the group like this, without taking notes. At the end, write down as much information as you can remember. Were other group members easy to listen to? Did anyone use non-verbal communication? Was the exercise affected in any way by *noise*? How would taking notes transform this exercise?

Speaking

Speech takes place between people in close proximity to each other or at the other end of a telehone line. Provided the listener (i.e. receiver) is attentive, ambiguity can be removed by **questioning**. Questioning is a very important process because it can clarify meanings and points of view.

For speech to be an effective means of communication it is important that an individual be aware of:

- his or her own role as a communicator
- the receptiveness of the listeners
- the listeners' own knowledge of the subject.

Writing and reading

Written messages vary from the very simple to the very complex. The following are some examples of situations where written communications are appropriate:

- the information needs to be received by several people in different places
- the information is highly complex, requiring extensive study
- the information needs to be referred to over a period of time.

The written word in some circumstances can be open to **ambiguity** if the receiver is not immediately able to question the sender. For this reason, even informal notes need to be accurate, clear in their meaning and easy to read. Documentation systems are widely used in industry to reduce elements of ambiguity and, very often, drawings and sketches are used to support the written text.

Some types of written communication are more easily read than others. For example, company accounts and other financial and quantitative information may be complex and require the reader to have specialist background knowledge. The target audience and the nature of the information are very important factors to take into consideration when deciding how to present data.

Information technology skills

IT skills are the 'penmanship' of the future. The revolution in information technology has transformed the way in which information is handled, processed and distributed – using desktop computer terminals. The result is that information quality can be improved. It can be accessed more quickly, sent more effectively and can contribute to more effective decision making and subsequent competitive advantage.

Body language

It is possible for some messages to be transmitted even without using the spoken or written word. Non-verbal communication or **body language** can be used on its own or to reinforce the spoken word. We all use physical gestures and show our feelings with facial expressions. Sometimes a gesture or expression on its own can say more than a verbal message – a nod or frown can convey its own special meaning. Being able to observe such signs is an important communication skill.

★Shaking hands	★Folding your arms	★Placing yourself in relation to others
★Shrugging your shoulders	★Leaning backwards or forwards in your chair	★Clenching your fists
★A slap on the back	★An arm around the shoulder	★Nodding your head
★Body posture		

Figure 5.3 *Examples of physical gestures*

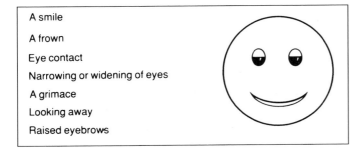

A smile
A frown
Eye contact
Narrowing or widening of eyes
A grimace
Looking away
Raised eyebrows

Figure 5.4 *Physical gestures may be supported by facial expressions*

Non-verbal communication can provide strong support for any message – it goes beyond the words themselves and gives a clearer view of what the sender really means.

During your next group task, make a point of observing body language – the physical gestures and facial expressions of members of the group. Explain how the use of such body language helped (or hindered) them in communicating their messages.

A man of influence

Jean Peyrelevade is chairman of the *Union des Assurances de Paris* (UAP), France's biggest insurer and cornerstone of the country's *mixed economy*. A banker by background, he was made chairman in the summer of 1988 by France's newly elected socialist government. Monsieur Peyrelevade is perhaps best known for having been economic advisor to President Mitterand's first Prime Minister in 1981.

A journalist of the time characterised Jean Peyrelevade's role: 'In the socialist party . . . he adopted the habit of expressing, in a very strong and serious voice, certain simple truths which often provoked uproar.'

Since those times M. Peyrelevade has continued to be viewed as an influential figure. Many feel that there is a certain refreshing directness about him. He always takes pains to explain his position clearly and he does not evade questions but tackles them head on.

There are two ways of reading Jean Peyrelevade's mind. The first is to listen carefully to what he says and the second is to look at what he does. Instead of looking at takeovers and acquisitions to expand UAP, he would like to see the creation of large groups of European insurers – he feels that co-operation would help to provide expansion for all those involved in such an operation. Given the nature of his approach there is good reason to believe all that he says.

1 Identify certain key communication skills used by Jean Peyrelevade.

2 How important is it for influential figures to have such skills?

3 Explain why a good speaker can make listening easy.

Figure 5.5 *Feedback from a message*

· COMMUNICATING THE MESSAGE ·

Before communicating any information the sender needs to think clearly about what is to be achieved. The objective or goal should influence the way the message is communicated. The sender should therefore ask himself or herself a few simple questions:

- What do I hope to achieve by the message?
- With whom am I communicating and how will they react to my message?
- What is my relationship with the receivers, and will this influence the way they react to my message?
- What information should be included in the message?
- What techniques should I use to communicate this particular message?

Task

Imagine that the assignment you intended to hand in this week has not yet been completed. Write a short note to the appropriate member of the staff explaining why it is late and what you are going to do about it. Use the questions in the text to help you to complete the message.

Feedback

Most messages generate some form of response. For example, a verbal message may provoke a non-verbal shrug or a frown, or another might lead to either a long-winded verbal response or a more formal written answer. These responses to the message are known as **feedback**. Feedback generally indicates how the recipient has interpreted the original message and whether the information has been understood.

The nature of the feedback can reflect the *type* of organisation in which the message is directed. In an **authoritarian** structure the sender may not expect a response from the receivers. Managers may issue commands or instructions or make statements to subordinates. This communication is a one-way process. The sender does not expect instructions to be questioned and, as a result, misunderstandings may occur. Conversely, in a **democratic** structure, managers will want to avoid misunderstandings and will positively encourage feedback. By examining the response to a message the manager can assess how it has been received and more closely monitor the feelings of employees.

· INTERNAL COMMUNICATIONS ·

Internal communications are communications **within** an organisation. The purpose of most forms of internal communication is to transfer information or to initiate some action. Figure 5.6 explains this is more detail.

★ **To present facts/information** – Informing employees may affect their responses to day-to-day decisions or keep them aware of changes in procedures connected with health and safety, breaks etc.
★ **To give instructions** – These may influence how employees carry out their duties.
★ **To provide a basis for negotiation** – Conflict exists in all organisations and internal communication may provide a basis for resolving disputes.
★ **To present findings** – These may be the result of a piece of research.
★ **To motivate employees** – Communication may be used to increase the involvement of employees in the organisation's activities.
★ **To improve teamwork** – It allows employees to work more closely together.

Figure 5.6 *Objectives of internal communication*

Internal communication may flow:

- downwards – from higher to lower levels
- upwards – from lower to higher levels
- horizontally – between people and departments at the same level
- multi-directionally – in all directions.

A **grapevine** will throw information out in all directions to all interested parties.

Task

Analyse the internal communication methods in an organisation known to you. What sorts of internal communication can you identify (provide examples)? What do these internal communications try to do? How do they flow?

Verbal communications

Verbal communications involve the transmission of information effectively by word of mouth. Speaking is often a vastly underrated skill. It can be used to communicate ideas, reasons and conclusions. A good speaker is likely to have a far greater impact on the receiver of a message than a poor speaker and can provoke a far better response (see Figure 5.7).

1 Express your ideas clearly, using language that is appropriate for your listeners
2 Say exactly what you mean – speak accurately using reliable information and never generalise with statements that go beyond the facts
3 Show empathy with the listeners, and convey enthusiasm
4 Try to be sincere and not put on an act – relax and talk naturally
5 Use tone, expressions and some body language (not too much)
6 Use appropriate pitch and volume
7 Articulate and enunciate well – a regional accent does *not* affect good diction if you speak clearly

Figure 5.7 *How to be an effective speaker*

Task

Think of anyone you know with good speaking ability. What makes him or her a good speaker? Make a complete list of the qualities of a good speaker. Discuss your conclusions with others in a group situation.

For many people at work, verbal communications tend to be **face-to-face exchanges** for the purposes of relaying messages, personal discussion, giving advice, providing instructions and guidance etc. Such exchanges are particularly appropriate for discussing personal matters and for conveying feelings or confidential facts where information should not be divulged further. Face-to-face contact can create a less formal relationship and allow communicators to get to know each other. Feedback can be instant, so that disagreements can be sorted out quickly. The main disadvantage of face-to-face contact, however, is that it is a time-consuming exercise which usually provides no permanent record of the message unless notes are written. Discussion may lack precision, and this can lead to misunderstandings.

Another area where verbal communications are important is in **meetings** (see Chapter 11). Nearly all employees at all levels in an organisation will spend some time attending meetings; administrative staff and managers will use a large proportion of their time in this way. Meetings are held to deal with issues, problems and areas of concern for an organisation. They provide an opportunity for a group of people to use their specialist backgrounds, experiences and knowledge to contribute to a range of matters.

Perhaps the most frequently used means of verbal communication, after face-to-face contact, is the telephone. Telephones are involved in both internal and external communications – they make it possible to communicate directly with people within the organisation, and throughout the country and internationally. Over recent years there has been a massive expansion in telecommunications services which have provided a global connection/highway provided by a single organisation (Cable & Wireless). There are information services (e.g. Prestel), video-conferencing, mobile phones and a very extensive range of other specialised business services.

The massive expansion of **telecommunications** over recent years is not just about new services. An employee's time costs an organisation money. Letters and memos are time-consuming – and therefore expensive – to write; they often then have to be processed before being despatched, and after that a reply must be awaited. With the use of a telephone a reply can be obtained in the shortest possible time – and in fact many systems will allow a number of users into the conversation simultaneously.

It does not always follow, however, that a telephone call saves time. According to one recent estimate, more than a half of all telephone calls fail simply because they do not result in direct communication with the person intended. Another possible drawback of using the telephone is that once a conversation starts it is all too easy for the parties to become sidetracked, and then forget some of the reasons for the call.

Task

Comment upon your own experiences using a telephone. How effective is your telephone style? Are there any situations when you find conversation difficult? How could you improve your technique?

Case Study

Darlo Holdings

John Hoskins is Group Personnel Manager for Darlo Holdings, a company which owns and coordinates the activities of a range of subsidiaries in the rapid-transit parcel and courier industry.

At the group's headquarters in the North East of England, over 200 staff are employed in a modern well-equipped office block in Newton Aycliffe. Over the last twelve months there have been a massive number of changes within the group office. Five directors, including the managing director, have retired and there have been a number of consequential managerial movements – including John's appointment.

The 'new blood' in the boardroom are concerned that their approach to the running of the organisation should be identifiably different from that of their predecessors. They are acutely aware that for a long time the organisation operated as a *power culture*, under the authoritarian rule of the former MD. Their view is that during the early development phase this type of management was successful. However, over recent years the organisation has grown considerably by acquisition, and some

managers now feel that such a regime is leading to a lack of motivation and high staff turnover.

At the heart of proposed changes designed to motivate staff at Darlo is the perceived need to create a mechanism which allows staff to be listened to and have their views and contributions taken account of. With these objectives in mind, the directors want to create more face-to-face contact between managers and employees at all levels. *Quality circles* and working groups/meetings have been suggested (see Chapter 11). There is confidence from the new management that, once developed, the system will help to generate new ideas and create an improved atmosphere within the organisation. John Hoskins has been entrusted with the responsibility of introducing these proposals.

1 *Advise John Hoskins in detail on the likely advantages and disadvantages of the new proposals.*
2 *Explain the importance of staff training to help employees to develop verbal skills at meetings if the proposal is to be a success.*

Written communications

Written communications are used within an organisation to convey information and ideas to others. They are also used to confirm important verbal messages.

For many people, putting pen to paper implies creating something rather permanent, and there can be fear of being misunderstood, particularly if the document is directed 'upwards' or is to be viewed by a number of other colleagues. Confidence is important, as is the need to read through the message to make sure that you get the message right.

The word **memorandum** (nearly always shortened to 'memo') derives from the Latin *memorare* which means 'thing to be remembered'. Today memos have a wider business use than just as memory aids, having become the most frequently used form of written communication within organisations. They are used to communicate information, instructions and enquiries. Though they are the internal equivalent of letters, there are one or two minor differences. An organisation's name does not normally appear on a memo for internal use, and it is not necessary to have a salutation or complimentary ending.

Memos should be kept as short as possible and ideally deal with only one item. Copies of the same memo are often distributed to a number of recipients.

The style of memoranda varies considerably. Instructions from senior management are likely to be written in relatively impersonal language, while a quickly scribbled message on a memo sheet to a close colleague may be in conversational English. It is often necessary to be more careful and diplomatic when writing memos up the ladder, rather than down. On all occasions it is important to take account of people's sensitivities and the position you hold.

MEMORANDUM

To: All staff   **Ref:**   BW/JK
From: B Watson   **Date:** 12th April 199_
        (Personnel Manager)

REVISED HEALTH AND SAFETY REGULATIONS

It has come to my attention that there have been a
number of minor accidents in the last few weeks
which has been recorded in the Accident Book.

It is important that all accidents are logged. The
company wishes to maintain a safe working
environment for all its employees and can only do
this if it is aware of defects.

Please make sure you are aware of your duties
under the HASAW Act, now outlined in the revised
Staff Handbook.

Figure 5.8 *A specimen memorandum*

Reports are another form of internal written communication. In simple terms, a report is a written communication from someone who has collected and studied some facts to a person who has asked for the facts (and possibly a recommendation) because he or she needs them for a particular purpose or to help with making a decision. It is therefore a basis for some form of action.

Reports may, for example, supply information for legal purposes (e.g. as a result of an incident or accident) or may be presented to shareholders. A report may attempt to assess the consequences of changes in company policy.

A well-written report is concise and does not contain anything the reader does not need to know. It should be clear and logically arranged but, at the same time, should not exclude anything that the reader needs.

Informal reports may be most suitably written or typed on a memo form, as in Figure 5.8. It is important to start with a title, and possibly a brief introduction, before going on to the body of the report. Recommendations for action should be clearly identified if these have been requested.

Formal reports will have many of the features listed below:

- Title page (subject matter, name and position of writer, date etc.)
- Contents page
- Terms of reference (explaining the reason for the report)
- Procedure (how the task was completed)
- Findings
- Conclusions and/or recommendations.

When preparing a formal report, decisions have to be made on aspects such as language and style, circulation, and the presentation (including whether the report should have a cover and binding).

Task

Imagine that you are a college administrator. Write a short memo addressed to the relevant personnel, indicating the term-time college dates for the coming year.

Task

Imagine that you are asked by the National Union of Students to write a formal report on the facilities available for students at the college or other place of tuition you are attending.

Your report should be based on *research* covering areas such as library and IT facilities, recreational and social facilities, guidance and counselling, refectory etc., and the strain (if any) put on these facilities by the numbers of students at the college.

Your conclusions and recommendations, clearly identified, should refer to the way in which the availability of facilities affects the working patterns of students at the college.

Minutes are a detailed record of a **meeting** and are often used as a form of internal communication. Such details, displayed on noticeboards or sent to key staff, inform people about decisions taken in various parts of the organisation. For example, in a school, copies of minutes of departmental meetings provide a useful guide to the headteacher on how staff might react to certain decisions. The same headteacher might put details of his or her meetings with deputies on a noticeboard so that other staff are kept up to date with developments. The minutes usually state who is responsible for specific actions arising from the meeting.

Before a meeting takes place, an **agenda** will list the items of business to be discussed and the order in which they will be taken. If an agenda is displayed on a noticeboard, a member of the organisation who is not invited to attend the meeting – and who might be concerned about a particular issue – will have the opportunity to have a prior word with someone who is invited.

Notices are another common form of written communication. They are placed in prominent positions and used to publicise any changes in policy, dates to be remembered, functions, events taking place etc. Notices are usually short and related to a single subject. They might be supported by artwork to catch the attention of staff.

House magazines, journals and newspapers are a useful way of communicating policies, information, events and public relations activities to employees throughout an organisation. They are a particularly useful form of internal communication in large organisations where they can be used to help staff to develop their identity within the group and feel a sense of belonging.

Case Study

St Michael News

Marks and Spencer is a company that has always attached great importance to the care and training of its staff. According to Lord Rayner, Chairman of M & S from 1984 to 1991, 'the continued development of our business depends upon the calibre of our people'. The company provides training, personal development and motivational packages which recognise the contributions of all the employees.

The senior management believes that the commitment of staff is greatly enhanced when they feel involved and consulted. Communications groups have been operating in stores for some time. Training encourages staff to use their communication group as an effective vehicle for two-way communication. Another aspect of partnership is the suggestions scheme – called the 'Good Ideas Scheme' – which produces many contributions designed to improve efficiency and save money. A further device to keep employees informed is the staff newspaper called 'St Michael News'.

St Michael NEWS
THE STAFF NEWSPAPER OF MARKS & SPENCER

St Michael News is a bi-monthly glossy newspaper made available to all Marks &Spencer staff. It provides an opportunity for senior managers to communicate overall group strategy, successes and achievements and economic matters of interest to all employees – such as profits, store expansions, new systems and company policies. As well as this the newspaper acts as a forum for other events in the group – for example, the introduction of new collections of clothes, new food ranges, homeware products, financial services etc. Other articles cover information on the group's overseas activities, staff profit sharing, community involvement, long-service awards, retirements, and competitions such as crosswords and 'Young Environmentalist of the Year'.

The newspaper helps to reflect the changing culture of the organisation from paternalism to partnership to ensure that values within the organisation are shared and not imposed. With more than 75 000 employees working for

Marks & Spencer worldwide, it is generally felt that good communications will improve involvement and help to create a working environment in which everyone wants to contribute.

1 Comment upon why the Marks & Spencer management today places so much emphasis on partnership with the employees.

2 How important is a good internal communication system for creating such a partnership?

3 What methods, other than those indicated in the study, could be used to enhance internal communications in a large organisation?

Visual communications

Visual communications within an organisation may take many forms. Presenting data by means of charts, graphs, drawings or photographs helps to reinforce a message. It also enables complex information to be communicated in a way that is readily acceptable to more people and easier to take in.

Although some visual information within an organisation will have a place on its own, most will be used to support verbal and written communications. For example, during an oral presentation various types of visual aid can be used to support the talk – flip-charts, magnetic boards, overhead projectors, videos, closed-circuit televisions etc.

Charts and diagrams can also be used to support internal written communications, as in a report or house magazine. The graphics in Figure 7.6 on page 196 are examples.

Task

Walk through the school or college you are attending. Make a list of the different types of visual communications.

· EXTERNAL COMMUNICATIONS ·

External communications are concerned with how an organisation is viewed by others. All of the actions of and communications from an organisation are encompassed. Every organisation has a public face or image, and this conveys a message which affects or influences everyone who has dealings with the organisation – customers, shareholders, suppliers, competitors, governments, communities, international agencies, environmental groups. Providing a positive image through external communication creates a better external environment for the organisation. Successful manipulation of **public relations** convinces others that the organisation is worth dealing with, and might provide it with a considerable strategic and competitive advantage.

Task

Collect a range of external communications from a number of organisations. Comment briefly upon the image created by each item.

As with internal communications, external communications can be divided into verbal, written and visual.

External verbal communications

The most frequently used form of **external verbal communication** is the **telephone**. Its great benefit is that it is fast and allows people who would find it difficult to meet to converse.

A telephone call may be the first point of contact an outsider has with an organisation. If a bad impression is created through this first call, it may be difficult to correct. Developing a telephone technique which makes the caller feel at ease and which creates the impression of efficiency is always important. There are, therefore, basic rules for answering the telephone (see Figure 5.9).

★ Answer calls promptly
★ Greet the caller with 'Good morning' or 'Good afternoon'
★ Be courteous – your tone of voice is crucial
★ Be brief but not abrupt
★ Speak clearly and slowly
★ Be resourceful and *think* of ways you might be able to help
★ Remain calm, even when under pressure
★ Have pencil and paper handy in case you have to take a message (don't forget to record the date and time of the call)

Figure 5.9 *How to answer the phone*

If you have to make a telephone call yourself, make sure that:

● you have all the necessary information to hand
● you know who you want to talk to
● you are prepared to leave a message on an answering machine if necessary
● you speak clearly.

It may be necessary to have a **face-to-face** exchange with somebody from outside the organisation. In many administrative jobs employees are constantly in situations where they are meeting customers, members of the public, representatives from suppliers, visitors, candidates for jobs etc. Dealing with people on a daily basis requires a degree of sensitivity. It is a bit like being an ambassador – no matter what the response of the person you are dealing with, you need to remain in control of the situation and resolve any dispute or problem using common sense. In fact, many organisations insist that their employees should conduct themselves in all their dealings with the public as if they were rendering a service.

Task

Imagine that you work for a government department as a civil servant. Make out a list of rules for dealing verbally with the public on a daily basis.

Another form of external verbal communication is an **interview** with somebody from outside the organisation, who may be interested in something the organisation has done (e.g. press, radio or television). Part of a public relations strategy in such circumstances is to build up a positive perception and image of your organisation. Your response should therefore be designed to improve public understanding of your organisation's actions.

Business letters

The **business letter** is still the most widely used form of external communication. It may be used, for example, to:

● make arrangements without the need for parties to meet
● provide both parties with a permanent record of such arrangements
● confirm verbal arrangements.

A well-written business letter conveys its message while maintaining goodwill. If a letter is sent promptly, is well set out and conveys its message accurately, the recipient will develop a favourable impression of that organisation, and is more likely to want to have further dealings than if the letter is tardy and inaccurate.

Task

Make a list of the advantages of using written communications outside the organisation, rather than some other means. Draw up another list covering the disadvantages.

To write an effective letter requires adequate **preparation**. It might be necessary to investigate the background to the letter by searching through previous correspondence, which may be stored in a file. As you research your letter, its necessary contents will become apparent to you. For example, you might have to:

● seek information as the result of an enquiry
● express an opinion
● deal with a problem or a fault
● place an order
● confirm an order
● seek references
● check credit-worthiness
● obtain quotations
● quote a price
● seek payment for a debt
● convey a personal message.

Collect examples of business letters you or your family have received from a variety of different organisations. What was each letter for? Comment upon the impression conveyed by each letter.

HEINEMANN EDUCATIONAL

Halley Court, Jordan Hill
Oxford OX2 8EJ

Telephone Oxford (0865) 311366
Telex 837292 HEBOXF G
Facsimile (0865) 310043

Our ref : PJ/bw

12 April 199

Mr J Saunders
18 First Close
Sutton Coldfield
West Midlands
B73 7DH

Dear Mr Saunders

Manuscript for BTEC publication

Thank you for sending me the BTEC manuscript so promptly. I read it over the weekend and was impressed with its content.

Over the next few weeks the manuscript will be out for review, after which I may have some suggestions for amendments.

Could you please send us a list of acknowledgements, and any photographic materials you may wish to include. If there are any further requirements I shall be in touch.

Yours sincerely

Peter James
Editorial Assistant

A division of Heineman Educational Books Limited
Part of Reed International Books
Registered Office, Michelin House, 81 Fulham Road, London SW3 6RB
Registered in England No. 677944

Figure 5.10 *An open-punctuated fully blocked business letter*

The layout, style and appearance of business letters – and even the envelope – varies from organisation to organisation. Most will endeavour to create a good impression, particularly by giving attention to the heading and layout. Organisations often have a house style which they encourage all clerical staff to follow. Business letters are usually typed on A4 or A5 paper, and a fully blocked open-punctuated style is now the most common form of display.

A typical business letter will have the following features:

- a heading or **letterhead** (Heinemann Educational in Figure 5.10)
- a **reference** – enabling the letter to be filed and traced later
- a **date**
- the **inside address** – which is that of the recipient
- the **salutation** (Dear Mr Saunders)
- the **subject heading** (Manuscript of BTEC publication)
- the **body** of the letter
- the **complimentary close** (Yours sincerely . . .)

There is a convention about pairings of salutation and complimentary close. When the name of the recipient is not known, so that 'Dear Sir/Madam' is used, this should be paired with 'Yours faithfully'. When the name is known and 'Dear Mr/Mrs . . .' is used, this should be paired with 'Yours sincerely'. If the recipient is addressed by his or her first name, this may be paired with 'Kind regards . . . Yours sincerely'.

When a letter is sent with **enclosures**, this is denoted by the letters 'Enc' or Encs' at the foot of the letter to alert the recipient to this fact.

When writing a business letter always plan what you are going to say beforehand. Organise your information into a logical sequence and try to keep your language simple. Be courteous yet direct. After you have written the letter, check it for spelling mistakes and grammatical errors.

You have just received a batch of 50 reams of headed stationery from Monsons Press Ltd. Unfortunately the printer has used the wrong size paper and has used an out-of-date heading. It is generally unsuitable for office use. You have checked that the printer was given the correct information.

Draft a letter of complaint, open a file on a word-processor, type in your letter and print a copy.

A form of external communication which has experienced massive expansion over recent years – and which is capable of sending both written and visual information – is **facsimile** ('fax'). Fax machines send information electronically over telephone lines.

As an alternative to writing letters, organisations today may occasionally use **electronic mail**. The 'mail-box' is a computer terminal linked to a telephone network; it can put messages into the system and store messages that have been sent through the system. Every user has a password to allow him or her to use the system. A message can be sent to several recipients at once. The message is stored in a terminal's memory until the mail-box is 'opened'. There are now a number of subscriber-based systems, such as Telecom Gold. The main advantage over ordinary mail is speed of transmission.

NORTHERN ELECTRIC

NORTH YORKSHIRE REGIONAL OFFICE
DUNDAS STREET
THE STONEBOW
YORK
NORTH YORKSHIRE
YO1 2PQ
TELEPHONE: (0904) 628941

19 Dec 90

Dear Customer,

INTERRUPTIONS TO ELECTRICITY SUPPLIES - December 1990

I am writing personally to you, a valued customer of Northern Electric, to apologise for any inconvenience caused when there were widespread interruptions of electricity supplies following the severe winter weather during the weekend of 7/8 December 1990.

I am aware of the hardship and distress that has been endured by many of our rural customers in North Yorkshire and I felt that it was appropriate for me to express the concern which the Company had for all during this emergency.

Weather conditions were extremely severe and a combination of high winds, low temperatures and wet snow caused a large build up of ice on the conductors of overhead power lines. The weight of the ice on the line caused conductor breakages and pole failures. The damage was extensive throughout North Yorkshire and some 30,000 customers were off supply for varying periods ranging from a few hours to in excess of one week in some isolated rural locations.

The substantial task of repairing the damage and restoring supplies was given top priority and additional resources were drafted in from other Regions of Northern Electric. Some 350 linesmen and engineers worked long hours in the field and in the Depot Control Centres co-ordinating arrangements for the major repair operations.

They were supported by Customer Information Staff who manned telephones around the clock to deal with customers' calls and to provide the best information available at the time. Up to 9 helicopters were brought in to assist in repair work as soon as flying conditions were possible and the Army provided valuable assistance in flying in men and materials to troubled areas.

The extent of the disruption caused by the storm in respect of electricity supplies was the most severe that we can recall in North Yorkshire and I was surprised to see the degree of devastation when I visited the Region and toured some of the affected areas after the storm. As always in occurrences such as this there may be lessons to be learnt and action will be taken if appropriate to improve the service to our customers and our ability to deal with extremes of weather.

I have written in general terms because although all rural customers were not directly affected by supply interruptions you may have found other services disrupted as a result of loss of electricity supply. May I take the opportunity to thank you for your patience and tolerance in these difficult circumstances.

Yours sincerely

R Dixon

R Dixon
Managing Director - Power
Northern Electric plc. Registered Office: Cariol House. Market Street. Newcastle upon Tyne NE1 6NE
Registered in England Number 2366942

Figure 5.11 *A letter of explanation and apology*

Case Study

Interruptions to electricity supplies. See Figure 5.11.

1 Why was it important for the Managing Director – Power to write this external communication?

2 How difficult would it have been to write such a letter?

3 Have you any criticism of this communication?

Other means of communicating externally

Advertising is a form of external communication. At the heart of advertising lies the knowledge of how consumers will respond to different strategies and how these strategies might affect the image of the organisation. Assessing the effectiveness of advertising is difficult because it goes beyond just selling products.

Many large organisations send out an **annual report** to shareholders and the news media. The document, as well as publishing information required under the Companies Act, often contains non-financial reports covering overall strategies, social and environmental objectives etc. Some of these documents are lavish, with coloured illustrations to enhance the image and help to convey information.

Magazines, publicity literature and educational

services, in both the public and private sectors, provide strong informed links between organisations and their various publics. For example, organisations send out brochures in response to enquiries in order to indicate what their activities, functions, beliefs and objectives are. Large organisations such as BP, the banks, British Rail, Shell and the Inland Revenue have their own educational services which supply packs of information and resources to schools and colleges on request.

Corporate videotapes have become increasingly popular over recent years as a method of providing a variety of interested parties with visual information about an organisation's activities. **Visits** and **open days** are another popular method of giving people a 'window' into an organisation – the Sellafield Visitors Centre claims to provide a 'window into a nuclear world' and has become a top tourist attraction in the North West of England. By means of exhibitions, organisations provide outsiders with a clearer understanding of their activities.

Point-of-sale displays and demonstrations attract the attention of consumers, generate interest and encourage them to approach and inspect a product before making a decision to purchase.

Videoconferencing allows organisations to hold face-to-face meetings between groups of people at two or more locations, nationally and internationally. Everyone can see and hear what is going on. British Telecom has eleven videoconferencing centres in cities and towns through the UK, and over 100 rooms are presently available worldwide with new locations being added all of the time. They can be booked in advance on a half-hourly basis. Videoconferencing can be used for meetings, product launches, press announcements and training sessions.

Videoconferencing

was worth around £121 million. A two-hour videoconferencing call from London to New York with six people at both sides costs about £1500.

BT is aiming to develop further its facilities through product innovation. For example the 'videophone' – a miniature camera and screen attached to the telephone system and a personal computer–which has just been launched. This would turn videoconferencing into desktop conferencing.

1 *How might videoconferencing save organisations money? (Hint: Consider the costs of time and travel.)*
2 *Comment briefly on the other benefits provided by videoconferencing.*
3 *How might such benefits provide organisations with a competitive advantage?*

Case Study

Videoconferencing coming of age in the Gulf war

While the Gulf war crucified the airline industry, it provided a real boon to other businesses. Videoconferencing saw its prospects improve. People still had to meet and, if travel was too risky, an interactive TV link would be just as good. Said Steve Gaudy, marketing and sales manager for BT's Visual and Broadcast Services arm: 'The Gulf crisis was a watershed. Turnover has doubled since the Gulf conflict and revenue is now growing at 30–40% year-on-year.'

While the technology for videoconferencing and corporate TV networks has been around for almost thirty years, it is only in the last ten that it has begun to take off. The UK is catching up fast. There are now ten permanent networks in Britain, seven using British Aerospace's Satellite Management International (SMI) and three with BT. The total figure is expected to double soon.

Recent reports suggest that the videoconferencing market worldwide will grow ten-fold by 1995. Last year the market

Case Study

British Nuclear Fuels PLC

Nuclear energy now accounts for about one-fifth of the electricity produced in Britain; in Scotland the proportion is almost one-half. Fuel for all the nuclear power stations in Britain is produced by British Nuclear Fuels PLC (BNFL), which offers the complete nuclear fuel cycle service from uranium enrichment, through fuel manufacture and transport to spent fuel reprocessing and waste management. To counter adverse public images, the company encourages understanding of its operations

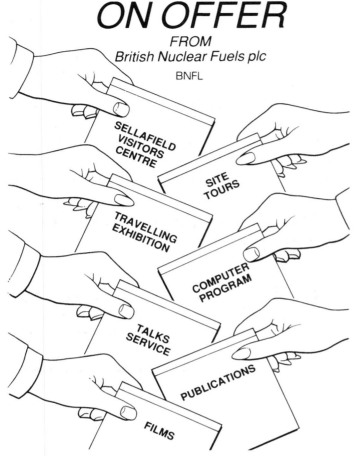

ON OFFER
FROM
British Nuclear Fuels plc
BNFL

Figure 5.12 *BNFL's external communications*

by providing a range of publications and by offering a variety of public relations functions and activities.

1 Why are external communications of fundamental importance to BNFL?

2 Comment on the range of communications available. In each case, state whether it is verbal, written or visual.

Element assignment

Organising effective meetings
This assignment can help you provide evidence for assessment, or claim the following Core Skills:

Communication
Communcate in writing
Participate in oral and non-verbal communication

Personal skills
Transfer skills gained to new and changing situations
Treat values, beliefs and opinions of others with respect
Relate to and interact effectively with individuals and groups
Work effectively as a member of the team

You work in the customer services department of a local branch of a company selling electrical appliances through high street showrooms. You have been asked to chair an important meeting in your workplace.

It is essential that all employees present the quality image of the company in all dealings with customers. The importance of the 'public image' of the company must be made clear to all employees in the showroom at which you work.

You have recently read an article about meetings which made the following points:

'All meetings have one thing in common: role playing. The most formal role is that of the "chair". The chair is in a good position to set the agenda and a good chairperson will keep the meeting running on time and to the point. This rarely happens because other players at the meeting often gain the upper hand.

'The chief distractors are the "constant talkers", who just love to hear their own voices. Constant talkers judge their own success by the percentage of time for which they can grab the limelight.

'Another distractor is the bureaucrat. This is the "dot the i and cross the t" type, the kind of person who bores everybody present.

'Then there are the "can't do" types, the people who always find reasons why something can't be done, usually based on some minor technical problem. The "can't do" types are cunning, wanting to preserve the status quo. They have often been in the organisation a long time and quote historical incidents to back up their arguments.

'Then there are the "red herring" types. They seem to enjoy meetings so much that they find the slightest excuse to keep the meeting going.

'Then there will be a group of people, "the disagreers", who will disagree with nearly every point that is made by the chair or the general consensus of the meeting. They tend to dislike authority of any kind.

''In addition, there will be "silent types" who hardly say

anything. Often it is because they are shy, insecure or bored.

'Meetings provide a forum for people to play power games. Ambitious people may try to say a lot in order to impress senior managers. Meetings can be used as a means of displaying power relations within a company. Senior members can impress on juniors their relative importance in the organisation.'

In recent meetings at your workplace it has seemed that some members of the organisation have obstructed the decision making process. Jane Brown a young sales assistant continually tries to take over the meeting. Phil Davies an experienced sales person tends to move away from the main issues being discussed. Jill Smith the assistant manager always picks up on minor points and labours 'what can't be done'. The end result is that there is a lot of talking and very little gets done.

Task
Prepare a set of notes which will help you to run the meeting effectively.

You will need to cover the following points:

1 What are your objectives?
2 How will you make sure that all members of the meeting are aware of these objectives?
3 How will you make sure that the agenda is kept to?
4 How will you deal with particular individuals or groups who might try to hijack the meeting?
5 How will you ensure that all group members are able to contribute to the meeting?
6 How will you monitor whether your objectives are being met?

Task

In a group of four role-play the above meeting. A fifth person should make notes on how the chairperson coped.

chapter **6** USING INFORMATION TECHNOLOGY IN ORGANISATIONS

In this chapter we look at ways of handling information in the office of a modern organisation. All organisations process a great deal of information, so information systems lie at the heart of effective data management. The chapter therefore looks at different types of information, and the processes involved in handling it.

We go on to explore many important features of modern information technology (IT), including word-processing, databases and spreadsheets – as well as more elaborate packages such as 'expert systems' and some of the very latest developments. The emphasis is on using *appropriate* technology rather than using technology for its own sake.

The activities are designed to encourage you to think about your own IT competence, and what you may need to do to improve your existing skills.

A few years ago the **'electronic office'** was regarded as a radically new idea. Today most organisations include some elements of the electronic office, and indeed in many organisations such developments have been steadily upgraded to new levels of 'hi-tech'.

The range of office activities that can be automated is increasing all the time, as is the number of ways of automating them. On the computing side – as opposed to telephony, photocopying and other elements of the electronic office – word-processing, electronic message handling, financial modelling and computerised personal organisers are commonplace.

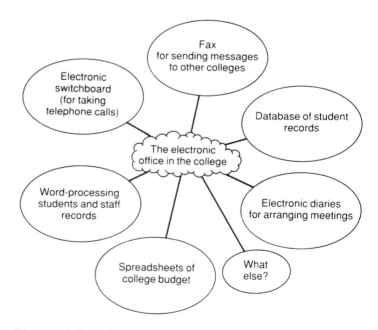

Figure 6.1 *Some IT inputs*

Task

What elements of the electronic office are used in your college, or in another organisation with which you are familiar? Draw a diagram like Figure 6.1 to show the range of applications.

Many people working during the 1980s felt that **information technology** (IT) was adopted by many companies for the sake of appearing 'with it'. The organisations that were really successful with their office automation were those that implemented the product rather than simply installing it. When installing new information technology it is best to look at the needs of the organisation first. It may be most appropriate to gear the IT towards the existing physical and human systems in the organisation.

At the end of this chapter there is a task that asks you to look at your own IT skills. Perhaps there will be some areas you would like to improve upon.

· INFORMATION TECHNOLOGY SKILLS ·

Information technology is now so widespread that it is useful to distinguish between:

- **general IT skills** needed across a range of jobs
- **specialist IT skills**, mainly at the professional level, needed for the development of sophisticated technology software and systems.

General IT skills

Very few jobs have been unaffected by information technology. Virtually all types of employees need some familiarity with the technology and its application in their particular working environment.

- *Managers* need sufficient understanding of the latest developments to spot new business opportunities and to carry out changes.
- *Technicians, maintenance and craft workers* need to deal with IT components in plants and vehicles of all types.
- *Clerical workers* have to be familiar with a variety of word-processing, spreadsheet, database and similar applications.
- *Professionals* need to use specialist IT applications – including 'expert systems' – as an aid to their decision-making.

Over the past decade at least, the rapid spread of microcomputers – and more recently of computer networks – has been matched by a good level of competence by a large proportion of the country's workforce. Over the next ten years, many organisations will be trying hard to catch up with the 'leading-edge' businesses of the 1980s.

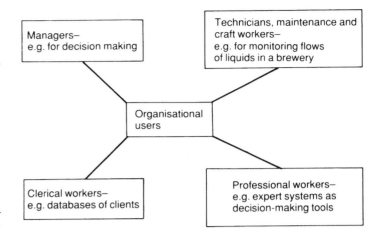

Figure 6.2 *Users of IT in the workplace*

People in the leading-edge businesses will in turn be developing their IT skills to work effectively with increasing integration between separate IT systems. They will be finding effective ways of using 'expert systems' and searching out the new opportunities and products from major telecommunications advances and new uses for robotics. We will be describing many of these changes in this chapter.

Specialist IT skills

Many of the readers of this book will become (if they are not already) generalist users of IT. In particular you will make use of the range of IT skills (as well as others) shown in Figure 6.3.

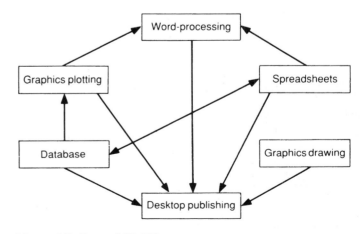

Figure 6.3 *General IT skills*

Some of the readers of this book may also become specialist users of IT skills. About one per cent of the working population (approximately a quarter of a million people) are in one of the IT professions. The numbers have grown by about 20 per cent since 1985. Despite the slowdown of the British economy in the early 1990s, numbers of recruits to this industry are expected to continue growing by up to 5 per cent a year for the rest of the century. The growth of this job sector is therefore one of the fastest in the country.

Task

Can you identify a business process in an organisation with which you are familiar? How are tasks passed on in a flow from one department to another?

HOW IT CAN CHANGE THE RUNNING OF AN ORGANISATION

A traditional business is often organised into **functional specialisms**. Each person in the organisation carries out one step before passing the job on to someone else. Often a job is passed from one department to another. Figure 6.4 shows this sort of flow – work starts on the left of the diagram. For example, market research is carried out by a few people in the marketing department, who pass the results to the technology department. The technology department comes up with some proposals which are passed to production . . . and so on.

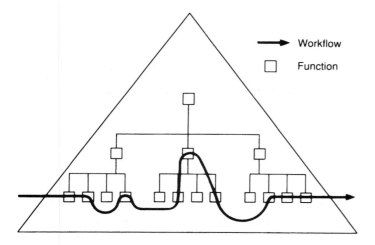

Figure 6.4 *In a functional organisation the work flows step by step*

The departments shown in the diagram have worked together in a flow on a particular 'business process', which is simply a set of work activities arranged logically to realise a business objective.

Transformed businesses

Today many business writers use the term 'transformed business'. Such an organisation is run according to business processes rather than functional specialisms. The business processes are handled by teams of people from different functions, working together to achieve the aim of the process.

In a 'transformed business' people involved in particular processes are given more freedom to make decisions and have more information at their finger-tips by virtue of information technology. Instead of having to get permission from their line manager, they are allowed to make important decisions. Senior managers then become more concerned with external matters than with running the internal system.

Organisations based on business processes put a high premium on information and on sharing IT facilities. IT has a very important role to play. Groups working together

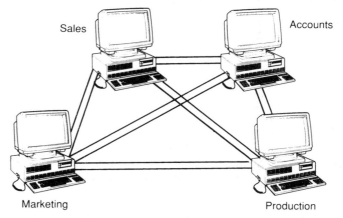

Figure 6.5 *A network of information can be made available to the process team*

in a team will need to share information, and computer terminals of different specialists are linked so that information is available to all.

One major benefit is a cost reduction as a result of simplifying the work flow. A job stays with one individual or team instead of passing in batches from specialist to specialist. The team is given the authority to make decisions, as well as the information and tools needed.

Another benefit is the improved responsiveness to customers' needs. Front-line staff are given powers to act rather than pass problems up to line managers.

Improved job satisfaction can be a result. Staff can share customer satisfaction with a job well done. They are more challenged and more fulfilled. The staff are part of a learning, adapting organisation focused on the customers' requirements.

Task

Study an organisation which uses IT widely. To what extent is information shared in the organisation? What are the effects on decision-making? Can decisions be made more easily by individuals, or do they still need to be passed to supervisors or senior managers?

Make lists of what you consider to be the major advantages and disadvantages of

a traditional functional organisations
b process-based transformed organisations.

• COMPUTER USABILITY •

It is not long since a high proportion of the population was frightened by computers. The machines appeared to be highly complex, came with daunting manuals, and seemed to stop co-operating at the most inconvenient times. Modern computers have become more consumer-orientated, and a lot of thought has gone into making sure that they are **'user-friendly'** and that they meet organisational needs.

Computers rely on end-users to tell them what to do, but the biggest problem many new computer owners face is discovering how to get the equipment to do what it is asked.

A major breakthrough came with the development of **graphical user interfaces** (GUIs, or 'gooies'). GUIs are making the technology easier to understand and to use – they are literally changing the face of computers. Instead of sitting there with a blank screen, a GUI presents you with a series of small pictures, called icons, which represent the various options available to you. A pointing tool, such as a 'mouse', is used to move an arrow around the screen and to select the icon for the desired action. At the press of a key the screen then redraws itself to show the next set of options. If the user has selected 'word-processing', for example, the screen will change to show him or her a second series of options; each option chosen leads to a further series of choices.

Figure 6.6 *Icons*

Windowing systems go one stage further, giving the same type of graphical interface but allowing the user to carry out several tasks simultaneously. He or she can be writing a document in the word-processing window, while an address list, stored in the system, can be sorted at the same time. As with everything else in the computer industry, a variety of different windowing systems is available, depending on the machine type.

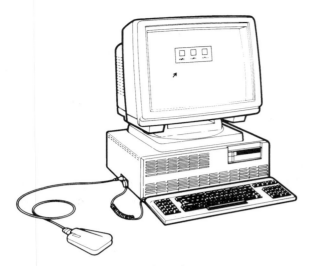

Figure 6.7 *Selecting an item from the menu*

Task

Design icons which would help a computer user to identify the following facilities:

a word-processing   **c** spreadsheet
b database   **d** drawing and artwork.

· WHAT CAN BE DONE WITH DATA? ·

In a modern office a number of operations make use of **data**. One way of looking at an organisation is as an 'information processing system'. As in any system there will be a means of transforming **inputs** into **outputs** by a number of processes. Today many of these processes are carried out with the support of information technology.

Here are a number of processes which take place in modern organisations, all involving data:

- recording
- checking
- classifying
- sorting
- summarising
- calculating
- storing
- retrieving
- reproducing
- communicating.

An example

We will demonstrate the kind of things we might want to do with data by using an example. An electricity company keeps records of customers and their outstanding accounts. It may keep a record of the amount owned by the Patel family who live at Greenlawns.

The company will keep a regular record of amounts owing for electricity used, the amounts paid by the family and the balance owed. Every now and then it will want to **check** on this information – for example, when the Patels have a query on their account.

The company may want to **classify** the information about the Patel's account into various subheadings – for example, into totals of electricity used at peak and off-peak times.

The information can be **sorted** in many ways – for example, into date order to show how much electricity the Patels used at different times of the year. The electricity company can sort out which customers have unpaid balances; and at the end of a quarter all the figures can be **summarised** to show the total amounts outstanding.

Calculations can be done with figures – for example, adding amounts owed and subtracting payments made.

All of the details relating to the Patel's account can be stored on files and **retrieved** from these files when required. This information can be **reproduced**, perhaps by making a copy of the Patel's records to send to them as a statement of account. This information can then be quickly **communicated** to them.

Simply by looking at one account we have been able to point to a wide range of **data processing** activities.

Task

1 Describe how each of the data-processing activities outlined in the text can be related to:
   a your own student records
   b your bank or building society statement.

2 Show how you use data processing to keep personal records – for example, in budgeting or keeping a diary.

WORD-PROCESSING, DATABASES AND SPREADSHEETS

The most common information processing in modern offices carried out using information technology are word-processing, databases and spreadsheets.

Word-processing

Word-processors are used to manipulate text. They display on a screen and record in memory the text that a person enters on a keyboard. However, the word-processor can do far more. For example:

- New text can be put on to the screen while existing text moves to create space for it.
- Blocks of text can be moved around on the document that is being created.
- The text can be spaced out to fill the whole line.
- A word or phrase can be searched for, and if necessary it can be removed or replaced by another word or phrase.
- A header or footer (a piece of text that is printed at the top or bottom of each page) can be added.

You will know from your own use of word-processors that there are many other exciting features. For example:

- Different printing styles (such as italics, underlined text and so on) can be shown on screen either as different colours or as they would appear when printed. This is referred to as WYSIWYG (pronounced 'wizzywig'), which stands for 'what you see is what you get'.
- Text can be written in more than one column, as in newspapers.

- Graphics can be put into the text.
- A number of similar letters can be produced, with information added from a database on each letter. For example, if a company has a database of its suppliers and wishes to contact the local ones, the database can be used to select all suppliers who are situated in the same county. The word-processor will then print a letter for each supplier, adding the individual information such as the name and address and salutation. This is called 'mailmerge'.
- A spelling checker can be used. This checks all the text against a dictionary and points out any word that it does not recognise, perhaps because it is spelt incorrectly. However, if you have used a technical word that the computer is not aware of, you can enter the new word into the computer's memory.

Desktop publishing

The improvements in word-processing systems and their ability to produce graphics and to operate with great efficiency, has made **desktop publishing** (DTP) possible. Special **computer programs** (also called **software packages**) make it possible to produce pages of text and graphics combined, to a very high quality of finish.

Different typefaces can be used, diagrams can be placed on pages with text flowing around them, and so on. Pictures can be introduced into the document and stretched or shrunk to fit a space. DTP is being used to produce items such as reports, company newsletters, training books and advertisements.

Task

Using a word-processor, draft a letter to the person responsible for your work experience placement, thanking him or her for the help and support you have received. Print the first draft and discuss it with your tutor. Then do several redrafts of the letter until you are happy with the final format. Save and print the document at each stage so that you can discuss progress with your tutor.

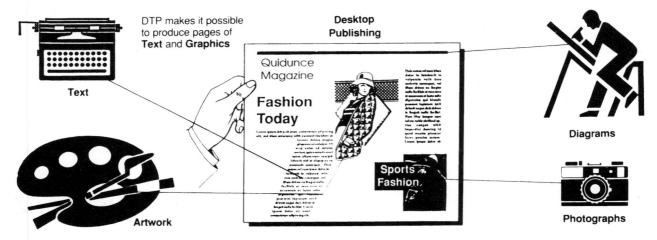

Figure 6.8 *A layout produced by DTP*

Task

If you have access to a desktop publishing system, use it to produce a cover sheet that can be adapted for each of your Business Studies assignments. The cover should be designed so that you can quickly amend it to word-process the new title of each assignment.

Databases

A **database** is a store of facts that can be called upon to provide information. A database may be used, for instance, in a bank or building society to store information on the state of all accounts. A database may be kept by a church to keep a record of all members of the congregation and their addresses. One may be used by a football club to keep a record of all tickets sold to various matches, and so on. Data (that is, information) is fed into the base in a clear form.

For example, a supplier might have a record of the account of Amin Stores. It would store the information in a number of fields – such as address, value of goods supplied, payments received, and balance of the account. If Mr Amin rings up asking for the state of his account, the supplier can simply order the computer to produce the appropriate information and display it on the screen.

Under the provisions of the **Data Protection Act**, companies wishing to store any personal information on a computer system must register with the government-appointed Data Processing Officer. It is necessary to indicate the type of data being stored and the use made of it. Individuals have the right to request (on payment of a small fee) details of any information held about them by any firm, and to require mistakes to be corrected.

Task

The students in your group may need to work together from time to time. If you were to compile a database of information about members of your group, what would you include in it? Bear in mind that the database should make it easier for the group to work together, and the data will be available for all students to consult at any time. Is there any information you should definitely *not* put in?

Using a database

Any work with a database needs careful planning. Once you have decided what you want to investigate you need to think:

- What questions do I want to ask?
- What information needs to be collected to answer the questions?

When using a database it is important to be consistent. For example, when entering figures you should not put 1.50 metres in one place and 150 cm in another place (they are of course the same thing). If you use NAME, decide whether you mean first or second name. If you use GENDER, decide whether you will use male/female or man/woman, and so on.

Figure 6.9 shows a printout of information collected from one particular respondent to a market research questionnaire.

NAME	:	JONES
GENDER	:	MALE
BOVRIL	:	YES
CHEESE	:	NO
SALT/VIN	:	YES
ONION	:	NO
PLAIN	:	YES
TOMATO	:	NO
FAV	:	SALT/VIN

Figure 6.9 *A section of printout*

When information is extracted from a database you can present it in a variety of different forms, including pie-charts and bar-charts (see Figure 7.6 in Chapter 7). A database can be a very useful means of doing research, particularly if you are working in a group. You can work together to enter information into the base. However, make sure that you are aware of the purpose of the database and how to enter information consistently.

Spreadsheets

A **spreadsheet** is a table of numbers which can be organised and altered on a computer. A spreadsheet is used when making forecasts and doing calculations – the computer does the work for you. Spreadsheets are used extensively in financial forecasting.

For instance, a firm will make a forecast of all the money that will come in and go out of the firm over a twelve-month period. The person using the spreadsheet can then alter the inputs to calculate the effect, for example, of lowering a heating bill by a certain amount each month. The computer will automatically recalculate the columns to change the heating figures, total cost figures and profits for each month. It will also recalculate the total profit.

In this way a managing director, accountant or any other user of a spreadsheet can quickly carry out business calculations – such as working out the effects of minor changes.

Task

Imagine that you are responsible for the financial management of a service station, and you need to plan your *budget* for the coming year. A budget is a series of figures indicating the possible income of your business (i.e. the money that you expect to take) and the outgoings (the money you have to spend). You think that the possible *sales income* for the year of your service station may consist of the following:

	£
Petrol	1 440 000
Lubricants	15 600
Confectionery	48 000
Fast foods (sandwiches and drinks)	8 400
Groceries	10 800
Accessories (such as torches,batteries)	14 400
Newspapers/magazines	12 000
Toys/greetings cards	3 600
Books/tapes	4 800
Cigarettes/tobacco	78 000

You estimate outgoings for the year to consist of the following:

	£
Staff wages	36 000
Insurance	1 500
Heat/light/power	4 500
Security charges	1 200
Rent/rates	4 200
Maintenance/repairs	2 100
Office supplies	5 400
Depreciation (estimated amount by which your assets decline in value during the year	3 600

Petrol	1 080 000
Lubricants	12 000
Stock for the shop	150 000

Your first task is to prepare a computer spread sheet to cover a twelve-month period, assuming that incomings and outgoings are spread evenly over all months of the year. Figure 6.10 below can be used as a guide.

When your spreadsheet is completed, you can experiment with some 'what if?' situations:

a What if petrol sales were twice your original estimate –

How would that affect overall profit? You would obviously have to pay more for your stocks of petrol from the depot, but would you also have to spend more money on wages?

b What if wages increase by 10 per cent in June? How does this affect the end-of-year profit figure?

c What if rent and rates on the site are increased by 20 per cent from 1 March?

d What if the cost of petrol and lubricants rises by 10 per cent in November with no corresponding increase in prices to motorists?

INCOME	JAN	FEB	MAR	APR	ETC.
Petrol					
Lubricants					
Confectionery					
Fast food					
Groceries					
Accessories					
Newspapers/magazines					
Toys/greetings cards					
Books/tapes					
Cigarettes/tobacco					
TOTAL INCOME					
OUTGOINGS					
Staff wages					
Insurance					
Heat/light/power					
Security charges					
Rent/rates					
Maintenance/repairs					
Office supplies					
Depreciation					
Petrol					
Lubricants					
Stock for shop					
TOTAL OUTGOINGS					

Figure 6.10 *The spreadsheet*

· USING THE RIGHT TECHNOLOGY ·

Changes in information technology go on at a tremendous rate. Today's growing product may next year be in decline. One way in which a small business can get an edge on bigger companies is through the appropriate use of technology. **Personal productivity** is one key to small business profitability. The link between time and money is very strong.

Two current methods of increasing productivity are through portable computers and cellular telephones. There is hardly a plumber, electrician, gardener or carpenter who can afford to miss a telephone call from a prospective customer. Employees on the move can now take a cellular phone with them. For a travelling office worker a portable microcomputer can make time spent in airport lounges and hotel rooms productive. Some portable machines are now just as powerful as desktop computers.

Hot competition in the personal computer market has produced a wide variety of products at low prices. These include easy-to-use word-processors, coupled with inexpensive but sophisticated laser printers which can make the correspondence of a small business look as slick as that from a large organisation with an inhouse typesetter. Nowadays paperwork from a number of modern personal computers can be sent by facsimile (faxed) directly to offices around the world.

The typical small business office will have a telephone, photocopier, fax machine, computer printer and telephone answering machine. Today there are many new products that combine all or just some of these functions.

· COMMUNICATIONS ·

The telephone network and other telecommunications networks make communication between computers possible in a number of ways. Here are some examples:

- Direct communication of data between organisations or between branches of the same organisation.
- Use of an 'email' (electronic mail) service such as Telecom Gold. To use this, a subscriber sends a message using the telephone line addressed to another subscriber; when the other subscriber calls the service he or she receives the message. The advantage over ordinary mail is speed.

- Using **remote databases**. Several large computer databases have been set up for specialist use, covering rapidly changing areas like case law, information on companies and medical knowledge. For a fee, individuals can call up and do a search on specific topics. Searches can specify a combination of factors. For example, an enquiry can be made for medical information referring to 'Aids' and 'Cardiff' to find only those items referring to both – the information is found rapidly and should be up to date.

Up-to-the-minute information is of tremendous benefit to a wide range of organisations.

Task

Describe how up-to the-minute database information helps the following organisations:

a the police
b hospitals
c oil companies.

Networking

If an organisation is using a number of personal computers, it is likely that some of the information on one will be useful to another user. It is possible to connect the machines together using a **local area network** (LAN), and this allows data to be transferred between machines.

There are two basic ways of using a LAN. In one, the computers work using their own programs and their own data, but can exchange data when required. In the other, the program and data are held on one machine, called a **file server**, and the others act as 'terminals', updating the data on the file server.

· FURTHER IMPORTANT IT · APPLICATIONS

As well as the more general uses of IT we have outlined, we should consider some of the more specialist uses that aid decision-making.

Project planning

Computers and their databases can be used to assist in *project planning*. Packages are used to plan and monitor a project consisting of a number of interrelated stages called activities. First the activities are defined and the time taken by each is estimated. Then the way in which the activities depend on each other is defined. The computer calculates the total time for the project and shows the activities which must be completed on time for the project not to be delayed.

A very simple example is the building of a new office. The activities and times may be:

1 Prepare land and build foundations	30 days
2 Build walls	30 days
3 Build roof	15 days
4 Install equipment	30 days
5 Equip office	20 days

Activity 1 must be done first, then 2, then 3. However, 4 and 5 – although they must come after 3 has finished – can be done at the same time. Therefore the total time for the project is only 105 days (30 + 30 + 15 + 30), not 125 days. The computer output will also tell you that activity 5 is not critical; that is, it can start late or take longer than planned without delaying the project.

This IT tool helps the project manager to determine the tasks that must be given top priority.

Most versions of this computer program can also plan the use of resources on activities, record costs and produce a

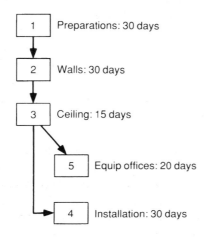

Figure 6.11 *Planning the building of an office*

variety of reports. While this example would be too simple to require a program, we can see how useful such a facility could be in developing a project involving, say, 1000 or more activities.

Expert systems

Expert systems are becoming increasingly popular. They are computer programs consisting of a set of rules based on the knowledge of experts. These rules can be used to form conclusions on information the program is given. Imagine, for example, that you feed into the computer all the rules that experts know about a particular field – geology. Geologists could feed in all the information they know about conditions in which particular minerals are likely to be found. The program can then be used to support researchers looking for new mineral fields. One oil exploration company's geological experts have formulated the rules they use in deciding whether a certain area is likely to contain oil deposits. Data on different areas can then be fed in to the program and it will assess the chances of oil in a similar way to a human expert.

These programs are of particular use where a human expert is not available at the time. One interesting use is in medicine where a program is being tested to aid diagnosis. It is used by the patient, not the doctor, the idea being that for personal and intimate problems a patient may answer questions more easily from a machine than from a person. It also means that trivial problems can be diagnosed without using the doctor's time.

One big problem with setting up expert systems is that it is often surprisingly difficult for experts to define exactly how they reach decisions.

Task

Describe three situations in which you think an expert system would assist decision making.

· ERGONOMICS, HEALTH AND SAFETY ·

Office systems were the subject of a European Commission directive to be implemented by the end of 1992; attention to safety aspects is increasing.

Enlightened self-interest makes this subject important to all organisations. Attention needs to be paid to **ergonomic factors** in offices if key personnel are not to be lost through injury or illness. Also, injured parties may make claims against organisations.

The main difficulty facing employers is that many of the ills associated with office technology are not well understood. For example, it used to be thought that orange characters on a brown screen were the last word in comfort for the eyes of a computer operator; now black on paper-white is widely favoured. Ergonomics in this context is still an imprecise science. Screen flicker is clearly harmful in the long run, and flicker-free monitors are becoming available. The reaction of the body to electromagnetic fields and to extra-low-frequency radiation is poorly researched. Employers have also to consider the environment in which equipment is used – the lighting, heating, ventilation and use of space – and the working practices followed.

Away from the computerised side of office automation, **conservation** is gaining ground. The **paperless office** is no more realistic a prospect than it ever was, but the nature of the paper is changing – many companies are now promoting recycled paper.

Case Study

The arrival of book computers

A new generation of computers, designed to be as simple to use as a notebook and pen, arrived in 1992. Users operate a book computer with an electronic pen and pad and enter data or commands in their own handwriting.

The main advantages of book computers are portability and ease of use, and so the new machines are initially being targeted at mobile workers such as sales representatives, doctors, accountants, solicitors and the police, who often make notes or fill in forms away from their base. Book computers could be used in almost any situation where data are recorded.

Two further advantages of the book computer are:

- the ease with which it can be used in a meeting without offending other people (in contrast to the laptop computer) – it is a bit like bringing in a notepad and pen
- privacy – the flip-up screen forms a barrier to prying eyes.

Files can be selected by simply pointing the electronic pen at them. Most devices also include 'gestures' – shorthand-type symbols that can be used to alter or manipulate text.

Their key feature is the ability to recognise and store clear handwriting. This involves the user writing a series of words and then checking to see whether the computer has learnt them. At present, handwriting recognition is the main weakness of book computers. Each letter needs to be clear if the computer is to be able to decipher it.

1 What do you consider to be the main advantage of book computers?

2 How widely are they being used?

3 How do you think they can be used in the modern office?

· THE CHANGING FACE OF OFFICE TECHNOLOGY ·

In the 1960s, big and expensive **mainframe computers** were introduced by large organisations to handle major data-processing operations – such as payrolls, stock and inventory control. These machines were housed in large, spotlessly clean (dust-free) rooms, and were managed by computer experts using systems that were difficult to operate. Keying in data was a monotonous task performed by semi-skilled staff, requiring accuracy and concentration but no knowledge of computers.

There have been great changes in the last 25 years. The development of **integrated circuits** led to the smaller, cheaper but equally powerful **minicomputer**. Hard on its heels came the tiny silicon-chip **microprocessor** carrying a vast number of electronic circuits. These chips make it possible to build sophisticated electronic control systems into very small spaces.

By 1990 personal computers (PCs) with equivalent power to the 1960s mainframes were to be found on desktops throughout the land, in offices large or small. These machines, costing sometimes less than a thousand pounds, can be used to run a range of software. Non-specialists can use PCs for many essential clerical and administrative tasks – word-processing, stock control, accounts, planning and so on. **Software** is widely available and becoming increasingly easy to use.

As we have seen, these machines become even more useful when linked together in networks. These range from three or four machines within the same office, to networks of several hundreds of computers across the country connected to each other by the existing telephone system.

Changes in the organisation of clerical and administrative work

When mainframe computers were introduced they led to **centralisation** of functions. As networking and PCs take over, **decentralisation** is following. Now different departments can use their own terminals to call up and update centrally held records. Typing is no longer carried out in the 'typing pool' – today word-processing can be carried out in any part of a building.

Low-cost microcomputers with user-friendly interfaces (keyboards, menus, mouses . . .) mean that staff can routinely work on **word and number crunching** (electronic textual and numerical processing), information storage and retrieval (database applications) and manipulating and analysing information (spreadsheets).

PCs are invaluable for a lot of management functions including data analysis and forward planning. It is unfortunate that too many senior managers rely on 'chauffeured' use of this vital business tool, content that junior staff – often their secretaries – operate the computer terminal for them.

Trends in office automation in the next decade are likely to lead to a reduction in keyboard data entry, resulting in fewer junior clerical jobs.

IT in finance and service industries

Senior clerks are starting to take over some functions of managers. This could lead to an increase in senior clerical jobs and a reduction in the junior or middle managers.

Bank clerks have become 'personal bankers', using **on-line computers** to enable them to answer questions on financial services.

Expert systems can permit insurance clerks to answer questions formerly the province of expert underwriters.

Building society clerks have become adept at using spreadsheets to provide customers with instant details of financial options.

Database marketing

Marketing is clearly an area of business life that needs the use of IT competence. **Electronic** marketing is already well established.

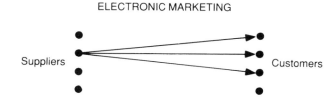

Figure 6.12 *Electronic marketing*

Information technology is used to improve the marketing of many products, even if there is no 'electronic link' with the customer. For example, **precision marketing** is a form of direct mail which targets customers using computerised databases; this is more selective than **carpet bombing** with so-called junk mail. Sites for new supermarkets are chosen using maps which show areas by type of housing, average household income, propensity to buy certain type of products, and lifestyles. This is all part of **database marketing**.

American airlines pioneered electronic marketing – they gave travel agents terminals which provided access to their computerised reservation systems. This meant that seats could be booked without the travel agent having to make several phone calls to check if seats were available.

Simulations of travel agent operations are now available from many **software houses** and are a useful way of learning about database marketing.

In the UK, the Bank of Scotland pioneered 'Hobs' – a home and office banking system. This enables users with simple videotext terminals to do their own banking by dialling into the bank's computers; and it meant that the bank could reach customers outside its geographical stronghold, without opening lots of expensive branches. The Midland and other banks now make similar software available to colleges and schools that want to set up their own students' banks.

Task

As a group, undertake a piece of research using *database marketing* to find out about consumer preferences in relation to cinema attendance in your area. Collect data about age, frequency of visits, type of films favoured, mode of transport used, and other details. Use the evidence from your research to make recommendations about whether the cinema should invest in a new screen, what sort of films should be shown, how the cinema service could be improved in other ways.

• CONCLUSIONS •

A modern office lies at the heart of any organisation's information system. Like any system it needs to run well; in fact it needs to run in the best possible way. Inputs of raw data and semi-finished data need to be converted into finished information by using the most effective processes that are appropriate. It would be ridiculous for a small company to make a computer database out of sparse data relating to just three customers. It would be equally ridiculous nowadays for a large company to rely purely on pen and paper records for dealing with thousands of orders. Organisations therefore need to use **appropriate technology** to meet their needs. This often means obtaining specialist advice about systems available to solve the problems. No two organisations are alike – every one has its own needs for an effective information system.

When you develop your own IT competency it is important that you think about how new knowledge, skills and attitudes will help you. Get advice from your tutor, supervisor or careers adviser to find out what new areas you need to master. There is nothing more pointless than learning skills which are not required, or in using IT to do things that could be done more quickly in other ways. We have all heard of colleges where students are provided with elaborate computer timetables only to find that the rooms are all wrong, the times given are incorrect, and that the named lecturer left three years ago.

In short, make sure you know why you are learning new information skills, use the most appropriate information processing methods, and use them well!

Case Study

IT at use in a service station

A modern service station can be viewed as a complex office administering a range of buying and selling operations. This case study looks at the range of IT applications used by a service station.

Figure 6.13 illustrates the IT links between a service station and its business partners.

Information technology facilities in a service station can carry out all the following procedures:

- transfer details of fuel withdrawals from the pumps to the central console
- monitor the amount of fuel left in the underground storage tanks
- issue the correct payment request and receipt
- accept cash, cheques or credit cards
- check and process the credit card transactions
- record the credit card transactions
- for daily 'polling' by a bureau acting for the credit card companies
- debit a customer's bank account directly
- record shop sales and monitor remaining stocks (broken down into product and package size)
- provide screen or printed management reports on sales and stock levels.

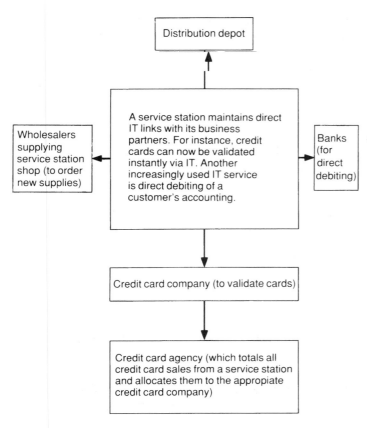

Figure 6.13 *IT links between a service station and its business partners*

Some service stations have IT facilities to carry out every one of these procedures – and integrate them on to one database. Others have IT facilities that can carry out only some of them.

1 *Produce a database of information about the range and variety of IT facilities in use at service stations in your local area. The database should include basic data about each service station, including address, brands and types of fuel available, number of pumps, and facilities such as car-wash, shop and toilets.*

2 *Use the database to list the IT procedures that are carried out at each service station in turn.*

3 *Word-process a report on the range of IT facilities in use at the service stations in your area.*

Looking at your own IT skills

In this chapter we have looked at a range of IT skills which you might be asked to use in a modern office. Now use the profile printed here to chart your own IT skills. Discuss with your tutor or supervisor ways of upgrading your skills.

IT SKILLS CHECKLIST

Indicate by a tick in the appropriate boxes what, in your opinion, is your level of **experience** with respect to the skills mentioned:

1 I am experienced at this.
2 I have some experience of this.
3 I have no experience of this.

Indicate by a tick in the appropriate boxes what you feel to be your **success** with the skills mentioned:

1 I was successful at this.
2 I was reasonably successful at this.
3 I was rarely successful at this.

	Experience 1 2 3	Success 1 2 3
Using a microcomputer in any way		
Using a simple word-processing package		
Using a more complex word-processing package		
Using a drawing/painting package		
Using a desktop publishing program		
Using a multimedia program (sound/animation/graphics)		
Using a data-retrieval system		
Using a spreadsheet		
Using a printer		
Using a colour printer		
Using a plotter		
Other experiences (specify)		

Element assignment

Reviewing software

This assignment can help you provide evidence for assessment, or claim the following Core Skills:

Communication

Receive and respond to a variety of information

Communicate in writing

Information technology

Use a range of technological equipment and systems

Personal Skills

Use information sources

Identify and solve routine and non-routine problems

Using information technology in business is tremendously important.

When looking for software to use in business there are a number of criteria to bear in mind. Questions to ask, to identify these criteria include:

- Can I use it on my existing system?
- How much does it cost?
- How much money will it save me?
- How much time will it save me?
- Is it easy to operate?
- Will things go wrong when I use it?
- etc. (What other criteria do you think are important?)

The most popular business applications programs are word-processors, spreadsheets and databases. Nowadays all users of these programs want them to be simple to operate, fast and efficient.

The pressure is therefore on software manufacturers to come up with user friendly software.

Let us look at the latest product from the US computer giant Microsoft. The company has a near-monopoly in operating systems such as MS-DOS and Windows – programs that turn dumb electronic circuits into computers. However, it is only recently that Microsoft has begun to expand into the software market, obtaining a market share of nearly 30 per cent by the end of 1992.

Microsoft has just launched a new database product on to the market called Access. Many people feel that it is one of the most ambitious pieces of software ever to be launched. Access is aimed at the average user who wants a database which is simple to operate. Access aims to provide the user with 'information at your fingertips'. The software employs 'wizards' – a computer term likely soon to become as widely used as a 'mouse'. The wizards act like intelligent advisers that pop up on screen to help construct forms, reports and graphs. Answer the wizard's questions, and up comes the result.

Task

You have been asked by a local estate agent to recommend to them

- a database program
- a spreadsheet program
- a word-processing program.

The software needs to meet a number of criteria:

1 Most importantly it needs to be easy to operate.

2 It should be competitively priced.

3 It should be suitable for the following functions:
- producing details of properties for sale
- sending out letters to clients
- producing advertising leaflets
- producing budget for forecasts and cash-flow projections
- keeping records of properties and customers.

The estate agents are shortly to buy a new set of computers which will run the software that you recommend.

You will therefore need to review existing software (with advice from your tutor). Make suggestions about which software would be appropriate. Outline the characteristics of the software and comment upon its suitability for the purposes suggested. Explain to what extent its functions are integrated.

You must then demonstrate appropriate software and show how it can carry out each of the functions listed above.

Produce a word-processed review explaining why it is so important for software to be easy to operate.

chapter **7** MARKET RESEARCH

Market research helps members of an organisation to understand the operation of their market. In doing so it enables them to answer questions such as:

- Who makes up the target audience?
- What goods and serv ices will they require?
- When will they need them?

- Where will they sell best?
- How should they be distributed?
- What trends are likely to take place in the future?

The answers to these questions will help an organisation to plan ahead rather than to rely upon guesswork

. THE IMPORTANCE OF THE . CUSTOMER

All organisations, whether in the public sector or in the private sector, have **customers** (sometimes called users or clients). A customer may be either a person or another organisation. In most cases the recipient of the good or service being provided has to pay for what is on offer, but in other cases there is no charge. For example, whereas a customer in a newsagent's shop is clearly a person buying the goods on offer, in the public sector it might be an organisation asking for *advice* from the Department of Trade and Industry. You yourself – in your capacity as a student – may be a customer of a school, college or other training institution.

Organisations never operate in an unchanging environment, because outside **influences** and **customer preferences** are constantly changing. If an organisation ever hopes to succeed it has to take these changes into account. It has to find out what goods or services its market requires now and in the future, and become **customer orientated.**

Assessing customer needs is therefore a process of **discovery**, so that an organisation can **direct its activities** towards supplying customers with the good-quality, reliable products and services they want.

A classic example in the United Kingdom of the failure to monitor customer needs comes from the motor-cycle industry. Twenty-five years ago British roads seldom saw a foreign motorbike. Great names such as BSA, Triumph, Ariel and Norton graced the roads with heavy, slow-revving, large-capacity machines. Imports from Italy in the form of lightweight, high-revving machines were hardly given a second glance by British manufacturers – they did not make them so customers could not have them! Someone *had* noticed these machines, however, and thousands of miles away research and development programmes were under way – Japan was about to enter the market-place. Today the transformation is complete; motorbikes on British roads are nearly all Japanese and there are very few British manufacturers left. If the British had researched their market and found out what their customers really wanted, the position might be very different today.

· DEFINITION OF MARKETING ·

The process of discovering and assessing customer needs is called **marketing**. The Chartered Institute of Marketing has a definition for this:

> MARKETING is the anticipation and fulfilment of a consumer need - profit.

The implication is that for an organisation to pursue its objectives *and* continue to make a profit, it has to discover in good time what its customers want to buy and then set out to meet their needs.

Case Study

What do customers really want?

Corky Ra is an entrepreneur who likes a challenge and feels that he knows what his customers really require. In the 1970s he bet his father that he could open a vineyard in Utah, the American state where the mainly Mormon population consider drink and the devil to be cousins. He won his wager by building a 12-metre-high pyramid in Salt Lake City, making sacramental wine in it, and selling the produce to religious groups!

Seeking to diversify, Mr Ra moved into an industry ripe for some innovative marketing – the funeral business. Until his company arrived, burial and cremation were the two choices, but his research indicated that some potential 'clients' wanted something different – they wanted a way of preserving their remains so that they could be remembered.

Mr Ra's answer was a type of mummification. For around $7700 clients can be pickled for eternity. Another $26 000 buys a bronze sarcophagus filled with an inert gas which does not allow body-eating bacteria to survive. One client has even specified a bejewelled interment costing $150 000. To help offset the expense to customers, Mr Ra has managed to persuade the US tax authorities that, unlike conventional funerals, mummification funerals should be tax-deductible.

There is, however, a snag – none of his clients has yet died. So far only his dog and cat have succumbed and sit mummified in his headquarters!

1 To what extent did Corky Ra find out what his customers really wanted?
2 What does it mean, he 'moved into an industry ripe for some innovative marketing'?
3 Working in groups if possible, try to identify a good or service that does not appear to be offered by any organisation. Discuss your findings with other groups.

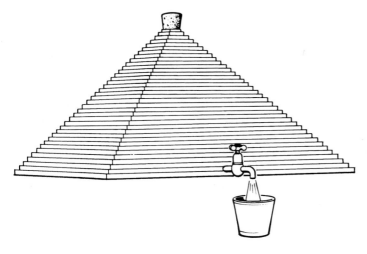

· MARKET RESEARCH ·

As we have seen, an organisation must be aware of changes in its external environment as well as changes in the needs of its customers. It requires **information**. The gathering of such information helps it to plan its activities and reduce uncertainty.

The American Marketing Association uses a simple working definition of market research:

> MARKET RESEARCH is the systemic gathering, recording and analysis of data about problems related to the marketing of goods and services

We can break this definition down into its important ingredients:

● *systematic* – in other words, using an organised and clear method or system

- *gathering* – knowing what you are looking for, and collecting appropriate information
- *recording* – keeping clear and organised records of what you find out
- *analysing* – ordering and making sense of your information in order to draw out relevant trends and conclusions
- *problems related to marketing* – finding out the answers to questions that will help you to understand your customers and other details about the market-place.

It is the responsibility of the market research function within an organisation to find out as much as it possibly can about customers, markets and products. This is essential for all organisations if they are to meet the needs of their customers and remain competitive and profitable. It is an organised way of finding answers to questions or solutions to problems and *should be an on-going activity*.

n order to sell to people *what* they want to buy, *when* they want to buy it, it is essential to build up a profile of customers – what they do, when and why they do it, and what would encourage them to use your products and services. In other words, you have to study their habits and motivations.

Market research also needs to find out what might make customers choose a rival product in preference to your own. For example, might falling sales be as a result of changes in demand, the existence of an aggressive competitor or poor service on your part?

Case Study

Researching consumer needs

For Procter & Gamble (a major international manufacturer of detergent, personal care, cosmetic and food products), market research surveys are a way of life. In fact, they never stop. Over 200 000 consumers respond to their questions each year, resulting in a research report virtually every day.

The changing patterns they reveal are fundamental to the firm's core business activities.

For example, in the immediate post-war years only 3 per cent of households had any form of washing machine, and these were not automatic. Today 80 per cent have one, and automatic machines account for more than four out of every five machines bought. Sales of low-suds powders and liquids necessary for automatic washing machines grew for several years at a rate of around 20 per cent a year.

Over the last 25 years the cotton content of fabrics has halved, and today man-made fibres account for over half of fabrics sold and around 80 per cent of articles washed are coloured. In response, washing products have had to be developed which don't eventually bleach out colour and which wash as well or better at lower temperatures.

There has also been rapid change in the social patterns which affect the clothes-washing task. Today's variations across family sizes, occupations, leisure pursuits and so on are considerable. Sophisticated research techniques are required to build up an accurate picture of washing habits.

All of these different consumer needs have to be met by products which, though highly sophisticated and chemically complex, are easy and quick to use and relatively inexpensive. Only 20p of every £100 of household expenditure goes on washing products.

1 Describe briefly what has happened to the market for washing materials over the last 25 years.
2 Explain how market research helps P & G to meet consumer needs.
3 What might have happened to their core business activities if P & G had not sufficiently researched the market?

Internal information

Much of the information that an organisation requires about the market-place is already held within its various departments. A lot of this **internal information** might be in filing cabinets, and at least some of it will be out of date. The secret is to know what you need, to discover where to find it, and then to retrieve it.

Nowadays, a lot of internal information is held on **computer files**. Computers have revolutionised the way information is stored, analysed and retrieved, and this has made the task of dealing with internal information much easier.

For example, in the past it was often difficult to get regular and reliable feedback from **sales representatives**, because their 'paperwork' was kept in their vehicles, was disorganised and bulky, and was rarely filed. This information was potentially enormously valuable as it represented **feedback** from first-hand experiences with customers – it is often said that a sales force is an organisation's 'eyes and ears'.

Computers have provided the means whereby information of this nature can be recorded in a simple manner, and contacts with each customer can be 'processed' so that information can be retrieved very quickly and then displayed in a way that is easy to understand, perhaps with the aid of a graphics software package. Techniques like this improve the quality of the market research process and enable organisations to direct goods and services to those customers who are most likely to make a purchase.

Task

What sort of information are sales representatives likely to find out from customers?

In organisations using computerised records, files of information are stored on a **database**. This is a large amount of information which is stored in such a way that it can easily be found, processed and updated. The database may be central so that it can be accessed by users from all parts of the organisation.

Case Study

The electricity distribution company

We can show how one type of database works by looking at the activities of an electricity distribution company. Customers are given a

customer reference number (CRN). To the CRN the electricity company can then attach a vast array of information which tells it about the consumer. For example:

Tariff type – The price a customer pays for electricity can vary according to whether they are a home or business, a large or small customer.

Consumption – The company can track the *amount* of electricity a customer uses, and *when* it is used.

Method of payment – Some customers prefer prepayment rather than credit, others prefer to pay monthly rather than quarterly.

Change of tenancy – The company knows when customers move out of and into a property.

New buildings – The company knows when and where new buildings that use electricity are being erected, because an electricity supply is applied for.

From such information it is possible to obtain answers to an almost endless list of questions, such as:

- What is the size of the market?
- What type of user uses the most/least electricity?
- How do customers prefer to pay?
- What is the average credit period?
- What type of customers are bad payers?
- How many new users are coming on-stream?
- How many users is the company losing?
- What is the average consumption per user?
- What is the profitability for each type of customer?
- How does the use of electricity vary during the day?
- Where is the market expanding/contracting?

1 How will the answers to the sort of questions indicated here improve the way the electricity company manages its business?

2 What other questions might be answered from this type of database?

External information

The internal information that has been collated needs to be put into context, since on its own it simply provides a snapshot of the organisation and its customers. In particular it tells the organisation nothing about how effective its performance is relative to that of its competitors, nor how the business could be threatened by those competitors.

external information is more commonly called **secondary data** because it is often in the form of published materials, collected by somebody else. It can provide a broader dimension to data previously collected and can be used in two main ways.

Firstly, external information can **enhance** the company's existing knowledge. For example, postcodes help the computer to group customers geographically. By identifying and labelling certain characteristics of its customers, a company can make assumptions about their needs. Two examples of useful external sources are:

- *Domestic socio-economic data* – Customers are classified by their house type, the assumption being that a certain lifestyle is associated with that type of house.
- *Industrial classification* – Organisational customers can be classified according to the nature of their activities. Certain types of organisations can then be expected to have predictable demands for services.

Secondly, external sources can complement an organisation's own information by providing direct comparison with competitors, by putting performance within the context of the economy as a whole, and by identifying markets offering potential.

Task

Imagine that you are the owner or manager of a small shop selling sports equipment in your local neighbourhood. What sort of information might give you a better understanding of the decisions you have to make?

Government statistics

The government's statistical service is coordinated by the Central Statistical Office (CSO). Government departments prepare statistics and the CSO publishes both a monthly

and an annual analysis. In addition, *Business Monitor* is published quarterly to provide a range of information about various markets. Information on particular groups of industries is identified by a code which relates to their Standard Industrial Classification (SIC) – for example, 'agriculture, forestry and fishing' and 'energy and water supply industries'. As the SIC is the government's official way of classifying organisations and markets, it is frequently used in market research.

Another useful source of information, particularly for industries selling in consumer markets, is **census data** published by the Office of Population, Censuses and Surveys. A full census is carried out every ten years, the last one being in 1991. This office also carries out two continuous surveys on Family Expenditure and General Households, which might also be useful for organisations to analyse for market research purposes.

Other sources of information

Mintel is a **commercial research organisation** which, in return for a fee, provides a monthly journal containing reports on a variety of consumer markets – for example, bread, alcoholic drinks, insurance. The **Mintel reports** are up to about 20 pages long, with information such as market size, main competitors, projected growth, market share of main producers, advertising spend of main brands, trends etc. Mintel also produces in-depth reports on certain markets.

Task

How might the information published in a Mintel Report be useful?

Another research outfit which operates in a similar way to Mintel is **Euromonitor**. Key Note Reports cover a range of businesses and, at around 75 pages long, provide a good introduction to markets.

Some research establishments work exclusively in one particular sector. For the food industry, for example, there is the Leatherhead Food Research Association and the Food Policy Research Unit. **Business-to-business reports** are available for many sectors.

A. C. Nielson and **Retail Audits** are research outfits which collect data of retail sales through supermarkets and large chains, and sell the figures to organisations wishing to buy them. These figures enable manufacturers to work out their share of the market, the sales of different products, and the effects of any recent strategy such as a price change or a promotion campaign. These audits therefore offer a window directly onto the market-place.

Another way of finding out what is happening in the market-place is to set up **panels**. These are groups of consumers who record their purchases and/or media habits in a diary. The purpose of the diary is not just to record purchases but also to provide research information which relates purchasing habits with social status, occupation, income, demographic details, neighbourhood etc.

There are many sources providing **information about the media** which might be of use to organisations wishing to look at how to get their promotional messages across to customers. Benn's *Media Directory* gives details of TV and radio companies, newspapers and magazines. *British Rate and Data* (BRAD) provides comprehensive coverage of virtually all the media selling advertising space, together with rates. *The Advertisers Annual* makes detailed comparisons of advertising agencies.

Information about companies is available from several sources. **Kompass** publishes two volumes of products and services listed by the SIC codes mentioned earlier. **Extel** provides details extracted from the published accounts of all the public companies and from many of the larger private companies. The annual publication *Who Owns Whom* gives details of the ownership of subsidiary companies.

Task

Visit both the reference section and the periodicals section of your college library or your local library. Identify which sources of information may be of use for market research purposes. Ask the librarian for help if necessary.

PRIMARY SOURCES OF INFORMATION

Internal and external data may not answer all the questions an organisation wants to ask. It may be out of date or it may not cover exactly the right market sector. Then, to meet an organisation's specific needs, **primary research** has to take place.

Primary data is first-hand knowledge, 'straight from the horse's mouth'. Information a company compiles from its own research efforts is called primary.

Surveys are the most common method used to collect primary data; they involve contacting **respondents** to find out how they react to a range of issues contained in a **questionnaire**. There are two types of survey, a census and a sample. A **census** involves questioning everybody in a particular market – but, unless the market is very small, this is unlikely to be practicable. Taking a **sample** involves questioning a *selection* of respondents from the target market. In order to ensure that the results of a sample survey are accurate, the market research process must identify a representative group of consumers. If the selection of the sample is fair and accurate, then information should be **statistically reliable**. If the sample is incomplete and does not accurately represent a group of consumers, misleading data are obtained – the sample is said to be **biased**.

Choosing a sample

One way to ensure that a selection is free of bias is to use **random sampling**. Individuals and organisations are selected from a 'sampling frame', which is simply a list (usually numbered) of all the members of the market or population due to be surveyed. We shall consider several popular forms of sampling.

Simple random sampling

With this method the researcher chooses the size of the sample required and then picks the sample on a random basis. The sample must be selected in such a way that every item in the sampling frame has an equal chance of being selected. One way of doing this is to use a computer to draw names or numbers from the list at random.

Another way is to use **systematic sampling**, which involves selecting items from the list at regular intervals after choosing a random starting point. For example, if it is decided to select a sample of 20 names from 1000, then every 50th name (1000 divided by 20) should be selected, after a random start in the first 50. If 18 is chosen as the starting point (possibly by using a table of random numbers), then the sample series would start:

18 . . . 68 . . . 118 . . . 168 . . . etc.

Stratified random sampling

If some customers are more important than others, then simple random sampling can distort the results. **Stratified random sampling** therefore weights the sample on the basis of the importance of each group of customers in the market.

For example, if an organisation has 5000 small users of products accounting for sales of £1 million, 4000 medium users accounting for £1 million, and 1000 big users accounting for £2 million, a random sample of 200 would not be representative of the whole market. To make the sample more representative would involve allocating the big users half of the sample because they make up half the sales, with a quarter of the sample to medium users and a quarter to small users. The stratified random sample would then include 100 big users, 50 medium users and 50 small users, all randomly chosen from their respective categories.

Cluster sampling

With **cluster sampling** the population/customers are divided up into small areas, but instead of sampling from a random selection of these areas, sampling is carried out in a few areas which are considered to be typical of the market in question. For example, you might divide the city of Newcastle into 200 segments and then, because of the nature of your survey, decide that you will only sample from a segment which contains at least one school, one church and one shopping centre, and any segments without these facilities are avoided.

Quota sampling

Although random sampling, if properly conducted, produces the best results, it can be expensive and time

consuming, and in some situations it is not possible to identify a random sample. **Quota sampling** is more commonly used.

Interviewers are given instructions as to the number of people to interview with certain characteristics – such as sex, age, socio-economic group or other demographic detail. For example, if the interviewers are asked to investigate housewives aged 36–50, they will quiz every housewife 'fitting the bill' (possibly in interviews in the high street) up to their maximum quota. The problem is that there is no assurance that the housewives interviewed are typical of housewives in that band, and the statistical accuracy of such sampling is questionable.

Convenience and judgement sampling

Convenience sampling involves gathering information from anybody available for the interviewer to survey, no matter what their background. **Judgement sampling** involves selection of the respondents by the interviewer based on his or her judgement that they seemed to be and looked representative of the group of customers in the market being researched.

Task

Study each of the sampling methods described and then comment on which methods you feel would provide:

a the greatest accuracy, and
b the greatest cost-efficiency.

Preparing a questionnaire

When the sampling problems have been settled, the researcher must design a questionnaire. This is a systematic list of questions designed to obtain information from people about:

● specific events
● their attitudes

- their values
- their beliefs.

Questionnaire design is probably the most crucial part of a survey. Though it is easy to design questions, it is difficult to produce a good questionnaire – and a badly designed questionnaire may lead to biased results. For instance, if the people completing the questionnaire are unaware of its purpose, they may place the wrong emphasis on the questions. Another problem may arise if very few completed forms are returned, or if those returned are only partially completed. In addition, if the questionnaire is being administered by an interviewer, there is always a danger that the interviewer may misinterpret the questions and introduce his or her own personal bias in a way which prompts certain answers from respondents.

Task

Think back to any questionnaire or form which you have recently had to answer.(If necessary, use your course enrolment form as an example.) What was the purpose of the questionnaire? Was it simple and easy to understand? Do you feel that it was well designed? If not, why not?

A good questionnaire will:

- ask questions which relate directly to information needs
- not ask too many questions
- not ask personal questions
- fit its questions into a logical sequence
- have unambiguous questions.

It will also have been extensively tested, possibly with trial interviews, before being administered.

The questions in a questionnaire may be 'open' or 'closed'. **Open questions** allow the person answering to give an opinion and may encourage him or her to talk at length. **Closed questions** usually require an answer picked from a range of options (which may be simply yes/no). Most questionnaires used closed questions, so that they can be answered quickly and more efficiently, and the answers are easier to analyse (see Figure 7.1).

The purpose of a closed question is to get people to commit themselves to a concrete opinion. If you ask an open question, the likelihood is that your survey will prompt a wide range of answers which are very difficult to analyse. Closed questions tie respondents down so that they have to make a decision within a range of choices.

To help interviewers operate a questionnaire, sometimes a **prompt card** is used. This means that, if several or all of the questions in the questionnaire have the same range of set answers, these can be numbered and then the respondents' answers can be recorded as numbers (see Figure 7.2).

Do you like the layout of our new shops?

(Tick one box)

Very good	Good	Satisfactory	Poor	Very poor

How would you rate our restaurant?

(Tick one box)

Very good | | | | | | Very poor

Which one of the following banks do you have an account with?

(Tick the relevant boxes)

- ☐ National Westminster
- ☐ Barclays
- ☐ Lloyds
- ☐ Midland
- ☐ Abbey National
- ☐ Yorkshire
- ☐ Others

Figure 7.1 *Three examples of closed questions*

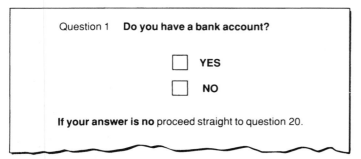

National Westminster	01
Barclays	02
Lloyds	03
Midland	04
Abbey National	05
Yorkshire	06
Others	07

Figure 7.2 *An interviewer's prompt card for the third example in Figure 7.1*

Question 1 **Do you have a bank account?**

☐ YES

☐ NO

If your answer is no proceed straight to question 20.

Figure 7.3 *An example of a 'skip'*

Some questionnaires are designed so that respondents can concentrate on the questions that are relevant, and then skip over questions which do not relate to them (see Figure 7.3).

Case Study

Jus-rol Ltd

As a manufacturer of frozen food, Jus-rol Ltd is conscious of the need to take into account the views of its customers. The company is also aware of the valuable information that its customers might hold. The questionnaire on page 193 was recently sent to a sample of known consumers of frozen fillo pastry. Read through the questionnaire and then answer the questions that follow.

1 Stating specific examples, explain how the answers provided to questions in the questionnaire will help Jus-rol to market its products.
2 Comment on the nature of the questions (open/closed, easy to understand etc.).
3 How easy (or difficult) would it be to analyse information from the questionnaire?
4 How would you suggest that this information be recorded?
5 Why do you think the questionnaire asks for the names and addresses of respondents?

Task

Set out a questionnaire (with at least ten questions) to find out whether members of your group have ever thought of setting up their own business and, if they have, what lines of business they would like to follow. Apply the questionnaire and keep the results, which will be used in a later task.

Administering the questionnaire

There are three different ways of using the questionnaire:

● with a face-to-face interview
● by telephone
● through the post.

Face-to-face tends to be the best form of contact. It allows two-way communication between the researcher and the respondent. It is flexible and also allows gestures, facial expressions, signs of impatience and boredom all to be noted.

A questionnaire put to a person in the street is likely to be less friendly and detailed than a group discussion in the home. A street interview is brief, impersonal and uses a broadly defined sample group, whereas a home discussion can be exactly the opposite – detailed, personal and with a tightly defined sample group. Different results can be expected.

JUS-ROL LIMITED 21ST MARCH 1991

1 HAD YOU EVERY PURCHASED FROZEN FILLO PASTRY PRIOR TO BUYING THE JUS-ROL BRAND OF FROZEN FILLO? (PLEASE TICK THE APPROPRIATE BOX)

YES	
NO	

2 HOW OFTEN DO YOU BUY JUS-ROL FILLO PASTRY? (PLEASE TICK THE BOX WHICH IS NEAREST TO YOUR PURCHASE)

FORTNIGHTLY	
MONTHLY	
EVERY 3 MONTHS	
ONCE A YEAR	

3 HAVE YOU PURCHASED JUS-ROL FILLO PASTRY ONLY THIS ONCE? IF SO, WHY IS THIS? (PLEASE EXPLAIN BRIEFLY)

4 IS JUS-ROL FILLO OBTAINABLE IN THE STORES YOU NORMALLY SHOP AT? (PLEASE TICK THE APPROPRIATE BOX)

YES	
NO	

5 WHERE DO YOU NORMALLY SHOP? (IT IS LIKELY YOU SHOP AT SEVERAL STORES. PLEASE PUT A TICK AGAINST THE STORE YOU NORMALLY VISIT AND THE RELEVANT FREQUENCY)

STORE	WEEKLY	MONTHLY	FORT-NIGHTLY
SAINSBURY			
TESCO			
SAFEWAY			
ASDA			
ICELAND			
CO-OPS			
GATEWAY			
OTHERS			

6 WHICH PRODUCTS DO YOU NORMALLY PREPARE USING FILLO PASTRY? (PLEASE TICK RELEVANT BOXES AND PROVIDE ANY ADDITIONAL INFORMATION IN THE SPACE BELOW)

SAMOSAS	
STRUDELS	
SAVOURY SNACKS	
SAVOURY MEALS	
DESSERTS	
OTHER	

7 FOR WHAT MEAL OCCASION DO YOU NORMALLY USE PRODUCTS MADE WITH FILLO PASTRY? (PLEASE TICK APPROPRIATE BOXES)

BREAKFAST	
MAIN MEALS – lunch	
MAIN MEALS – dinner	
SNACK OCCASIONS – day	
SNACK OCCASIONS – evening	

8 WHICH OF THE FOLLOWING CATEGORY ARE YOU? (PLEASE TICK THE APPROPRIATE BOX)

FULL TIME EMPLOYED	
PART TIME EMPLOYED	
HOUSEWIFE/ HOUSEHUSBAND	

9 IF EMPLOYED, WHAT IS YOUR OCCUPATION? PLEASE SPECIFY

10 IS THE TEXTURE AND TASTE OF JUS-ROL FILLO TO YOUR SATISFACTION? (PLEASE TICK THE APPROPRIATE BOX)

YES	
NO	

11 DO YOU FIND JUS-ROL EASY TO USE (PLEASE TICK APPROPRIATE BOX) IF NOT, WHAT IS THE PROBLEM?

YES	
NO	

12 WHAT IS YOUR VIEW ON THE PACK SIZE OF JUS-ROL FILLO I.E. 300G (PLEASE TICK THE APPROPRIATE BOX)

ABOUT RIGHT	
TOO LARGE	
TOO SMALL	

13 AT PRESENT THE SIZE OF EACH JUS-ROL FILLO SHEET IS 12" × 6". WHAT IS YOUR VIEW ON THIS SIZE? (PLEASE TICK THE APPROPRIATE BOX)

ABOUT RIGHT	
TOO LARGE	
TOO SMALL	

14 IF YOU FELT AN AMENDMENT TO THE PACK AND SIZE OF SHEETS IS DESIRABLE, WHAT WOULD YOU RECOMMEND? (PLEASE TICK PREFERRED WEIGHT AND SIZE)

WEIGHT: 400G	
WEIGHT: 250G	
WEIGHT: 200G	
SIZE: 20" × 10"	
SIZE: 12" × 12"	
SIZE: 15" × 12"	

15 DO YOU HAVE A COPY OF JUS-ROL'S FILLO RECIPE BOOKLET (PLEASE TICK THE APPROPRIATE BOX)

YES	
NO	

16 IF YOU HAVE A JUS-ROL FILLO RECIPE BOOKLET, DO YOU USE IT . . . (PLEASE TICK THE APPROPRIATE BOX)

OCCASIONALLY	
OFTEN	
NEVER	

17 PLEASE WRITE YOUR NAME AND ADDRESS IN THE BOX PROVIDED.

Telephone interviewing is usually more appropriate for business surveys as the respondents are often busy people and unavailable for group discussion. However, this method is often regarded as intrusive since it catches people unawares, especially in the home. This means that the respondent can start the interview with a negative view, which questioning will not necessarily help to overcome. However, it is a cost-effective means of reaching people, and the replies received are likely to be truthful. The rate of response will probably be higher than with the third method, the **postal technique**.

The level of response to a questionnaire sent through the post will vary enormously, depending on its relevance to the reader and his or her interest. Response rates are often as low as 10 per cent, so that answers are not particularly representative – they might just be representative of those who like filling in forms! The way to avoid this outcome is to ensure that the questionnaire is brief, succinct and sent only to those for whom it is directly relevant. A good postal questionnaire can achieve a response rate as high as 70 per cent.

Other primary sources

Another simple primary source is **observation** – for example, looking at how consumers behave when shopping. Information obtained like this can help to decide on packaging, or suggest offers which seem to attract the attention of consumers.

Discussion groups are an inexpensive method of obtaining useful qualitative information from consumers. For example, under the guidance of a chairperson, a group of users of the same product may be invited to give opinions upon its use.

Opinion polls are often used to find out about consumer awareness, opinions and attitudes. Perhaps the most famous organisation in this field is **Gallup**, but there are others. Questions are short and are designed to find out how consumers respond to issues such as image, product lines etc.

Electronic interviewing is a market research technique based on an interactive system with a telecommunications network. A respondent need only be a television and telephone subscriber and can respond instantly with a range of answers while a television campaign is actually being carried out.

Task

Make sure you know the difference between *qualitative* information and *quantitative* information.

· ORGANISING THE DATA ·

When an organisation has completed the important task of gathering information, it has to decide what to do with it. There are three stages involved:

- sorting and storing the information
- presenting the information
- making sense of the information.

Each of these three stages has been transformed by the use of information technology.

Today, compilation, storage and analysis of market research may be undertaken using **specialist software**, of which examples are the Statistical Package for Social Sciences (SPSS) and Minitab. Use can also be made of information received from **bar code analysis** derived from electronic checkout and scanning systems located at the point of sale.

Electronic data processing (EDP) is frequently used for compiling and then categorising and summarising the results of market research. Questionnaire answers can be numerically coded for data entry. EDP makes it easy to deal efficiently and quickly with the results of lengthy questionnaires.

Task

Use the information obtained from your questionnaire in the task on page 192 to create a database. Interrogate your database by asking your own questions, and then comment on the conclusions you draw from the results.

Presentation of data

Once statistical data has been obtained from all sources, it needs to be broken down and presented in such a way that its significance can be appreciated easily. Information can be displayed as text, tables, charts, or graphs.

A **table** is just a matrix of rows and columns defining the relationships between variables; it summarises information into a form that is clear and easy to read. With suitable computer software, a table can be shown on a screen in the form of a **spreadsheet** – a grid of columns across the screen and rows going down the screen (see Figure 4.8). It can also be manipulated through a series of calculations to show what would happen if alterations were made to any of the figures. As a result, one of the great benefits of spreadsheets is that they allow '**what if?**' questions to be asked and answered quickly.

Pictorial **charts** are eye-catching and enable information to be presented in a form that can be readily understood. For example, in a **pie chart** each slice of the pie represents a component's contribution to the total amount. A circle is divided up in proportion to the figures obtained and, in order to draw the segments accurately, a protractor is necessary to mark off the pieces. The following formula can be used to find the angles (in degrees) for each segment:

$$\text{Angle for segment A} = \frac{\text{Amount of A} \times 360°}{\text{Total}}$$

Task

A company's sales are made up as follows:

	Sales (£million)
Home	15
USA	4
Australia	3
EC	8
Middle East	10
Total	40

Draw an accurate pie-chart to present these sales figures. Label the chart.

In **bar charts** the areas for comparison are represented by bars – which can be drawn either vertically or horizontally. The lengths of the bars indicate the relative importance of the data.

Task

Look at the bar chart in Figure 4.9, which shows the proportions of men and women in each job category in the marketing industry. Comment on:

a the nature of the information, and
b the form of presentation.

OUTPUT	FIXED COSTS	VARIABLE COSTS	TOTAL COSTS	AVERAGE COSTS
10	300	20	320	32
20	300	120	420	21
30	300	200	500	16.6666667
40	300	260	560	14
50	300	300	600	12
60	300	320	620	10.3333333
70	300	390	690	9.85714286
80	300	460	760	9.5
90	300	620	920	10.2222222

Figure 7.4 *A spreadsheet*

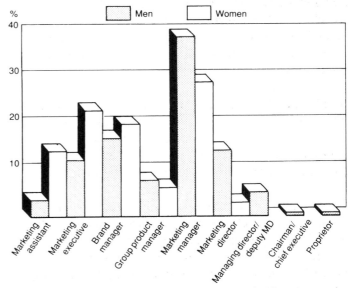

Figure 7.5 *Proportion of men and women in each job category*

Graphs are another visual way of displaying data. They show the relationship between two variables either in the form of a straight line or in the form of a curve. In particular, a graph shows how the value of one variable changes given a shift in the value of another. A graph may, for example, be constructed to show:

- sales over a time period
- the way the total cost of production varies according to the units of output produced.

If a computer is being used it can be applied as a powerful tool to present information using **graphics packages** (programs) – drawings or pictures stored in a computer are known as graphics. A graphics package might be able to show a 'three-dimensional' shape as well as reduce and enlarge an image. Some programs allow bar charts, pie charts, graphs and other characters to be built up. Figure 4.10 shows a simple set of information displayed in three different ways, for comparison.

Making sense of the data

Statistical analysis of the hard-won information enables forecasting to take place. Decision-making techniques applied to the data allow decisions to be taken with greater precision and probability of success. Statistics are, therefore, a **tool of management** which tell managers what has happened in the past and what is happening now, thus providing a more secure direction for the future.

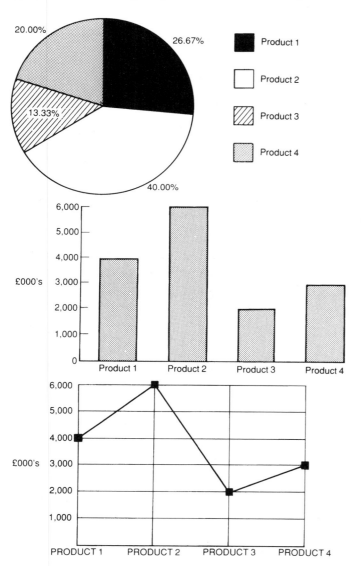

Product 1
Product 2
Product 3
Product 4

Figure 7.6 *Sales figures for four products shown as a pie chart, a bar chart and a graph, using a computer package.*

Case Study

Mintel on personal savings

Tessa – the tax-exempt special savings account – has prompted feverish promotional activity by many banks and building sociFeties. Judging by Mintel's findings (summarised in the pie chart) their efforts appear to have paid off; but whether anyone is saving more of their income than before is less than certain as many of those opening Tessa accounts have simply transferred funds from an existing savings vehicle.

1 What is meant by AB consumers?
2 Why would Mintel produce a report on Tessas?

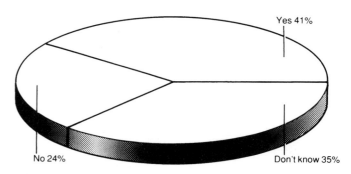

Figure 7.7 *Mintel's findings on the percentage of AB consumers intending to open a Tessa account*

3 Comment briefly on the way the results have been presented.

Market research reports

Tourists desert Mediterranean – British tourists are deserting the Mediterranean beaches and many are turning their attention to locations such as the Caribbean and the Far East.

SOURCE: *UK Tourism and Holiday Travel*, Key Note Publications, £295.

Sober reading – Consumption of low-alcohol and alcohol-free beers were set to triple by 1991: sales were to grow from 0.5 to 1.6 million barrels.
SOURCE: *Leisure Futures Report* (Quarterly), Henley Centre, £875 per annum.

Increases in home shopping – Home shopping in the UK is set to grow.
SOURCE: *Homeshopping UK* (Databrief), MSI, £110.

PR agencies need a PR job – Advertising agencies are thought to make the most genuine contribution to clients' marketing strategies and PR consultancies the least.
SOURCE: Mintel Report, £650.

1 To whom might each of the reports mentioned be of interest?
2 How might these reports be useful to them?
3 Comment on the price tags attached to each of these reports.

The preserves market

A market research company recently audited the preserves market (jam, marmalade, lemon curd and others) and calculated it to be worth £130 million a year. This agency is a retail audit organisation that collects data on items sold through supermarkets by analysing till rolls etc. It then sells the figures to interested organisations. Such figures provide a window onto the market place and enable manufacturers to work out their market share, where there are areas of growth, the performance of different products as well as to see the effects of recent marketing strategies.

The preserves market is a relatively traditional, mature market that has been suffering a 2 per cent yearly decline in volume, but it has recently begun to grow in value by about 9 per cent per year.

Preserves	% of market
Jam	55
Lemon curd	5
Marmalade	38

Division of the preserves market

Jam is divided into three categories:

- *Standard* with a minimum of 35 per cent fruit and over 60 per cent soluble solids.
- *Extra* with a minimum of 45 per cent fruit and over 50 per cent soluble solids
- *Reduced or no added sugar* with a minimum of 35 per cent fruit and 30–35 per cent soluble solids.

The most important sector of the jam market is standard jam, currently with a 76 per cent share of the total market. Extra jam is by far the most dynamic and is growing in share at 6 per cent per annum. This reflects consumers' increasing demands for premium and luxury products.

Jam market	% of market	% Trend
Standard jam	76	−1
Extra jam	15.5	+6
Reduced or no added sugar	8.5	+1

Current trends in the jam market

It is expected that the preserves market will continue to perform well. We are beginning to adopt the eating habits of the Continent, where they consume twice as many sweet preserves as we do. As the drive towards healthy, low sugar products continues, so the market for higher value premium jams will increase.

Assume you work for a preserves manufacturer.

1 Why might the type of quantitative information in the case be useful to your organisation?

2 Explain why your organisation buys information from a retail audit agency.

3 Using information extracted from the case study, construct:
- a pie-chart showing the percentage of the market taken by each type of preserve, marking the 2 per cent not accounted for as 'others'
- a bar chart showing the percentage of market attributed to each type of jam.

4 Put up a spreadsheet showing the current trends in the jam market. In five years' time, if current buying patterns continue, what will be the market share for each type of jam?

5 How might the information in the case study influence decisions?

6 To what extent does this case illustrate the importance of quantitative information to a business?

Unit assignment

Market identification

This assignment can help you provide evidence for assessment, or claim the following Core Skills:

Communication
Receive and respond to a variety of information
Present information in a variety of visual forms
Communicate in writing

Application of number
Apply numerical skills and techniques

Information technology
Use a range of technological equipment and systems

Personal skills
Use information sources
Identify and solve routine and non-routine problems
Use a range of thought processes

Before one opens a new enterprise or before a company launches a new product, it is necessary to identify the target market. This is so one can:

- Set out a marketing policy.
- Put this policy into action through action plans and targets.

Market identification is the setting up and use of research to get quantitative answers to the following questions:

1 Who are the prospects for the product? For example, they may be other businesses, men, women, children, the youth market, etc.

2 What are their characteristics? For example, age, social class, marital status, income group, wholesaler, manufacturer, retailer, etc.

3 Where do they live? For example, country, district, urban, rural, north/south/east/west, etc.

4 What are their buying habits for this type of product? For example, shops, mail-order, co-operatives, super-markets, etc.

5 How often do they currently buy or will they buy? For example, daily, weekly, monthly, yearly, etc.

6 What will they expect? Eg, after-sales service, delivery, guarantees, packaging, terms, etc.

7 How can one communicate with them? What media are they likely to see or read? Local or national coverage?

8 What is the total potential market? What percentage can be captured and over what period?

The list above highlights many of the important quantitative areas that you will need to look at when researching into market identification.

Task

You are just about to set up a small business of your own selling pizzas. You want to start off by producing three or four popular pizza toppings for deep pan and short crust pizzas. You must identify the market for pizzas by considering in depth each of the eight factors highlighted above. You will need to do some primary research of your own interviewing potential prospects for the product. You should also so some library research to look at the wider market for pizzas and fast food. You will also benefit from interviewing existing owners of pizza and other fast food premises.

In your assignment use your research to identify:
- the size of the market for pizzas (value and volume)
- the type of customer likely to buy a pizza
- the price which consumers will pay for a pizza
- the costs of producing a pizza
- your projections for turnover and profitability.

Use a spreadsheet and graphics to show how demand for pizzas would be affected by changes in the price charged to consumers.

Present your findings as a written report, incorporating print-outs from the spreadsheets and graphics.

chapter **8** UNDERSTANDING CUSTOMER BEHAVIOUR

I n this chapter we set out to show that no modern organisation, whether it be in the private or the public sector, can afford to disregard the preferences or views of its customers. In order to achieve objectives, the organisation has to discover what existing and potential customers really want. This requires a thorough understanding of human behaviour patterns and trends, coupled with a logical approach to market research activities.

Little more than forty years ago – immediately following the Second World War – there was rationing of food and many other goods. There was not much choice, and incomes were generally low. Since then there has been a massive expansion of product ranges, and the average income has risen faster than prices of the basic necessities of life. We have entered the 'age of the consumer'.

· UNDERSTANDING CUSTOMER BEHAVIOUR ·

The process of buying a good or service is not as simple as it might at first appear. A customer does not usually make a purchase without thinking carefully about his or her requirements. Wherever there is choice, **decisions** are involved and these are influenced by complex motives. An organisation that understands *why* customers make particular decisions, *who* buys, *what* they buy, and *how* they buy, can design products to attract the attention of consumers, cater more closely for their needs – and thereby become more profitable.

Task

Think of the last item or service you purchased. Describe *what* you bought, *why* you bought it and *how* you bought it. Why might the knowledge of this be useful for the supplier?

Customers can be divided into two distinct types:

● consumers, and
● organisations.

Consumer markets are made up of individuals who purchase items for personal or domestic consumption, typically from **retailers**. The purchases can, for example, be goods with a short 'shelf life', manufactured for immediate consumption (such as food and confectionery) or durable goods with a longer life and which are bought less frequently (such as cars and video recorders).

Organisational markets consist of buyers who purchase goods and services to use towards the production of other goods or services. In this category we can mention goods with a pattern of frequent purchase but limited life (such as chemicals, stationery and lubricants) and durable goods with a longer life (such as machinery and equipment). These are, of course, just examples.

Some organisations provide goods or services for both consumer and organisational markets. A motor retailer may sell cars to private customers as well as commercial vehicles (vans and trucks) to businesses.

Consumers

If an organisation is to match appropriate products with a group of consumers, it must have fairly detailed knowledge of **economic**, **social and cultural differences** in consumer behaviour. For example:

- Different consumers are able to afford different types of products.
- Some consumers might be offended if offered particular products.
- Products vary considerably between the regions.

Case Study

Party, party, party

At a time when airlines are struggling to win passengers, an older rival is building up steam. Sea cruising, once the province of the leisured rich, is booming.

The typical passenger booking a cruise today is successful, in his or her mid-thirties and looking for a good time. In response to this trend, ships have been transformed into floating fun palaces. Discos with laser lights and lavish floor shows have replaced a game of whist on the sun-deck. Gambling is an additional attraction. Customers also want shorter breaks – three to five days is the fastest growing segment of this holiday market.

1 If you were a cruise operator, given the nature of the market indicated, how and where would you reach this particular type of consumer?

2 Where else is there a market for cruises? Are there other groups of consumers for whom you could gear particular types of cruises? How would you do this?

Economic factors

A group of factors which clearly affect consumer behaviour are the **economic determinants** of **consumer demand**.

At the top of the list of determinants is probably the **real disposable incomes** available to consumers to spend on goods and services. An increase in real incomes (that is, after inflation has been taken into account) generally increases the demand for goods and services.

A second economic determinant is the relative price of a **substitute product** whose purchase might be preferred or seen as better value for money.

Thirdly, the **size of a population**, or its composition, can affect the demand for products. For example, how many elderly people are there in the market-place, and how many infants?

Tastes, fashions and habits, too, constantly influence the pattern of demand for goods and services. Think of how the markets vary for beverages such as instant tea and chocolate drinks, 'green' products, satellite televisions, CDs, frozen confectionery products, and so on.

Finally, **government measures** in areas such as credit controls and safety requirements influence the demand for a host of commodities.

Task

Think of a number of products that are currently in fashion. Comment briefly on the intended market for each, and how they are promoted.

Social factors

A provider of products or services must be interested in what inspires a customer's **individual motivation** to purchase a particular type of commodity. In Chapter 13 we looked at the work of Abraham Maslow who developed a hierarchical picture of human needs. As well as relating such needs to motivation and behaviour at work, it is also possible to relate them to purchasing behaviour. Let us look at the five broad categories of need:

- *Physiological needs* are concerned with acquiring food, shelter and clothing.
- *Safety and security needs* are concerned with physical

well-being and the need for protection. If these needs are threatened by events such as increased car-thefts and burglaries, then manufacturers can develop appropriate products.

- *Love needs* centre on the desire for acceptance. Purchases are linked to wanting to belong to a community, and examples are a barbecue apparatus or a football strip.
- *Esteem needs* stem from a desire for status, for a sense of achievement and for respect for one's accomplishments. This might lead to a lavish life-style and the possession of prestigious items such as an expensive car, a sauna, a swimming pool, a box in a stand at a football ground etc.
- *Self-actualisation needs* are concerned with full personal development and individual creativity. To achieve this level individuals try to use all their creative skills and capacities.

The implications of Maslow's system are easy to perceive as different products and services are related to different needs. It is noticeable that in Western societies there are far more products and services related to higher needs than in poorer countries. Such a theory also helps to bear the consumer more closely in mind when undertaking advertising and marketing activities.

Task

Identify two products which you feel would appeal to each of the needs in Maslow's hierarchy.

Another theory which seeks to explain the behaviour of consumers is the **self-image theory**. The 'self-image' is an individual's thoughts about himself or herself as a person of a certain type. There are various ways to maintain and enhance this image, and in particular the individual makes choices of car, music, clothing and places to shop which fit into his or her perception of 'self'. By discovering how consumers wish themselves to be perceived, organisations can design, promote and retail goods that are consistent with the image sought. For example, the Rover Group recently altered the nature of its advertising to try to match its

products (that is, the way they are perceived) more closely with the 'self-image' of the prospective purchasers.

Task

Identify a number of products that you have recently purchased which match your own self-image.

Closely related to self-image is the **personality** of the consumer. Considering customers with similar personalities, it may be possible to divide up the market on the basis of such stereotypes. For example, various models of cars, records and fashion products all reflect the personality traits of customers.

Task

Which newspaper you read regularly tends to reflect your personality. Make a list of national papers and indicate the sort of personality to which you feel each paper is likely to appeal.

Cultural factors

Culture encompasses standard patterns of behaviour and plays an important role in shaping our purchasing patterns. It stems from the traditions, beliefs and values of the community in which we live. For example, our religious beliefs, our attitudes towards alcohol, the food we eat and the importance of the family are all part of our culture. Though a nation may be characterised by one dominant culture, there may be a series of sub-cultures existing within it. Sub-cultures are important for organisations that wish to target their output to those who share the values of that particular sub-culture – for example, youth markets, ethnic groups and senior citizens.

Socio-economic factors

One way of meeting customer choices is to divide the customers into **socio-economic groupings** based on the types of jobs they do. Dividing people into classes is called **social stratification** and is a controversial issue. The underlying assumption is that, as particular jobs tend to have certain life-styles attached, if the market can be divided, more appropriate products and services can be targeted towards particular groups.

One of the best-known classifications used to divide the UK is shown in Figure 8.1. In this scheme, an exclusive product would be advertised to groups A and B because they would be more likely to be able to afford it.

Whatever one may think of the fairness or correctness of socio-economic grouping, it does provide a reliable picture of the relationship between occupation and income for the purposes of marketing. Members of each group have similar priorities which influence their wants and needs. For example, we could expect those in groups A, B and C1 to spend some of their income on private education, private health care, a new car, antiques etc.,

whereas those in groups C2, D and E spend a significantly higher proportion of their income on necessities.

Over recent years organisations have paid increasing attention to the life-styles of their consumers. A life-style is a behaviour pattern adopted by a particular community or a sub-section of it. Products can be developed and targeted to support such a life-style. For example, someone upwardly mobile and ambitious would be seeking an affluent life-style and a higher material standard of living. The UK 'yuppy' is reputed to be young (24–35), well-educated, professional and upwardly mobile.

Case Study

Launching new products

A feature of all markets is the development and launch of new products. Here are a few examples.

Cadbury introduced 'Strollers' as an 'adult, functional' product in the bagged chocolate 'selfline' sector of the chocolate market.

Whitbread launched Boddington's Draughtflow, a draught ale in cans, and is planning a similar product for Murphy's Irish Stout. A successful launch opens up other possibilities for Whitbread's wide range of cask-conditioned ales.

Pepsi-Cola is selling 1.5 litre plastic bottles in six-bottle crates for the first time, to match the industry trend to package colas in larger units.

Socio-economic group	Social 'class'	Most likely types of occupation	Examples
A	'Upper' or 'upper-middle'	High managerial Administrative Professional	Surgeon Director of large company
B	'Middle'	Intermediate managerial Professional Administrative	Bank manager Headteacher Surveyor
C1	'Lower-middle'	Supervisory Junior managerial Junior administrative Clerical	Bank clerk Nurse Teacher
C2	'Skilled working'	Skilled manual workers	Joiner Welder Foreman
D	'Working'	Semi-skilled Unskilled	Driver Postman Porter
E	Lowest subsistence level	Low-paid Unemployed	Casual worker State pensioner

Figure 8.1 *An example of a socio-economic classification*

Wander, makers of Ovaltine, is offering Cafetino, a complete coffee drink available in mint chocolate and orange blends with milk and sugar. It only needs hot water.

Alfa Romeo launched its fastest ever car – the 164 Cloverleaf. This completed their range and was designed to become the flagship of Alfa Romeo's saloon range.

1 *Comment on the consumer needs intended to be met by each of the products outlined above. In each case mention the economic determinants of consumer demand, appeal to motivation, self-image, the personality of the consumer, culture, social stratification and life-style.*

2 *Briefly explain why consideration of each of these factors is important before launching a new product.*

Organisational behaviour

In an organisational market, organisations buy products and services which are used directly or indirectly in the production of other goods or services or which are stocked in order to be resold.

Think of a complex manufactured product such as a motor car. It is made up of numerous parts obtained from several suppliers. We tend to think of a product as a single item when, in fact, it really represents the culmination of a process that has brought together a vast number of items. A car typically has about 12 000 parts in it, and probably only half of these are produced by the car manufacturer, who buys the other 6000 from other companies. The organisations supplying these parts will also have suppliers from whom they buy raw materials and components.

Whereas a consumer market might have a potential 56 million users, the total number of organisations in the UK is fewer than three million and the likelihood is that the product on offer will appeal to only a very small number of organisations. However, items to be used in a production line may be ordered in large quantities.

The demand for organisational products and services is called **derived demand** because the amounts purchased are determined by the demand for related goods and services. For example, the amount of flex required by a manufacturer of electric lawnmowers depends on the demand for new lawnmowers, which must therefore be estimated by the flex manufacturer. The organisational supplier is aware that he is supplying goods to help produce someone else's product so that the demands of the final consumer can be met.

Being dependent on derived demand can have serious consequences for a business. Organisational markets are subject to business cycles, and the demand for industrial products and services may fluctuate violently when the pace of business activity changes. The recessionary business conditions in 1991, for example, saw severe cutbacks in the derived demand for inputs, and this led to a record number of business failures, with rising unemployment as a result. (See also Chapter 3.)

Companies supplying goods in organisational markets face constantly changing circumstances which are often called **contingency factors**. Organisations need to be constantly aware of these factors. Here are a few examples:

- The supplier is usually expected to provide credit facilities for the customer.
- There is a risk of a takeover by the customer.
- Buyers deliberately exercise their buying power to influence the conditions of supply – such as discounts.
- Large companies often use small companies as suppliers simply in order to exercise their buying power.
- Buyers in any size of company may deliberately pursue a policy of delaying payment for goods and services received.
- There is a risk of a supplier becoming dependent on one customer.

Task

Working in groups, discuss the dangers associated with each of the contingency factors mentioned in the text.

Vertical and horizontal markets

Organisational markets are described as either vertical or horizontal. Where a product or service is used by only a small number of buyers, it has a **vertical market**. For example, there are very few buyers or passenger aircraft or electric locomotives. A product has a **horizontal market** if it is purchased by many kinds of organisations in different industries – examples are stationery and lubricants.

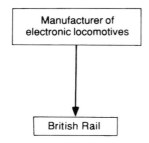

Figure 8. 2 *A vertical market*

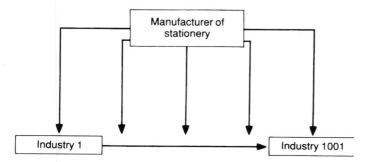

Figure 8.3 *A horizontal market*

Ikangi Products

Ikangi Products is a large multi-national electronics business which was founded in South Korea some 15 years ago. It is supported by considerable investment from a variety of south-east Asian interests, which includes widespread Japanese involvement. Ikang,i today, is one of the major players in the electronics business and has developed strong market shares in a variety of product sectors.

Ikangi produces many different types of electronic products, some of which are sold under brand names which are recognised by and found in every household. Apart from a small factory in Portsmouth which produces personal stereos, all Ikangi's production is overseas.

With so much competition in the electronics industry, only a slow prospect of growth, and with the UK exchange rate falling. Ikangi is seriously considering its strategies for the UK. One option which the company is considering, and which would help with the exchange rate problem, is to take the competition head-on by establishing a large manufacturing base in an area of economic need within the UK. This could then be used as a base for European operations.

Though the recent recession has clearly changed the trading situation for many companies within the UK, Ikangi believes that it would be more appropriate to project trends for the next ten years by looking at the period from 1980 to 1990 rather than considering figures which relate to just the last two or three years. The following figures about national income have been researched:

	1980	1985	1990
Gross National Product (GNP) £ billion	200.8	309.4	481.8
Population – million	56.3	56.6	57.4
GNP per head – £	3567	5466	8394
GDP volume – 1985 = 100	90.7	100	116.2
% shares of GDP			
Primary industry	11.8	12.5	6.6
Secondary industry	32.9	29.8	30.0
Tertiary industry	55.3	57.7	63.4

Ikangi has also identified various elements of consumer expenditure and quality of life within the UK which they feel it would be useful to analyse further. These include:

	1980	1985	1990
Dwellings per '000 population	381	394	407
TV sets (licences) per '000 pop	325	331	342
Private cars per '000	269	298	344
Telephone connections per '000	312	363	434
Refrigerators per '000	94.8	97.6	98.0
Consumer expenditure per head at 1990 prices:			
food	712	714	730
alcohol	368	368	379
durable goods	340	444	582
energy	335	357	388

From 1986–1990 annual volume growth in the UK as an average per year was 2.4 per cent which compared with 2.4 per cent in France, 2,6 per cent in Germany, 2.5 per cent in Italy, 2.3 per cent in the US and 4.1 per cent in Japan.

You work in the marketing department of the distributors for Ikangi Products in the UK. The distributors are part-owned by Ikangi. You have been asked to use the information to answer the following questions.

1 Use the economic information to comment upon the changing nature of the UK economy between 1980 and 1990. What does such information indicate about opportunities for manufacturers?

2 Look at the figures which relate to consumer expenditure and quality of life. Analyse the percentage levels of change and growth. What implications would the period from 1980 to 1990 have on the prospect for growth for the mid to late 90s?

3 Choose an appropriate format (report, memo, verbal presentation) and tell Ikangi about the conclusions that can be drawn from the figures.

Element assignment

London Zoo

This assignment can help you provide evidence for assessment, or claim the following Core Skills outcomes:

Communication
Present information in a variety of visual forms
Communicate in writing

Personal skills
Identify and solve routine and non-routine problems
Apply a range of skills and techniques to develop a variety of ideas in the creation of new/modified products, services or situations

Imagine that you work for an advertising agency that has been commissioned to produce an advertisement for London Zoo. The following notes give you some background information showing why the zoo needs to be advertised. The brief that follows gives you guidance on how to design the advertisement.

The following newspaper article appeared in the popular press.

LONDON ZOO – safe, but for how long?

London Zoo is safe for the near future, thanks to a gift of one million pounds and a further £330 000 from the Save Our Zoo campaign.

However, according to the Director of the zoo, 'there is still a long way to go to turn the zoo's survival into a permanent reality.'

Visitors to the zoo have steadily dropped over the last five years, reflecting the declining popularity of zoos in general.

The Chairman of the zoo commented: 'If we could only double the number of visitors, our long-term future would be secure. There are many exciting things to see and do at the zoo, that people are just unaware of. The zoo closure can only be prevented by an effective advertising campaign.'

Task
The senior executive of your advertising agency has asked you to handle the London Zoo account. She has set out some clear guidelines for you to follow. You will need to produce:

- A brief written report (two sides of A4) showing the thinking behind the promotion. This should include:
  a Target market
  b Market segmentation
  c Media type
- The advertisement itself.

Use the following flow-chart to help you with your work:

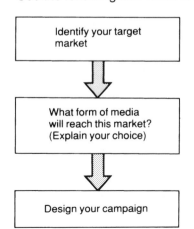

Who are you trying to attract to the zoo?
– What type of person?
– What age?
– Where will they come from?

Choose from:
– Poster campaign
– TV advert
– Radio advert

Think of and design an appropriate advertisement (Transcript or sketch and slogan)

chapter **9** THE MARKETING ENVIRONMENT AND PRACTICAL MARKETING ACTIVITIES

Organisations operate in a broad environment in which they have to respond sensitively to social, political, economic and consumer issues. At the same time they have to satisfy the expectations of their shareholders and respond with appropriate action to counter competitive influences.Marketing must therefore not only take into account ethical issues such as consumerism and environmentalism but also satisfy the objectives of the organisation and the demand of the market.

In this chapter we look at competition and competition policy. In doing so we look at the legal framework relating to competition. The chapter also proceeds to analyse the responsibilities that organisations have to consumers, ecological and environmental responsibilities and other influences upon marketing activities.

This chapter concludes by looking at the practical aspects of marketing activities. Marketing is the essential point of contact between every organisation and its clients. It is the key strand of the business fabric – it runs through everything an organisation does. Using information from the market-place, organisations segment the market into different groups of customers and then use the ingredients of the marketing mix to suit the precise requirements of each market segment. As markets are dynamic, the marketing mix requires constant adjustment and management to suit the changing requirements of each group of customers. Throughout this chapter tasks and case analysis encourage you to relate the marketing activities highlighted to your own experience of the market-place.

· COMPETITION POLICY ·

Organisations in modern society frequently have to compete. Petrol stations compete to make sales, as do fast food outlets, cafes and pubs. Colleges compete for students and hospitals compete to provide patient services.

Competition is an essential element in the efficient working of markets. It encourages enterprise, productivity and choice. In doing so, it enables consumers to buy the goods they want at the best possible price. By encouraging efficiency in industry, competition in the domestic market also contributes to our international competitiveness.

The overall aim of United Kingdom competition policy is to encourage and enhance the competitive process. When that process is adversely affected, the law provides a number of ways in which the situation can be examined and, if necessary, altered.

Task

Do you think that competition should operate freely in all markets? Can you think of exceptions to the general principle? Explain why you think these exceptions should exist.

Competition is not regarded as an end in itself. With some exceptions, there is no assumption that a particular type of action or a particular situation is necessarily wrong. The legislation provides for case-by-case examination, and only when a matter is found to be, or likely to be, against the public interest can it be prohibited.

Task

Search the national press for examples of cases where actions by companies were thought to be anti-competitive. Why were the actions regarded as against the public interest? What were the government rulings in each case?

The administrative framework

Overall responsibility for competition policy is in the hands of the **Secretary of State for Trade and Industry**. Working with the Secretary of State are two bodies specifically set up to deal with matters affecting competition. They are the **Office of Fair Trading** (OFT) and the **Monopolies and Mergers Commission**. Both organisations are given specific roles and responsibilities by Act of Parliament. The **Restrictive Practices Court** also has an important role.

The Director General of the OFT acts very much as a watchdog, keeping an eye on commerce as a whole, carrying out initial enquiries, calling for in-depth investigations by the Commission and, depending on the response of the Secretary of State to the Commission's recommendations, asking companies for specific undertakings and then watching them. He or she also maintains a register of **restrictive trading agreements** and may refer these agreements to the Restrictive Practices Court.

The Commission has no power to initiate enquiries. It investigates specific markets or the actions of companies in detail and decides what is and what is not in the public interest.

The final authority to prohibit actions rests either with the Secretary of State or with the Restrictive Practices Court

in the case of restrictive agreements or the imposition of minimum resale prices.

• RESPONSIBILITIES TO CONSUMERS •

Any product or service that is provided to the market-place must meet certain standards. Some of these standards are established by law, some by voluntary codes of practice within an industry, and others are set by individual businesses.

Before the 1960s, consumers had very little protection under the law. They had to rely on their own common sense. The Latin expression *caveat emptor* – 'let the buyer beware' – applied.

Businesses supply goods or services for consumers in return for payment. The legal system exists to provide a framework within which transactions can take place, and to provide a means of settling disputes. Large or well-developed organisations often deal with relatively small consumers, so there is a need for the law to make sure that this inequality in bargaining power is not abused.

Task

When did you last make a complaint to a shop about something you had bought? How did you make the complaint? What rights were you aware of? What was the outcome of your complaint?

How do disputes arise?

Damaged or poor quality goods. It quite often happens that purchased goods do not function properly. They may have been damaged in transit or they may be of poor quality and not suitable for the purpose for which they are intended.

Goods not matching descriptions. Goods may not be as described on the packaging or in an advertisement.

Manufacturer's negligence. Faulty manufacturing processes or bad design might lead to the personal injury

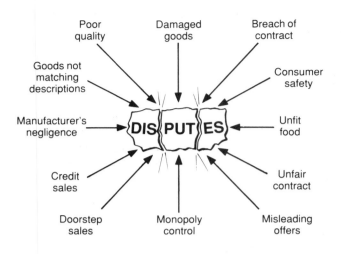

Figure 9.1 *Some causes of disputes*

of the consumer or damage to other goods. For example, a faulty electrical component might cause fire.

Breach of contract. This could include the failure of the supplier to supply, a failure to meet the required quality, or a failure to supply by a given date. For example, a shop selling bridal gowns might fail to supply the dress by the agreed date.

Consumer safety. Goods may not be safe and could cause injury to consumers.

Unfit food. Eating unfit food can have particularly unpleasant consequences and consumers need to be protected against this.

Misleading offers. Consumers can easily be misled by offers, bargains and their rights concerning sales items.

Unfair contracts. Contracts may contain exclusion clauses or disclaimers which might make the relationship between the buyer and the seller unreasonable. It would be unacceptable for a company to disclaim responsibility for an injury caused by its own negligence.

Doorstep sales. There need to be guidelines to protect clients who might have been intimidated into buying goods from doorstep salespeople, particularly if these goods are expensive and have been bought on credit.

Credit sales. Customers 'buying now and paying later' over an extended period leave themselves open to abuse. They could well be charged excessive interest rates, pay large administration costs or be tied to an expensive maintenance agreement.

Monopoly control. Monopolies and mergers produce a situation where one or just a few companies control a market. Lack of competition can be to the disadvantage of consumers in terms of quality and prices.

Task

Interview a selection of 20 consumers to find out the sorts of disputes they have been involved in with sellers. Do most complaints fit into a small number of headings, or do their complaints go right across a wide range of areas? What actions did consumers take in each case? Is there scope for more consumer protection? If so, what form should it take?

Legal processes of consumer protection

The consumer may need help to ensure that he or she gets a fair deal when making an exchange with an organisation. Various Acts of Parliament set out to ensure that organisations keep to their responsibilities.

The **criminal justice system** deals with cases where the laws of the country have been broken. These laws attempt to protect members of society and to punish offenders whose actions have been harmful to the community. Cases might, for example, be brought to court for dishonesty and for selling unhygienic foodstuffs. Punishments could be fines, imprisonment or both.

The **civil law** is concerned with disputes between individuals and groups. Laws have been built up over the years dealing with buying and selling activities. Laws related to contracts set out the obligations that individuals have to each other every time they enter into an agreement, while the law of **torts** protects individuals and groups from each others' actions, particularly if an individual or

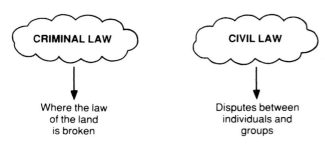

Figure 9.2 *Criminal and civil law*

group suffers injury as a result of these actions. Individuals and groups enforce their rights by suing in the civil courts.

Consumer laws

Numerous Acts of Parliament are concerned with consumer protection. Although it is not possible to know each Act in detail, it is necessary to understand the reasons for the more important Acts, and their general effects. They all create legal responsibilities for organisations.

We shall look at these Acts under three main headings (see Figure 9.3). **Competition** laws, which are concerned with creating a healthy climate of competition within the economy, are the subject of a separate section later in this chapter.

Figure 9.3 *The three divisions of consumer laws*

The provisions of credit laws cover most forms of credit transactions. Under the **Consumer Credit Act** all businesses involved in some way with credit have to be licensed by the Office of Fair Trading. Advertisements offering credit have to state the annual percentage rate of interest (APR) so that consumers can compare the true cost of one credit offer with another. It is illegal for traders to send you a credit card that you have not asked for and, if you are refused credit, you can ask for the name and address of the credit reference agency that has reported you as a bad risk. You can then put the matter to rights if the refusal has been based on false information.

We now turn to Acts covering the quality of goods or services.

The Sale of Goods Act

Sellers must provide goods that are of '**merchantable quality**' – that is, they must not be damaged or broken. Goods sold must also be **fit for the purpose** intended. If you bought a pair of shoes and they fell apart at the seams within a week, they would not have been fit for the purposes for which they were sold – serving as footwear.

Figure 9.4 *Unfit!*

Under this law you can ask for replacements if goods do not meet the requirements you specified to the seller. For example, if you bought spare parts for your car from a garage on the understanding that they were for a Mini, and found that they would only fit a larger car, you would be within your rights to ask for your money back or replacements.

The Trades Description Act

The description given of the goods forms part of the contract that the buyer makes with the seller. This Act makes it a criminal offence for a trader to describe goods falsely. A type of case frequently prosecuted under this Act is the turning back of mileometers on used cars to make them appear less used.

The main objective of the Trades Description Act is thus quite straightforward – descriptions of goods and services must be accurate. Terms like 'waterproof' and 'shrinkproof', if used, must be genuine.

sausage if it contains a certain amount of meat. Similar rules apply to items like Cornish pasties and beefburgers.

The contents of medicines are strictly controlled by this Act. Certain substances are not allowed at all.

Figure 9.5 *Won't fit!*

The Weights and Measures Act

The aim of this Act is to ensure that consumers receive the actual quantity of a product that they believe they are buying. For example, pre-packed items must have a declaration of the quantity contained within the pack. It is an offence to give 'short weight'.

The Food and Drugs Act

This Act is concerned with the contents of foodstuffs and medicines. The government needs to control this area of trading so that the public is not led into buying harmful substances. Some items have to carry warnings – tins of kidney beans, for example, must have clear instructions that they need to be boiled for a fair length of time before they can be eaten.

The Act lays down minimum contents for various foodstuffs. For example, a sausage can only be called a

---

Case Study

Food safety

Safety laws are passed both to protect employees at work, and to provide safety standards for the users of particular products.

Workers in a modern food processing plant are used to following strict procedures aimed at ensuring hygienic (i.e. germ-free) working conditions. For example, they must usually take off watches and rings, put on a hairnet and hat, a coat that is laundered daily and a pair of wellington boots. Any dressings on cuts or grazes must be replaced by metal-lined plasters that can be found by metal detectors should they fall off. There are several other rules that have to be followed.

Despite these precautions, between 1982 and 1989 the number of reported cases of food poisoning tripled to 52 700. Food manufacturers' sales and profits were hit by scare after scare, from salmonella to listeria, from botulism to bovine spongiform encephalopathy ('mad cow disease').

In January 1991 the government brought in a new Food Safety Act, giving environmental health officers the power to shut down offending premises immediately, and to seize suspect food before it reaches shops. Regulations on refrigeration temperatures, chemical residues in food and the use of certain technologies have been tightened, and from now on all food premises will be compulsorily registered. Staff training has to improve. Ministers have the power to oversee the introduction of new technologies such as irradiation. Perishable foods must carry 'eat by' rather than 'sell by' dates.

The EC has decreed that member governments must achieve adequate standards of inspection at the point of production by 1993.

1 *Why is food safety so important?*
2 *Could it be left to manufacturers and retailers of foodstuffs to regulate their own trades and industry?*

---

3 Why is it necessary to update good laws constantly?

4 Comment on the likely effect of the new laws on:

a the production of food

b the sale of food

c the quality of food

d the price of food

e consumers

f the number of food producers in the industry

g the use of new technology in food production.

Sources of consumer help and advice

There are numerous sources of help and advice for consumers, providing opportunities for people to follow up complaints and grievances. It is therefore important to consider carefully the circumstances of each grievance before deciding on the most appropriate way forward. Through these channels, consumers and bodies representing consumer interests are able to put pressure on organisations to meet their responsibilities in full.

The **Office of Fair Trading**, a government body, was set up to look after the interests of consumers and traders. It publishes a wide variety of information, and encourages businesses to issue codes of practice to raise the standards of their service. A trader who persists in breaking the law must give an assurance that he will mend his ways. As we saw in Chapter 2, the OFT also keeps an eye on anti-competitive practices, monopolies and mergers and might suggest changes in the law.

The **National Consumer Council** represents the consumer to the government, nationalised industries, public services and businesses. It also carries out research and publishes its recommendations.

Citizens' Advice Bureaux, of which there are some 900 in various parts of the country, cover many aspects of day-to-day life. A CAB will often agree to act as a 'go-between' in disputes between traders and consumers.

Local authorities have **trading standards departments** that investigate complaints about misleading offers or prices, inaccurate weights and measures, and consumer credit.

Environmental health departments enforce legislation covering health aspects of food – for example, unfit food, or unhygienic storage, preparation or serving of food.

Nationalised industries are vast monopolies with the potential to put consumers in a weak position. **Consumer and consultative councils** represent consumers and aim to prevent the misuse of monopoly power.

Standard setters

The **British Standards Institution** is financed by voluntary subscriptions and government grants. Its primary concern is with setting up standards that are acceptable to both manufacturers and consumers. Goods of a certain standard are allowed to bear the BSI kitemark, showing consumers that the product has passed the appropriate tests.

Professional and trade associations promote the interests of their members as well as the development of a particular product or service area. In order to protect consumers their members often agree to abide by voluntary codes of practice. These codes aim to keep up standards and will often set up funds to safeguard consumers' money. For example, the Association of British Travel Agents (ABTA) will refund money to holidaymakers should a member company fail.

Independent consumer groups and the media

The **Consumers' Association** examines goods and services offered to the public and publishes the results of its research in *Which?* This magazine was founded in 1957 and has developed a circulation of over half a million. It has become an invaluable source of information for consumers.

The National Federation of Consumer Groups is a coordinating body for voluntary local consumer groups. Local groups survey local goods and services, publish reports and campaign for changes.

There is no doubt that, when consumers' rights and obligations are abused or when dangerous goods are brought into the market-place, feelings run high. The media – newspapers, television and radio – increasingly become involved in campaigns for changes. High TV viewing figures, in particular, clearly demonstrate the public's interest.

Case Study

Ice-creams found to contain bacteria

The report below is adapted from an article in *The Independent* newspaper on 4 August 1989.

'Nearly half of the ice-creams tested by a consumer group contained levels of bacteria which were unsafe. Eight could have caused food poisoning.

'In the study, published by *Which?* magazine, 21 ice-creams were unsatisfactory. Seven soft ones, sold from vans, had bacteria counts way over the government safety standards.

'Inspectors bought ice-cream cones from 23 vans and 24 shops and cafes. The ice-cream included scoops, wrapped blocks and soft ice-cream. The soft ice-cream was the most contaminated. Twelve out of twenty-eight soft ice-cream cones had high bacteria levels. Nineteen of the scoops failed the bacteria count test. Wrapped ice-cream caused no problems, passing the test with flying colours.'

1 *Name the organisation that publishes* Which?
2 *What does this organisation do?*
3 *How did* Which? *magazine:*
   a *collect information about different types of ice-cream*
   b *make the public aware of the findings?*
4 *How is the* Which? *report likely to affect:*
   a *ice-cream consumers*
   b *ice-cream retailers*
   c *ice-cream manufacturers?*
5 *How does government try to maintain standards in the food industry?*

· OTHER INFLUENCES UPON MARKETING ACTIVITIES ·

The **Advertising Standards Authority** is an independent body that exercises control over all advertising except that on radio and television. The Authority draws up its own codes which it uses to ensure that advertisements are 'legal, decent, honest and truthful.' Advertisements should be prepared with a sense of responsibility to both consumers and society and conform to the principles of fair competition. For example, a number of complaints were made to the ASA over a campaign by Rover to extol the virtues of wood panelling on the Rover 820 Se. Suspended by the main body of the text appeared a box with the words 'A woman, a dog and a walnut tree, the more you beat them, the better they'll be'. At Rover they insisted that the advertisement was only put there to inject humour!

The ASA were unconvinced of the cholesterol-reducing properties of the showpiece launch of Common Sense Oat Bran Flakes. It brought in a team of top nutritional scientists amidst fears that the product and the advertisement might create needless worry for consumers.

The **Chartered Institute of Marketing** has its own Code of Practice which members are required to adhere to as a condition of their membership. The code refers to professional standards of behaviour in securing and developing business, and demands honesty and integrity of conduct. The **British Code of Advertising Practice** is supported by advertisers, agencies and the media whose representatives make up the Code of Advertising practice Committee. The Code sets out the rules which those in the advertising industry agree to follow. It also indicates to those outside advertising that there are regulations designed to ensure that advertisements can be trusted.

Voluntary and statutory controls, and the formation of active and strong pressure groups which often gain popular support from the media, have helped to develop a changing climate for marketing activity. Organisations today can no longer disregard groups of consumers or wider environmental issues in which they should be involved. They have to show greater sensitivity to their many publics.

Task

Here is a task that is best tackled by a group. It involves looking closely at a particular product, finding an appropriate market and deciding how to sell the product in that market. Material has been kindly supplied by East Midlands Electricity PLC.

Introduction

Everyone knows that East Midlands Electricity sells electricity to firms and households, but do you realise that it also sells appliances which use electricity?

Can you list ten products which are likely to be sold from East Midlands Electricity shops?

In this activity you are asked to help East Midlands Electricity to promote **one** of its popular products – either cordless kettles or satellite dishes.

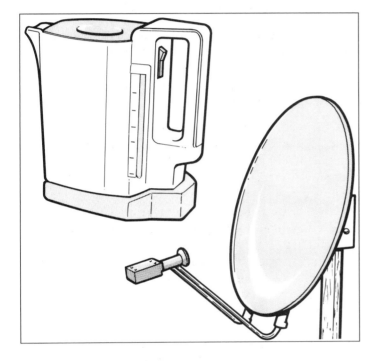

First you must do a SWOT analysis of one of the products. Then you must decide who you are going to sell the product to and how you will reach them. Lastly, you may like to produce a creative advertisement for the product.

What is a SWOT?

SWOT stands for:

- strengths
- weaknesses
- opportunities
- threats

When you are marketing a product you should work out what are its **strengths** and **weaknesses** – then try to work out what are the **opportunities** that will help you to promote the product and the **threats** likely to be faced by your product in the near future.

For example, if Rowntree wanted to do a SWOT analysis of its product Smarties, it might say that:

- *its strengths include* – the fact that everyone knows what a Smartie is; that children love the different colours; that they are not expensive; the packets look attractive in the shop, and so on
- *its weaknesses might include* – they are primarily a children's sweet, rather than for adults; they have been around a long time (perhaps people are getting bored with them)
- *its opportunities are* – new European markets for Smarties are opening up, not just in the European Community, but also in Poland, Hungary and so on; blue Smarties are new and exciting
- *its threats might include* – the wide range of new sweets being sold; the arrival of M&M's and competition from European chocolate manufacturers, and so on

What Rowntree needs to do then is promote and improve strengths, play down and cut out weaknesses, make the most of opportunities, and be aware of and respond to threats.

Do your SWOT analysis

Do your SWOT analysis for EME cordless kettles **or** satellite dishes. Can you list **three** strengths, **three** weaknesses, **three** opportunities and **three** threats? Decide how you will:

- maximise the strengths
- minimise the weaknesses
- make the most of the opportunities
- reduce the threats.

Use the SWOT analysis sheet on page 214.

Who are you selling to?

You need to be able to identify your **target** market. This is the group of people you think will be interested in your product or service and who have the money to spend on it.

- Try to identify the target audience for your chosen product. You will probably target two or three groups to concentrate on. An example of a target group might be single women in the 18–24 year age-group on high income.
- What type of media will be most suitable for reaching the target audience you have chosen?

Guidelines for promotions

To help you choose the most effective media for your promotions, consider the following guidelines. You will have detailed costs of these media outlets, and you should

TARGET CUSTOMERS
PRODUCT

STATUS	AGE	INCOME H–HIGH L–LOW	TARGET AUDIENCE	SUITABLE MEDIA
MALE (MARRIED) NO CHILDREN	18 – 24	H / L		
	25 – 45	H / L		
	OVER 45	H / L		
FEMALE (MARRIED) NO CHILDREN	18 – 24	H / L		
	25 – 45	H / L		
	OVER 45	H / L		
MALE (MARRIED) + CHILDREN	18 – 24	H / L		
	25 – 45	H / L		
	OVER 45	H / L		
FEMALE (MARRIED) + CHILDREN	18 – 24	H / L		
	25 – 45	H / L		
	OVER 45	H / L		
MALE (SINGLE)	18 – 24	H / L		
	25 – 45	H / L		
	OVER 45	H / L		
FEMALE (SINGLE)	18 – 24	H / L		
	25 – 45	H / L		
	OVER 45	H / L		

MEDIA PLAN
PRODUCT

MEDIA		£ COST	JAN	FEB	MAR	APR	MAY	JUN	JUL	AUG	SEP	OCT	NOV	DEC	SUB-TOTAL COSTS	COMMENTS
TELEVISION (CENTRAL AREA)	30 SECOND TV COMMERCIAL OFF PEAK	600														
	30 SECOND TV COMMERCIAL ON PEAK OCT, NOV, DEC, MAR, APR, MAY	4,000														
	30 SECOND TV COMMERCIAL OFF PEAK	400														
	30 SECOND TV ON PEAK JAN, FEB, JUN, JUL, AUG, SEP	3,000														
LOCAL RADIO	30 SECOND SPOT	100														
NATIONAL PRESS	ONE INSERTION PER NEWSPAPER	5,000														
LOCAL PRESS	ONE INSERTION PER NEWSPAPER	500														
FREE TRADE PRESS	ONE INSERTION PER NEWSPAPER	200														
ELECTRICITY ACCOUNT INSERTS	ONE FOR EACH DOMESTIC CUSTOMER PER QUARTER	30,000														
DIRECT MAILING	1000 PACKAGES DELIVERED BY THE POST OFFICE (SELECTED ADDRESSES)	450														
	1000 PACKAGES HAND-DELIVERED (SELECTED AREAS)	300														
TELEPHONE SALES	PER HUNDRED CALLS	10														
EXHIBITIONS	SMALL	250														
	MEDIUM	1,500														
	LARGE	4,000														
LEAFLETS	PER THOUSAND	250														
SHOP DISPLAYS	76 SHOPS	10,000														

SWOT ANALYSIS
PRODUCT

STRENGTHS	WEAKNESSES
OPPORTUNITIES	THREATS

make a sensible selection to suit your chosen product. This will be your **media plan**.

Television. In order to have a meaningful TV campaign you need at least ten on-peak and twenty off-peak spots in any one month. Some months are cheaper than others. Do you feel that spots during particular programmes are more desirable (e.g. Coronation Street)?

Local radio. For maximum effectiveness you need 50 spots per month. This medium is particularly effective with the 16–25 years age-group and has high listening ratings during 'drive time'.

Press. Which newspapers and magazines would you use?

Electricity account inserts. Each quarter of the year, 1.8 million customers receive an electricity bill, which gives an excellent opportunity to include promotional literature (the postage is already paid by the accounts department).

Direct mailing. This is an excellent means of communicating with small customer groups (e.g. recent purchasers of cars, videos, microwave cookers) whose addresses can be readily obtained from existing sources. Hand delivery of direct mail can be employed. These will not be personally addressed, but posted through letter-boxes of everyone in a selected area. This is therefore suitable for products that have a wider appeal.

Telephone sales. A member of staff is employed to phone direct to the customer.

Shop displays. This is a facility in all 76 shops to display products.

Exhibitions. The company may take part in local or national exhibitions, building its own stands, staffed by trained advisers who can promote the various appliances featured.

Leaflets. These are a very useful promotional aid which a potential customer can take home, to help their decision whether to buy after visiting a shop or an exhibition.

Producing a creative advertisement

Can you, as a group, produce an advertisement for a newspaper or magazine?

Preparing a media plan

Now that you have a clear idea about who your customers are, you should prepare a Media Plan for the next 12 months.

You can either do this on a copy of the 'MEDIA PLAN' sheet or set out your media plan on a spreadsheet.

Here are your media guidelines:

You have a budget of £750 000 to spend over 12 months. If the campaign is going to be a success you will need to use several different types of promotion. You would almost certainly use the power of television as part of your campaign. Show on your chart or spreadsheets:

- During which months you will spend your money.
- How much you will spend.
- Remember to put in your sub-totals.
- Your total spending should not exceed £750 000.

Finally you need to produce a creative advertisement

How will you present your ideas? To finish off this activity you will do a presentation to the rest of your class. This presentation should be rounded off by a Creative Advertisement – a poster, a video, a talk, or some other creative advert.

The presentation time will be divided as follows:

2 minutes To set up.
2 minutes To explain your SWOT analysis and to discuss your media plan, explaining how it will effectively communicate with your target customers.
4 minutes To present your creative execution in any way, shape or form, using chosen media.
2 minutes To pack away.

You should explain during your four minute presentation how you expect to maximise the strengths and overcome the weaknesses of the product which you have identified in the SWOT analysis.

You should also indicate how your presentation may relate to the target audience you have previously identified.

Points to consider:

- Do I need a personality? If so who?
- Do I need music? If so, what type?
- Do I need any promotional offers, e.g. interest-free credit, buy now pay later, etc?
- How do I make it interesting, amusing, memorable, credible and original?

Element assignment

Promoting a racecourse

This assignment can help you provide evidence for assessment, or claim the following Core Skills:

Communication
Receive and respond to a variety of information
Participate in oral and non-verbal communication

Information technology
Use a range of technological equipment and systems

Personal Skills
Transfer skills gained to new and changing situations
Identify and solve routine and non-routine problems
Apply a range of skills and techniques to develop a variety of ideas in the creation of new/modified products, services or situations
Use a range of thought processes

You work for the promotions department of a small racecourse. Recently profits have deteriorated due to (a) the general economic recession and (b) the continued high level of taxation, including VAT on racing.

However, the general manager has recently been heartened by a survey produced by the Racecourse Association (RCA). The 20 000 questionnaires revealed that 60 per cent of the RCA's customers think racing provides good value for money, and that 70 per cent approve of the 'quality of general facilities and view of racing'.

The survey revealed that only football has drawn a higher proportion of the public through its turnstiles and women would rather watch racing than football, golf or motor racing.

The survey also revealed that evening racing would be popular – 78 per cent said they would prefer more evening meetings.

The survey also showed that 15–34 year olds form a smaller proportion of the racing audience than for other sports.

The survey did however destroy the myth that race going is only for the rich. The survey showed that, in fact, racing is patronised equally by people from all social classes.

Task
The racecourse general manager calls you into his office. 'Look here' he says, 'If we promote the course to a wider range of people I think we will get more support. I want you to carry out a new promotion for the racecourse using the information from the RCA survey.

Decide:

1 Who the promotion should be aimed at.
2 The best way of reaching them.
3 What we should be saying to them.
4 Any special promotions we should launch to attract a wider audience.'

'In addition, I want you to look at the results of the survey on satisfaction levels from a day at the races. These reflect closely what people think about us. Come up with a list of suggestions as to how we can improve on any weak areas. I think we also need to stress the value for money aspect. After all, we charge £20 to see six races. Compare this with £14 to see the Open or £70 to watch the British Grand Prix. Heaven knows how much it costs to watch a Premier Division football match! I would like you to come up with some ideas, covering the points outlined above. I would like to see some advertising copy or some other means of promoting the racecourse that will get these key messages over. In fact, do a 20-minute presentation to the senior managers. Make the presentation punchy and attractive.'

Carry out the task outlined above.

· THE NATURE OF COMPETITION ·

An organisation must at all times be aware of its competitors and the nature of what they are doing. There is **competition** when two or more organisations act independently to sell their products to the same group of consumers. In some markets there may be a lot of competition, signified by an abundance of products and services so that consumers have a massive choice. These markets are characterised by promotional activities and **price competition**. In other markets, competition is limited and consumers are able to choose from a limited range of products and services on offer – perhaps only one. In these circumstances consumers may feel that prices are too high – they are not getting value for their money.

Task

Look at the market for one particular type of product (e.g. cars, electricity, insurance, beer, confectionery). Comment briefly on how the organisations supplying this market behave. In particular, is there a link between the numbers of competitors in this market and prices, promotional activities and choices being offered?

Direct competition exists where organisations produce similar products and appeal to the same group of consumers. *The Daily Star* directly competes with *The Sun*; and if you want to have a wall built, all the builders in your area looking for this type of work are in direct competition.

Even when an organisation provides a unique end-product with no direct competition, it still has to consider **indirect competition**. Potential customers might examine slightly different ways of meeting the same need. Instead of buying a car they might buy a moped; instead of buying a bag of sweets they could buy a box of chocolates from a different supplier.

It is frequently argued that competition is good for consumers and organisations alike. It forces organisations to act reasonably, stimulates the market-place, increases **choice** and boosts sales. Organisations have to become **more efficient** and offer **better products** at prices acceptable to the market. As a result customers have a wider selection of goods and services and better value for money. Without competition customers would have to accept a limited range of goods and services at higher prices.

Case Study

Computers in schools

Acorn Computers recently commissioned a survey of the computer market in schools from market research company Taylor Nelson. The survey revealed that the best selling computer was the Acorn A3000 with about 30 per cent of the

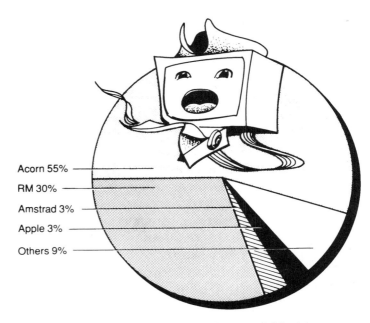

Acorn 55%
RM 30%
Amstrad 3%
Apple 3%
Others 9%

Figure 9.6 *Schools market share based on research by Acorn*

market of 106 000 classroom computers sold in 1990. Second was the Nimbus 186 selling about 20 per cent. The BBC Master was third at around 15 per cent. Nimbus came fourth again with its PC-clone 286 range capturing about 10 per cent, and fifth was Acorn with the Archimedes 400 series with around 8 per cent.

The survey was based on a telephone sample of 600 schools throughout the UK covering primary, secondary, independent and special schools banded by size, and the results are consistent with a Department for Education survey recently undertaken.

Acorn's survey showed that its market share in the last three quarters of 1990 was 55 per cent. In other words, 55 out of every 100 computers sold into schools in the UK between 1 April and 31 December 1990 were Acorn machines (see Figure 9.6). In the 'others' category, no company had more than 1 per cent of the market.

Acorn estimated that at the time of the survey there were 430 000 computers in the UK's 34 000 schools, and that 106 000 were bought in 1990.

1 *Working in groups if possible, comment on the nature of the market for school computers. Analyse:*
   a the features of Acorn machines
   b reasons for their success
   c possible reasons for the absence of major competitors other than RM

d the benefits of such a large market size for Acorn

e the direct and indirect competition for Acorn.

2 How might Acorn use the results of this survey?

3 Estimate the annual market value of the school computer market.

Market share will constantly change as new competitors and products come into the market-place. Spain used to be the most popular destination for UK tourists overseas, but in recent years its popularity has been affected by, for example, Miami, EuroDisney and Legoland. The Spanish tourist industry has had to respond to change by providing better packages to entice customers. Competition thrives upon such changes and provides consumers with greater benefits through better products.

Competition and market share can also be affected by changes in an organisation's **external environment** which may be completely beyond its control. Some changes may be cosmetic and almost imperceptible, while others – such as the takeover of a competitor, technological discoveries, high interest rates or the creation of a single European market – can have a dramatic affect on the behaviour of organisations. Every organisation should be aware not only of its own market, the actions of its competitors and new ideas and products, but also of changing business conditions within a wider environment. It should be prepared to respond with appropriate measures.

If the competitive forces within a market lead to a **trade war** between rivals, they sometimes call for a 'ceasefire' if the competition is so fierce as to make their activities virtually unprofitable. To cite a famous example, the cigarette card war was ended by mutual consent of the tobacco companies in the late 1930s. Competition may also be overcome by taking over (that is, buying) a rival – Iceland took over Bejam, Nestlé took over Rowntree Mackintosh. Competition may be reduced by engaging in joint-ventures with rivals – Courage, the Australian brewing company, recently signed a host of lager brewing and distribution agreements with the brand leaders Carlsberg.

Task

In your local library, scan the newspapers for an example illustrating competition deliberately reduced by agreement, takeover or a joint-venture in a market. Why do you think this has taken place? Indicate to what extent consumers might be affected.

· MARKET SEGMENTATION ·

Customers exhibit different needs, wants, likes and dislikes. Not every person likes the same make of motor car or has the same taste in clothes. If cost and production time were of no importance, manufacturers would make products to the exact specifications of each buyer. Unfortunately, this is not at all practicable – an organisation cannot provide a different product for each customer. On the other hand, neither can it serve its customers successfully if it groups all of their needs and wants together.

Instead of trying to serve all consumers equally, an organisation may focus its efforts on different parts of the total market-place. Within the total market-place it is possible to group customers with similar characteristics into market segments. Market segmentation is therefore a process of separating a total market into parts so that different strategies can be used for different sets of customers.

If you attempt to market a single product to the whole population, this is sometimes said to be like using a blunderbuss, firing shots to pepper the whole market-place. When it is not possible to satisfy all its customers' needs with a uniform product, an organisation will use market segmentation to divide consumers into smaller segments consisting of buyers with similar needs or characteristics, so

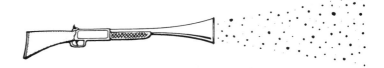

Figure 9.7 *Marketing by blunderbuss*

Figure 9.8 *Marketing by rifle – hitting the target segment*

that marketing becomes like firing a rifle instead of a blunderbuss. A rifle with an accurate sight will hit the target more efficiently, without wasting ammunition.

Case Study

Credit card services

National Westminster Bank has widened its range of credit cards, as have many other financial institutions. By dividing the market up into segments the bank is now able to provide a credit card specifically geared to the needs of identified groups of customers and, at the same time, give customers a choice. A few years ago the only credit card this bank offered was an Access Card.

National Westminster now offers four different cards:

- the regular credit card (Access or Visa) with a credit limit to suit the customer's circumstances, and an annual fee
- a Visa Primary card, with a lower annual fee and a fixed credit limit of £500
- a Mastercard, which is similar to Access and Visa but offering the facility of converting an outstanding credit balance into a fixed-term loan at any time
- a Visa Gold card, with a *minimum* credit limit of £2500.

So National Westminster has created a range of products, each providing different benefits to cater for each group of customers. Having created such a portfolio of products, the bank now has to monitor and develop each one to ensure the success of each in the market-place. It needs a **range strategy**.

1 What are the benefits of dividing a market into segments for:

Figure 9.9 *A range of credit cards is available*

a the National Westminster Bank?
b the bank's customers?
2 Explain the difference between a blunderbuss strategy and one that carefully targets a specific group of customers.
3 Chapter 8 dealt with 'assessing customer needs'. Using examples, explain how knowledge of consumer behaviour helps an organisation to segment its product range.
4 Why must an organisation monitor the success of its range strategy? What might happen if it failed to do so?

Positioning

Segmentation enables an organisation to follow **marketing objectives**. It also provides a means whereby an organisation can position its brands and product varieties in the market-place. The marketing department can, by suitable promotion, establish a particular position in the market for each brand (e.g. up-market, mid-market or down-market) and then tailor selling strategies for each position.

· THE MARKETING MIX ·

By splitting the market-place and developing strategies to position products, an organisation can choose an appropriate **marketing mix** for each target segment.

The marketing mix comprises a complex set of variables which an organisation combines in order to ensure that objectives are achieved. It includes strategic, tactical and operational elements and techniques.

The concept is usually analysed on the basis of the four P's. To meet customer needs an organisation must develop **products** to satisfy them, charge them the right **price**, get the goods to the right **place** and make the existence of the product known through its **promotion**.

'Mix' is an appropriate word to describe the marketing process. A mix is a composition of ingredients blended together to fulfil a common purpose. Every ingredient is vitally important and each depends on the others for their contributions. Just as with a cake, each ingredient is not sufficient on its own – but blended together it is possible to produce something very special. In the same way that there are a variety of cakes to suit various tastes, a marketing mix can be designed to suit the precise requirements of the market.

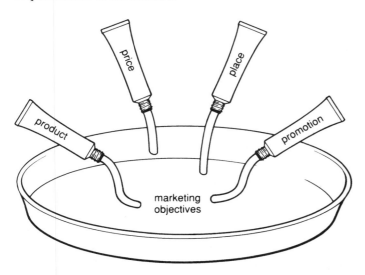

Figure 9.10 *The marketing mix*

The marketing mix must have a **time scale**. An organisation must have a plan that indicates when it expects to achieve its objectives. Some objectives will be set to be attained in the near future. Others might be medium-term (one to five years), and yet others might be visionary objectives for attainment in the longer term.

The mix must have **strategic elements**. These will involve the overall strategy of the organisation. They require considerable use of judgement and expertise and are only made by senior managers. Such decisions might involve the development of a new product or a new market strategy.

The mix must also have **tactical** or **medium-term elements**. The business environment has to be constantly monitored and decisions have to be taken according to whatever changes take place. External events might affect pricing strategies, product modifications or amendments to marketing plans.

There must also be **short-term operational elements**. These involve predictable everyday decisions such as contacts with customers, analysis of advertising copy and minor decisions about packaging.

The commitment and support of a programme of planning with sufficient resources will underlie the manipulation of the marketing mix and will ultimately determine how capable an organisation is of achieving its objectives.

Task

Choose a product you use regularly and comment briefly on:

a the nature of the **product**
b its **price**
c its availability (**place**)
d how it is **promoted**.

If you were given overall responsibility for this brand, how would you use the marketing mix to develop its core strength?

· THE PRODUCT ·

The **product** is the central point on which all marketing energies must converge. Organisations have to analyse what their products mean to their customers. People and organisations buy goods and services for a variety of reasons, and a wide range of characteristics influence the decision to buy. For example, on the surface there are often clear and tangible benefits such as:

- shape
- colour
- size
- design
- packaging
- appearance.

The intangible features are not so obvious. They may include the reputation of the producer on certain issues, such as:

- after sales service
- availability of spare parts
- customer care policy
- guarantees.

Turtle Beach, Jamaica

Task

Choose a product. List both its tangible and its intangible benefits.

At a basic level, people buy woolly jumpers to keep warm. They buy umbrellas to keep dry in the rain, and watches to tell them the time. However, human behaviour is a complex process. It is not uncommon to hear someone say 'I wouldn't be seen dead wearing one of those'. In other words, for many of us it cannot be any old jumper, umbrella or watch – it needs to be an item that fits in with a particular perception or self-image.

Products are not usually purchased to meet a single need; the ownership and use of a product involves a whole range of factors that make up the product concept.

For example, it may appear that a person chooses to holiday in the West Indies because he or she is attracted by the sand, sun and surf. However, it may come to light that the person is more concerned with 'image' – friends and associates will become aware that he or she is able to afford to holiday in the West Indies. Holidaying in the West Indies is therefore associated with a particular life-style. In the public imagination it may represent being rich and able to afford exotic things.

Product benefits can be broken down into a number of important dimensions, of which we shall consider three:

- **Generic dimensions** are the key benefits of a particular item. Shoe polish cleans shoes. Freezers store frozen food. Deckchairs provide a comfortable seat on a sunny day. Hairdressers cut and style hair.
- **The sensual dimensions** of a product are those that provide sensual benefits. These include design, colour, taste, smell and texture. A ring doughnut has a shape, appearance, texture, taste and smell all of its own. The sensual benefits of products are frequently highlighted by advertisers.
- **Extended dimensions** of a product include a wide range of additional benefits. Examples are servicing arrangements, credit facilities, guarantees, maintenance contracts and so on.

Research and development

Many people associate the **research and development** function of an organisation with the invention of new products. Whilst this is very important, the development of existing products is also significant. The task of product research and development is to combine with marketing activities to cater for the changing preferences of consumers and come up with the goods and services that will meet the needs of tomorrow's customers. Product research and development therefore goes hand in hand with market research, and considerable liaison is required between these two areas. For example, researchers will attempt to investigate all of the questions in Figure 9.11 before a final decision is made to go into production.

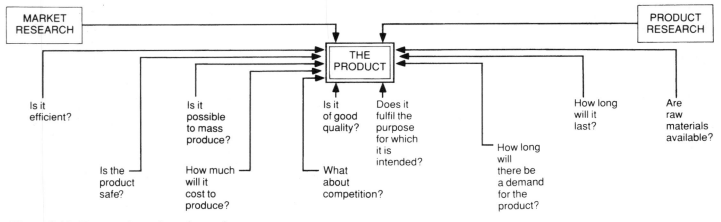

Figure 9.11 *Key questions about the product*

Imagine that you have come up with the idea of a mailbox which opens at the top, for the delivery of newspaper and post to households. The idea is that the box will be attached to the outside of front doors. Highlight areas of market and product research that will need to be covered before going into final production of the boxes at a factory unit. What are the key questions that you will need to consider? What are the key tasks that will need to be carried out?

Product researchers use marketing information to help them develop well-designed products. **Design** involves developing goods and services in a form which both attracts customers and serves the intended purpose. The layout of a department store, for example, must be designed so that a customer is able to find the item he or she wants quickly – the right use of space is vital to ensure profitability. Product researchers must also consider production costs, ease of manufacture and selling price.

A company might be reluctant to change an existing design, particularly if it provides status (e.g. the radiator grill on a BMW car). Conversely, small changes may be made to products to give them a more up-to-date feel. A company logo may be updated to give it a 'modern look'.

Built-in obsolescence

Built-in (or planned) obsolescence can be, and frequently is, a feature of many products. Fashion clothes are designed to last for a season, and cars are built to last for only a few years. A manufacturer is able to sustain long-term market demand by limiting the life-span of a product. Some commentators argue that this leads to a huge waste of resources, while others see it as boosting demand, employment and output in the economy.

Draw up a list of arguments an environmentalist might put forward against built-in obsolescence. How might a major manufacturer respond to such arguments?

The product mix

Many organisations produce more than one product. One advantage of **diversification** is that it enables the company to spread its risks. The **product mix** is the complete range of items produced by an organisation. These products have to be managed and positioned in appropriately targeted market segments. The mix comprises all the brands, line extensions, sizes, and types of packaging on offer.

Design three charts to show the product mixes of three well-known companies.

The key to a good product mix is having an effective balance of products in line with the organisation's strategy. Effective management involves creating this balance. If a product is losing pulling power, it may need to be revamped, relaunched or replaced.

Case Study

New product development in Japan

WESTERN companies are supposed to be the masters of innovation, marketing and incisive management. Japanese firms have a reputation for borrowing ideas from abroad, making painstaking improvements and then, when everything is ready, churning out better-quality products in huge volumes at low prices. This reputation may still be partly true for Japanese companies abroad. At home almost the opposite is the case, as many American and European companies trying to compete in Japan have been shocked to discover.

Foreign firms entering the Japanese market with a four-year technical lead have seen their products quickly matched – not copied, mind, matched – and then left behind. Once Japanese manufacturers relied on slick production techniques to make them into awesome competitors. Today their most effective weapon is rapid innovation.

Take Sony's best-selling CCD-TR55, a miniaturised video camera and recorder ('camcorder') that weighs a mere 790 grams (1.5 lb). To make the product palm-sized, Sony had to shrink 2200 components into a space one-quarter the size they occupy in a conventional camcorder. Yet only six months after introducing the CCD-TR55 in June 1989, Sony had people. Matsushita, followed by its stablemate, JVC launched even lighter look-a-likes. Within a year, Sanyo, Canon, Ricoh and Hitachi were selling palm-sized camcorders as well.

The process of rushing out instant imitations is known in Japan as **product covering**. Rival manufacturers rush to produce their own versions just in case the pioneer's should prove to be a best-seller. With a target to aim at, the coverers know that the innovation is at least technically feasible. Reverse engineering – taking the product apart to see how it works – provides shortcuts. The top priority of companies is to prevent distributors and retailers from deserting their own camp.

Product covering is really just a part of an even more formidable Japanese process known as **product churning**. When developing a new product, western firms use a 'rifle' approach, testing the market constantly and revising the product each time until it exactly meets the customer's needs before launching it. Japanese manufacturers, by contrast, tend to use a 'shotgun' approach. For instance,

around 1000 new soft drinks appear annually in Japan, though 99% of them vanish within a year. New-product ideas are not tested through market research, but by selling the first production batch.

Kevin Jones, a consultant in McKinsey's Tokyo office, points out that nobody could imagine why people would want a hi-fi with not one, but two, compact-disc players. The doubters included Sharp, the firm that launched the machine. Nevertheless teenagers bought the machines to mix tracks from separate CDs onto tape. Within months both Sanyo and JVC followed with their own twin-CD machines.

Firms also engage in **parallel development** – developing second-and-third-generation products along with the initial version. As soon as the pack catches up, the original innovator has a replacement for its own hit product ready to go. Only weeks after Matsushita launched a rival to Sony's palm-sized camcorder. Sony hitback with two new models – one even lighter, the other with yet more technical features. Companies that fail to ride each successive wave of innovation risk being washed away.

This looks wasteful. But according to a study by McKinsey, Japanese companies develop new products in a third to half the time spent by their western counterparts, at a quarter to a tenth of the cost. Three factors help Japanese companies pull off this feat:

● **Japan's army of engineers**. Japanese companies are reaping the benefits of the country's enormous investment in education, especially in engineering schools. Technical literacy is now more widely diffused throughout Japanese business than anywhere else in the industrial world. Japan has 5000 technical workers for 1 million people. The comparable figure for America is 3500, for western Germany 2500; no other country comes close.

● **Catalogue design.** Instead of designing every component of a new product from scratch, Japanese engineers reach instinctively for the parts catalogue. By using off-the-shelf components wherever possible, they devote their most creative engineering skills to fashioning a product that is 90% as good as a product designed from scratch might be – but only half the price of a completely original version.

● **Free flow of information.** Unlike western firms, which tend to hand their

His master's CD

suppliers the skimpiest of specifications when seeking a price quotation for a new component, Japanese manufacturers share their most secret plans, send their top staff to help out and hand over any proprietary know-how needed. They then leave the supplier to get on with the job of developing the part needed for the new product. With so much trust and exchange of staff, product-development information can flow between a company and its suppliers while a new product is still only a gleam in an engineer's eye. The lack of job-hopping among Japanese engineers limits the leakage of information to competitors.

Even Japanese firms have not been able to transfer all these practices abroad. Flooding the market with new products, even imitations, is important in Japan because firms are determined not to lose access to scarce, and often rigid, dealer and distribution networks. Abroad, this matters less. Tarnishing their reputation with a poor product is also less of a concern because many new versions are aimed at a small core of sophisticated consumers who will try anything new. The extraordinary appetite of all Japanese consumers for new gizmos can also make an ageing product-line fatal to a firm's prospects, as many failed camera manufacturers discovered in the 1980's.

Abroad, new products still have to be chosen and developed more carefully. A single dud can damage a carefully nurtured image. And falling a small step behind is not so threatening once brand loyalty has been established. Nevertheless, the new-product treadmill Japanese companies face at home has already given them an enviable prowess in foreign markets. Moreover, any western firm hoping to grab a chunk of the huge Japanese market will have little choice but to step on to the new-product treadmill too.

Source: The Economist Newspapers Ltd

1 Explain why it is difficult for many American and European companies to compete in Japan.

2 What are the dangers of rushing out instant imitations too quickly?

3 Explain what is meant by:

a product covering

b product churning

c parallel development.

4 How do the Japanese benefit by using off-the-shelf components?

5 Identify the areas of new product development in Japan which, in your opinion, use:

a good marketing practices

b poor marketing practices.

6 How is the Japanese consumer affected by such activities?

· THE PRICE ·

Of all the aspects of the marketing mix, price is the one which creates sales revenue – all the others are costs. The Oxford English Dictionary has the following definition:

THE PRICE is the sum or consideration or sacrifice for which a thing may be bought or attained.

However, to produce a watertight definition of pricing which gives a clear indication of its importance in the marketing mix is like trying to define the length of a piece of string. In some contexts a particular definition will be appropriate, in others it will not. The problem stems from the fact that 'price' has different meanings for different groups of people:

- For **buyers**, price may be regarded as an unwelcome cost. Price involves sacrificing the next-best alternative that could be bought This is sometimes referred to as the **opportunity cost**. Price can also be used as a measure of the **value** of an item.

- For **sellers**, price is a key element in the marketing mix. It is an important selling point. 'Getting the price right' is an important tactical decision and as such it is a key factor influencing revenue and profit. We all know of a business that sold wonderful products which were just a little too expensive – it went bust. We also know of

businesses that sold themselves too cheaply – not enough revenue was generated to cover costs adequately.

- For the **government**, the price of individual products is an influence on the general price level – and hence votes!

The importance of price within the marketing mix varies from one market to another and between different segments in the same market. In low-cost, non-fashion markets, price can be critical (for example in the sale of white emulsion and gloss paint for decorating). In fashion markets, such as fashion clothing, it can be one of the least relevant factors. Certain products are designed to suit a particular price segment (e.g. economy family cars) whilst others perform a specific function regardless of cost. For consumers with limited budgets, price is a key purchasing criterion, whilst for others for whom 'money is no object', price is less important.

Task

Identify a range of similar products or services. Comment briefly on the differences and similarities in their prices.

Pricing objectives

There are many possible objectives in establishing prices. A key assumption of many business theories is that **profit maximisation** is the most important pricing target. Studies of actual business behaviour, however, reveal a wide range of objectives other than short-term profit maximisation.

A **competitive price** is one that gives a competitive edge in the market-place. It is not necessarily lower than that of a rival because other elements of the marketing mix add to the competitive edge. For example, it is possible to argue that Gillette razor blades are better quality than those of rivals, giving scope to charge a higher yet more competitive price than those applying to other blades.

A further aim of competitive pricing is to set a price that deters new entrants in a particular market. Large organisations with some degree of monopoly power may be inclined to keep prices relatively low in order to secure their long-term market dominance. From time to time you might hear the owner of a small organisation say: 'Of course we would like to diversify into producing X but we simply cannot compete with the prices being offered by the big boys.'

H.A. Simon put forward the view that a business may want to **satisfice** – that is, achieve given targets for market share and profits from sales which may not maximise profits but which instead inflate boardroom egos. This can arise when the managers of an organisation are clearly different from the owners. If the managers can provide sufficient profits to keep the shareholders satisfied, then a proportion of the profits can be diverted to provide more perks for managers and large departments.

There are many other possible objectives in establishing prices. For example, a company might feel that it is important to **maximise sales** to create **brand leadership**, or it might want to establish a high price to create a **reputation for quality**.

Pricing strategies

Once a pricing objective has been established, it is necessary to establish an appropriate strategy. Three broad strategies can be considered: low-price, market-price and high-price.

A **low-price strategy** should be considered when consumers respond positively to small downward changes in price. In technical terms we can measure this response by calculating the **elasticity of demand** (see pages 116 and 117 in Chapter 3). Elasticity of demand can be used to express the changes in quantities purchased as a response to price changes. In Chapter 3 we saw that demand is said to be *elastic* if the change in quantity demanded is of a greater proportion than the change in price that initiated it. If the price of a brand of washing powder were to fall by 10 per cent and there was an increase in sales of 20 per cent, then the demand for the product would be said to be elastic – the change in price leads to a more than proportionate response in quantity demanded. In this example:

$$\text{Elasticity of demand} = \frac{20\%}{10\%} = 2.$$

Products with a value greater than 1 are said to have an elastic demand. However, it needs to be remembered that elastic demand does not always mean that a producer will benefit from price reductions. If a company in a **price-sensitive** market lowers its price, there is a strong chance that other producers will follow suit. Another consideration is cost – if a company lowers its price, and sells more, it will have to pay out more in expenses and other variable costs.

A low-price strategy is important wherever it is easy for consumers to compare competitive products. When brands of similar washing powders sit side by side on the shelves of a supermarket there is a strong incentive to set a lower price.

In many situations organisations will tend to set prices at the **market-price level.** This will happen where:

- products are bought frequently
- competitive products have very similar characteristics
- a few large organisations dominate the supply in a specific industry.

In any of these situations, an organisation could quickly lose all its business if it set its price above those of the competition. Conversely, if it lowers its price the competitors may be forced to follow. Organisations tend to set prices at market-price level so that the role of the price is neutral.

A **high-price strategy** can be a long-term or a short-term policy. A long-term policy implies that the firm seeks to sell a high-quality product to a small, select market, high prices being an essential feature of up-market products. A short-term policy is based upon the advantages gained by selling a patented product (when there is also heavy investment in new equipment) or when there is some form of barrier to others entering the market.

Task

Give two examples of situations where it would be appropriate to use:

a low-price strategy
b a market-price strategy
c a high-price strategy.

Pricing techniques

How are prices set in practice? Important influences upon pricing techniques include:

- cost
- demand
- competitors' prices.

Practical pricing involves elements of all three. Below we explore some commonly used pricing techniques.

Any study of how organisations price products or services inevitably reveals a very high proportion using no other basis than a mark-up. This is known as **cost-plus pricing**. Information about costs is usually easier to piece together than information about other variables such as likely revenue. The unit cost is the average cost of each item produced; if a company produces 800 units at a total cost of £24 000 the unit cost is £30. The price is then arrived at by adding on a certain percentage of the unit price.

Contribution pricing involves separating out the different products that make up a company's portfolio, in order to charge individual prices appropriate to each product's share in total costs. Two broad categories of costs can be identified:

- **Direct costs** vary directly with the quantity of output produced – for example, costs of materials and wages.
- **Indirect costs** are amounts that have to be paid irrespective of the level of output – for example, the salaries of permanent staff and the cost of maintaining a plant.

When an organisation produces a range of individual items or products it is easy to determine the direct costs of each, but not the indirect costs. For example, in a food processing plant producing 100 different recipe dishes it is easy to work out how much goes on each line in terms of raw materials, labour input, and other direct costs. However, the same cannot be said of indirect costs, and the organisation has to decide on a policy of allocating reasonable amounts of the total indirect costs to each product line in order to calculate prices.

Contribution is the sum remaining after the direct costs of producing individual products have been subtracted from revenues. Figure 9.12 makes clear how this works.

Demand-orientated pricing involves reacting to the demand for a product, so that high demand leads to high prices and weak demand leads to low prices even though unit costs are similar.

When an organisation can split up the market in which it operates into different sections, it can carry out a policy of price discrimination. This involves selling at high prices in sections of the market where demand is intense and at relatively low prices where demand is elastic. Price discrimination may be carried out in the following circumstances:

- **In a customer-orientated situation**. Some customers may have a high demand for a product while others may have only a weak demand. Discrimination would involve selling the same type of product to the first type of customer at a high price and to the second type at a lower price.
- **In a product-orientated situation**. Slight modifications can be made to a product to allow high-price and low-price strategies.

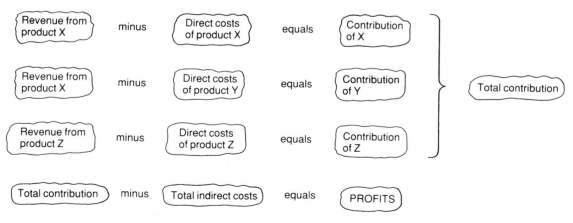

Figure 9.12 *Calculating profits using contribution pricing*

- **According to time**. Sellers are able to discriminate between customers at different times of the day or according to seasons or the time of year.
- **According to situation**. Prices can vary according to the situation associated with the product. For example, house prices vary according to the area of a town or city in which they are located.

Task

BT uses discriminatory pricing according to time. Find out in detail how BT currently applies this policy. List and explain examples of other forms of price discrimination according to customer, product and situation.

Competition-orientated pricing is frequently adopted in extremely competitive situations. If a product is faced with direct competition from highly similar products in the market-place, this may constrain pricing decisions so as to keep them in line with the actions of rivals. In contrast, when there is only indirect competition in other sectors of the market, there will be more scope to vary price.

Markets are sometimes classified according to the level of competition. One extreme is called **perfect competition** (it exists in theory rather than in practice). In perfect competition there would be no limitations to new firms entering the market-place, and buyers would know what was on offer and have to accept the ruling market price. The other extreme is monopoly, where a single company dominates a market-place, giving it considerable powers

to set high prices – to be a **price maker**. In the real world, most markets lie between these extremes and involve some level of imperfection.

Task

Identify one market in which there is little competition, and one in which there is a lot of competition. Comment on prices in these two markets.

Short-term pricing policies

Pricing can be used as an incentive to pursue short-term marketing and selling targets for an organisation. Typical attack-based policies include:

- skimming pricing
- penetration pricing
- destroyer pricing
- promotional pricing.

Skimming pricing is used when there is little competition in the market. It involves setting a relatively high initial price in order to yield a high initial return from those customers willing to buy the new product. Once the first group of customers has been satisfied, the seller can then lower prices in order to make sales to new groups of customers, and this process continues until a large section of the total market-place is catered for. This sort of pricing often takes place when new electrical products are launched.

Figure 9.13 *Decreasing levels of competition*

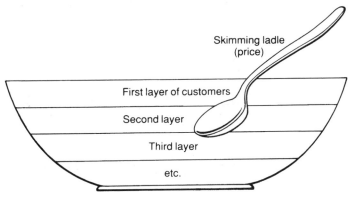

Figure 9.14 *Skimming*

Penetration pricing is appropriate when the seller knows that demand is likely to be elastic. A low price is therefore required to attract customers to the product. Penetration pricing is normally associated with the launch of a new product for which the market needs to be penetrated. Because price starts low, the product may initially make a loss until consumer awareness is increased. As the product rapidly penetrates the market, sales and profitability increase and prices can creep upwards.

Task

Identify examples of penetration pricing – products or services that have been launched at low prices to establish themselves in markets.

A policy of **destroyer pricing** can be used to undermine the sales of rivals or to warn potential new rivals not to enter a particular market. Destroyer pricing involves reducing the price of an existing product or selling a new product at an artificially low price in order to destroy competitors' sales. This type of policy will almost certainly lead to short-term losses.

Prices can be lowered from time to time to promote a product or service to new customers. **Promotional pricing** can be used to inject fresh life into an existing product or to create interest in a new product. Supermarkets frequently use a loss-leader to boost sales of other items.

Case Study

Car wars

The plunge in car sales in 1991 cost the motor trade more than £2.5 billion in the first half of the year and sparked a savage price war. Nissan fired the first volley with the announcement of price cuts across its entire range. Ford, the market leader, followed with a dramatic move which led to it slashing list prices on many of its models by up to £2000. Vauxhall, down from number two in the car market to third place behind Rover, came in with a cash-back offer to pay a refund of up to £1500 to customers taking delivery of a new car within a three-month period. Fiat cut showroom prices by between £500 and £2000 across its range.

The reason for the price battle became clear when the latest monthly sales figures were released by the Society of Motor Manufacturers and Traders. New car sales for June were the lowest for 21 years and served to confirm the dismal trend. Car sales were running 24.8 per cent down, with registrations barely scraping past 800 000, compared with well over a million in the previous year. The deep depression throughout the motor industry is also having a serious knock-on effect upon component manufacturers.

The action of four major car manufacturers in slashing prices inevitably set the scene for a dramatic price war. Soon after the price cuts there was evidence that business warmed as a result. One motor retailer said: 'There seem to be people around in a buying mood who have been holding back, not quite confident enough to take the plunge, and the price reductions might just tip the balance.' He also pointed out that customers coming into showrooms were much more aggressive – they knew there were discounts to be had and were determined to push for them.

Few car manufacturers have escaped the icy draught blowing through the car market. For manufacturers in 1991, every customer counts.

1 Comment generally on the nature of the car market in 1991.
2 Look at the pricing techniques outlined in this chapter. Which of the pricing techniques contributed to the actions of motor manufacturers in 1991? Explain why they used these techniques.
3 Make a list of those who benefit from a price war in the car market.
4 What techniques other than price could motor manufacturers use to sell more new cars?
5 What knock-on effect might the recession and a price war for new cars have on the market for second-hand cars?

• THE PLACE •

Though figures vary widely from product to product, roughly a fifth of the production cost of an item goes on getting it to the customer. The issue of place deals with various methods of transporting and storing goods, and then making them available to the customer. Getting the right product to the right place at the right time involves the distribution system. Distribution is the process of moving goods and services to the places where they are wanted. It may involve a single step or any number of steps. The local baker might supply bread directly to customers. In contrast, the furniture store might supply chairs and tables produced in Scandinavia which have passed through a number of hands and have been stored two or three times before arriving at their final destination.

Transport

Transport can be a key cost component in many products. Choosing the 'best' possible transport system involves weighing up and 'trading off' a number of key elements. What forms of transport should be used – road, rail, air, sea? Can these forms of transport be integrated? What are the best possible routes? Do you use your own fleet or outside carriers? How do you maximise safety? How do you minimise costs? How do you make sure that products arrive on time and in the best possible condition?

Task

Imagine you are the transport manager for an organisation that manufactures and delivers fresh cream cakes from Shildon, in County Durham, around the North East of England – particularly to Darlington, Sunderland, Durham, Newcastle and Consett. Work in groups to research and then discuss each of the transport issues mentioned in the text.

Different forms of transport have their own distinctive advantages and disadvantages. Pipelines are expensive to construct, cheap to run and expensive to repair. Roads give door-to-door delivery, are fast over short and some long distances, and make it possible to use your own fleet relatively cheaply. However, road travel is also subject to traffic delays and breakdowns, and drivers may only drive their vehicles for a certain number of hours in a day. Rail

transport is relatively cheap and quick over long distances, particularly between major cities. However, it is not always appropriate for reaching out-of-the-way destinations and is costly for guaranteed speedy deliveries. Air is very fast between countries, provided the ultimate destination is not off the beaten track. Air is generally used for carrying important, urgent, relatively light and expensive loads. Sea transport is a cheap way of carrying high-volume bulky loads when speed is not of the essence.

Containerisation of loads has made possible the integration of these different forms of transport. Routes and services have been simplified to cut out wasteful duplication. Special types of vehicles have been developed to carry certain loads. Direct motorway connections between major cities have proved to be of major importance in determining factory location decisions, as have fast intercity rail services and air links. Different methods of transport may prove to be more or less cost effective in different situations depending on the cost of transport relative to the type of good being transported, the price of the good, or the speed with which it is needed.

Channels of distribution

Distribution is not just concerned with moving goods physically from manufacturers to consumers. It is also concerned with choosing the appropriate channel of distribution – for example, whether to sell direct to the consumer or to sell primarily to wholesalers or retailers (see Figure 9.15).

Choosing appropriate channels for distribution involves highly significant policy decisions which can have an

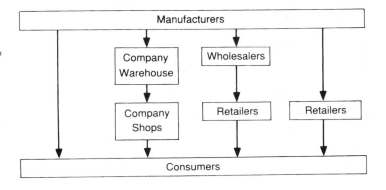

Figure 9.15 *Some of the many channels of distribution*

important effect on other areas of the marketing mix. For example, if you choose to distribute through a chain of readily accessible cut-price stores this will have obvious implications for the public perception of your products.

Modern commerce uses thousands of channels and methods of distribution. The traditional way of distributing goods from a manufacturer to a market is through a small number of wholesalers who then sell the goods to a large number of retailers. In this way a wholesaler is a go-between who buys in bulk from manufacturers and breaks the bulk down into small units for retailers. Wholesalers often provide a variety of services which benefit both manufacturers and retailers, such as warehousing, credit arrangements transport and packaging. However, the involvement of a wholesaler adds to the selling price.

If a manufacturing company sells to a retailer directly, it can exert firmer control over its sales, and the manufacturer and retailer can work together on sales promotion schemes. Selling direct to retailers involves a larger sales force and increased transport charges when sending smaller consignments. If circumstances allow, it can be possible for manufacturers to sell directly to consumers, particularly if the product is a high-cost one and has a good reputation within the market.

Case Study

Developing a fast answer to fashion fads

Britain's chain stores are working to eliminate their risk from the notoriously high-risk clothing industry. Alarmed by almost unprecedented volumes of unsold stock caused by recession, high street fashion chains are trying to solve this costly problem by working more closely with the manufacturers. In order to reduce losses from marking down clothes, they have developed a solution: a **quick response** to changes in fashion.

'Quick response' means developing a system of working which produces a much closer relationship between demand and supply. Methods of achieving QR vary at each stage of the clothing supply chain. The aim is to provide the right product in the right quantity in the right place in the quickest possible time, with minimum inventory and costs.

QR has profound implications right down the supply chain. It helps to eliminate some of the complacency in the modern fashion market which developed in the late 80s when the consumer boom kept factory order books full. Today fashion has become much more unpredictable and retailers and manufacturers can no longer anticipate what their customers will want to buy a year in advance. They recognise the need to respond quickly to the uncertain twists of fashion. They no longer want to have to guess customer requirements months in advance of the season.

Marks & Spencer, the UK's biggest clothing retailer, is expected to step up its QR programme in coming months. From 1993 the company wants its suppliers to replenish clothing lines twice weekly instead of once a week. Woolworths is introducing QR throughout its children's wear divisions and plans to reduce **lead times** to under ten days on some lines that currently stand at five to ten weeks.

Domestic clothing manufacturers believe QR is an essential tool for fighting competition from the Far East. Suppliers to the Burton Group say buyers want greater flexibility and want merchandise fast. Research suggests that QR can develop a 7.5 per cent increase in sales for retailers and improve margins through reduced mark-downs. The development of QR seems to be transforming the industry.

1 *Explain what is meant by quick response (QR).*
2 *How will QR benefit the 'place' ingredient in the marketing mix?*
3 *Make a list of the groups who benefit from QR.*
4 *Investigate how retail technology might help an organisation to implement QR.*
5 *What other 'unpredictable' markets might benefit from QR?*
6 *Imagine you are responsible for clothing sales in a large chain. How would you attempt to introduce QR?*

· PROMOTION ·

Since early days individuals have used hand signals, vocal patterns, symbolic drawings and facial expressions for the purpose of communicating. Today, the exchange of information takes place through sophisticated media in order to accomplish the same goal. An efficient network of communications is essential for successful promotional activity.

The **promotional mix** comprises all the marketing and promotional communication methods used to achieve the promotional objectives of the marketing mix. These methods can be broken down into two distinct areas: non-controllable and controllable.

Non-controllable methods are marketing messages which take place on the basis of word-of-mouth, personal recommendations and a consumer's overall perception of a particular product or service. For example, consumer opinions are influenced by a number of factors, such as whether their family has regularly used the product. A brand heritage, character, colour and image will also have helped to create brand loyalty and influenced regular purchasing patterns. On the other hand, public displeasure with a particular organisation, country or range of products might influence purchases; examples are CFCs in aerosols and 'dolphin-unfriendly' tuna.

Controllable methods are marketing messages which are carefully directed to achieve the objectives of an organisation's promotional campaign. We shall consider four main areas.

Advertisements

Advertisements are messages intended to inform or influence the people who receive them. A message is paid for by an advertiser in order to sell a product or service or to seek support or participation. This category includes adverts on TV, radio and in magazines, but does not include promotional materials supplied with a product, promotional events, branding or company brochures.

To plan a campaign, an advertiser usually consults an **advertising agency**. Such an agency is a vital link between the advertiser and the consumer. The role of an advertising agency is to create, develop, plan and implement an advertising campaign for a client. The extent to which an agency does so will vary according to its type. Some agencies offer all kinds of services while others specialise, for example, in creative work.

The interaction of ideas with creativity forms a major factor in the success of an advertising campaign. The message might be a combination of words, symbols, characters, colours, sounds and gimmicks. It must be conveyed to the right people in the right place at the right time, as 'good' advertising will not work if it is misdirected.

At the heart of advertising is identification of where the interests of the consumers lie, and knowing how they will respond to different messages. Good copywriting is important. Buzz words such as 'new' and 'free' try to encourage the consumer to do something. Straplines are associated with a brand name and can help to develop an image – for example, 'Once driven, forever smitten' or 'Ralgex has the muscle'. Sometimes a character is used to identify the qualities of the brand – for example, Mr Sheen and Mr Kipling. A brand's heritage is often an area that advertisers like to build upon. Artwork, sex appeal, humour and repetition all help to communicate the identity of the brand as well as provide a foundation for the other areas of the promotional mix.

Case Study

Using sex to promote ice-cream

Combatants in Europe's $7 billion a year ice-cream war are using sex to turn on the public. The use of naked flesh to market new products is nothing new, but fierce competition in the 'adult' market is inspiring advertisers to new heights. In Britain, campaigns by two manufacturers in the gourmet market have raised eyebrows as well as brand awareness. The UK's television watchdog, the Independent Television Commission, recently banned from national TV a series of erotic advertisements for ice-cream, saying they were 'too hot' for British viewers. The Advertising Standards Authority has also received complaints about ice-cream adverts, all expressing surprise that sex should be used in such a blatant way to sell ice-cream.

Unilever's best-known adverts featured the pan-European Cornetto gondola. It, too, has recently turned to sex appeal with the girl-licks-lolly formula to help it to double the sales of Magnum, the chocolate covered ice-cream on a stick. With predicted sales of £200 million in Europe this year, it shows that the proof of the pudding is in the eating!

1 Why might using sex-appeal to sell ice-cream sometimes be considered to be against the public interest?

2 Outline the benefits of using such a strategy for:
  a advertisers
  b consumers.

3 What other methods of promoting ice-cream might also be successful? Working in groups, consider what themes you would emphasise if you had to promote a new ice-cream product in the luxury 'after-dinner' segment of the adult market.

A key element in advertising is media selection. Media selection will depend on the target audience – that is, the number of **potential customers** the advertiser will wish to reach (**coverag**e) – as well as the number of times the advertiser wishes the message to be transmitted to customers (**frequency**).

Task

List as many types of media as you can think of. Comment on the advantages and disadvantages of using each to reach a *carefully selected target audience*.

Advertising is an essential part of the promotional mix and requires particularly large levels of expenditure. It is therefore crucial that organisations try to analyse the effectiveness of their investment. The success of a campaign will depend upon the way it appeals to the attitudes of its target audience.

Sales promotion

Sales promotion describes a set of techniques designed to encourage customers to make a purchase. It usually complements advertising, personal selling and publicity, and might include point-of-sale materials, competitions, demonstrations and exhibitions. The essential feature of a sales promotion effort is that it is a short-term inducement to encourage customers to react quickly, whereas

advertising is a much more long-term communication process involving the building of a brand image.

Promotions into the pipeline are techniques used to sell more stocks into the distribution system. Examples are 'dealer loaders' such as thirteen for the price of twelve (the baker's dozen), point-of-sale materials, dealer competitions, extended credit to dealers, sale-or-return and promotional gifts.

Promotions out of the pipeline assist in promoting and selling products to the end-user. These might include free samples, trial packs, coupon offers, price reductions, competitions, premium offers, demonstrations, charity promotions and point-of-sale displays.

Task

Do some fieldwork. Interview a retailer to find out more about sales promotions into the pipeline. Also look at those offered out of the pipeline. Which are the most common? How effective do they seem to be?

The effects of individual sales promotions vary widely. Though most promotions using free samples lead to an immediate (if temporary) increase in sales, sales promotions are a short-term measure on the whole and have little effect on brand loyalty over a longer period.

Personal selling

Personal selling involves persuasive communication between a seller and a buyer which is designed to convince the consumer to purchase the products or services on offer. The objective of personal selling is therefore to obtain a sale and is the culmination of all the earlier marketing activities. It involves matching a consumer's needs with the goods and services on offer – the better the match the more lasting the relationship between the seller and the buyer.

Personal selling is important in both customer and organisational markets. In consumer goods markets, advertising is often the driving force which has pulled a product through the distribution network so that most consumers know what they want to purchase. In organisational markets, the purpose of a sales force is to push the product through the market.

The sequence of events used in personal selling is often described as the **five Ps** (do not confuse with the four Ps of the marketing mix!). They are:

- *Preparation* – Sales staff should be adequately trained and familiar with the product, customers, competition and the market.
- *Prospecting* – Prospective customers (prospects) are identified before the selling can take place.
- *Pre-approach* – Learning about the projected customer.
- *Presentation* – Use of active selling skills.
- *Post-sale support* – Following up the sale to create repeat business.

Task

In what ways is personal selling likely to be easy? In what ways is it likely to be difficult?

Those involved in personal selling operate as an information link between the suppliers and their customers. As a result, personal selling involves a boundary role – being at the boundary of a supplying organisation as well as in direct and close contact with its customers. The role is often one not only of selling but

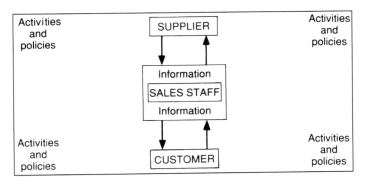

Figure 9.16 *The information link between customer and supplier*

also of interpreting the activities and policies of supplier and customer.

The role of personal selling has changed considerably in recent years. However, despite database management and changing patterns of distribution, personal selling continues to play an essential role in the promotional mix.

Public relations

Public relations (PR) encompasses all of the actions of and communications from an organisation. The forces in an organisation's **external environment** are capable of affecting them in a variety of ways. The forces might be social, economic, political, local or environmental and could be represented by a variety of groups such as customers, shareholders, employees, special interest groups and by public opinion. Reacting to such elements in a way that will build a positive image is very important.

The purpose of public relations is therefore to provide an external environment for an organisation in which it is popular and can prosper. Building goodwill in such a way will require sound organisational performance and behaviour and the communication of such actions and attitudes to its many publics.

The direct selling of products or services is *not* an objective of public relations. Whereas advertising is about relatively short-term objectives, public relations is long-term; it works by sending free messages to various groups through the activities of the organisation in order to improve its reputation and maintain its positive image.

PR can be used as a strategic device to develop a more positive public perception and image of an organisation. Activities might include charitable donations and community relations, hospitality, press releases, visits, event sponsorship, free literature etc.

Public relations can provide an organisation's many publics with information about what it does and how it responds to different circumstances. It can help to build confidence in its activities, develop goodwill in the community and provide benefits for its publics.

Ski uses rock 'n' roll for cerebral palsy

Yoghurt brand Ski recently pledged £200 000 in its biggest programme for the cerebral palsy charity the Stars Organisation for Spastics (SOS). To mark SOS's tenth anniversary, Eden Vale, the parent, will sponsor a single title 'The Spoken Word of Rock 'n' Roll', featuring seventeen SOS celebrities. The proceeds will go to the Dame Vera Lynn Children's Project. Each record contains an SOS information leaflet and a coupon for 20p off a pack of four Ski yoghurts. At the same time an on-pack promotion will ask consumers to take part in a competition with cash prizes by calling a Ski hotline and identifying some of the voices on the record. Ski will donate 10p for every call.

The £65 million Ski brand has backed the charity – whose supporters include founder Dame Vera Lynn, Michael Grade and Martyn Lewis – for a decade.

1 *Why do organisations such as Eden Vale take on the responsibility of supporting a charity?*
2 *It has been suggested that all organisations should make a minimum annual charitable donation. Comment upon this.*
3 *Describe how the Ski contribution will help the brand in:*
   a *the short-term*
   b *the long-term.*

· USING THE MARKETING MIX ·

As we have seen, the marketing mix is a carefully constructed combination of techniques, resources and tactics which form the basis of a marketing plan geared to achieve both marketing and corporate objectives. Whenever objectives or external influences change, so the blend of ingredients will have to be varied. No two mixes

Figure 9.17 *Undifferentiated marketing*

in similar types of organisation will ever be the same. Each will represent a unique approach to developing a strategy for the resources available.

In **undifferentiated marketing**, a single marketing message is offered to the total market-place. This is unlikely to be successful as markets are made up of buyers with different wants and needs.

Differentiated marketing is the strategy of attacking the market-place by tailoring separate product and marketing strategies to different sectors of the market. For example, the car market may be divided into an economy segment, a luxury segment, a performance segment etc.

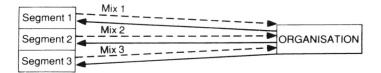

Figure 9.18 *Differentiated marketing*

Concentrated marketing is often the best strategy for small organisations. This involves choosing to compete in one segment and developing the most effective mix for this sub-market. Jaguar, for example, concentrates on the luxury segment of the car market.

Although companies try to select and dominate certain market segments, they find that rivals are engaged in

Figure 9.19 *Concentrated marketing*

similar strategies. They therefore try to create a **differential advantage** over rivals. A positioning strategy will involve selecting a market segment and creating a differential advantage over rivals in that area.

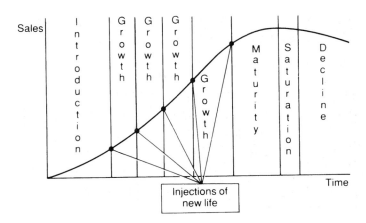

Figure 9.21 *Periodic injections into the product life-cycle*

Task

Look at two similar products. Comment on the similarities and the differences of their marketing mixes. To what extent are these due to positioning strategy? What are the differential advantages each product has over its rival?

The product life-cycle

An important aspect of the marketing mix is its use in managing the life-cycle of a product or brand. The **product life cycle** is an essential mechanism for planning changes in marketing activities. It recognises that products have a finite market life and charts this through various phases. The sales performance of any product introduced into the market will rise from nothing, reach a peak, and at some stage decline.

The life-cycle can be broken down further into distinct stages. In the **introductory phase**, growth is slow and volume is low because of limited awareness of the product's existence. Sales then rise rapidly during the period of growth. It is during this phase that the profit per unit sold usually reaches a maximum. Towards the end of this phase, competitors enter the market to promote their

own products, which reduces the rate of growth of sales of the first product. This period is then known as maturity. Competitive jockeying – such as product differentiation in the form of new flavours, colours, sizes etc. – will sift out the weaker brands. During saturation, some brands will drop out of the market. The product market may eventually decline and reach a stage when it becomes unprofitable.

The life-cycle may last for a few months or for hundreds of years. To prolong the life-cycle of a brand or a product an organisation needs to readjust the ingredients of its marketing mix. Periodic injections of new ideas are needed – product improvements, line extensions or improved promotions.

A readjustment of the marketing mix might include:

- changing or modifying the *product,* to keep up with or ahead of the competition
- altering distribution patterns, to provide a more suitable *place* for the consumer to make purchases
- changing *prices* to reflect competitive activities
- considering carefully the style of *promotion.*

The product portfolio

Most large organisations produce a range of products, each with its own life-cycle. By using life-cycles, companies can plan when to introduce new lines as old products go into decline. The collection of products that an organisation produces is known as its **product portfolio**.

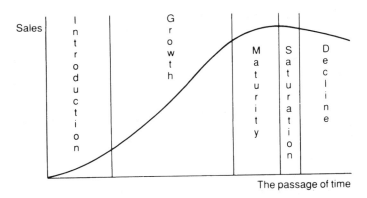

Figure 9.20 *Stages in the product life-cycle*

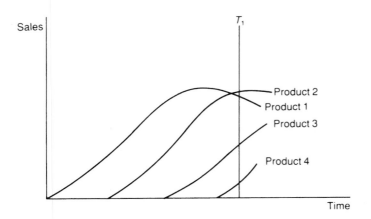

Figure 9.22 *A product portfolio*

In Figure 9.22, T_1 represents a point in time. At that point product 1 is in decline, product 2 is in maturity, product 3 is in growth and product 4 has recently been introduced.

Task

The organisation you work for or attend will have a portfolio of products or services. Identify the elements of the portfolio and try to determine where they stand in their life-cycles.

If an organisation's products are launched at just the right time, it is likely to benefit from a continuous period of growth. Most organisations today are multi-product and provide a portfolio of products *at different stages in their life-cycles*. This helps to avoid serious fluctuations in profit levels and ensures that the most profitable products provide support for those that have not yet become quite so profitable.

Case Study

Using market segmentation techniques to create defined services for different types of customer

Businesses of all kinds need efficient financial services, but the right financial package for one type of business may be the wrong type for another. The banks are aware of this and have started a process of market segmentation to ensure that the right company gets the right service at the right times.

An example of this is the division by Midland Bank of its UK business customers into Enterprise (organisations with annual revenues of up to £250 000) and Corporate (revenues of between £250 000 and £250 million). Companies larger than this are handled by the bank's international and investment banking wing, Midland Montagu.

The idea is to enable the bank to concentrate its specialist resources on clearly defined groups of customers, which then allows branch managers to spend more time on personal customers.

Whichever category a business falls into, it has access to a business centre, staffed by bankers especially trained for that particular field of industry. The idea of segmentation is one which complements that of 'one-stop-shopping' – the customer's needs can all be met under one roof. Both segmentation and one-stop-shopping are weapons in the bank's armoury against competition. Businesses today, more than ever before, want to deal with a bank that understands their needs and provides them with the services they want.

1 Explain why Midland Bank segments its market for business customers.
2 Identify other organisations that segment their products. Show how they apply market segmentation.
3 How might segmentation complement one-stop-shopping?
4 How do you as a bank customer respond to segmentation?

Case Study

Bringing Kettle Chips to Britain

Kettle Foods is Britain's newest and, arguably, most fragile potato crisp maker. In just two years the organisation has obtained a £5 million slice of Britain's £1.4 billion snacks market. At the start it was told the situation was hopeless, but with luck, a neat distribution deal and hard work it has established itself as the UK's fastest growing food business.

The big manufacturers long ago realised the benefits of premium-priced snacks aimed at adults rather than children. Despite a continually large advertising spend by the larger organisations the premium sector of the market had begun to flatten out. Nirbhao Khalsa and Tim Meyer, the founders of Kettle Foods, perceived there was a real opportunity for something different. Kettle Chips are made from potatoes with a high natural sugar content so that they turn brown during frying; they are cooked in batches on a conveyor and flavoured with natural ingredients. Larger companies would be horrified at the hand-cooked processes, the labour content of the crisps and the price of the ingredients (the potatoes cost three times as much as those used in traditional crisps).

Kettle Foods has neither a sales force nor an advertising budget. Instead, distribution deals have taken the product into all the big retail chains. The company knows that such deals are essential if it is to survive.

The managers at Kettle Foods feel that new ideas and quality will help to secure the company's future. They have recently launched Kettle Poppins – popcorn flavoured with white cheddar cheese and packaged in black bags.

1 Using an example, explain what is meant by a premium priced product.

2 How important is distribution for the future of Kettle Chips? Does this mean that the company should have invested more in other ingredients in the marketing mix?

3 Working in groups, suggest new product ideas to extend the Kettle range. Comment briefly on the ingredients in the marketing mix you would emphasise for your new products.

4 Comment on whether it is possible for Kettle Foods to establish itself over a long period in the adult snack market.

Element assignment

Direct selling – the way forward?

This assignment can help you provide evidence for assessment, or claim the following Core Skills:

Communication
  Receive and respond to a variety of information
  Participate in oral and non-verbal communication

Personal Skills
  Transfer skills gained to new and changing situations
  Relate to and interact effectively with individuals and groups
  Work effectively as a member of a team
  Use information sources
  Apply a range of skills and techniques to develop a variety of ideas in the creation of new/modified products, services or situations
  Use a range of thought processes

In this assignment you will be required to present the case (to an organisation) for direct selling.

Direct-selling companies which use door-to-door salespeople or party plans, continue to boom. According to the Direct Selling Association (DSA), the industry enjoyed unbroken growth of 10–14 per cent per annum in the period 1988–93.

One reason for this imperviousness to recession is that direct-selling companies offer low prices. Low overheads allow direct-sales companies to offer goods more cheaply than retailers or mail order firms.

One of the fastest growing companies is Betterware, whose sales rose by 44 per cent to £41 million in 1992. Betterware sells a range of more than 400 household goods, from mops to microwave dishes. The average price of one of its products is £3.40 with only around a dozen items costing more than £10. The average value of a transaction is about £8.

Cheap products are not the only reason for the success of direct selling. *Encyclopaedia Britannica*, for instance, costs between £1000 and £4000 depending on the binding.

Part of the reason for the enduring popularity of direct sales may be that, while postponing buying a car or a television, women are still prepared to allow themselves the luxury of a perfume or a body lotion.

In a 1992 Mori poll, carried out on behalf of the National Consumer Council, 40 per cent of shoppers complained of unhelpful and uninterested shop staff treating them with ignorance and rudeness. Many people say that personal service is where direct selling scores over other forms of retailing.

Task

The company that you work for is a major manufacturer of perfumes which it sells to large high street retailers of cosmetics. However, because of recent disappointing sales figures it would like to explore the option of direct selling using door-to-door salespeople and party selling. The idea of party selling is particularly attractive because of the opportunities it provides for market research through direct consumer contact.

You have been given the responsibility of presenting the case for direct selling. You will need to canvas the views of potential customers through primary research. You will also need to look at current direct-selling companies for cosmetics, such as Avon, and the techniques of party-selling operations such as Ann Summers.

Working in a small group of not more than three, undertake the above research, compile the results and then make a presentation of your findings to the rest of the group. Use OHPs and statistics, if available, to support your case. Your aim is to persuade your listeners that direct selling is the way to counter the current slump in sales.

chapter **10** INVESTIGATING HUMAN RESOURCING

This chapter introduces important aspects of human resource management. People are often the most expensive resource of an organisation. Organisations are human creations. They are made up of people rather than material assets such as buildings and machinery. It is the individuals working within an organisation who produce the product, make the decisions and devise strategies.

Over the last fifteen years, employment in manufacturing has dropped by over 20 per cent. This erosion of the nation's manufacturing base has meant that the economy has become more dependent on the growth and strength of service industries. Service organisations have become more people-intensive and increasingly dependent on skills and expertise.

In this chapter we look at the responsibilities of organisations for recruitment, redundancy, discipline, health and safety, employee consultation, training and professional development. We also look at key laws in the areas of equal opportunities, equal pay, and health and safety at work. We cover ways in which individual employees can take up issues and problems at work through industrial tribunals, and court action. The impact of new technology on people at work, and working relations, are examined. In particular we look at developments such as robotics, electronics, telecommunications, computer-aided design and computer-aided manufacture.

An organisation's most valuable resource is its **workforce** – the people who work for it. Managers therefore need to give careful thought to the needs of employees. An organisation can have all the latest technology, and the best physical resources, but unless it looks after its people it will never thrive and achieve optimum results.

▪ THE 'EMPLOYMENT PROCESSION' ▪

The **personnel** department of an organisation has the prime responsibility for recruiting and looking after employees – the human resource. A key part of this function is administering what is known as the **employment procession**.

Employees have needs from the time of their selection for employment until they cease working for the organisation. The employment procession starts with the **recruitment** process – finding potential new recruits and choosing whom to take on. New staff then need to be helped to 'fit in', so they go through a period of **induction.** During their employment they will need to be **trained** to upgrade their skills and knowledge. Then, when the need arises, they can be **transferred** to other jobs or areas. When they finish working for the organisation they need to have their jobs **terminated** in a satisfactory way – this includes making sure that pension and other matters are dealt with according to the law.

Among the personnel department's other functions, it is responsible for:

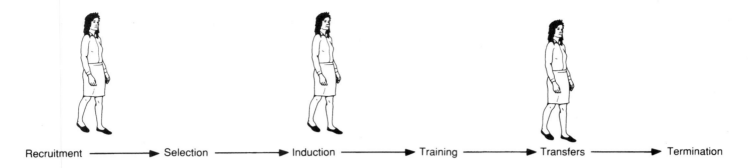

Recruitment ⟶ Selection ⟶ Induction ⟶ Training ⟶ Transfers ⟶ Termination

Figure 10.1 *The employment procession*

- health and safety
- equal opportunities
- bargaining
- appraisals
- discipline
- payment systems.

▪ RECRUITMENT ▪

From the personnel department's point of view, the purpose of recruitment is to buy in and retain the best available human resources to meet the **organisation's** needs. Hence the first requirement is to define and set out what is involved in particular jobs.

This can be done by carrying out a job analysis, which leads on to an outline **job description**. For example, the job of a trainee manager in a supermarket could be described under the following key headings:

- title of post
- prime objectives of the position
- supervisory/managerial responsibilities
- source(s) of supervision and guidance
- range of decision-making
- responsibility for assets, materials etc.

Task

Imagine that you are a personnel officer with a large high-street retailer. Currently you do not have enough shop assistants to meet the demands of customers, particularly at weekends. There are long queues at the tills, and it has become impossible to stack shelves neatly or to price all items accurately. Set out a job analysis for a shop assistant, by answering the following questions:

a What tasks need to be performed?
b What skills and qualities are required?
c How can these skills be acquired?

Once the appropriate managers in the organisation are happy with the outline job description, the personnel department can use this outline to produce a fuller job description to be applied in advertising the job vacancy.

A **job specification** goes beyond a simple description of the job, by highlighting the mental and physical **attributes** required of the job holder. For example, a recent Prison Service advertisement specified the following: 'At every level your task will call for a lot more than simple efficiency. It takes humanity, flexibility, enthusiasm, total commitment and, of course, a sense of humour.'

Summary of job			
Attributes	**Essential**	**Desirable**	**How identified**
Physical			
Qualifications			
Experience			
Training			
Special knowledge			
Personal circumstances			
Attitudes			
Practical and intellectual skills			

Figure 10.2 *Layout for a person specification*

The personnel department may therefore set out, for its own use, a 'person specification' using a layout similar to the one shown in Figure 10.2.

The job specification can be used to:

- make sure that a job advertisement conveys the qualities that prospective candidates should have
- check that candidates for the job have the right qualities.

Case Study

A job at Mothercare

The display below shows the essential information contained in a recent advertisement for a job vacancy at Mothercare.

1 What do you think the job analysis for the Mothercare vacancy indicated to the personnel department?

AREA MANAGER

Southern England

£24–28k + car + benefits

The concept of Mothercare is unique in the world of retailing. With over 250 stores nationwide and a clear market leadership in its chosen field, it is an essential part of life for nearly all of Britain's parents-to-be and new parents.

We are seeking an Area Manager to operate in the South with responsibility for around 20 stores. Your role will be to maximise sales, working closely with your Store Managers and appreciating the individual needs within your area . . .

Imagination, flair, an entrepreneurial attitude and problem-solving skills are just some of the qualities you will need, as well as the ability to lead and motivate your team. Our culture is changing and our Area Managers are at the forefront of this. Substantial retail experience is obviously essential . . .

---

2 What are the key ingredients of the job description?
3 How appealing do you find the job description?
4 What other details might a prospective recruit be interested to know?

Other uses for the job specification

The job specification can, in addition to serving as a recruitment instrument, be used in **staff appraisal**. Appraisal is a widely used means of monitoring staff performance and is a feature of promotion assessment in modern organisations. In some organisations – such as hospitals, schools, and profit-making businesses – employees and their immediate line managers discuss personal goals and targets for the coming period (e.g. the next year); the appraisal then involves a review of performance during the previous year, and the setting of new targets. Job details thus help to focus discussions.

Job descriptions can be used to arbitrate on who should be doing what in an organisation, and job analysis can serve as a way of setting standards.

Internal recruitment

Organisations can recruit internally or externally. A decision has to be made as to whether to select an existing employee to fill a job vacancy or to find a suitable outsider (see Figure 10.3).

An insider knows the culture of the organisation, and his or her qualities are already familiar to the managers. On the other hand, an outsider may introduce a lot of new

Advantages	Disadvantages
1 You know what you are getting	1 No new ideas are brought to the organisation
2 It saves on recruitment costs	2 There is no buzz of efficiency that follows an external appointment
3 It saves on induction costs	3 The person moved to a new position will need to be replaced
4 Promotion is seen as an incentive for all members of the organisation to work harder	4 Promotion of one person may upset someone else who is 'overlooked'

Figure 10.3 *Advantages and disadvantages of internal recruitment*

ideas which he or she has picked up elsewhere, but the person is very much an unknown quantity. Job references can be very deceptive.

External recruitment

The way in which external recruitment takes place depends on the type of job involved. Generally speaking, the more junior the position the less elaborate will be the means of recruitment. For example, the post of a junior mechanic may be advertised in a local newspaper, whereas a senior management position may be advertised in national media, including specialist magazines and newspapers.

Task

Why are some jobs advertised only locally and some nationally? (Hint: Your answer should mention skills and costs.)

Recruiting through newspaper and magazine advertisements

Job **advertisements** form an important part of the recruitment process. An organisation is able to communicate job vacancies to a selected audience by this means. Most job advertisements are written (or at least checked) by the personnel department, involving the same skills as marketing a product. Advertisements must reach those people who have the qualities to fill the vacancy.

Job advertisements therefore take many forms, according to the current requirements. Good advertisements contain at least the following information (check the list against Figure 10.4):

- *Job title* – This should form the main heading, possibly in bold print.
- *Job description* – This should highlight the major requirements of the job in a concise format.
- *Organisational activities and market-place* – There should be a brief description of the environment in which the organisation operates.

New Globe Theatre Company
DIRECTOR
London
Basic £20k + car + bonuses

The New Globe Theatre Company is a new group which will be staging productions in major London theatres. The Director will receive an initial salary of £20 000 but can expect to progress steadily to higher rates as the size of the company increases and the scale of operations expands.

We are looking for someone with extensive experience of theatre production and management who will probably have worked in a similar capacity for at least five years in regional theatre productions.

If you wish to take the opportunity of pioneering this new and exciting venture, please forward a letter of application to:

Director of Personnel,
The New Globe Theatre Company,
1001 The Strand,
London WC2 0NG
Telephone 071 900 1234

Figure 10.4 *Advertising a job nationally*

- *Location* – Applicants need to know the location of the organisation and the location of the job (which may be different).
- *Salary expectation* – Figures are not always necessary, but an indication of the salary level (or a recognised grade) should always be given.
- *Address and contact* – This should appear, with a telephone number if appropriate.
- *Qualifications* – Certain jobs require a minimum entrance qualification, which should be clearly stated.
- *Experience* – This should be quantified as it will have a bearing on the expected salary level for the job.
- *Fringe benefits* – The advertiser may wish to mention a company car, a health scheme, and so on.
- *Organisation identity* – This may be in the form of a logo (or simply the name of the organisation).

A good job advertisement, while providing prospective candidates with helpful information, also helps to deter people who do not have the required qualifications for the job.

Presentation of the advertisement is very important as it gives prospective employees a first impression of the organisation.

Task

Cut out three newspaper job advertisements and highlight what you consider to be the strengths and weaknesses of each.

Task

Think about the features of what you would consider to be an ideal job for you. Try to make out a realistic job advertisement to describe this job. You may need to carry out some research to find out such features as a realistic wage and the experience required.

Commercial employment agencies

A number of commercial agencies recruit employees for organisations in return for a fee. These agencies often specialise in particular areas of employment (e.g. office, manual, technical, managerial).

Agencies are widely used in the field of recruiting temporary secretarial help. A secretary signs to work for an agency. The agency then finds a temporary appointment for that person with a company. The company pays the wages direct to the agency, which takes a commission from the pay packet before handing it on to the worker.

Government-run employment agencies

Government-run **employment agencies** play a major part in finding jobs for people who are unable to do so by other means. The job-finding agency established to help school-leavers is the **Careers Service**. Every school has a careers officer who interviews all potential school-leavers. The careers officer works from a local careers office where a list of local job vacancies is displayed. The careers officer puts school-leavers in touch with the personnel departments of organisations in which they are interested.

The **Employment Service** has brought together the Jobcentre network and the network of unemployment benefit offices. The Employment Service aims to:

- give encouragement and help to unemployed people, particularly those who have been unemployed for a lengthy period
- make accurate and prompt benefit payments to claimants, at the same time ensuring that payments are made only to those who are entitled to them.

Jobcentres are to be found in prominent places in many towns. Cards advertising jobs are on open display, and members of the public can ask Jobcentre staff to make appointments for interviews with appropriate personnel departments.

· SELECTION AND INDUCTION ·

Recruitment and selection are closely tied together. Selection is the process of choosing people to work in an organisation. The selection system should attempt:

- to get the best people within existing budgets – that is, those with the most appropriate skills, experience and attitudes
- to select people who will stay with the organisation for a reasonable time
- to minimise the cost of recruitment and selection relative to returns.

Selection **interviews** should be well organised. They should be arranged at convenient times and at convenient locations, and should present to candidates a realistic picture of what the job entails and what working for the organisation will be like.

Before selecting candidates for interview, the organisation should have a clear picture of the 'ideal' candidate. Preparatory work should be done through careful job analysis, description and specification. It is then a matter of sifting through all the applications to find candidates who best meet the organisation's requirements, and drawing up a 'shortlist'.

As part of their interviews, candidates may be given **tasks** to complete to test their aptitude. Also, to check whether applicants are likely to stay with the organisation, it is important to ask them about their future intentions, and to show them the working environment. While the organisation needs to select suitable employees, it is also important that employees select the organisation.

Case Study

Recruitment and selection of older employees

At the B&Q do-it-yourself store in Macclesfield, the average age of the sales staff is 57. The store works very efficiently and consistently achieves profits that are 30 per cent ahead of the targets.

B&Q now has a policy of aiming job advertisements at older people. A national advertisement prompted 7000 replies, and more than 600 over-50s applied for 57 job vacancies at Macclesfield.

The scheme was started because of B&Q's difficulties with the youngsters it employed – in some areas the staff was turning over faster than the stock, so senior management decided to see whether older people would stay longer. Research has indicated that they do, and they take fewer days off for sickness. Employee turnover at Macclesfield is nearly one-sixth that at similar stores, and absenteeism is 40 per cent less. Shoplifting is also low.

As a result of this experiment, B&Q's target is to have 10 per cent of its national workforce aged over 50. The company feels that older staff are prepared to work harder. In addition, many have had a lot of experience of using the materials that the company sells, so that they can give useful advice to customers.

1 What qualities do you think B&Q looks for in its sales staff?
2 Set out these qualities in the form of a job specification for a sales person.
3 Would older people fill this job specification better than younger workers?
4 What disadvantages will there be to B&Q from employing older sales staff?

Interview assessment

An interview assessment form like the one in Figure 10.5 is a useful tool for summarising all the quantities of candidates interviewed.

Factors	INTERVIEW ASSESSMENT					
	Rating					Remarks
	A	B	C	D	E	
Appearance Personality Manner Health						
Intelligence Understanding of questions						
Skills Special skills Work experience						
Interests Hobbies Sports						
Academic						
Motivation						
Circumstances Mobility Hours Limitations						
OVERALL						

A = Exceptional B = Above average C = Satisfactory
D = Below average E = Unsuitable

Figure 10.5 *An interview assessment form*

Work in groups. Choose a job advertisement from your local newspaper, and draw up the appropriate job specification. Decide on the questions that an interviewer would be most likely to ask. You can use the interview assessment form in Figure 10.5 to hold mock interviews for this post.

Handling job interviews

Interviews can be nerve-racking. In a short space of time the candidate must convince the interviewer that he or she is the person the organisation needs. Both the interviewer and the candidate need to be prepared. The candidate can prepare by practising answers to the questions likely to be asked, possibly with the help of a friend who takes the role of the interviewer.

It must be remembered that interviews are a two-way activity. The candidate has a chance to ask questions and find out if the organisation and the job are suitable. Questions can, for example, be asked about training, promotion prospects and social facilities.

Induction

New members of an organisation need to have an induction period – a time during which they are 'shown

DO ✔	DON'T ✘
Find out about the firm before the interview	Be late
Dress smartly but comfortably	Smoke unless invited to
	Chew gum or eat sweets
Speak clearly and with confidence	Answer all questions 'yes', 'no', or 'I don't know'
Look at the interviewer when speaking	Be afraid to ask for clarification if anything is unclear
Be positive about yourself	Say things which are obviously untrue or insincere
Be ready to ask questions	

Figure 10.6 *A candidate's interview checklist*

the ropes'. This might involve a short familiarisation course, following an experienced employee around, part-time working, or some other means of gentle induction. However, in some organisations it may be considered more appropriate for new recruits to be thrown in 'at the deep-end' – to swim or to sink in the organisation according to their ability.

▪ TRAINING ▪

Many organisations develop schemes to enable training to be carried out 'in-house'. At the same time staff may be encouraged to attend college courses to learn new skills. Thus training can be divided into two sorts:

- **on-the-job training** – learning new skills through experience at work
- **off-the-job training** – learning through attending outside courses.

There are various government-sponsored training schemes. For example, the government currently subsidises organisations to employ and train school-leavers. Promotion within an organisation often depends on gaining qualifications to do higher grade jobs.

Skilled workers will be more in demand in the 1990s because of falling numbers of young people entering the job market. Some older people with suitable skills will be tempted back from retirement. Changes in work and child-care patterns will enable more women to combine motherhood with having a career – women will confidently tackle jobs which have been dominated by men in the past, and men will share responsibilities in the home.

Flexibility at work will be vital. Boundaries between traditional trades are breaking down as 'multi-skilling' – the ability to do different jobs – becomes more and more desirable. Workers with transferable skills will be the ones able to train or re-train as new markets develop and expand.

Opportunities are expected to abound for people trained and skilled in technology, in electronics, in science, in management and in the service industries.

Training and Enterprise Councils (TECs)

In the 1990s, **TECs** are expected to play an important role in encouraging training in particular skills. Training and

Enterprise Councils are employer-led independent local bodies whose aims are to foster economic growth and regeneration. TECs arrange training and enterprise programmes in local areas to meet the needs of the local business community. The TECs receive start-up funds from central government, but are expected to become increasingly financed by the local businesses they serve. While this idea might be effective in some densely populated areas where there are concentrations of industries, it may not be so effective in sparsely populated areas with a diversity of small businesses.

Task

Find out about your local TEC. How is it financed and run? What is it doing about training in your area? Is it getting a favourable or an unfavourable press?

National Vocational Qualifications (NVQs)

An **NVQ** is the expression of a person's ability to do a job satisfactorily, and is awarded by a combination of exams and an assessment of competence at the workplace.

It is important for everyone starting work or training to check that they are being given the opportunity to obtain a relevant NVQ.

These are well established in service industries, and in construction, engineering, clerical jobs, clothing manufacture, retail sales, agriculture and horticulture and many more sectors.

It is now possible for older people with experience but no qualifications to have their experience assessed. If they are judged to be competent, they will be awarded an appropriate qualification.

Reforms of training and education

The government has introduced a series of reforms aimed at providing TECs with the opportunity to work in

partnership with local education authorities and the Careers Service, and to equip young people with stronger basic skills and more higher level skills. The key changes are as follows:

- More NVQs have been introduced.
- New diplomas have been developed to record achievements in academic and vocational areas.
- Schools are to be allowed to admit part-time and adult students to their sixth forms.
- Employer influence in the education system has been extended through TECs.
- By 1996, Training Credits will be offered to every 16- and 17-year-old leaving full-time education. These credits may be used to buy training.
- Careers and vocational work in schools have been strengthened.
- More places have been made available in higher education.
- All pupils aged 16 have to stay in school to the end of the summer term.
- Further-education and sixth-form colleges have been given the freedom to expand and respond to their markets.
- Introduction of GNVQs.

· TRANSFER OR RETIREMENT ·

From time to time, a member of an organisation may need to be transferred from one section to another. This may be for the purpose of promotion or to widen experience, or for disciplinary or other reasons.

Retirement

When people reach retirement age they still need to be looked after. Some large organisations, such as Shell UK, prepare employees for retirement by running special courses. Members are given advice and support in preparing for retirement. Their rights and entitlements can be ensured. Once they have retired they can still be looked after by the organisation. It is also possible to look after the dependants of personnel.

· INVOLUNTARY TERMINATION ·

Redundancy occurs when all or part of an organisation closes down, or when particular types of employees are no longer required. It should be noted that it is jobs that are made redundant, not people.

Dismissal

Over the years an elaborate system for the **dismissal** of staff has developed as a result of the large number of cases that have been before industrial tribunals or other courts. The heart of the matter lies in the difference between what is termed **fair** dismissal and what is regarded to be **unfair** dismissal.

The **period of notice** that an employee must be given when being dismissed is stated in the contract of employment, which is a legal document.

Task

Study your own contract of employment or that of a friend. How long a period of notice must be given before employment can be terminated? What does it depend on?

Fair dismissal

If a dismissal is disputed, it may be up to an **industrial tribunal** to decide on the fairness of the action (see page 265). An organisation member can be fairly dismissed under certain circumstances, including the following:

- wilful destruction of the organisation's property
- sexual or racial harassment
- continuous bad timekeeping
- a negligent attitude at work
- inability to do the job which the employee was appointed to do
- sleeping on the job.

Some circumstances may lead to instant dismissal where there has been gross misconduct (e.g. theft from a factory). It is usual for an employee to receive a written warning before being dismissed.

Unfair dismissal

Dismissal for the following reasons would be judged to be unfair.

- *Pregnancy* – A pregnant woman can be sacked only if she is unable to do her job properly (e.g. as a shelf stacker).
- *Race* – A worker cannot be sacked on the grounds of his or her race.
- *Homosexuality* – If an organisation member is a homosexual, that is no reason why he or she should be sacked unless it can be proved that it affects his or her standard of work, or leads to sexual harassment.
- *Union membership* – An employer cannot sack a worker for belonging to a trade union.
- *Criminal record* – If an employer does not find out about an employee's criminal record until some time after employing him or her, the employer cannot sack the worker on these grounds unless it was a very relevant crime (e.g. a cashier who has a record of stealing the petty cash).
- *Religion* – An employee cannot be sacked on grounds of religion.

Task

During your time at work you will go through a number of important phases of self-development. At first you will have few skills and little experience. As time passes you will build up more skills, confidence and experience. It is helpful to review your own progress in a particular job: by looking at where you are now you can get a better picture of where you want to go. Here is a useful review sheet to help you to do this:

The purpose of my job is . . . . . .
I moved into this job because . . . . . .
I believe I am effective in my present job because . . . . .
One aspect of my job that I do well is . . . . . .
The part of my job that I get most satisfaction from is the same/different from what I do well, because . . . . . .
The area of my job that I do least well is . . . . . .
And I believe I could improve on this by . . . . . .
An area of training and development that I would really like to pursue is . . . . . .
The teams I work in/lead are . . . . . .
As a team member I am . . . . . .

I feel I make my best contribution when . . . . . .

The times I contribute least are . . . . . .

The particular skills that I bring to work are . . . . . .

One area I need to be more skillful in is . . . . . .

Some evidence of my success (or lack of success)
*   includes . . . . . .*

Some ways in which I have personally developed over the last
*   two years are . . . . . .*

other. The aims of a business organisation may be to win more orders and to make sales and profits; employees working for that business, on the other hand, may be more concerned with having a longer holiday break, job security and improving their wages and conditions of service. A forum of some description needs to be set up to make these different viewpoints known. Employers and employees need to come together to discuss their needs and problems. Arrangements for such industrial bargaining vary a lot.

· OTHER PERSONNEL FUNCTIONS ·

In this chapter we have so far focused on 'employment procession'. In addition, the personnel department plays an important role in managing health and safety laws, equal opportunities policy, and appraisal and disciplinary procedures. The personnel department is responsible also for representing the management side of organisations in industrial relations matters.

Employers and employees need to have a system for communicating their views and requirements to each

· TRADE UNIONS ·

The media's reporting of **trade union activities** can easily give the wrong impression of the full role of unions in modern industries. Unions are, in fact, involved in all aspects of industrial relations.

A trade union is an organisation of employees, which aims to protect and promote the interests of its members. A trade union is therefore a **promotional pressure group** and a **protective pressure group**. It exerts pressure by means of **collective bargaining** with employers.

Figure 10.7 *Viewpoints require a forum*

Trade unions are organisations formed, financed and run by their members in their own interests, and several have existed for over 100 years. Trade unions today consist of many groups, from bank managers to bank clerks, from school caretakers to school teachers, and from lorry drivers to civil servants.

In British law, a union must be 'independent' – that is, it must not rely on an employer for funds, facilities or organisation. It must show that it can provide adequate services to its members and is able (if necessary) to sustain itself during disputes.

In the United Kingdom there are over 200 certified independent trade unions, although the vast majority of members belong to the largest few unions. They can be divided into three main categories:

- manual worker unions
- white collar unions
- managerial/professional unions.

Task

Using newspapers, library sources and your memory of news programmes, write out the full names of the unions listed in Figure 10.8.

	Initials	Full name of union
Manual	ASLEF	
	NUM	
	TGWU	
	NUPE	
	EETPU	
White collar	NUT	
	APEX	
	NALGO	
	NASUWT	
Managerial and professional	NATFHE	
	BALPA	

Figure 10.8 *Some familiar unions*

Decline of the unions

During the 1980s and 90s there has been a decline in union membership. However, the fall in numbers has not been fastest in the UK under a Conservative government – it fell faster in France with a Socialist government. Indeed, union membership as a proportion of the workforce fell in *every* major industrial country. In the UK the proportion in 1988 was 41 per cent and in France 12 per cent. By 1991 it was down to 37 per cent in the UK.

The central causes of union decline are the changes in industrial structure and the nature of the workforce that have been taking place across the industrial world. These changes include the decline of numbers employed in 'heavy' industries such as coal and steel, the shift of manufacturing employment from production to design and marketing, the increase of women in the workforce, the shift to part-time work, and the growth of small companies and self-employment. Lower inflation in the eighties may also have contributed because people did not have to fight so hard to keep their pay up with price rises.

Internationally, the main area where unions have kept their memberships – though not necessarily their influence – has been the public sector. Where unionisation is lowest, as in France or the United States, the public/private sector balance of union membership is even more heavily skewed towards the public sector.

It is likely that union memberships will continue to decline as the factors which created the unions become less significant. It is possible that trade unions will, by the beginning of the twenty-first century, be seen as having had a natural life of a little more than 100 years, for the conditions that led to their growth will no longer apply. The appaling abuse of workers by industrial management that made the unions necessary rarely occurs today in the developed world, and the ineffective management that operated in the public sector will no longer be tolerated. As industry in the developed world increasingly shifts production (though not design, finance and marketing) to less developed countries, where labour costs are lower, union memberships will be further eroded. This shift is already widespread in the USA and Japan.

Task

A new freight company has been set up, and the management is approached by a trade union official expressing a desire to represent the employees. In your opinion, which union is most likely to approach the company? Think of reasons for and against recognising the union from the points of view of employees and the management.

Some major union aims

A trade union tries to protect its members' interests in a number of ways, including:

- protecting their levels of wages and other payments
- negotiating their hours of work and other working conditions
- keeping an eye on health and safety at work
- protecting promotion opportunities and seeing that employees get fair treatment
- providing benefits for members who are ill, unemployed, retired or injured
- representing members in disputes at work.

However, trade unions do not concern themselves simply with matters related to employment. They also debate issues such as education, political freedom and the international economy, as well as running their own educational courses and giving cash donations to various causes.

Recognition

Prior to 1971, if a trade union wanted to be **recognised** in an organisation, it had no legal backing. Disputes about recognition were resolved by negotiation or a trial of strength between the parties.

However, the Industrial Relations Act 1971, and subsequently the Employment Protection Act 1975, gave a trade union the option to apply to the Advisory, Conciliation and Arbitration Service (**ACAS**) if it was being denied recognition, and therefore bargaining rights.

ACAS has a legal duty to encourage collective bargaining, and will put pressure on an organisation to recognise a union. It cannot force the organisation to agree, it can only encourage recognition. It may take a ballot of employees' wishes, and will usually accept a vote of 30 per cent in favour as grounds for recognising the union.

The objectives of a **recognition policy** are:

- to negotiate bargaining procedures that will be effective and viable in the long term
- to minimise the need for intervention by a third party in disputes
- to ensure that bargaining procedures are consistent with the decision-making structure of the organisation
- to negotiate arrangements conducive to the orderly and peaceful settlement of disputes.

Task

This activity continues with the freight company example of the previous task. After studying the recognition objectives outlined in the text, decide what issues should be included in a recognition policy, and prepare a presentation from either the management or union point of view.

a At what level of support should the union be recognised?

b Should there be only one union?

c How much involvement should the union have in decisions on pay and conditions?

d Should the union have to promise not to call for a stoppage of work?

Your presentation should form the basis for a discussion document. You may wish to adopt a hard stance on some issues at first in order to compromise during negotiations. In a classroom situation you could role-play the negotiations.

Trade union representatives

In medium-sized and large organisations it is not really possible for each employee to negotiate individually with management on every issue or grievance that arises. Instead, trade unionists elect or appoint **representatives** who negotiate on behalf of all the members. These representatives can be divided into two groups.

Shop stewards are elected by union members at their workplace, their task being to represent the views of trade unionists on day-to-day issues. They are not paid a wage by the union since they work at their own job when not involved with union business. However, they are trained by the union to carry out their union duties.

Full-time officials of a union are either elected by the members or appointed by the union's executive team. They are paid out of the union's funds.

To do their jobs well, trade union representatives need skill in talking to members and in gaining a clear view of their problems. They must be able to organise and speak at meetings and present arguments to management, and have an understanding of accounts, production levels, the market and basic economics. They must also have a good knowledge of present laws concerning health and safety, dismissal, redundancy and employment in general. The job of a trade union representative is therefore an extremely demanding one.

The show must (not) go on

Task

The National Union of Students represents the interests of students. Write out a job specification for a union representative at the college you attend.

Case Study

Out of tune

The Royal Opera House in London has experienced some industrial problems. The management offered the musicians a 5.5 per cent increase in payments, but the musicians wanted 20 per cent spread over two years. The Musicians' Union wanted to avoid strike action by using other methods to force the management to negotiate.

For example, the orchestra played some performances in casual dress instead of full evening dress, and the musicians planned to add extra intervals, to make the performances up to 45 minutes longer.

The director of the ROH told the musicians to stay away from work unless they were prepared to work normally. The musicians failed to attend a final dress rehearsal, and the ROH had to cancel all performances until further notice. The Musicians' Union said that this was a 'management lockout' – that is, not their responsibility.

The union said: 'Our members have been staging a limited action because they didn't want to jeopardise productions.'

The management said: 'The musicians' action was in breach of their contracts and threatened the security of their jobs and those of other employees.'

1 *If you were the director of the ROH, what action would you take to avoid the disruptive actions of the musicians?*
2 *What other actions could the musicians take in support of their claim?*
3 *Do you think that this dispute should go to arbitration, or can the management and the union come to an agreement?*

Running a trade union

Full-time union officers in most unions are in three or four grades (see Figure 10.9).

At the top is the general secretary who is an elected official. Next come the national officers, who are usually recruited internally and operate from their union's headquarters. A third band of officers run the union in regions or districts, and they are responsible for the first-line officers who not only organise the union at local level, but also are closely involved with the union membership at the place of work and the local branch. The first-line officers make up the vast majority of all full-time officers.

The annual conference

National officers are responsible for arranging the annual general meeting (often called the annual congress) of the union. At this meeting delegates from the regions meet to discuss issues and pass resolutions setting out the future policy of the union. This annual meeting is very important because, if the union is to truly represent its members, it must listen to and then carry out their wishes.

Unofficial action

Disputes often boil up very quickly at the workplace, and the official union structure may be too slow in moving to deal with such problems. Employees are therefore represented at the workplace by a shop steward who deals with these local matters. Sometimes a shop steward will ask the employees if they want to take industrial action

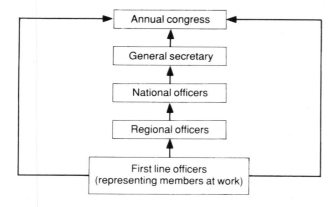

Figure 10.9 *A typical union structure*

without first getting the union's permission. This is known as unofficial action, for which the union will not offer financial or other support unless the action is subsequently made official.

In large factories and other workplaces, there will be a committee of shop stewards supervised by a leading shop steward called a **convenor**.

Task

In a factory making cast-iron pipes all the workforce are in the 'GMB Union'. There are four divisions in the factory – the melting shop, the pipe spinning shop, the pipe coating shop and the despatch department. Draw a diagram showing how the GMB could be organised in this factory.

Case Study

Changes in the labour force

Over the next few years there will be dramatic changes in the structure of the labour force. These will stem from shifts in the population structure, advances in technology, and changing attitudes at work, as well as other factors.

Figure 10.10 shows the projected changes up to the year 2001.

1 *What impact are these changes likely to have on the size, structure and influence of trade unions in the UK?*

2 *How should trade unions adjust their recruitment policies to accommodate these changes?*

Trade unions and disputes

The mass media often give the impression that trade unions set out to create industrial disputes. In the UK the number of disputes is low when compared with other

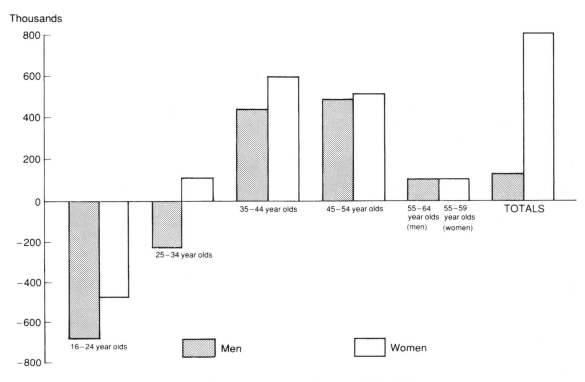

Figure 10.10 *Projected changes in the UK civilian labour force of working age, 1989–2001*

countries. Many trade unionists have never been involved in industrial action.

Trade union representatives help to ensure the smooth running of industry. Wherever people work or meet together, disputes and grievances will occur, and in industry the problems of new technology, complicated payment systems and work that lacks stimulation are bound to create occasional dissatisfaction. Many of these everyday problems are easily dealt with by meetings, discussion and bargaining.

It is the trade union representative who expresses the views of employees. Shop stewards often complain that, while most of their activity is concerned with preventing disputes or strikes, such information is not reported in the newspapers.

Disputes usually occur when all the available channels of discussion and negotiation have been tried. Reasons for disputes are usually very complicated, and one needs to be cautious about saying that one party is 'wrong' or 'right'. If the causes of disputes were that simple, then they would rarely occur.

Negotiation

The way in which negotiation takes place varies from plant to plant. **Collective bargaining** means that representatives of employers and employees get together to discuss and bargain. At one extreme, negotiation may involve just two people. This is a very common arrangement – the personnel manager and a representative of each trade union will have short meetings every week. Most collective bargaining over major issues, however, involves inter-party negotiations. These can range from fairly small groups on each side of the bargaining table to over twenty representatives from management and a similar number from different trade unions. It is important to remember that discussion is the major tool of industrial relations, not industrial action.

Types of industrial action

Non-co-operation. This can take the form of working without enthusiasm, a go-slow or a work-to-rule. Working-to-rule means sticking firmly to the rule book, elements of which might normally be set aside to speed up procedures.

A P&O picket line

Overtime ban. This is a weapon that needs to be used carefully because employees lose earnings while employers pay out less in wage and production costs. It can be most effective when management has important orders to meet.

Strike. A strike is the ultimate weapon of a trade union and occurs when employees withdraw their labour. A strike will normally involve some form of **picketing** action. A picket is a union representative who stands outside the place of work to explain to people why the strike is taking place and why they should not go into the workplace.

Sit-in/work-in. In response to their jobs being made redundant, employees may continue working and 'lock out' the management until negotiations take place.

Types of employer action

Employers and management can themselves take industrial action to put pressure on employees. Actions can include the withdrawal of overtime, mass suspensions, changes in working standards and payment rates, locking employees out, the closing down of enterprises and the removal of plant and machinery at the workplace. The withdrawing of overtime or mass suspensions, for example, are sometimes used by the management to put over the point to union negotiators that it proposes to stand firm on a particular point.

The Trades Union Congress

The trade unions as a group have their own organisation known as the Trades Union Congress (TUC). Every year delegates from the separate unions meet together at a conference to discuss and vote on general union policy. The TUC itself has a permanent body of national officials under the leadership of a president. The TUC puts forward the unions' collective point of view to the government and others. It has a major interest in employment laws, training and conditions at work.

Trade unions in a changing environment

Earlier in the chapter we saw that the number of people in trade unions has declined. There are many challenges and changes which trade unions must face in their environment today, not least of which is the increased affluence of the general labour force.

There has been the decline of manufacturing industry – the traditional base for large unions – and its replacement by the supremacy of the service sector of the economy. Large factories and plants have increasingly been replaced by smaller units of employees, but where large concentrations of employees still work together they tend these days to be

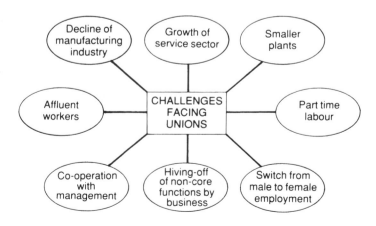

Figure 10.11 *Challenges*

part-time or unskilled workers with limited bargaining powers.

The separating-off of non-core service functions by large businesses means that individual employees have closer contact with their immediate managers.

There has been a move towards increased co-operation between managements and employees. A new style of management increasingly stresses the importance of including employees in decision-making processes, and in return employees are expected to take on wider responsibility for their own actions. For example, **multi-skilling** involves employees being prepared to do many different jobs rather than concentrating on a single job skill. At the same time many employers have introduced single-union deals – rather than bargaining with many individual trade unions they recognise and bargain with a single union.

Case Study

A single-union deal

In November 1991, engineering union leaders and Toyota signed a single-union agreement that was heralded at the time as likely to give the company the lowest labour costs in the motor industry. Five unions competed for the prize of recognition for up to 3300 workers to be employed at Toyota's new plants at Burnaston in Derbyshire and on Deeside. The deal offered workers 'stable employment' in exchange for total flexibility between skills and a commitment to maintain production goals.

Wage levels offered were at a high level for the time. Employees were expected under the agreement to work a 39-hour week despite the Amalgamated Engineering

Union's successful campaign for the introduction of a 37-hour week throughout the engineering industry.

The Japanese owners wanted to establish productivity levels comparable to those of Japanese plants. The agreement also sorted out arrangements for industrial action. If the two sides could not be brought together in their thinking by an independent third party, then a ballot of members would need to be called before any industrial action could take place. The expected output from the plant is 200 000 cars a year from a tiny labour force compared with that of domestic competitors. Workers will have representatives on the company board and they have also been given the strongest commitment to job security in the car industry.

1 *What have the management at Toyota contributed to make this deal a success?*
2 *What contribution has the Amalgamated Engineering Union made?*
3 *How will each side benefit from the deal? Who else might benefit?*
4 *What weaknesses can you see in this deal?*
5 *What ingredients of this arrangement do you see as 'forward looking'?*

Case Study

Union structure in Germany

The German union structure has been shaped by the country's history. In the 1920s the German economy was racked by huge inflation and strikes. In reaction, a new concept known as *Mitbestimmung* (co-determination) grew up. This was based on the radical idea that workers and managers should have equal power in a company. Under Hitler, unions were suppressed but the movement came back after the Second World War. Ironically it was the British who were largely responsible for the shape of the post-war unions in Germany. As the occupying power they saw the need for a stable industrial relations set-up, and brought in experts to create the structure that still survives.

A small number of unions were created (there are now sixteen, headed by the engineers' IG Metall, the biggest union in the world) and a one-plant-one-union rule was

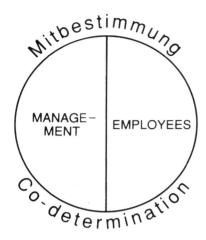

established. With everyone from cook to toolmaker in the same union, there was never any possibility of **demarcation** (who does what job) disputes.

Mitbestimmung took on a definite legal form. It was introduced first in the steel industries and later spread to all large companies. Its basis was a two-level board system, with the workforce and employers equally represented on the supervisory board. If it came to the crunch, employers could always get their way, but the set-up did have a calming effect. Management was able to find out the wishes of labour early on in negotiations.

In addition a **works council** – a non-union body that represents the workers' interests (except on pay) – has been in place since 1972. Conflict is illegal. The principle of co-determination sets the scene for the whole industrial relations atmosphere, which is remarkably free from confrontation. But the other leg of the system – the legal framework – ensures that even if the unions do want to push wages up, their actions are strictly limited.

Wage talks are carried out between unions and employers' organisations. Some are countrywide, while IG Metall negotiates state by state. One state will be chosen by the union; the battle will be fought there, and other states will fall into line.

The idea is to thrash out collective deals which set basic pay levels for different grades of employee. These are binding and, as individual companies are not involved in the negotiations, there is no scope for one company to offer bigger wage increases than another.

The basic wage level is, however, rarely paid, because virtually every company adds a top-up that can boost basic pay by perhaps 25 per cent. These top-ups reflect local skill shortages, and tend to be more generous in large companies. So the idea of the centralised coordinated pay settlement in Germany is really a myth.

1 *What are the main differences between the union structures in Germany and in the UK?*
2 *How and why did the differences develop?*
3 *Which do you think is the better system?*
4 *Why do companies in Germany pay more than the negotiated basic wage levels?*

· EMPLOYERS' ASSOCIATIONS ·

Just as employees have formed and joined trade unions in order to protect their common interests, so employers have formed and joined their own groups. Examples are the Confederation of British Industry (**CBI**) and the National Farmers Union. These associations have two main functions:

● to represent employers in dealings with trade unions
● to give help and advice to employers on a wide range of issues, such as training, calculating tax, etc.

In some industries an employers' association will bargain with trade unions to establish a minimum wage for a given period of time. Individual employers then negotiate additional payments at a company, plant or workplace level with shop stewards.

Most employers' associations today operate principally at a regional rather than a national level.

The Confederation of British Industry

This body was set up to provide a national organisation giving the views of employers. The CBI acts as a mouthpiece for the employers to present their opinions and feelings to trade unions, government, the media and other interested parties.

The CBI collects and makes known information on a wide range of matters. Its *Industrial Trends* survey, published quarterly, gives up-to-date information on the state of business. It also produces a magazine, *CBI News*, giving employers up-to-the minute information on a wide range of business issues.

The CBI has a permanent staff involved in collecting statistics, processing information, publishing articles, and dealing with queries from industrialists. It is led by a Director General.

Professional associations

A **professional association** offers exclusive membership for suitably qualified people in order to enhance the status of their work. There are many types, reflecting the wide range of **professions**, and many were established under the Companies Acts or by the granting of a Royal Charter. Their functions include:

- acting as examiners of standards and providing study facilities and guides (for example, prospective bankers take exams organised by the Chartered Institute of Bankers)
- controlling entry into the professions
- preserving high standards of professional conduct in order to protect the public
- providing members with technical information and keeping them in step with new knowledge.

With more specialisation in the professions, and more people working in the service sector, professional associations have increased in number in recent years.

THE GOVERNMENT AND INDUSTRIAL RELATIONS

ACAS

The Advisory, Conciliation and Arbitration Service (**ACAS**) was set up in the 1970s to act as a 'third party' in industrial disputes. It can do this in a number of ways.

Conciliation is a process through which an independent outsider, such as an ACAS official, tries to act as a channel of communication between an employer and a union. The conciliator will usually meet the parties separately before trying to bring them together.

Mediation is a stronger process whereby an independent outsider proposes the basis for a settlement. However, the parties involved do not have to accept it.

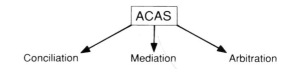

Figure 10.12 *The functions of ACAS*

Arbitration involves both parties agreeing to accept the recommendations of an independent body like ACAS.

New initiatives

Smooth industrial relations are an important ingredient in a prosperous economy. The government meets frequently with representatives of employers and employees to discuss issues of national importance. The government will actively seek the co-operation of trade unions and employers in launching **initiatives** such as training schemes and new health and safety laws.

The government establishes the general framework in which industrial relations is set.

Throughout the 1980s the government established a comprehensive set of new laws limiting the actions of trade unions. Important pieces of legislation have been the banning of secondary picketing (i.e. the picketing of premises not directly involved in a dispute), establishment of the right of individuals and groups to sue unions for damages (including lost business) caused by illegal industrial action, and provisions for balloting members on strike action.

The general feeling is that during the 80s the powers of the unions were increasingly restricted, and that unions became more fully accountable under the law. In 1991 the government published a fresh **Green Paper** (a discussion

☆ Members of the public to have a new right to seek injunction to halt unlawful industrial action disrupting public services

☆ Seven days' notice of any industrial action

☆ The right for an individual to join the union of his or her choice

☆ The right for workers not to have union deductions made from their pay without their individual consent

☆ Rights to information about their union's affairs, including the salaries of principal officers

☆ New rights to combat fraud and vote-rigging in union elections, including the right to inspect voting registers

☆ The right to an independently scrutinised postal ballot before strikes

☆ Postal ballots on union mergers

☆ Collective agreements to be legally binding unless they include provision making them unenforcable

☆ New powers for the government-financed Certification Officer to investigate mismanagement of union finances

☆ Higher penalties for union leaders failing to keep proper accounts

Figure 10.13 *Main proposals of Industrial Relations in the 1990s*

document) setting out some ideas for the future. The title was *Industrial Relations in the 1990s*. The main proposals are shown in Figure 10.13.

Case Study

European social policy

The major changes introduced in 1987 by the Single European Act included giving the community wider powers in the social field to create a European social policy. The social dimension is a vital part of the single market project. It stresses the need to make full use of resources and to distribute benefits more fairly.

After all, the Single Market would be pointless if it weakened people's living standards and levels of protection. People are now free to move and work within Europe. The European Commission is also working to raise training standards, with the focus on encouraging

schemes for further training and the rapid integration of young people into working life. Improving health and safety at work is another major problem being tackled by the Commission, the emphasis here being above all on rules for the protection of workers exposed to hazardous substances.

The main focus for social policy is dealing with **unemployment**, and in particular fighting long-term unemployment and helping young people to find work. Projects assisted by the Social Fund range from training in new information technology, to aid for migrant workers and vocational training for the disabled.

Article 119 of the Treaty of Rome requires men and women to be given equal pay for equal work. Women can insist on these rights through their national courts. In the mid-1970s women's rights were strengthened by three Directives which extended the legal guarantees of equal treatment at work beyond the field of equal pay to include access to employment, vocational training, working conditions and promotion, and social security.

The European Commission aims to underpin the foundations of community social policy by means of a **Social Charter** of basic rights which will reflect the European model of society, social dialogue, and the rights of each and every individual in the community.

The Social Charter is still being developed. It is a package of new measures planned to harmonise working conditions and protect employees throughout the EC. One of the key proposals being debated is to restrict the working week to a maximum of 48 hours. Other suggestions are: a minimum period of four weeks' paid holiday guaranteed to all employees; a rest period of at least eleven continuous hours every day; a maximum eight-hour shift of 96 hours per fortnight for night staff; and, in principle, every Sunday off. Under the charter, part-time workers would have to be given a proportion of full-time workers' benefits (such as paid holidays, pensions and sick pay).

1 Explain what you think might be the consequences of the proposals for:
   a part-time workers
   b full-time workers
   c small businesses
   d large businesses
   e the British economy.
2 You will be able to discover the most up-to-date information about the Social Charter from newspapers and TV and radio news broadcasts. Have the proposals outlined above come into being? Have they been modified?

THE ORGANISATION'S RESPONSIBILITY TO ITS PEOPLE

An organisation is like an organism made up of many parts, of which the most important is probably the **people** who work for it. Other elements of the organism are the processes and procedures that take place within the organisation.

Running an effective organisation with dissatisfied employees is difficult. Most people would rather work for an organisation that they can be proud of, rather than one which embarrasses them in some way. Employees will therefore try to put pressure on an organisation to reflect their own values and ambitions. Of course, some employees have more power and influence than others – a managing director has more than a young trainee. However, a business that ignores a young trainee's views is very short-sighted.

The modern idea of **quality circles** is spreading. Small groups of employees meet together to talk about problems, possible improvements and ideas for change.

Shareholders are another important internal pressure group. As part owners of an organisation they can voice their opinions by making comments at shareholders' meetings, proposing motions for discussion and voting in the way they see fit. Unhappy shareholders can withdraw their support from a company by selling its shares.

The **Board of Directors** is intended to represent shareholders' wishes. It has the crucial responsibility of appointing the managing director of a company.

Trade unions and staff associations exert internal pressures. Groups of employees within a company or plant are formed to represent the wishes of all employees, and much of their influence comes from informal discussions with the managers. More severe pressure can be applied through strike action or other means of removing full co-operation.

If an organisation is of the type to have **members**, these also have an important influence. For example, members of the Church of England may express views about the role of women in the church's ministry. Supporters of a football club may call for the directors to sack the manager, and members of a film club may show their preferences for certain types of film.

Task

What organisations do you belong to? Set out your answer in the form of a diagram like the one shown here for Howard Sykes.

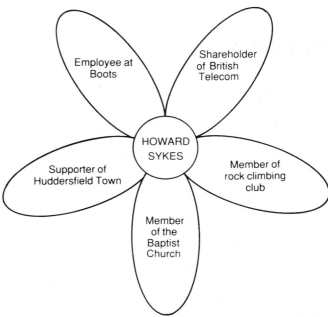

Figure 10.14 *The organisations to which Howard Sykes belongs*

Now consider in turn each organisation that you belong to, and set out a list of some of the internal and external pressures.

It is, of course, not just people that exert pressures – we also have to consider organisational processes. For example, every organisation must generate a cash flow – financial controllers need to ensure that every day there is sufficient cash available to meet the payments it is necessary to make that day (as we see in Chapter 20). Production planners look at the demands that production flows and the operation of machinery make on the way in which a company operates (Chapter 24). Marketing people assess the needs and wants of consumers and relate these to the capabilities of an organisation (Chapter 7), and so on.

Responsibility is two-way

One of President Kennedy's well-known sayings was: 'Do not ask what your country can do for you; instead think of what you can do for your country!'. This remark expresses the idea that responsibility is a two-way affair. Yes, any organisation that you belong to will have responsibilities towards you, but you too will have responsibilities to that organisation.

Task

Choose one organisation of which you are a member. What responsibilities does this organisation have towards you? What responsibilities do you have? You may need to do some research to find out more about these responsibilities. Who can you ask? Are there any leaflets or other documents that set out your rights and obligations?

Case Study

Exploration and production by Shell UK

The following extract is taken from a Shell UK company report for 1991, describing the activities of the exploration and production division (Expro).

'For Shell, the year not only marked the twenty-fifth anniversary of the start of North Sea exploration but, significantly, also saw new "low-cost" oil and gas fields brought on-stream ahead of schedule at a time when a programme was being put in hand for rejuvenating many of the original platforms.

'Oil sales fell by 13 per cent to 208 thousand barrels a day, the lowest for nine years. Gas sales were similarly depressed by 10 per cent.

'Expenditure on exploration and capital investment in production was £495 million, the highest level for some years. In the harsh environment of the North Sea, safety must be given the highest priority, and the improvement of performance in this area is a prime concern of management. It was a matter of the deepest regret, therefore, that ten fatalities occurred in our operations in 1990. These included six people killed when an S61 helicopter crashed while attempting to land on the Brent Spar tanker loading facility.

'Although the sector's performance gives no cause for comfort, there were signs that the company's commitment to safety has begun to yield some general improvement. In 1990, the frequency of lost-time incidents amongst employees and contractors improved from 6.3 to 5.1 per million man-hours worked. In particular, a third year of operation without a lost-time incident was completed on Brent Alpha, demonstrating that substantial further improvement of the safety record is achievable. Strenuous efforts are being made to enhance the effectiveness of safety management.

'Lord Cullen's report on the Piper Alpha disaster, published in November, made 106 recommendations for the improvement of safety on offshore installations. Our staff were prominent in presenting technical evidence on safety management to the Cullen enquiry. Along with other operators, we welcomed the recommendations, many of which had been adopted ahead of the report. Among the physical changes recommended in the report, the most significant were the installation or relocation of emergency shut-down valves, nearing completion in early 1991.

'Our normally good relations with contractor employees offshore were disrupted by a period of unofficial industrial action which affected maintenance programmes on a number of installations.

'Recognising the need for a motivated, stable and skilled contractor workforce offshore, we introduced forward-looking approaches. These give contractors more responsibility for the work and enable them to offer improved terms and job security to their employees. Rather than purchasing services on a job-by-job basis, the five-year engineering services contract provides long-term engineering support and design; the four-year modification and maintenance services contract will enable the contractor to assemble and train a core team of workers who will become part of the platform team.

'A prime target is to minimise the impact of our activities on the environment, including the reduction of emissions during operations and plans for dealing with environmentally hazardous accidents. An inventory of all discharges and emissions was completed, providing a quantitive basis for achieving further improvement and monitoring progress. In August, staff took part in a mock oil-spill exercise, which successfully tested all aspects of our response.'

1 Identify the groups highlighted in the extract to whom Shell Expro has responsibilities.

2 Explain why it is crucial that these responsibilities are met.

3 How can internal and external individuals and groups influence the activities of Shell Expro?

· RESPONSIBILITIES TO EMPLOYEES ·

New employees must be given a written contract of employment within thirteen weeks of starting a job. However, the employer and the employee are said to have formed a contract even before the written contract has been drawn up and signed. This contract is recognised in law when the employee agrees to work for the employer, and the employer agrees to pay the employee a wage or salary.

By law the contract of employment must include the following:

- the title of the job
- the date the job starts
- hours of work
- the rate and method of pay
- holiday arrangements
- the period of notice that must be given
- pension scheme arrangements
- rights concerning trade unions
- the organisation's rules concerning discipline.

New employees agree a date for work to start, and the contract becomes binding from this date.

Task

Obtain a copy of a contract of employment (your own or that of someone else) and identify its various parts.

Imagine that you have to write a contract of employment for an apprentice hairdresser. You may need to carry out some research into rates of pay, and other terms of employment for a hairdresser.

Health and safety at work

Task

Look at the pictures in Figure 10.15. Can you spot the dangers illustrated? List them, and suggest possible action to be taken in order to ensure a safer working environment in each case.

Health and **safety** at work are the responsibility of the **personnel department**. Official regulations covering these topics occupy thousands of pages of text. The details are very important. We shall examine the three main laws that apply.

Figure 10.15 *Hazards at work*

The Factories Act

The Factories Act covers most businesses that use machinery. It therefore applies to a wide range of premises, including garages, printing works, and engineering works, as well as building sites. Note that it does not apply just to 'factories'. Some of the important details of this Act are:

- Adequate toilet and washing facilities must be provided.
- The inside of buildings must be properly heated and ventilated.
- Floors, stairs and passageways must be free from obstructions such as boxes and furniture.
- Floors must not have slippery surfaces.
- Machinery such as presses must have fenced screens to prevent serious injury.
- Fire escapes must be provided and kept in good order. Fire doors should not be locked or obstructed.

The Offices, Shops and Railways Premises Act

This Act is particularly important in relation to office and shop conditions.

- Temperatures must not fall below 16 degrees centigrade in places where people work for any length of time.
- There must be adequate supplies of fresh or purified air.
- Toilet and washing facilities must be adequate for the number of employees and kept in a clean state. There must be running hot and cold water with soap and clean towels.
- Suitable lighting must be provided wherever people walk or work.
- The minimum amount of space for each person is 12 square metres of floor area.

The Health and Safety at Work Act

This Act establishes a responsibility for both employers and employees to provide safe conditions at work. The employer's duty is to ensure, so far as is reasonably practicable, the 'health, safety and welfare at work of all employees'. The employee's duty is to take reasonable care to ensure both his or her own safety and the safety of others who may be affected by what he or she does or does not do. Employers or employees who do not abide by these rules can be punished in a court of law.

An example of an area covered by the Act is protective guards for cutting machines such as food-slicing machines and industrial presses. Accidents occur if the guards are faulty or if they are removed. Generally the workplace must be designed in such a way as to minimise the risk of accidents.

The Act also lays down training standards for employees in potentially hazardous occupations.

This Act is backed up by a Health and Safety Executive which includes representatives of employers, employees and local authorities. Inspectors make sure that the law is being observed.

The safety officer of an organisation must be aware not only of general laws, but also of specific laws and codes relating to particular industries. For example, there are laws relating to workers in mines, the explosives industry, and textiles. On top of this, many industries establish their own safety regulations, often in conjunction with trade unions. A firm's safety officer will normally attend conferences and refresher courses on safety as a regular feature of his or her work.

Task

Investigate the health and safety features that apply either to you in your place of work, or to a parent or friend at their place of work. Set your findings out as a written report.

If you have the facilities, work in a group to produce a video to highlight the health and safety lapses that affect the members of your college. This video could be a short 'commercial' lasting no more than 45 seconds. You should first construct a story board to clarify your ideas, before you shoot the video.

Welfare responsibilities

Many organisations nowadays provide **social facilities** for employees, with special functions at Christmas. The organisation may subsidise a canteen and provide premises for a sports and social club. There may be

Name:	
Salary grade:	
Relationships:	Responsible to: Supervises: Others:
Purpose of job:	
Responsibilities:	These should not exceed eight in number. The responsibilities will cover tasks which the postholder does not necessarily do, but must ensure are done to fulfil the job purpose.
Key tasks:	These should not exceed eight in number. They are tasks to be done by the postholder, each task crucial to the fulfilment of the purpose of the job.
Context of the post:	Facts, factors and circumstances which have a bearing on the fulfilment of the job.

Figure 10.16 *Suggested framework for devising an agreed job description*

company 'outings'. A good personnel manager will keep an eye on the well-being of employees and their families.

Although **staff appraisal** is usually seen primarily as a means of assessing employees' skills, it is also a useful tool to find out the ambitions, concerns and interests of employees. Regular meetings can be arranged between employees and their line managers to discuss how things are going, and possible pathways for job enhancement and promotion.

A common starting point for appraisal is a **job description**, for which a suggested framework is shown in Figure 10.16. The job description will aim to:

● achieve a shared understanding of the job, working relationships and needs and requirements
● bolster co-operation and teamwork by encouraging discussion on the basis of agreement and common acceptance of areas of responsibility
● provide a means of self-assessment
● provide a useful management document for recruitment, selection, organisational review and development, appraisal of training and career developments and requirements.

Every employee should have a job description, which is negotiated between the employee and his or her manager.

Using Figure 10.16 as a basis, draw up a possible job description for your business studies lecturer. Discuss your description with others.

The advertisements in Figure 10.17 appeared in a local newspaper. Do you think that they discriminate in any way?

Discrimination at work

Discrimination against anyone on the grounds of their sex, race, colour or national origin is illegal, whether it be in recruitment, conditions of work, promotion, training or dismissal. Job advertisements must clearly not discriminate. It is then necessary to make sure that interviews are fair, pay is equal for similar work, and that there is no sexual or racial harassment.

There must be no discrimination of any sort. Alleged cases of discrimination can be taken to an **industrial tribunal** or a body such as the **Race Relations Board**.

The **Sex Discrimination Act** set out rights for both men and women. Unlawful discrimination means giving less favourable treatment to someone because of their sex or because they are married or single, and can be either direct or indirect. The Act also covers victimisation.

Direct sex discrimination means being treated less favourably than a person of the opposite sex would be treated in similar circumstances. For example, a policy to appoint only men to management positions is clearly illegal.

Direct marriage discrimination means being treated less favourably than an unmarried person of the same sex. A

SALES REPRESENTATIVE
Get in the fast lane with one of the fastest growing frozen food firms.
PILGRIM FROZEN FOODS
Pilgrim Frozen Foods need a Sales Representative for the area bordered by Leicester, Loughborough, Stamford and Grantham.
You should be presentable and articulate, able to assimilate the latest marketing strategies and be able to develop new sales outlets. Experience of the food trade would be helpful.
In return we offer an attractive remuneration package and company car.
Send your CV together with a hand written letter explaining why you should fill this demanding position to:-
Philip Parker
Sales Manager
Pilgrim Frozen Foods
Blue Street
Boston
Lincs PE21 8UW

RESPONSIBLE PERSON
required to deliver the

in Denton
Tel. (0476) 71739

MERES STADIUM POWERSPORT
require
One Full Time and
One Part Time
FITNESS INSTRUCTOR
Must have a sporting background, good communications and first aid certificate. Experience as a fitness advisor would be advantageous but training will be given.
Salary negotiable upon experience.
Apply in writing to Box No. 339
c/o Grantham Journal
46 High Street, Grantham,
Lincs NG31 6NE.

Figure 10.17 *Job advertisements*

policy not to recruit married people for a job that involved being away from home would not be allowed.

Indirect sex discrimination is less easy to identify. It means being unable to comply with a requirement which on the face of it applies equally to both men and women, but which in practice can be met by a much smaller proportion of one sex. For example, organisations may be indirectly discriminating against women if access to certain jobs is restricted to particular grades which in practice are held only by men.

Victimisation means being treated less favourably then other people because you have in good faith made allegations about discrimination in relation to the Sex Discrimination Act or any other regulation.

A person who thinks he or she has been treated unfairly with regard to sex discrimination can lodge a complaint with the Central Office of Industrial Tribunals within three months of the alleged wrongdoing.

An industrial tribunal is a relatively informal 'court' which will usually meet locally. It consists of a legally qualified chairperson and two ordinary members of the public with experience of industry and commerce. A complainant can either present his or her own case to the tribunal or seek help from the Equal Opportunities Commission.

Figure 10.18 *An industrial tribunal panel*

If the tribunal finds in your favour it can do any or all of the following things:

- make an order declaring your rights
- order that you be paid compensation, which could include lost earnings, expenses, damages for injury to your feelings or damages for future loss of earnings

- recommend that the person or organisation you complain against should take a particular course of action within a specified period – for example to consider you for promotion within the next year.

The **Race Relations Act** makes it unlawful to discriminate against a person, directly or indirectly, in the field of employment on the basis of race, colour or national origin. **Direct discrimination** is treating a person, on racial grounds, less favourably than others are or would be treated in the same or similar circumstances. Segregating a person from others on racial grounds constitutes less favourable treatment.

Indirect discrimination consists of applying a requirement or condition which, although applied equally to persons of all racial groups, is such that a considerably smaller proportion of a particular racial group can comply with it. Examples are:

- a rule about clothing or uniforms which disproportionately disadvantages a racial group and cannot be justified
- an employer who requires higher language standards than are needed for safe and effective performance of the job.

The **Commission for Racial Equality** has produced a code of practice for the elimination of racial discrimination and the promotion of equality of opportunity in employment. This code aims to give practical guidance which will help employers, trade unions, employment agencies and employees to understand not only the provisions of the Race Relations Act and their implications, but also how best they can implement policies to eliminate racial discrimination and to enhance equality of employment. This code covers a variety of areas including recruitment, training and appraisal.

· MANAGING PEOPLE ·

The successful operation of an organisation's activities depends ultimately on its people. The abilities of the labour force are the result of training, background and experience. Managers who wish to obtain the most from their labour force treat them as a valuable resource and keep them motivated. As many of an organisation's labour force tend to work in operational activities providing

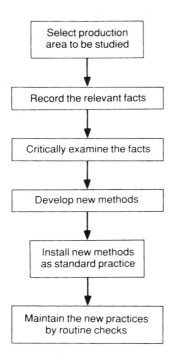

Figure 10.19 *Stages of a method study*

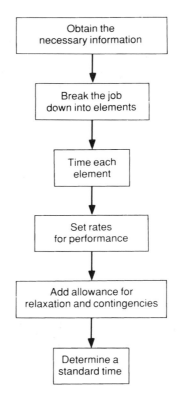

Figure 10.20 *Stages of a time study*

goods or services, operations managers need to be involved with policy decisions affecting employees within their area of responsibility.

Organisation and methods (O&M) (quite commonly called work study) has developed as a managerial science to help managers to use their labour force more effectively. Its primary concern is to analyse efficiency in order to maximise the use of resources. By looking at the ways in which activities are carried out by human and material resources, O&M tries to ensure that the techniques used create the maximum possible benefits for the organisation. Its objectives are:

- to reduce costs by establishing the most cost-effective methods of doing a job
- to standardise such methods
- to establish a time pattern of working
- to install the findings as standard working practices.

Work study consists, therefore, not only of a study of *methods*, but also *measurement* in order to achieve higher productivity.

Method study involves examining both existing and proposed methods of undertaking a job, in order to find a

way to do the job more easily and therefore increase output. The steps are shown in Figure 10.19.

Work measurement is the establishment of techniques to time activities so that they can be carried out with a defined level of performance – for the purpose of improving worker motivation, creating incentives and improving future performance. The steps are shown in Figure 10.20.

Task

In this activity you should look at how you manage your studies. First conduct a method study of your techniques to discover whether you could work more efficiently. Then conduct a form of work measurement to analyse what you should be expected to undertake over certain periods of time.

After a method study and work measurement process have been carried out, management must decide what changes, if any, need to be made. The information available will cover the placement of machinery, ergonomics, the main communication channels and how they interact, the way in which people work, their incentives, facilities, problems and motivation.

Work study can make its practitioners unpopular because of its association with sensitive areas such as payments, incentives and working methods and speeds. Success in handling the exercise depends upon the extent of the trust between managers and those involved in producing the goods or services. Some organisations run **appreciation courses**.

THE EFFECT OF NEW TECHNOLOGY ON THE HUMAN RESOURCE

Technology involves the use of scientific discoveries to solve problems, and putting ideas into practice. New technologies lead to new goods and services, as well as changing the ways in which existing ones are made or offered. New jobs are created, because new production methods and new markets are opened up. At the same time new technology does has negative effects. For example, old ways of life and methods of production become outdated, so some plant and products are replaced, and people have to look for new occupations.

Task

Name three ways in which new technology has improved existing products or led to the development of completely new products. In each case make a list of all the benefits created by the new technology, and another list of all the negative effects. Do the benefits to society of the new technologies that you have mentioned outweigh the costs? Why might different people have different views on this subject?

New Technology in production processes

Computer-aided design

Twenty-five years ago designers spent a lot of time at drawing boards. The skills brought to the job included:

- creativity (thinking up ideas, styling, etc.)
- analysis (calculating strengths, quantities, etc.)
- mechanical drawing (putting the ideas on paper).

Although the central role of the designer was to carry out creative and analytical work, much of the time was spent on drawing and redrawing. Today, with the coming of computers, it is possible to use a computer screen instead of a drawing board. This saves considerable time and effort.

A designer employing a CAD (**computer-aided design**) program uses a keyboard, a screen and a graphics pad. The designer is able to program the computer to perform many quick calculations of angles, volumes, dimensions etc. Having drafted the design, the designer can see a view of the item from different positions, and view it as a solid object instead of merely as a series of lines. The computer can then be asked to calculate all the important features of the design, and to show how these change when, for example, one dimension is altered.

CAD in industry has revolutionised almost every area of industrial design, from wedding dresses to supertankers.

Control

The word '**control**' means the ability to direct or restrain. A controller carries out a function automatically. For example, in a washing machine, once a program has been set, the controller takes over, switching the heater on and off, regulating the water supply and outlet, and switching the motor that rotates the drum (Figure 10.21).

Robotics

Robots are really an application of automatic control. They are of special benefit for jobs that are repetitive and where human manipulative skills are not required. Another application is in dangerous or unpleasant work areas.

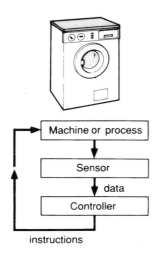

Figure 10.21 *Basic features of control*

Robots vary in the method of programming. Some are programmed by keying in instructions, but this is laborious and liable to error. In other cases the robot can learn to copy movements carried out by a human operator. (It is ironic that the operator teaching the robot is the person likely to be replaced by it.) As robots become more 'intelligent' they increasingly also have some system for checking progress (e.g. an electronic eye or camera).

The benefits of robots are therefore:

- People can be replaced by robots in mundane jobs where human intelligence is not required (e.g. routine assembly work).
- Robots can be used where working conditions are difficult or dangerous (materials may be heavy, hot or radioactive, or deep underground or under water).

The disadvantages of employing robots are:

- Further erosion of craft skills may result.
- Greater levels of capital investment increase pressure for shift working.
- A new danger is introduced into the workplace – the first fatality from an accident involving a robot has already happened.

CADCAM and CIM

Over recent years many developments have taken place in production industries. As well as computer-aided design (CAD), developments have taken place in machine tools. Many are now controlled numerically by a computer (computer numerical control – CNC). Other developments have taken place in robotics. With CADCAM (computer-aided-design/computer-aided-manufacturing), data from the CAD system is used to drive machines, making the CAD system part of the manufacturing process.

A more recent development is called computer integrated manufacturing (CIM). Not only is the product designed on a CAD system, the software also orders materials, drives CNC machine tools and has its own control system which provides data for purchasing, sales, etc.

Task

Investigate human resourcing in two contrasting business organisations (e.g. small/large, private-sector/public-sector, local/regional, college/business, etc.). Show how the management of human resources in these organisations affects the quality of work. Present your findings in the form of a written report. In addition you should show how legislation regarding employee rights, health and safety, and equal opportunities affects working practices. Comment on how changing technology in the workplace affects work patterns.

Case Study

Artificial intelligence

In the 1970s and 80s great things were expected of the development of 'artificial intelligence' (AI) through computers. It was hoped that their tremendous ability to calculate would enable them to 'think' at a higher level than mere mortals. The aim was to produce a machine able to analyse data and reason for itself. It was hoped that the knowledge of an expert could be recreated within a machine using a system of rules and facts.

Why has AI failed to live up to expectations? One of the reasons is that researchers underestimated how difficult it was to encode expert knowledge and ordinary wisdom into rules. They also failed to recognise how time-intensive and expensive it would be to keep such devices up to date, and how people are reluctant to rely solely on a machine for important answers. Although such expert systems are successful in specialised fields of engineering and finance, forecasts that we would all be using them in everyday life have never come true.

Now, in the mid-90s, rather than trying to out-perform human beings in problem-solving skills, there are signs that AI applications are earning their keep by processing routine tasks, enabling people to concentrate on more demanding work.

Typical of the new approach is work at the Veterans Medical Centre in Dallas, to produce a cost-effective assistant for doctors in specialist clinics. The aim is not to increase expertise but to cut costs and time. A recent device developed by the hospital is called Epileptologist Assistant, and is used by nurses in a follow-up clinic to question epiletpic patients before their examination by a doctor.

A doctor can spend 60–80 per cent of his or her time on relatively trivial matters. About 20 per cent of the time is spent on interesting and exciting cases, and just 1 per cent on treatment that needs special research or consultation with a colleague. Rather than concentrate on that 1 per cent (the original idea of developing an expert system), it is possible to provide the best assistance to manage the 60–80 per cent of routine work.

The 'Assistant' prompts the nurse to ask between 30 and 50 set questions from a choice of 300. Each line of questioning is dictated by more than 200 rules, and at the end the program delivers a full report of patient responses as well as suggesting changes in treatment which the doctor can adopt or alter during consultation.

1 *What was the original view of the value of expert systems?*
2 *What is the new view of the value of artificial intelligence highlighted above?*
3 *What other areas of organisational life could benefit from the use of AI?*
4 *Think of familiar situations in which AI could be used routinely. What would be the chief benefits resulting from its implementation in these cases?*

Element assignment

Reducing absenteeism

This assignment can help you to provide evidence for assessment, or claim the following Core Skills outcomes:

Communication
Receive and respond to a variety of information
Communicate in writing

Personal skills
Transfer skills gained to new and changing situations
Identify and solve routine and non-routine problems
Use a range of thought processes

Background
Superior Foods Meat Group is the largest producer of meat products in the country. Its meat products are sold to all major retailers, as well as small independent retailers and the catering industry. The Group employs 7000 people. Within the Group there are 15 companies. Each company is run as a separate business being responsible for its own management and profit.

The managers and employees in each company within the Group are encouraged to identify with their own company. A lot of 'red tape' is avoided by allowing each company to be independent.

Superior Foods Meat Group now feel that it is important to keep absenteeism within the group to a minimum if it is to maintain a competitive cost position.

There are two main reasons why absenteeism is regarded as an important issue.

1 The working environment in meat factories contributes to higher than average absence rates. Meat products need to be kept chilled, and working areas and equipment need to be regularly washed down. Working in a meat factory is therefore less pleasant than say, a confectionery factory. The meat factory is by comparison cold, wet and drafty. The smell of meat can also be unpleasant.
2 Absence makes scheduling difficult. If people go absent at short notice it is difficult to plan adequate cover. In other factories it is possible to have buffer stocks of products that can make up for any shortfalls in a particular production line. However, because meat goes off so quickly it is impossible to create stockpiles.

For the purposes of this assignment, absence is defined as follows:

- Absence due to illness – during the first seven consecutive days of sickness it is not necessary for an employee to obtain a doctor's certificate to establish that he or she is ill. This is 'self-certificated sickness'. Thereafter a doctor's certificate is required ('certificated sickness').
- Non-authorised absence – absence that is not certificated, where the employee has provided no explanation, or an explanation that was unacceptable to the employee's supervisor.
- Authorised absence – absence approved by the supervisor usually in advance, including jury service, public duties, bereavement, leave and other extenuating circumstances.

The following 'fast facts' about absenteeism may be helpful:

- The average length of sickness absence is two days. seventy-five per cent of all absence is for fewer than three consecutive days.
- An absence rate of 8–9 per cent is equivalent to an employee's annual leave entitlement plus statutory days combined. Employees with such an absence rate (holidays included) would not be available for work for 11 weeks of the year.
- While all sites have a personnel department, most older sites have limited occupational health facilities (usually one or two full-time nurses, with a doctor visiting twice per week).

The following data refers to absence in 1992.

	Self-certificated sickness	Certificated sickness	Non-authorised absence	Authorised absence
Meat Group Average	7.2%	3.8%	1.2%	0.4%
'Worst' Factory	15.0%	4.2%	2.2%	0.8%
'Best' Factory	5.3%	3.1%	0.4%	0.3%
Meat Industry	5.8%	3.5%	0.7%	0.5%

Figure 10.22 *Fast facts about absenteeism*

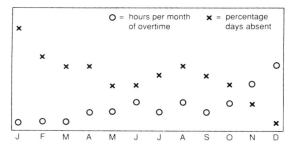

Figure 10.23 *Availability of overtime in relation to absence rates*

- The majority of shop floor workers are represented by the Transport and General Workers Union.
- Employees with more than six months' service who are absent due to illness receive 'sick pay' at the full hourly rate from and including the first day's sickness absence, up to a total of 60 days per annum (thereafter at the company's discretion).
- Docking of pay for non-authorised absence is at the discretion of supervision.

In the graph in Figure 10.23, the circles represent availability of overtime and the crosses show average absence rates (hours per month, and percentage days absent respectively).

Task

Because of the importance and sensitivity of the absence issue, the Group has set up a group-wide management/trade union working party which has the following aims:

- to develop a common action plan to reduce absenteeism and its effects on production and quality.
- to establish specific absence controls that could be implemented at shop floor level to promote good attendance.

You are a member of the personnel department. You need to produce a short report setting out Personnel's point of view to the working party at the first meeting. The objective of this first meeting is to set out Personnel's overall policy towards absence and to make this clear to the working party.

You should consider the following points in your report:

- specific initiatives that you feel could be worthwhile
- realistic 'target' levels for the progressive reduction of absenteeism
- the roles and responsibilities of companies':
  - production line management
  - personnel departments
  - occupational health departments
  - trade unions
- the desirability of introducing incentives for good attendance (bonuses etc).

chapter **11** INVESTIGATING JOB ROLES IN ORGANISATIONAL STRUCTURES

C hapter 4 looked at organisational structures in different types of business organisation. In this chapter we go on to look at job roles and at the nature of group and team working in modern organisations. We also build on work in the previous chapter, looking more closely at job and person specifications.

In modern organisations managers place great emphasis upon understanding the needs of employees. Valuing the workforce also helps to defuse problems caused by changes in the employment market – the 'demographic timebomb'. Ways of achieving co-operation and improving contributions from the workforce include teamwork, meetings, quality circles and extensive training and development.

▪ WHO DOES WHAT IN AN ▪ ORGANISATION

Some organisations are very small while others are very large. On the whole, the larger an organisation the more complicated its organisational structure. Large organisations often require several 'layers' of command. Some people spend a lot of time making important decisions while others are mainly involved in carrying out routine tasks and following set procedures. Different types of business organisations are discussed in Chapter 3 and the operation of organisational structures is analysed in Chapter 4.

Management

Managers have the job of deploying an organisation's resources and making policy decisions. Managers use and develop systems for 'organising the organisation'.

Strategic (senior) managers

Strategic managers make top-level decisions concerning the scope of an organisation's activities. These decisions

set out what the managers want an organisation to be like and to be about. Strategic decisions are therefore vital for the development and welfare of an organisation. They require detailed analysis and considerable use of skilled judgement. Examples of strategic decisions include deciding to develop a new product, to open up new markets, or to carry out major investment projects.

Middle managers

Middle managers organise and control the resources of an organisation within established guidelines. Middle managers do, however, usually have considerable scope for using their own judgement and for bringing in new ideas after consultation with senior management. Examples of middle management decisions include setting out and controlling a departmental budget, organising a sales force, and changing prices of products in response to changes in the market.

Junior/supervisory management

Junior managers are usually concerned with short-term operational decisions. These are routine and frequently recurring tasks that can be carried out by following straightforward decision rules. Examples include managing stock, arranging schedules for the delivery of goods, and organising hours worked by staff.

Unfortunately the title 'junior manager' or 'trainee manager' is sometimes used by organisations to encourage people to work hard for relatively low pay, because the title 'manager' seems to give a certain status. Anyone taking on a job described as a junior manager should check the opportunities for promotion.

Task

Study one organisation with which you are familiar. What is the management structure within the organisation? Are there distinct layers of senior, middle and junior management? Determine the nature of the decisions made at each level, and give examples.

Supervisors

Supervisors are quite often the backbone of an organisation. They are people who know how things should be done at 'ground level'. They work with middle and junior managers to put plans into practice at an operational level. Supervisors know the capabilities of all the resources (machines, people and materials) because they work in among them every day.

Supervision is a skilled and demanding job. The supervisor is like a sergeant major in the army giving orders to the ground troops. He or she will be first in line to deal with day-to-day problems as and when they occur.

Organisations therefore look for people with good qualifications to fill supervisory roles. They are likely to have mathematical and communication skills as well as a good knowledge of the technology of their industry. Supervisors may have risen 'through the ranks' of their organisation by hard work and the ability to cope with responsibility, so they need to have their skills periodically upgraded through training courses.

Tasks

Figure 11.2 shows the specification for a supervisor in a large office.

Attributes	Essential	Desirable
Physical		
Health	General good health	
Grooming	Well dressed and good presentation	
Voice		Well spoken, friendly
Attainments		
Job experience	Experience with administration work, reports, memos, and documentation	
General education		4 GCSEs including Maths and English
Job training	Willing to be trained to required level	
Special aptitudes		
Skill with words		To a good standard of written and spoken English
Skill with figures		Good level of numeracy
Interests		
Social	Able to socialise with staff and customers	
Intellect	Common sense and a good level of intelligence	
Disposition		
Leadership	To be responsible for staff and to be responsible to management	
Self reliance	To be punctual and to act in mature and reliable way	
Other points	To follow and abide by company rules and to help other staff	

Figure 11.2 *Specification for a supervisor*

Figure 11.1 *A supervisor's operational duties*

Sets daily schedules

Oversees work being carried out

Identifies and sorts out operational problems

Introduces new staff to work tasks

Gives advice and guidance

Keeps check on levels of production

Applies expert knowledge of job

Liaises with management

SUPERVISOR

1 What does the person specification tell you about the qualities that a prospective employee would need to have to fill the post? How clear is the specification?

2 Now produce your own person specification for two different roles within an organisation. One of the roles should be a management position and the other for a supervisor.

3 Produce a job description for the two posts that you have outlined. (Refer back to Chapter 10 for more details.) Explain the purpose of job descriptions and show how they help organisations.

Operators

Whilst operational activities may be routine, they need to be done with great care and precision. There are many different types of **operators**. In a supermarket there are shelf fillers and checkout staff; in a textile company there are cutters, stitchers and packers, etc. Operators need to be made to feel that they are valued, and there should be opportunities for them to learn new skills, so that they can move on to higher grade work.

· VALUING EMPLOYEES ·

If an organisation's activities seem to run smoothly it is easy to take the employees for granted. If something goes wrong, it is equally easy to blame them. Such an approach ignores the needs of employees and fails to take into account *why* something is or is not taking place. All organisations must plan for and manage effectively the people they employ to achieve the most from the skills and experiences they possess. An organisation's most valuable asset is its people and the work they do; each is indispensible to the other.

Think what might happen if a certain manager failed to manage his or her employees and organisation effectively. Initially, this might cause bottlenecks, inefficient procedures, possibly poor communication channels. Staff would be put in difficult and uncomfortable situations. They might lose time, not know what to do, be put under pressure unnecessarily, have to apologise to customers, and so on. How would employees react to these events? In the early stages many would put up with the inefficiencies of management in the hope that things would improve. If

the weak management remained, morale would start to wane, some employees might become resistant to events taking place, and become more time-conscious about the hours they worked. After a period many might leave, and some of those leaving might be key members of staff with important functional responsibilities – for which they have never been properly recognised and rewarded. Replacing them with staff of an equal calibre could be impossible without extensive delay and training costs. The organisation would, therefore, have suffered an **own-goal**.

Over recent years the concept of **human resource management** has become increasingly recognised. Human resource management places more emphasis upon people in the working environment and how their activities and needs should be understood, provided for, maintained and satisfied.

Case Study

Using the workforce properly

Using the workforce properly is a key to Australian industry becoming truly competitive, according to Dr Michael Deeley, the chief executive of ICI Australia.

Dr Deeley believes that improved competitiveness requires a fundamental shift in direction in relationships with employees: 'We need to move from seeing employees as an undesirable and variable cost, to seeing them as an important investment; as the key to improving performance through fully utilising their talents.' Dr Deeley thinks that this can be achieved by moving away from a workplace where employees are controlled, to a workplace designed to encourage them to become more committed: 'This is where employees are trusted and empowered, where management provides support and motivation by focusing on performance and outcome.'

This idea would create a workplace based upon commitment. An individual would have a job that was flexibly defined within a career structure and with opportunities for further advancement and training. Dr Deeley feels that 'where people have control over their jobs, where they have freedom to act and an ability to influence their working environment, they have job satisfaction and an outlet for their creativity. This in turn leads to more committed employees with secure and satisfying jobs.'

In support of these views is the Institute of Personnel Management of Australia (IPMA), which launched its annual Human Resources Week with the theme 'Our Workforce – Use It or Lose It', designed to raise public awareness of the importance of people to Australia's future. During the week the role of human resource management in Australia was discussed and debated.

1 How will using the workforce more effectively help Australian industry?

2 What fundamental shift in attitudes did Dr Deeley suggest?

3 Why did Dr Deeley suggest more participation by the workforce?

4 How might a Human Resources Week improve the ways in which organisations manage people?

· THE DEMOGRAPHIC TIME-BOMB ·

Over recent years organisations have been hit by recession, shortages of people with suitable skills, increasing competition as well as a massive range of changes requiring them to manage their human resources more effectively. Never before has the requirement to recruit, train and retain suitable staff been quite as important.

As we move through the 1990s, however, these challenges will not only continue, but will also become more intense as the pace of change increases even further and the **demographic time-bomb** affects the availability of skilled labour.

The demographic time-bomb refers to changes in the employment market. It is estimated that the numbers of young people entering the employment market will fall drastically by the end of the century. By 1999 the number of people between 16 and 19 years of age will fall by a quarter, or 850 000. Organisations will therefore face growing problems recruiting suitable young people and trainees. There will be too many organisations competing for too few people with the right skills. The solution to this problem seems to be for organisations to reassess completely the whole range of their recruitment, retention and training policies.

Consider what happens if an employee leaves:

- Skills are lost to the organisation and may take a long time to replace.
- Specialist knowledge of how the organisation operates leaves with the employee.
- Those who leave may join a competitor.
- Quality of the organisation's output can be adversely affected.
- Pressure can be put on other employees to do more work.
- The recruitment, induction and training of another team member can be expensive.
- There can be a demotivating effect upon those who remain with the organisation.

The demographic time-bomb can be defused by maximising the contributions from existing employees through efficient human resource management designed to improve retention, and by looking to groups such as women who have previously stayed at home, the disabled, the over-50s and the long-term unemployed, who can be re-trained.

Task

Explain in detail how you might feel if you worked in a small section with four staff, and within a six-month period the other three staff left. (Your answer will obviously depend on whether all or any of the three people were replaced!)

· ACHIEVING CO-OPERATION ·

The successful organisation in the 1990s will be the one which has a **clear vision** of the future and of the resources it requires to take it there. This vision must relate to the future of employees and emphasise their role in achieving corporate goals. To attain such goals an organisation's:

- culture
- structure and communications system
- management
- policies and actions

must all be in line with this mission.

At the heart of reaching stated goals is the co-operation of all employees. Most want to do a good job, be recognised for what they do, feel adequately rewarded for their skills, learn more, develop their skills and be able to contribute their ideas and efforts. Managers achieve co-operation by providing a **secure environment** for employees. This involves them in having to make decisions and solve problems, but at the same time they must elicit commitment from employees by treating them with respect, providing them with a flow of information and a sense of involvement with the organisation. The remainder of this chapter looks in detail at ways of achieving this.

· TEAMWORK ·

Teamwork and the development of a **team spirit** can go a long way towards increasing the sense of satisfaction people obtain from their working environment, and to providing them with a sense of purpose. For example, imagine what it would be like if you played in a rugby team in which the scrum-half did not like passing the ball, or if you were in a play in which the actors were competing with each other to impress the audience. In both situations confusion would arise. The group or team would not perform well because individuals would be working against each other – teamwork would be lacking.

Task

Choose one example of a team or group situation in which you operate. How important is it that you co-operate with other members of the group to perform the activity? What would happen if you did not?

At work, lack of teamwork might lead to a job not being completed or, if it is completed, it might be finished badly. Working relationships might be fractious. People might not listen to each other or respect others' views. They would be working as individuals and not heeding advice or providing suggestions. Group values, pride and purpose would not exist.

A team can be defined as 'a collection of people with a common purpose who communicate with each other over

Figure 11.3 *Working together for a common purpose*

a period of time'. In a team the contributions of individuals are complementary. At the very centre of team operations is **collaboration**. See Chapter 3, page 89 for an introduction to Teams.

Whenever a team undertakes a task, there are three elements involved in making decisions about its completion:

- The **task** is the content of the work. For example, the team may be involved in a project or in the provision of a good or service.
- The **process** is all of the interaction which takes place between the different members of the group. It involves people working together, the relationships they establish and the feelings they generate within the group. One test of a good team is how well its members can contribute to a sequence of activities when they work apart.
- The **action schedule** is how the team is organised to undertake a particular task. It will set out who does what and all the procedures necessary for completing the task.

Outward Bound is one organisation which enables people to discover what they can achieve by teamwork, mutual support and co-operation with others. Their courses provide opportunities for people to learn by actually doing rather than simply watching or listening. Lever Brothers sends apprentices on Outward Bound courses to teach them about themselves and each other – by learning about self-reliance, assertiveness, consideration and the ability to think, the company feels that the trainees will be able to contribute more to a team and be of greater value to the company.

Task

In *Making It Happen*, Sir John Harvey-Jones says: 'When I took over as chairman of ICI one of my first actions was to arrange for the executive directors and myself to spend a week away together in order to discuss how the board should lead the company, and how we should organise our work.'

How does this statement by Sir John relate to the *task*, *process* and *action* schedule discussed in the text?

Case Study

Howtown Outdoor Education Centre

Early in 1991, three members of the business studies staff at Darlington College of Technology took a group of twenty-five BTEC National students in Business and Finance away to Howtown Outdoor Education Centre by the side of Lake Ullswater. The education centre, run by Durham County Council, is staffed and managed by teachers with expertise in outdoor activities.

The main reasons for taking the students to Howtown were to find out (1) how practical problem-related activities could relate to the BTEC National course, (2) whether working away from college would help the students to work together more closely, and (3) if it would be possible to build an assignment around the activities.

Upon arrival at the centre students were divided up into groups/teams and introduced to their instructors. Almost immediately the emphasis was placed upon allowing each group, wherever possible, to take responsibility for its actions. The groups were presented with a timetable of activities with the only criterion being that they had to spend a night away from the centre. Wherever possible, with any of the activities chosen, students would be encouraged to develop skills and be provided with feedback and support not only from staff but also from the group.

The key concept underlying the process was that, by putting students through a series of challenges, the experience would help them to understand their own strengths and this would show them how to relate more closely to others. It was hoped that building such awareness would assist them to develop personally in areas such as:

- self-confidence
- leadership
- working with others
- making decisions
- developing trust in others
- independence
- tackling problems as a group
- taking into account the feelings of others.

Whereas some of the activities were specifically for outdoors (e.g. skiing and climbing), others could be developed with a business application. For example, the raft-building exercise involved classroom work in which students were provided with a budget; they then designed and later built a raft with the materials they could afford. Quality control involved testing the raft – and the inevitable ducking!

Throughout the course activities were supported by good humour. Wherever someone struggled, others in the group were quick to respond with help, guidance and encouragement. Friendships and support for each other characterised the week. Given a purpose, a team and a problem to solve or a task to undertake, each of the groups responded well. In fact many of the students were surprised at how they could work with others and just what they could do if they belonged to a team. The course seemed to make them more aware of themselves and built up their self-confidence. Back at college it was felt that the programme of activities had helped the group to interact better and this was borne out by other members of staff.

1 Why was it important to allow each group to take responsibility for its actions?
2 Imagine you are a member of a group building a raft. Identify:
  a the task
  b the process
  c the action schedule.
3 What importance would an employer attach to staff being able to work effectively in a team?

Forming teams

The ability to work in a team is an important element in the learning process. When employers look for new staff, they do not just concentrate upon those with the right qualifications, important though these are. They look for people with the right personality for the job, who can cope with the work involved and also work with others. Smith Kline Beecham Pharmaceuticals recently advertised a management post in a daily newspaper. As the following extract from the advertisement shows, the company was looking for someone with both technical and business skills who could work well with others:

'You will lead a small team which is involved in all stages, from negotiation with key suppliers to the provision of first-class user support services. The implementation of new technology in the scientific environment presents special challenges, and you will need to combine a confident and persistent approach with tact, diplomacy and excellent communication skills. We are looking for someone whose high level of technical expertise is matched by business and management skills.'

The success of any project usually depends upon all the members of the team. For example, imagine a group of workers building a house. The completion of the project and the quality of the final product depends upon when each specialist turns up and how well they carry out their task. If anyone fails to pull their weight the success of the project is affected. Or imagine a group of people putting up a marquee: if they do not work together and pull on the ropes at the same time, it is not possible to erect the tent.

In an organisation, groups or teams may be formed by people who share workstations, who have a similar specialism or who work on the same project. This sometimes involves working with others from different departments or from other areas.

Before any team can be put together a number of issues have to be addressed. These include:

- the size of the team
- the nature of the project
- the requirements of the group
- the roles of members of the team
- the abilities of the group members
- the norms of the group.

Case Study

Ignore teamworking at your peril

Heslegrave Gill, a Yorkshire-based consultancy, recently claimed that UK companies are ignoring one of their greatest assets by failing to harness the talents of the people working for them. They feel that giving more attention to teamworking would enable UK firms to emulate the success of the Japanese and they point to several examples to prove the case.

Teams of shift workers at the Scunthorpe Rod Mill in South Humberside were looking at ways of achieving greater levels of productivity. Team leaders were instructed in skills such as time management, identification of training needs and problem solving. The teams were given scope to manage their own work and introduced initiatives to improve both product quality and customer service.

At Penine SCS, a small Halifax firm supplying pneumatic equipment to British Steel and British Coal, the teamworking approach was used to involve employees in the running of the business. Mel Westwood, the company's Managing Director, commented: 'We have now installed what we call profit centre managers. These are people from the workforce who are in charge of each department. They are provided each month with a profit and loss report and have set up their own budgets. We have introduced a profit-sharing scheme and they know exactly what the financial position of the company is. We don't hide anything.'

The employees at Penine SCS became so committed to the best interests of their company that they insisted on

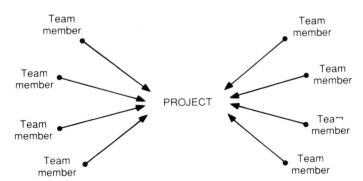

Figure 11.4 *Working together as a team*

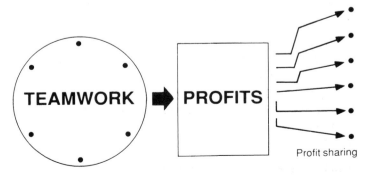

Figure 11.5 *Benefiting from teamwork*

postponing the profit-sharing scheme for a year so that a reinvestment programme could lay a solid foundation for the future. They showed that they wanted rewards in the future and not in the short-term.

1 *Why do you think that many UK companies have ignored the talents of their workforce?*
2 *What are the benefits of teamworking?*
3 *Comment briefly on how teamworking has helped:*
   a *Scunthorpe Rod Mill*
   b *Penine SCS.*

A **strong team** is one having a sense of purpose, with clear objectives and goals. Within the group there will be norms of attitude, behaviour and discipline. Individual team members will be open about their views, be prepared to confront where necessary but will be prepared to co-operate with decisions made by the group. Support and trust are important in a team, as are good relationships across the whole group.

Task

Work in teams of four to design and build a spaghetti bridge to span a gap of half a metre and be capable of supporting the weight of a boot. The bridge should be supported at each end by a tower constructed from a sheet of cardboard. Glue and sticky tape may be used. Summarise the following:

a how you planned the bridge
b how the team worked together
c the role undertaken by each member of the team.

Team roles

Within every team, various roles can be identified. In general there are four types or functions:

● leaders
● doers
● thinkers
● supporters.

A **leader** is someone who influences others with his or her actions or words in order to pursue the goals of the organisation. Many leaders have great strength of personality or charismatic qualities, while others are quietly forceful or persuasive.

A **doer** is a more practical person who gets things done and wants to get on with the job once decisions have been taken. A doer will quite often side-step problems rather than spend time trying to find the best solution.

A **thinker** inspires others by providing solutions to problems. A thinker is capable of deep thought, is inventive and can be a constant source of ideas.

A **supporter** is somebody who creates harmony in the team by looking for ways to overcome any problems or destructive undercurrents. A supporter can be particularly useful in a crisis.

Task

Imagine that you have been asked to form a small team consisting of yourself and a few of your friends. The team must contain a leader, a doer, a thinker and a supporter. What role would you give yourself, and which friends would you ask to fill the other roles? What leads you to believe that they fall into the categories you have assigned to them?

Group dynamics

For members of a team to work together effectively it is vital that they understand the corporate objectives of their organisation and how the tasks they are undertaking serve to fulfil such objectives.

In the modern world people at work need to feel involved and informed about processes and decisions that affect them. Being in a team provides a **sense of belonging** and enables employees to establish friendships which help to make the workplace a more attractive place.

Advantages of groups

Teams are capable of carrying out a far wider range of activities than is an individual. Where some form of division

278

of labour is required, teams can work better by allocating separate tasks or components of tasks to each member. Teams, properly organised, are also better at tasks requiring creativity and judgement as 'several heads are better than one'.

Another aspect of teamwork is greater impartiality. Humans, by their upbringing, have a certain bias in their opinions and outlook, whereas in a group such views are offset by a wider range of backgrounds and experiences.

Groups also seem to be able to make more courageous decisions than individuals alone. A risky decision is difficult for an individual to make, whereas group members sense that the overall responsibility will be shared.

Disadvantages of groups

There are several possible disadvantages of groups. One is **time-wasting** – groups require careful coordination, without which time is wasted. For example:

- time can be wasted pursuing just one issue
- members may persist with discussion about irrelevant points
- members may repeat statements made by others.

The presence of others sometimes inhibits group members and makes them feel that they ought to go along with what the others say rather than express their own views, particularly if a dominant character seems to be influencing the group. This is called **group-pressure**.

Another drawback to groups is delays. An organisation may not be able to make decisions quickly because of the need for group discussion, and so delays may ensue in dealing with an important issue.

Finally, groups may talk too much and do too little. A group may discuss a problem but not actually do anything about solving it – there is then **lack of action**.

Task

Weigh up the advantages and disadvantages of groups. Make lists of issues you feel that groups would be:

a good at dealing with
b bad at dealing with.

Figure 11.6 *Factors affecting group dynamics*

Factors affecting group dynamics

Many factors affect the way in which a group operates. All are interconnected and therefore influence each other.

The size of the group affects members in different ways. Some feel confident speaking to a large group, while others may find it difficult to contribute unless they know the group members well. With groups of under five people, often there is insufficient breadth of experience; whereas with a group of more than ten people, low participators stop talking, the group becomes more formal and discussion is stifled. The ideal size of a group is often between five and eight.

Task

What size of group do you prefer to belong to? Explain your answer.

The **physical location** of the group meeting affects interactions. A large room, or seating arrangements which separate members of the group from others according to status, both discourage interactions. If the group meets in

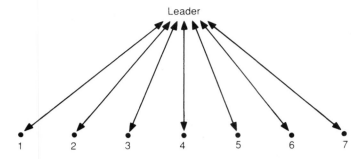

Figure 11.7 *Autocratic leadership style*

the office of a senior member of staff the status relationships are likely to be reinforced, whereas if it meets on neutral ground members will tend to feel less inhibited.

Leadership style affects the way the group functions. If the leader is **democratic** and only guides where needed, members will tend to make extensive contributions to decisions. If, on the other hand, the leader is autocratic, then the group will be driven to agree to the beliefs and goals of the leader – and dissatisfaction of the other members.

Interaction will largely depend upon the style of leadership. With an autocratic style interaction will be centralised (see Figure 11.7), and with a democratic style it will be decentralised (see Figure 11.8).

The nature of the **task** will affect the way in which the group works. A group may be expected simply to share information or to sanction some suggested action. On the other hand, the activities of the group may be more

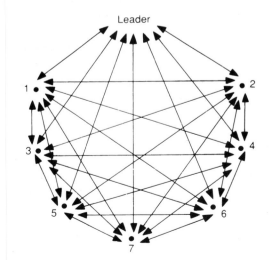

Figure 11.8 *Democratic leadership stlye*

creative, in which case it will be expected to come up with ideas designed to solve problems, or to work together to complete a defined task.

The **behaviour of group members** will depend upon factors such as:

- perceptions of the leader
- atmosphere
- morale
- the need for recognition
- influence
- conflict/consensus
- competition.

In order to overcome any problems caused by the above factors, it may be necessary for the group leader to indulge in group-building. This can involve:

- encouraging contributions, recognising and praising them
- making it possible for all members of the group to make a contribution
- providing the group with a direction designed to avoid conflict
- constantly summarising the feelings of the group.

Each member of a group is there for a reason, which determines the **role** they will undertake. For example, he or she may be there because of expertise or because of seniority. The individual's behaviour will be determined by these parameters.

Finally, members of the group will approach the task with **different beliefs**. Some might come with preconceived values, while others will come with no notion of what contribution they can make. Some may come simply to defend the area they represent or to cover up errors or even to use the platform for amusement. As a generalisation, groups where members have similar beliefs tend to be more harmonious and satisfying for their members, whereas groups where members have widely differing beliefs tend to be more productive.

Task

This task will only be possible if you are studying in a class. Form a circle of eight people in the centre of the room, and elect a group leader. The rest of the class should sit outside the circle as observers. The task of the central group is to design a student magazine. The observers should look at the process and make comments under the following headings:

a How did the appointed leader control the activities of the group?
b Did the group work well together?
c Who tended to lead the discussion?
d Was everyone involved?
e Did anyone block progress?
f Who seemed to listen and who did not listen?

You should allow ten minutes at the end of the session for comparison of notes.

· MEETINGS ·

Meetings provide one type of opportunity for organisations to consult employees. They bring together interested parties who can express their views and help to develop a common policy designed to achieve the organisation's objectives.

Meetings are therefore an important administrative activity; information can be exchanged, ideas passed and opinions expressed. They also play an important part in communicating information, providing a forum where problems can be solved and where decisions can be made.

Aims of meetings

People tend to be more committed to a decision if they are **consulted** and are involved in some way in the decision-making process. If they understand why a decision is necessary, they are more likely to accept all that it entails.

Some meetings are called to generate ideas. Individuals have different backgrounds and the number of ideas being put forward tends to increase with group size. One popular problem-solving technique is **brainstorming**, which was originally used in the advertising industry with the object of coming up with new ideas. In a brainstorming session, the problem is stated and participants to the meeting are encouraged to produce as many ideas as they can, out of which the best can be selected.

Meetings can be called to give people information or spread **knowledge**. These are particularly important if a lot of people need to be informed or if the information is confidential.

Meetings allow parties from both sides of an issue to **negotiate an agreement**.

Often meetings are used to get **collective decisions** from members by democratic means. If an individual does not have the authority to make a decision, he or she might call a meeting so that others can agree to some proposals. Sometimes when a decision is made by a senior member of staff, it then needs ratification (confirmation) by others in a meeting.

Finally, meetings can be called to **investigate** something that has happened – for example, an accident or a series of thefts.

Task

Working with a group of others, try a *brainstorming session* to come up with an idea for a new garden tool.

Informal and formal meetings

Meetings range from **informal** unstructured gatherings between a few people to **formal**, heavily structured meetings controlled by rigid rules and procedures.

Informal meetings involve the gathering together of individuals, often at short notice and without any set procedures. Informal meetings are flexible and can be called to respond to any issue, or can be used to share responsibility for a decision.

On the other hand, the rules and procedures for a formal meeting may be contained in a company's Memorandum and Articles of Association or in an organisation's standing orders or written constitution. The features of a formal meeting are:

● The meeting is called by a **notice** or **agenda**.
● Conduct in the meeting depends on the formal rules of the organisation.

- Decisions are reached by voting.
- Formal meeting terms are used.
- The proceedings are recorded in **minutes**.

Task

Give some examples of formal meetings and informal meetings.

Procedures for formal meetings

Formal meetings must be properly conducted according to legal requirements or a written constitution. It is usual to

---

NOTICE OF MEETING
CROWTHORNE FOOTBALL CLUB

The Annual Meeting of the Selection Committee will be held in the upstairs room of The Buckshot Inn on Monday 18th August 199_ at 7.45 pm. Any items for inclusion in the Agenda should reach me no later than 18th July 199_.

Secretary:

Figure 11.9 *A notice of meeting*

AGENDA
CROWTHORNE FOOTBALL CLUB

Annual Meeting of the Selection Committee
to be held on Monday 18th August 199_ at 7.45 pm in The Buckshot Inn

1 Apologies for absence
2 Minutes of the last meeting
3 Matters arising from the minutes
4 Reports: Treasurer's report
          Team Secretary's report
          Chairperson's report
5 Proposal to redecorate clubhouse
6 Proposal to increase match fees
7 Any other business
8 Date of next meeting

Secretary:

Figure 11.10 *An Agenda*

give **notice** of the meeting to every person entitled to attend according to the rules and regulations. The notice should be signed by the issuer and should specify the date, time and place of the meeting.

A notice of a meeting will be accompanied or followed by an **agenda**, which is a list of topics to be discussed at the meeting. It will normally be sent to all those entitled to attend the meeting so that they can consider the topics in advance of the meeting.

Task

In your role as Secretary to the Richmond Squash Club, prepare an agenda of a meeting to be held next Friday in the clubhouse at 8.00 pm. As well as the regular items, include the following: entry fees; bar takings; redecoration of the clubhouse.

A **chairperson** has certain duties and powers in a meeting. He or she makes sure that the meeting is properly constituted, preserves order, works through the agenda preventing irrelevant discussion, and ascertains the views of the meeting by putting **motions** and amendments to those attending.

Often a chairperson will have a special copy of the agenda known as the **chairperson's agenda**. On this, further information is provided for the chairperson's guidance, and space is provided on the right-hand side for notes to be made.

Shortly before the time a meeting is designated to start the chairperson makes sure that there is a **quorum** – this is the minimum number of people required for the meeting to go ahead according to the rules. He or she will also ensure that everybody has an agenda and that all new members are introduced.

The **secretary** then states whether any apologies have been received for absence, and reads through the official record – the minutes – of the last meeting. If the minutes have already been circulated, it will be assumed that they have been read! Members are asked to approve them as a correct record of the last meeting and, if necessary, the secretary will amend them before they are signed by the chairperson.

At this stage any **matters arising** from the minutes will be discussed. For example, if the last meeting suggested that

certain individuals undertake certain actions, these may be mentioned.

The chairperson then works through the business of the meeting according to the agenda. If **reports** are to be read (again, circulated reports are assumed to have been read) the writers may be asked to speak briefly about their reports. If a **motion** is proposed the chairperson will ask for a proposer and a seconder, allow for discussion of the motion making sure that all sides are heard, and then call for a vote. The chairperson usually has a casting vote if the voting is tied.

Any other business is normally limited to non-controversial issues, because if it is felt that something deserves further attention it must be put on the agenda for the next meeting. At the end of the meeting a decision may be made about the date, time and place of the next meeting.

While a meeting is taking place, the secretary records the proceedings with a series of notes – the minutes. These should provide an accurate and clear record of what has taken place at the meeting. They are usually written up immediately after a meeting and are in the past tense.

- **Narrative minutes** include details of discussion and the decisions reached.
- **Resolution minutes** record only details of the decisions agreed.
- **Action minutes** have a column which indicates who is to follow up and take action upon any decision reached.

Whichever version is produced, the secretary only summarises the main points.

The secretary will usually have a folder containing agendas and minutes from previous meetings. It is important that such documents be kept as they provide a permanent record of issues that have been discussed and decisions that have been sanctioned.

CROWTHORNE FOOTBALL CLUB

Minutes of the Annual Meeting of the Selection Committee held on Monday 18th August 199_ in The Buckshot Inn at 7.45 pm.

Present
Mr A James (Chairperson), Mr D Smith (Team Secretary), Mr R Pitt, Mrs H Johnson, Mr N Rees (Secretary), Miss E Walters (Treasurer)

1 Apologies	Apologies for absence were received from Mr R Cook and Mr S Turner.
2 Minutes	Minutes of the last meeting were taken as read, approved and signed.
3 Matters arising	Mrs Johnson reported that, since last season she had taken on the task of writing the press releases and match reports that had regularly appeared in local newspapers.

4 Reports	Miss Walters presented the Treasurer's report. The club had a good season and finances were healthy. A copy of the audited accounts was distributed.
	   Mr Smith presented the Team Secretary's report. The first team squad last season was strong and this was reflected in performances. The second eleven, however, struggled to attract players, and this was reflected in several dismal performances.
	   Mr James thanked everybody for their hard work last season. Sponsorship had increased for the season ahead, and they had received a record number of enquiries from new players.

5 Clubhouse redecoration	Mr Rees said that this was long overdue and was conveying a poor image of the club to visiting teams and supporters. After further discussion it was agreed that this was a priority and the secretary was asked to obtain quotations and to bring these to the attention of the committee as soon as possible.
6 Match fees	Miss Walters pointed out that match fees had not increased over the last 3 years. Mr Smith expressed that if match fees increased too much this might deter new players from joining the club. It was agreed to increase match fees by just 50p per game.
7 Any other business	Mrs Johnson expressed that a small gift should be sent to Jim Robinson for running the line last season. Mr Pitt volunteered to visit local businesses to increase sponsorship.
8 Date of next meeting	It was decided to hold a short meeting of the committee on 5th September 199_ at 8.00 pm at the same location to discuss clubhouse redecoration.

Chairman
21st August 199_

Figure 11.11 *Minutes of a meeting*

The entertainments committee

Peter Jones, Dawn Williams, Tony Peters, Alison Sharpe, Donna Thomas, Alison Piper, Michael Sherbourne and Roger Hanson are all interested in setting up an entertainments committee at their local Community Centre. The centre's administrator has agreed to their request to set up a committee and has indicated that they can use the centre's hall on a trial basis on the last Friday of each month. He has, however, set certain conditions:

- Events should not make a loss.
- There will be no hire fee for the hall but half the profits from each event must be contributed to the centre's funds.
- Events must not disturb local residents.
- Events should attempt to cater for as wide a range of residents as possible.
- The entertainments committee must have a chairperson, a secretary and a treasurer.
- All meetings of the entertainments committee must have a proper notice of meeting and an agenda, and minutes must be taken.

1 *Consider whether you feel that the committee could be successful.*
2 *Have a preliminary meeting of the committee with seven colleagues. Make arrangements for a notice of meeting, agenda and items for inclusion to appear for the next meeting. Stage the meeting and take minutes.*
3 *Analyse your role in the meeting. What sort of contribution did you make? How could it be improved?*

Contributing to meetings

At the majority of meetings you attend you will be a participant rather than the chairperson, secretary or treasurer. In such circumstances the sort of contribution you wish to make will rest on your shoulders. Raising a point at a meeting is something that many people do not feel comfortable about doing. The following might act as a useful guide:

- Scrutinise agenda items before you attend the meeting to see if there are any areas that may be of interest to you.
- Research such areas of interest and obtain any associated reading materials.
- Plan out, either in your mind or by making notes, what you might wish to say.
- Listen to what others have to say before speaking yourself.
- Timing is important – make sure the point you make fits into the discussion.

- Do not ramble on.
- Be tactful, and do not deliberately upset someone.
- Be assertive.
- Make your contribution coherent.
- Be ready for some sort of opposition by trying to anticipate the response you might receive to the points you are making.

· QUALITY CIRCLES ·

Making the most of what employees have to offer and valuing their contributions is becoming increasingly important for industries wishing to remain competitive today. The old-fashioned notion that employee involvement was about collective bargaining through trade unions is steadily disappearing. Today's ideal form of consultation tends to be by means of groups or teams of employees in **quality circles**.

Quality circles originally came from Japan in the early 1960s. They were developed in order to improve quality and productivity in manufacturing. It was not, however, until the early 1980s that they started to appear in Western industry. Originally they captured the attention of management specialists as they brought together workers in a **consultative process** which involved group dynamics.

As a result, over recent years quality circles have attracted a lot of attention and thousands of companies have established them. To coordinate the diverse activities of quality circles, the International Association of Quality Circles has been formed.

Quality circles comprise small groups of employees engaged on any sort of problem affecting their working environment – for example, safety, quality assurance, efficiency. They are a medium for employees to improve their working life by bringing forward their points of view on day-to-day issues. They are therefore a form of indirect consultation designed to meet both employee and management needs. They also allow employees to identify their actions more closely with the success of the organisation and this increases their degree of job satisfaction.

Like many management theories the quality circle is easy to understand. A typical circle consists of between eight

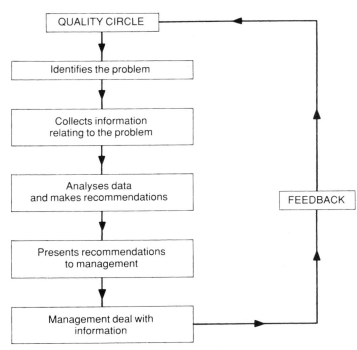

Figure 11.12 *How a quality circle works*

and twelve people from similar working backgrounds. They meet perhaps once a week, usually during working hours, and each circle has a leader. Figure 11.12 indicates what a quality circle does.

Form a quality circle of between eight and ten people. You have been asked by management to suggest practical ways of improving the quality of your course. Discuss your ideas and make recommendations.

A great benefit of quality circles is that an organisation can use line specialists, who know their jobs and understand how they work, to resolve problems without having to call in management consultants. Furthermore, the management's support of quality circles implies that the employees are trusted to solve problems and their contributions are valued. This helps to develop stronger links between managers and employees and improves morale, as well as the quality of performance.

Quality circles in management accounting

Managements are beginning to realise that the principle of quality circles can be applied to accounting personnel as well as to production workers. Quality circles offer accountants an opportunity to identify areas of working which could be improved and made more productive.

A quality circle consultancy exercise was carried out by a major UK manufacturer with the establishment of a quality circle management accounting group. The group broke down its activities into two main areas: quantitative and qualitative.

The quantitative areas were capable of measurement:

- The production of management reports to time schedules improved from 86 per cent to 94 per cent over a two-year period.
- The accuracy of accounting data being entered into the computer improved. Whereas in the past 2 per cent of entries had errors, as a result of the quality circle errors fell to 0.4 per cent. Fewer miscodes into the computer reduced overtime by 45 per cent.
- There were reduced errors in inventory records from 30 per cent average error to 1.7 per cent.
- Late payments to suppliers were reduced from 5 to 0.027 per cent.

Savings made by such improvements were thought to be substantial.

On the qualitative front, the quality circle had a major impact on the suggestions scheme. The numbers of suggestions increased by a half and the number of people participating by a quarter. Savings resulting from suggestions went up by three-quarters.

It was also felt that improved quality had raised morale. An opinion survey revealed that employees felt their general satisfaction with the company had improved, their skills were being better utilised, and they had developed personally from the experience.

1 What degree of improvement took place in accounting data input after the introduction of a quality circle?

2 Why did the establishment of a quality circle improve morale?

3 To which other parts of the organisation could quality circles be applied?

· TRAINING AND DEVELOPMENT ·

Training is an investment in the workforce. It is used not only to meet short-term organisational objectives but also to develop employees personally and create a long-term future for them. This can help them to achieve their ambitions, undertake responsibilities and, at the same time, increase their sense of belonging to the organisation.

In **on-the-job training**, an individual is placed into a job position and trained to perform the task under close supervision. This is training for a specific function, but an increasing amount of training today is directed towards improving employees' understanding of how the organisation operates. Induction training also fulfils this aim.

Staff development provides skills and qualifications for promotion. This is often off-the-job training acquired by attending courses.

Some training is directed towards developing employees personally so that they can fulfil personal needs. This type of training is based on the belief that it will benefit the organisation in the long-term.

Certain questions arise when considering training requirements. Training is a **cost**, and while staff are being trained, unless the training is on-the-job, they are absent from the workplace and not contributing to output. Another consideration is who should undertake the training – should an organisation train in-house or should it use an external agency?

The immediate tangible benefit of training is improved standards or work. However, there are other benefits and these are usually not quite so visible. As a result of training employees generally feel more involved, so that morale should improve and labour turnover be reduced. Also, staff who are developed and prepared for promotion become motivated to undertake further responsibilities; indeed, some would argue that without preparation for higher

levels of responsibility employees could become promoted beyond their true level of competence.

Though many organisations today still direct their attention primarily towards organisational training needs, there is an increasing recognition of the need for genuine employee development.

Management discovers training

The tendency of management in the UK to regard training simply as a cost rather than also as an investment is well-known. When a recession occurs it tends to be one of the first areas to suffer cutbacks. This weakens the ability of organisations to hold and recruit staff and undermines their ability to cope with problems. For example, a recent study by the Small Business Research Trust suggested that lack of management training was a significant factor in the reluctance of small firms to pursue a growth policy.

Professor David Ashton from Lancaster University believes there has been a significant change in attitude in recent years by larger companies, though the old weaknesses persist amongst smaller companies. Among larger businesses he has seen increasing interest in management qualifications rather than training alone. This has led to a provision by business schools of a range of programmes tailored to the requirements of business, such as the Master of Business Administration. Projects on which managers work in such programmes are often viewed as key to future business success. Companies themselves have also responded to the demands of managers and seem to view management development as a valuable strategy for retaining personnel.

Professor Ashton's findings are supported by a survey carried out by Harbridge Consulting Group. This indicated that today a more thoughtful approach is taking place in management development. More organisations feel that training should take place entirely on individual needs, and management development is also being discussed more frequently at board level than ever before.

Management development is, however, usually planned on a one-year basis in most companies. The Harbridge report indicates a need to bring an understanding of long-term issues into the process of planning for management development. This will enable organisations to cope with demographic changes in the structure of the workforce.

1 Why is training sometimes regarded simply as a cost rather than as a benefit?

2 How might training help to retain personnel?

3 Express your views as to whether or not training should be based upon organisational needs or individual needs.

Case Study

Gaps in training threaten growth

In some circles there is a strong feeling that training in the United Kingdom for too long has been regarded as a second-rate activity. Some statistics suggest that competitor countries spend between three and ten times as much on training as we do in the UK. France and Germany, for example, produce two to three times the number of craftsmen and ten times the number of individuals obtaining middle-ranking vocational qualifications.

The recent White Paper, 'Education and Training for the 21st Century', is an attempt to pull together education and training. Yet despite the passing on of responsibility to Training Enterprise Councils (TECs), the Construction Industry Training Board recently reported a 10 per cent drop in craft trainees.

The real problem is trying to encourage employers and individuals to take part in training. Unfortunately, many employers have in recent years been under pressure to cut back. Individuals may be more willing to pay for training if they can see a tangible reward, leading to a vocational qualification which will enhance their job prospects.

Over recent years the National Council for Vocational Qualifications has developed NVQs. An NVQ is a statement of competence relevant to work which is intended to facilitate entry into or progression further in employment, education and training. The hope is that the new qualifications will be quickly understood by teachers, pupils and parents and that employers use the qualifications as a basis for recruitment and view them as an essential way of motivating their employees. If employers fail to take on this responsibility, there is a strong likelihood that Britain's economic fortunes may take a further downward turn.

1 Do you feel that the case study exaggerates the plight of training in Britain?

2 Who do you feel should pay for training?

3 How should NVQs help to simplify vocational qualifications?

Case Study

Problems as opportunities

The following is an extract from an article by Tony Colman published in *Purchasing and Supply Management*.

'As a manager it always seemed to me that it was a good thing to be surrounded by problems. After all, I tried to convince myself, perhaps one reason for my continued employment was that my boss (poor misguided chap) rated me an effective problem-cracker. Far from it in reality, although it would have been wonderful to have been endowed with near-infallible "over the horizon" anticipation of the oncoming problem.

'Of course my mistake was not seeing problems as opportunities. Eventually, persuaded by academics and management gurus to "think positive", I finally came to see the profound truth underlying this concept.

'Soon I was able to welcome disasters. A sudden supplier bankruptcy became an opportunity to find a better source, a demand from Sales to double next month's output appeared as a welcome challenge, while a late engineering design change offered scope to develop one's persuasive power with disgruntled suppliers.'

1 How does the author of the article approach problems?

2 To what extent should being able to deal with problems be part of a training programme?

3 Do you agree with the author that problems should be viewed as opportunities?

Element assignment

Can you re-organise an organisation?

This assignment can help you to provide evidence for assessmentr, or claim the following Core Skills outcomes:

Communication
Receive and respond to a variety of information
Communicate in writing

Personal skills
Transfer skills gained to new and changing situations
Identify and solve routine and non-routine problems
Apply a range of skills and techniques to develop a variety of ideas in the creation of new/modified products, services and situations
Use a range of thought processes

Members of an organisation should feel proud to belong to it.

- They should feel a sense of responsibility for what they produce in that organisation.
- They should feel that they are involved in decision making processes.
- They should feel that the 'culture' of the organisation is one that they can relate to.

Let us look at these three ideas in more detail:

1 External and internal customers
The external customer is the person who pays for the products or services supplied.

The internal customer is the person to whom another person in the organisation supplies products or servies.

The 'products' may be half-finished products (as on a production line) or tools/equipment of one kind or another. The services include such items as secretarial assistance or site security.

Unless the products or services supplied to the internal customers are of the right quality, it is unlikely that those supplied to the external customer can be of the right quality.

The concept of the internal customer helps create a feeling of independence and worth among employees ('it's my responsibility'). It also encourages teamwork ('we can only be successful as individuals if we treat each other as valued customers').

2 Delegation (or subsidiarity)
This is the principle of pushing decision- making authority down to the smallest possible unit compatible with efficiency and cost-effectiveness.

In general, the smaller the unit, the greater the capacity to respond to change, and the higher the morale within the unit.

3 Company culture
A business organisation has some similarities to a living organism. It can, to an extent, accumulate experience and expertise which can be made available to all employees.

This experience and expertise may be stored in conventional databases, printed or electronic; it is also stored in people's minds and passed down by word of mouth to succeeding generations of employees. There is also certainly a metaphysical dimension – 'something in the air' – which motivates an employee of a particular company to act in a way that is typical of that company.

Task
For this task you will need to focus closely on an organisation that you work for or one that you know about. To start the assignment you should carry out some research into the following areas.

1 What scope is there for teamwork in the organisation?
2 How are employees encouraged to see each other as part of a team?
3 Is there an emphasis on the internal customer? For example, how are employees encouraged to work for each other?
4 How are employees encouraged to feel 'responsible' for their work?
5 How much delegation of authority is there in the organisation?
6 How does delegation affect the smooth running and flexibility of the organisation?
7 What is the culture of the organisation? Is it a culture that encourages people to work hard for the organisation?
8 Is the culture of the organisation one in which its members take pride?

When you have carried out your research you should be in a position to make some recommendations about beneficial changes that can be made.

Make a list of recommendations in the following areas:

1 *ways of fostering and improving the internal customer principle*
2 *ways of improving existing methods of delegating authority so that all organisation members are given more responsibility and a sense of ownership*
3 *ways of developing and improving the 'organisational culture' so that organisation members feel proud to belong.*

chapter **12** # EVALUATING JOB APPLICATIONS AND INTERVIEWS

In this chapter we look at why it is important for organisations to recruit the workforce carefully. Letters of application and curriculum vitae are described. It is shown how an applicant for a job can best prepare for an interview. The chapter looks at the interview process and encourages you to practise your interview techniques. Finally, some of the legal and ethical obligations involved in recruitment are explained.

▪ THE IMPORTANCE OF SELECTION ▪

An organisation is only as good as the people it employs. However, choosing the right people involves more than just identifying the skills and qualifications needed to perform the various jobs and then recruiting the candidates most likely to possess those skills.

The main reason for saying this is that work nearly always takes place in a **group setting**. Individuals need to 'fit in' with other employees, with the work environment, with the style of work and with the organisational culture. Working as a lecturer in a large college in central London, for example, may require quite different attributes from working in another college in outer London.

The costs of poor selection can be very high. Expenditure on training courses can be completely wasted if the wrong people are chosen. (The cost of training a policeman, for example, is at least £30 000.) The costs of employing an unsuitable technician to work on aircraft maintenance could be astronomic. If an organisation has people working in an environment that does not suit them, they will be dissatisfied, will lack commitment to the organisation and may feel under stress. The individuals concerned and the organisation both suffer.

Despite this, many organisations still tend to recruit on the basis of a short interview of perhaps 30 minutes. Indeed, research has shown that often a selection decision is made within the first four minutes of the interview – and for the rest of the time the interviewer concentrates exclusively on information that reinforces the initial 'reject' or 'accept' decision. Research has also suggested that **unstructured interviews** are a poor guide to future job performance. This is why it is important for interviewers to know exactly what they are looking for and to be guided by a structured set of questions. It is also possible to give personality and intelligence tests to interviewees.

It may also be helpful to give the interviewee a short task to perform – for example, many colleges ask would-be lecturers to give a 15-minute talk on the day of their interview.

Figures 12.1 and 12.2 identify stages in the **selection process**. The first chart shows the process from the point of view of the recruiting organisation and the second from the point of view of the applicant.

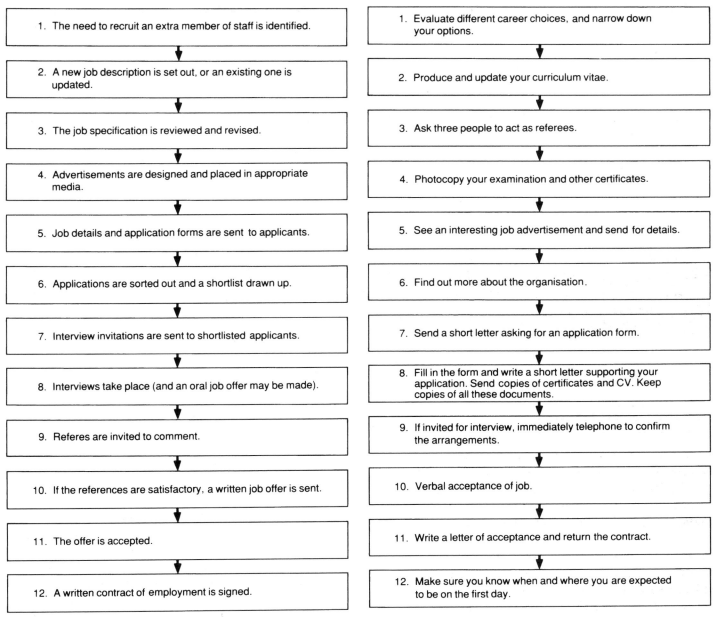

1. The need to recruit an extra member of staff is identified.

2. A new job description is set out, or an existing one is updated.

3. The job specification is reviewed and revised.

4. Advertisements are designed and placed in appropriate media.

5. Job details and application forms are sent to applicants.

6. Applications are sorted out and a shortlist drawn up.

7. Interview invitations are sent to shortlisted applicants.

8. Interviews take place (and an oral job offer may be made).

9. Referes are invited to comment.

10. If the references are satisfactory, a written job offer is sent.

11. The offer is accepted.

12. A written contract of employment is signed.

Figure 12.1 *Job selection... the employer's schedule*

1. Evaluate different career choices, and narrow down your options.

2. Produce and update your curriculum vitae.

3. Ask three people to act as referees.

4. Photocopy your examination and other certificates.

5. See an interesting job advertisement and send for details.

6. Find out more about the organisation.

7. Send a short letter asking for an application form.

8. Fill in the form and write a short letter supporting your application. Send copies of certificates and CV. Keep copies of all these documents.

9. If invited for interview, immediately telephone to confirm the arrangements.

10. Verbal acceptance of job.

11. Write a letter of acceptance and return the contract.

12. Make sure you know when and where you are expected to be on the first day.

Figure 12.2 *Job selection: the applicant's view*

▪ WRITING A LETTER OF APPLICATION ▪

A letter should have a clear structure, with a beginning, a middle and an ending. It should state:

- your reason for applying for the job
- the contribution you can make to the organisation
- how you have developed your capabilities through training and education
- skills and knowledge that you have acquired that would help you to do the job well.

The letter needs to be *interesting* – you are writing about (i.e. selling) yourself! It should contain just enough information to support your application form and CV (see below), highlighting the most relevant evidence. You will know that you are writing effective letters if they lead to interviews.

Here are some important rules to remember:

- Use good English with accurate spelling. *Always* check in a dictionary if you are unsure of a spelling.
- Use your own words rather than simply copying those in the advertisement.
- Do not try to be 'too clever' by using long words.
- Keep the paragraphs short.
- Try not to use the word 'I' too much.
- Word-process letters if possible. Failing this, draft a handwritten copy before producing the final typed copy.
- Follow the correct convention of addressing people. 'Dear Sir/Madam' should be ended with 'Yours faithfully', whereas 'Dear Mr Ramprakash' should be ended with 'Yours sincerely'.
- Keep a copy of what you have written.

Task

The following letter was sent by an applicant for the post of trainee accountant with British Rail. What weaknesses can you spot?

<pre>
                                    21 Wade Park Avenue
                                           Market Deeping
                                            Peterborough
                                                PE6 8JL
</pre>

20th September 1993

BR Finance Manager, Anglia Region
Room 109
East Side Offices
Kings Cross Station
London
N1 9AP

Dear Sir,

I noticed in my local paper that you have a job avalable for a junior accountant. I am very interested in the post because I see it as presenting a good opportunity. I have always been very interested in accounts. I am also studing accounts at collage. I understand that on your accountancy training scheme there will be good oppertunities for promotion. I am also studying GNVQ course in Business. This is a very interesting course and I have had good reports from all my tutors on the course. As part of the course I am studying accounts. I have found the accounts to be the most exciting and interesting parts. I am also interested in train spotting.

   I am working at the Anglia Co-operative Society. This is a part time post but it involves a lot of responsibility. I have to check the stock and make sure that shelves are well organised. I also have had my EPOS training.

   I am currently working on my cv and will send it to you next week. Many thanks for your interest in my application.

Yours Sincerely,

Norman Major

Task

Write a letter of application for the post described below.

The position: Trainee manager at Marks & Spencer.

The company: One of the top ten companies in the UK by turnover and a leading retailer. The company employs over 50 000 people and continues to grow.

A manager: Managers at all levels are expected to show responsibility. The company is looking for people who are tough and talented. They should have a flair for business, know how to sell and be able to work in a team.

The training: The first year's training will introduce the new manager to the stores and to working in a management team. In the second year trainees can specialise in personnel, selling or administration.

Salaries: £8000–£11 000 p.a.

▪ PREPARING A CURRICULUM VITAE ▪

A **curriculum vitae** (usually called simply a 'CV') is a summary of your career to date. There are three stages you should follow when setting out your CV:

- Assemble all the facts about yourself.
- Draft the CV.
- Edit the document several times.

Try to create a favourable impression (but always be truthful). Omit negative statements about yourself. Do not be vague.

Always use a word-processing package with an impressive yet conservative font.

Assembling the facts

At this initial stage you are trying to get together as many relevant facts as possible about your career to date. It does not matter if you put down too many to start with – so make a list of all your educational, work-based and leisure achievements, as well as training activities and courses you have been on. Make brief notes about each of these as well as about projects and assignments that you have been involved in.

Drafting the CV

A CV should be divided into headings and sub-headings as follows:

PERSONAL DETAILS
EDUCATION AND QUALIFICATIONS
TRAINING
CAREER HISTORY
RESPONSIBILITIES
ACHIEVEMENTS
OTHER INFORMATION
INTERESTS AND HOBBIES

Remember that the key part of the CV is the **career history**, so the bits that go before should not be too long. For example, when dealing with training list only the most important and relevant training courses, and then if necessary include some of the others under 'Other information' (see Figure 12.3).

When you set out your responsibilities and achievements, decide whether it is necessary to put some of them under sub-headings. It is normal practice to start your career history with your most recent job and work backwards in time, because employers are usually most interested in your recent experience.

If some of your experience is of a technical nature, try to present it in a way that can be read easily by the general reader (rather than only by a specialist).

Try to use dynamic words in your CV. Here are some good examples:

Accomplished	Achieved	Conducted
Completed	Created	Decided
Delivered	Developed	Designed
Directed	Established	Expanded
Finished	Generated	Implemented
Improved	Increased	Introduced
Launched	Performed	Pioneered
Planned	Promoted	Redesigned
Reorganised	Set up	Solved
Succeeded	Trained	Widened
Won	Work	Wrote

CURRICULUM VITAE	
Name:	Prakesh Patel
Home address:	50 Palmerston Road Reading RG31 9HL
Date of birth:	1.3.76
Place of birth:	Reading
Nationality:	British
Education:	Waingels' Copse School, Reading *Sept 1988–July 1993*
Qualifications (GCSE):	Mathematics (B) English (C) Business Studies (A) French (C) Technology (D) History (D) *All July 1993*
Interests and activities:	Swimming, reading, Venture Scouts
Work experience:	Assistant at Marks & Spencer on Saturdays
Referees:	Mr P. Marks Rev. K. Engels Waingels' Copse School St Jude's Denmark Avenue Church Street Woodley Reading R4 7QT Reading R3 8SL

Figure 12.3 *A skeleton CV*

Editing the CV

You may need to alter your CV slightly for each job application, so that it concentrates as closely as possible on the requirements of a particular job. Look at the details of the job and ask yourself whether your CV suggests that you have the requirements for the post. Imagine yourself in the employer's shoes: what qualities do you think the organisation is looking for?

Task

Produce your own up-to-date CV. Ask someone else to evaluate your CV against the following checklist:

1 Have you set out clearly a good impression of your skills, knowledge, experience and personality?

2 Are these set out in a concise and readable fashion?

3 Do significant achievements stand out?

4 Have you eliminated confusing terms, jargon and obscure abbreviations?

5 Are all words spelt accurately, have you used correct grammar, and is the layout clear and organised?

6 Does the CV have a good 'feel'?

7 Would the person reading it understand it easily?

· THE INTERVIEW ·

Chapter 10 provided some useful tips to bear in mind when going for a job interview. Any job interview involves a certain amount of luck and the outcome depends on 'how you do on the day'.

A recent study reported that the person who is first on the interviewer's list is three times less likely to be hired than the last name on the list! Monday is the worst interview day because managers are under pressure on the first day of the week, while Friday offers the distraction of a looming weekend. Early morning interviews are not recommended because managers are too preoccupied, while those after 4 pm are unhelpful because interviewers are anxious to get home!

At the interview it is important that you adopt the right **body language**. Look alert and eager. Look the questioner in the eye. Avoid nervous movements, and try not to cross your arms in a defensive position. Try not to threaten the interviewer by pointing your finger or making sudden violent movements. Sit up straight and try to look confident and at ease (not apathetic and too laide back). Do not give brief one-line answers, but try to expand on your answers so that the interviewer can see you at your best. Smile, and at all times try to appear interested and enthusiastic about what is being discussed. You do not have to stand for being pushed around by an aggressive interviewer – be assertive by standing up for yourself, without taking it to the extreme by becoming heated and argumentative.

Task

In groups, carry out mock interviews for an imaginary post. Before the interviews take place the interviewing panel will need to establish the qualities they are looking for in the successful applicant. The interviewing panel will also need to establish a set of questions. The same questions need to be asked of each applicant if the interviews are to be fair.

The 'applicants' will each need to produce a CV and a written application. They will also need to research the nature of the organisation and the post.

After the interviews, all interviewers and interviewees should fill in an evaluation sheet containing the following questions:

1 How did you feel before the interview?

2 How did you consider that the interview went?

3 What impression do you think you gave?

4 What did you think of the interviewers'/interviewee's:
   a planning and organisation
   b preparation for the interview
   c performance at the interview?

· EQUAL OPPORTUNITIES ·

In Chapter 10 we looked at the importance of **equal opportunities** in the workplace. This concept is particularly important in the interview and selection process. Consider the following interview questions from the equal opportunities stance. Commentary is provided in *italics*.

● Mrs . . . . . I see you are married. Do you intend to start a family soon?

*The question is not relevant to whether the interviewee is capable of doing the job. It also shows direct **sex discrimination** because a man is not likely to be asked the question. This question cannot be asked.*

● What will happen when your children are ill or on school holidays? Who will look after them?

The question has no relevance as to whether the interviewee is capable of doing the job.

- Your hair is very long Mr . . . . If offered the job are you prepared to have it cut?

This question is only relevant if a safety aspect of a job can be brought in (e.g. use of machinery). Otherwise the standard of dress expected by the company could be discussed (e.g. the correct image for dealing with customers).

- Mr . . . . . , as you are 55 do you think it's worth us employing you?

This question may not be relevant because, at this age, it might not stop the person from doing the job. However, if the interviewee was 60 years of age, the company might feel that any necessary training would not be worth while.

- Miss . . , as a women do you think you are capable of doing the job?

This question cannot be asked as it discriminates on the grounds of sex.

- Do you think your disability will affect you doing the job?

This question can be asked but might be better phrased 'Do you have any health problems that may affect you in this job?'

- How do you feel about working with people from a different ethnic background to yourself?

This question cannot be asked on the grounds of race discrimination.

- As a woman returner, Mrs . . . , do you feel you will be able to cope with the new technology in the office?

This question cannot be asked on the grounds of sex discrimination. Also, it should be accepted that as a woman returner Mrs . . . will probably need some retraining.

- As a man, Mr . . . , you will be working in a department consisting mainly of women. Are you easily distracted?

This question is not relevant as it will not affect the way the applicant performs the job.

- Miss . . . , don't you think your skirt is rather short?

This question should not be asked on grounds of sex discrimination.

ETHICS OF APPLICATIONS AND INTERVIEWS

When you fill in an application form you must sign it to certify that the details you have provided are accurate. Failure to disclose certain information, or including information you know to be false, is an offence in law and will mean that any contract you sign is not legally binding.

In a similar way, the job description and details provided by the organisation have to be described accurately and honestly. For example, a job advertised as involving a 30-hour week which actually involves working 40 hours can be said to be unfairly described.

When you are at an interview you must talk honestly about yourself and your qualifications. The interviewer should also provide an honest description of working conditions and the nature of the job.

Element assignment

Methods of recruitment

This assignment can help you to provide evidence for assessment, or claim the following Core Skills:

Communication
Receive and respond to a variety of information
Present information in a variety of visual forms
Communicate in writing

Personal skills
Use information sources
Identify and solve routine and non-routine problems
Use a range of thought processes

Tasks
You are required to select two jobs of different types in order to investigate in detail appropriate methods of recruitment of staff to fill these positions.

Background work
In order to select two jobs for study, use local newspapers, freesheets and available specialist papers, and advertising at Job Centres and employment agencies. Keep a selection of advertisements for the jobs you

choose, or copy details from the cards on display. If you know an employer or employee with inside knowledge of a job that you are considering, ask whether they will talk to you. This might be particularly helpful in compiling a job description and deciding on the type of personality and qualifications required.

Details to look for
For each post determine:

a what business or other organisation would require this type of work
b a suitable job title
c the job description
d the type of personality that would be required
e what qualifications and previous experience would be needed
f the closing date for applications.

Documents to prepare

- An advertisement.
- An application form – if appropriate.
- Further details for enquirers. Include any part of the job description that does not appear in the advertisement.

The final report

You should include as much as possible of the following:

1 A statement of the questions you are considering.
2 The choice of jobs you decided to investigate.
3 Sample advertising of similar positions.
4 A summary of the interview with employer or employee (if you do one).
5 A description of the recruiting methods used by a firm, if you have visited one.
6 For each job you chose in turn:
   a your advertisement
   b where you would place it and why you chose that media/agency
   c further details for enquirers
   d how you would proceed when applications were received
   e how many people you would expect to interview
   f how you would choose a shortlist
   g questions you would ask the applicants.
7 A summary of the differences between your procedures for the two jobs, with reasons for the differences.

I n this chapter we look at the changing nature of employment in modern society in the United Kingdom and in the European Community. There has been a change in the pattern of employment in different business sectors. A particularly important trend, for example, has been the growth of the service sector of the economy at the expense of manufacturing. The chapter therefore explores some of the important economic factors that have brought about changes in the demand for labour and in its supply.

▪ THE LABOUR MARKET ▪

Labour can be defined as human mental and physical efforts to make goods or deliver services. The demand for labour is said to be **secondary** (or **derived**). In other words, employers do not employ people simply because they like to have them around – they employ people to create goods and services which are sold for money. The secondary demand for labour is therefore derived from the primary demand for goods and services.

Labour is bought and sold in the market-place. Employers demand labour and employees supply labour. The price of labour (the **wage rate**) depends on the relative strengths of supply and demand. If there is a high supply of unskilled labour, for example, then wages for this labour are likely to be relatively low. Similarly, when there is scarce supply of skilled labour, then wages for that are likely to be relatively high.

The supply of labour

The supply of labour depends, first, on the **total population** of a country. Factors such as birth and death rates, and the ease of migration into and out of the country, alter the total population and hence the total supply of labour.

Second, the size of the **working population** also depends on the birth and death rates and on the **age structure** of the population. In Britain the working population includes all people between the ages of 16 and 65 who are available for work.

Third, the supply of labour also depends on the working populations preference for **leisure.** Generally speaking, as people become more affluent they prefer to swap leisure for work.

When considering the supply of labour one should also take into account skills and training. A highly skilled and trained labour force is clearly more valuable than a poor-quality one.

Tasks

1 Give three examples of groups of people between the ages of 16 and 65 who are not available for full-time work.
2 Explain how the age structure of the population affects the size of the working population.

3 Why might people want to:
  a work longer when wage rates increase
  b work less when wage rates increase?
4 Explain how the birth rate, death rate, emigration and immigration may affect the size of the working population.

The demand for labour

Because the demand for labour is secondary or derived, its level changes with the demand for goods and services. In a period of *boom* the demand for labour will increase, whereas in a period of *slump* the demand for labour will fall. It follows that the total wage bill will increase in a boom and fall in a slump. Unemployment will fall in a boom and rise in a slump (see Figure 13.1).

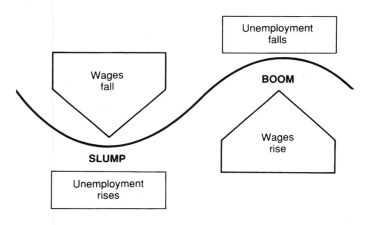

Figure 13.1 *Slump and boom*

Illustrating the market for labour

Figure 13.2(a) shows the supply and demand lines for labour (i.e. it depicts the market for labour). A rise in the demand for labour will lead to an increase in the number of people employed, and to a rise in the wage rate (Figure 13.2 (b)). A fall in the demand for labour will lead to more unemployment and a fall in the wage rate (Figure 13.2 (c)).

Particular labour markets and immobility

In the real world (i.e. in the real economy) there is not just one labour market but many. There is the market for

computer programmers, the market for fashion designers, the market for teachers, and so on. There are also regional labour markets: the market for computer programmers in

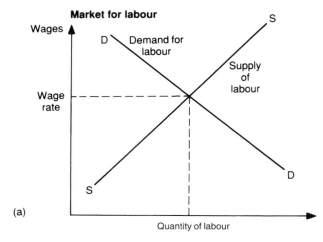

(a)

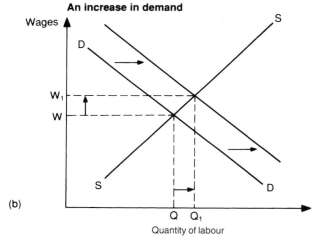

(b)

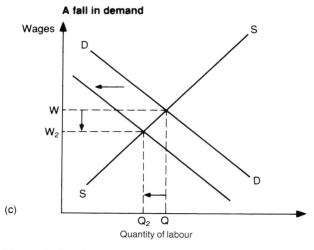

(c)

Figure 13.2 *The dynamic market for labour*

central Scotland, the market for computer programmers in the North East of England and so on. Wage rates *in each of these markets* depend on demand and supply conditions.

Of course, there is **overlap** between these markets. If the wage rate of computer programmers in Scotland doubled, then programmers might move from the North East of England to work in Scotland. If the wage rate of fashion designers doubled, then a teacher might retrain to become a fashion designer. However, there is always considerable **immobility** between different labour markets. Regional immobility exists when people are not prepared to move from one region of a country to another. Occupational immobility exists when people in one occupation are not prepared to retrain to do another job.

Task

List six reasons for geographical immobility of labour, and six reasons for occupation immobility.

Factors limiting the supply of labour

In an ideal world there would be an abundant supply of labour possessing all the skills and capabilities required by employers. In the real world the supply of labour is limited in many important markets. Some natural skills are rare. Other skills can be developed through study, practice and training. By following a GNVQ in Business you are acquiring skills and knowledge that will make you an effective employee, and the harder you work the more skilled you will become. The more employees trained and educated to higher levels, the more skilled will be the labour force.

It is therefore essential that the education and training system of a country develops people to meet the requirements of the modern labour market.

Factors that tend to restrict the supply of labour therefore include:

- the natural skills of the population
- limitations of the education system
- the non-availability of training opportunities
- the unwillingness of employers and employees to take advantage of training opportunities
- restrictions on importing skills from other countries and regions
- limitations resulting from trade unions and other groups controlling the supply of labour.

If labour becomes more *productive* (see later) this has the effect of moving the supply curve of labour to the right (Figure 13.3 (a)). A given quantity of labour can now produce more output. The technical term for this is an increase in **productivity.**

When restrictions are placed on the supply of labour this will have the effect of increasing the price of labour (Figure 13.3 (b)). For example, when trade unions and professional

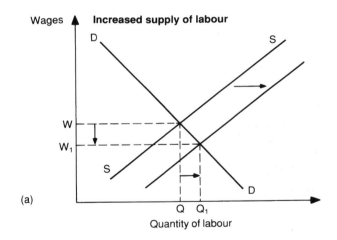

(a)

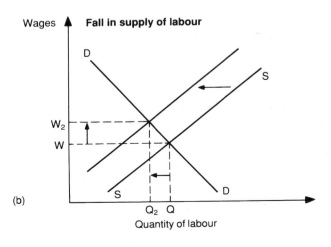

(b)

Figure 13.3 *The effects of changes in supply*

bodies insist on long apprenticeships and periods of training this reduces the possible supply of labour. Those already trained can benefit from the generally higher wages (e.g. doctors, solicitors, accountants, etc.).

Factors influencing the demand for labour

We have already seen that the total (**aggregate**) demand for labour in an economy will contract during a slump and rise during a boom.

In a period of slump many people will be dismissed because there is no work for them to do, and there will therefore be a surplus of skilled labour.

During a boom period, however, more and more workers will be in employment. Moreover, they will be in a strong position to gain pay increases because employers have to compete for labour. In a period of boom, unemployment will be falling and there will be a shortage of skilled labour in many occupations.

Task

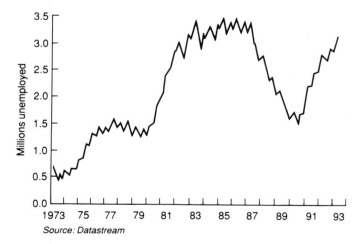

Study the two charts in Figures 13.4 and 13.5. Can you make any connections between trends shown in the two charts? How would the skills shortages affect wages in the economy over the period shown?

Figure 13.4 *Total unemployment in the UK*

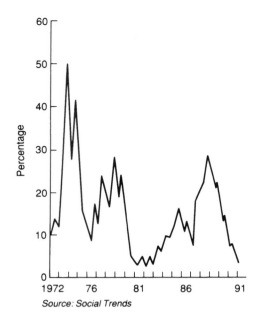

Source: Social Trends

Figure 13.5 *Skills shortages*

THE GROWING IMPORTANCE OF SERVICE SECTOR EMPLOYMENT

As manufacturing has become better (not just in improving quality and efficiency but also in responding to environmental concerns and other challenges), it has also become smaller. In every advanced nation, industry employed a smaller proportion of the workforce in 1990 than it did in 1980, and in virtually every nation it also contributed a smaller proportion of their gross national product (GNP). Everywhere the 'slack' has been taken up by services. It was in 1959 in the United States that, for the first time, the service sector of a nation became larger in terms of its GNP than the industrial sector. In 1992, the service sector in every country was much bigger, contributing 69 per cent to the GNP in the United States, Britain and France, 63 per cent in Italy, 59 per cent in Germany and 56 per cent in Japan.

There are three broad reasons for the shift. One is that as societies become richer, people choose to spend a higher proportion of their income on buying services rather than things.

The second reason is that it has so far proved very much harder to wring additional **productivity** out of services than out of manufacturing. Greater productivity in a car plant comes from more robots on the production line: the product does not suffer (indeed, probably the reverse). However, if greater productivity in a school means fewer teachers in the classroom, quality of education suffers immediately.

The third reason for the shift to services is that, as countries become richer, they are able to 'export' their profits in the form of investments in manufacturing in other, less developed, countries. It is evident that a number of countries have invested in manufacturing in new developing industrial countries. In turn, the rewards are returned in profits, interest and dividends that can be spent on leisure and services.

There are no signs at all that the present shifting of demand towards services will cease. Indeed, there is a powerful reason to expect it to accelerate – namely, the ageing population in industrial societies. The proportion of people aged over 60 will continue to rise in every developed country for at least a generation. By the year 2020, more than 30 per cent of the population of Germany and Italy will be over 60. Elderly people are more likely to spend their income and savings on health care, holidays and domestic services, rather than on consumer goods. The countries that increase living standards most quickly in the future will be those that can improve the way they run service societies.

Services can be divided into four main groups. *Financial services* and *distribution* tend to be in the private sector, while *health* and *education* tend to be in the public sector. Technology can be used to transform each of these areas. In financial services, for example, we will see, more than ever before, the development of 'paperless money'. Also, financial services are becoming increasingly tailored to the needs of individual customers. In distribution services, the benefits of bulk retailing are likely to be grafted on to much wider swathes of the industry, with resultant cost-cutting. In health care, technological advances have led to people living longer, and the focus will now shift to raising the quality of care and fitness throughout people's lives. Education, too, will become a continuous process, involving people of all ages. Workers can expect to be retrained to take on completely different skills several times during their careers.

Is it possible to absorb the growing supply of labour?

Making products involves combining capital and labour. A football club needs turnstiles and stands as well as its players and officials. A factory needs machines as well as its managers and process operatives. In these circumstances capital and labour complement each other. However capital and labour can also be seen as *substitutes* for one another. Machines can be used to replace labour: in the car industry robots can do jobs previously done by workers, and in the coal mining industry modern cutting machines reduce the need for thousands of miners.

When we look at the growth in the labour force in Britain we see that more people are available for work than ever before (see Figure 13.6). At the beginning of 1990 the workforce in employment stood at nearly 26 million. More and more jobs need to be created to absorb this potential labour force.

However, as we have seen all too painfully in the recession of the early 1990s, when a downturn comes in the economy then labour is **shaken out.** Some people argue that high unemployment rates will come to be seen as a normal state of affairs, but that is probably to pessimistic. The emphasis must be on providing relevant training (and retraining) for employment. The labour force needs to become increasingly **flexible.**

On a GNVQ course you can expect to develop general skills, such as communication and IT skills. These can help you in a variety of jobs. Flexibility will be the key to successful careers in the future.

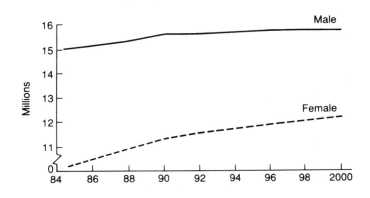

Figure 13.6 *The British labour force projected up to the year*

Make a list of the core skills that a GNVQ course sets out to develop. Suggest how these generic skills can be used in a variety of jobs.

Employers prepare to ditch equal opportunities at work

A confidential report that was leaked to the press in March 1993 suggested that the Confederation of British Industry, the employers' organisation, was preparing to abandon support for equal opportunities for women and the ethnic minorities. Other disadvantaged groups – the disabled, long-term unemployed, the over 50s and ex-offenders – would also be sacrificed.

The report argued that rising unemployment had reduced the need for employers to concern themselves with getting previously under-represented groups into the labour force and improving their level of skills. Unemployment was thought unlikely to fall below 2.5 million during the 1990s. It was suggested that some of the business reasons for employing previously excluded groups and for training them had become irrelevant. The document – entitled *Economic Growth and the Prospects for Employment* – concluded that the 'demographic timebomb', which had been expected to lead to a shortage of young people in the labour market, was effectively 'defused'.

1 *What is meant by 'business reasons for employing previously excluded groups'?*
2 *What is (or was) the demographic timebomb?*
3 *How had the market for labour altered between 1989 and 1993? (Refer to Figure 13.7.)*
4 *How might business reasons and ethical reasons for employing minority groups differ?*
5 *If you were managing a business, what arguments would you put up in favour of an equal opportunities programme?*

At the end of the 1980s a major worry for employers was the ability to recruit enough skilled labour to fill existing vacancies. At a time when the number of young people was falling this was a major concern. In 1990 it was estimated, for example, that one major insurance company in Norwich would be able to absorb all the school-leavers coming on to the labour market in the area. A report published at the time entitled *Defusing the Demographic Timebomb* showed:

- Employment was at its highest level ever and unemployment was continuing to fall. Employers were increasingly looking for staff who were both highly skilled and flexible.
- The number of women in employment was continuing to rise.
- The strongest growth was in the service sector and self-employment.
- As the number of young people fell, employers would need to extend their recruitment to include the longer-term unemployed, older workers, women returners, ethnic minority groups and people with disabilities.
- The number of small businesses was increasing as well as vacancies for skilled labour in Job Centres.

Clearly the situation outlined in 1989 was one of a 'seller's market'. There was a shortage of supply of labour (particularly of the skilled kind) coupled with high demand. However, by 1993 the picture had changed considerably (see Figure 13.7).

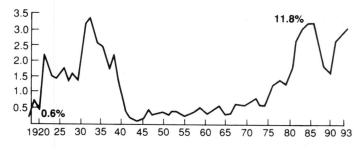

Figure 13.7 *The fall and rise of Britain's unemployment*

• THE CONCEPT OF PRODUCTIVITY •

A productive system can be thought of as a whole economy or simply a group of people working together. The productivity of the system is the amount of output that can be produced from a given set of inputs:

$$\text{Productivity} = \frac{\text{Output}}{\text{Input}}$$

The productivity ratio therefore measures how *efficient* a system is in converting inputs of resources into useful outputs.

Increases in productivity can be gained by:

- output increasing while input remains the same
- output increasing while input increases at a smaller rate
- output staying the same while input decreases
- output falling while input falls at a slower rate.

Measuring the productivity of labour

If we wanted to find out how productive the employees in a food processing plant were, we could do so by studying the following ratio:

$$\text{Productivity} = \frac{\text{Number of units of good produced per month}}{\text{Average number of people employed per month}}$$

The manager of the plant would need to measure the number of units produced in the plant each month and compare it with the average number of employees. Clearly this process is fairly simple if the plant is producing a standard item (e.g. loaves of standard white bread). However, in most manufacturing operations different types of outputs are produced. It may therefore be necessary to measure the value of outputs:

$$\text{Productivity} = \frac{\text{Value of food items produced per month}}{\text{Average number of people employed per month}}$$

Multi-factor productivity ratios

Outputs are not produced by labour alone. We also need to take account of machinery and raw materials. A multi-factor productivity ratio like the one shown below takes into account other inputs:

$$\text{Productivity} = \frac{\text{Output}}{\text{Labour + materials + fixed assets etc.}}$$

In the real world the most common calculation made is of labour productivity. This is because labour is the most commonly used factor of production. Industries that use a great deal of labour are said to be **labour-intensive**. Today, however, with the introduction of new technology, capital is becoming more and more intensive. Many new industries are employing more and more capital – that is, they are becoming increasingly **capital-intensive**.

Task

List four types of manufacturing that are still labour-intensive, and explain why they are so. List four types that are capital-intensive and give reasons. Finally, list four types that are becoming less labour-intensive but more capital-intensive, and explain why these changes are happening.

Task

What do the pie-charts in Figure 13.8 tell us about the changing importance of labour in manufacturing?

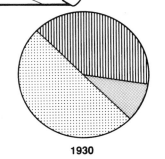 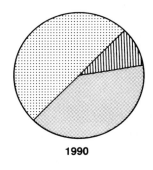

1930   1990

Materials   Direct labour   Overheads

Figure 13.8 *The breakdown of manufacturing costs*

Measuring productivity over time

It is important to be able to monitor productivity trends over a time period to see whether an organisation is becoming more efficient or less efficient. Clearly, if a company increases the training of its workforce, increases the automation of its plant, or successfully reorganises the production process, it will expect to see an increasing productivity ratio. This can be tracked over time.

Productivity figures for different industries appear from time to time in national newspapers, and are available on request from the Department of Employment. Study the productivity figures for a particular firm or industry and observe how these vary over time. Try to give reasons for the changes.

Changes over time can also be measured by means of an **index** (see Chapter 2):

$$\text{Productivity index} = \frac{\text{Productivity ratio in time period}}{\text{Productivity ratio in base year}} \times 100$$

Useful comparisons can then be made between firms in the same industry, and between the economic systems in different countries.

Measuring productivity of inputs by value

As we have already seen, it is possible to measure productivity by value. For example, we can use a multi-factor measure of productivity:

$$\text{Productivity} = \frac{\text{Sales revenue}}{\text{Labour} + \text{materials} + \text{overheads}}$$

A manager can break this down further to measure the productivity of particular inputs:

$$\text{Labour productivity} = \frac{\text{Sales revenue}}{\text{Wages}}$$

$$\text{Capital productivity} = \frac{\text{Sales revenue}}{\text{Value of capital items}}$$

$$\text{Materials productivity} = \frac{\text{Sales revenue}}{\text{Value of materials used}}$$

Productivity of the national economy

We could try to measure the productivity of the national economic system in a similar way, by using the formula:

$$\text{Productivity} = \frac{\text{Total national output}}{\text{Land} + \text{labour} + \text{capital}}$$

However, this is almost impossible to measure. (Why?) Economists therefore use a quantity known as the **gross national product** (GNP). This involves measuring the outputs of each of the industrial sectors that make up the economy manufacturing; energy and water; agriculture, forestry and fishing; services; construction; …).

When calculating these individual outputs it is necessary to look at the value added by each sector of the economy. This is so as to avoid double-counting certain outputs. For example, a book on sale in a shop has been sold by a publisher to the bookshop, the publisher bought in raw materials such as paper, binding, glue etc.

· EDUCATION AND TRAINING ·

A considerable proportion of the British workforce does not have any form of qualification. The proportion in 1990 was 28 per cent according to the *Labour Force Survey*. The sector 'agriculture, forestry and fishing' had the highest proportion without qualifications (42 per cent), followed by 'distribution, hotels and catering' (37 per cent). 'Metal goods, engineering and vehicles' and 'construction' both had around 30 per cent with no qualifications.

The development of **NVQs** and **GNVQs** should simplify the national system of qualifications, and a major aim of the government, trade unions and CBI is to make sure that all young people have access to these.

Figure 13.9 shows the number of school-leavers expected to enter the labour market up to the year 2000. If these leavers are to have productive careers they will need access to further education and training.

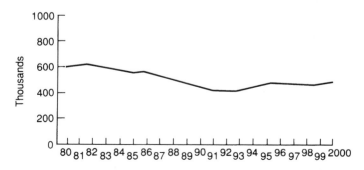

Figure 13.9 *School-leavers available to enter the labour market in Britain*

Study Figure 13.10. What does it tell you about the importance of getting qualifications?

2.4% — Degree or equivalent or above

1.2% — Higher education below degree level

17.3% — GCE A-level or equivalent

8.9% — GCE O-level or equivalent/CSE grade 1

5.4% — CSE other grades

6.6% — Foreign/other qualifications

57.0% — No qualifications

Also: Qualifications not stated, 1.2%

Figure 13.10 *Ladder of Qualifications of those looking for work for over six months*

Training

Training is the process of systematically teaching employees so that they acquire and improve job related skills and knowledge. Lack of training may lead to a reduction in the possible production level, to errors and to waste. Potentially good employees may decide to leave in frustration.

It would be quite foolish to expect a teacher to instruct a class of pupils without an extensive period of preparation, so that skills and abilities can then be quickly applied to the job. Poor preparation costs an organisation time and money. It can also lead to injury in hazardous environments.

Training is a key part of working life. Not only does it add to the skillfulness and abilities of labour, and thus increase its supply; it is also a great motivator. Training helps to give employees a sense of purpose.

Training for future needs is a long-term investment. Unfortunately it is an area of expenditure that is easy to cut back in difficult times without immediately affecting productivity. Expenditure in the UK on training is quite low by European standards.

· MOTIVATION ·

Motivation is what causes people to act or do something in a particular way. By understanding why people behave in the ways they do, managers can improve the designs of jobs, rewards and the working environment to match more closely the economic, social and personal needs of the employees.

We all have different motives for the things that we do. For example, some people strive for achievement status and power while others strive for money. Our personality, our expectations and our social backgrounds strongly influence the way we act. Managers must understand the needs of employees.

Identify your personal goals. To what extent are these goals influencing the things that you do now?

Understanding managerial commitment

A recent survey supplied evidence of a critical lack of motivation affecting the leadership and management of many major British companies.

The survey found that modern organisations tend to allow managers greater freedom to work within a smaller, separately budgeted unit, but that many found it difficult to work in such an environment and would prefer a more tightly controlled hierarchy. They were often experiencing stress and were finding it difficult to adapt to the new demands of their managerial roles. Stress was reducing their commitment to their organisations. Their views were reinforced by a feeling that they were under-paid and that there were limited opportunities for promotion. As a result many managers were developing their personal sources of motivation and satisfaction outside rather than inside work.

The survey concluded that management potential was being wasted because of a lack of attention to motivation, and this was affecting the quality of leadership in British companies.

1 Why did many of the managers in the survey lack motivation?

2 How could the commitment of managers be improved?

Satisfying needs

There has been extensive research into motivation and the behaviour of people at work. One of the leading theories is that of **Maslow** which provided an insight into people's needs. Maslow's study of human behaviour led him to devise a hierarchy of needs with basic needs at the bottom and higher needs at the top (see Figure 13.11).

Maslow claimed that people want to satisfy a lower level of need before moving on to a higher need.

- *Physiological needs* are basic. Food, shelter and clothing are required to meet the needs of the body and for

physical survival. This basic level of need will be typically met at work by the exchange of labour for a wage packet or salary and by the physical conditions of the working environment.

- *Safety and security needs* involve protection from danger and the provision of a predictable and orderly work space. Security of employment, and pension and sick-pay schemes, are also relevant here.

- *Love needs* are concerned with the individual's need for love and affection. This involves relationships and a feeling of 'belonging'. At the place of work these needs can be satisfied by the companionship of fellow workers, working in a group or team, and company social activities.

- *Esteem needs* are based on an individual's desire for self-respect and the respect of others. Employees have a need to be recognised as individuals, to have a job title or some form of status or prestige, and to have their efforts noticed.

- *Self-actualisation needs* are concerned with personal development and individual creativity to achieve one's full potential. In order to meet these needs at work individuals need to be provided with the opportunity to use their creative talents and abilities fully.

Maslow felt that as an employee moves up the hierarchy he or she becomes more 'complete', someone who enjoys work and feels a direct involvement in it. However, the theory has its critics who question the realism of a hierarchy where needs are structured in such an ordered way. Maslow has also been criticised for producing a theory which only reflects middle-class values in American society.

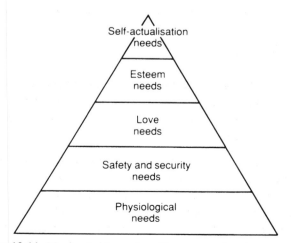

Figure 13.11 *Maslow's hierarchy of human needs*

Task

Can you recognise the needs in Maslow's theory in your own behaviour? If so, at what point in the hierarchy are you currently concentrating? How does society influence the way you satisfy these needs?

Job satisfaction

Another famous theory of motivation is that of **Herzberg**, and this in many ways complements Maslow's findings.

Herzberg investigated how satisfied people were at work. Following a series of interviews he came to the conclusion that certain factors tended to lead to job satisfaction while others frequently led to job dissatisfaction.

Factors which give rise to satisfaction Herzberg called **motivators** or **satisfiers;** those tending to give rise to dissatisfaction he called **hygiene factors** or **dissatisfiers**.

The most important motivators or satisfiers are:

- a sense of achievement
- recognition of effort and performance
- the nature of the work itself
- responsibility
- the opportunity for promotion and advancement.

Hygiene factors or dissatisfiers include:

- company policy and administration
- supervision and relationship with supervisor
- working conditions
- salary
- relationships at the same level in the hierarchy
- personal life
- relationships with subordinates
- status
- security.

The main difference between motivators and hygiene factors is that motivators *bring satisfaction* whereas hygiene factors can at best only serve to *prevent dissatisfaction*. The theory thus makes a distinction between factors causing positive satisfaction and those causing dissatisfaction.

Task

Look at Herzberg's motivators and hygiene factors. If you were a manager or employer, how useful would a knowledge of these be if you wanted to improve the morale and commitment of your workforce?

Enrichment and enlargement

The work of Herzberg has led to considerable research on **job enrichment** and **job enlargement**. Job enrichment involves loading a job *vertically* to maximise responsibility, achievement and recognition. This may mean increasing the variety of individual tasks an employee undertakes at different levels of responsibility. It could also mean increasing his or her area of supervision so that the person's contribution is perceived as more highly valued. Other possibilities are to upgrade the job, give more control over the job, provide more challenging tasks, provide feedback etc. Herzberg did, however, recognise that not every job can be enriched with other levels of responsibility, and that some employees feel happier in conditions of predictability.

Job enlargement, on the other hand, involves loading a job *horizontally* with more tasks of a similar nature. The idea behind this is to increase the challenge and variety of the work and provide employees with a broader range of skills to cover work at that level. Increasing the variety of an individual's tasks can satisfy more work needs and allow him or her to see their contribution to the whole.

Task

Interview someone who has employment. To what extent is the job horizontally loaded or vertically loaded? Explain how the job could be enriched or enlarged.

Quality circles

An organisation can attempt to motivate employees by developing special groups or teams (see Chapter 11). For example, quality circles have been a particularly important motivator in recent years.

Quality circles are typically small groups of seven or eight people who voluntarily meet on a regular basis to identify, investigate, analyse and resolve quality-related matters or other work-related arrangements using problem-solving techniques. Members tend to be from the same work area or do similar work.

Quality circles are about participation, teamwork, job satisfaction, self-esteem and organisational commitment as well as resolving work and quality-related problems. They have been particularly effective in Japanese industry where they have been responsible, it is claimed, for loyalty coupled with high productivity.

Case Study

Nissan Motor Manufacturing (UK) Ltd

On 1 February 1984, Nissan and the UK government signed an agreement to build a car plant near Sunderland in the North East of England. Within months the company had appointed its first British employee, the personnel director. Since then their short British tenure has been a success story, with forecast production of 270 000 cars by 1993, 70 per cent of which will be exported to continental Europe and the Far East.

Nissan's philosophy is to build profitably the highest-quality car sold in Europe. The company also wants to achieve the maximum possible customer satisfaction and ensure the prosperity of the enterprise and its staff. To assist in this, Nissan aims to achieve *mutual trust* and *co-operation* between all people in the company and to make Nissan a place where long-term job satisfaction can be achieved.

Nowadays, '**kaizen**' is a word much used in Sunderland. It is Japanese, the literal translation being simply '*continuous improvement*'. The improvement is gained by slow and steady change, and once achieved it is maintained at that level until such time as the next step of improvement takes place.

During the 1950s, Japanese industry made great efforts to improve the image of its product quality. These efforts were assisted by two prominent American specialists who visited Japan. Their influence caused Japanese industry to take a fresh look at its strategy, and in 1962 the first *quality circles* were formed and registered. By the mid-1960s most of the larger Japanese companies were supporting a great many quality circles, and currently Nissan in Japan has over 3900 active circles. Throughout the whole of Japan there are over 10 million members of some 1.2 million quality circles covering manufacturing industries, service industries and commerce. Such circles

Final assembly area – Nissan Sunderland

have been viewed as a powerful force for promoting a company-wide quality awareness and for encouraging contributions from an organisation's greatest resource – the workforce.

At Nissan's UK plant the 'kaizen' programme has been developed as a replacement for periodic quality circle activity. It encourages constant quality awareness and is better suited to the needs and aspirations of the British workforce. 'Kaizen' assumes the total involvement of all employees but recognises that participation depends on individuals genuinely feeling part of the Nissan team. The company policy is that:

- all staff have a valuable contribution to make as individuals, and this contribution can be most effective within a team environment
- 'kaizen' team activity helps develop leadership and presentation skills as well as enabling people to understand, acknowledge and learn from others
- 'kaizen' is one way in which employees may participate in issues that affect their workplace.

The 'kaizen' philosophy may be applied anywhere at any time. Everyone is encouraged to participate in the activity and, as members of a team, learn how to analyse situations logically and factually and discuss issues meaningfully and efficiently. People who contribute to the activity include:

- leaders who receive special training in the 'kaizen' process and then apply these skills to team activities
- members who participate in the activities, often from the same work unit or area
- specialists who assist a team with a particular project.

A steering committee develops the policies and guidelines under which the activity operates.

The 'kaizen' process is designed to enable a team to move on from the stage of dealing with current problems or areas in need of improvement to a stage where sources of concern are dealt with in advance of their actual occurrence.

1 Explain how and why 'kaizen' activity or the process of participation through quality circles might motivate employees.
2 Refer to a group or team activity with which you have been involved (e.g. sports, hobbies, clubs). Explain how membership of the group or team affected your approach to the activity.

· MONETARY AND OTHER REWARDS ·

Monetary and non-monetary **rewards** should be designed to attract, maintain and motivate employees. They should also be designed to meet the objectives of the organisation. The reward system is one of the key ingredients in motivation. Careful thought needs to be applied to structuring a payment system in a way that encourages motivation and performance.

In establishing a system of rewards an organisation will agree a policy for salaries and benefits. It will then evaluate jobs and place them into levels and scales. Assessment of the effectiveness of this policy of rewards will take place through some form of **staff appraisal.**

The policy of rewards

The **policy** of rewards should:

- ensure that the organisation can recruit both the quality and the quantity of staff it requires
- foster staff loyalty

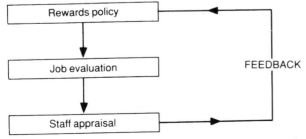

Figure 13.12 *A system of rewards*

- provide rewards for good performance as well as incentives
- create differentials between jobs
- reflect market rates for different skills
- be easy to understand
- be cost-effective.

Task

Interview someone who is in employment. To what extent do they feel that their reward system matches the aims listed in the text? Do you feel that any other factors ought to be added to this list?

Job evaluation

Job evaluation aims to:

- establish the rank order of jobs within the organisation
- evaluate the differences in value of jobs and place them into an appropriate pay structure
- ensure that judgements about jobs are made on objective grounds.

Ranking is the process of analysing all jobs and determining their relative positions in terms of importance by comparing one job with another. For this purpose an office manager would be ranked above a typing pool supervisor but below a director. The purpose of ranking is to collect jobs of comparable responsibility into broad bands before pricing the structure by attaching rewards and salary brackets to the bands.

Task

Name ten jobs or positions which appear in the organisation you either work for or attend. Rank them by dividing the jobs into bands or grades of comparable responsibility. Indicate what you think each grade is worth in terms of monetary and non-monetary rewards. If possible, compare your answers with others in a group.

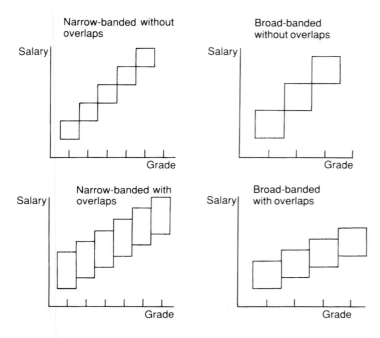

Figure 13.13 *Examples of graded salary structures*

Graded salary structure

A **graded salary structure** consists of a sequence of salary bands, each with a maximum and a minimum amount of reward. The structure gives an indication of the different levels of importance of jobs in the organisation. It also establishes differentials and helps to create some form of career path.

Organisations vary in the number of grades, the widths of grades and the overlaps between them. Some examples are shown in Figure 13.13.

Task

Find out details of two different graded salary structures. Into which category does each fall? Comment on any other differences between the two structures. In particular, refer to the effect each grade structure might have on staff motivation.

Incidental (or occasional) rewards

Incidental rewards are often linked with certain grades of job. They may also be given to encourage commitment to the organisation or to reward any special efforts made. They might include:

- a bonus scheme in the form of a lump sum related in some way to either individual or group performance
- the availability of overtime for extra monetary reward
- a profit-sharing scheme in the form of shares or special payments.

Other 'perks' that can be mentioned are pension schemes, insurances, sick pay, private health care, redundancy cover, extra holiday entitlement, bridging loans, relocation assistance, credit cards, fees to professional bodies, subsidised product purchase, a company car, payment for courses, and luncheon vouchers. The list is literally endless and stretches the imagination of the employer.

Case Study

Why industry thrives on the carrot

Industry in the UK spends at least £1 billion a year on staff motivation. Though some of the money is spent on involving the workforce in improving productivity, quality and level of customer service, most is spent on more obvious rewards such as holidays, gifts and bonuses for meeting performance targets.

As companies are reluctant to divulge information about incentives it is difficult to estimate the exact value of the incentive market. There are, however, four main areas – cash, travel, merchandise and bonus shares (vouchers or bonds). All incentives have their own limitations. For example, cash is subject to taxes and it soon gets forgotten as a reward, and there are limitations with merchandise – how many video recorders will a high-flying salesman need?

Not every company thinks it is necessary to offer a vast array of material rewards. TGI Friday, the Whitbread-owned restaurant chain, operates on the principle that the greatest benefit is *recognition*. Staff are awarded merit pins for technical ability, sales acumen and leadership qualities.

A project was recently completed on behalf of Ireland's state-owned electricity board. As prices were frozen from 1989 to 1992, even though the organisation expected to have increased fuel bills, a cost-saving programme called Bright Ideas was designed to motivate staff. Nine out of ten staff responded to the scheme when they were offered one-third of the saving in its first year. Massive savings were made and staff felt they had made gains in teamwork, staff communications and achieving their sense of 'belonging'.

The indications are that, for the 1990s, motivation programmes in industry will move away from short-term incentives towards more long-term methods of investing in people.

1 *What are the advantages of providing employees with short-term rewards for the efforts they make?*

2 *Of the four main reward types mentioned, what in your opinion would provide the greatest incentive?*

3 *How important is recognition as a motivator? If you were running a small chain-store, explain how you would try to recognise the efforts of your staff.*

4 *Comment on the Bright Ideas scheme, and outline any ideas you have for providing a more permanent long-term method of motivating employees.*

Staff appraisal

Staff appraisal, while designed primarily to assess an employee's performance, also provides an opportunity to judge the effectiveness of a policy of rewards. Such appraisals concentrate not on jobs but on *individuals*. A manager can discuss an employee's needs on a one-to-one basis.

Task

If you, as a manager, wanted to find out more about the needs of your staff, what questions would you ask them on an appraisal form?

Case Study

Finding the vital motivation

A senior director of a large company was surprised by the poor performance of an employee who had been with his company for only a short time. This man had all the right qualities for the job, including the relevant technical skills, but was not doing as well as expected.

He was running a technical department with 30 highly qualified specialists, and his role was to lead and motivate the team in order to pursue the company's objectives. Despite a generous salary, help with relocation costs, free health insurance, a company car and a pension scheme, the employee's heart did not seem to be in the job and, instead of taking a real pride in running his department, he busied himself in technical work where he could see the fruits of his labours.

When the man was asked to comment on this observation, it was discovered that he felt the role was no longer challenging. Though he had been recruited on the basis of his technical competence and management potential, the company had not realised that he needed to be constantly involved in challenging projects that used his technical skills. As a result he had started to lack motivation in the management role.

A theory of human behaviour relevant to this case is the one devised by **Professor McClelland**, who sought to produce a theory of practical use to companies and individuals in search of job satisfaction and fulfilment. He identified three primary social motives which govern our behaviour:

- *Group energy* – the need to establish and maintain good relationships, often as part of a team
- *Influence energy* – the need to have an impact, be perceived as influential and accomplish tasks through the efforts of others
- *Task energy* – the need to improve one's performance and accomplish tasks through one's own efforts, often in innovative and entrepreneurial ways. People high in task energy are motivated by challenging goals.

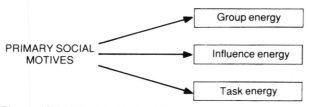

Figure 13.14 *The McClelland theory*

The man discussed above was found to be particularly high in group and task energy. Whereas his new job had initially satisfied both 'energies', his task energy has become unfulfilled. Subsequently, therefore, he was put in charge of a smaller team of project design experts where he could see the direct results of his efforts.

1 *Apart from monetary and incidental rewards, what do people look for at work?*
2 *How high are you in each of the three energy types?*
3 *Interview two or three people in different types of employment. How closely do their 'energies' seem to match their involvement at work? Do you think this is a good theory?*

Element assignment

Building a team

This assignment can help you provide evidence for assessment, or claim the following Common Skills outcomes:

Communication
Participate in oral and non-verbal communication

Personal Skills
Undertake personal and career development
Treat others, values, beliefs and opinions with respect
Relate to and interact effectively with individuals and groups
Work effectively as a member of a team
Deal with a combination of routine and non-routine tasks
Identify and solve routine and non-routine problems

In this assignment you will choose a leader for a team of students. As part of the assignment you will need to reflect on the process of team leadership in order to improve your own leadership skills. There are six stages:

1 As a group decide on a project (assignment) that you can work on together.
2 Somebody is chosen as group leader (by the tutor or by election).
3 Plan your project together.
4 Review the project as it develops.
5 When the teamwork assignment is complete the group reflects on the process.
6 Each member of the group writes an action plan for the next time he or she acts as leader.

Carrying out the assignment
1 Choose the project
As a group decide on an area of study that you can tackle together. You should consider:

● Why do we need to work together as a team on this project?
● What problems will be caused if we don't share our work together?
● Who is committed to the idea of sharing?
● Who is affected?
● How will the environment affect the outcomes of our work?
● How will we review progress?
● How can we measure success?

2 Choose a leader who is prepared to lead

3 Produce a plan
The plan needs to set out to answer the questions outlined above. Answers to the questions might include.

a Why do we need to work together?
  to set clear objectives
  to manage time better
  to get feedback about our performance
  to make better decisions
  What else can you think of?
b What problems will be caused if we don't work together?
  What will happen if the group does not collaborate?
  Who will suffer?
c Who is committed?
  Has everyone been consulted?
  Does everyone feel involved?
  Who will do what?
d Who is affected?
  Make a list of all students and non-students;
  How are they affected?

e What effect will the environment have on outcomes?
How will physical location affect the project (e.g. with respect to time management, communication, consultation)?
How will other groups affect the project?
What power will the leader be able to use?
Do you need to get permission from anyone to carry on with the work/use resources?

f How will you check on progress?
external assessment to given criteria
tutor assessment
peer group assessment

g How can success be measured?
by completing objectives by a certain time
Are objectives/outcomes measurable?
external evaluation
Can changes be observed?

4 Reviewing the project

Look at the objectives that you established in your plan, and any subsequent changes that you have made. List the objectives that should have been achieved by a given time. Are you working to plan?

If any objectives have not been achieved try to work out why. Do you need additional resources to get the plan back on target? What are the likely consequences of increasing resources (e.g. spending more hours on the project)? Does the time period of the project need to be altered? Have there been any unexpected objectives that have been achieved? What new decisions need to be made? When should the next review take place?

5 Reflection on the process

Every member of the group should now draw up a review sheet similar to the one opposite and complete it, analysing the performance of the leader. It should be filled in honestly in order to help the leader develop leadership skills.

Feedback to help the leader:

The qualities of your leadership that helped me the most were

1
2
3

The qualities of your leadership that caused me the most problems were

1
2
3

In order to strengthen your leadership qualities I would suggest that you do the following

1
2
3
4
5

You can check that you are developing these skills by reviewing your progress in the following ways

1
2
3

Step 6

As a member of the group reflect on what you have learnt from the activity. You should now be in a better position to write your own action plan. This will set out the steps you will take next time you have to take the part of leader in a group activity.

14 INFLUENCES ON EMPLOYMENT

T his chapter sets out to highlight some important decisions and steps in decision-making that are relevant to organisation of the workforce. We have already seen that conditions in the labour market alter frequently because of changes in demand and supply. The employment market also operates in an environment of change resulting from government actions and the policies of trade unions and employers' groups.

To develop an understanding of changes in the employment market it is necessary to investigate important information sources. You need to know why this information has been collected. You will then be able to use it to understand and explain why businesses take certain decisions.

▪ MANPOWER PLANNING ▪

Every organisation must know *how many* employees it will need to take on in the short, medium and long term, and the availability of appropriate employees and how they can be recruited. It must assess their *training* requirements.

The **manpower plan** must match the objectives of the organisation which are established in its corporate plan. All sorts or internal and external factors therefore need to be considered in setting out the manpower plan.

Internal factors include:

- plans to introduce new machinery and equipment
- the availability of finance
- expected labour turnover and absenteeism
- wage rates in comparable firms and industries.

External factors include:

- national and local population trends
- government policies on labour market issues (e.g. maximum number of hours that can be worked by individuals, health and safety regulations, etc.)

- the expansion or contraction of rival firms, and other firms competing for the same supply of labour.

What should be included in the manpower plan?

A manpower plan should look at an organisation's employment policy over a period of several years. The following details might be included:

- changes to the numbers employed
- changes in job tasks to be performed
- training and retraining schemes
- recruitment and redundancy plans
- considerations of industrial relations
- changes in the management and supervision of labour
- possible changes in corporate objectives in line with changes in manpower policies.

In the *short term*, manpower planning is concerned with making sure that enough employees are available to meet production targets (e.g. by altering overtime patterns in line with current orders). Perhaps extra part-time staff need to be recruited in order to meet a Christmas rush, or extra staff may need to be trained to operate a new machine that has just been installed.

▪ SOURCES OF INFORMATION ▪

Many sources of statistics on the labour force and employment trends are produced regularly by government departments. Two examples are:

● *Quarterly Labour Force Survey*, produced by the Department of Employment
● *Employment Gazette*, produced by the Department of Employment.

In addition the Confederation of British Industry (CBI) produces its *Quarterly Industrial Trends Survey.*

These surveys (and others) provide a wealth of really useful and detailed information. You may want to look at them. However, the *Labour Market Quarterly Reports,* available from the Department of Employment (Training Agency), give wonderful summaries of nearly all of the relevant information.

You should also study a good-quality national newspaper (and possibly a magazine like *The Economist*) to find references to employment trends. Because the labour market changes so frequently you need to obtain the very latest information. Information about employment trends is particularly relevant to all young people, who need to know what skills are in demand and what new opportunities are arising.

Task

Study some information sources showing changes in the labour market. Identify some sectors of the job market that are expanding, and those that are contracting.

▪ EDUCATION AND THE NEEDS OF INDUSTRY ▪

A report published in March 1993 (*Educational Provision: Educational Attainment and the Needs of Industry,* by the National Institute of Economic and Social Research) showed that the number of French and German 16-year-olds

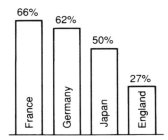

Figure 14.1 *Sixteen-year-olds' exam achievements compared (1991)*

gaining the equivalent of GCSE A, B or C grades in maths, their national language and a science subject is more than double the figure for England and Wales (see Figure 14.1). The report's authors pointed out that the most striking disparity between the attainments in Britain and those in other countries was in the lower half of the ability range.

Surveys carried out in a wider range of countries in the 1960s and 70s by the International Association for the Evaluation of Educational Achievement showed that, in maths and science, England and Wales had the largest percentage of pupils with a score of five or less (out of a maximum of 70). Only 8 per cent of the Japanese pupils attained scores below those achieved by the lowest quarter of English pupils. England came tenth out of fourteen countries in maths achievement.

In considering why Britain lags so far behind, the report says: 'It would appear that in high-achieving countries teachers generally have high public esteem.' Such countries 'have a "learning culture" in which parents and teachers have high expectations.'

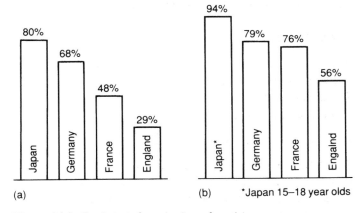

Figure 14.2 *Statistics of continuing education*

A further weakness in Britain's position is the relatively small number of young people **continuing** their education and training. Figure 14.2(a) shows the proportions of young people obtaining entry-requirement qualifications for further education. For England, it shows school-leavers or further-education students up to the age of 19 years with two or more passes at A-level or with National Diplomas. (The equivalents in Germany are the Abitur and Berufsabschluss and in France the Baccalaureate.) Figure 14.2(b) shows the 'staying-on rate' in different countries. This is the proportion of young people in the range 16–19 in full- or part-time education and training.

The growth of GNVQs and NVQs and their availability should help to increase the capability of young people in Britain. Targets established by the CBI and supported by the government are for 50 per cent of young people to be educated and trained to GNVQ level 3 by the year 2000.

production systems foolproof because they cannot dispense with unsatisfactory workers. Downtime (time when production lines are not working) is greater than on the continent because workforces are unable to repair faults and have to await specialised skilled maintenance and repair teams. Stocks have to be higher to avoid bottlenecks.

1 What is meant by:
   a productivity
   b a shortfall in intermediate skills training
   c a bidding war that aggravates inflation?
2 What is the difference between output per head and output per employee? Why is the difference between output per employee smaller than the difference in output per head between the UK and Germany?
3 What evidence is given that relatively poor education and training in this country holds back the economy?
4 Why is this weakness particularly a problem in times of boom?
5 What solutions would you suggest for these problems?

Case Study

Education and training and national output

Many commentators in the United Kingdom feel that if we can improve our education and training then the output of goods and services will increase because employees will become more productive.

People are often surprised that we are not further behind in our productivity. Our *national output per head* in 1990 was 87 per cent of that in the former West Germany and 92 per cent of that in France. (One explanation of the small gap is that workers in this country work longer hours.) *National output per employee* in 1990 was 83 per cent of the German level, but this was made up by more people at work, and longer hours.

Training in crafts and technology in this country lags behind that in France and Germany. Britain awarded 30 000 mechanical and engineering qualifications in 1989 compared with 98 000 in France and 134 000 in Germany. The shortfall in intermediate skills training leads to the familiar problems suffered by British businesses near the peak of any boom. They cannot find enough skilled people, and therefore enter into a wage bidding war that aggravates inflation. British managers have to make

Case Study

The German system of vocational education

The German education system is based on dividing schools into three groups: grammar, technical and vocational.

The vocational group is put through a methodical system of apprenticeship training – 70 per cent of Germany's labour force has passed through this system. If is firmly based in the private sector. Teenagers leaving school between the ages of 15 and 19 sign with an employer, who trains them for two or three years in one of 380 occupations. They become craftworkers, machinists, secretaries, sales assistants, etc.

The system is administered by chambers of commerce, which register the apprentices, certify the trainers, regulate the programmes, and organise the exams. The qualifications are recognised throughout Germany and increasingly throughout Europe.

The trainees receive not more than a quarter of the wage paid to qualified employees. The training is based in the workplace. The apprentices are among adult workers, so they have models to emulate. And their reward for completing the course is clear – their wage is tripled.

However, major weaknesses of the German technical schools are that they lack good libraries and study space. They are overcrowded and there is little assignment or project work.

1 What aspects of technical education in Germany outlined above can we benefit from?

2 What are the major weaknesses outlined?

3 Try to find out more about German technical education, perhaps by interviewing German visitors to this country, or people with experience of working in Germany.

▪ MORE ON TRAINING ▪

It is important that employers train their existing workforces in order to improve their productivity and remain **competitive.** The major responsibility for training rests with employers, not with the government. Unfortunately, in periods of recession employers are likely to cut back substantially on their training budgets. It then becomes cheaper to recruit skilled labour from the pool of the unemployed.

Employers can benefit from:

● supporting the development of employer-led Training and Enterprise Councils (TECs) and the initiatives created by TECs to deliver training schemes

● offering placements on employment training schemes.

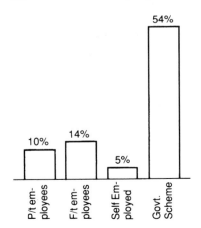

Figure 14.3 *Job-related training according to employment status (1990)*

The availability of job-related training varies according to employment status and age. Part-time employees are less likely than full-time employees to be offered training, and the self-employed are significantly less likely to get training (see Figure 14.3). The older an employee, the less likely it is that he or she will be offered job-related training (Figure 14.4). The figures also vary according to the industrial sector (Figure 14.5).

Tasks

1 Study the bar-charts in Figures 14.3–14.6 (which are from the Labour Force Survey for 1990) and write some key comments on each.

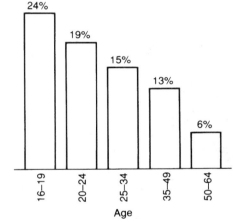

Figure 14.4 *Job-related training according to age (1990)*

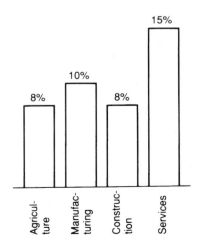

Figure 14.5 *Job-related training according to industrial sector (1990)*

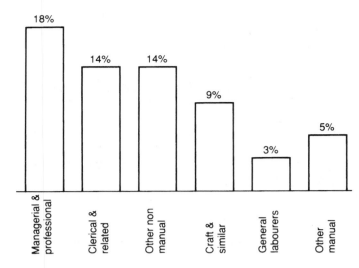

Figure 14.6 *Job-related training according to type of employment*

2   Compare the opportunities for training of the following three people:
  a Bob Jones is a 55-year-old full-time employee working in agriculture as a general labourer.
  b Barbara Davies is a 35-year-old part-time clerical assistant working for a building firm.
  c Jennifer Philips is a 37-year-old marketing manager of a large insurance company.
3   With others in a group, carry out your own survey to find out how training varies with occupation, industrial sector, age and nature of work. Record this information in a database. Set out your findings as bar-charts.

· WAGE LEVELS ·

The ability of an organisation to pay high wages depends on the value of the output of employees and the price at which the organisation can sell its products. The same is true of a whole economy.

A **high-wage economy** is one that produces products that command premium prices. A **low-wage economy** is one that produces basic items at prices that have been forced down to a low level by competition.

Figure 14.7 shows that there is a substantial difference between the pay received by some categories of employees (e.g. doctors) and others (e.g. hairdressers). The chart relates to the spread of pay in 1992. We can also see that within an occupational group there is a considerable spread in pay – some doctors were earning about £20 000 while others were getting nearly £50 000. In 1992 the average salary of doctors was £32 100, but 10 per cent of all doctors earned less than £19 292, and 10 per cent earned more than £48 229.

The figures shown in the chart were produced by the New Earnings Survey. The survey broke occupations down into the following ten categories according to earning power:

● Bottom tenth – hairdressers, beauticians, kitchen porters
● Second to bottom tenth – dry-cleaning staff, waiters, cleaners
● Third tenth – assistant nurses, receptionists, packers

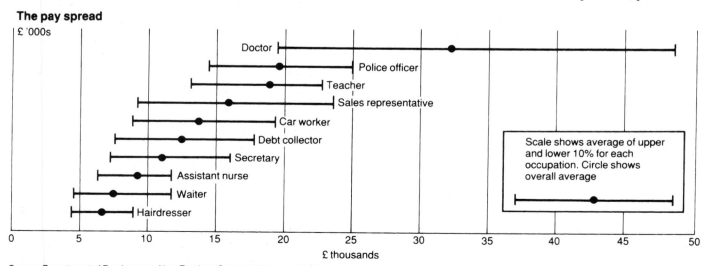

Source: Department of Employment, New Earnings Survey 1991 parts (A&D)

Figure 14.7 *The pay spread*

318

- Fourth tenth – caretakers, stores clerks, secretaries
- Fifth tenth – debt collectors, factory workers
- Sixth tenth – laboratory technicians, car workers
- Seventh tenth – librarians, sales reps
- Eighth tenth – teachers, electricians, scientists
- Ninth tenth – accountants, production managers
- Top tenth – bank managers, doctors.

Task

Explain how and why the differences in earnings outlines in the above table come about. Also try to explain why there are such big differences within an occupational group (e.g. between a poorly paid and a well paid doctor).

· CLASSIFICATION OF EMPLOYMENT ·

In the New Earnings Survey outlined above, people were grouped into tenths of the population according to the amount they earned. In survey work people are often graded according to the occupations they do. The simplest division is that between **manual** and **non-manual** work. Jobs that require physical effort of some kind, such as in a mine or on a building site, are distinguished from those that involve working at a desk. This is mainly because considerable differences often exist in the level of wages, of skills, or working conditions, or attitudes and prestige attached to manual and non-manual occupations.

In a factory, for example, it is not unusual for manual and non-manual workers to use a different entrance, to work different hours, and to use different facilities.

The most commonly used classification of occupations is that produced by the Registrar General. This divides occupations into five classes:

1 Professional and higher administrative, such as lawyers, architects and doctors.
2 Intermediate professional workers and administrative personnel, such as shopkeepers, farmers and teachers.
3 Skilled:
   a Non-manual such as shop assistants, and clerical workers in offices

   b Manual such as toolmakers and electricians.
4 Semi-skilled, such as bus conductors and farm workers.
5 Unskilled, such as general labourers on building sites.

Task

What are the similarities and what are the differences between the gradings of occupation groups by the Registrar General and the New Earnings Survey? Explain the trends that you have observed.

Since the 1950s there has been a steady decline in the numbers of low-skilled jobs and a great increase in the numbers of professional and lower and middle management positions. There are now more high-status jobs around. Commentators refer to the 'new working class' which is particularly concentrated in the South of England. These workers have more spending power and access to goods and services.

However, another quite distinct group has emerged during the recession, labelled the 'underclass'. These people can be found in pockets all over the country. They lack any power and receive the worst of everything. The group includes some youngsters with poor qualifications, pensioners, some single-parent families, and some members of ethnic groups. For example, a report in 1993 by the charities Barnardos and Youthaid reported that there were 100 000 16- and 17-year-olds with no job and no training place. Hardship payments of £33.60 were available for youngsters awaiting training places. The number of payments made rose dramatically from just over 10 000 in 1988 to nearly 80 000 in 1992.

Professional workers are a loose group of people who generally have to learn a body of knowledge in order to carry out their work. Doctors and lawyers are professionals. They tend to earn high incomes and enjoy a good standard of living but have to work long hours.

Many traditional working-class jobs have disappeared with the decline of manufacturing and the growth of the service sector of the economy. As a result far more opportunities have opened up for white-collar workers. Whereas the old factory system would be characterised by people 'clocking on' in the morning and 'clocking off' at the end of the day, many of the new offices and workplaces operate a flexi-time system: all employees are expected to be 'in' at certain key times, but they have the flexibility to work the remainder of their contracted hours at times of their own choice. This has made it increasingly possible for people with family responsibilities to find and keep rewarding work.

· INCREASING PRODUCTIVITY ·

In business that employs just a few workers there is little scope for specialisation of jobs. On the other hand, a firm that employs more people is able to organise production to make the best use of its labour inputs.

As an organisation adds more labour to its capital equipment, there is at first an increase in output. However, if it employs too much labour then decreasing returns will set in.

We can illustrate the **returns to labour as** more hands are added to a production process in the form of a table (see Figure 14.8). This shows that total output increases as more employees are added, up to the nineteenth employee in this case. However, when we organise production we are more concerned with average output *per employee* than with changes in total output. We can see from Figure 14.8 that at first each new employee increases average output successfully. For example, the second employee increases

average output from 100 (with one employee) to 125 (with two employees). Note, however, that the eighth employee actually *reduces* average output (from 171.4 to 171.2).

When planning production, a key figure to look out for is **marginal product.** The marginal product is the addition to total output that comes from employing an additional employee. In Figure 14.8 we see that when nine people are employed the total output is 1531, but with ten people it is 1682. The marginal product of the tenth employee is therefore 151 units. The twentieth and twenty-first employees actually have negative marginal products in this case.

Task

Complete the following table showing the output of a factory as it increases its labour force.

Number of employees	Total output	Average output	Marginal product
1	200		
2	300		
3	380		
4	440		
5	480		
6	500		
7	500		
8	480		

Illustrating average and marginal product

When we come to illustrate the average product and marginal product curves of a business they should have the typical shape shown in Figure 14.9. At first the average and marginal products increase. This is called **increasing returns to labour** (labour is used more efficiently). Eventually, however, the marginal product starts to fall – this is **diminishing returns to labour.** When the marginal product falls below the average product it will pull the average product curve down.

The law of diminishing returns states that *as the proportion of one factor* (e.g. labour) *in a combination of factors* (e.g. labour, building and machinery) *is increased, after a point the marginal and average product of the factor will diminish.*

Number of employees	Total output	Average output	Marginal product
0	0	0.0	0
1	100	100.0	100
2	250	125.0	150
3	450	150.0	200
4	646	161.5	196
5	837	167.4	191
6	1022	170.3	185
7	1200	171.4	178
8	1370	171.2	170
9	1531	170.1	161
10	1682	168.2	151
11	1822	165.6	140
12	1950	162.5	128
13	2065	158.8	115
14	2166	154.7	101
15	2252	150.1	86
16	2322	145.1	70
17	2375	139.7	53
18	2410	133.9	35
19	2426	127.7	16
20	2422	121.1	–4
21	2397	114.1	–25

Figure 14.8 *Product of labour (in units)*

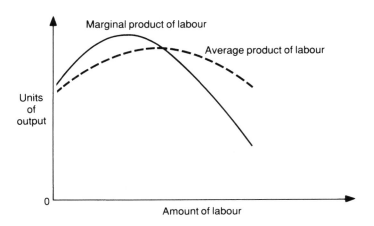

Figure 14.9 *Returns to labour*

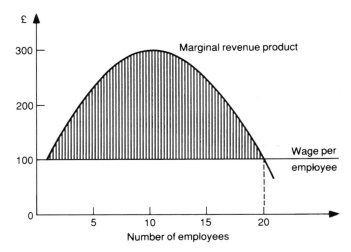

Figure 14.10 *Marginal revenue product*

Marginal revenue product

We have seen that marginal product is the extra physical output produced by adding more labour to the production process. For example, in a tailoring business the first employee might be able to produce ten shirts and the second employee may be able to produce an extra twelve shirts (total 22). The third employee may be able to produce an extra fifteen shirts (total 37). The marginal revenue product is the value of the product measured in money terms. If a shirt sells for £10 we could set out the following table.

Number of employees	Total output	Marginal physical product	Marginal revenue product
1	10	10	£100
2	22	12	£120
3	37	15	£150

An employer will employ more labour as long as the marginal revenue product of employing an extra employee is greater than the marginal cost of employing that employee.

We can illustrate this in the form of a diagram. Let us assume that all employees in a particular industry receive a standard wage of £100 per week. This is represented by a straight line in Figure 14.10 (the wage rate, or cost of employing an extra employee). The curve represents the marginal revenue product of employing more people. Clearly in this case the employer should keep on employing extra people until the twentieth employee.

The effect of increasing productivity

If the labour force becomes more productive (perhaps as a result of training) then the marginal revenue product of labour increases. Alternatively, if the demand for the product increases the marginal revenue product will increase. When the marginal revenue product increases it becomes possible to increase employment (and/or wages). In Figure 14.11, 25 employees can profitably be employed instead of the 20 in Figure 14.10.

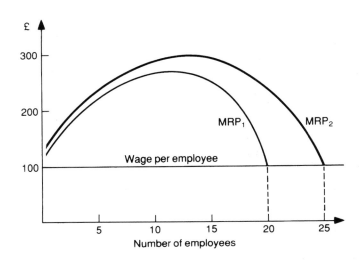

Figure 14.11 *The effect of increasing labour productivity*

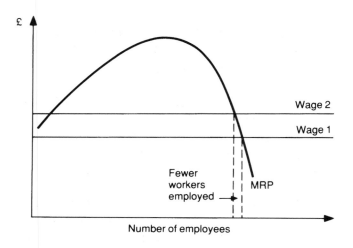

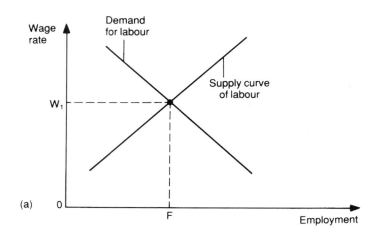

Figure 14.12 *The effect of a wage increase without increasing productivity*

Wage increases not matched by increases in productivity

One criticism levelled against trade unions is that sometimes they force wages up with no corresponding increase in productivity. The impact can be to reduce the quantity of labour employed (see Figure 14.12).

Similarly, a criticism of imposing minimum wages in an industry is that they may lead to a reduction in the quantity of labour employed. A criticism levelled at the European Community's Social Chapter is that it establishes minimum wages. If Britain has to establish minimum wages this could lead to job losses, particularly for low-paid workers.

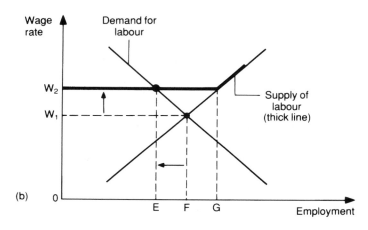

Figure 14.13 *Showing the effect of imposing a minimum wage*

· TRADE UNIONS AND THE · SUPPLY OF LABOUR

Economists who favour free market conditions use economic theory to show how the actions of trade unions and/or the creation of minimum wages can restrict the supply of labour, and hence cause unemployment.

Figure 14.13 (a) illustrates a competitive market for labour. The wage rate is $0W_1$ with $0F$ people employed. This is determined by the point at which the demand and supply curves for labour meet. However, if unions

manage to raise wages to $0W_2$, then employers in the industry cannot hire workers below this rate. (This would be exactly the same if the EC insisted on minimum wages of $0W_2$ being imposed on a free market.) The supply curve then needs to be represented as a horizontal line over the employment range $0G$ (as in Figure 14.13 (b)). Notice, however, that employment has reduced to $0E$.

Free market economists can thus argue that trade unions can increase wages for their members but at the expense of creating unemployment. They can also argue that imposing minimum wages will create unemployment in a similar way.

1 Are minimum wages in low-paying industries a good thing? Discuss the arguments for and against.
2 Is it always a good thing for trade unions to raise the wages of union members?

The power of trade unions

In this section we list the important factors that influence the ability of a trade union to increase the wages of its members and to improve working conditions.

- The demand for labour is derived from the demand for the product. Employees producing a product that is in strong demand are well placed to secure higher wages.
- As employees become more productive they become better placed to secure wage increases. They can become more productive as a result of improved training, harder work, better organised work and improved technology.
- A union with a high membership of key workers is more likely to be successful than one with few members, or one with part-time workers.
- The commitment of members to their union is crucial. When employees are strongly behind their union officials, the union is likely to be powerful. The union needs to be well organised, with a clear structure and policies.

Study an example of a pay dispute in the national press. How many of the factors listed above are present? Is the union in a strong or weak position to gain wage increases for members? What other factors (not listed above) influence power relations in the dispute?

OPPORTUNITIES FOR EUROPEAN · UNIONS AND MANAGERS TO WORK · TOGETHER

It is increasingly recognised that managers and employees need to co-operate on shared interests. The use of the phrase **human resource management** is recognition that the human resource is very valuable to any organisation and that good working relations will lead to the best results.

Within Europe, the trade unions of Sweden are probably the most 'integrated' into the political system and the economic–industrial system. The unions have always been represented at boardroom level, in management committees and on management bodies, and they play an active part in the decision-making process. Germany has also introduced a system of worker co-management.

In Japan, in contrast, a trade union is simply a body for voicing the opinions of employees. As soon as they begin to work for a company, workers take an oath of loyalty to the company. In a number of companies in Japan the daily ceremony of flag-hoisting and reciting the company prayer is still adhered to. Workers often wear achievement armbands that are given to the worker in each group who has the best productivity record, and these are worn with pride. Many employees are given responsibilities in the workplace. 'Production islands', for example, are individual production units staffed by several workers, an engineer and a manager. The employees have absolute responsibility for a certain sector of work. All employees of any rank may change 'islands' when they wish to and when they consider it advisable in view of the general aims of the company. The system of organising work into 'islands' is at the root of the Japanese success in all sectors of industry, particularly cars.

In other countries, such as Italy, France and the UK, there is a strong tradition of conflict between management and unions. This stems from the days when unions were set up to combat the worst excesses of management – such as low wages and inhuman working conditions. Because unions were the product of conflicts, confrontational attitudes became the norm. In times of slump, working people have tended to suffer.

Today, relations throughout the industrialised world are going through a period of transformation. This is partly a response to new ideas of human resource management. In Italy, the huge labour confederation, the CGIL, is the most powerful union in Europe. In 1991 it changed its policy, accepting the need for worker participation in management – this was a rejection of the old principle that company policy decisions were the bosses' problem. The unions now accept that everyone should have a say in their future.

In the UK the decline in the power of unions has been reinforced by laws that made pre-strike ballots compulsory and severely limited the ability of unions to mount 'sympathy' action. One union has sought to carve out a niche for itself by being politically moderate and mounting a campaign to sell itself to employers as much as to workers. The Electrical, Electronic, Telecommunications and Plumbing Union (EETPU) sought to militate against the increasing anti-unionism by signing 'no-strike' deals, largely with incoming Japanese companies. The agreements seek to replace the confrontational nature of industrial relations with a framework for consultation and joint decision-making. Other groupings of unions have created larger unions with a commitment to joint consultation. For example, in the public sector in a new public service union Unison (made up of employees in town hall, health, water and electricity unions) will represent about one-third of the remaining 7.7 million trade unionists. Such a union is trying to move away from the old 'them and us' view.

It would be unrealistic to say that managers and trade unionists today share a commonality of interests; there are still many old-fashioned employers exploiting poorly paid labour in poor working conditions. A continuing form of frustration for employees is disagreement about salaries and wages between one occupation and another and the large number of unions in some workplaces. The historical pattern of union growth showed long upward and downward swings. Despite the wider adoption of human resource management, it is possible that factors such as European integration may help the unions to confront the globalisation of production and company power.

PREPARING THE WORKFORCE FOR CHANGE

Faced by conditions of 'constant upheaval', organisations have to recognise and respond to the need for change. This might lead to a change in a range of organisational activities and practices, including:

- changing corporate policies and marketing strategies
- developing new products
- introducing new technologies, systems and procedures
- restructuring the organisation
- combining with other organisations.

All of these changes will have profound effects on the labour force and upon people's working lives. The new ideas will be effective only if they have the acceptance of employees, because changes bring with them uncertainty and anxiety. It is therefore very important to *manage* changes in the culture of an organisation, and this requires clear leadership.

Case Study

New jobs for old

If we look at 'who does what' in Britain today we get a picture of the types of job that are disappearing and new jobs that are growing in importance.

	Employment in 1987	Net change 1987–95
		(thousands)
Agriculture	558	−38
Mining	207	−34
Utilities	291	−22
Metals, minerals	443	−23
Chemicals	345	−17
Engineering	2239	−91
of which:		
Mechanical	737	−25
Electrical	567	−32
Motor vehicles	245	0
Food, drink, tobacco	581	−61
Textiles and clothing	563	−39
Other manufacturing	1102	+5
Construction	1569	+201
Distribution	5268	+414
of which:		
Distribution	3972	+97
Hotel and catering	1295	+317
Transport, communication	1500	+18
Business services	2631	+602
Other services	2420	+615
Manufacturing	5362	−230
All industries	19 807	+1523
Health and education	3001	+265
Public administration	2178	−66

Figure 14.14 *Forecasted employment changes in the UK*

1 Does the table tell us that more jobs will be created than lost in the period 1987–95?

2 What types of job are being created? What type are being lost?

3 What does the table tell us about the changing nature of employment in the UK?

4 Look at five categories of jobs that are in decline and five categories that are increasing. Try to explain why these trends are taking place.

5 How does the national picture relate to your local picture? What jobs are declining in your area? What jobs are expanding? What types of job are being offered in your local employment market? Carry out some research – look in the local press, Job Centre, Employment Office, etc.

ORGANISATIONAL RESPONSE TO CHANGING MARKETS

We have seen that there are some industrial divisions that are growing and some that are in decline. Some new products are being researched, others are in a period of infancy or growth, while still others are mature.

In Chapter 9 we looked at this in terms of life-cycles. The product life-cycle suggests that all products have a limited life. Of course, the rates at which their cycles proceed will vary. For some the life-cycle may last just a single year (e.g. a new fashion item such as 'loon pants' or 'hot pants'). For others the life-cycle is much longer (e.g. hearing aids, hot-water bottles, Ribena). There is, however, growing evidence that the lengths of product cycles are tending to become shorter. So, in order to continue to grow and to continue to make profits, businesses need to innovate on a regular basis. There are several ways of doing this.

Figure 14.15 illustrates three ways of maintaining sales. One way is to introduce a new product as the existing one becomes obsolete, so that there are **overlapping cycles.** This is a common practice with motor vehicles. A second alternative is to **modify** the existing product in order to extend its life-cycle. This is the case with many modern desktop computers – improved models with more memory, a wider range of applications and greater speed continually update old models. A third option is to change the **production technology** itself to make the product

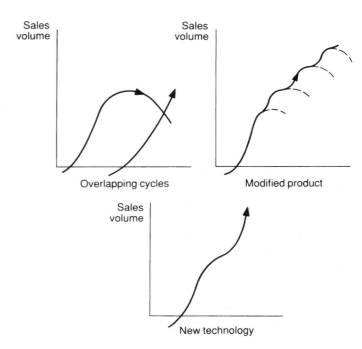

Figure 14.15 *Three ways of extending product life-cycles*

more competitive – for example, by employing better production technology in the textile industry.

In fact most business organisations today employ a mixture of three ways of extending product life-cycles.

Product and process innovation

In modern competitive markets it is essential for businesses to be able to innovate. Freeman, in a book *The Economics of Industrial Innovation* (Penguin), argued that for a large business organisation, 'not to innovate is to die'. Indeed, such organisations are trapped on an 'innovation treadmill'. Inevitably, therefore, employees who work for these organisations need to be prepared for changing practices. They need to adjust to new styles of operation and management.

As industries become more mature the emphasis on change is placed on the **processes of production** as opposed to the products themselves. In their early days, new products can set their markets alight with their flair and product originality. As time passes other businesses will copy, so that if companies want to remain as market leaders they need to re-think their methods (see Figure 14.16).

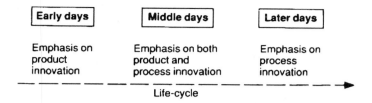

Figure 14.16 *Moving the emphasis of innovation*

Two major trends have become more noticeable in the production process in recent years. The first is increasing specialisation so that the processes can be split into many separate operations. The second is increasing standardisation of these separate operations so that they can be done by semi-skilled and unskilled labour. This is particularly so during the mature phase of a product's life-cycle.

Many of the declining industries are therefore characterised by more old-fashioned working practices, lower-paid workers and resistance to change.

Hirsch produced an interesting picture to show the relative importance of different factors of production during the life-cycles of products. This is presented as Figure 14.17.

It is important to remember that different products have different production methods. Also, although many modern products are made in automated plant this does not necessarily mean that they have to be produced on a large scale. Traditional automation is geared to high-volume standardised production, but newer flexible manufacturing systems are quite different. With flexible manufacturing

different products can be produced on the same line. Flexible manufacturing means that economies can be achieved for both large-scale and small-scale production. A flexible automation system can turn out a small batch or even a single copy of a product as efficiently as a line geared to producing a million identical items.

Task

Make a study of changing industrial processes in a local industry. What changes have taken place in recent years? Have the changes been in the products or the processes, or both? What new products have been developed? What new processes? How have the processes affected the organisation of work? How have employees in these organisations had to adjust? What have been the effects of these changes? What further new changes, if any, need to take place?

Case Study

Changes in the textiles industry

Figure 14.18 shows changes in employment in the UK textiles industry in recent years. During the 1990s there was a steady drip of closures which sapped the lifeblood of what is still Britain's fifth largest industry. The British textiles industry

Life-cycle phase			Factors of production
NEW	GROWTH	MATURITY	
2	3	1	Management
3	2	1	Scientific and engineering know how
1	2	3	Semi-skilled and unskilled labour
3	2	1	External economies
1	2=	2=	Capital

Figure 14.17 *Relative importance of factors of production at different stages of product life-style*

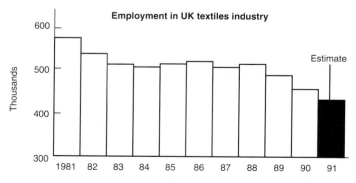

Source: Apparel, Knitting and Textiles Alliance

Figure 14.18 *Employment in UK textiles industry*

has been in decline for so long, people could be forgiven for thinking it no longer exists. In fact, it has an output of more than £13 billion and employs close on half a million workers. It was the country's first major industry.

During the 1980s the textiles industry seemed to be recovering from years of decline. Between 1980 and 1988 productivity rose by more than 40 per cent, and companies invested more than £4 billion in new plant and machinery. Exports rose by more than 50 per cent in this period, and the level of home demand increased with rising incomes and people spending more of their incomes on clothes. However, in 1988 the textiles industry was the first to slump into recession. It was hit by falling demand at home, particularly in household fabrics. The industry was hit again by a weak dollar – US and Far Eastern exports are priced in dollars.

A lot of the new investment of the 1980s has been wasted. Investments in cutting costs have been effective, but investments in increasing capacity have not.

Today the market for UK textiles rests around flexibility. As fashions change faster, and as shops look to sell a wider range of new products, manufacturers have had to deliver their products faster. UK manufacturers find it difficult to compete with Far Eastern suppliers, particularly on price. Their only main advantage is closeness to the market. UK manufacturers therefore have to concentrate on delivering products to the market quickly. Shortening lead times and being flexible require considerable managerial skills and the sort of machinery that can be quickly adapted to new products. It also needs a skilled and flexible labour force.

1 *Outline three major changes in the textiles industry in the 1990s.*
2 *What skills and attitudes are needed to respond to these changes?*
3 *What restraining forces can you identify that might hold back change?*
4 *How do you think change can be brought about in British textiles to give the industry a competitive edge?*

CONSTRAINTS ON THE EMPLOYMENT MARKET

Employers are faced with a variety of external contraints in the employment market. For example, in some situations it is easy to recruit labour because there is an abundant supply with appropriate skills. At other times it is difficult to recruit labour with appropriate skills.

Task

Make a list of situations in which the recruitment of labour with the required skills is easy. Make a list of other situations in which it might be difficult to recruit labour with appropriate skills.

Conditions in the employment market are constantly changing. Sometimes these changes take us by surprise. For example, in the first quarter of 1993 the economy moved out of a recession more rapidly than people had expected. Commentators looked for the reasons employers were more willing to take on extra labour so quickly. One of the popular explanations was that employment legislation made it easier to lay workers off in a period of recession. It follows that when orders start to pick up again employers will be prepared to take on extra staff knowing that they can be dispensed with if bad times set in again. Government employment legislation is therefore an important external influence on the employment market.

Other factors include health and safety requirements and equal opportunities policies – both arising from Government legislation. Giving due care and attention to both health and safety and equal opportunities costs money in the short term. However, in the longer period it leads to a healthier workforce, a more highly motivated labour force, and a workforce that has fewer accidents. It also makes the best use of scarce labour resources. Equal opportunities and health and safety policies cost money to introduce and administer. However, they add to productivity, and therefore reduce long-term costs.

Case Study

Health and safety in a college

The Health and Safety at Work Act covers all places of work including schools and colleges. It places a general duty on an employer to ensure, as far as is reasonably practicable, the health, safety and welfare of his or her employees. It goes further than this as it stipulates that persons, other than those at work, but who may be at risk due to activities of persons at work should also be protected. In this way, students are protected at college.

A schoo or college will make certain demands of its students in order to provide a safe and healthy environment for all. What is required of students?

- On college premises, students must take reasonable care for their own health and safety and that of other persons who may be affected by what they do (or do not do).

- Students should co-operate with college staff in fulfilling the requirements of the Health and Safety Act.

- Students must not intentionally interfere with, or misuse anything that has been provided in the interests of health, safety or welfare.

- Students should be advised of particular safety requirements.

- Students must report any accident, no matter how trivial, to a member of college staff.

- Students who do not comply with the requirements should be disciplined.

1 How can Health and Safety requirements be seen to raise costs for an employing organisation such as a college?

2 How can keeping to Health and Safety requirements reduce the costs of an employing organisation such as a college.

Task

Find out what your college regulations are for Health and Safety in each of the following categories:

- if you work or study in a workshop or laboratory
- if you come to college by car or on a motorcycle
- around the college
- in case of an emergency evacuation.

Produce a booklet for students outlining in clear language what these key requirements are.

Case Study

An Equal Opportunities Policy Statement

Every school and college should have an Equal Opportunities Policy Statement. Here is an example:

'Broxtowe College is committed to the development of positive policies which will promote equal opportunities in student access and in staff employment regardless of race, colour, nationality, ethnic or national origin, creed, age, disability, sex, marital status or sexual orientation.'

In particular this applies to:
- the implementation of an Equal Opportunities Policy and Code of Practice
- student recruitment, selections and admissions practices and polices
- programme and curriculum development
- course and learning opportunity, evaluation and review process
- guidance, counselling and student support
- marketing and publicity
- staff development and training
- employment practices and conditions of service.

Positive action

The College is committed to operating an effective system of data collection, monitoring, evaluation and review to aid in planning processes.

We recognise that certain groups have been disadvantaged in the past and we have undertaken

- to improve access for these groups
- to review every aspect of College life and to make whatever changes are necessary
- to consult and take advice from the College community

1 Why might setting up and running an equal opportunities policy increase the costs of running Broxtowe College?

2 Why might setting up and running an equal opportunities policy decrease the costs of running Broxtowe College?

3 Why is running an equal opportunities policy an ethical imperative?

4 How can: students, lecturers, the wider community, the national economy each benefit from such a policy?

5 Find out about equal opportunities policies and how they affect employment and recruitment in your college or school. Are there any differences between formal written policy statements and the actual operation of that policy? Explain.

Element assignment

Human resource issues
This assignment can help you provide evidence for assessment, or claim the following Core Skills outcomes:

Communication
Receive and respond to a variety of information
Communicate in writing

Personal Skills
Use information sources

Human resource management and planning are ongoing activities. A business needs to review constantly the internal and external factors influencing its operations. It needs to ask:

- Should we be recruiting or laying off employees in the current economic climate?
- What scope is there for wage increases?
- How much would we be spending on training?
- To what extent is the demand for our product going to influence our demand for labour?
- How would the adoption of the European Community Social Chapter affect working practices in our business?

Task

Choose a particular human resource issue to investigate. The issue will involve business decisions and actions that relate to the workforce. You may want, for example, to compare and contrast the decisions and actions of two businesses operating in different sectors. Carry out some detailed research into the issue. For example:

1 How are wages and conditions negotiated in the two businesses?

2 What provisions are made for training in the two businesses?

3 Has the ratio of capital to labour costs changed (perhaps as a result of automation)?

You will need to bear in mind that some of the human resource issues that you investigate may be viewed from different perspectives. For example, in a wage dispute the representatives of employees and managers may have different views about what can be afforded. If you are researching a particular issue using newspapers and magazines, look for possible bias in the articles. You will need to make it clear why some of the information that you have used has been collected.

chapter **15** EVALUATION OF BUSINESS AND WORKFORCE PERFORMANCE

n this chapter you are provided with an opportunity to focus on the evaluation of business performance as it relates to workforce performance.

The writer Mike O'Neill has used a canoeing analogy to look at the employment market. He talks about being faced by 'permanent white water' – i.e. a continual state of testing and unpredictable conditions in which the canoeist needs to be constantly on the alert and prepared to cope with changes. Individuals and organisations today need to be prepared for such an environment of change. A modern workplace may be characterised by the need for flexibility and multi-skilling, whereby an employee is prepared to do a variety of tasks.

We therefore start this chapter by looking at managing personal change in preparation for the labour market. We go on to look at organisational change and factors creating change in the organisational environment. Finally we examine the important areas of leadership and direction, culture of an organisation.

Changes take place all the time. Some are almost unnoticeable because they occur over a long period of time, and only when we look back is it clear that they have taken place. For example, many of the changes involved in growing up happen so slowly that they go unnoticed at the time. Other changes are dramatic and obvious – for example engagements or bereavements.

Of course, both slow and quick changes are important, and one should be aware that change is ever present. Any organisation that you work for will experience changes. People who work for the organisation will need to alter the ways in which they operate, the skills they use, and knowledge will need to be updated and attitudes adjusted. As a member of an organisation you will need to be flexible.

Task

First think of changes that happened as you grew up. Which of these were dramatic and obvious and which were almost unnoticeable?

Then think of changes that have taken place in an organisation with which you are familiar. Answer the same question about these changes.

Lastly, identify if you can which of the changes were of greatest importance in each case.

• MANAGING PERSONAL CHANGE •

Some of the changes we experience in our lives are **inevitable**, such as growing older. Others can be **controlled**. For example, you can decide to go on a training course, to learn to drive a car, or to alter your appearance. Attitudes to change vary from one individual to the next. This is because individuals have certain driving forces within them, which we refer to as 'wants', 'needs', 'urges', and 'fears'. One person may feel the need to 'play it safe' all the time, while another may actively seek risky situations.

When we looked at Maslow's hierarchy of needs in Chapter 13, we saw that the needs of individuals are not always fixed. At certain times particular needs are all-important, but once these have been satisfied they may be replaced by new needs.

It is appropriate to start our discussion by looking at ways of **managing change**, particularly so that you can take responsibility for changing the way you operate in an organisation.

Force field analysis

Force field analysis is commonly used to look at problems that have restraining forces as well as driving forces (see Figure 15.1). Analysing a problem in this way helps you to arrive at a strategy for bringing about changes that deal with the problem.

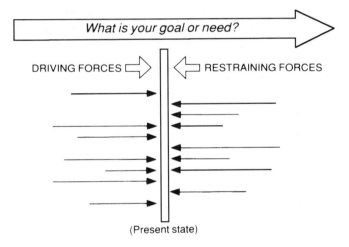

Figure 15.1 *Force field analysis*

Task

First think of a problem or difficulty that you are faced with at the moment. Copy Figure 15.1, and write a short title for the problem in the top (large) arrow.

On the right side list all the forces (reasons) that are preventing the change from taking place – these are the restraining forces. On the left side list all the driving forces that are encouraging change (e.g. Maslow's motivational drives).

After you have filled in your force field chart and thought about it, set out an action plan that will help you to:

a increase the driving forces
b reduce the restraining forces.

In planning for personal change you will need to:

> KNOW WHERE YOU ARE NOW

> KNOW WHERE YOU WANT TO BE

> HAVE SOME MEANS OF KNOWING IF YOU HAVE ARRIVED

In other words you will need to set out some clear **objectives**. At the same time you will need to decide on ways of measuring whether these objectives are being met.

Setting out objectives

When you write down your objectives, make sure that they are:

- worthwhile and consistent with your own values
- clear (not vague)
- realistic and attainable
- measurable
- time bound (e.g. to be achieved by the end of the year).

Here is an example of a possible format:

Objectives:	To improve my performance when being interviewed
	To appear more confident when being interviewed
	To prepare answers to the questions I may be asked
Measurement:	I can check on improvements in my performance by studying videos of my mock job interviews
	I can ask advice from friends and tutors on how well I did
	I will be able to judge how confident I feel as time passes
	Ultimately I can see whether I am

Time period: successful in being offered jobs
I will need to improve my skills by the
end of May for interviews in June

Another way of setting out a framework for personal
change is to use three categories:

Performance
Conditions
Standards

Performance is the actual objective, *conditions* are the
environmental context your objectives need to be set
against, and the *standards* are the ways in which you will
measure success. Under the standards heading you should
include the time scale and ways of measuring
competencies. This is made clear by the example in
Figure 15.2.

PERFORMANCE	CONDITIONS	STANDARDS
Study effectively for GNVQ Level 3 Business	Within the present course environment	Satisfy myself that I have learned. and obtained the necessary competencies

Figure 15.2 *A framework for personal change*

Set out three of your major objectives
for the coming year in a framework of
performance, conditions and
standards.

Self-assessment

When managing changes it is essential to know how
successful we have been. We can more effectively develop
these skills by looking at ourselves more critically.

The profile form in Figure 15.3 gives the opportunity for
self-assessment in terms of the personal and social skills
required to operate as a member of a group. The form can
be adapted to self-assessment in other areas. The tick

boxes are intended to be filled in according to the
following pointers:

1 = I am experienced at this.
2 = I have some experience of this.
3 = I have no experience of this.

and

1 = I was successful at this.
2 = I was reasonably successful at this.
3 = I was rarely successful at this.

Complete the questionnaire in Figure
15.3. Try to base your answers on
specific experiences at school,
college, in the family, at work or in
voluntary organisations .

When you have finished the
questionnaire you may want to
consider which aspects you would like to improve on. You
could then set out some objectives (with your tutor) to
develop realistic plans to improve on these areas as part
of your course.

· ORGANISATIONAL CHANGE ·

Like individuals, organisations need to monitor
continually where they have come from, where they are
and where they are going. The **planning process** lies at the
heart of preparation for change.

The planning process
translates
PURPOSES
into
POLICIES
into
PLANS
to ensure
IMPLEMENTATION, FEEDBACK and REVIEW

As a member of any group have you experience of:	Experience			Success		
	1	2	3	1	2	3
*Contributing ideas						
*Listening to other people's ideas and making use of them						
*Compromising when your opinion was not shared by others						
*Taking notes of what went on in the group						
*Carrying out an agreed task in co-operation with others						
*Carrying out part of a task assigned to you as an individual						
*Showing flexibility						
*Asking for things to be explained even though you could have looked silly						
*Getting the task finished						
*Choosing a person to do a particular task						
*Keeping a check on how far the group had got in carrying out a task						
*Chairing a meeting						
*Giving instructions to others						
*Trying to influence others in a group						
*Contributing ideas to a group discussion						
*Making a formal presentation to a group						
*Producing visual material as part of a presentation						
*Helping to organise a major event						
*Deciding on the best solution and planning a way forward						
*Encouraging people to carry on even when they were uninterested						
*Getting the group to finish on time						
*Sharing any praise						

Figure 15.3 *A self-assessment questionnaire*

Implementation is making sure that policies are carried out, *feedback* means that actions, successes and failures are recorded, and *review* entails looking at successes and failures with a view to planning future steps.

. RESPONDING TO CHANGE: . AN EXAMPLE

A service station provides a good example of a working environment. There is always plenty of action to be seen at a successful station, with customers continually coming in for the products and services they want.

There is plenty of action behind the scenes too. The people working at the service station must:

- maintain stocks in good condition (and order more when necessary)
- keep all the equipment in first-class condition
- monitor and control the finances
- ensure that publicity is up to date and effective
- see that the whole site is kept clean and attractive
- adhere strictly to safety and security procedures.

This list shows that there is a lot of work to be carried out to keep the service station simply ticking over. Each day certain stocks need to be replenished, and this involves

keeping track of what is going out and making sure that it is re-ordered in good time. Each day a lot of money comes in for petrol, oil, foodstuffs, the car wash, maps, and many other facilities and services. If an accurate record is not kept straight away, then the whole financial record-keeping system will become a mess.

Litter must be cleared from the site, water replenished in cans and buckets, spillages dealt with straight away, lights repaired and toilets cleaned. Activity within the station is therefore continuous, and change will continually be taking place (remember that many service stations are open 24 hours each day).

In addition to these daily fluctuations there are seasonal changes – more people take to the roads during holiday times, and fewer during bad weather. There are changes in response to the economy – for example, in a period of recession there are fewer vehicles on the roads, and before the Budget there may be a rush in demand for petrol if motorists think taxes will rise. Then there are legal changes affecting the way service stations operate – for example, in the late 1980s it became compulsory for all service stations to have toilet facilities, and health and safety laws have been considerably tightened up. Changes in social attitudes constantly affect people's expectations about the way in which service stations

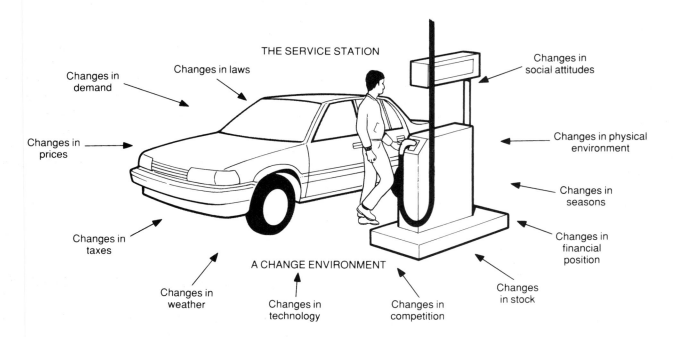

Figure 15.4 *A change environment*

operate – for example, fewer people today expect attendant service, and most people have switched to lead-free petrol.

The pace of activity in a service station demands that many of the operations involve information technology. Staff need to be constantly updated in IT operations and in many other areas of running a dynamic business.

Working for such an organisation therefore involves an ability to respond to change. One day employees at a service station may have to respond to lengthy queues of motorists rushing to buy fuel before an expected price rise. The next day they may be working flat out to keep the station running smoothly in a snowstorm – keeping entrances clear, water mopped up from floors, dealing with stranded motorists and so on.

· THE CHANGING INDUSTRIAL STRUCTURE OF THE UK ·

	1870	1913	Late 1920s
Britain	31.8	14.0	9.4
USA	23.3	35.8	42.2
Germany	13.2	15.7	11.6
France	10.3	6.4	6.6
Japan	0	1.2	2.5

Figure 15.5 *Percentage share of world industrial output*

In the nineteenth century the United Kingdom was known as the 'workshop of the world'. This is not surprising when one looks at the statistics. As a result of early industrialisation, Britain led the world in manufacturing. However, during the last quarter of the nineteenth century several other Western nations not only came to be core industrial producers, they even overtook Britain. This process continued into the twentieth century with the rapid development of the United States, Germany and then Japan, and more recently many other countries. This change of world leadership in industrial production in the early part of the twentieth century is clear from Figure 15.5.

Britain must now be considered an industrial dwarf compared with several other countries. Today manufacturing is concentrated largely among the big three (the USA, Germany and Japan), which account for about a half of all world manufacturing output. In the United Kingdom, many of the early pace-setting industries – coal, iron and steel, engineering and shipbuilding – are in an advanced stage of decline. Manufactured goods traditionally exported by Britain have declined as a proportion of all production in the country for a long time, and by 1984 Britain was importing more manufactured goods than she was exporting.

When manufacturing industry goes into relative decline and the service industries become more important, this process if often called **de-industrialisation**.

For statistical purposes industries are normally grouped together under a major heading or division in what is called the Standard Industrial Classification (SIC). The divisions were shown in Chapter 1 (see the task on page 6).

(see the task on page 6)

Task

Endeavour to obtain from your local Employment Office a breakdown of the numbers of people in your area who work in each of the divisions of the Standard Industrial Classification.

Alternatively, carry out some research of your own. You could, for example, work in groups to do street interviewing to find out the sorts of jobs people do. You would need to plan carefully how and when you would do this research. You would need to decide on which day of the week you would get a representative sample of people in your area on the high street. How large would your sample need to be to give a reflection of the typical population of your area? What problems would you be likely to encounter in setting up and carrying out the research?

· CHANGING ATTITUDES TO LEISURE ·

Today many people have more leisure time than used to be the case. Employees' representatives have managed to secure reductions in the working week, and in the working day. Standards of living are also rising, so that people can afford to spend more time on leisure, and it is more socially acceptable to have free time. A range of new leisure pursuits has developed.

Employers are beginning to realise more the importance of leisure to a happy and fulfilled workforce. Going back to Maslow (Chapter 13), we can see that individuals can satisfy their needs through their leisure activities as well as their working activities. If it becomes possible to combine the two in a fulfilling lifestyle, then all well and good.

Task

How you spend your spare time can provide an insight into what is important to you. Try to identify what it is about the activities you do that attracts you to them. Consider keeping a record of your leisure activities, adding information about benefits (such as diplomas, music grades etc.).

Then think about objectives you can set yourself to improve your leisure time. How can you go about achieving these aims? You should refer back to the notes earlier in this chapter on managing change.

What information do you need to find out more about leisure opportunities? What skills and attitudes do you need to improve your experience and enjoyment of leisure?

Case Study

Work and leisure

Study the data in Figures 15.6 and 15.7, which show some information about work and leisure in the United Kingdom. In Figure 15.7, 'essential activities' covers essential domestic work and personal care, including shopping, child care, washing and getting up and going to bed.

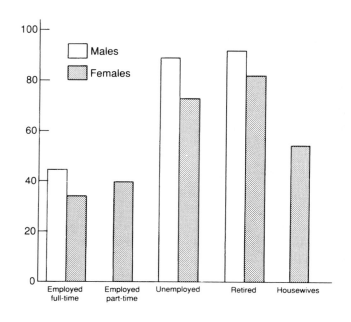

Figure 15.6 *Leisure time in a typical week (hours)*

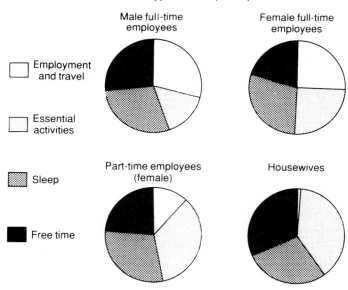

Figure 15.7 *Time use in a typical week (hours)*

1 *Which groups seem to have the most leisure?*
2 *How does your own leisure pattern fit in with those shown?*
3 *Do you think that the groups will have different attitudes to leisure?*

4 *What interesting features do the pie-charts show about how different groups divide their leisure time?*

5 *How do you think the use of leisure affects people's attitudes to their work?*

6 *How can organisations cater for the leisure needs of their members and employees? Should they?*

BUSINESS RESPONSE TO A CHANGING LABOUR MARKET

Throughout this book one of the main themes has been the changing nature of the employment market. But the employment market is just one aspect of a competitive environment in which businesses operate. If the human resource is to be used effectively, it needs to be used productivity and competitively. Clearly this involves providing work that is rewarding and motivating, and which results in high productivity levels and maximises long-term profitabilty.

We need to identify examples of 'best practice' in other countries and transfer them to our own industries. Faced with the challenge of Japanese productivity levels, for example, many Western companies are trying to learn from and use successful Japanese practices.

Just-in-time manufacturing

Just-in-time production is a very simple idea:

1 Finished goods are produced just in time for them to be sold, rather than weeks or months ahead.

2 The parts that go into a finished product arrive just in time to be put together to make the final product, rather than being stored (at some cost) in a warehouse.

The idea is to run a company with the smallest possible levels of stock and work-in-progress. Clearly this needs careful planning:

- All sources of uncertainty must be removed from the manufacturing process. There must be absolute reliability of production targets, supplies, and levels of output achieved.
- The time to set up machines must be reduced to a minimum so that components and finished products can be produced in small batches as and when required.
- Bottlenecks must be eliminated.

Using a JIT system requires a complete reorganisation of the traditional factory. Factories have traditionally been organised into 'shops', each working at a particular stage in producing a final product. With a JIT system the factory is reorganised so that people are grouped together around the products they produce. They may need to have access to a family of machines (e.g. a lathe, a milling machine, a drill and a grinder, as in Figure 15.8).

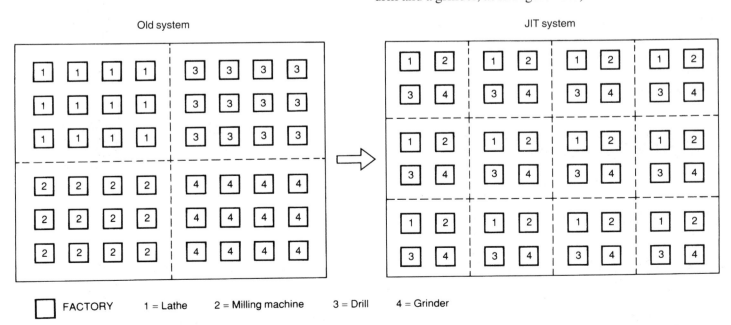

FACTORY   1 = Lathe   2 = Milling machine   3 = Drill   4 = Grinder

Figure 15.8 *Adopting the JIT system*

A recent survey has shown that two-thirds of Western manufacturing companies are trying to use JIT. However, the ability to make JIT successful may depend on the organisation and environment in which the idea is applied.

Task

In Japan, just-in-time production is widely used by business organisations. However, in that country the business environment has the following characteristics:

- There is lifetime employment in many large corporations, so that labour mobility between companies is limited.
- Unions are based around companies and not on trades or occupations.
- JIT relationships between firms and their suppliers have built up over a long period.

1 How many of the above apply in British companies?
2 Which would be easy for British companies to adopt and which would be more difficult?
3 What factors are likely to influence the success of British companies in adopting JIT practices?
4 List six main recommendations that you would make to a company developing JIT practices in this country.

Total quality control

Traditionally, quality has been checked by inspecting finished products after they have left the production line. The identification of faulty products then leads to the activity of tracing the weak area of the production process. However, this leads to wasted products and time taken in tracing the fault.

Total quality control involves building in quality inspections at each stage of the production process. The emphasis is on *preventing* errors from happening. The Japanese practice has therefore been to give operators the authority and resources to control their own quality of output. For example, operators are able to stop a production line if and when they detect a problem.

Task

How could total quality control be built into the running and organisation of a GNVQ Business course?

Flexibility and multi-skilling

A past feature of the British industrial scene was demarcation disputes. These were arguments over 'who should do what'. The trade union movement insisted that only members of a relevant union could be asked to do particular tasks (e.g. mend a broken machine). This led to a great waste of time and other resources.

Multi-skilling involves training employees to do a range of tasks in the workplace. A machine operative can be trained in the art of performing routine maintenance work and in doing straightforward repairs. This can be a great motivator because it gives a job variety, as well as opportunities for higher pay. It means that a plant can be continuously productive, more competitive, and therefore possibly better able to provide good wages and conditions (because the demand for labour is derived from the demand for the final product).

Task

In the new Japanese Toyota and Nissan car plants in the UK, the managements have agreed single-union deals. Only one union operates in each plant, and operators are flexible and able to do a number of different tasks. When Nissan started its car plant in Sunderland there were only three job classifications, whereas in the past some British car plants have had as many as 500 different job classifications!

1 Why might managers prefer to have multi-skilled workers in a narrow range of job classifications?
2 Why might employees prefer such a scheme?
3 Why might some employees and trade unions oppose such a scheme?
4 What are the benefits and drawbacks to the economy of allowing these schemes to operate?

· ABSENTEEISM ·

In a typical working year (i.e. 250 days) an average employee may be away from work for 20 per cent of the time. There will be authorised times (e.g. attending a conference) and there may be non-authorised times (skipping work to have an extra holiday).

Case Study

Absenteeism

A survey carried out by the Industrial Society, the results of which were reported in March 1993, showed that workers in Japanese-owned firms took fewer days off through 'sickness' than workers in companies with a British ownership.

The working days lost per year were 2.35 and 3.9 per cent respectively.

The survey also showed that Japanese managers are more likely to ask job applicants about their attendance records. Furthermore, 55 per cent of Japanese managers will interview workers after every day off sick, compared with only 38 per cent in other firms. Japanese companies have smaller working groups, so absence is more likely to be noticed. They are also more likely to communicate absence rates to employees on noticeboards.

Workers take 200 million days off with sickness every year at a cost of £9 billion – this is far more than through industrial stoppages. The highest absence rate is in the public sector (4.5 per cent), with the health service suffering the most (5.9 per cent). Companies that provide healthy food in their canteens, and those which ban smoking, have absence rates below 3 per cent.

Employers said 'stress' was the second-highest reason for absenteeism after 'cold or flu'. 'Low morale', 'childcare problems' and 'Monday morning blues' were also cited.

1 *Name three factors that may encourage absenteeism from work.*
2 *Name three factors that might discourage absenteeism.*
3 *Outline a series of steps that might encourage higher attendance in a particular type of workplace. Choose a local organisation with which you are familiar (e.g. a supermarket).*

· STAFF TURNOVER ·

Firms need to attract and retain a good and reliable labour force. It is wasteful to recruit and train someone only for that person to leave the organisation to work for someone else. It is therefore important to make working for the organisation an attractive proposition, by providing rewarding work with good career prospects.

Inevitably, though, employees do leave, and this is called **staff turnover**. The turnover of labour can be calculated by using the following formula:

$$\text{Turnover of labour (\%)} = \frac{\text{Number of leavers}}{\text{Number of employees}} \times 100$$

Task

Make a study of one business organisation with particular reference to its workforce related performance. You will need to use a range of information sources, which can include the organisation's policy statements of training, pay and conditions, benefits and equal opportunities. You may be able to glean information from newspapers and journals, and employer and labour organisations.

1 How is work performance measured in the organisation?
2 How does the organisation week to motivate its employees?
3 How has the organisation responded to changing conditions in labour and product markets?

4 What employment practices exist in the company (e.g. multi-skilling, opportunities for training, working in teams, rewards, etc.)?

5 What measures can be used to quantity the effectiveness of such policies (e.g. labour turnover, absence rates, productivity per employee)?

THE EC'S SOCIAL CHARTER AND CONDITIONS IN THE WORKPLACE

The Social Charter has been mentioned in Chapter 2. In negotiations on the Maastricht Treaty the UK Conservative government managed to side-step the **Social Charter** on the ground that it would restrict the free operation of the labour market. However, it is vitally important that you appreciate the nature of the charter and how it influences working conditions and practices in the European Community.

The Social Charter sets out the following rights:

i to work and to fair remuneration for work carried out;

ii to the improvement of living and working conditions;

iii to social protection, particularly for those excluded from the labour market (including migrant workers);

iv to eduction and training throughout life;

v to freedom of association and negotiation (the right to trade union membership and to participate in free collective bargaining);

vi to freedom of movement in the Community, equal treatment between Community workers, and recognition of professional qualifications;

vii to information, consultation and participation of workers in their enterprises;

viii to health, particularly in the field of prevention and health care;

ix to protection of health and safety at work;

x to protection of children and young people (notably a minimum working age and protection against physical and moral dangers), the elderly (including pension rights and minimum incomes) and the disabled;

xi to consumer protection, including the right to information and to protection from environmental risks.

Of course, most of these principles are enshrined in existing UK law. However, the UK government did not want to be bound by regulations on such things as minimum wages. The fear was that having workplace legislation dictated by directives from Brussels would reduce the ability of the UK to create competitive labour market conditions that would enable us to sell our products in competitive world markets.

THE CULTURE OF AN ORGANISATION

Organisations are as individual as nations and societies. They have vastly different **cultures**, reflected by their own values, ideals and beliefs. The culture influences the way an organisation operates, so that it is necessary to understand the culture before deciding how people might contribute to the organisation's success or failure.

Organisational cultures, therefore, determine the way in which things get done. This might involve:

- the ways in which people interact
- the way they dress for work
- the image of the organisation
- the way in which employees are treated
- the general environment of the organisation
- organisational rules
- goals and objectives
- the use of technology.

Case Study

Comparing two organisations

In Organisation A, ideas are considered from individual employees. The staff are responsible, motivated and capable of governing themselves, and decisions arise through consultation. Members of the organisation see themselves as a family who take care of each other.

In Organisation B, ideas are considered from older and high-status individuals. There is loyalty and discipline, and relationships are well defined, so everyone has a niche. The organisation takes care of its members.

In Organisation A there is a general air of informality, whereas in B formality permeates everything. Neither of these organisations is wrong in its approach to employees – they are just different.

1 Make lists of the advantages and disadvantages of working for each of the two organisations.
2 Which of the organisations would you prefer to work for, and why?
3 Why do organisations differ so widely?

Types of organisational culture

Cultures are founded and built over years by the dominant groups in an organisation. We shall consider the four main types of culture.

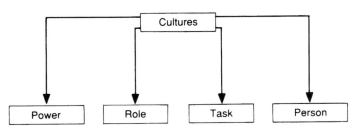

Figure 15.9 *Types of culture*

The power culture

Centralisation of **power** is the key feature of this type of culture. It is frequently found in small entrepreneurial organisations where control rests with a single individual or a small group of individuals.

Its structure is best pictured as a web (see Figure 15.10). There is a central power source and rays of influence spread out from that central figure. In this type of organisation the emphasis is on individuals rather than group decision-making, enabling it to move quickly to make decisions and react well to threat or danger.

However, the danger of this sort of culture is that, because it is autocratic, there can be a feeling of suppression and lack of challenge in the workforce. Size is also a problem

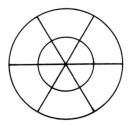

Figure 15.10 *A simple way to visualise the power culture*

for power cultures, and the web can break if it tries to support too many activities. Power cultures tend to suffer from low morale and high staff turnover in the middle management layers.

Apricot Computers

One of the organisations to receive the attentions of Sir John Harvey-Jones's expertise in his television series 'Troubleshooter' was Apricot Computers, which was run by Roger Foster, its flamboyant founder. In his investigation Sir John found that Roger Foster wanted to get involved in almost every aspect of the business – often with quite trivial decisions – a technique which was appropriate when the company was small but no longer appropriate as the company grew.

1 Speculate on how important a power culture was for Apricot Computers in its earlier years.
2 Why does a power culture tend to become less important as an organisation grows?
3 Outline the advantages and disadvantages of working within a power culture.

The role culture

The **role culture** is typical of bureaucracies. An organisation is arranged according to a set of functions which are determined by formal rules and procedures concerning the way in which the work is to be conducted. The culture works by logic and rationality, and the simple diagram depicting this type of culture bears a resemblance to the temple of Apollo, the Greek god of reason.

In a role culture, power is hierarchical and derived from the employee's position in the organisation. Its strength lies in its pillars or functions – such as the finance department or the purchasing department. The interaction

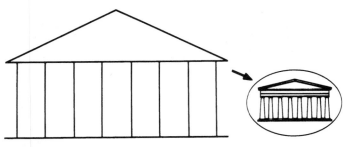

Figure 15.11 *The role culture*

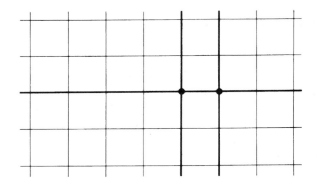

Figure 15.12 *The task culture*

of these pillars is determined by job descriptions and defined communication procedures. Indeed, in this culture the job description is often more important than the person who fills it, and performance over and above the role is not required. 'Position' is the main source of power, and 'rules and procedures' are the main source of influence.

Role cultures tend to offer security and predictability, a good example being the civil service. Their efficiency depends on the allocation of work rather than individual personalities. They can encourage a more-than-my-job's-worth approach and be slow to respond to change.

position or personal power. The matrix relies on the unifying power of the group to complete a specific task. Teams are formed for specific purposes and then abandoned, allowing the system to be flexible to short-term needs.

In a task culture workers have considerable freedom, and the opportunity to be flexible makes them rewarding environments to work in. However, lack of formal authority and a considerable number of strands can make management and control of the task culture difficult.

Task

Explain how an employee benefits from working in a role culture.

The task culture

A **task culture** is job- or project-orientated and places emphasis on completing a specific task. It is a team culture. The task determines the way in which the work is organised, rather than either the individuals or the formal rules of operation.

A task culture is best represented as a net, with some strands thicker and stronger than others. Much of the power and influence lies at the interstices of the net at the knots.

The **matrix** is a form of task culture. It brings together people and resources and is based on expertise rather than

---

Case Study

Introducing the matrix into colleges

Over recent years many colleges of further education and colleges of technology have introduced the task culture through some form of matrix. As a result many heads of departments who formerly engaged in traditional role cultures have become assistant principals with college-wide functions. At the same time new levels of management have been created with cross-college responsibilities for areas such as information technology, school liaison, resources, client support and research and development.

1 Explain the advantages of working in an organisation which operates some form of task-orientated matrix. Relate your answer to the college situation.
2 For a large organisation operating a matrix, such as a college, explain how this could make the organisation more difficult to manage.

The person culture

In a **person culture**, individuals are central. The organisation only exists to serve the interests of those within it. Not surprisingly, person cultures are more likely to be found in communities such as kibbutzim rather than in profit-motivated enterprises. Other examples may be co-operatives, barristers' chambers and architects' partnerships, where there is a cluster of individuals or a galaxy of stars all operating at the same level.

In a person culture, hierarchies are impossible except by mutual consent. An individual may leave the group but the organisation does not have the power to evict the individual. In this sort of culture the individual has almost complete freedom to adopt any direction and to do as he or she pleases. Given the opportunity many people would have a preference for this sort of culture.

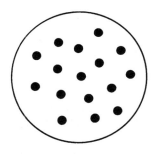

Figure 15.13 *The person culture*

Cultural changes

Most organisations start with power cultures. Then, as they mature and become less dependent upon the founder, they tend to become role cultures. When the role culture needs greater flexibility, there might be a further change towards a task culture to fit the requirements and needs of each part of the organisation.

Culture and commitment

There is a strong relationship between culture and the level of **commitment**, job satisfaction and stress felt by individuals at work. Many employees prefer to know where they stand by working within a rigid framework, rather than in an organisation that gives them too much responsibility for decisions (see Figure 15.14).

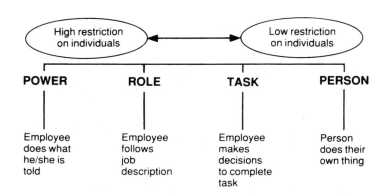

Figure 15.14 *Effect of culture on employees*

Task

Find out what sort of culture prevails in the organisation you work in or attend. Try to discover why the organisation has this sort of culture and comment on how effective it is in terms of commitment and job satisfaction.

· LEADERSHIP ·

Individual workers have their own goals and needs. The closer the work of the organisation meets the needs of the employees, the greater their satisfaction will be. Managers are people who decide what should be done and then get others to do it. They must satisfy the needs of each employee while also meeting the goals of the business. Being able to do so involves **leadership**.

The activities of managers cover many areas, but perhaps a manager's most important function as a leader is to encourage employees to produce their best work in order to improve the performance of the organisation. Leadership therefore involves more than just policy-making, planning, organising, control and coordination – it also involves achieving results by working with other people using **human relations skills**.

Explain why a good manager must also be a leader. List five powerful and influential figures alive today whom you would describe as leaders. What special qualities do these people have?

Margaret Thatcher

Categories of leadership

A leader, as we have seen, is someone who exercises influence over other people in order to achieve organisational goals. Being able to exercise leadership depends entirely on the *opportunity* to be able to do so. Many people have 'leadership qualities' but never have the opportunity to use them, while others become leaders by virtue of inheritance or an accident of birth.

A **charismatic leader** is someone with exceptional personal qualities who influences others by sheer strength of personality. Examples from history include Napoleon, Churchill and Hitler.

Case Study

Margaret Thatcher's leadership

Whatever one's political beliefs, there is no doubt that one has to describe Margaret Thatcher as a charismatic leader. During her years in office as Prime Minister she articulated her vision and gave strong expression to her beliefs in such a way that others in her party accepted her ideas and pursued the common objective of 'Thatcherism'.

Margaret Thatcher has also been described as a **transformational leader** – one who seeks and brings about radical change. Such leaders are capable of being ruthless in pursuit of what they believe to be right and can be willing to take huge risks. Margaret Thatcher's strong sense of direction ('This lady's not for turning') and her

ruthless determination earned her the label Iron Lady. Huge risks – such as those taken in the Falklands war – as well as her personal charisma generated strong feelings amongst colleagues and the electorate.

Some of the Thatcher qualities were her high energy level (long hours and little sleep), her mental power (ability to absorb, digest, retain and recall information, to keep in touch with details and to focus on major issues), her courage (the Brighton bombing) and the conviction that she was right. This conviction has, however, been described as her Achilles' heel. If you are completely convinced of the correctness of your own views this often stirs up challenges.

Another of her weaknesses, it has been said, was her inability to build a cohesive and stable team. Theorists tend to believe that transformational leaders should transform and then move on to look for fresh challenges – and that Margaret Thatcher's mistake was to stay too long. It is often argued that 'nothing is so dangerous as yesterday's success'.

1 *How important is it for a head of government to be a charismatic leader?*
2 *Why should transformational leaders move on?*
3 *Make up your own lists of other charismatic and/or transformational leaders. Give a short explanation of why you believe them to be so.*

A **traditional leader** is someone whose leadership is determined by their birth and inheritance. Members of the royal family adopt a role of traditional leadership.

Situational leaders provide leadership of a temporary kind by being in the right place at the right time. We hear of the courage and valour of people who make crucial decisions in times of disaster or natural crises.

At work, leadership is often exercised by an **appointed leader** whose influence arises from ambitions and promotion. The person's power stems from his or her position within a hierarchy.

Another type of leadership at work is functional. This leadership is determined by the particular skill or expertise of an employee – for example, a building surveyor, an accountant or a solicitor. The person's behaviour will adapt to the needs of each situation he or she advises on.

Theories of leadership

Most people have some leadership qualities, but such qualities vary considerably from person to person. **Personality** is an important influence, as is position at work and the opportunities arising to demonstrate leadership. To be an effective leader you have to have a **positive self-image** and the ability to face many obstacles.

Task

Assess your own leadership qualities by answering the following questions:

a Do you tend to lead or to follow others?

b How frequently do people look to you for guidance?

c Are you an 'ideas' person?

d Do you often put ideas into action?

e Do you try to build upon your strengths?

f Are you aware of your weaknesses?

g Do you have objectives?

h Do you learn from your mistakes?

j Are you a confident person?

k Do you ever speak to large groups of people?

l Are you a good communicator?

m Are you respected by others for what you do?

n Are you a dependable person?

o Could you deal with people effectively?

p Could you delegate?

q Are you a good organiser?

r Can you use your initiative?

Leadership must be seen against a background of one or other of the organisational cultures, and this will have important implications for the level of power exercised by the leader as well as the style of leadership. There are three main categories into which theories of leadership can be placed (see Figure 15.15).

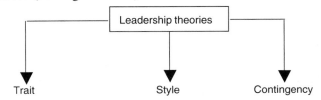

Figure 15.15 *Categories of leadership*

Trait theories

Trait theories assume that to get others to perform well requires certain personal characteristics in the leader. Some examples are physical stature, social background, intelligence and energy. One American study identified the following 15 attributes for leadership:

- judgement
- integrity
- energy
- human relations skills
- dependability
- fairness
- dedication
- co–operation
- initiative
- foresight
- drive
- decisiveness
- emotional stability
- ambition
- objectivity

Having these traits (or most of them) will not always ensure that a person becomes a good leader, because leaders also must understand the work that needs to be done, and work for an organisation that is efficiently run. Each leadership situation differs and requires more or less of a certain trait.

Leadership traits are an important aspect of the working world. Managers are often employed and periodically appraised on the basis of such traits. With extensive training people can develop traits and improve the quality of their decision-making.

Style theories

Style theories focus on *what the leader does* and the way in which he or she treats and directs employees, handles problems and makes decisions, rather than on individual traits. Leadership style can be influenced by numerous factors, and all managers are different.

Since the 1960s many style theories have been put forward. Often they have been expressed in terms of autocratic versus democratic, or people-orientated versus task-orientated. One such theory is that of **D. McGregor** who looked at leadership and motivation at work. He came up with two contrasting approaches to management which he labelled 'Theory X' and 'Theory Y'. A Theory X manager is tough and autocratic, supporting tight controls with punishment/reward systems – this person is authoritarian. A Theory Y manager is benevolent and participative, with a belief in self controls – the democrat.

Task

What experiences have you had – either in education or at work – of autocratic and democratic leadership styles? What sort of leader would you prefer to work for?

Case Study

Two contrasting styles

When Sir Kit McMahon resigned from Midland Bank in 1991 after unveiling poor results for the previous year, his place was taken by *Sir Peter Walters*, the former chairman of British Petroleum. Sir Peter revels in his 'hardman' image and does not deal in half-measures. He compares business to military situations and does not believe in waiting for the enemy to appear. He has often rid himself of managers because he has lost faith in their ability. He also believes in absolute power and is prepared to 'lead but not to drive'.

Paul Judge was the chairman of Premier Brands – the Smash, Marvel and Typhoo Tea company – which was forced to sell the business to Hillsdown Holdings, a food conglomerate. Paul was described by his colleagues as 'professional, analytical and nice'. His tutor at university thought of him as pleasant, sensible and quiet, and likely to be a conformist. When Paul sits down at meetings he suggests measured and practical solutions. He resigned after the sale to Hillsdown because he felt that staff commitment would be damaged by the sale.

1 To what extent do the two leadership styles of Paul and Sir Peter indicate contrasting approaches?
2 Explain why each type of approach represents an effective style of leadership.

Rensis Likert devised another model of leadership style. This highlights four types:

- *System 1 – the exploitive, authoritative system.* This epitomises the authoritarian style. Threats and punishments are employed and communication and teamwork are poor.
- *System 2 – the benevolent authoritative system.* This is paternalistic and allows some opportunities for consultation and delegation.

- *System 3 – the consultative system.*
  This moves forward to greater democracy and teamwork. Rewards are used instead of threats.
- *System 4 – the participative group system.*
  This is the ultimate democratic style, leading to commitment to organisational goals.

Task

If you were given a leadership role, where would you fit into Likert's four management systems? Give a supporting reason for your answer.

Task

Place the following leading figures in the managerial grid:

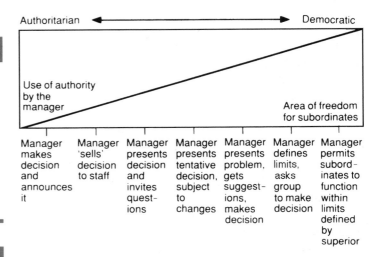

Paddy Ashdown
Ron Atkinson
Richard Branson
Brian Clough

Edwina Currie
Princess Diana
Graham Gooch
Neil Kinnock

John Major
Anita Roddick
Clare Short
Margaret Thatcher

Tannenbaum and Schmidt came up with a continuum of leadership styles which fall between the authoritarian and the democratic. This is easier to understand when looked at in diagrammatic form (see Figure 15.16).

| Authoritarian | | | | | | Democratic |

Use of authority by the manager

Area of freedom for subordinates

| Manager makes decision and announces it | Manager 'sells' decision to staff | Manager presents decision and invites questions | Manager presents tentative decision, subject to changes | Manager presents problem, gets suggestions, makes decision | Manager defines limits, asks group to make decision | Manager permits subordinates to function within limits defined by superior |

Figure 15.16 *The continuum of leadership styles*

Task

How does Tannenbaum and Schmidt's continuum relate to your own personal experiences?

The **managerial grid** is a matrix model of management which, instead of concentrating on autocratic versus democratic styles, looks at 'concern for people' and 'concern for production'. Again, this is easiest to understand in a diagram (see Figure 15.17).

Of the five styles of management shown in the grid, only 'Team' is the ideal style because it combines concern for people with concern for production, gets things done and keeps everybody happy. Looking at the others:

- 'Country Club' is too concerned with people and gets very little done.
- 'Task' is too concerned with production and creates an

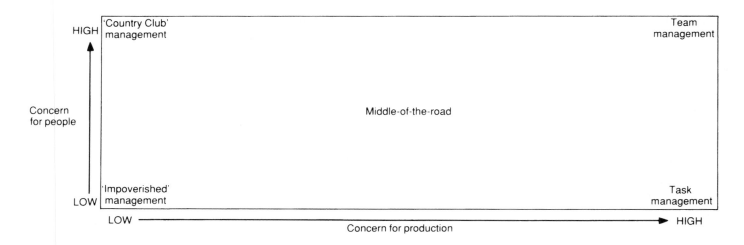

Figure 15.17 *The managerial grid*

atmosphere of low morale.

● 'Impoverished' has no concern for people or output.
● 'Middle-of-the-road' shows some concern for people and some concern for production.

A manager can study the grid, assess where his or her leadership style lies, and consider where improvements are possible.

Contingency theories

Contingency theories argue that the most appropriate style of leadership depends largely on the nature of the situation into which a leader is put.

One modern theory along these lines is due to **Fielder**. He pointed to three variables which appear in any situation to determine the leader's approach. These are:

● leader–member relations
● the degree and structure of the task
● the power and authority of the leader's position.

Another contingency theory is represented by **Adair's functional model** of leadership. Adair sees three main variables at work which determine how a person behaves in a leadership situation – task needs, group needs and individual needs. Effective leadership involves creating the right balance between the three sets of needs in the light of the total situation. The circumstances of each situation (urgency, danger etc.) affect the priority due to each area of need.

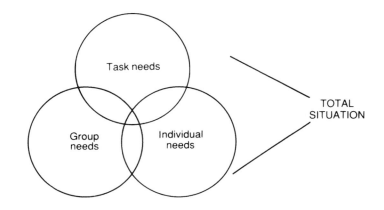

Figure 15.18 *Functional model of leadership*

Case Study

A British cure for a German company

As many British firms wallowed in the trough of recession, fork-lift truck manufacturer Lancer Boss of Leighton Buzzard was buying into Europe. In the process it revived a German manufacturer with a dose of management discipline.

Lancer Boss had itself suffered from a crisis in its recent past and had trimmed back at a time other UK companies had kept their ample layers of blubber. This meant that when times of high interest rates and an exchange rate crunch came they were well prepared. At that time they were looking for a European partner, and Steinbock – a Bavarian lift-truck maker – became available because of poor trading results.

The Germans were surprised by a British takeover, and even more so at the recovery plan which was brutal and swift. A factory was shut down, a production line was cut to half capacity and the workforce was reduced. Sir Neville Bowman-Shaw, the Lancer Boss chairman, found that the Germans were amenable to strong management disciplines 'because they were well educated and well trained'.

As the British company used leadership skills to turn the company round, confidence was restored. From the seventh month after the takeover Steinbock was back in profit, and Lancer Boss had the European partner it wanted. Since then investment in the German plant had contributed to a doubled market share in Germany.

1 Explain why the situation of the takeover in this case required a particular type of contingency leadership.
2 Were there any alternatives to a strong dose of management discipline?

Summary of leadership effects

Trait, style and contingency theories of leadership all have considerable merit when trying to understand how a leader should operate. No organisation chart or job description will ever be able to specify every action that a leader has to perform. Effective leadership goes above and beyond a job description – it provides direction for the organisation as it works towards goals and, at the same time, helps to build relationships, affects morale and improves the motivation of employees.

Element assignment

Women can manage – equal opportunities for all?

This assignment can help you provide evidence for assessment, or claim the following Core Skills:

Communication
Identify and solve routine and non-routine problems

Personal Skills
Treat the values, beliefs and opinions of others with respect

Appy a range of skills and techniques to develop a variety of ideas in the creation of new/modified products, services or situations

You are the personnel officer for a large, well-established building society. You have been set the task of reducing the turnover of female staff in the building society.

Artt, Davies and Deaves Building Society
The Artt, Davies and Deaves Building Society has branches all over the country. The society was founded in 1938 by Messrs N. Artt, D. Davies and L. Deaves, all of whom are still active in the management of the organisation.

Concern has recently been aroused within the Society following the completion of a five-year study by the personnel department. The study has highlighted an increasing turnover of female staff. In addition to the study, a recent survey within the organisation has shown that there is a feeling that women are discriminated against.

Staff Level	Male	Female
Executive Officer	74	6
Principal Officer	220	100
Administrative Officer	50	910

(from sample of 80 branches across UK)

Figure 15.19 *Male/female breakdown according to career grade*

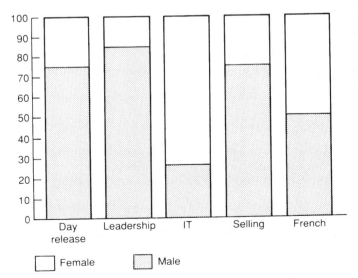

Figure 15.20 *Male/Female breakdown of staff sent on training courses*

Task

As personnel officer you have been given the following task brief.

Produce a report for discussion within the personnel department covering the following areas:

1 What does 'equal opportunities for all' mean?
   a Set out a series of objectives in the form of a diagram which could be set out as in Figure 15.21.

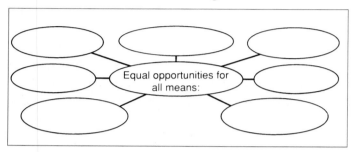

Equal opportunities for all means:

Figure 15.21

b How can Artt, Davies and Deaves communicate these objectives to all members of the organisation?
c How can Artt, Davies and Deaves keep a check that these objectives are being applied?

2 From the evidence provided in the text, suggest possible reasons why there has been an increasing turnover of staff.

3 Suggest possible ways of reducing this turnover.

4 In your report you should highlight the laws which Artt, Davies and Deaves need to comply with in providing equal opportunities.

5 In your conclusion you should put forward some hard hitting suggestions for future policy. Set out a programme of suggestions for future changes in a series of clear action steps.

chapter **16** FINANCIAL TRANSACTIONS

All organisations are required to keep records of their activities. By keeping such records accurately and up-to-date, organisations can measure their performance, improve their overall financial control and take action whenever problems arise.

In this chapter we look at the purpose and use of business documentation for generating accounting data which can then be used to create accounting information. In doing this we look at a range of business documents which originate from accounting transactions.

Despite the advent of information technology, paper documents and recording procedures are still an essential part of business life. Although most records today are stored on computer databases, we need to identify the types of documents that records relate to.

Whenever we buy goods from a shop there is rarely a need for much documentation. We might pay directly by cash or, if we pay by cheque, credit card or debit card, we will have to sign a receipt. Large organisations, however, require a lot more documentation to cover the requirements of a transaction. One reason for this is that their purchasing requirements might be highly specified, but a more important reason is that nearly all of their transactions will be on credit. Payment is then made at a month-end or later.

Source documents are documents that relate first-hand to transactions between customers and organisations. Their importance should never be underestimated. Imagine the sort of confusion that might arise if a source document is mislaid. For example:

- Goods might be sent to the wrong customer.
- The wrong goods might be despatched.
- Payment could be delayed.
- General confusion might arise, leading to complaints and loss of further business.

There are many types of business documents, several of which we look at in this chapter. Business documents required for transactions capture the details of accounting events, are necessary as proof of business dealings, and are a way of checking goods ordered and received.

Business documents are also used for **internal planning and control**. For example, documentation may relate to a specific job which a team of workers undertakes, or to the amount of materials used in the manufacturing process. Documentation is also required for wages or salaries, petty cash, stores requisitions and so on. Organisations often design documentation for their own purposes to cater for such specific requirements.

Case Study

Monitoring and controlling your business

The following key points appear in a Barclays Bank business advice booklet *Monitoring and Controlling your Business.*

- Keep all your records and write them up promptly and regularly. Do not allow invoices and receipts to accumulate in a drawer.

- Have a look at various ready-made record systems that are on the market. They could simplify matters for you. Larger and more complicated businesses may find a computer package helpful, but first discuss this with your accountant.
- As always, get good professional advice if you are in any doubt about your records.
- Remember that the Inland Revenue and Customs & Excise are interested in your records. Do not try to mislead them or yourself.
- Accurate and up-to-date records can help your business to avert a crisis as well as saving money with your accountant.

1 Give at least two reasons why a small business should not allow documents to accumulate.

2 Identify two benefits of keeping accurate and up-to-date records.

3 Who will be interested in such records?

3 The posting of data from source records into a more permanent record of data called **the ledger**.

4 The presentation of accounting reports from ledger information.

Data-flows from source documents are today, more often than not, channelled through a **management information system**, known as an MIS. An MIS is used to meet the needs of managers for planning and control. Source documents provide the raw data for such purposes.

Task

Find out if your college or organisation has an MIS. Find out what it does.

INFORMATION GENERATION FROM SOURCE DOCUMENTS

Financial information is the end-result of a process involving the following stages:

1 The preparation of source documents.
2 The entry of data from source documents into source records.

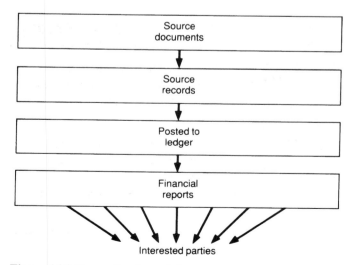

Figure 16.1 *Generating financial reports*

SOURCE DOCUMENTS FOR CREDIT TRANSACTIONS

Whenever a credit transaction takes places, the transaction creates a **debtor** and a **creditor.** A debtor is a person or an organisation owing money to you or your organisation. A creditor is a person or organisation to whom you or your organisation owe money. So, if you buy goods on credit, you owe that organisation money and it is your creditor. From that organisation's point of view, because you owe it money, you are a debtor.

Figure 16.2 identifies many source documents that may be needed for a business transaction.

It is usual for source documents to be headed with the name of the organisation. Most medium-sized or large organisations nowadays use computer-generated records, which means that documents are printed rather than written on by hand.

Letter of enquiry

A letter of enquiry may be sent to several suppliers to find out what they can offer, and so that various details and

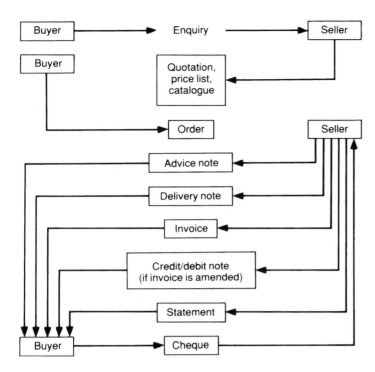

Figure 16.2 *Types of transaction source documents*

specifications can be compared. A buyer will wish to find out many things before placing an order – for example, prices, details about the goods, delivery dates and times, as well as discounts.

Quotation/price list/catalogue

In response to an enquiry the potential seller may supply a quotation or a catalogue with a price list. The buyer will then compare quotations or analyse details from the catalogues. A quotation provides details of availability and of terms being offered. For example, '5%–30 days' indicates that if the bill is paid within 30 days, the buyer can deduct a cash discount of 5 per cent.

An order

Once a buyer has decided upon the best quotation or has scrutinised a series of catalogues, the next step may be the issuing of a purchase order. Order forms are numbered and dated so that they can be traced easily (see Figure 16.3). Upon receipt of the order, the seller will check all the details, such as price and date of delivery.

ORDER NUMBER
2693 / /0-43 /

FROM: _____

TO: _____

ADDRESS: _____

DATE: _____

TITLE: _____

When invoicing please quote title and ORDER NUMBER. Failure to quote this will delay payment. Please send your invoice addressed to

INSTRUCTIONS:

DATE WORK REQUIRED BY: _____

SIGNATURE: _____   DATE: _____

Please sign both copies (before commencing work), and return the duplicate copy to:

HEINEMANN EDUCATIONAL

Halley Court, Jordan Hill
Oxford OX2 8EJ

Telephone Oxford (0865) 311366
Telex 837292 HEBOXF G
Facsimile (0865) 310043

Figure 16.3 *A specimen order*

Task

Look closely at the specimen purchase order which appears in Figure 16.3, and then answer the following questions.

1 Explain why failure to quote the order number might lead to delayed payment.

2 Why does the 'date work required by' appear on this order?

Advice note/despatch note

Before despatching the goods the seller may send an advice note to say that the goods are being sent and that they will arrive shortly. If the goods do not arrive, the buyer can then contact the seller to find out why the delay has arisen.

Delivery note

A delivery note is usually sent with the goods. This lists the items that have been sent. The buyer can use it to check that all the goods have arrived (see Figure 16.4).

Goods received note (GRN)

A goods received note is used internally to inform various departments about the arrival of orders. For example, copies will be sent to the department that ordered the goods; a copy will also go to the accounts department where it will be checked against the invoice before the supplier is paid.

An invoice

The invoice is the official request for payment and is therefore an important document in any transaction. It shows the details of the transaction, the amount charged and the terms. The following details might be found on an invoice:

- *Order number* – This can be used to check the goods delivered against those ordered.
- *Terms* – This shows how much time the buyer has to pay for the goods, and the cash discount which may be given for quick payment.
- *Carriage* – If this appears it will show how transport costs should be paid for. 'Carriage paid' means that the seller will pay for the transport and 'Carriage forward' means that the buyer is expected to pay.
- *E & O E* – this stands for 'errors and omissions excepted', which means that the seller can correct any mistake on the invoice at a later date.
- *Trade discount* – This may be given for a variety of reasons. It will be deducted from the invoice price.
- *VAT* – if a good or service is subject to value added tax, this will be added to the amount appearing on the invoice.
- *Invoice number* – This makes it easy for the accounts department of both the buyer and the seller to identify the invoice quickly.
- *VAT registration number* – Most organisations print their VAT number on their invoices for convenience.

ATHENÆUM PRESS LTD.

Unit 3, Mill Lane Ind. Est., Newcastle upon Tyne NE4 6TD
Tel: (091) 273 7737

DELIVERY NOTE   3587

TLE: MODULAR SCIENCE.   DATE:

PUBLISHER: HEINEMANN.   SP 1593/1c 2NG/0435 ORDER NO: 57597X/0001

DESCRIPTION OF GOODS: Collated Book Block Packs.

QUANTITY: 20.

NO. OF PACKAGES/PALLETS: 1

DELIVERY ADDRESS: STEPHEN PEGG — HE PRODUCTION
HEINEMANN EDUCATIONAL
HALLEY COURT
JORDAN HILL
OXFORD
OX2 8EJ.

VIA: RECEIVED BY:

Figure 16.4 *A delivery note*

Task

The blank Heinemann sales invoice shown as Figure 16.5 is extracted from a pack of continuous stationery.

1 Name two advantages of handling invoices by computer.
2 On the sales invoice identify the VAT number, the invoice number, the address where the invoice is to be sent, payment details, and the column which refers to trade discount.
3 Explain why the invoice address might be different from the delivery address.
4 What details mentioned in the text do not appear on this invoice?

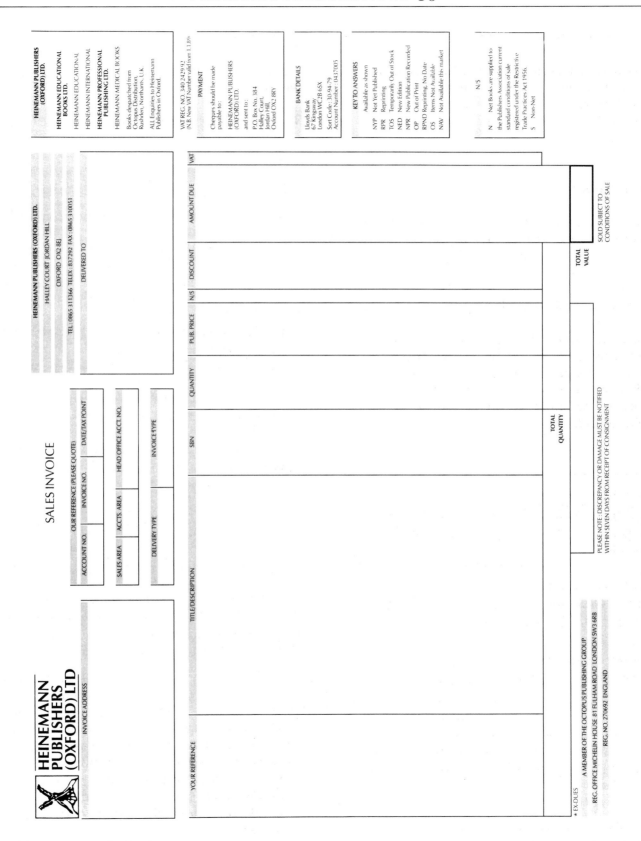

Figure 16.5 *A specimen sales invoice*

If the seller has not transacted any previous business with the buyer, or perhaps if the buyer has been late with payments in the past, the seller might send the buyer a *pro forma invoice*. This document is sent to the buyer before the goods are delivered and sets out the charges which then have to be paid in advance. The goods are then delivered after the payments are made.

Credit notes and debit notes

These may be sent by the seller to adjust the amount which appeared on an invoice.

A credit note *reduces* the invoice price. The invoice price might be reduced because a mistake has been made, or because goods have been found to be faulty or damaged, or simply because the wrong goods have been delivered. A credit note is sometimes printed in red.

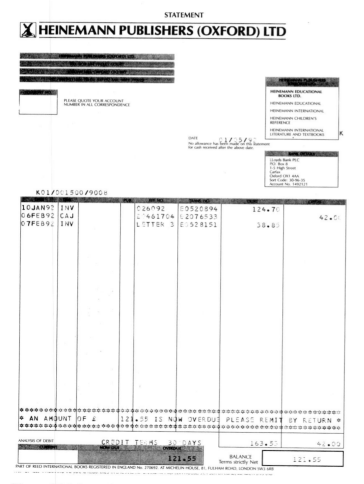

Figure 16.6 *A specimen statement*

A debit note *increases* the invoice price. This might happen where a mistake has been made on the invoice or too many goods have been sent.

Statement of account

The seller will send all regular customers a statement of account at the end of every month. This is simply a copy of the customer's account in the sales ledger and usually contains a record of all transactions with the customer during the month. The debit column shows the sales by the seller to the buyer and will include anything which increases the debt, such as a debit note. The credit column shows any payments, credit notes and anything which reduces the debt (see Figure 16.6).

Case Study

Working as an auto-electrician

Peter Birch recently set up in business as an auto-electrician in York. Peter's business is located in an area that has a large number of garages, many of which have expressed an interest in using Peter's specialist services. Peter also hopes to attract a lot of work from personal customers. He has paid for an advert in *Yellow Pages* and has advertised in local newspapers. Peter has been surprised by the extent of the documentation he has to handle in the day-to-day running of his business. He has opened accounts with several local suppliers of parts and has already received an assortment of documentation, including advice notes, delivery notes invoices and statements. Peter is also concerned about the type of documents he should provide.

1 *Explain briefly the purpose of each of the types of documents mentioned above.*
2 *Advise Peter on the sort of documentation he should be providing for his customers. Though all of his personal customers will be paying by cash, garages will expect to be allowed to pay by credit.*
3 *Advise Peter on the benefits of using a computer or some form of information technology to help with the documentation process.*

356

▪ PAYMENTS DOCUMENTS ▪

Most business transactions involve at some stage a transfer of money from one person or organisation to another. Whereas in the past transactions involved payment by notes and coins, today most involve the use of automated systems which transfer money directly from one place to another without any direct movement of cash.

The most significant document used for payment and transferring funds is clearly the **cheque,** which is issued through the mechanism of the **banking system**. Though cheques are not legal tender, their use and acceptability today is widespread.

A cheque is an unconditional order in writing drawn on a bank, signed by a drawer, which requires a bank to pay on demand a sum of money to the order of a named person or to the bearer.

Figure 16.7 *A specimen cheque*

The meanings of the various parts of the above definition of a cheque are:

- *Unconditional* – Payment cannot be dependent upon certain conditions being met.
- *Writing* – A cheque must be in ink or print.
- *Signed* – A cheque must be signed by the drawer who is the person paying the money.
- *On demand* – The cheque will be paid when presented to the bank.
- *A sum of money* – This must be written on the cheque in words and figures.
- *Named person or to the bearer* – The cheque must be payable to someone by name or to the bearer (the person in possession of the cheque).

Task

Make a list of the advantages of using cheques in preference to cash.

It is estimated that more than eight million cheques are processed through the banking system each working day. Dealing with such large volumes of documentation has become a very expensive process. Banks have therefore increasingly sought to use information technology to reduce costs and increase the efficiency of the system. In doing this bankers and the banking system have opened up and developed other methods of payment transfer. Examples are:

- *Standing orders* – Customers can advise their banks to make regular payments on certain dates for fixed amounts. If the amounts or the dates are to be changed, the customer simply advises the bank of such changes.
- *Direct debits* – With this system the customer tells the bank what to pay and when. The receiver provides the documentation requiring payment, and this system can deal with variable payments.
- *BACS (Bankers Automated Clearing Services)* – This system was set up to deal with bulk electronic clearing for payments purposes. It removes the need to send vast amounts of paper around the system and is used for standing orders, direct debits and salary credits. The user of the system provides the bank with data in the form of magnetic tape, diskette or disk and this is then sent to the BACS computer centre for processing. If the information is sent down the telephone line, it is known as BACSTEL. The input is processed and debits and credits are made to relevant accounts.

For many organisations the largest payment commitment is to their employees. The employer will keep an **individual pay record** for each employee (se Figure 16.8) and provide each with a **pay advice/slip** (Figure 16.9) on each payment date.

The individual pay record contains all of the relevant details for each employee with regard to pay (tax codes, National Insurance contributions etc.). National Insurance

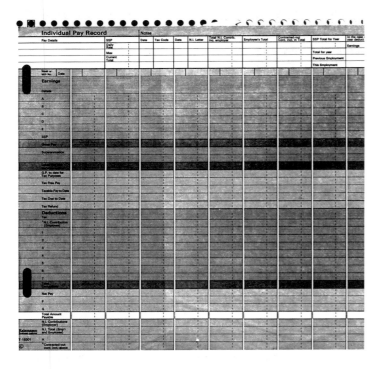

Figure 16.8 *An individual pay record*

contributions are regular contributions to the government which go towards pensions and benefits.

Figure 16.9 *A pay advice slip*

Petty Cash Voucher

Folio _____
Date _____ 19 ___

Requested by	VAT Amount		Amount including VAT	
Description	£	p	£	p

Signature _____

Passed by _____

Figure 16.10 *A petty cash voucher*

The pay advice slip is prepared from the pay record. 'Gross pay' is the total amount earned by an employee before deducations are made, and 'net pay' is the actual amount received after deductions. 'Superannuation' is the contribution to the company/organisation pension scheme. Tax is then deducted. Each employee is entitled to some tax-free pay, and then tax is paid on the remainder. Other deductions might include union fees or sports and social club membership.

Another regular form of payment which most organisations will have to make is that of **petty cash**. A petty cash book is usually set up to record low-value payments made by members of staff for relatively small purchases such as travelling expenses, items of stationery etc. Such small items are not entered in the main accounting system; instead, a petty cashier will control the money and make the necessary payments. Payments of petty cash are usually made against a petty cash **voucher** (see Figure 16.10) – the voucher is then authorised and payment is made in cash.

· RECEIPTS DOCUMENTS ·

As well as documents associated with making payments, documents are also used to record **receipts**. The most basic and common document used to show a receipt of

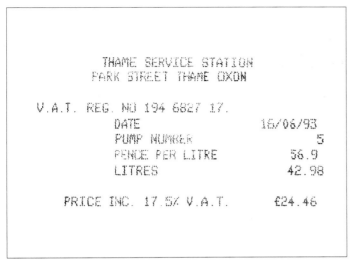

Figure 16.11 *A sales receipt*

payment is simply a **sales receipt**. This is evidence that money has been received and may show the various elements comprising the transation. For example, Figure 16.11 shows a sales receipt for petrol. Note the VAT number, the date and the total value of the receipt.

Make a list of the information shown in the sales receipt of Figure 16.11. How might this information be used?

Another document associated with receiving or transferring payment is a **paying-in slip** or a **bank giro credit** (see Figure 16.12). These allow for the credit transfer of money into a bank account and may be used for putting takings into an account, for the payment/receipt of bills and payment of salaries. Credit clearing works in a similar way to cheque clearing – it involves the transfer of money between accounts.

Banking documents are source documents of entry for an organisation's cash book. See Chapter 17 for details of books of prime entry. It is from these books that company accounts are drawn up – both management accounts which project and analyse business performance and financial accounts which record past performance, many of which are required by law.

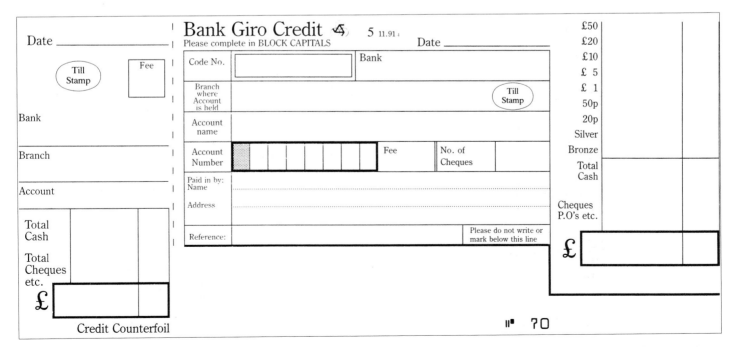

Figure 16.12 *A bank giro credit*

· THE CASH BOOK ·

The cash book is used for recording receipts and payments of both cash and cheques. The most common form is the two-column cash book which has two columns on the left-hand side of the page and two columns on the right-hand side. The first left-hand column is for the receipts of cash and the second left-hand column is for the receipts of cheques. The first right-hand column is for the payments of cash and the second right-hand column is for the payments of cheques. The cheque columns are usually labelled 'bank'.

Often there is a need for a transfer between the bank columns and the cash columns – for example, when putting cash into the bank. This is known as a contra transaction and requires two entries (a withdrawal or payment of cash and a receipt of money into the bank account – see Figure 16.12).

In Figure 16.12, note that the contra entry is indicated by the letter 'C' and, in the situation indicated, requires £100 to be taken from the cash column on the payments side and then paid into the bank account on the receipts side. Note also that, at the end of the month, the balances left in cash and in the bank account are calculated by adding up the columns and taking the columns with the least from the columns with the most. The balances are then brought down for the start of the new month.

CASH BOOK

		RECEIPTS				PAYMENTS		
DATE	DETAILS	CASH	BANK	DATE	DETAILS	CASH	BANK
199_		£	£			£	£
1 Jun	Balances brought down	200	1200	2 Jun	Rent		50
3 Jun	Sales	50		3 Jun	SMP Ltd		200
7 Jun	Sales	150		4 Jun	Purchases	200	
16 Jun	R. Peters		430	17 Jun	Bank C	100	
17 Jun	Cash C		100	21 Jun	Wages		500
22 Jun	Sales	200		23 Jun	R. Smith		125
				24 Jun	Electricity		50
				30 Jun	Balances carried down	300	805
		600	1730			600	1730
1 Jul	Balances	300	805				

Figure 16.13 *Entries in the cash book*

Imagine that you are working for I. M. Lucky Ltd as a cashier, and one of your duties is to maintain the two column cash book. Prepare the cash book from the details below and balance it at the end of the month:

01 Aug Balances cash £265, bank £1657
02 Aug Received £278 cash from sales
03 Aug Payment of motor expenses £44 by cheque
04 Aug Received £125 cheque from A. Bennett
07 Aug Payment for stationery £10 cash
08 Aug Received £400 cash from sales
10 Aug Payment to R. Sid Ltd £76 by cheque
17 Aug Put £350 cash into the bank
22 Aug Received cheque from A. Pridgeon for £65
25 Aug Pay B. Nasty Ltd £322 by cheque
27 Aug Received £30 cash from sales
28 Aug Pay wages £476 by cheque
29 Aug Payment for stationery £33 with cash

Checking the cash book

At the end of every accounting period the **closing balances** in the cash book should be checked. The actual cash in hand should be counted and checked to ensure that if agrees with the figure in the cash column. If it does not, this may be due to one of the following:

● an incorrect entry into the cash book
● figures totalled incorrectly
● loss or theft of cash
● loss of a source document such as a receipt.

The bank reconciliation statement

Checking the bank columns of the cash book is not quite so easy since the money is deposited with the bank. It is therefore important that the cashier always checks the cash book records against the organisation's bank statements. This matching of the cash book balances with the balances shown in the bank statements involves the preparation of a bank reconciliation statement. Preparing such a statement is vital to ensure that mistakes have not been made either in the cash book or in the bank statement.

However, it is quite common – *even if a mistake has not been made* – for a bank statement balance to differ from the balance in the bank column of the cash book. This may be due to items that have appeared in the cash book but which do not yet appear on the bank statement. These are known as timing differences. Timing differences may result from:

- cheques that have been issued and been recorded in the cash book, but which have not been paid into the recipient's bank account
- cheques that have been received, recorded in the cash book and paid into the bank but, because they have not yet cleared, have not been recorded in the bank statement.

Furthermore, items may appear on the bank statement but not appear in the bank columns of the cash book. These may include

- payments such as standing orders, direct debits and bank charges
- receipts such as interest, dividends received by the bank, and bank giro credits or credit transfers received by the bank.

Stages in preparing a bank reconciliation statement

- Tick (in pencil) all the entries appearing in the cash book against those appearing in the bank statement.
- If items appear on the statement but do not appear in the cash book, then the bank columns of the cash book should be brought up to date. The bank columns of the cash book should be balanced with the new figure.
- Timing differences which appear in the bank columns of the cash book and which do not appear in the bank statement should now be used to prepare the bank reconciliation statement.

DATE	DETAILS	BANK	DATE	DETAILS	BANK
RECEIPTS			**PAYMENTS**		
199_		£			£
1 Aug	Balance b/d	525	8 Aug	J. James Ltd	65
12 Aug	P. Jamieson	16	17 Aug	R Nettle Ltd	20
21 Aug	R. Tree	122	22 Aug	P. Green	38
28 Aug	N. Bell	165	28 Aug	J. Smith	15
			31 Aug	Balance c/d	690
		828			828
31 Aug	Balance b/d	690			

Figure 16.14 *Cash book bank columns of A. Jones Ltd*

DATE	DETAILS	PAYMENTS	RECEIPTS	BALANCE
199_		(£)	(£)	(£)
01 Aug	Balance b/d			525
03 Aug	Standing order P. Proby	50		475
11 Aug	J. James Ltd	65		410
13 Aug	Credit		16	426
14 Aug	Credit transfer		85	511
15 Aug	Direct debit	34		477
19 Aug	R. Nettle Ltd	20		457
23 Aug	Credit		122	579
28 Aug	Bank charges	4		575

Figure 16.15 *Bank statement of A. Jones Ltd*

Let us look in detail at an example. The cashier of A. Jones Ltd needs to reconcile the bank columns of the cash book and the bank statement shown in Figures 16.13 and 16.14.

Having checked all the entries appearing in the cash book against those appearing in the bank statement, and vice versa, the cashier will amend the cash book so that it looks like Figure 16.15.

DATE	DETAILS	BANK	DATE	DETAILS	BANK
RECEIPTS			**PAYMENTS**		
199_		£			£
31 Aug	Balance b/d	690	3 Aug	Standing order	50
14 Aug	Credit transfer	85	15 Aug	Direct debit	34
			28 Aug	Bank charges	4
			31 Aug	Balance c/d	687
		775			775
1 Sept	Balance b/d	687			

Figure 16.16 *Amended cash book bank columns of A. Jones Ltd*

The amended cash book balance would then be used to draw up the bank reconciliation statement, as shown in Figure 16.16.

```
                    A Jones Ltd
      Bank Reconciliation Statement as at 31 August 199-

                                                        (£)
Balance at bank as per cash book (amended)              687
Add: cheques drawn but not yet presented for payment
       P. Green     38
       J. Smith     15                                   53
                                                        740
Less: cheques deposited but not yet cleared
       N. Bell                                          165
Balance as per bank statement                           575
```

Figure 16.17 *The reconciliation statement*

Task

Imagine you are the cashier of C. More Ltd. Prepare a bank reconciliation statement from the bank columns of the cash book and the bank statement in Figures 11.17 and 11.18.

RECEIPTS			PAYMENTS		
DATE	DETAILS	BANK	DATE	DETAILS	BANK
199_		£			£
1 Sep	Balance b/d	931	2 Sep	R, Joyce Ltd	54
7 Sep	N. Smith	25	9 Sep	H. Fawcett	338
8 Sep	R. Peterson	15	18 Sep	N. Ray	55
20 Sep	N. Jones	30	21 Sep	P. Bryan	82
27 Sep	R. Mink	58	27 Sep	J. Jewel	151
			30 Sep	Balance c/d	379
		1059			1059
30 Sept	Balance b/d	379			

Figure 11.17 Cash book bank columns of C. More Ltd

DATE	DETAILS	PAYMENTS	RECEIPTS	BALANCE
199_		(£)	(£)	(£)
01 Sep	Balance b/d			931
04 Sep	Credit transfer		25	956
07 Sep	R. Joyce Ltd	54		902
08 Sep	Credit		25	927
09 Sep	Credit		15	942
15 Sep	H. Fawcett	338		604
16 Sep	Bank transfer	12		592
18 Sep	Credit transfer		39	631
21 Sep	N. Jones		30	661
24 Sep	Standing order	50		611

Figure 11.18 Bank statement of C. More Ltd

Element assignment

Business documents

This assignment can help you to provide evidence for assessment, or claim the following Core skills:

Communication
Receive and respond to a variety of information

Communicate in writing
Application of Number
Apply numerical skills and techniques

Personal Skills
Use information sources

Task 1
Obtain either an original copy or a photocopy of a major source document. Explain the purpose of the document. Who sent it and who received it? Label the main features of the document.

Task 2
Find out more about the sort of business documentation used by a local business. Interview somebody who works for the business and then present your findings in a short report.

chapter ## 17 CONTROLLING DOCUMENTATION

Almost every employee within an organisation will come across various types of business documentation within the workplace. In the last chapter we looked specifically at the purposes and use of such documentation. In this chapter we move a stage further to analyse how to handle business documents so that you can develop an understanding of the processes in which they are involved and how the information they provide is eventually recorded and used.

This chapter begins by looking at the various procedures for purchasing and selling goods. Payment and receipt processes and the documents they create are then analysed and then, finally, this chapter looks at how such documents relate to double-entry bookkeeping and books of prime entry.

· THE PURCHASING PROCESS ·

Procuring materials is a key management function for any organisation. The importance of this role can be fully appreciated when one realises that an average manufacturer spends about one half of its income on supplies of raw materials and services.

An efficient purchasing department will aim to provide the organisation with a steady flow of materials and services, and with continuity of supplies. It will also aim to provide the best value for money.

The starting point for any purchasing transaction involves the identification of a need to obtain raw materials, equipment or supplies. A department within the organisation might have sent a request to the purchasing department on a **requisition form**. This form will state the type of goods required as well as the quantity and will be signed by an authorised person.

An alternative way of obtaining goods would be to send a

stores requisition to the storekeeper to release certain items (see Figure 17.1). If goods are not in stock the process shown in Figure 17.2 has to be followed.

STORES REQUISITION	
Materials required for: _____ Job Number _____	Requisition number: _____ Date _____
Quantity	**Description**
Section Supervisor _____ Required by: _____	Storekeepers initials _____

Figure 17.1 *A stores requisition*

Identify how goods and materials are obtained by staff either in the place you work or the place you attend. If you can, obtain a copy of a stores requisition. How similar or different is it from the one shown in Figure 17.1?

Following the requisition, it might then be necessary to order the goods, parts or materials. The purchasing department will obtain quotations or scrutinise price lists and catalogues. A **purchase order** will be sent to a suitable supplier outlining:

- product descriptions
- quantities
- delivery dates
- details regarding despatch (see Figure 17.3).

The purchase order will refer to the quoted price of goods or to the supplier's catalogue – though these prices are not

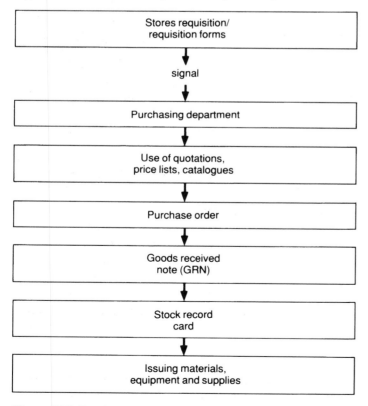

Figure 17.2 *Purchasing goods*

CLEANQUICK LTD
45 Greenbank Road
Frodsham
Cheshire
CH3 9HP

Telephone 0352 867567
Fax   0352 867568

To: R & S Supplies Ltd
    Bolton Road
    Burnley
    B3 2SP

Please supply:

PURCHASE ORDER
Number 35/568

Date 2nd July 199–

QUANTITY	DESCRIPTION	CAT NO	PRICE
500	Tins of polish	RG/345	£4.75 per tin

Please deliver to the above address within 10 days of this order.

P.Wilks _____ (Buyer)

Figure 17.3 *A purchase order*

binding on suppliers. It will contain a reference number and the name of the person responsible for ordering the goods. Copies of the order may be distributed to the receiving department, to the stock control department (to advise on the impending arrival of the goods), as well as to the accounts department for checking of prices and discounts.

Upon delivery of the goods, the receiving department will check that the goods delivered correspond in every detail with the purchase order. A **goods received note** (GRN) is then prepared which contains details of the goods received, such as quality, quantity and description. A copy is sent to the accounts department as well as to the department responsible for the order. If the **stock control** department is responsible for the storage, distribution and control of the goods, details will be recorded on a **stock record card** such as the one illustrated in Figure 17.4.

Shortly after the goods are received, the supplier will send an **invoice** which will state the price of the goods ordered, the date of despatch and the amount owing. The invoice will be **checked** by the accounts department against the goods received note, to ensure:

STOCK RECORD CARD

Description: Tins of polish
Code No: RG/345
Re-order no: 500 tins

Bin No: 25
Maximum: 700 tins
Minimum: 100 tins
Ordering level: 150 tins

Date	Receipts		Issues		Balance
	GRN No	Qty	Req No	Qty	
1993–					
May 1					300
May 25			451	70	230
June 7			493	80	150
July 10	793	500			650

Figure 17.4 *A stock record card*

- that the prices are correct
- that discounts have been calculated correctly
- that VAT has been applied correctly
- that all of the other details on the invoice are correct.

If there are no queries, the invoice is cleared for payment.

Task

Imagine that you work for Jevons General Maintenance Co. Ltd and that you have been asked to design a suitable goods received note to be used within the company. Use a word-processor to help you with your design. Aim to make the design simple and effective.

Task

Look carefully at the order in Figure 17.5 and then answer the following questions.

1 How is the number on the order to be used?
2 Why does the order require confirmation of delivery date?
3 Why does the order contain instructions regarding:
   a delivery
   b packing
   c invoicing?

ORDER NUMBER
1828 / /0-43 /

REF YOUR ESTIMATE

TO:
TITLE:

DATE:

HEINEMANN EDUCATIONAL

Halley Court, Jordan Hill
Oxford OX2 8EJ

Telephone Oxford (0865) 311366
Telex 837292 HEBOXF G
Facsimile (0865) 310043

MATERIAL ENCLOSED:
(Please show proofs/imposed ozalids)

PRINT QUANTITY: _____ x _____ pp TRIMMED PAGE SIZE _____ x _____ mm NO. OF COLOURS

PAPER:
QUANTITY:
SIZE _____ gm²
IN STOCK WITH YOU/WE TO SUPPLY/PRINT UP TO PAPER SUPPLIED
DELIVERY DUE

COVER: PRINT _____ COPIES
NO. OF COLOURS _____ UV VARNISH/LAMINATE
MATERIAL:

IN STOCK WITH YOU/WE TO SUPPLY BY

BINDING/PACKING:

IMPOSITION

DELIVERY DATE REQUIRED
CONFIRM BY RETURN

4 ADVANCE COPIES TO .... AT OXFORD

INVOICING – Invoices must include our Order Number (as above), together with details of our paper/cover material usage. Please send invoices to Finance Dept. at above address.

ARTWORK/CRC – PLEASE RETURN TO THE UNDERSIGNED

SIGNATURE:

DELIVERY INSTRUCTIONS – Bulk stock with advice note to Reed Book Services Ltd., Warehouse No. 2, Sanders Lodge Industrial Estate, Rushden, Northants NN10 9RZ.

PACKING INSTRUCTIONS
All books must be packed in binders parcels/cartons, each with a maximum weight of 10 kilos per parcel/carton.

Each parcel to have label showing:- TITLE, ISBN, EDITION, QUANTITY, PUBLISHER, PRICE (if known). (pack in multiples of 10 where possible).

PALLETS
Use 1000 x 1110 mm
2 way entry
non-reversible
pallets as illustration
on the left.
Do not mix
titles on one
pallet.

No overhang on pallets. Maximum height including pallet 1250 mm. To avoid movement in transit, strap and shrink wrap each pallet.

Figure 17.5 *An order form for book printing and binding*

· THE SELLING PROCESS ·

The major responsibility of a sales department is to generate orders for products. The size of the sales department and the overall nature of its operations will depend largely on the type of industry in which the organisation operates. For example, selling to industrial markets will normally require a lot of personal selling, whereas in retail markets promotional activities stimulate sales and organisations will generally operate with smaller sales teams.

A sale is concluded when a customer completes an **order form.** When an order form is received for a credit sale a copy is usually sent to the **credit control** department for approval. This is because there are many dangers with credit transactions. Some customers may take too long to pay their bills or may even not pay their bills at all. The credit control department reviews all accounts, sets credit limits, ensures that limits are not exceeded, and tries to ensure that payments are made promptly. These actions constantly influence the cash flow and liquidity of the organisation. Before granting credit for the first time, a supplier may ask for a trade or bank reference. A **trade reference** is provided by a supplier who has previously given credit to a business and may vouch for the reliability of their custom.

The selling process might involve a series of stages as in Figure 17.6.

An **advice note** is sent to the customer either shortly before or when the goods are despatched, to advise the customer on the date of despatch and the mode of delivery. Goods will normally be accompanied by a **delivery note** which simply provides a description of the goods being delivered. The customer acknowledges receipt of the goods by signing the delivery note.

When goods have been despatched to the customer by the stock control department, a copy of the sales order stating the date of despatch is sent to the sales invoice section of the accounts department, who then prepare the **invoice.**

WORKWISE LTD 4 Cottingham Street HULL HU8 7YT				Invoice No. 7643 Order No. 93/876 Account No. 89/78
To: Watchet Works Ltd 4 Sonnet Corner PICKERING YO13 5FK				VAT No. 765 6543 9th July 199–

Code	Description	Quantity	Unit Price	Total
F300	Overalls	16	£12.50	£200.00
G567	Shirts	25	£9.50	£237.50
	Goods total Less 10% discount			£437.50 £43.75
	Add VAT 17.5%			£393.75 £68.91
	Grand Total			£462.66

Figure 17.7 *An invoice*

The invoice contains the relevant details of the transaction – such as the quantity and price of the goods ordered and the amount due from the customer. When the invoice is prepared, prices should be checked, discounts should be calculated, VAT should be added where necessary, and all other details should be checked carefully.

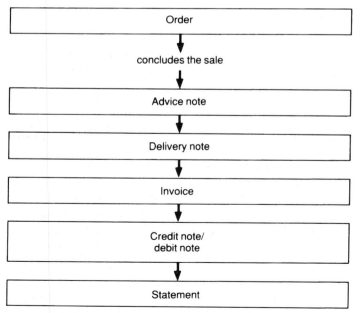

Figure 17.6 *Selling goods*

Order
↓
concludes the sale
↓
Advice note
↓
Delivery note
↓
Invoice
↓
Credit note/ debit note
↓
Statement

Task

Look at the invoice which appears in Figure 17.7. Check the details on the invoice and suggest where amendments should take place.

Details appearing on an invoice will include any or all of the following:

- name and address of seller
- name and address of buyer
- invoice number and date

- VAT number
- purchase order number
- details of goods supplied including code or catalogue or reference numbers
- total net price of goods
- trade discount (if any)
- VAT (if any)
- total amount due from customer
- date by which payment is required
- cash discount for prompt payment – terms (if any)
- E & O E (see Chapter 16, page 354).

Customers are usually required to pay within one month but this will depend on agreed credit terms. Some customers will, however, pay on receipt of the invoice while others will wait as long as possible before making any payment.

If a mistake has been made on the invoice, or if goods are faulty or damaged and have been returned, a **credit note** will be sent to the customer and this will decrease the invoice price (see Figure 17.8).

STATEMENT				NBC LTD	
To: Best Stores 5 High Road WIGAN L15 7GH				Queen Street **BROMSGROVE** **W14 5TR** VAT No 897 6544 11 March 199–	

Date	No	Details	Debit	Credit	Balance
			£ p	£ p	£ p
1993 5 July	456	Goods	135.00		135.00
19 July	CN 67	Credit Note		10.00	125.00

Figure 17.9 *A statement*

Alternatively, if a mistake has been made on the invoice which increases the invoice price, a **debit note** will be prepared and sent to the customer.

Many buyers, particularly if they deal regularly with the supplier, will not make payment against individual invoices but, instead, will wait for the supplier to send a monthly **statement of account**. This summarises the transactions between the buyer and the seller and shows monthly how much is owed by the buyer. When preparing a statement the following details should be checked:

- the name and address of the buyer
- the details of transactions (invoices sent, payments received, credit notes etc.)
- the balance owed by the buyer.

Most statements have three money columns: a debit column, a credit column and a balance (see Figure 17.9).

WILSONS STORES				**Credit Note** 93/45	
56 Curzon Street LIVERPOOL L13 7GH				Account No. 89765	
Telephone 051 876 9876 Fax 051 876 5487				VAT No. 876 6543 23 October 199–	
To: Rothman and Gould 4 Wilkinson Street BIRMINGHAM B3 7GH					

Code	Description	Quantity	Unit Price £ p	Total £ p
GH78	Overcoats	9	10.50	94.50
Reasons for credit:		NET TOTAL VAT		94.50 16.53
		TOTAL CREDIT		111.03

Figure 17.8 *A credit note*

Selling goods on credit

An office furniture manufacturer called Makingthings Ltd has been approached by a company which specialises in distributing office equipment. They have looked at the catalogue supplied by Making-things and are happy with the prices and terms quoted. In the near future they hope to place the first of what they expect to be a series of orders. The value of the orders could be high and represent regular business. Makingthings knows very little about this distribution company.

1 *What steps should Makingthings go through before allowing the company to purchase goods on credit?*

2 *Explain why Makingthings will set a credit limit for this new customer.*

3 *What action should Makingthings take if this new customer fails to make prompt payments?*

Task

Imagine that you work for a company called Smithers Ltd whose address is Unit 5, Tees Estate, Hartlepool, Cleveland, TS3 4GL. A customer called BSTI Ltd from 9 Chapel Street, Leeds, LS3 4DF, has sent you an order for the following:

7 tyre levers @ £34.90 each
3 batteries @ 54.80 each.

VAT is to be charged on both items and the customer is entitled to a 15% discount for being in the same trade. Prepare invoice number 93/87 dated for today.

· BANKING DOCUMENTATION ·

One of the most important jobs in a cashier's department is to record incoming **cheques.** Cheques are today the most widely accepted form of payment. The various parts of a cheque are illustrated in Figure 17.10.

When recording cheques it is important to make sure of the following:

- Cheques contain current dates.
- The amounts in words and figures are the same.
- The payee's name is correct.
- The cheque is signed.
- Any alterations are clear and have been signed.

A **paying-in slip** is used when paying cheques and cash into an organisation's bank account. A paying-in slip is illustrated in Figure 17.11. Where a number of cheques are paid in on one slip, they are listed on the reverse of the slip.

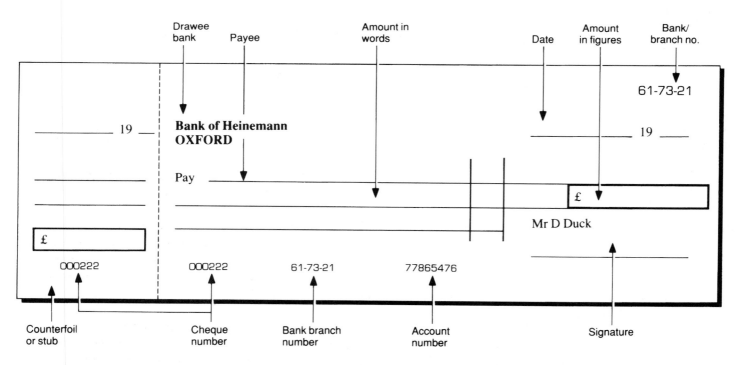

Figure 17.10 *The parts of a typical cheque*

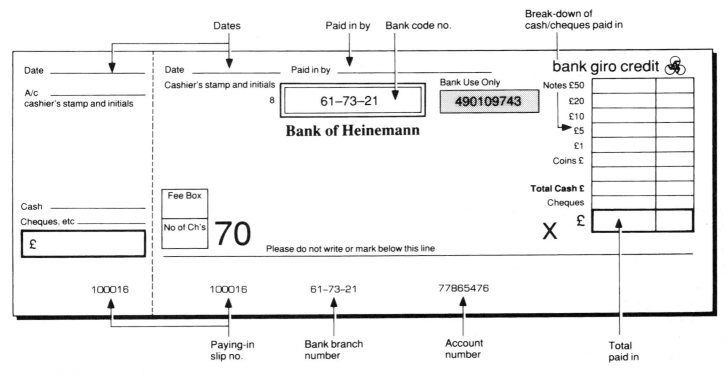

Figure 17.11 *A paying-in slip*

Imagine that you work in a cashier's department. In the morning post there are a number of remittances. These include:

a cheque for £8.76
a cheque for £7.89.

In addition, the following cash payments are received during the day:

8 × £10 notes
9 × £5 notes
8 × £1 coins

Prepare a paying-in slip for all of the above to be paid into the bank. Make up suitable account and code numbers.

· WORK AND PAY ·

For most organisations, particularly those involved with manufacturing, wages and salaries form the largest element of cost. It is important, therefore, that such organisations create a system which properly records labour and how it is used. Such systems should record:

- actual hours spent by employees at work
- hours spent by employees on specific activities.

To do this, organisations have to maintain records that relate to each individual worker.

Pay may be calculated by a number of different methods. For example, workers may have a flat rate of pay based upon a set number of hours. Work done over this number of hours may be at an 'overtime' rate. Sometimes, to provide incentives to work hard, piece-rate systems are used whereby payment is made according to the number of items produced. The problem with this is that it can be difficult to measure the output of some employees (for example, teachers or doctors). Bonuses can be used as an additional encouragement to effort, and for sales personnel commission can be provided which relates directly to the number of sales made.

In order to assess the time spent at work many employers use some form of time recording system such as **clock cards**. With this system employees 'clock on' when they arrive at work and 'clock off' when they finish (see Figure 17.12).

CLOCK CARD

No. 543
Week ending 14th July 199..   Name: Shirley Smith

DAY	IN	OUT	IN	OUT	TOTAL HOURS
Mon	0800	1203	1301	1700	8
Tue	0759	1202	1300	1702	8
Wed	0800	1204	1301	1603	7
Thu	0800	1200	1301	1705	8
Fri	0800	1203	1300	1500	6
		37 hours |£4.75 Overtime			£ 175.75
			TOTAL GROSS WAGE		175.75

Figure 17.12 *A clock card*

For detailed costing purposes a record is often kept of the time spent by employees on each job. This can be done using a **timesheet** or a **job card.**

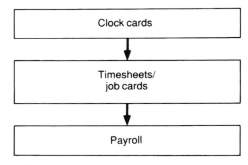

Figure 17.13 *Calculating labour costs*

Clock cards or an equivalent system provide the basic information for calculating wages. Timesheets or job cards may be reconciled with the clock cards.

After gross pay has been calculated from the clock cards or timesheets, it is then recorded on individual pay records. Pay advice slips are constructed to inform employees of their levels of pay and deductions for that period. Though pay advice will vary in form from organisation to organisation, most will include the information shown in Figure 17.14. The details are as follows:

Column 1	Column 2	Column 3	Column 4
Pay advice (1) TP PLC	NAME (5) M. SINGH	Ref. No (Quote on any query) 28 3567 12	27 NOV 93
BASIC PAY/ADDITIONS	DEDUCTIONS	PAY CUMULATIVES	YOUR NET PAY HAS BEEN CREDITED TO YOUR ACCOUNT AS STATED BELOW:
(2) BASIC PAY 1053.52 (3) OVERTIME 101.23	(6) TAX CODE 450H 201.65 (7) NAT.INS 78.21 (8) SUPERANNUATION 65.36 (9) UNION 4.00	THIS YEAR	(17) BANK NAT.WESTMINSTER SORTING CODE 71–36–02 ACCOUNT NUMBER 57468321
	(10) NAT.INSURANCE NO. YS 4565 A (11) DATE OF PAYMENT 28 Nov 92 (12) INCOME TAX YEAR 93/94 (13) PAY PERIOD 08 (14) ENTER 'X' IF FINAL PAY PERIOD IN TAX YEAR ☐		M. SINGH
TOTAL PAY (4) £1154.75 ADDITIONS	(15) TOTAL DEDUCTIONS £349.22	(16) NET PAY £809.93	

Figure 17.14 *A typical payslip*

Column 1

1 The name of the organisation.
2 The employee's basic month's pay.
3 Level of overtime worked.
4 If we add (2) and (3) we get gross pay.

Column 2

5 The employee's name.
6 Tax code.
7 Amount paid in National Insurance.
8 M. Singh's contribution towards a company pension.
9 Monthly trade union subscription.
10 National Insurance number.
11 The date on which the net amount will be transferred to M. Singh's bank account.
12 The income tax year runs from 1 April 1993 to 31 March 1994.
13 The pay period is the 8th month, i.e. November.
14 An X would appear in this box in March.
15 The total amount of deductions.

Column 3

16 Net pay is gross pay less deductions.

Column 4

17 This statement indicates that the money is being paid by giro into M. Singh's bank account.

In addition the pay slip might show the overall amount of gross pay, superannuation and National Insurance paid in the financial year up to that date.

· RECORDING PETTY CASH ·

In Chapter 16 we looked at the use of petty cash vouchers or requests for authorising payments for assorted minor purchases. Petty cash is usually handled by a trustworthy member of the office staff who will make payments as and when appropriate.

The system most commonly used for petty cash is the **imprest system.** With this, the petty cashier starts the week or month with a certain amount of money; requests are authorised during the period when vouchers are submitted, and then, at the end of the period, the 'float' is made up to the imprest amount again by the cashier. For example:

	£
Beginning of period imprest amount of	50.00
Petty cash vouchers submitted and paid	18.50
Cash held at end of period	31.50
Amount drawn to restore imprest	18.50
Balance at start of next period	50.00

PETTY CASH BOOK

RECEIPTS	DATE	DETAILS	VOUCHER No.	TOTAL PAYMENT	POSTAGES	TRAVEL	STATIONERY	OTHER
£	199_			£	£	£	£	£
70.00	01 Jan	Bal b/d						
	02 Jan	Stamps	67	3.50	3.50			
	02 Jan	Taxi	68	4.20		4.20		
	03 Jan	Meals	69	3.69				3.69
	04 Jan	Stationery	70	5.55			5.55	
	05 Jan	Envel	71	8.50			8.50	
	05 Jan	Post	72	6.25	6.25			
	05 Jan	Clean mat	73	5.39				5.39
	06 Jan	Petrol	74	10.00		10.00		
				47.08	9.75	14.20	14.05	9.08
47.08	07 Jan	Received						
	07 Jan	Bal c/d		70.00				
117.08				117.08				
70.00	08 Jan	Bal b/d						

Figure 17.15 *The completed petty cash page for the example*

To carry out his or her task, the petty cashier is responsible for keeping records of payments of petty cash in a **petty cash book**. Receipts are recorded in the far left-hand column and then there are columns for the date and details of transactions. All payments are analysed and, at the end of the period, the total of the analysis columns should equal the total of the 'total payments' column.

Example

A petty cashier starts the week of 1 January with an imprest of £70.00. The following vouchers are received during the week:

02 Jan	voucher 67	£3.50 for stamps
02 Jan	voucher 68	£4.20 for a taxi fair
03 Jan	voucher 69	£3.69 for meals
04 Jan	voucher 70	£5.55 for stationery
05 Jan	voucher 71	£8.50 for envelopes
05 Jan	voucher 72	£6.25 for postage
05 Jan	voucher 73	£5.39 for cleaning materials
06 Jan	voucher 74	£10.00 for petrol

See Figure 17.15.

Task

Imagine that you work for BC Chemicals Ltd. One of your duties is to work as a petty cashier. You use the imprest system and start each week with an imprest of £135.00. During the week beginning the 1 February you receive the following vouchers:

02 Feb	voucher 35	£4.25 for stamps
02 Feb	voucher 36	£8.29 for stationery
03 Feb	voucher 37	£7.65 for envelopes
03 Feb	voucher 38	£4.55 for a taxi fare
03 Feb	voucher 39	£9.75 for postage
04 Feb	voucher 40	£12.75 for petrol
05 Feb	voucher 41	£2.50 for staples
05 Feb	voucher 42	£3.60 for stamps
06 Feb	voucher 43	£12.00 for meals

Prepare the petty cash book for that week using suitable analysis columns.

· DOUBLE-ENTRY BOOKKEEPING ·

Accounting transactions are recorded in ledgers using the process known as **double-entry bookkeeping**. This system recognises that there are two elements to every transaction. For example, if you buy a bar of chocolate you *give* (i.e. pay) cash and *receive* chocolate. Under this system every transaction necessitates an entry into two accounts: one account is debited and another account is credited. A separate account is held for each element of each transaction and every debit entry is always matched by a credit entry.

Most organisations divide their double-entry accounting systems into four main areas:

- The **sales ledger** comprises the individual accounts of debtors, being people or organisations to whom goods or services have been sold on credit. They become debtors until they pay for the goods or services they have received or, if they fail to pay, until their debt is declared to be a bad debt.
- The **purchases ledger** comprises the individual accounts of creditors, being people or organisations from whom goods and services have been purchased on credit. Creditors remain in the ledger until they have been paid.
- The **cash book** records the organisation's receipts and payments (see Chapter 16).
- The **general ledger** comprises all of the other accounts – for example, expenses, assets such as land and buildings and machinery, sales and purchases accounts, an account recording the owner's capital, loan accounts etc.

Ledger accounts at one time were held in large leather-bound volumes which were then meticulously looked after. Today computer systems are extensively used to deal with the recording of ledger transactions. Changes brought about by information technology have improved the way in which information is captured, stored and processed.

· BOOKS OF PRIME ENTRY ·

As it is generally not practicable to enter each and every transaction individually into ledgers, books of prime entry tend to be used. These are used to record details of all business transactions, and then similar transactions are added together to provide totals which are entered into the ledgers at regular intervals.

Books of prime entry include:

- the sales daybook which is prepared from invoices issued and which gives sales totals
- the purchases daybook which is prepared from invoices received and which gives purchases totals
- returns books prepared from credit notes issued and received
- the cash book (which as we have seen is also a division of the ledger) which records receipts and payments.

The sales daybook

The **sales daybook** records all the credit sales made by the organisation from the invoices issued for each transaction made. It therefore provides a total for the credit sales made over a period, and this total is transferred at regular intervals to the **sales account** in the general ledger. Information for individual customer accounts is also transferred from the sales daybook, but this time to the sales ledger to list the organisation's **debtors**.

SALES DAYBOOK			
DATE	NAME	INVOICE NO	£
199_			
4 June	B. Hicks Ltd	10237	451.20
7 June	Gem Stones Ltd	10238	54.85
15 June	B. Sting PLC	10239	368.85
21 June	R. Donald	10240	21.50
27 June	J. Lowry	10241	82.25
30 June	Transferred to Sales Account		978.65

Figure 17.16 *Part of a sales daybook*

The purchases daybook

The **purchases daybook** records all the credit purchases made by the organisation and is prepared from all the invoices received from suppliers. It is used to provide a total made for credit purchases over a period, and this is transferred at regular intervals to the **purchases account** in the general ledger. Information about individual creditors is transferred to the purchases ledger.

PURCHASES DAYBOOK			
DATE	NAME	INVOICE NO	£
199_			
3 June	R. Thompson Ltd	B3456	34.50
18 June	M. Pillings Ltd	A789	78.40
21 June	E. Murphy Ltd	44544	125.70
28 June	A Donkey Ltd	R567	35.75
30 June	Transferred to Purchases Account		274.35

Figure 17.17 *Part of a purchases daybook*

Returns books

Often when goods are bought and sold **returns** are made – perhaps because the goods are faulty, or because the wrong goods have been delivered.

Goods that have been sold by the organisation and returned back from a customer are known as **returns inwards** or **sales returns**. Credit notes are issued when the returns are received, and these notes are used to compile the **returns inwards daybook**. The total from the returns inwards daybook is transferred to the **returns inwards account** in the general ledger. All of the accounts of each customer/debtor returning goods are also adjusted in the **sales ledger**, and the amounts they owe are reduced to cater for the returns.

RETURNS INWARDS DAYBOOK			
DATE	NAME	CREDIT NOTE NO	£
199_			
12 June	B. Hicks Ltd	CN525	10.00
19 June	B. Sting	CN526	18.50
30 June	Transferred to Returns Inwards Account		
28.50			

Figure 17.18 *Part of a returns inwards daybook*

On the other hand, goods that have been bought by the organisation but sent back to the suppliers are known as **returns outwards** or **purchases returns**. Credit notes are sent by suppliers when the goods are returned to them, and these are used to compile the **returns outwards daybook**. The total from the returns outwards daybook is transferred

RETURNS OUTWARDS DAYBOOK

DATE	NAME	CREDIT NOTE NO	£
199_			
21 June	M. Pillings Ltd	X33	21.00
28 June	E. Murphy Ltd	A21	5.50
30 June	Transferred to Returns Outwards Account		
26.00			

Figure 17.19 *Part of a returns outwards daybook*

to the **returns outwards account** in the general ledger. All of the accounts of each supplier/creditor to whom goods have been returned are also adjusted in the purchases ledger, and the amounts owed to them are reduced to cater for the returns.

Task

Imagine that you work as a clerk for A. Corn Ltd, which is a small electrical business in which all purchases and sales are on credit. You have just returned from holiday and find a boxfile on your desk containing invoices received from suppliers, copies of invoices sent out to customers, credit notes received from suppliers, and copies of credit notes sent to customers. From the detailed list which follows, enter the transactions into the appropriate daybooks.

01 August Invoice 1345 sent to R. T. Electronics Ltd for £45.40

02 August Invoice A230 received from Breman PLC for £1250.25

03 August Invoice 1346 sent to M. P. Electrics Ltd for £82.25

04 August Invoice X217 received from P. Thompson Ltd for £95.34

05 August Credit note P254 received from Breman PLC for £90.10

06 August Invoice 1347 sent to R. Bingley for £20.00

07 August Credit note CN121 sent to R. T. Electronics Ltd for £10.00

08 August Invoice 14279 received from A. Bognor Ltd for £324.76

09 August Credit note H20 received from P. Thompson Ltd for £12.30

10 August Invoice 1348 sent to R. T. Electronics Ltd for £27.59

11 August Credit note CN122 sent to R. Bingley for £5.00

12 August Invoice 18948 received from H. Charlton Ltd for £345.99

13 August Invoice 1349 sent to R. T. Electronics Ltd for £675.45

Element assignment

Buying and selling

This assignment can help you to provide evidence for assessment, or claim the following Core Skills.

Communication

Present information in a variety of visual forms

Communicate in writing

Participate in oral and non-verbal communication

Application of number

Apply numerical skills and techniques

Information Technology

Use a range of technological equipment and systems

Personal Skills

Relate to and interact effectively with individuals and groups

Work effectively as a member of a team

Deal with a combination of routine and non-routine tasks

The class should be arranged into an even number of groups with not more than four in each group. One half of the groups should be involved in the purchasing process and the other half should be involved in the selling process. One purchasing team should be appointed to deal with each selling team.

Selling team

You work for a company called Widget Supply Ltd which manufactures kitchen supplies for the retail trade.

1 Design a series of sales documents using a suitable computer package. (NB the first step is to produce a catalogue and a price list.)

2 Issue relevant documentation to the purchasing team at appropriate stages in this simulation. Keep copies of all documentation.

3 Make sure that your documentation corresponds with the price list and the catalogue.

4 Negotiate appropriate terms with the purchasing team.

5 Assume VAT at the current rate.

Purchasing t eam

You work for a company called Kitchen Supplies Ltd which buys and sells kitchen products. You are shortly to receive a catalogue and price list from a company called Widget Supply Ltd.

1 Using a suitable computer package, design a series of purchasing documentation.

2 Issue documentation at the relevant stages in this simulation.

3 Make sure that your documentation corresponds with the price list and catalogue.

4 Negotiate favourable terms with the selling team.

5 Assume VAT at the current rate.

chapter **18** BUSINESS PERFORMANCE

The performance of any organisation is in some way related to its stated objectives. In order to review the performance and assess whether such objectives have been achieved, an organisation requires financial information.

Financial information helps managers to plan and control activities. It is also required by outsiders – such as shareholders, creditors, the government, potential investors and others who have some interest in the organisation. The development and communication of such data is the role of an organisation's accounting system.

In this chapter we look at the need to monitor organisational performance. The type and nature of accounting information which can be drawn from an organisation is then explained so that judgements can be made about an organisation's activities.

▪ WHAT IS PERFORMANCE? ▪

Whether we are at school, at college, in an interview or meeting the parents of a new friend, we are concerned, to a greater or lesser extent, with how we get on, and how we might get on or perform in the future. In order to measure the results of such experiences we rely on **information** and **feedback.** Some of the information we receive might be precisely measured – for example, perhaps you achieved 64 per cent in an examination or took 2 hours 50 minutes and 25 seconds to run a marathon. This sort of information is described as **quantitative.** Other information may not be capable of precise measurement but may nevertheless support a view or a considered judgement – for example, somebody saying 'I liked that jacket', 'that colour is nice' or 'that car seems fast'. This sort of information is described as **qualitative**. Whether we like the information we receive will largely depend upon our **objectives** or **goals**. If, as above, you achieve 64 per cent in an examination and you expected or hoped to get 50 per cent, you would have exceeded your objectives. If you hoped for 70 per cent you would have been disappointed and not achieved your goal.

In the same way, organisations must be concerned with their performance and with what they are likely to be doing in the future. As we saw in Chapter 1, organisations do have goals and objectives which they strive to achieve. Just as we have to use quantitative and/or qualitative information to indicate a standard by which we can judge our success or failure, organisations are in exactly the same position.

Case Study

The world of British Airways

The following edited extracts are from a statement by Lord King, when he was Chairman of British Airways:

'British Airways is not only the world's largest international airline – it is also the world's leading airline, and one of the most profitable.

'Our corporate statement of objectives lists seven goals, and we have new information systems to track our progress in achieving them.

'First of all, we must be safe and secure. Safety has always been our paramount concern, and it must remain so. Safety and security are areas of no compromise.

'Our second goal is another overriding objective: to deliver a strong and consistent financial performance. As any business person knows, you must make profits if you are to maintain and expand your business. *The airline business is often regarded as cyclical.* We have to prove that we can produce good profits consistently.

'We aim to secure a leading share of air travel business worldwide with a significant presence in all major geographical markets. *Hence our global strategy.*

'We seek to provide overall superior service and *good value for money in every market segment* in which we compete, and we are out to excel in anticipating and quickly responding to customer needs and competitor activity.

'Any service industry's real strength is its staff. Our policy is to sustain a working environment that attracts, *retains and develops committed employees* who share in the success of the company.

'Finally, our intention is to be a good neighbour, concerned for the community and the environment.

'Overall, our aim is to be the best and most successful company in the airline industry. It is an objective that we are in no doubt we can achieve.'

1 Identify British Airways' seven goals.
2 Why do organisations require goals?
3 Explain the following:
   a 'The airline business is often regarded as cyclical.'
   b 'Hence our global strategy.'
   c 'good value for money in every market a segment'.
   d 'retains and develops committed employees'.
4 Comment briefly upon how the BA information systems might measure the company's success in achieving its stated goals.
5 What is an overriding objective?

Organisations use information to cover as wide a range of activities as possible. The more thorough and accurate the information, the more successful decision-making is likely to be and the better the performance. On the other hand, misleading information may result in poor decisions and poor performance.

Every level of management within an organisation has different information requirements for improving performance. For example:

- **Strategic** level managers deal with policy decisions and matters concerning the future of their organisation. They need summarised information from all parts of the organisation, as well as from outside.
- **Tactical** level managers make decisions based upon strategic policy decisions. They are invariably concerned with analysing issues *within* the organisation and often require information relating to time periods.
- **Organisational** decision- makers deal with the 'grass roots' – the day-to-day running of an organisation. They need information which helps them to solve short-term practical problems.

How does a manager know what information to concentrate on to achieve the organisation's objectives? Remember Coloroll, the home furnishings group. Coloroll collapsed in June 1990 with debts of around £400 million. The company's objective had been to build a solid base for expansion, and by 1988 the group had annual sales of around £300 million. The target set for 1995 was £1 billion, but this it was destined to miss: poor management, over-emphasis on market-share figures and neglect of cash income contributed to the group's downfall.

The lesson to be learned from Coloroll is quite clear. All organisations, whether large or small, in the private or public sector, have a common feature – they all have to deal with financial information. If an organisation wishes to pursue its objectives in order to improve performance, it must not neglect its management of financial resources.

· THE ACCOUNTING PROCESS ·

An accounting system consists of a series of methods and procedures which are used to keep track of financial activities and can be used to summarise activities in a form suitable for decision-making. In doing this accounting is acting as an **information system** by processing business data so that interested parties can be provided with the means to understand how well or badly the organisation is performing.

The three basic steps in the accounting process are:

- recording financial activities
- classifying information
- summarising data.

Recording financial activities. The first function of an accounting system is to create an organised record of business activities. For example, whenever a transaction takes place, even if it involves a credit purchase or sale, it has to be recorded. The recording of a transaction may be through a series of accounting books, by using a computerised accounting system, or on the basis of some form of scanning media.

Classifying information. A list of business transactions and records would be too large, diverse and unwieldy for decision-makers unless it was classified into a series of groups and categories.

Summarising data. For accounting information to be useful it must be summarised. For example, accounting information might be summarised by division, or according to products or departments.

It is quite possible that the investors of one company will want to compare the accounting information of one organisation with the accounting information of another. For example, they might wish to make comparisons to find out which organisation is financially stronger and might be a better investment. In order to do this they will have to *interpret the financial information* in order to help them to make the best decision.

Business data is the input into the accounting system, and the output is valuable **financial information**. Such information can then be passed to those who need it for decision-making and record-keeping purposes (see Figure 18.1).

For example, managers require information in order to run the organisation efficiently by monitoring the results of their decisions. Shareholders want to assess the performance of managers and need to know how much profit or income they can expect to take from the business. Suppliers need to know whether the organisation can pay its debts, and customers may wish to ensure that supplies will be

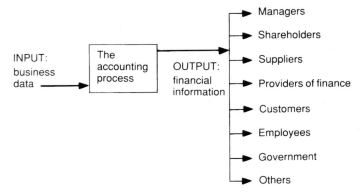

Figure 18.1 *The accounting process*

forthcoming. Any provider of finance for the organisation – such as a bank – will wish to know about the organisation's ability to make repayments of a loan. The tax authorities (Inland Revenue and Customs & Excise) require information so that they can make accurate assessments for tax. Employees have a right to know how an organisation is performing and how secure their jobs are. Financial advisors and brokers need to know about an organisation's activities so that they can advise their clients accurately.

Financial accounting

The process of accounting can be divided into two broad areas. **Financial accounting** is primarily concerned with the recording process and the information that can be extracted from such a process. It ensures that an organisation's accounts give a **true and fair view** of its activities and that they comply with the provisions of the Companies Acts.

At the end of a certain period, accountants prepare summary statements – called **final accounts**. By studying these, shareholders know how the directors or managers have performed on their behalf. From the final accounts, **ratios** and other figures can be extracted which provide fairly precise **indicators of performance.**

Financial accounting involves auditing, bookkeeping, advice on taxation, insolvency and many other areas.

Management accounting

Though the information from financial accounting is important, it deals only with the past and tends to view the organisation as a whole. **Management accounting** is concerned with providing information for managers so that they can plan, control and make decisions about future activities. It involves guiding an organisation in a particular direction so that it can achieve its objectives. Business operations can be closely monitored to ensure that processes, products, departments and operations are managed efficiently.

The accounting profession

The accounting profession is represented by a number of different bodies. For somebody to call themselves a **qualified accountant**, he or she must have passed examinations to have become a full member of one of these professional bodies. They include:

Institute of Chartered Accountants in England and
    Wales
Institute of Chartered Accountants in Ireland
Institute of Chartered Accountants in Scotland
Chartered Association of Certified Accountants
Chartered Institute of Management Accountants
Chartered Institute of Public Finance and
    Accountancy

Standards

If a number of accountants were presented with the same data and asked to present the accounts for an organisation they might well come up with different figures or arrive at different conclusions. This happens because estimates have to be made about future events, and this involves an element of opinion and guesswork. For example, in calculating depreciation – how an asset loses its value over time – estimates have to be made for the useful life of each asset; accountants will have different estimates.

The 1970s saw the appearance of the first Statements of Standard Accounting Practice (SSAPs), designed to ensure consistency and comparability between the financial statements of companies. These standards describe the approved methods of accounting which should be applied to all final accounts so that a 'true and fair' view is obtained.

Case Study

The Accounting Standards Board

On 1 August 1990 the Accounting Standards Board took over from the Accounting Standards Committee. Unlike the ASC which was a joint committee of the six major accounting bodies, the new Board is independent of the professional institutes and will set accounting standards in its own right. Creation of the Accounting Standards Board is a progressive step designed to produce a better world of accounting.

In the 1960s the growth of the accounting profession had gone unnoticed. However, this quiet progress was brought to an abrupt halt following the hostile takeover of Associated Electrical Industries (AEI) by General Electric Company (GEC). In 1967, AEI had forecast a profit of £10 million, and GEC based its takeover bid partly on this expected profit. But the actual results for 1967, revealed after the takeover had been completed, showed an AEI loss of £4.5 million. In the ensuing controversy it became clear that much of the difference arose because of different subjective judgements. This led to the formation of the Accounting Standards Committee and SSAPs.

In more recent years there have been further concerns about the ASC; for example:

- a general failure to respond to emerging issues
- a lack of timeliness in setting standards
- doubts over the independence of the standard setters
- concern over the flexibility of their pronouncements.

There is a feeling today that the Accounting Standards Board will have greater independence.

1 Why are SSAPs needed?
2 What were the criticisms of the ASC?
3 What are the benefits of an independent Accounting Standards Board?

A good example of one of these standards is SSAP2 which refers to the four fundamental concepts that should underlie financial accounts (see Figure 18.2). The **going concern** concept assumes that an organisation will persist with its current activities into the foreseeable future. The

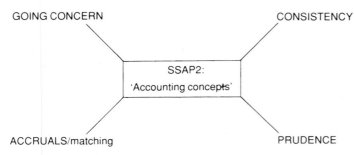

Figure 18.2 *Accounting concepts*

accruals/matching concept recognises that costs are incurred as soon as their liability is taken on, and not later as money is paid. Thus as the end of an accounting period all transactions relating to that period will appear in the accounts whether payments have been made or not.

The **consistency** concept is that the accounting treatment of similar items should be consistently applied within each accounting period and from one period to the next. Finally, the concept of **prudence** (or **conservatism**) is that businesses should not lay claim to profits unless they are sure they have been earned.

COMMUNICATING ACCOUNTING INFORMATION

The information an accounting user requires will usually depend on the types of decisions to be made. For example, the manager of a small department might want information on daily operating costs, whereas shareholders will require information on profitability over the last period so that they can assess the value of their investment.

As the nature of the accounting information required will vary according to each category of user, an accounting system has to cater for each need wherever possible.

Financial statements

Final accounts are financial statements produced at the end of each year's trading. Basic financial statements include:

- a trading account which simply shows how gross profit is arrived at
- a profit and loss account which uses gross profit as a

starting point and adds other income and deducts expenses until the net profit is calculated
- a balance sheet which shows what an organisation owes and owns at a particular point in time.

Managerial data and reports

In addition to financial statements, managers require more detailed accounting data for planning and controlling the operations of an organisation. Such information is tailored to their specific needs.

USING ACCOUNTING INFORMATION

Accounting goes further than just the creation of records and reports. The ultimate objective of accounting is to provide information in a form that will be useful, so that by analysing and interpreting it, better decisions can be made.

Interpretation of final accounts

An organisation's accounts can be analysed to pick out information that gives an indication of its performance and structure. The four major areas of interest are:

- profitability
- liquidity
- asset usage
- capital structure

and we shall look at each of these in turn.

Taken in isolation, figures in accounts have limited value. For example, what does it mean to say that a company has a profit of £6 million? It is better to look at how profits have risen or fallen since the previous year, how other similar companies have fared, how much the company has invested to make a profit of £6 million, and so on.

By reducing financial information to **ratios**, we can compare the performances of different companies and performances from year to year. However, ratios must be used with care and a good understanding of the sorts of questions they can answer effectively. Before using a ratio always ask yourself *why* you are using it and *what* it is likely to tell you.

Profitability

To assess the profitability of an organisation one can turn to the published accounts. We have seen that the balance sheet gives a snapshot view of the organisation; alternatively one can take the video view from the profit and loss account or look at the cash flow statement. If it is a public limited company (PLC) one can look at the Stock Exchange valuation – this reflects the stock market's view of how the company is doing, based on expert study of the accounts and other snippets of current information.

Frequently one will use accounting ratios – the relationship between two items in the accounts– to assess the health of a company. The figures used come directly from the final accounting statements. See Chapter 22 for details of final accounts.

Return on capital employed (ROCE)

A good indication of profitability is the relationship between the capital employed in the business and the profits the business has generated. This ratio is expressed as a percentage and is calculated in the following way:

$$\text{Percentage return on capital employed} = \frac{\text{net profit for year}}{\text{capital employed}} \times 100\%$$

(Note: capital employed = net assets before deduction of long-term debt.)

The figure for capital employed is usually taken as the figure at the beginning of the year as this is the capital that generated the profit in the following year. The best way to think about the percentage return is to compare it with other investments. For example, if you invest £100 with a building society and receive £10 a year in interest (before tax), then you can see that you are getting a return on your capital of 10 per cent. This is a good measure of how effective your investment is. ROCE is therefore a quick and useful way of calculating the effectiveness of an investment in the business: it relates profitability to other investments.

Gross profit percentage

The gross profit percentage is a ratio that is extracted from the trading account. It relates gross profit to sales revenue:

$$\text{Gross profit percentage} = \frac{\text{gross profit}}{\text{sales revenue}} \times 100\%$$

For example, if sales of £100 000 produce a gross profit of £25 000, then the gross profit percentage is 25 per cent. In terms of buying stock and selling it, this means that every £1 worth of sales gives a 25p gross profit.

The gross profit percentage should be calculated at regular intervals, and if it rises or falls the reason should be investigated. If the percentage falls this may indicate that stock is being stolen or damaged. Alternatively, it could mean that the cost of stock is rising and the increase has not been passed on to the consumer.

Task

Why might a small business constantly check its stock and keep a close eye on its gross profit percentage?

Net profit percentage

The net profit percentage is calculated as follows:

$$\text{Net profit percentage} = \frac{\text{net profit}}{\text{sales revenue}} \times 100\%$$

It should be similar from year to year and should be comparable with the ratios of other enterprises in the same field of business. It takes into account business expenses.

If the *gross* profit percentage is consistent from year to year, any changes in the *net* profit percentage could indicate an increase in overheads (costs) as a proportion of sales revenue, and a need to make economies or to adjust prices.

Liquidity

Liquidity defines the ability of an organisation to convert its assets into cash. Cash is *perfectly liquid*. Assets such as money in the bank and debtors are highly liquid, while assets such as buildings and machinery are clearly illiquid. It is always important to have a range of assets to meet the demands of any short-term creditors if required.

Current or working capital ratio

The **working capital ratio** is the ratio of current assets to current liabilities.

Clearly some assets are more liquid than others and the time factor involved in transferring them into cash is something an experienced manager should be able to estimate. A prudent ratio is sometimes said to be 2:1, but this might not necessarily be the case if stocks form the bulk of the value of the current assets. Companies have to be aware that bank overdrafts are repayable on demand and that figures extracted from a balance sheet might reflect the position of the current assets and liabilities at the time but not over the whole year. In practice most businesses operate with a slightly lower ratio than 2:1.

Quick ratio

The **quick ratio** (also called the **acid-test ratio** or the liquidity ratio) is the ratio of current assets to current liabilities *when stock value is taken off the current assets.*

The quick ratio is a tougher test than the working capital ratio because it excludes stocks, which as we have seen may not be immediately available as cash to meet short-term liabilities. A rule of thumb for the quick ratio is that it should be greater than 1.0. This will, however, depend upon the type of business, the relationship with suppliers and several other factors.

Debtor's collection period

This is calculated by the formula:

$$\text{Debtor's collection period} = \frac{\text{debtors}}{\text{average daily sales}}$$

It may be possible to improve a company's liquidity by reducing the debt collection period. Customers who are late in paying their debts are receiving free finance for their own activities. This ratio indicates the average number of days of credit received by customers before they provide a payment.

The average sales are calculated by dividing yearly sales by 365. The normal period of debt is between 30–60 days.

Period of credit taken from suppliers

This is calculated by the formula:

$$\text{Credit period} = \frac{\text{creditors}}{\text{average daily purchases}}$$

Now we are looking at the other side of the coin. Just as liquidity can be analysed by looking at the debt collection period, it could also be helpful to look at the average credit period taken from suppliers.

Task

The table shows a set of ratios calculated from the final accounts of a small laundry for 1992 and 1993. What might the figures indicate about the business? What questions would you want to ask to find out more about the changes that have taken place?

	1992	1993
Gross profits as a percentage of sales	10%	12%
Net profit as a percentage of sales	11%	10%
Net profit as a percentage of capital employed (ROCE)	12%	10%
Current ratio	2:1	1.5:1
Acid-test ratio	0.5:1	0.5:1

Asset usage

Asset usage ratios can be used to assess how effectively an organisation is using its assets and how its performance might be improved by using the assets more efficiently. Comparisons can then be made with similar companies.

Stock turnover

An organisation does not want to have its stock hanging around. **Stock turnover** is the average period of time an item of stock is held before it is used or sold. The adequacy of this ratio depends upon the type of business an organisation is in. For example, a jeweller may hold the same items of stock for a long period of time. It would be unwise for a fashion clothes retailer or baker to hold stock for the same period of time. Stock turnover can be calculated by the formula:

$$\text{Stock turnover} = \frac{\text{cost of sales}}{\text{average stock}}$$

In this formula the average stock is calculated by adding together the values of the opening stock and the closing stock and dividing the result by 2.

Many organisations today hold smaller stock levels than in the past. Often they operate a 'just in time' system – this means that they keep just enough stock to meet current demand. (See page337.) Consequently they have a higher stock turnover ratio.

Task

List six types of business which need to replace existing stock regularly. List six which would probably need to keep the same stock for a considerable length of time. Identify the problems associated with having a low rate of stock turnover.

Asset utilisation

This ratio shows how effectively fixed assets are used to generate sales revenue. It is measured by:

$$\text{Asset utilisation} = \frac{\text{sales}}{\text{fixed assets}}$$

This is really an efficiency ratio designed to show how well managers are using fixed assets to generate sales. However, as with all ratios we must be careful. Some businesses need only limited fixed assets (e.g. a market trader). Other businesses require substantial fixed assets (e.g. an oil company). The level of the ratio will depend upon the type of organisation.

Capital structure

Companies are financed by share capital, loans and funds from several other sources. The shareholders or owners receive dividends on their investments, and people or organisations which lend money receive interest. Both investors and suppliers of loan finance will want to ensure that their money has been invested wisely and that it brings in a secure return. In particular they might be interested in the ratio of share capital to loan capital.

Gearing

Gearing makes a direct comparison between the capital in a business provided by ordinary shareholders and that provided in the form of long-term loans and preference shares. It is calculated from the formula:

$$\text{Gearing} = \frac{\text{interest-bearing capital}}{\text{risk capital}} \times 100\%$$

It can also be represented by:

$$\frac{\text{prior charge capital (long-term loans and preference shares)}}{\text{equity (ordinary shares plus reserves)}}$$

A company is highly geared if the gearing is more than 100 per cent, or low-geared if the gearing is less than 100 per cent.

The higher the gearing, the higher the proportion of a firm's revenue that must be used to pay interest. This means that fixed costs are higher and, therefore, average costs are higher. Higher average costs put the firm at a competitive disadvantage when compared with rivals. Highly geared companies are more likely to fail particularly when there is a recession, or when high interest rates need to be paid.

If a highly geared company wishes to raise extra finance it may find it difficult to raise a loan. The great attractions to a company of raising money through loans are that loans do not carry voting rights, interest payments attract tax relief, and the reward to debt holders is generally lower than that required by shareholders.

A company may be highly geared because:

- it has just started up
- it is in a capital-intensive industry with many fixed assets which are secured against loans
- it has owners who wish to maintain control and so do not want outside shareholders
- the owners are not fully aware of the dangers of being highly geared
- total return on capital is expected to exceed the returns

required by debenture holders so that higher gearing will deliver super-returns to shareholders.

Gearing levels vary from organisation to organisation and from industry to industry. If a firm has a stable background, high gearing may be safer.

Case Study

The Maxwell legacy

The Maxwell publishing empire was created by the drive of Robert Maxwell, who died suddenly in November 1991 whilst on a yachting holiday. Robert Maxwell controlled many businesses around the world, including *The European* and *The Daily Mirror* in the UK. Finance for the various enterprises was raised not only through the sale of shares, but also on the basis of large-scale loans. Many of these loans were secured against shares in the companies. Despite the recession of the early 1990s the businesses continued to expand their interests.

At the time of Robert Maxwell's death, the Maxwell Communications Corporation (MCC) owed banks £1.4 billion. Though the businesses were mainly sound they borrowed at a time when money was not cheap to borrow and there was a general climate of recession. The general feeling in the industry was that the businesses had become too highly geared and had over-traded.

1 Make a list of the dangers of relying too heavily on loan capital.

2 Explain what you think is meant by 'over-trading'.

Interest cover is a measure of the risk of gearing. This ratio is calculated by the formula:

$$\text{Interest cover} = \frac{\text{profit before interest and tax}}{\text{interest paid in the year}}$$

If the ratio is less than 1:1 a company has not earned enough to cover interest charges. Some people argue that a sensible ratio is 3:1.

Dangers of using ratios

People studying an organisation's financial statements have to be careful when using ratios. Making comparisons can sometimes be unrealistic, particularly when so many organisations vary so considerably in size, structure and management style. For example, they may value their assets using different methods, and financial information may be distorted when we compare one year with the next because of the way in which inflation distorts prices.

Furthermore, financial information only provides a partial picture of what a business is trying to achieve. For example, it ignores the human relations aspects.

However, ratios are a useful means of spotting problems in a business and can provide a constructive guide as to profitability and financial strength.

· USING MANAGEMENT INFORMATION ·

Management accounting supports the managers of an organisation by providing them with vital information designed to help them with their decision-making processes. In doing this management accounting involves a cycle as shown in Figure 18.3.

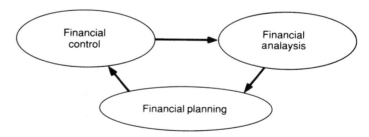

Figure 18.3 *The management accounting process*

Financial analysis is required to find out where an organisation is and to ensure that its objectives are realistic and can be achieved. The **planning process** involves developing a long-term strategy as well as a series of action plans which enable an organisation to achieve its objectives. **Financial control** involves monitoring the degree of achievement of objectives and then feeding this information back to decision-makers.

Management accounting is used by **insiders** within an organisation. As management accounting reports are used exclusively by managers they can be tailored in a way that suits these managers best.

For management decision-makers, **costs** represent money measurements that can be used to assess the performance of either the whole organisation or parts of it. Costs are collected for three main purposes:

1 To assist in planning decisions – for example, how many products to manufacture, which products to make and how to arrive at a selling price.

2 To assist in the control of operations by creating systems such as budgets which help to assess the performance of current operations against planned operations.

3 To help with the measurement of profits from parts of the organisation as well as the organisation as a whole.

Costs can be assessed in two main forms. **Responsibility accounting** uses costs and associates them with individual managers and their departmental responsibilities within the hierarchy. Costs can also be related to a **product** and the development of that product into a form which is acceptable for the market.

Chapter 21 describes the use of costs in the planning process. It looks at:

● *Marginal costing* – This is a technique that forecasts profits from different sales levels.

● *Total costing* – This method of costing helps managers to fix prices so that costs can be met and profits can be made.

● *Budgetary control* – This form of responsibility accounting puts an onus upon managers to perform in a pre-determined way.

Task

Find out how both responsibility-based and product-based accounting decisions are undertaken in either the organisation you work for or the institution you attend.

MEETING NON-FINANCIAL OBJECTIVES

For nearly all organisations, profitability or meeting cost targets are the overriding objectives. However, today many also specify non-financial objectives which they consider to be important goals. Such goals frequently impose an element of **social responsibility** on their actions.

The traditional view of social responsibility is that, by aiming to maximise profits, organisations generate wealth which benefits society as a whole. Many organisations today, however, realise that they have to balance the interests of their shareholders with those of society as a whole. By doing so they are creating a better external environment for the organisation in the long-term. Though profits should be maximised, the end result should be a satisfactory level of profit which is compatible with the attainment of a range of social goals.

Task

Make a list of non-financial objectives which you think a fast-food restaurant chain should have.

Case Study

Environmental accounting

Though accountants are not always noted for being dynamic, it may come as some surprise to find that the profession is right at the forefront of the environmental debate.

Environmental accounting involves organisations in assessing the environmental impact of their activities, such as increased pollution and the depletion of natural resources. At the recent environmental reporting awards held by the Chartered Association of Certified Accountants, Mike Bett, deputy chairman of award-winning British

Telecom, pointed out that BT's report had shattered the public delusion that BT was a clean company. In fact the company used CFCs, consumed 1.2 per cent of the country's electricity and burned 125 million litres of vehicle fuel annually. Mr Bett pointed out that BT had 'addressed the environment as a serious business issue'. Publication of this environmental report had helped to formalise BT's internal accounting systems across the company. It allowed for targets to be set, and put the company ahead of competitors in a market-place where environmental values were becoming of increasing importance. So far BT is just one of a handful of companies to have adopted this approach.

The European Commission has put environmental accounting high on its action programme for the environment. Their objective is for organisations to include full environmental costs to society for the production of goods or provision of services. To achieve this by the year 2000, the EC has asked the accounting profession for help.

The UK has taken a strong lead in this area. At present the government is considering its reply to a report published by the financial sector working group of its advisory committee on business and the environment. The group has made several recommendations designed to improve the quality and extent of environmental reporting, including a suggestion that the Stock Exchange should consider requiring environmental disclosures by companies as a condition for listing. It is hoped that such measures will mark a turning point after which all organisations will come to terms with their responsibilities to the wider community.

1 Why should all organisations be responsible for the impact of their activities?
2 List the benefits and costs of developing environmental values.
3 What are the arguments for and against companies making environmental disclosures in their annual report?

Element assignment

Analysing an annual report

This assignment can help you to provide evidence for assessment, or claim the following Core Skills:

Communication
Receive and respond to a variety of information
Communicate in writing

Application of number
Apply numerical skills and techniques

Personal skills
Use information sources

Using your library reference section, obtain the address of a large company listed on the main market of the Stock Exchange. Write to that company, explain what you are doing and ask if they could send you a copy of their annual report and accounts.

Task 1
Look through the report and, in particular, analyse the statement made by either the chairman or chief executive. Make a list of the objectives which you feel the organisation identifies, and then comment on the extent to which you feel that they have achieved these objectives over the last year.

Task 2
What financial statements appear in the report? Explain broadly the usefulness of each statement and what each attempts to show.

Task 3
Explain how ratios would help a user to understand the financial statements. Relate one ratio to the balance sheet and one ratio to the profit and loss account in support of your answer.

Task 4
Comment briefly on how the company you have chosen meets its social responsibilities.

chapter **_19_** SOURCES OF FINANCE

There are many issues to be considered before financing any proposition. Having set aims and developed objectives, an organisation has to engage in financial planning which is part of an overall business plan. Such a document is made available to a prospective lender and hence influences availability and cost of finance.

In this chapter sources of finance are identified for both individuals and organisations. In all cases borrowers have to consider how much money they need to borrow, how easily they can afford the repayments and how long they need the money for.

· SOURCES OF PERSONAL FINANCE ·

A crucial element in personal financial planning is to evaluate your **present position**. By carefully looking at your own resources as well as others which are available, you can then work out the most efficient way of using them to achieve your aims and objectives.

Sources of personal finance will vary for each individual according to their own circumstances. For example, those with a higher and more secure income will find it easier to use other sources of finance such as a mortgage or a loan.

Financial planning will help individuals to identify sources of finance to reflect such different circumstances.

Earnings

Most young people first earn an income with a part-time job such as a paper round, weekend work or holiday work. They might refer to their income as either a wage or salary. **Wages** tend to relate to hourly effort and are paid weekly while **salaries** are usually paid to people who have 'white-collar' jobs and are paid monthly.

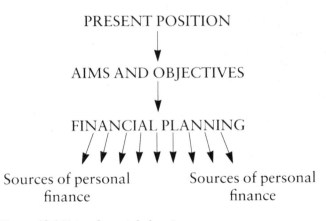

Figure 19.1 *Using financial planning*

Tax on earnings

For taxation purposes earnings subject to income tax may include:

- all wages and salaries, including tips, bonuses, benefits in kind such as company car, cheap loans etc.
- interest from banks and building societies
- dividends/profits from investments such as stocks and shares

- state benefits
- pensions by the state or by a former employer.

Employers have a responsibility to see that everybody pays their tax. They do this through the PAYE system. PAYE stands for Pay As You Earn. Employers deduct tax from wages and then hand it over to the Inland Revenue. This saves each individual from having to pay the tax themselves at once at the end of the tax year.

(Note: the tax year runs from the 6 April of one year to 5 April of the following year.)

Employees do *not* have to pay tax on all of their earnings. Everybody can earn or receive certain amounts of income during the tax year without having to pay tax. **Tax allowances** represent the amount of income an individual can receive before starting to pay tax.

The main tax allowances are:

- the personal allowance – every UK resident is entitled to a personal allowance
- the married couple's allowance –a married man who is living with his wife for any part of the tax year is entitled to a married couple's allowance as well as his personal allowance (From 6 April 1993 husbands/ wives can elect for the married couple's allowance to be given to the wife instead, or be split equally between them.)
- the additional personal allowance – mainly for single parents
- the widow's bereavement allowance
- the blind person's allowance.

As well as tax allowances there are tax reliefs. Tax reliefs are not allowances but they affect tax in the same way. This is because the amount of income an individual receives before paying tax can also depend upon outgoings (payments they make out of income). Tax reliefs may be obtained on the following:

- interest on loans to buy property. Most people get basic tax relief through the MIRAS system which automatically involves individuals making lower interest payments to their bank or building society. Tax relief is eligible on the first £30 000 of a mortgage.
- interest on other loans such as improving property to rent out or to buy a car or machinery necessary to carry out work
- donations to charity

- where expenses at work are incurred – this may include subscriptions to professional bodies
- against pension scheme contributions.

Task

Identify your main tax allowances and tax reliefs.

Taxable income is calculated by deducting personal allowances and tax reliefs from gross income. These are reflected by the tax code. Everybody's tax code will normally comprise a number and a letter. The number is the total amount of allowances, but with the last figure left off. For example, allowances of £3695 would give a code of 369. Most people who start their first job would have the letter L after the code number, which reflects the basic personal allowance. There are other letters for married men, single parents and people over 65 years of age.

Case Study

Calculating a tax code

EXAMPLE 1

Sally Nicholls works for a local plumber. She has a tool allowance of £90 a year.

<u>For the tax year 1992–93</u>

	£
Personal allowance	*3445*
Tool allowance	*90*
Total allowances	*3535*

Allowances to set against income £3535.

To turn these allowances into a tax code, the last figure is taken off and the letter L is added because Sally is single. So her tax code is 353L.

EXAMPLE 2

Ramesh Patel is 36 and married.

For the tax year 1992–93

	£
Personal allowance	3445
Married couple's allowance	1720
Total allowances	5165

Allowances to set against income £5165.

To turn these allowances into a tax code, the last figure is taken off and the letter H is added because Ramesh is married. So his tax code is 516H.

1 How much can Sally earn per year before having to pay tax?
2 Explain the difference between the code for a single person and the code for a married person with a married couple's allowance.
3 If Ramesh earns £12 000 per annum, calculate his taxable income.
4 If Ramesh is taxed at 25 per cent on his taxable income, how much tax will he pay over the year?

Everybody receives a notification of income tax coding on a form P2(T) (see Figure 19.2). Under PAYE the total of the allowances is spread equally among the number of pay days in the tax year. This would be 52 for weekly paid workers and 12 for employees paid monthly. If someone is not paid over a number of weeks, the tax-free pay then, of course, they would not have to pay tax.

In the year 1993/4 there were three rates of tax which could be applied to taxable income:

	£
Lower Rate 20%	1–2000
Basic Rate 25%	2001–23 700
Higher Rate 40%	over 23 700

If someone therefore earns more than £23 700, they will be taxed at 20 per cent on their taxable income under £2000, 25 per cent on their taxable income under £23 700 and at 40 per cent on their taxable income over £23 700.

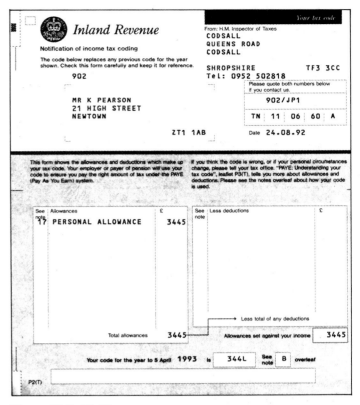

Figure 19.2 *P2 (T)*

Task

Identify two reasons for there being different rates of tax.

An employer will be provided with two sets of tables which will help them to work out the right amount of tax to be paid. Figure 19.3 – the Free Pay tables – will show the weekly and monthly free pay for each tax code. Figure 19.4 – the Taxable Pay tables – will show the tax due on taxable income at the basic rate.

Week 1
April 6th - April 12th

FREE PAY

Code	Total free pay to date £	Code	Total free pay to date £	Code	Total free pay to date £	Code	Total free pay to date £	Code	Total free pay to date £	Code	Total free pay to date £	Code	Total free pay to date £	Code	Total free pay to date £
0	NIL														
1	0·37	61	11·91	121	23·45	181	34·99	241	46·52	301	58·06	361	69·60	421	81·14
2	0·56	62	12·10	122	23·64	182	35·18	242	46·72	302	58·25	362	69·79	422	81·33
3	0·75	63	12·29	123	23·83	183	35·37	243	46·91	303	58·45	363	69·99	423	81·52
4	0·95	64	12·49	124	24·02	184	35·56	244	47·10	304	58·64	364	70·18	424	81·72
5	1·14	65	12·68	125	24·22	185	35·75	245	47·29	305	58·83	365	70·37	425	81·91
6	1·33	66	12·87	126	24·41	186	35·95	246	47·49	306	59·02	366	70·56	426	82·10
7	1·52	67	13·06	127	24·60	187	36·14	247	47·68	307	59·22	367	70·75	427	82·29
8	1·72	68	13·25	128	24·79	188	36·33	248	47·87	308	59·41	368	70·95	428	82·49
9	1·91	69	13·45	129	24·99	189	36·52	249	48·06	309	59·60	369	71·14	429	82·68
10	2·10	70	13·64	130	25·18	190	36·72	250	48·25	310	59·79	370	71·33	430	82·87
11	2·29	71	13·83	131	25·37	191	36·91	251	48·45	311	59·99	371	71·52	431	83·06
12	2·49	72	14·02	132	25·56	192	37·10	252	48·64	312	60·18	372	71·72	432	83·25
13	2·68	73	14·22	133	25·75	193	37·29	253	48·83	313	60·37	373	71·91	433	83·45
14	2·87	74	14·41	134	25·95	194	37·49	254	49·02	314	60·56	374	72·10	434	83·64
15	3·06	75	14·60	135	26·14	195	37·68	255	49·22	315	60·75	375	72·29	435	83·83

Figure 19.3 *Free pay*

Columns 1 and 2

(Tax at 25%)

Tax Due on Taxable Pay from £1 to £99

Total TAXABLE PAY to date £	Total TAX DUE to date £	Total TAXABLE PAY to date £	Total TAX DUE to date £
1	0.25	61	15.25
2	0.50	62	15.50
3	0.75	63	15.75
4	1.00	64	16.00
5	1.25	65	16.25
6	1.50	66	16.50
7	1.75	67	16.75
8	2.00	68	17.00
9	2.25	69	17.25
10	2.50	70	17.50
11	2.75	71	17.75
12	3.00	72	18.00
13	3.25	73	18.25
14	3.50	74	18.50
15	3.75	75	18.75

Tax Due on Taxable Pay from £100 to £23,700

Total TAXABLE PAY to date £	Total TAX DUE to date £	Total TAXABLE PAY to date £	Total TAX DUE to date £	Total TAXABLE PAY to date £	Total TAX DUE to date £	Total TAXABLE PAY to date £	Total TAX DUE to date £
100	25.00	6100	1525.00	12100	3025.00	18100	4525.00
200	50.00	6200	1550.00	12200	3050.00	18200	4550.00
300	75.00	6300	1575.00	12300	3075.00	18300	4575.00
400	100.00	6400	1600.00	12400	3100.00	18400	4600.00
500	125.00	6500	1625.00	12500	3125.00	18500	4625.00
600	150.00	6600	1650.00	12600	3150.00	18600	4650.00
700	175.00	6700	1675.00	12700	3175.00	18700	4675.00
800	200.00	6800	1700.00	12800	3200.00	18800	4700.00
900	225.00	6900	1725.00	12900	3225.00	18900	4725.00
1000	250.00	7000	1750.00	13000	3250.00	19000	4750.00
1100	275.00	7100	1775.00	13100	3275.00	19100	4775.00
1200	300.00	7200	1800.00	13200	3300.00	19200	4800.00
1300	325.00	7300	1825.00	13300	3325.00	19300	4825.00
1400	350.00	7400	1850.00	13400	3350.00	19400	4850.00
1500	375.00	7500	1875.00	13500	3375.00	19500	4875.00

Figure 19.4 *Taxable pay at 25%*

Weekly Pay

Week No.	Amount to subtract
	£
1	1.93
2	3.85
3	5.77
4	7.70
5	9.62
6	11.54
7	13.47
8	15.39
9	17.31
10	19.24
11	21.16
12	23.08
13	25.00
14	26.93
15	28.85

Figure 19.5 *Subtraction tables (to give the benefit of the lower rate band)*

We can see how these tables work by looking at two examples.

Example 1

Peter Jones is single and has a tax code of 365L. In week 1 (6–12 April) Peter earns £235. His pay is as follows:

	£
Week 1 pay	235.00
Less free pay	70.37
His taxable pay is:	164.63

(this is rounded down to £164.00)

Tax due on £164 =	£
on the first £100	25.00
on £64	16.00
	41.00
Less effects of the lower band in week 1	1.93
Tax to pay in week 1	39.07

Example 2

Rachel Miller is single and has a tax code of 370L. In week 1 (6–12 April) Rachel earns £280. Her pay is as follows:

	£
Week 1 pay	280.00
Less free pay	71.33
Her taxable pay is:	208.67

(this is rounded down to £208)

Tax due on £208 =	£
on the first £200	50.00
on £8	2.00
	52.00
Less effects of the lower band in week 1	1.93
Tax to pay in week 1	50.07

Task

Len Shoulder is single and has a tax code of 425L. In week 1 (6–12 April) Len earns £290. Calculate the tax due during that week.

Case Study

Why do we have to pay tax?

It is very easy either to say or think 'we are being taxed too heavily' or 'why should we have to pay for this?', but the effectiveness of our government in providing goods and services is really only dependent upon the ability of the tax-payer to supply them with adequate revenue to do so.

Imagine what it might be like if no-one paid a fair share towards the expenses of our country. We might immediately find ourselves threatened by other nations because we wouldn't have a defence budget. Many parents would not be able to afford to send their children to school. The protection from essential services such as the police or the fire brigade would not exist. If people could not afford health care their lives could be cut short. Each of these areas plus many more, such as consumer protection, housing, social services, a legal system, roads and sanitation ensure that we all enjoy a good 'quality of life'. Many of us take this quality of life for granted because we have always had it.

It is generally agreed by people of all political persuasions that everyone should pay a fair share towards the expenses of our country. For example, we all pay taxes when we purchase many of the articles which we buy in the shops in the form of VAT. There are also more than 26 million income tax payers in the UK. Total tax receipts in the UK exceed more than £140 billion. Each year the Chancellor of the Exchequer prepares 'The Autumn Statement' which includes an estimate of what the Government will spend in the coming year as well as an explanation of how the money will be raised.

1 Make a list of the services provided by the government and then number them in order of importance for you.
2 Express your views upon the amount of tax you are asked to pay. To what extent are these views dependent upon your political persuasion?
3 Identify areas where you feel that government spending should be (i) expanded or (ii) cut.

Other than the P2T mentioned earlier, two other tax forms are of particular importance.

a The **P45** helps an employer to work out the tax of a new employee. The form records the tax code, the total pay and the total tax paid to date. Part I of the P45 is sent to the Tax Office to inform them that an employee has left their job. Part II shows the starting point for tax deductions and Part III informs the Tax Office of the new employer.
b The P60 is received by all employees at the end of the year and provides them with a certificate of the tax paid in that year.

Case Study

The Taxpayer's Charter

In 1992 the Inland Revenue issued the following Taxpayer's Charter:

You are entitled to expect the Inland Revenue

To be fair
* *By settling your tax affairs impartially*
* *By expecting you to pay only what is due under the law*
* *By treating everyone with equal fairness*

To help you
* *To get your tax affairs right*
* *To understand your rights and obligations*
* *By providing clear leaflets and forms*
* *By giving information and assistance at enquiry offices*
* *By being courteous at all times*

To provide an efficient service
* *By settling your tax affairs promptly and accurately*
* *By keeping private affairs strictly confidential*
* *By using the information provided only as allowed by the law*
* *By keeping to a minimum your cost of complying with the law*
* *By keeping our costs down*

To be accountable for what we do
* *By publishing standards for ourselves and publishing how well we live up to them*

In response to the Taxpayer's Charter the Inland Revenue has worked hard to improve their levels of customer service. In doing this they have set up Mobile Enquiry Centres, produced a range of leaflets, reviewed their forms, initiated a system of Customer Service Managers in various parts of the country and set up a Minicom System to help the hearing impaired.

1 Explain briefly what the Taxpayer's Charter is designed to do.
2 Who benefits from the Charter?
3 Suggest two further ways in which the Inland Revenue could improve their levels of customer service.

Employees also have to make **National Insurance contributions** from their earnings. The payment of National Insurance enables an employee to claim a variety of benefits from the State such as a retirement pension and sickness benefits.

OTHER SOURCES OF PERSONAL FINANCE

Savings

These will include any amounts of money accumulated over a period of time. Saving money as cash under a mattress or in a teapot is clearly not wise because of risks such as fire and theft. At the same time it is important for savings to be effective and work on the behalf of their owner by generating interest.

There are four broad areas to consider with any form of savings. These are:

a The degree of *risk* involved with a savings investment. For example, savings with a bank or a building society will generally be safer than with stocks or shares.
b The *amount* will determine the return. Larger amounts invested will receive higher rates of interest.
c The degree of *access* to the savings. With instant access forms of saving there will be a lower rate of interest.
d The rate of *return* is the interest generated by the savings.

Types of savings

As well as the traditional bank or building society accounts, there are a number of alternative ways of maximising the returns from savings. For example:

- **Pensions** are a tax-efficient way of saving for the future. Tax relief can be obtained for contributions and a lump sum can be received as part of the pension.
- **Tax Exempt Special Savings Accounts (TESSAs)** were introduced in 1991. These provide the security of bank or building society accounts with the benefit of interest exempt from tax. The capital should not be touched for five years to gain the maximum tax advantage.
- **National Savings Certificates** provide competitive rates of interest but capital has to be tied up for five years. Moreover, though income from National Savings accounts is paid gross, it is taxable.
- **Personal Equity Plans (PEPs)** allow an individual to invest in the Stock Market and obtain tax-free and capital gains on investments. For example the Halifax Standard Income Advantage PEP quotes the following:

THE TAX FREE INVESTMENT

Tax free returns for faster growth

The Income Advantage PEP is an opportunity to obtain all your returns completely free from taxation. The income earned and the tax savings you make are invested back into your Plan, so that they can continue to grow. Over time, not paying tax can considerably increase the returns on your investment.

Please remember though, that as with all investments of this kind, nothing can be guaranteed. The value of your investment can go down as well as up.

Up to £6,000 may be invested in the Income Advantage Unit Trust within a Personal Equity Plan (PEP). Returns from this PEP are entirely free of income or capital gains tax giving a further boost to the rate at which your money can grow.

You can invest in an Income Advantage PEP – from as little as £50 per month, or a lump sum (minimum of £1,000), up to a limit of £6,000 in any tax year.

- **Stocks and shares** would include securities issued by companies, local authorities and central government. The return from these may vary widely and there is no guarantee that the investment would grow.
- **Unit trusts** are managed funds that buy and sell shares in a portfolio of shares on the investor's behalf.

Task

Look at the various savings schemes above and then answer the following questions:

1 Assume that you have been given *(i)* £1000 and *(ii)* £30 000. How would you invest each in order to maximise your return? Provide reasons why you chose each type of investment.

2 Explain the difference between a TESSA and a PEP.

3 Why are pensions a form of saving?

Borrowing

The main source of finance for many people is to borrow money so that they can be provided with goods or services *now* and pay for them *later.* Many different types of institutions compete for this type of business.

There are often a whole range of different prices and offers from lenders who try to make terms for their loans appear more attractive than those of their competitors. For example, advertisements for cars frequently seem to centre more on credit terms than on the vehicles themselves.

A wide variety of organisations offer different types of credit and borrowing facilities. These include banks, building societies, credit card companies, finance houses and retail stores. These organisations will, however, exclude applicants under the age of 18 as, in accordance with the Minors Contracts Act of 1987, any person under the age of 18 will not be legally bound to any contracts for money borrowed.

The **Annual Percentage Rate** (APR) is one figure which can be used to make comparisons with the true cost of

borrowing. The APR is the total annual cost to the borrower both in terms of interest *and* fees and is expressed as a percentage of the amount borrowed. As the APR includes fees it is not just a measure of the interest rate but is intended to be a measure of the full cost. Under the Consumer Credit Act of 1974 all loan and credit agreements, excluding mortgages and overdrafts, up to £15 000 have to be carefully documented and drafted in the form of a **Regulated Agreement.**

Task

Obtain details of either a form of credit you could select to purchase a specific article, or for a personal loan. Details of such credit arrangements could be found advertised in newspapers or magazines or in a bank or building society. Comment upon whether you feel that the credit being offered provides value for money. Support your answer with appropriate reasons.

When borrowing you need to ask the questions shown in Figure 19.6.

Before providing a customer with any form of credit a lender will almost certainly follow certain principles of lending.

For example, bankers who have the responsibility for advances of various types, frequently use different types

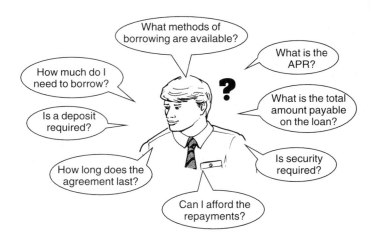

Figure 19.6 *Questions to ask before borrowing money*

of mnemonics to evaluate whether or not they should lend to a customer. One of these is IPARTS. This stands for:

INTEGRITY
PURPOSE
AMOUNT
REPAYMENT
TERM
SECURITY.

The **integrity** of the customer would determine whether the loan would be repaid or not. For example, some customers might stop repaying the loan if they ran into a cash crisis, while others would make numerous sacrifices to ensure that the loan was repaid.

Is the **purpose** of the loan a sensible investment, likely to benefit the customer and make repayments possible?

Is the **amount** requested likely to be sufficient? Will the customer come back because they might not have enough or conversely have they overestimated their requirements?

Can the customer make the **repayments?** The banker will pay particular attention to the pattern of their customer's income and expenditure.

Over what **term** is the loan to be repaid? Though a longer term loan is more profitable for the bank, it is also more risky.

What **security** has a customer got? Should some form of security be taken to insure against default by the customer?

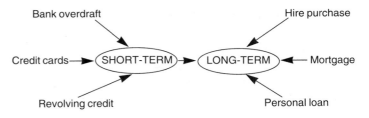

Figure 19.7 *Forms of short-term and long-term finance*

A **bank overdraft** is a form of borrowing on a bank account up to an agreed credit limit. Banks charge interest upon the amount borrowed, usually calculated at a set rate above base rate. Most banks calculate this on a daily basis and charge it to their customer's account quarterly.

Most people who arrange overdrafts use them for a temporary cash shortfall. Sometimes overdraft facilities are part of a current account package offered to customers. For example, the Midland Bank offer an interest-free overdraft of up to £300, available on request to students. Note that unauthorised overdrafts can be very expensive. National Westminster state that 'If you borrow more than £50 without our agreement (including borrowing above an overdraft limit) you will **pay an extra fee of £36 a quarter'**, and this is on top of overdraft interest!

One of the most convenient methods of borrowing is to use a **credit card** such as Access, Visa or a retail store credit card. With credit cards, customers can purchase goods or services and pay for them at a later date. Depending upon when they buy the goods, users of credit cards can receive up to eight weeks' interest-free credit. Each month they receive a statement of their transactions, and they can either clear the balance in full, pay what they choose or make a minimum payment. Interest is then charged on the amount not cleared. Interest charged on accounts not cleared is relatively high. A recent trend is for companies offering credit cards to set an annual charge to customers for this facility.

Many stores offer a **revolving credit** facility. Revolving credit involves transferring by standing order an amount from a personal customer's current account to that of the store. The customer is then granted a fixed credit limit which is usually based upon a multiple of this transfer. For example, if they transfer £20 a month and the multiplication factor is 30, then they can spend up to £600 in the store. Interest is added to the debt each month. This

Task

Using the credit information you obtained earlier, identify an item you might like to purchase and then apply the mnemonic IPARTS to your intentions. What conclusions can you draw? For example, if you were the provider of credit, how would you feel about lending yourself the money?

The different forms of borrowing are usually divided into short-term and long-term.

can also be quite an expensive form of borrowing and has the added disadvantage of limiting the choices of a customer to a particular retailer.

Task

Compare and contrast both the use, flexibility, benefits and the charges for each of the above methods of short-term borrowing.

At various times of their lives people need to buy expensive items for which they might find it difficult to save. People might also miss bargain opportunities if they wait too long to purchase an item. A personal loan is one of the main methods of borrowing money for such purposes. A personal loan is:

- usually for a fixed amount
- over a fixed period of time
- at a fixed interest rate
- usually unsecured for amounts up to £10 000
- repaid by monthly installments.

For larger sums with longer repayment periods, the lender will probably require some form of security such as a claim on a property. Most personal loans offer the option of a protection plan which cover problems or difficulties with repayments in the event of unemployment, accident or sickness. Protection is provided by a group of insurance companies and will cost extra (see Figure 19.8).

Case Study

Applying for a personal loan

Whenever a customer wishes to apply for a personal loan they have to fill in an application form such as the one on shown in Figure 19.9.

The form asks a range of questions which are then credit-scored by the lender to help them to make a decision about whether the application will be successful.

Decisions are quickly reached and then documented with a formal Loan Agreement which is signed by both the lender and the borrower.

1 Why does the form ask about previous addresses?
2 Explain why an application from an owner occupier might receive more favourable consideration than an application from a tenant.
3 Name three occupations and number them in order of job security.
4 How might the level of gross annual salary influence the amount borrowed?
5 Why is the lender interested in the credit cards held by the customer?

Mortgages

A **mortgage** is an important source of finance for anyone wishing to buy a property. It is usually people's biggest single borrowing commitment and most are arranged over a 25-year period. The mortgage is secured on the property, though it is possible to sell on the property or pay the mortgage off.

The lender of the mortgage has certain legal rights over the property, including a power of sale, if the borrower is unable to meet the repayments.

If a customer already has a property it is possible to raise finance by considering a re-mortgage. A re-mortgage simply replaces one mortgage agreement with another. By doing this it is possible to release money from the home to start a business, build an extension, pay off existing loans, etc.

Examples of Repayments for loans of £1,500 and over with Loan Protection Plan

	Amount of Loan £	Insurance Premium £	Total Amount Borrowed £	Monthly Repayment £	Total Repayment £
12 Months APR 22.6%	*500.00	33.00	530.00	49.25	590.05
	*1,000.00	70.00	1,070.00	99.43	1,193.05
	2,000.00	139.00	2,130.00	197.92	2,374.05
	3,000.00	208.00	3,200.00	297.34	3,568.04
	5,000.00	346.00	5,340.00	496.18	5,954.10
	10,000.00	692.00	10,690.00	993.28	11,919.30
24 Months APR 22.8%	*500.00	44.00	540.00	27.68	664.20
	*1,000.00	88.00	1,080.00	55.35	1,328.80
	2,000.00	175.00	2,170.00	111.22	2,669.10
	3,000.00	262.00	3,260.00	167.08	4,009.80
	5,000.00	437.00	5,430.00	278.29	6,678.90
	10,000.00	874.00	10,870.00	557.09	13,370.10
36 Months APR 22.4%	*500.00	52.00	550.00	20.55	739.73
	*1,000.00	103.00	1,100.00	41.10	1,479.50
	2,000.00	205.00	2,200.00	82.20	2,959.00
	3,000.00	307.00	3,300.00	123.30	4,438.50
	5,000.00	512.00	5,510.00	205.86	7,410.95
	10,000.00	1,023.00	11,020.00	411.72	14,821.90
48 Months APR 21.9%	*500.00	69.00	560.00	17.04	817.60
	*1,000.00	138.00	1,130.00	34.38	1,649.80
	2,000.00	275.00	2,270.00	69.05	3,314.20
	3,000.00	412.00	3,410.00	103.73	4,978.60
	5,000.00	687.00	5,680.00	172.77	8,292.80
	10,000.00	1,373.00	11,370.00	345.84	16,600.20
60 Months APR 21.4%	*500.00	88.00	580.00	15.23	913.30
	*1,000.00	175.00	1,170.00	30.72	1,842.75
	2,000.00	350.00	2,350.00	61.69	3,701.25
	3,000.00	525.00	3,520.00	92.40	5,544.00
	5,000.00	873.00	5,870.00	154.09	9,245.25
	10,000.00	1,749.00	11,740.00	308.18	18,490.50

Examples of Repayments for loans of £1,500 and over without Loan Protection Plan

	Amount of Loan £	Monthly Repayment £	Total Repayment £
12 Months APR 22.6%	*500.00	46.46	557.50
	*1,000.00	92.92	1,115.00
	2,000.00	185.84	2,230.00
	3,000.00	278.75	3,345.00
	5,000.00	464.59	5,575.00
	10,000.00	929.17	11,150.00
24 Months APR 22.8%	*500.00	25.63	615.00
	*1,000.00	51.25	1,230.00
	2,000.00	102.50	2,460.00
	3,000.00	153.75	3,690.00
	5,000.00	256.25	6,150.00
	10,000.00	512.50	12,300.00
36 Months APR 22.4%	*500.00	18.69	672.50
	*1,000.00	37.37	1,345.00
	2,000.00	74.73	2,690.00
	3,000.00	112.09	4,035.00
	5,000.00	186.81	6,725.00
	10,000.00	373.62	13,450.00
48 Months APR 21.9%	*500.00	15.21	730.00
	*1,000.00	30.42	1,460.00
	2,000.00	60.84	2,920.00
	3,000.00	91.25	4,380.00
	5,000.00	152.09	7,300.00
	10,000.00	304.17	14,600.00
60 Months APR 21.4%	*500.00	13.13	78.50
	*1,000.00	26.25	1,575.00
	2,000.00	52.50	3,150.00
	3,000.00	78.75	4,725.00
	5,000.00	131.25	7,875.00
	10,000.00	262.50	15,750.00

Figure19.8 *Examples of repayments*

PAB

Midland Personal Loan

Application Form

PLEASE COMPLETE IN BLOCK CAPITALS, WRITE 'NONE' WHERE
APPROPRIATE AND TICK ☑ WHERE APPLICABLE

Personal Details

Surname _____ Mr/Mrs/Miss/Ms

Forename(s) _____ Other name _____

(For joint account holders)

Surname _____ Mr/Mrs/Miss/Ms

Forename(s) _____ Other name _____

Postal Address _____

_____

_____ Postcode _____

Date moved to
present address Month _____ Year _____

Previous address (If at present address less than 2 years)

_____

_____

_____ Postcode _____

Date moved to
previous address Month _____ Year _____

Tel. No. Home _____ Business _____

Date of birth _____

Marital status: Married ☐   Single ☐   Separated ☐

Divorced ☐   Widowed ☐

Number of children _____ Ages _____

Your Home

Are you: An owner occupier ☐   A tenant ☐

Living with parents ☐   Other ☐

If an owner occupier:

Market Value of residence: £ _____

Amount outstanding on mortgage(s)   £ _____

Your Job

Employer's name _____

Address _____

_____ Postcode _____

Employer's business _____

Your occupation _____

Do you have a pension arranged?   Yes ☐   No ☐

Date started in
present employment   Month _____ Year _____

Date started in
previous employment   Month _____ Year _____

How paid: Cash ☐   Cheque ☐
Direct credit to your bank account ☐   Other means ☐

When paid: Weekly ☐   Fortnightly ☐
Monthly ☐   Otherwise ☐

Gross annual salary (joint salary if joint application)
Up to £5,000 ☐   £5,001-£10,000 ☐
£10,001-£15,000 ☐   £15,001-£20,000 ☐
£20,001-£30,000 ☐   £30,001-£40,000 ☐
over £40,000 ☐

Your Bank

Date you first opened a
Midland Current Account   Month _____ Year _____

Name of present branch _____

Current Account no. | | | | | | | | |

Name & branch of bankers if not
a Midland customer _____

Other accounts held (please specify) _____

Cards Held

Do you hold an existing:

Midland Access   Yes ☐   No ☐   Midland Visa   Yes ☐   No ☐

Midland Access Card Number | 5 | 2 | 2 | 4 | 0 | 0 | 4 | | | | | | |

Midland Visa Card Number | 4 | 5 | 4 | 6 | 3 | 8 | | | | | | | |

Cheque Card   Yes ☐   No ☐

Any other Cards

Midland Gold ☐   Barclaycard ☐   Other ☐
MasterCard

Figure 19.9 *Personal loan application form*

There are three basic types of mortgage:

a With a **repayment mortgage** the customer pays back the interest and the sum borrowed. As the interest element reduces so does the tax relief. Customers get most benefit from this mortgage in the early years.

b An **endowment mortgage** involves a customer taking out an insurance policy. At the end of the mortgage period the policy matures and the sum insured pays off the outstanding mortgage. Only interest is paid off during this type of mortgage and, though this is more expensive, customers receive tax relief throughout the period of the mortgage.

c A **pension mortgage** is similar to an endowment except for the fact that the mortgage is paid off at the end of the term by a lump sum from a pension plan.

Hire purchase

HP was the most widely used form of borrowing before the advent of credit cards. Hire purchase or instalment credit, as it is sometimes known, enables a customer to obtain goods and repay the cost of an item over a fixed period such as five years. It is widely available either direct from retailers or from a wide variety of specialist finance companies.

Terms for hire purchase or instalment credit vary from company to company. Though it can be a convenient way of purchasing an item and stores or garages might offer low interest deals, because some contracts are structured so that the interest is paid before the capital, if the agreement is terminated it is possible to have to pay back a higher proportion of the original sum than expected.

Task

What form of credit would you advise in each of the following situations? Provide explanations with each answer.

1 Robin requires £4000 to buy a motor car.
2 Sarah knows that next month is going to be difficult as she has to pay the road tax and insurance on her car. She is going to require at least £250 but can pay the debt off within six weeks.
3 Peter generally shops in the same store for clothes. He wishes to start paying for his clothes with some form of credit.
4 Karen would prefer a more flexible way of paying for purchases such as petrol and family shopping.
5 Ian is thinking of buying a house.

. SOURCES OF FINANCE . FOR ORGANISATIONS .

An organisation has to engage in a planning process to consider what its financial requirements are and how they are going to be met. This financial planning process involves looking at present financial resources, **forecasting** changes likely to take place in the future, and then ensuring that the plans match the organisation's objectives.

Usually, in order to obtain finance, an organisation has to draw up a **business plan**. As we shall see later in this chapter, a business plan provides essential information to the people whose support is needed.

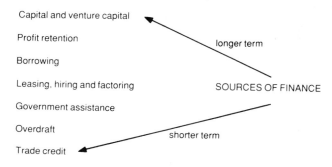

Figure 19.10 *Sources of finance*

The first important decision about any finance is for how long a period you require it. Though short-term funds tend to be the most expensive, they are also more flexible – and this benefit can offset the lower cost of **long-term funds**, which might not be fully employed if fluctuations take place in business activity.

Many organisations expand by using short-term finance and then replace this type with long-term finance through a **funding operation**. Funding in this situation therefore raises long-term finance to pay off short-term finance, so that further short-term finance is then made available for the organisation to expand again.

Capital and venture capital

The type of capital available varies according to the make-up of the organisation.

A **sole trader** business is easy to set up and is the most common form of business ownership. Though a sole trader has considerable flexibility, this type of business carries a lot of risk. Thus a sole trader often relies on finance from personal sources and additional sums can be difficult to raise.

Sole traders frequently expand by taking in **partners**. Partners can bring in further capital together with greater expertise. They are particularly suitable for the professions, but limitations on numbers can restrict capital-raising opportunities.

Task

List the possible drawbacks of bringing in a partner to develop a sole trader business.

Share capital

In order to achieve the benefits of **limited liability** and extend their capital-raising opportunities, many partnerships transform themselves by a legal process into a registered company, and issue shares.

As we have seen already, companies can be either **private** or **public.** A **private limited company** has certain restrictions on the rights of members to transfer shares, and there are limits on the ability of the public to subscribe for share ownership. Membership of the **Unlisted Securities Market** (USM) is often seen as a half-way stage between a small company and a company that is fully listed on the London Stock Exchange. The USM, which was created in 1980 by the Stock Exchange, has enabled many smaller companies to become public and raise finance for expansion before progressing to a full Stock Exchange listing. A fully listed public limited company has almost endless opportunities to raise fresh capital from the financial markets.

Task

Obtain a prospectus from a public company.

For example, a public limited company can create a **public issue by prospectus.** An issuing house (probably a merchant bank) organises the issue of shares by compiling a prospectus (a brochure), accompanied by an advertisement and an invitation to buy shares. This can be expensive – something like 7 per cent of the money raised by the issue can go to meet the costs.

Another method for a public company to raise finance is to make an **offer for sale**. The public company issues shares directly to an issuing house, which then offers them for sale at a fixed price. This too is an expensive method and is best used when the size of the issue is too small to need a public issue by prospectus.

A **rights issue** is a cheaper method of obtaining finance – existing shareholders are offered shares directly at an advantageous price. Another method which avoids the expense of 'going to the market' is a placing, whereby shares are placed with a number of investors through an intermediary (a share dealer).

In a public limited company most capital is held usually in the form of ordinary shares. An **ordinary share** is a fixed unit of ownership and gives the holder the opportunity to share in the profits or losses. Most ordinary shares carry voting rights at shareholders' meetings. Shareholders elect the Board and sanction the level of dividends proposed. **Authorised capital** is the maximum amount of share capital a company is empowered by its shareholders to issue, whereas **issued capital** is the nominal amount of share capital issued to shareholders.

Case Study

Burton wins approval for cash call

THE BURTON GROUP PLC

Sir John Hoskyns, Chairman of Burton Group, had to ride out a bumpy shareholders' meeting. He had to resist calls for the sacking of the entire Board, and so won over-whelming approval for the Board's £161 million cash call.

Sir John defended the group's strategy, controversial pay rises for senior directors and a one-for-one rights issue. Questioners at the meeting were mostly hostile. One called for the entire Board to be replaced. To applause, another said: 'It looks like the Board is looking after the interests of directors at the expense of shareholders.'

Several complaints were made about the directors' contracts signed just before the group announced the rights issue. The chief executive earned £375 000 and other directors more than £200 000 a year. Sir John rejected some analysts' suggestions that the group was close to ruin. In the end the rights issue was approved by the shareholders present by 108 votes to 10.

1 How does this case illustrate a division between the loyalties directors have to the company, the shareholders and to themselves?

2 Explain what is meant by a 'one-for-one' rights issue.

3 How would you feel about this rights issue if you were a Burton shareholder?

Another class of shares is **deferred shares** (or **founders shares**). These are issued to members of the family which built the business, and they sometimes carry enhanced voting rights so that a small group of people can maintain control of a family business.

Task

Identify the founders of some large companies. Comment upon how the organisations they founded have developed.

Preference shares are a less flexible class of share. Owners of these shares are not, strictly speaking, part owners of the company and their exact rights will be found in the company's Articles of Association. However, they do have preferential rights to receive dividends if profits exist and, in the event of a company winding up, will receive the face value of their shares before the ordinary shareholders are repaid. On the other hand, dividends on preference shares are limited.

Some companies issue **cumulative preference shares** and this avoids the difficulty of having to pay preference shareholders if profits are too small. The holder of the cumulative preference share will receive arrears of dividends accumulated from the past in later years. **Redeemable preference shares** are such that the company can buy back the shares from the shareholders. Redemption can be made from profits or reserves or it may be financed by a fresh issue of more shares. **Participating preference shareholders** receive dividends above the fixed rate when ordinary shareholders have been paid and if the company has done well in a particular year.

It should be noted that organisations in the **public sector** are publically owned and – unless they are going through the process of privatisation – cannot go to the Stock Exchange for capital. They can, however, use the financial markets for loans.

Venture capital

Venture capital is capital available from non-banking commercial organisations who offer investment for private customers for specific projects. The provider of the finance usually demands a strong element of control over the borrowing company.

Profit retention

A very important source of capital for British industry is profits that have been 'ploughed back'. Initially profits are subject to Corporation Tax payable to the Department of Inland Revenue. Then a proportion of the remaining profit is paid as dividends to shareholders. The directors recommend how much profit should be allocated as dividends. Whatever is left over is retained in the business as reinvested profit, and is shown in the balance sheet as **reserves**. The funds represented by the reserves are spread out amongst the assets of the business.

Borrowing

Financial institutions today try to provide a package of lending facilities designed to meet the needs of the market. **Borrowing** is considered an acceptable feature of commercial activity. The charge for borrowing is the loan × the interest rate. Risk is involved in setting the interest rate.

An organisation may negotiate a loan from a **high-street bank** such as National Westminster or Barclays. With these loans, repayments are usually credited to a separate loan account held by the organisation and are repaid in equal instalments. Alternatively, the **merchant banks** provide specialist business and financial services.

A long-term loan obtainable through the Stock Exchange market is called a **debenture.** This is an acknowledgement of a debt taken up by a company for a fixed rate of interest.

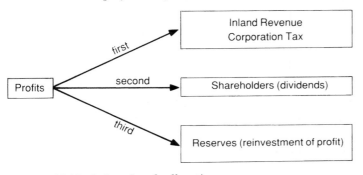

Figure 19.11 *Order of profit allocation*

A debenture is transferable – that is, it can be bought and sold like a share.

Other sources of finance include the government's small-firms Loan Guarantee Scheme, and loans from the Rural Development Commission.

Lenders always try to minimise the risks of loan finance. When providing finance for a limited company, it is possible for the lender to demand a **personal guarantee** of repayment from the main shareholder, and this effectively removes that shareholder's limited liability and puts him or her in a similar position to a partner or sole trader. Lenders also frequently ask for **security** or **collateral** against a loan. In this way certain assets are 'secured' and, if the business has to be wound up, the lender has priority over other creditors in claiming any money raised from the sale of these secured assets (office furniture and equipment, vehicles, machinery etc.)

Case Study

Japanese borrowers

The Japanese have had a reputation for being very careful and wise savers. However, a report from the Economic Planning Agency has raised many eyebrows, for its shows that Japanese consumers now owe more than Americans! Japanese

consumers now tend to borrow 20 per cent against their disposable income compared with 19 per cent for American consumers. The Japanese, who have only recently learned to spend, have certainly learned how to borrow.

1 *To what extent has borrowing today become a way of life for individuals and organisations?*

2 *What might happen if an organisation borrows too much in comparison with its income?*

Leasing, hiring and factoring

One way in which an organisation can obtain the *use* of an asset without having to pay for it outright is through **leasing**. The *lessee* uses the asset and makes regular payments to the *lessor* who owns it. An **operating lease** is for a small amount and a **capital lease** is for a large amount over an extended period. The procedure for leasing is for the lessee company to choose the exact equipment it requires, and this is then purchased and supplied by the lessor company. A contract determines the rent payable, maintenance, conditions and so forth.

Task

What are the advantages to an organisation of leasing equipment rather than purchasing it outright from profits, from a bank loan or from any other source of finance?

Finance houses, which often have links with banks, provide a variety of schemes which enable customers to receive goods immediately and make payments over an agreed period of time. Goods on **hire-purchase** remain the property of the finance company until the customer has made all of the payments, whereas other **credit purchasing** schemes permit the goods to belong to the customer from the time of the first payment.

Factoring can provide finance for an organisation by making use of the amounts of money owed to the organisation by its own **debtors.** Factoring companies 'take over' the debts – they invoice the customers, collect the money due and pur-

sue any slow payers; in the meantime the organisation has the benefit of the payments from the factoring company.

Government assistance

A range of schemes is made available by central and local government to help organisations requiring finance. Many of these schemes are directed specifically at small organisations. Examples are Regional Selective Grants, Regional Enterprise Grants, and the government's Loan Guarantee Scheme.

Overdraft

A bank **overdraft** is the most frequently used form of short-term finance and is often used to ease a cash-flow problem. An arrangement is made between the customer and the bank to agree a limit up to which a customer can draw funds over and above what is deposited. Interest is calculated on the level of overdraft on a daily basis. Since overdrafts are repayable on demand, organisations must make sure that they are in a position to pay back the money owed.

Trade credit

A useful form of finance for all organisations is that of trade credit allowed by suppliers. The credit period is the time between receiving the good or service and being obliged to make payment for it. Credit periods are usually governed by the type of business and the relationship between the purchaser and the supplier. Although no rate of interest is attached to trade credit, cash discounts may be forfeited if payments are not made within the agreed time. Organisations trying to extend trade credit in order to improve their short-term cash situation endanger their reputation with suppliers.

Element assignment

Working as a cashier

This assignment can help you to provide evidence for assessment, or claim the following Core Skills:

Communicating
Receive and respond to a variety of information
Communicate in writing

Application of number

Apply numerical skills and techniques

Personal skills

Use information sources

Identify and solve routine and non-routine problems

You have recently been appointed as a cashier to a newly set up business.

Task 1

During your first month you have been asked to record the following transactions in the two-column cash book:

1 Jan – Started business with £10 350 in the bank and £655 in cash

2 Jan – Purchased computer equipment £1450, paying by cheque

4 Jan – Received £867 cash from sales

6 Jan – Transfer £600 cash into bank

8 Jan – Pay wages £150 cash

9 Jan – Pay office rent £150 by cheque

11 Jan – Purchased goods for resale £350, paying by cheque

13 Jan – Payment for stationery £25 by cash

14 Jan – Payment of travel expenses £32 by cheque

17 Jan – Received £67 cash from sales and banked £255 of cheques from sales

18 Jan – Pay B. Hasty £680 by cheque

21 Jan – Pay £9200 for business vehicles

25 Jan – Receive £490 cash from sales

27 Jan – Bank £400 cash

Note these transactions and balance the cash book at the end of the month.

Task 2

You have been asked to reconcile your cash book with the bank statement at the end of each month. Explain why you have been asked to do this.

Task 3

You have been asked to attend a meeting of all the employees next week. One of the items on the agenda is a discussion of possible sources of finance for the business so that it can:

a buy/lease more suitable premises

b purchase more machinery

c deal with a cash-flow problem during March when few sales are expected.

Before the meeting prepare notes on various sources of finance for these situations.

chapter **20** CONTROLLING CASH

All individuals and organisations have to analyse their cash flows so that they can plan for events which are expected to take place in the future. With cash planning or budgeting it is possible to forecast flows of cash into and out of an account in the future so that actions can be taken to overcome any shortfall that may occur.

The art of successful cash planning is being able to calculate future receipts and expenditures accurately. For example, goods may be bought in January and then sold in May. The money for the goods might be received in August. In this chapter we look at the matching of personal finance with personal expenditure and then we move on to forcasting the financial requirements for a business.

• MATCHING SOURCES OF PERSONAL • FINANCE TO PERSONAL EXPENDITURE

Successful control of personal finance involves matching sources of finance with personal expenditures. In an ideal world everybody would have a regular income which would match neatly against a series of bills which are

spread evenly throughout the year (see Figure 20.1). In practice, however, this rarely happens as most people find that bills pile at certain times of the year. For example, the car tax and insurance might have to be paid at the same time as the electricity bill and the gas bill (see Figure 20.2)..

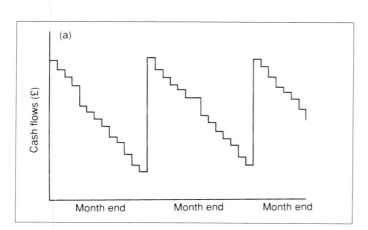

Figure 20.1 *Regular income and regular cash flows*

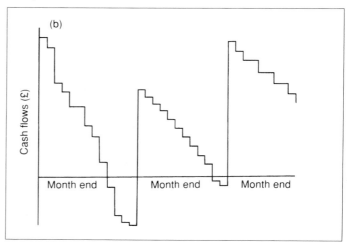

Figure 20.2 *Regular income and irregular cash flows*

Case Study

The budget account

Most banks offer their customers a budget account service which can be used to spread the effects of bills which appear at irregular intervals during the course of the year. A customer simply estimates the total of their bills which they expect to arrive during the year and then divides the total amount by 12. This provides a monthly amount which can then be either paid or transferred to the budget account.

For example, if a person's total bills for the year are estimated to be £4800, the monthly payment or transfer to the budget account would be £400. If, let's say, several bills arrived in the same month, they could still be paid from the account. This means that in some months the account would be in credit and in other months it would not. The budget account is, therefore, a mechanism which enables a bank customer to account for the irregular pattern of their bills during the year and avoid having to go to the bank at certain key stages of the year and ask for overdraft facilities.

1 *Explain how a budget account could help with the planning of personal finance.*
2 *Identify one other key benefit of having a budget account.*
3 *Imagine that you intend to open a budget account. Work out your monthly transfer figure.*

An important element in controlling personal finance is that of personal **budget planning** or **personal cash flow**. Personal budgeting or cash flow involves matching cash flows in with cash flows out. Using these techniques to **forecast** cash flow will help an individual to:

- work out what money is coming in and when they expect it to come in
- identify weeks or months when expenditures are heavy
- identify when they might have cash-flow problems
- cater beforehand for any anticipated cash-flow problem by trying to cut down on expenditure or by arranging some form of short-term credit facility such as an overdraft.

We can understand how personal budget planning works by looking at an example. On 1 January Patricia Williams has £225 in the bank. She receives take home pay of £850 per month and is determined to save £2000 to pay for a car in June. To see if this is possible she is preparing a cash-flow forecast. She predicts that her cash flows will be as follows:

- Council Tax £400 per annum with payments to be made in April and October.
- Electricity £150 payable at the end of each quarter.
- Mortgage £200 per month, payable monthly.
- Travelling expenses £50 per month, payable monthly.
- Insurances/assurances total £60 per month, payable monthly.
- Food £150 per month, payable monthly.
- Car £2000 in June.
- Inheritance – she expects to receive £400 from her late aunt's estate in March.

Patricia's cash-flow forecast would therefore be as shown in Figure 20.3.

The forecast shows that not only could Patricia afford to buy the car in June, she could in fact afford to purchase it earlier than she anticipated at the end of May.

	JAN £	FEB £	MAR £	APR £	MAY £	JUN £
RECEIPTS						
Take home pay	850	850	850	850	850	850
Inheritance	0	0	400	0	0	0
Total receipts	850	850	1250	850	850	850
PAYMENTS						
Council Tax	0	0	0	200	0	0
Electricity	0	0	150	0	0	150
Mortgage	200	200	200	200	200	200
Travelling expenses	50	50	50	50	50	50
Insurance/assurance	60	60	60	60	60	60
Food	150	150	150	150	150	150
Car	0	0	0	0	0	2000
Total payments	460	460	610	660	460	2610
Opening balance	225	615	1005	1645	1835	2225
Add receipts	850	850	1250	850	850	850
	1075	1465	2255	2495	2685	3075
Less payments	460	460	610	660	460	2610
Balance carried forward	615	1005	1645	1835	2225	465

Figure 20.3 *Cash-flow forecast of Patricia Williams*

Task

Rob Richards has £385 in the bank on 1 January. His take-home pay from work is £600 per month. He is going on an expedition holiday to Greenland during August but will have to pay £1500 for the holiday in February. Though he expects to overdraw at that time and will arrange an overdraft facility to do so, he wants to know by which month he can pay back his overdraft. He predicts that his cash flows will be as follows:

- Council Tax £300 per annum with payments in April and October.
- Electricity and gas £100 payable each quarter.
- Mortgage £180 per month, payable monthly.
- Transport costs £50 per month, payable monthly.
- Food £150 per month, payable monthly.
- Entertainment £100 per month, payable monthly.
- Overtime – he has been guaranteed at least £300 of overtime in February, £250 in March, £400 in April and £400 in June.

a Prepare Rob's cash-flow forecast for the first six months of the year. When will he be able to pay back his overdraft?

b Put the cash-flow forecast on to a computer spreadsheet and then use the spreadsheet to answer the following questions:

1 If the cost of the holiday was £1000, when would Rob be able to pay back his overdraft?

2 How would the cash-flow forecast be affected if the overtime was withdrawn?

3 How would a 50% reduction in mortgage cost and entertainment costs affect the forecast?

Case Study

An Action Plan for dealing with debt

It is all too easy to allow your financial circumstances to get out of control and find yourself in debt. Imagine what it is like to be in a situation in which you just cannot pay your bills. The procession of letters for gas, electricity, rent,

mortgage and so on may seem endless. You may have missed credit payments. Everything will just seem like a mess. The *worst* thing to do is to do nothing and try to ignore the problems in the hope that things will get better. The sooner those in debt face the problems, the sooner steps can be taken to improve the situation. The first thing to do is to contact the creditors. The Office of Fair Trading publish 'Debt – A survival guide' which is a six-step action plan for those people unlucky to be in debt. Their six stages are as follows:

Step 1 – Work out your income
This involves finding out how much money is coming in on a weekly or monthly basis.

Step 2 – Where your money goes
Expenditures should be calculated on a weekly or monthly basis. Luxury items should be distinguished from essential items. Credit arrangements should be noted. Total expenditure should be compared with total income.

Step 3 – Still more going out than coming in?
If this is still the case, is it possible to make cutbacks, and sacrifices particularly on non-essentials?

Step 4 – Can you increase income?
Some people find that they are paying too much tax or are not receiving all of the income to which they are entitled. Is there a possibility of part-time work?

Step 5 – Find out how much is owed
Arrears payments, loans and credit commitments should be listed. Debts likely to cause problems such as rent/mortgage, fuel debts, hire-purchase debts should be prioritised.

Step 6 – Talk with creditors
This involves sending creditors a financial statement and then making a fair offer to pay off the debt, making sure that priority debts are dealt with first.

1 Why is ignoring the problems the worst thing to do?
2 What is an action plan?
3 What mechanism could be used to compare the flow of income against the flow of expenditure?
4 List (i) three essential goods and (ii) three non-essential goods.
5 How should a person in debt deal with their creditors?

Case Study

The Banking Ombudsman scheme

The leaflet reproduced as Figure 20.4 (on page 408) is published by the Council of the Banking Ombudsman. The following banks appear in the same scheme.

Abbey National	Allied Irish Bank
Bank of Ireland	Bank of Scotland
Barclays Bank	Clydesdale Bank
Co-operative Bank	Coutts & Co.
Girobank	Lloyds Bank
Midland Bank	National Westminster Bank
Northern Bank	The Royal Bank of
TSB	Scotland
TSB Scotland	Standard Chartered Bank
TSB Northern Ireland	Yorkshire Bank
Ulster Bank	

The Council is independent of the banks, and the Ombudsman is responsible to the Council, not the banks.

1 *Identify two possible situations in which you might wish to complain about the services provided by your bank.*
2 *What steps should an individual take if they have a complaint against their bank?*
3 *What is the purpose of the Banking Ombudsman?*
4 *Why is it not possible to complain about banking interest rate policies or other general policy matters?*
5 *How will the Ombudsman deal with each complaint?*
6 *What other industries do you feel should have an Ombudsman?*

Case Study

Late payers deal the fatal blow

This account is now overdue for payment

The UK recession has claimed many casualties. Among the victims are many small and medium-sized businesses; many blame their plight on more than economic downturn and high interest rates. They claim that having supplied goods or services to large companies, late payments by those customers are often the final fatal blow. It is a common accusation that, by deliberately withholding payments for months on end, many well-known public companies greatly enhance their own cash positions, but at the same time squeeze the life out of weaker, more vulnerable suppliers who find it difficult to fight back – and might lose business if they did.

A nationwide survey of 250 financial directors of large, small and medium-sized companies by accountant Pannell Kerr Foster found that 70 per cent believed that late payment was making the recession worse, and an overwhelming 96 per cent said it was adding to their business problems. Nine out of ten companies said that small firms were hit hardest by late payments. The survey also revealed that 76 per cent of firms had to wait a staggering three months or more for their bills to be paid, while only 14 per cent received their money within the widely accepted contractual credit period of 30 days.

Richard Pearson, the Chairman of Pannell Kerr Foster, commented: 'The message we have to get across is that companies – small, family-run firms – need to adopt a much tougher attitude towards credit control and take active measures to ensure that they are paid what they are owed on time.'

Various other surveys show that, on average, companies take 75 working days to pay suppliers' invoices. Late paying seems to have become a culture in the UK. Companies seem to think it is common sense for them to delay payment for as long as possible, but many feel that late payments are putting certain categories of business organisation at a considerable competitive disadvantage with foreign businesses. It seems likely, however, that the little organisation at the end of the payment chain will continue to suffer the brunt of late payments.

1 *Explain why late payments by debtors may cause a fatal blow to a business.*
2 *How might withholding payments improve an organisation's cash flow?*
3 *In your opinion, what is a reasonable credit period?*
4 *What is meant by credit control?*
5 *Why is late payment causing a competitive disadvantage?*

WHO CAN USE THIS SCHEME?

Any individual person, or groups of individuals such as partnerships or clubs, who have a complaint against any of the banks listed overleaf. The scheme is not available to companies.

WHAT DOES THE SCHEME PROVIDE?

If you have a complaint against a Bank which is not settled to your satisfaction, you can in most cases appeal to the independent Banking Ombudsman. This service is free of charge.

WHICH COMPLAINTS CAN BE DEALT WITH BY THE BANKING OMBUDSMAN?

As a rough guide, the Ombudsman will deal with complaints about all types of banking business normally transacted through bank branches, and also with complaints about bank credit cards, and some bank executor and trustee services. He can also deal with some complaints about bank services relating to taxation and insurance.

WHICH COMPLAINTS CANNOT BE DEALT WITH?

Broadly speaking, the Banking Ombudsman *cannot* deal with your complaint if:

— Your complaint is not against one of the member Banks (see overleaf).

— Your complaint is about something which happened before 1 January 1986 (unless you could not reasonably have known about it until after then).*

— Your complaint is being, or has been, dealt with by a Court or similar body (unless your Bank gives written agreement to it being investigated by the Ombudsman).

— Your complaint comes within any of the complaints procedures set up to deal with investment matters. If in doubt ask the Ombudsman.

— Your complaint relates to a Bank's *commercial* judgement in decisions about lending or security.

— Your claim is for more than £100,000 (or is part of a claim for more than that amount).

*12 July 1989 for Abbey National

— Your complaint is about the way a Bank has exercised its discretion under a will or trust, or about any lack of consultation in exercising that discretion.

— Your complaint concerns your Bank's general interest rate policies or other general policy matters.

— Your complaint concerns a guarantee or charge given to a Bank to support a company.

— Your complaint concerns a banking service provided abroad. The Ombudsman scheme covers bank services provided in England, Wales, Scotland or Northern Ireland but not the Channel Islands or the Isle of Man.

WHEN TO SEND YOUR COMPLAINT TO THE BANKING OMBUDSMAN

If you have a complaint against a Bank your first step should be to try to sort it out with the local branch. The Banking Ombudsman cannot help until you have reached the end of the road in trying to obtain satisfaction through the Bank's own complaints procedure. This will usually involve taking your complaint as far as the Bank Head Office, although you can write to the Ombudsman if you feel your complaint has got bogged down.

The Bank should tell you when your complaint has reached deadlock at the highest level. If you then decide to take it up with the Ombudsman you will need to do so within six months.

WHAT HAPPENS NEXT?

The Ombudsman will check that your complaint is one that he can deal with, and that deadlock has been reached. He will ask you to send him any relevant letters etc., to agree to your complaint being dealt with under the Scheme and to authorise the bank to supply any relevant information it holds. Normally he will then try to sort out your complaint informally, for example by pointing out any misunderstanding on either side.

If that fails he will usually ask for more formal presentations of the case from both sides and then make his recommendation. He can make an award (of up to £100,000) if he concludes that you are right. You do not necessarily have to accept his decision, and retain your right to go to court instead.

All complaints will normally be dealt with in writing and will be treated in confidence.

Figure 20.4 *The Banking Ombudsman Scheme*

. FORECASTING FINANCIAL . REQUIREMENTS

Whereas profit is a **surplus** from trading activities, cash is a liquid asset which enables an organisation to buy the goods and services it requires in order to add value to them, trade and make profits. It is therefore possible for an organisation to be profitable while at the same time creditors have not been paid and liquid resources have not been properly accounted for.

On the other hand, an organisation must look carefully to see that its use of cash is to its best advantage. For example, if it holds too much cash in the bank it might be sacrificing income it could otherwise earn.

An organisation must therefore ensure that it has sufficient cash to carry out its plans, and ensure that the cash coming in is sufficient to cover the cash going out. At the same time it must take into account any cash surpluses it might have in the bank. The organisation is said to have a certain **cash-flow** position.

Looking carefully at the availability of liquid funds is essential to the smooth running of any organisation. With cash planning or budgeting it is possible to forecast the flows into and out of an organisation's bank account so that any surpluses or deficits can be highlighted and any necessary action can be taken promptly. For example, overdraft facilities may be arranged in good time so that funds are available when required.

Case Study

When the numbers fail to add up

Every year thousands of businesses fail as a result of cash-flow problems. The root cause of these problems seems to be weak financial management, which is frequently identified when the businesses are wound up. Today it has become one of the key reasons for business failure.

The paramount importance of effective cash management is touted again and again in booklets, guides and starter packs. For example:

'Finance . . . is where your numbers stand up and be counted.' (Price Waterhouse)
'The banker is far more concerned by the cash flow that trading generates.' (Ernst & Young)
'Many businesses fail to make profits or to have enough cash at the right time, because the management has not planned ahead.' (National Westminster Bank)
'The big question in cash flow is: what would happen if … …? (Barclays Bank)
Despite these points being made in every booklet and guide, the message concerning weak financial management seems slow to penetrate.

Lee Manning, a senior manager at Buchler Phillips, says that 'weakness in company management and the information available to it' is a common theme running through reports of business reviews carried out for lenders. He identifies five principal components within that theme:

● Most companies which suffer long-term financial difficulties are victims of inadequate and insufficient management information, with particular emphasis on up-to-date cash-flow information.
● Cash-flow forecasts are generally prepared at the start of the business period and not reviewed again until the period has elapsed, thus defeating the object of cash-flow analysis.
● Cash-flow forecasts are generally highly optimistic.
● Management tends to ignore the quality of debtors and tends to look at the face value of invoices rather than how easy it is to get the money in.
● Companies are often brought down by large speculative projects which represent a move away from their core business.

According to one firm of accountants, businesses often reach crisis conditions before thinking about their cash flow. The major lesson to be learnt from accounting is that 'cash is king'.

1 Explain why an organisation's cash flow is considered important by its bank.
2 What does Barclays Bank mean when its representative says 'The big question in cash flow is: what would happen if … …?'
3 Why, in your opinion, do so many businesses ignore cash flow?

Preparing a cash-flow forecast

In order to prepare a cash-flow forecast, it is necessary to know or to estimate what receipts and payments are likely in the future and when they will happen.

Suppose that C. Moon Ltd has £500 in the bank on 1 January. The owner, Christine Moon, anticipates that her **receipts** over the next six months are likely to be as follows:

JAN	FEB	MAR	APR	MAY	JUN
£2300	£1400	£5300	£6100	£4700	£1400

She has also worked out what her **payments** are likely to be over the next six months:

JAN	FEB	MAR	APR	MAY	JUN
£1400	£4100	£5600	£5000	£3100	£900

Christine Moon is concerned about whether she needs an **overdraft facility** and, if so, when she is likely to need it. Her cash-flow forecast for the six months would look like Figure 20.5. It is possible to match receipts to payments to forecast her expected cash position at the end of each month. Note that whenever the cash balance is a negative, brackets are put around the figures. C. Moon Ltd therefore requires an overdraft from February to the start of May.

	JAN £	FEB £	MAR £	APR £	MAY £	JUN £
Cash balance	500	1400	(1300)	(1600)	(500)	1100
Add receipts	2300	1400	5300	6100	4700	1400
	2800	2800	4000	4500	4200	2500
Less payments	1400	4100	5600	5000	3100	900
Balance carried forward	1400	(1300)	(1600)	(500)	1100	1600

Figure 20.5 *The cash-flow forecast of C. Moon Ltd*

Task

In the example above, what would be the consequences if C. Moon Ltd's actual receipts for January, February and March were each £1300 higher than expected? Assuming that all other receipts and payments remain the same, how would this affect the overdraft requirements, and the cash position at the end of June?

Task

Prepare the cash-flow forecast of S. Todd Ltd. The business has £250 in the bank and the owner anticipates that his *receipts* over the next six months are likely to be as follows:

JAN	FEB	MAR	APR	MAY	JUN
£1400	£1600	£1500	£1000	£900	£700

He has also worked out his *payments* and expects these to be:

JAN	FEB	MAR	APR	MAY	JUN
£1100	£700	£900	£1400	£1000	£900

The cash-flow forecasts we have considered so far have shown monthly totals. In real life, however, the information is likely to be broken down into specific components. It is useful to ascertain when each of these components needs to be applied and what the effect of each is. It is therefore possible to modify the cash-flow forecast by making it more detailed.

For example, Andrew Nut sets up in business as a manufacturer of string vests by putting £28 500 into a business bank account on 1 January. For the first six months of the year he anticipates or **budgets** for the following situations.

- His forecasts for the purchase of raw materials and sales receipts for finished goods, based upon extensive market research, are as follows:

	PURCHASES (£)	SALES (£)
January	6 500	5 500
February	7 000	7 100
March	7 300	8 000
April	7 500	14 000
May	6 100	17 000
June	6 500	14 300

- Andrew Nut has arranged one month's credit from suppliers, so raw materials purchased in January will have to be paid for in February.
- He expects one-half of sales to be for cash and the other half on credit. He anticipates two months on average to be taken by credit customers; i.e. sales made in January on credit will not be settled until March.

- Wages are expected to be £1000 per month, paid in the same month.
- Machinery must be purchased for £15 500 on 1 January and must be paid for in the same month.
- Rent for his factory is £6000 per annum, payable in equal instalments at the start of each month.
- Other costs (**overheads**) are £1500 per month, and these are assumed to be paid in the month following that in which they are incurred.
- In April, Andrew Nut expects to receive an inheritance from his Auntie Kitty of £8000, which he will put straight into the business bank account.

Andrew Nut's cash-flow forecast for the first six months would therefore be as in Figure 20.6.

Amending the forecast

We have seen that it is essential for any organisation, particularly one starting up in business, to prepare a cash-flow forecast. It is also important for the organisation to amend the forecast as events take place. It is possible for a business, as we mentioned earlier, to be quite profitable but still not have sufficient cash for its needs. To be in a position to draw up an accurate forecast an organisation must be able to predict the flows of cash coming into and leaving the business and the **timings** of these flows.

	JAN £	FEB £	MAR £	APR £	MAY £	JUN £
RECEIPTS						
Sales – cash	2 750	3 550	4 000	7 000	8 500	7 150
Sales – credit	0	0	2 750	3 550	4 000	7 000
Other receipts	0	0	0	8 000	0	0
Total receipts	2 750	3 550	6 750	18 550	12 500	14 150
PAYMENTS						
Raw materials	0	6 500	7 000	7 300	7 500	6 100
Wages	1 000	1 000	1 000	1 000	1 000	1 000
Machinery	15 500	0	0	0	0	0
Rent	500	500	500	500	500	500
Other overheads	0	1 500	1 500	1 500	1 500	1 500
Total payments	17 000	9 500	10 000	10 300	10 500	9 100
Opening balance	28 500	14 250	8 300	5 050	13 300	15 300
Add receipts	2 750	3 550	6 750	18 550	12 500	14 150
	31 250	17 800	15 050	23 600	25 800	29 450
Less payments	17 000	9 500	10 000	10 300	10 500	9 100
Balance carried forward	14 250	8 300	5 050	13 300	15 300	20 350

Figure 20.6 *The cash-flow forecast of A. Nut Ltd*

Albert Spanner sets up as a manufacturer of machine tools by putting £17 400 into the business bank account on 1 January. For the first six months of the year he anticipates or budgets for the following:

- His forecasts for the purchase of raw materials and sales receipts for finished goods, based upon market research, are as follows:

	PURCHASES (£)	SALES (£)
January	3200	2000
February	3350	4000
March	4185	6200
April	5500	7000
May	5700	8200
June	5900	8400

- Albert Spanner has arranged two months' credit from suppliers.
- He expects one-quarter of sales to be for cash and the other three-quarters to be on credit. He anticipates two months credit on average to be taken by credit customers.
- Wages are expected to be £800 per month, paid in the same month.
- Machinery is to be purchased in January for £2500 and in April for £3500. On both occasions the owner anticipates making payments in the month following purchase.
- Rent for his factory is £3000 per annum, payable in equal instalments at the start of each month.
- Other overheads are £1000 per month, to be paid in the month following that in which they are incurred.
- In May, Albert Spanner will take out a loan for £4000, which he intends to put straight into the business bank account.

Prepare A. Spanner's cash-flow forecast for the first six months of the year.

Setting up home

This assignment can help you to provide evidence for assessment, or claim the following Core Skills:

Communication
Present information in a variety of visual forms
Communicate in writing

Application of number
Apply numerical skills and techniques

Information technology
Use a range of technological equipment and systems

Personal Skills
Deal with a combination of routine and non-routine tasks
Identify and solve routine and non-routine problems

Peter and Rachel are both 24, have had a steady relationship for the past two and half years and are planning to get married early next year. Rachel's parents are paying for the wedding and Peter's parents are going to give the couple £3000 as a wedding present which they intend to use towards setting up their new home.

Peter is an Assistant Store Manager for a large retail chain. His job involves him travelling up to 50 miles for work daily, visiting branches, acting as a relief manager to cover holidays, sickness, etc., and to gain new experiences. Peter currently drives a seven-year-old Vauxhall Cavalier which he intends to replace with a newer model during the next twelve months. He receives a mileage allowance from work of 20p per mile. Peter's salary is £9200 gross per annum and, apart from tax and national insurance, he has no other deductions from his pay. At present Peter lives with his parents, pays his 'keep', but has no savings at all. He has no other financial commitments.

Rachel is a Warehouse Manager at a large unit on a local industrial estate. She earns £10 000 gross per annum and

lives in a furnished flat. Apart from tax and National Insurance she has no other deductions from pay. Rachel also does some part-time bookkeeping work for which she earns about £30 per week. She walks to work and has accumulated £5000 in savings which is deposited with a local building society.

The most important decision which the couple have to make is to consider where to live. They do not know whether to live in Rachel's flat or whether to buy a flat or a house. At present Rachel's current expenses are as follows:

Rent £250
Council Tax £300
Telephone £60 per quarter
Gas £45 per quarter
Electricity £75 per quarter
TV rent and licence £150 per annum
Housekeeping £200 per month

If they do decide to purchase a house they will require furniture. They also estimate that a decent honeymoon will cost them at least £1500. Peter's car (tax, servicing and insurance, etc) is costing £500 per annum plus cost of petrol. Last year he drove just over 18 000 miles.

Task
Imagine that you are in the position of either Peter or Rachel. Carry out the necessary research to determine how they will manage financially during their first year of marriage. Your findings should:

- involve an estimate of their net earnings (with research of current tax allowances)
- take into consideration their wish to purchase a property and the associated costs
- account for the replacement of the car (if necessary this should involve careful research of an appropriate method of paying for the car)
- identify current figures for the Council Tax
- involve basic research of the housing market
- lead to a budget plan/cash-flow forecast for their twelve months – this will involve the use of a spreadsheet.
- suggest possible use of savings if any are identified.
- identify any other factors which might influence the decisions they have to make.

chapter **21** USING COSTS FOR PLANNING

Nearly all business managers have to deal with costs, sometimes on a day-to-day basis. A knowledge of costing techniques is, therefore, an essential part of the process of business planning. Costing techniques help managers to work out what they should be doing and provide a series of measures which help them to control various activities.

This chapter looks at the areas into which all costs fall.

Marginal and absorption costing techniques are explained, and there follows an analysis of budgetary control. Making decisions is rarely an easy process and the quality of information and the way it is handled will ultimately affect the risks an organisation takes. Techniques used in this chapter help managers to forecast events as part of the planning process.

The word **cost** has several meanings, even in everyday language. The cost of items we purchase is something we come across daily – it is a money sacrifice we have to make for the things we want. Organisations frequently refer to calculating the cost of an event or an activity – managers talk about **costing an activity.** Within this context they are using a knowledge of costs together with a knowledge of revenues to determine whether or not something they are planning will ultimately reap the rewards they desire. Today **cost accounting** and the use of costing techniques provides a useful source of data for management accountants.

Nearly all of an organisation's activities involve some sort of cost. A sound knowledge of these costs and their influence is fundamental for assessing profitability, as profits are only a reflection of income over and above such costs. Costs from the past – which therefore have already been incurred – often provide a guide to likely costs in the future.

There are two broad areas into which costs can be allocated. **Fixed costs** are those that *do not increase as the total output increases*. For example, if an organisation has

the capacity needed it might increase its production from 25 000 units to 30 000 units. Its rent, rates and heating bills will be the same, since they also had to be paid when the organisation was producing 25 000 units.

Variable costs are those that *increase as the output increases*, because more of these factors need to be employed as inputs in order to increase the output. For example, if you produce more items you will need more raw materials.

▪ MARGINAL COSTING ▪

Marginal costing is a commonly used technique which uses costs to forecast profits from the production and sales levels expected in future periods. The great benefit of marginal costing over other costing methods is that it overcomes the problem of allocating fixed costs – only variable costs are allocated, as we shall see.

The difference between an item's selling price and the variable costs needed to produce that item is known as the contribution (that is, its contribution to the whole profit).

Contribution = selling price per unit LESS variable costs per unit

By producing and selling enough units to produce a total contribution that is in excess of the *fixed* costs, an organisation will make a profit.

For example, Penzance Toys Ltd manufactures plastic train sets for young children. It anticipates that next year it will sell 8000 units at £12 per unit. Its variable costs are £5 per unit and its fixed costs are £9000. From the above formula we can deduce that the contribution is £12 minus £5, which is £7 per unit. Therefore – for each unit made – £7 will go towards paying off fixed costs. We can also show this using totals to show how much profit will be made if the company sells 8000 units (see Figure 21.1).

The problem can also be looked at by constructing a table as in Figure 21.2.

```
                                               (£)
Sales revenue (8000 × £12)                  96 000
less marginal costs (8000 × £5)             40 000
Total contribution                          56 000
Less fixed costs                             9 000
Net profit                                  47 000
```

Figure 21.1 *Profit statement for Penzance Toys Ltd*

Marginal costing is particularly useful for making short-term decisions – for example, helping to set the selling price of a product, or deciding whether or not to accept an order. It might also help an organisation to decide whether to buy in a component or whether to produce it themselves.

Break-even analysis

Break-even analysis is an extension of marginal costing. Breaking-even is the unique point at which an organisation makes neither profit nor loss. If sales go beyond the break-even point profits are made, and if they are below the break-even point losses are made. In marginal costing *it is the point at which the contribution equals the fixed costs.*

To calculate the break-even point there are two stages:

- Calculate the unit contribution (selling price less variable costs).
- Divide the fixed costs by the unit contribution:

$$\text{Break-even point} = \frac{\text{fixed costs}}{\text{unit contribution}}$$

Task

Rovers Medallions Ltd produces a standard size trophy for sports shops and clubs. It hopes to sell 2000 trophies next year at £9 per unit. Its variable costs are £5 per unit and its fixed costs are £4000. Draw up a profit statement to show how much profit it will make in the year. Also construct a table to show how much profit it will make at each 500 units of production up to 3000 units.

Units of production	Fixed costs (£)	Variable costs (£)	Total costs (£)	Revenue (£)	Profit (loss) (£)
1 000	9 000	5 000	14 000	12 000	(2 000)
2 000	9 000	10 000	19 000	24 000	5 000
3 000	9 000	15 000	24 000	36 000	12 000
4 000	9 000	20 000	29 000	48 000	19 000
5 000	9 000	25 000	34 000	60 000	26 000
6 000	9 000	30 000	39 000	72 000	33 000
7 000	9 000	35 000	44 000	84 000	40 000
8 000	9 000	40 000	49 000	96 000	47 000
9 000	9 000	45 000	54 000	108 000	54 000
10 000	9 000	50 000	59 000	120 000	61 000

Figure 21.2 *Profit table for Penzance Toys Ltd*

For example, in Penzance Toys Ltd (see opposite) the contribution per unit is £7 and the fixed costs are £9000. The break-even point would therefore be:

$$\frac{9000}{7} = 1286 \text{ units (to nearest unit)}$$

The **sales value** at the break-even point can be calculated by multiplying the number of units by the selling price per unit. For Penzance Toys this would be:

$$1286 \times £12 = £15\,432$$

Penzance Toys has covered its costs (fixed + variable) and broken-even with a sales value of £15 432. Anything sold in excess of this will provide it with profits.

If an organisation has a **profit target** to aim at, break even analysis can be used to calculate the number of units that need to be sold and the value of sales required to achieve that target.

For example, we can imagine that Penzance Toys wishes to achieve a target of £15 000 profit. By adding this £15 000 to the fixed costs and dividing by the contribution, the number of units can be found which need to be sold to meet this target. Thus:

$$\frac{£9000 + £15\,000}{£7} = 3429 \text{ units (to nearest unit)}$$

The difference between the break-even point and the selected level of activity designed to achieve the profit target is known as the margin of safety.

Cost/volume/profit analysis

Cost/volume/profit (CVP) analysis is a term sometimes used to show changes in the relationship between costs, production volumes and various levels of sales activity. This sort of information can be shown in the form of a **break-even chart.** This is the procedure to construct a break-even chart (you may find it helpful to look forward to Figure 21.3):

- Label the horizontal axis for units of production and sales.
- Label the vertical axis to represent the values of sales and costs.
- Plot fixed costs. Fixed costs will remain the same over all levels of production, so plot this as a straight line parallel to the horizontal axis.
- Plot the total costs (variable costs + fixed cost). This will be a line rising from where the fixed-cost line touches the vertical axis. It is plotted by calculating total costs at two or three random levels of production.
- Sales are plotted by taking two or three random levels of turnover. The line will rise from the intersection of the two axes.

The break-even point will be where the total-cost line and sales line intersect. The area to the *left* of the break-even point between the sales and total-cost lines will represent losses, and the area to the right of the break-even point between these lines will represent *profit*.

As always, an example will make this clearer. Eddie Bowen plans to set up a small restaurant. In doing so he knows that he will immediately incur annual fixed costs of £10 000. He is concerned about how many meals he will have to sell to break even. Extensive market research indicates that a typical customer will pay £8 for a meal, and Eddie knows that variable costs – such as cooking ingredients and the costs of serving customers – will amount to about £3. Eddie has set himself a profit target of £14 000 for the first year of operation. Our task is to advise Eddie on the number of meals he has to sell and to indicate to him his margin of safety.

Eddie's unit *contribution* is:
£8 − £3 (selling price − variable costs) = £5 per meal

His *break-even point* in units will be:
£10 000 (fixed costs) ÷ £5 (unit contribution)
= 2000 meals

The *sales value* of the meals will be:
2000 meals × £8 (selling price) = £16 000
His *profit target* will be achieved by:

$$\frac{£10\ 000\ (\text{fixed costs}) + £14\ 000\ (\text{profit target})}{£5\ (\text{unit contribution})} = 4800\ \text{meals}$$

The *margin of safety* will be the difference between the selected level of activity and the break-even point. It will be between 4800 meals with a turnover of £38 400 and 2000 meals with a turnover of £16 000.

The three random levels of variable costs and sales chosen for the purpose of plotting the break-even chart are at 1000 meals, 3000 meals and 5000 meals:

	1 000 meals (£)	3 000 meals (£)	5 000 meals (£)
Variable costs (£3/meal)	3 000	9 000	15 000
Fixed cost	10 000	10 000	10 000
Total cost	13 000	19 000	25 000
Sales	8 000	24 000	40 000

We can now plot the break-even chart (Figure 21.3) which shows graphically the break-even point of 2000 meals with a sales revenue of £16 000. The margin of safety can be seen on the chart if we identify the selected level of profit (at 4800 meals) and the targeted turnover (of £38 400), and compare this point with the break-even point.

The break-even chart is a simple **visual tool** enabling managers to anticipate the effects of changes in production and sales upon the profitability of an organisation's

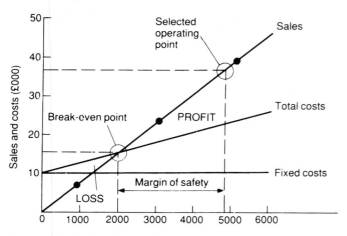

Figure 21.3 Eddie Bowen's break-even chart

activities. It emphasises the importance of earning revenue and is particularly helpful for those who are unused to interpreting accounting information.

Case Study

Taking over the family business

John Smith had a visit from an aged relative who wanted advice. For many years she had run a small hotel in a market town in the Thames Valley. After careful consideration she had decided to 'call it a day' and retire, but she was keen to see the business continue and wished to retain her ownership in it.

John is interested in a proposition she has put forward, which involves running the hotel on her behalf. The hotel has been allowed to deteriorate over the years and, in John's opinion, it is obvious that extensive refurbishment is necessary before he could realistically consider her proposal. The hotel is, however, in a prime spot, was extensively used little more than ten years ago, and John feels that with hard work it has the potential to become successful again.

He arranged for a number of quotations to be made for building works. The most favourable quotation received was for £180 000, which involved extensive interior redecoration and refurbishment as well as completely reorganising the reception and kitchen areas.

John's intention is that the finance for the building work should come from a five-year bank loan with a fixed annual interest rate of 10 per cent, payable each calendar month, and based upon the original sum. The loan principal would be paid back in five equal annual instalments.

He has estimated the following fixed and variable costs:

Fixed
Annual loan repayment (£36 000)
Annual interest on loan (£18 000)
Business rate and water rates (£7000 p.a.)
Insurance (£4500 p.a.)
Electricity (£1300 per quarter year)
Staff salaries (£37 000 p.a.)

Variable
These include direct labour such as cleaners and bar

staff, as well as the cost of food, bar stocks etc. After careful research John has estimated these to be £2000 for each 100 customers who visit the hotel.

John has had a local agency conduct an extensive market research survey and feels confident that the hotel will attract about 100 customers per week, who will each spend on average (including accommodation, food and drinks) about £70 in the hotel.

1 *Work out the break-even point for the hotel in both numbers of customers and value.*
2 *Work out the number of customers required to make a gross profit of £35 000.*
3 *Draw a break-even chart showing the break-even point, the profit target and the margin of safety.*
4 *What other information might John Smith require before deciding whether to go ahead with the project?*

Limitations of marginal costing

Marginal costing is often considered to over-simplify organisational behaviour by reducing it to an equation: how to generate sufficient contribution to cover fixed costs and provide a surplus (profits). Its limitations are several:

● It can be argued that, in real situations, fixed costs actually vary with different activity levels, and so a stepped fixed-cost line would provide a more accurate guide.
● Many organisations fail to break even because of a limiting factor restricting their ability to do so (e.g. shortage of space, labour or orders).
● The variable-cost and sales lines are unlikely to be linear (i.e. straight). Discounts, special contracts and overtime payments mean that the cost line is more likely to be a curve.
● Break-even charts depict short-term relationships, and forecasts are therefore unrealistic when the proposals cover a number of years.
● Break-even analysis is (like all other methods) dependent upon the accuracy of forecasts made about costs and revenues. Changes in the market and in the cost of raw materials could affect the success of the technique.

Task

Think about a business activity you might like to engage in. Describe the activity and what it involves. Anticipate the selling price you would expect to set and then work out your variable costs per unit and your overall fixed costs. Use the marginal costs technique to work out whether your project could be successful. Comment in detail on the outcome.

· USING COSTS FOR TOTAL COSTING ·

One limitation we identified of marginal costing was that it reduced accounting behaviour to an equation: how to generate sufficient contribution to cover fixed costs and provide a surplus in the form of profits.

An alternative approach to costing is to look at all of the costs incurred in producing a single product. This is known as absorption costing. With this method all costs – **both fixed and variable** – are absorbed into the cost of a product. The absorption unit cost is calculated by dividing total costs (both fixed and variable) by the total production in order to obtain a unit cost. In order to price the product, a profit margin is added to the cost to obtain a selling price.

For example, take a structure as in Figure 21.4. Although there is an absorption rate for fixed overheads, these overheads are fixed and, for example, might be £6000. If 1000 units are sold the fixed overhead absorbed will be 1000 × £3 or £3000 and stated profits under absorption costing will be 1000 × £2 or £2000. In reality there will be a net loss of £1000 because £3000 of the overhead has not been absorbed.

	Marginal		Total absorption	
	£		£	
Direct materials	5		Direct materials	5
Direct labour	3		Direct labour	3
Variable overheads	2		Variable overheads	2
			Fixed overheads (absorption rate)	3
Marginal cost	10		Unit cost	13
Contribution	5		Profit margin	2
	15			15

Figure 21.4

Classification of overheads

Whereas direct costs such as materials and labour are relatively easy to identify, to use the absorption process an analysis of overheads must take place.

An overhead comprises the 'total cost of indirect materials, wages and expenses'.

As we saw earlier in the chapter direct costs can be divided into those which are fixed and those which are variable. (See page 413.) Overheads can also be fixed and variable. Variable overheads will vary in some way with output whereas fixed overheads will *tend* to vary over a period of time. Having a good knowledge of the organisation will help to identify where overheads should go. Overheads are usually divided according to whether they are incurred in the factory or by selling or in administration (see Figure 21.5).

Type of overhead	Factory	Selling	Administration
Variable	power, maintenance, indirect wages.	commission vehicle costs, warehousing.	
Fixed	rent and rates, depreciation of machinery, management salaries.	advertising, reps' salaries, promotional expenses.	stationery, postage, insurance.

Figure 21.5 *The classification of overheads*

Information about overheads may be extracted from various parts of the organisation. For example:

- Stores – non-direct material requirements can be analysed.
- Payroll – this can be broken down between different cost centres.
- Journal entries – will record items of cost for which no payment is made such as depreciation.
- Cash book – overheads can be identified and analysed.
- Purchase day book – invoices received for items other than direct materials and direct expenses can be placed into the relevant overhead category.

For most organisations much of the above information, if not all, will be held on computer. A **coding system** for overheads will then allow further analysis to take place.

Whereas selling and administration overheads are relatively simple to account for, production is more complex and may involve allocation and apportionment.

Allocation and apportionment

Allocation is the allotment of complete overhead items to cost centres. For example, if there was a quality inspector in each of five departments, the wages of each inspector would be allocated to the department in which each worked.

Apportionment is the allotment of only parts or proportions of an overhead item to cost centres. For example, if only one quality inspector supervised the work of the five departments then a way of apportioning the overheads would have to be found. This might be done on the basis of the time spent in each department.

There are several methods of apportioning overheads:

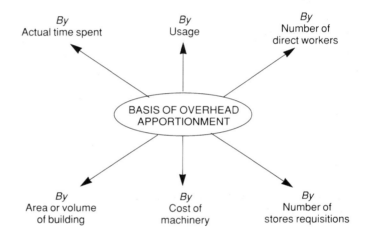

Figure 21.6 *Methods of apportioning overheads*

The basis for apportionment can be arrived at using simple ratios. In the following example overheads are apportioned using each of the above methods:

Basis of overhead apportionment	Overhead	Ratios for each production department		
		Dept 1	Dept 2	Dept 3
Time spent (hours)	Maintenance	2000	2000	1000
Area (square metres)	Rent	500	300	200
Usage (machine hours)	Power	8000	5000	7000
Direct workers	Canteen	12	10	10
Machine cost (£)	Depreciation	20 000	15 000	5000
Requisitions	Storekeeping	10	20	20

By now looking at the total cost for each overhead the overhead can be apportioned between departments:

Overhead	Total Cost (£)	Dept 1 (£)	Dept 2 (£)	Dept 3 (£)
Maintenance	2500	1000	1000	500
Rent	3000	1500	900	600
Power	2000	800	500	700
Canteen	1200	450	375	375
Depreciation	4000	2000	1500	500
Storekeeping	1500	300	600	600

Task

Using the ratios below apportion overheads to each department:

Dept 1	Dept 2	Dept 3	Overhead	Basis for apportionment
60	90	90	Quality control	hours spent
140	70	70	Maintenance	hours spent
600	1200	600	Power	machine hours
4	5	11	Wages office	direct workers

The total costs of each overhead was as follows:
- quality control   = £5400
- maintenance   = £6000
- power   = £5000
- wages office   = £7500

Overhead absorption rate

Having analysed all factory overheads and apportioned them to production departments, the final step is to charge these overheads to cost units. By doing this it is possible to identify how much of the overheads are **absorbed** in each period of the year as and when this happens, and then be able to relate this to forecasts of total overheads and output. There are two stages of calculation:

- calculating the overhead absorption rate
- applying this rate to the cost units.

The two most common methods of doing this are the units of output method and the direct labour hour method.

1 Units of output method. With this method overheads are absorbed for each unit of output.

$$\text{Overhead absorption rate (OAR)} = \frac{\text{Total overheads}}{\text{Total units of output}}$$

This rate is developed by **forecasting** total overheads and output for the forthcoming year. Overheads will be absorbed by applying this rate to **actual** output achieved in each period.

Overhead absorbed = actual units of output × OAR.

For example, Department S has the following:

Budgeted annual output   = 12 000 units
Budgeted annual overheads   = £48 000
Actual output for Jan   = 1200 units

$$\text{OAR} = \frac{£48\,000}{12\,000} = £4 \text{ per unit}$$

$$\text{Overhead absorbed in January} = 1200 \times £4 = £4800$$

2 Direct labour hour method. With this method, overheads are absorbed per direct labour hour.

$$\text{OAR} = \frac{\text{Total overheads}}{\text{Total direct labour hours}}$$

This rate is developed by forecasting total overheads and direct labour hours for the forthcoming year. Overheads will be absorbed by applying this rate to actual direct labour hours worked in each period.

Overhead absorbed = actual direct labour hours × OAR

For example, Department T has the following:

Budgeted annual direct labour hours   = 43 200 hours
Budgeted Annual Overheads   = £108 000
Actual direct labour hours for Jan   = 3000 hours

$$\text{OAR} = \frac{£108\,000}{43\,200} = £2.50 \text{ per direct labour hour}$$
Overhead absorbed in January = 3000 × £2.50 = £7500

Over- and under-absorption

As absorption rates are based upon budgeted figures which involve forecasts of overheads and units of output or direct labour hours, they are pre-set for the forthcoming accounting period. It is quite likely during the year, possibly because of seasonal variations in demand, for actual output or actual direct labour hours not to be used at consistent rates each month. Where this happens there is some degree of over- or under-absorption.

For instance, using the two examples above we can illustrate the following:

1 Actual overhead absorbed in January = £4800
   Budgeted overhead for Jan 1000 (units)
   × 4 (OAR) = £4000
   Therefore in January actual overheads over-absorbed £800.
2 Actual overhead absorbed in January = £7500
   Budgeted overhead for Jan 3600 (hours)
   × 2.5 (OAR) = £9000
   Therefore in January actual overheads under-absorbed £1500.

· BUDGETARY CONTROL ·

Budgetary control is the technique of looking into an organisation's future in order to anticipate what is going to happen and then trying to make it happen. It is considered to be a system of **responsibility** accounting because it puts an onus upon managers to perform in a way that has been outlined for them, and its success will depend upon the quality of information provided.

In Chapter 20 we looked at how to forecast financial requirements with a cash budget or cash flow forecast. We saw that a cash budget ensured that an organisation would have sufficient cash to cater for any **plans** it might have, and that it would help the organisation to highlight any problems at an early stage so that managers could take the necessary action.

Organisations that fail to produce a budget are likely to be uncertain about what is happening. When their financial accounts are drawn up and presented the owners or managers may be pleased or upset with the results. This is uncertain and undisciplined. Management should not have to wait for the financial statements to understand how they have performed. Budgeting helps them to understand how they are performing as well as how they are likely to perform in the future. Budgets can cover every aspect of an organisation's activities – production, cash, overheads,

labour, purchases, debtors, creditors etc. Information drawn from these separate budgets can then be used to forecast the final accounts for the end of the following year.

Case Study

The born-again IBM

The UK subsidiary of IBM, the world's largest computer manufacturer, has been shaken to the core as drastic measures to improve efficiency and effectiveness have been put into action. These include:

- the loss of many jobs
- a pay-incentive scheme which depends upon customers' opinions
- a futuristic plan to manage individuals' workloads through a computerised control system.

There is scarcely an employee left at IBM at any level who has been unaffected by the changes. IBM is going through this corporate transformation as it fights with increased competition, declining profit margins and overweight bureaucracy. Mr Nick Temple, IBM UK's general manager, who was recently appointed for planning and overseeing the shakeup of the UK operation, describes it as 'a renaissance: a rebirth of a local company'. His mission was to create a blueprint for a lean, flexible organisation able to respond to its customers' requirements speedily and efficiently.

The 'Temple Plan' involved a powerful attack on expenses – with an across-the-board 8 per cent reduction. It also involved measures which not only change people's jobs but also their careers and ideas. To measure the success of the renaissance IBM UK today has a series of criteria, such as:

- a computer model of the company which shows how successfully resources are deployed and the extent to which overheads are being reduced
- an accreditation process which measures the level and variety of skills acquired by IBM staff

- opinion surveys to measure whether the corporate culture is changing fast enough
- quality surveys against both US standards and customer opinions
- business performance measured by sales and pre-tax profits.

1 Given the problems at IBM UK, how important is forecasting to the company?
2 How might budgeting help IBM UK to become a 'lean, flexible organisation'?
3 Comment on the prospect of a pay-incentive scheme dependent upon customers' opinions.
4 How might the computer model manage the company's budgetary activities?

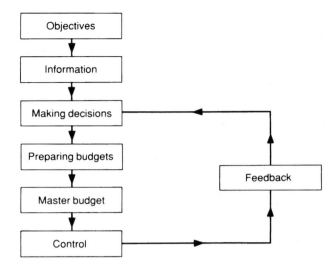

Figure 21.7 *Preparing a budget*

We all budget to some extent. Our short-term budget is probably our plan to survive the month, meet all our commitments and do all the things we intend to do. Our longer-term budget might involve planning for Christmas presents or for how we are going to pay the car insurance. In exactly the same way organisations try to dig deep into their future, to plan ahead and forecast their commitments. Budgets enable an organisation to prepare for the year ahead and include all activities as part of a longer plan, perhaps over three or five years.

The budgeting team

An organisation may appoint a **budget controller** to coordinate the budgetary activities, and the **budgeting team** then consists of representatives from various areas of activity within the organisation. The task of the team can be considered under headings (see Figure 21.7):

- *Considering objectives.* The team will undertake activities designed to enable the organisation to meet its objectives (e.g. profit maximising, improving market share, improving product quality).
- *Providing information.* The team will also look at figures from previous years so that new budgets can to some extent be based on past results. A clear knowledge of the environment in which the organisation is competing is also important.
- *Making decisions.* Whenever forward planning takes place it will highlight the need to make decisions.
- *Preparing budgets.* Detailed budgets are then prepared for all areas of the organisation's activity.

- *Preparing a master budget.* The individual budgets, when linked together, can be used to forecast a set of final accounts.
- *Controlling.* Even though budgets are drawn up, this does not always mean that such plans are successful. Managers try to use their budgets as a guide to achieving certain results. If there is a difference between actual performance at the end of a year and budgeted performance, action can be taken.

Variance analysis

Variance analysis can be used to quantify the difference between the budget and the actual outcome, and feedback from such an analysis can affect decision-making in subsequent years.

Variance analysis detects problems and enables managers to take prompt action to improve efficiency and profitability. For example, there could be a sudden upturn in expenditure on raw materials, caused perhaps by one of the following:

- increased wastage
- inefficiency by operators
- materials damaged in transit
- inefficient buying.

The list is not exhaustive, but the variance analysis has indicated a problem and the manager can use experience to find out the cause.

What a budgetary system can do

Each year the way the organisation functions is reviewed by the budgeting team, and this provides a **better understanding** of the organisation as a whole. In addition, budgeting increases co-operation between various parts of an organisation and lowers departmental barriers.

When a budget is drawn up, non-accountants from various parts of the organisation become more aware of the **importance of costs**. This helps them to work to achieve the budgeted targets. It also helps individuals across the organisation to become aware of **profitability**.

Sometimes, however, there are problems with a system of budgetary control:

- If the actual results are completely different from the targets, the budget can lose its significance as a means of control. Whereas a **fixed budget** is not able to adapt to such changes, a **flexible budget** will recognise changes in behaviour and can be amended to fall into line with changing activities.
- Following a budget too rigidly can restrict an organisation's activities. On the other hand, if a manager realises towards the end of the year that his or her department has *under*spent, he or she might go on a spending spree.
- If budgets are *imposed* upon managers without sufficient consultation, they may be ignored.

Task

Interview someone who has responsibility for a budgeted area of activity. Find out how the budget helps and hinders the ways in which the person supervises his or her area of operations.

· PREPARING A BUDGET ·

Budgets are prepared for a set time period known as a **budget period** (quite often a year). Sometimes the budget period is broken down into shorter **control periods**, such as months. Each part of the master budget is the responsibility of an individual manager, and the part of the organisation for which each budget is prepared is known as a **budget centre**.

In looking at budgets we shall start by drawing up **cash budgets**, and take them through to final accounts. Then we shall look at budgets for other activities.

Example 1 – P. Rogers (sole trader)

Peter Rogers has recently been declared redundant by a large industrial component manufacturer in the North East of England. However, he had been worrying about the prospect of redundancy for some time and had been making plans for such an eventuality. In his spare time he had been repairing cars for friends, and this led him to decide to use his redundancy money to start a garage business locally. Peter has found a suitable site.

Drawing up the opening balance sheet

The purchase price of the existing garage is £130 000. It comprises a small filling station with two pumps, a small office, toilets and a service area of 200 square metres containing an inspection pit and other facilities. This has been valued at £100 000, and the remainder of the selling price is for equipment and tools valued at £25 000, and petrol and oil stocks of £5000.

	(£)	(£)
Fixed assets		
Land and buildings		100 000
Equipment and tools		25 000
		125 000
Current assets		
Stocks – petrol and oil	5 000	
Bank	10 000	
Working capital		15 000
		140 000
Less **Long-term liabilities**		
Bank loan		40 000
		100 000
FINANCED BY:		
Capital		100 000
Capital employed		100 000

Figure 21.8 *Opening balance sheet of P. Rogers' garage at 1 January 1992*

Peter received £40 000 redundancy money. He has surrendered two life insurance policies for a further sum of £30 000, and has remortgaged his house and obtained £30 000. He intends to borrow another £40 000 from a local bank. Hence, when he has paid the £130 000 purchase price he will have £10 000 left in the bank account.

His **opening balance sheet** will therefore be as shown in Figure 21.8.

Drawing up the cash budget

Peter has put together estimated *sales figures* for the first six months based upon the records of his predecessor. In the list below, the left column shows Peter's projected sales of petrol and oil, and the right column shows expected income from repairs and servicing:

Jan	8 000	3 100
Feb	9 800	2 100
Mar	12 300	1 700
Apr	11 200	1 800
May	8 100	2 300
June	8 300	3 100
	57 700	14 100

All *sales* of petrol and oil will be for cash, with immediate payment. It is anticipated that one half of the receipts for repairs and servicing will be in cash, received immediately, and one half will be on one month's credit terms.

Deliveries for January to March inclusive will involve £8000 of petrol and oil delivered on each occasion, and from April to June will involve £7000 of petrol delivered each month. One month's credit is given by the supplier.

Other *expenses* each month will be £200 for wages, £90 for insurance, £100 for the business rate, and £30 for advertising. These are all to be paid at the end of each month.

Peter *draws* £800 from the business each month for personal use. It is estimated that the *stocks* of petrol and oil at the end of the six-month period will be valued at £4400. Peter intends to *purchase* a pick-up truck in March for £21 000 and a van in June for £10 000.

Peter's **cash budget** (the cash-flow forecast) for the first six months will therefore be as shown in Figure 21.9.

Drawing up the master budget

Debtors for repairs and servicing are £1550 at the end of June, and *creditors* for petrol supplies are expected to be

	Jan (£)	Feb (£)	Mar (£)	Apr (£)	May (£)	Jun (£)
Receipts						
Sales – cash	9 500	10 850	13 150	12 100	9 250	9 850
Sales – credit	–	1 550	1 050	850	900	1 150
Total receipts	9 550	12 400	14 200	12 950	10 150	11 000
Payments						
Petrol and oil	–	8 000	8 000	8 000	7 000	7 000
Wages	200	200	200	200	200	200
Business rate	100	100	100	100	100	100
Insurance	90	90	90	90	90	90
Advertising	30	30	30	30	30	30
Drawings	800	800	800	800	800	800
Motor vehicles	–	–	21 000	–	–	10 000
Total payments	1 220	9 220	30 220	9 220	8 220	18 220
Opening bank	10 000	18 330	21 510	5 490	9 220	11 150
Add receipts	9 550	12 400	14 200	12 950	10 150	11 000
	19 550	30 730	35 710	18 440	19 370	22 150
Less payments	1 220	9 220	30 220	9 220	8 220	18 220
Balance c/f	18 330	21 510	5 490	9 220	11 150	3 930

Figure 21.9 *P. Rogers' cash budget*

	(£)	(£)
Sales		71 800
Less cost of sales		
Opening stock	5 000	
Add purchases	45 000	
	50 000	
Less closing stock	4 400	45 600
Gross profit		26 200
Less expenses:		
Wages	1 200	
Business rate	600	
Insurance	540	
Advertising	180	2 520
Net profit		23 680

Figure 21.10 *P. Rogers' financial operating statement*

	(£)	(£)
Fixed assets		
Land and buildings		100 000
Equipment and tools		25 000
Motor vehicles		31 000
		156 000
Current assets		
Closing stock –		
petrol and oil	4 400	
Debtors	1 550	
Bank	3 930	
	9 880	
Less **Current liabilities**		
Creditors	7 000	
Working capital		2 880
		158 880
Less **Long-term liabilities**		
Bank loan		40 000
		118 800
FINANCED BY:		
Capital		100 000
Add net profit		23 680
		123 680
Less drawings		4 800
		118 880

Figure 21.11 *P. Rogers' forcasted balance sheet*

£7000 at the end of June. From this information, and the totals in the cash budget, the **financial operating statement** for the six months ending on 30 June 1992 can be drawn up as shown in Figure 21.10. The **forecasted balance sheet** at 30 June is shown in Figure 21.11. These two documents constitute P. Rogers' **master budget** for the first six months of operation.

Task

Rachel Salt set up in business as a grocer on 1 January 1994. She spent £100 000 on land and buildings and £5000 on fixtures and fittings. She started with stocks of £1000. She also put £14 000 from her bank account into the business. Rachel has forecast the following figures:

- She expects sales over the next six months to be:

	(£)
Jan	2100
Feb	1800
Mar	1800
Apr	2100
May	1800
June	2000

All sales are for cash with immediate payment.

- Deliveries of stock to her shop from January to June will be made monthly. She expects to purchase:

	(£)
Jan	1400
Feb	1200
Mar	1700
Apr	1800
May	1200
June	1200

Two months' credit is given by suppliers.

- Other expenses each month will include:

	(£)
Wages	400
Business rate	70
Insurance	30
Transport	20
Advertising	20

- Rachel draws £600 each month for her personal use.
- It is estimated that stock at the end of June will be worth £4300.
- Rachel intends to purchase a new till in March for £400.

1 Show Rachel's opening balance sheet.
2 Forecast her likely cash flow over the first six months.
3 Produce a financial operating statement, and a forecasted balance sheet for the end of the period.

Example 2 – Meashams Ltd

In this example we look at an exercise which produces:

- a **raw materials budget** showing figures for each month
- a **production budget** showing figures (in units) for each month
- a **production cost budget** showing cost figures for each month
- a statement showing total **debtors** and **creditors** at the end of a six-month period
- a **cash budget**
- a **forecasted operating statement**
- a **forecasted balance sheet**.

```
                              (£)        (£)        (£)
Fixed assets
Premises                                           90 000
Plant and machinery                               105 000
Office equipment                                    9 000
Motor vehicles                                     50 000
                                                  254 000

Current assets
Stocks - finished goods              26 000
Stocks - raw material                 2 000
Debtors                              87 000
Bank                                  4 000
                                    119 000
Less Current liabilities
Creditors for fixed expenses  3 000
Creditors for raw materials
  (Mar 28 500, Apr 25 500)   54 000  57 000
Working capital                                    62 000
                                                  316 000

FINANCED BY:
Share capital: Ordinary shares                    250 000
               Preference shares                   46 000
Reserves                                           20 000
                                                  316 000
```

Figure 21.12 *Balance sheet of Meashams Ltd at 30 April 1994*

Alison Bicknell, the accountant of Meashams Ltd, has been asked to set up a budgetary system to forecast the next six months' activities. As budgetary controller she has met representatives from various departments before putting together her budgetary estimates. On the 30 April 1994, Meashams' balance sheet was as shown in Figure 21.12.

The plans

Meashams' plans for the next six months are as follows:

- After lengthy consultations, a sales price of £15.00 per unit has been agreed. By carefully analysing the market the *number* of sales are expected to be:

May	June	July	Aug	Sept	Oct
6500	7750	8000	8200	8550	9000

All of the sales are on credit, and debtors usually pay their outstanding balances one month after they have received the goods.

- In order to satisfy production requirements it has been agreed that purchases of raw materials will be:

May	June	July	Aug	Sept	Oct
£23 700	£24 300	£24 500	£27 500	£28 250	£24 750

All raw materials are bought on credit, and the creditors for raw materials will be paid two months after purchase.

- It has been decided that production will be 8000 units per month from May to August and 9000 units per month in September and October.

- Production costs will be (per unit):

	(£)
Direct materials	3.00
Direct labour	4.00
Variable overheads	6.00
	13.00

- Fixed expenses average £3000 per month and these are always paid one month in arrears.

To forecast the sales income the selling price of £15.00 is multiplied by the number of units for each month. For example, in May the value of sales is expected to be £97 500, June £116 250, July £120 000, August £123 000, September £128 250 and October £135 000. The total sales figure for the six months is therefore £720 000. As debtors pay one month after they have received the goods, the debtors from the balance sheet in April will pay in May; May debtors will pay in June etc. When Alison produces her cash budget these will be entered as *receipts*.

The raw materials budget

The **raw materials budget** is intended to ensure that there is always an availability of resources to move on to the production line and that levels do not dwindle. Decisions about minimum stock levels have already been taken. The

	May (£)	June (£)	July (£)	Aug (£)	Sept (£)	Oct (£)
Opening stock	2 000	1 700	2 000	2 500	6 000	7 250
Add purchases	23 700	24 300	24 500	27 500	28 250	24 750
	25 700	26 000	26 500	30 000	34 250	32 000
Less production materials	24 000	24 000	24 000	24 000	27 000	27 000
Closing stock of raw materials	1 700	2 000	2 500	6 000	7 250	5 000

Figure 21.13 *Meashams' raw materials budget*

	May	June	July	Aug	Sept	Oct
Opening stock (finished goods)	2 000	3 500	3 750	3 750	3 550	4 000
Add production	8 000	8 000	8 000	9 000	8 000	9 000
	10 000	11 500	11 750	11 750	12 550	13 000
Less sales	6 500	7 750	8 000	8 200	8 550	9 000
Closing stock (finished goods)	3 500	3 750	3 750	3 550	4 000	4 000

Figure 21.14 *Meashams' production budget (in units)*

raw materials budget involves adding purchases to the opening stocks materials for each month, and then deducting those used in production each month (see Figure 21.13).

It must be remembered that creditors for raw materials are paid two months after purchase. This means that those for March (as shown in the balance sheet in Figure 21.12) will be paid in May, those from April in June etc. In the cash budget these will be payments.

The production budget

The **production budget** links production volume with sales volume. The production budget is therefore normally produced in units. The opening stock of finished goods is added to anticipated production levels for each month, and then the monthly sales are deducted. This is shown in Figure 21.14.

The closing stock of finished goods is therefore 4000 units at the end of October. As stocks are valued at their cost price, the value of the closing stock of finished goods – to be transferred to the balance sheet – will be 4000 units × £13 production cost, which is £52 000.

The production cost budget

The **production cost budget** supplies the costs of production on a month-by-month basis and gives the total cost of goods completed, which can then be transferred to the trading section of the forecasted operating statement. It involves multiplying the unit production costs of direct materials, direct labour and direct overheads by the number of units produced month by month. This is shown in Figure 21.15.

Debtors and creditors

Alison now works out the **debtors** figure for the end of October. As debtors pay their outstanding balances one month after they have received the goods, the debtors figure for the end of October will be the sales figure for *September*, that is £128 250. She knows that **creditors** for raw materials are paid two months after purchase. The creditors figure for the end of October will therefore be made up of *September's* and *October's* purchases of raw materials of £28 250 and £24 750, totalling £53 000.

	May (£)	June (£)	July (£)	Aug (£)	Sept (£)	Oct (£)	Total (£)
Materials cost	24 000	24 000	24 000	24 000	27 000	27 000	150 000
Labour cost	32 000	32 0000	32 000	32 000	36 000	36 000	200 000
Variable cost	48 000	48 000	48 000	48 000	54 000	54 000	300 000
	104 000	104 000	104 000	104 000	117 000	117 000	650 000

Figure 21.15 *Meashams' production cost budget*

	May (£)	Jun (£)	Jul (£)	Aug (£)	Sept (£)	Oct (£)
Receipts						
Sales	87 000	97 500	116 250	120 000	123 000	128 250
Total receipts	87 00	97 500	116 250	120 000	123 000	128 250
Payments						
Raw materials	28 500	25 500	23 700	24 300	24 500	27 500
Direct labour	32 000	32 000	32 000	32 000	36 000	36 000
Variable o/h	48 000	48 000	48 000	48 000	48 000	54 000
Fixed expenses	3 000	3 000	3 000	3 000	3 000	3 000
Total payments	111 500	108 500	106 700	107 300	117 500	120 500
Opening balance	4 000	(20 500)	(31 500)	(21 950)	(9 250)	(3 750)
Add receipts	87 000	97 500	116 250	120 000	123 000	128 250
	91 000	77 000	84 750	98 050	113 750	124 500
Less payments	111 500	108 500	106 700	107 300	117 500	120 500
Balance c/f	(20 500)	(31 500)	(21 950)	(9 250)	(3 750)	4 000

Figure 21.16 *Meashams' cash budget for May-October*

	(£)	(£)	(£)
Fixed assets			
Premises			90 000
Plant and machinery			105 000
Office equipment			9 000
Motor vehicles			50 000
			254 000
Current assets			
Stocks – finished goods (4000 units)		52 000	
Stocks – raw materials		5 000	
Debtors		135 000	
Bank		4 000	
		196 000	
Less **Current liabilities**			
Creditors for fixed expenses	3 000		
Creditors for raw materials			
(Sep 28 250 + Oct 24 750)	53 000	56 000	
Working capital			140 000
			394 000
FINANCED BY:			Share capital
			250 000
			Ordinary shares
			46 000
			Preference
shares			
			98 000
		Reserves (£20000 + retained profit)	

Figure 21.17 *Meashams' forcasted balance sheet as at 31 October*

	(£)
Sales	720 000
Less cost of sales:	
Opening stock of	
finished goods 26 000	
Add cost of goods supplied 650 000	
676 000	
Less closing stock of	
finished goods 52 000	
	624 000
Gross profit	96 000
Less overheads:	
Fixed expences 18 000	
Net profit	78 000

Figure 21.18 *Meashams' forecasted operating statement*

The cash budget, forecasted operating statement and balance sheet

Alison now has sufficient information to work out the **cash budget**. This is shown in Figure 21.16. With all sectional budgets completed, she can finally draw up a master budget in the form of a balance sheet and forecasted operating statement . These are shown in Figures 21.17 and 21.18.

Information from the sectional budgets and master budget can now be fed back into departments. The budgetary system has coordinated the revenue and expenditure areas and organised them into an overall plan.

▪ USING ACCOUNTING INFORMATION FOR FORECASTING ▪

The main problem with any information system is that is reflects data from the past and present, and will only enable *predictions* to be made about the future. At the same time, numerous pressures in their jobs may impose constraints upon managers which affect the quality of information they collect. The problems can be numerous. Clearly nothing can be forecasted with absolute certainty. No matter what financial and marketing research takes place, every organisation has to take risks. Though accounting information may reduce the unpredictability of events in the future, it will never eliminate it.

The economic recession of the late 1980s and early 1990s claimed some notable scalps. For example, during 1992 and 1993 such well-known businesses as Lyon's Maid, Dan Air and the Queen's Moat House hotel group either went into receivership or were rescued at the last minute by a take over. In fact business failures in 1992 were at their highest level for many years.

Many organisations found their forecasts completely out of line with their plans when they became sandwiched between a falling market for their products and high interest rates on debts they took on during the boom years of the mid-1980s. Companies which were highly geared – with a high proportion of loan capital to share capital – were often particularly vulnerable to the climate. Late payments by larger organisations, and tough action by the banks over loans and overdrafts, also contributed to many failures.

The early signs of a business's failure appear long before it crashes. Initially, profits start to fall, gearing starts to increase and then losses are reported. The beginning of the end is when trading in shares is suspended. **Liquidation** occurs when it is considered that a company can no longer pay its debts – liquidation is ordered by a court, usually at the behest of a creditor. In many cases the next step is **receivership** – this involves the appointment of an independent accountant to supervise the sale of the company. Over the whole period that the company is struggling to survive there is always the possibility of a **white knight** attempting to launch a rescue for it. For example, over the eleven years that the newspaper *Financial Weekly* existed, it had four different proprietors who collectively lost about £11 million. It was rescued from extinction twice, had two management buyouts and was in a permanent state of crisis. Against the recent background of notable business failures, there always seem to be many thousands of budding business entrepreneurs willing to put their ideas into action – and many will undoubtedly do so with their redundancy money!

1 *List five possible causes of business failure.*
2 *What measures might an organisation take to avoid failure?*

3 What are the various stages of a business failing?
4 Find examples of business failures reported in the national newspapers. Can you find a white knight?

Case Study

Britain's twilight homes

At Tony Acton's elegant mews house there is nothing to betray his role as chairman of a conglomerate with products ranging from kitty-litter to nursing homes. Acton is one of a growing band of corporate executives who are keen to pursue demographic changes which will see Britain's over-85 population increase by 40 per cent by the year 2000. Welfare subsidies and the spur of the Community Care Bill have recently encouraged more development of nursing homes in the private sector.

However, according to the industry's trade associations, nursing and residential homes are closing at the rate of four a week, sunk by high interest rates, rising staff costs and falling occupancy rates. The nursing home sector, previously dominated by husband-and-wife teams, had become ripe for rationalisation and for large organisations to move in. One such organisation is Takare. Takare's blueprint is to build nursing homes to its own specifications. All except one are in single-storey 30-bed units built round a central management facility. The company believes it can benefit from greater economies of scale. The chairman feels that the company's proven formula enables it to 'give twice the care for half the cost'. Where others seem to be failing Takare seems destined for success.

1 Explain how larger organisations are able to run nursing homes more efficiently than smaller organisations.
2 If you were running a small nursing home, in the sort of market indicated here, how would you attempt to manage the finances of your business? What decisions might you have to make?

Element assignment

The importance of selling in high volumes

This assignment can help you to provide ev idence for assessment, or claim the following Core Skills:

Communication
Receive and respond to a variety of information
Present information in a variety of visual forms
Participate in oral and non-verbal communication

Personal Skills
Transfer skills gained to new and changing situations
Relate to and interact effectively with individuals and groups
Work effectively as a member of a team

You are a trainee accountant working for the regional office of a large petrol company. You have been presented with the following memo from your senior accountant.

MEMORANDUM

TO: *Trainee Accountant*   REF: RD/BC
From: Rita Daines   DATE: 10 APRIL 19–3
     (Senior Accountant)

PRESENTATION TO LOCAL SERVICE STATION MANAGERS

I want you to prepare a presentation for six service station managers which will take place in the Boardroom on 15 May. You will need to show the managers the importance of selling high volumes of petrol in order to keep down unit costs. Please prepare four overhead transparencies to support your presentation.

You must also work with Jane Johnson the Sales Manager to come up with at least six clear suggestions as to ways in which more motorists can be encouraged to buy petrol.

You will need to calculate how much the margin is at each of the three retail outlets shown in the pie charts (see my notes below) using the figures given for sales. Also explain why retail outlet No 3 will be in the best position to improve its premises and equipment.

You may use my notes to develop some ideas for the first part of the presentation.

                              RD

Working in groups prepare the presentation requested in the memo. The notes (below) provided by the senior accountant give some useful background information.

Volume

The quantity of product that you sell is a critical factor in the success of every kind of business. The reason for this is that every business has to pay two different types of cost: fixed costs and variable costs.

Fixed costs

So-called because they remain the same no matter how many units of product you sell. For instance, a shop still has to pay the same rent, rates, heating and lighting, staff wages, insurance and much else no matter how large or small its sales are in a particular month. The same applies to a factory, or any other kind of business. (Of course, if sales remain low over a long period, say a year, then the owners of the business will have to think of reducing its fixed costs, by taking smaller premises, for instance, or employing fewer people.)

Variable costs

These are those that vary with the number of units you sell. For instance, if your shop sells confectionery, the more units of confectionery you sell to customers, the more you have to buy from the wholesaler; if your factory makes furniture, the more units of furniture you make, the more wood and other materials you have to buy from your supplier. In other words, your costs vary directly with the number of units you sell.

What is the margin?

The difference between the variable costs of each unit of product and the price paid by the customer is called the 'margin'.

The proportion of fixed costs to the margin changes with the number of units you sell. For instance, if your fixed costs are £1000 a year and you sell 100 units, then each unit has to carry £10 of fixed costs. If the margin is £20 then the fixed costs represent 50 per cent of the margin.

If you sell 500 units, then each unit has to carry only £2 of fixed costs – which is 10 per cent of the margin.

Fixed and variable costs

Fixed costs at a service station include: staffing, insurance, heat/light, security, business rate and office costs.

Variable costs are the costs paid by the service station to the refinery for bulk supplies of petrol, diesel and lubricants, plus items such as stationery and sales promotion.

The left-hand side of Figure 21.19 shows a typical value for the total fixed costs of a typical service station. The right-hand side shows a typical value for the variable costs. The table has been simplified for the sake of clarity, and of course the figures given are examples only.

Fixed Costs		Variable Costs expressed in pence per litre (ppl)	
Staff	£35 000	Fuel	30.00ppl
Insurance	£2 000	Bank charges	0.30ppl
Heat/light/		Sales promotion	
power	£5 500	& advertising	0.15ppl
Security	£1 500	Postage &	
Business rate	£6 000	stationery	0.03ppl
Maintenance			
& repair	£2 000		
Office	£6 500		
Depreciation	£3 500		
Total	£62 000	Total	30.48ppl

Figure 21.19 *Typical fixed and variable costs of service station.*

Note: To cover fixed costs of £62 000, a service station selling 500 000 litres a year must add 12.4 per litre (£62 000 divided by 500 000) to the variable costs.

A similar sized but more successful service station selling 3 million litres a year would only have to add 2.06p per litre (£62 000 divided by 3 000 000). In other words, the minimum price per litre (before profit) that the lower volume station must charge its customers is 42.88p (30.48p + 12.4p). The higher volume station can cover all its costs, fixed and variable, by charging only 32.54p (30.48 + 2.06p).

The higher volume station can afford to charge less per litre, and still make a bigger margin – to be used for further investment and distribution to shareholders.

These figures are examples only. There is a further fact to remember: the variable cost of fuel (the price the service station has to pay) can go up or go down (because of currency fluctuations or bulk deals) over a period.

The pie-charts show how the per-unit ratio between fixed costs and variable costs changes with the number of units sold.

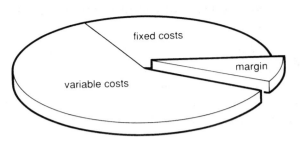

**Retail outlet No 1
sells 150 000 units per annum**

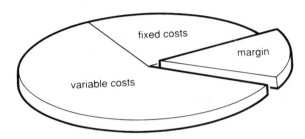

**Retail outlet No 2
sells 200 000 units per annum**

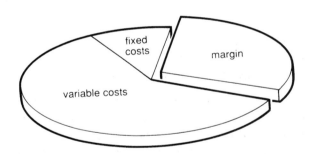

**Retail outlet No 3
sells 500 000 units per annum**

Cost amd margin per unit sold

The more units sold, the lower the proportion of the unit price taken by fixed costs.

Assume:

- each unit has a retail price of £1
- variable costs per unit are 60p
- fixed costs are £50 000 per annum
- each of the three retail outlets (1, 2 and 3) have the same fixed costs (rents, rates, staff, depreciation, etc.).

chapter **22** UNDERSTANDING FINANCIAL STATEMENTS

With the increasing complexity and diversity of information available to managers and administrators across the working environment, it has become important today for more employees to be able to read and understand financial statements. Such statements help to provide the basic information necessary to make decisions.

In this chapter we look first at the basic financial statements of a sole trader and then at those of other organisations. We consider what these statements mean and how they can be interpreted. The chapter provides a series of tasks related to each area to enable users to develop basic accounting skills.

What sort of statements do you know about? You have probably seen a bank statement, and may even have been asked to give a statement to the police about an event you have witnessed or have been involved in. While these statements are quite obviously different in kind, they do have some things in common. Each provides a summary

of events, and it may be possible to use these to find out:

● about something that has happened
● the current state of events
● likely developments in the future.

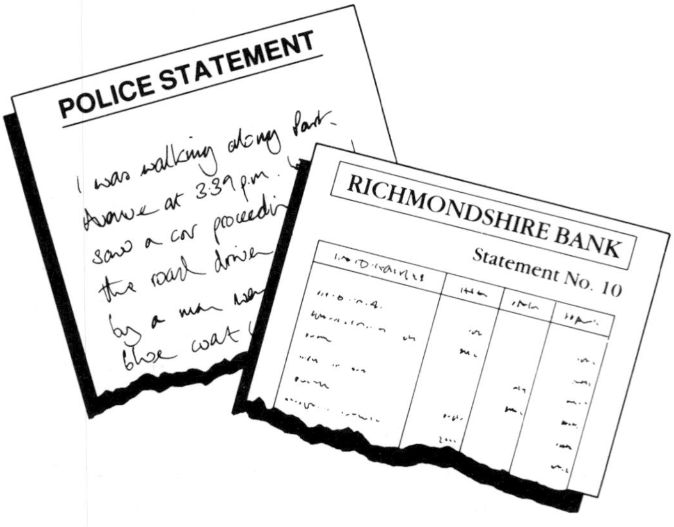

Final accounts

Accountants use information from the **trial balance** to draw up an organisation's **final accounts**. Final accounts are the summary financial statements produced at the end of each year's trading. Different types of organisations will need different types of financial statements. We start by looking at the financial statements of a sole trader, and then look at those of a limited company.

· FINAL ACCOUNTS OF A SOLE TRADER ·

The basic financial statements of a sole trader include:

● a trading account
● a profit and loss account
● a balance sheet.

Figure 22.1 *Two kinds of statements*

The trading account

The **trading account** can be likened to a video giving ongoing pictures of an organisation's trading activities. For many businesses trading involves buying and selling stock. The difference between the value of the stock sold (sales) and the cost of producing those sales – which is the production costs of manufactured goods for a manufacturing company, or the cost of purchasing the supplies for a trading company – is known as **gross profit**. The trading account simply shows how gross profit is arrived at:

> **Sales – cost of sales = gross profit**

'Cost of sales' has to take into account the value of **stocks**. 'Opening stocks' is effectively a purchase as these will be sold in the current trading period. On the other hand, 'closing stocks' must be deducted from purchases as these will be sold next year. The true cost of sales is therefore found by applying the following formula:

> Cost of sales = opening stocks PLUS purchases
> LESS closing stocks

The profit and loss account

The **profit and loss account** may be drawn up beneath the trading account and covers the same period of trading. The gross profit figure from the trading account becomes the starting point for the profit and loss account.

Some organisations receive income from sources other than sales. There may be rents received, commission received, discounts received, profits on the sale of assets etc. As these are **extra income** they are added to the gross

> Net profit = gross profit PLUS income from other sources LESS expenses

profit. In addition, every organisation incurs **expenses** and a range of overheads, and these are deducted to show the true net profit of the business. The expenses might include:

- rent of premises
- gas
- depreciation
- bad debts

- electricity
- stationery
- cleaning costs
- insurances
- business rates
- interest on loans
- advertising costs
- sundry expenses
- motor expenses
- accountancy and legal fees.

Figure 22.2 shows how the final account might look. The part of the account up to and including the gross profit is the trading account, while the remainder is the profit and loss account. Net profit is the final profit in the business and will belong to the owner.

	(£)	(£)
Sales		27 500
Less cost of sales:		
Opening stock	9 000	
Add purchases	15 000	
	24 000	
Less closing stock	3750	
		20 250
Gross profit		7 250
Add other income:		
Profit on sale of plant		2000
		9 250
Less expenses:		
Electricity	510	
Stationery	125	
Business rate	756	
Interest on loans	159	
Advertising	745	
Depreciation of motor vehicles	1000	
Insurances	545	
Sundry expenses	124	
		3 964
Net profit		5 286

Figure 22.2 *Trading and profit and loss account of E. Blyton for year-ended 31 May 199_*

Responsibility for the accounts

Most sole traders employ an accountant to draw up their accounts. Nevertheless, whoever prepares them, it is the sole trader who remains responsible for their accuracy and for correctly declaring the amount of the profits. The **tax authorities** will need to be satisfied that the accounts supplied to them represent the true results of the business.

It is essential to keep full and accurate records from the start of a business. Well-kept books make the preparation of the annual accounts easier, and save the accountant's time (so keeping down the fee charged).

Case Study

Assessments and payments of tax

The following is an edited extract from a booklet *Starting in Business*, issued by the Inland Revenue (IR28).

'If you cannot give your Inspector an accurate statement of your profits, they will have to be estimated and you will then have to pay tax on the basis of this estimate. If you consider the estimate is too high, it will be up to you to prove it. So it is in your own interests to keep accurate records.

'You are required by law to make a true return of your income each year. This, of course, includes your business *profits*. If possible you should send in a copy of your business accounts, either with your return form, or – if your accounting year ends some time before the return is due – in advance of the return.

'If your business makes a loss there are four main things you can do with it, and it is up to you to decide which of the various alternatives to adopt

You can:

- set the loss against future profits from the same business, starting with the earliest profitable year first
- claim relief for the same income tax year as the year of the loss
- claim relief for the income tax year following the year of the loss
- claim relief for the three income tax years before that in which you make the loss.

'The Small Firms Service is an information and business counselling service to help managers of small businesses with their plans and problems. It also acts as an advisory service to those thinking of starting their own business.'

1 Why do sole traders need to inform the Inland Revenue of their activities?

2 How important is it for sole traders to keep accurate records? What might happen if they did not?

3 Briefly explain what might happen if the business makes a loss.

4 Why does the Inland Revenue provide a Small Firms Service?

Task

A business sells £100 000 worth of goods during 1993. Its stock at the beginning of the year is worth £10 000. During the year it makes purchases worth £50 000 and its stock at the end of the year is worth £20 000. It has three main expenses: rent of £5000, rates of £5000 and advertising costing £10 000. Show a trading/profit and loss account for the year-ended 31 December 1993.

The balance sheet

Whereas the trading account gives an ongoing picture, a **balance sheet** is a snapshot of what an organisation owns and owes *on a particular date*. It is a clear statement of the assets, liabilities and capital of a business at a particular moment in time (normally the end of an accounting period).

Looking at the balance sheet can thus provide valuable information because it summarises a business's financial position at that instant in time.

The balance sheet does balance simply because the accounts record every transaction twice. For example, if you give me £100 we can say that:

- I *owe* you £100 (a liability or debt)
- I have now got £100 (an asset, something I *own*).

Look at Figure 22.3. Does it seem odd to you that 'capital' is *owed* by the organisation? This will become clear as you read on page 436.

Assets are what an organisation OWNS or is OWED

Liabilities or capital are what an organisation OWES

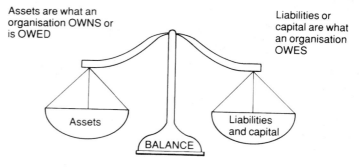

Figure 22.3 *Assets equals capital plus liabilities*

At the end of a trading period a business will have a number of assets and liabilities. Some of these will be for short periods of time, while others will be for longer periods. Whatever the nature of the individual assets and liabilities, the *balance sheet will balance*.

Task

Make lists of six probable assets and six probable liabilities of a small corner-shop. Do the same for a public house.

The parts of a balance sheet

Every balance sheet has a heading, which contains the name of the organisation and the date at which the snapshot is taken. You will find it helpful to refer to Figure 22.5 on page 437 as you read this section.

Assets

The **assets** side of the balance sheet is normally set out in what is called an **inverse order of liquidity**. This means that items which may be difficult to convert into cash quickly (and are therefore **illiquid**) appear at the top of the list of assets. By looking down the order it is possible to gauge the ease with which successive assets can be converted to cash, until we come to the most liquid asset of all, cash itself.

Task

A small bakery has the following assets. Try to put them into an *inverse order of liquidity* with the most illiquid at the top and the most liquid at the bottom:

- cash in the tills
- bread in the shops
- supplies of flour
- money in the bakery's bank account
- a bakery van
- the bakery oven
- money owed to the bakery by firms
- the baker's premises

Assets can be divided into fixed assets and current assets. **Fixed assets** tend to have a life-span of more than one year. They comprise items that are purchased and generally kept for a long period of time. Examples of fixed assets are premises, machinery and motor vehicles. When a business buys fixed assets it does so by incurring capital expenditure.

Case Study

Brand accounting

Some of the most valuable assets owned by many organisations are the brands they have developed and nurtured. Despite this, the Market Accounting Research Centre at the Cranfield School of Management discovered from a survey that a majority of businesses do not place a price on their portfolio of brands. It could well be argued that an accountant cannot create a 'true and fair view' of the business if they are not included.

The survey found that brand support and other marketing costs are rarely treated as an investment to achieve competitive advantage in the long-term. Furthermore, the strategic benefits of including brands in the accounts are not recognised by managers.

1 *Using examples to support your analysis, comment on whether a brand could be included in a balance sheet as an asset. What sort of asset might it be?*
2 *What are the advantages and the disadvantages of including brands within the balance sheet?*

Current assets are sometimes called 'circulating assets' because the form they take is constantly changing. Examples of current assets are stocks, debtors, money in the bank, and cash in hand.

A manufacturing business holds **stocks** of finished goods in readiness to satisfy the demands of the market. When a credit transaction takes place, stocks are reduced and the

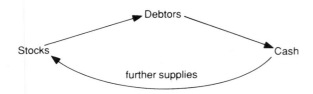

Figure 22.4 *The cash cycle*

business gains **debtors**. These debtors have bought goods on credit and therefore owe the business money; after a reasonable credit period payment will be expected. Payments will have to be made on further stocks, so that the business has a **cash cycle**. 'Cash' or 'bank' changes to 'stock', then to 'debtors', back to 'cash' or 'bank' and then to 'stock' again.

Task

Identify (giving reasons) which of the following items should be considered as a current asset of a newsagent:

- the fixtures and fittings of the shop
- cash in the tills
- money in the bank
- money owed by the newsagent to the suppliers.
- money owed by customers for newspaper bills
- the delivery bicycle
- stocks of newspapers in the shop

Current liabilities

Current liabilities are debts which a business needs to repay within a short period of time (normally a year). Current liabilities include **creditors**, who are suppliers of goods on credit for which the business has been invoiced but not yet provided any payment. They might also include a **bank overdraft** which is arranged up to a limit over a time period and is, technically, repayable on demand. Other current liabilities might include any short-term loans and any taxes owed.

Working capital

The balance sheet is set out so as to show **working capital** because this is always an important calculation for an organisation. The working capital is the current assets less the current liabilities.

The **working capital ratio** is the ratio of current assets to current liabilities:

Working capital ratio
= current assets : current liabilities

It is important for an organisation to maintain a sensible ratio. The level of ratio necessarily depends on the type of business, and the likelihood that funds will be required quickly to meet liabilities (e.g. creditors demanding repayment quickly). For most businesses a ratio of 2:1 is regarded as a sign of careful management, but some businesses have lower ratios.

Working capital is important because it provides a buffer to 'keep the wolf from the door'. Many businesses have suffered the consequences of having too many of their assets tied up as illiquid assets.

Long-term liabilities

A **long-term liability** is sometimes called a **deferred liability** as it is not due for payment until some time in the future. By convention, in a set of accounts, this means longer than one year. Examples for a sole trader might include a bank loan or a mortgage.

Capital

Capital is provided by the owner of the business and is therefore deemed to be *owed to the owner by the business* (look again at Figure 22.3). The balance sheet keeps an updated record of the amount owed by the business to the owner.

During a year's trading the owner's capital may be increased by the inflows of **profits** and decreased by outflows of **drawings** (money or other assets taken out of the business for personal use). Having taken these into consideration a new capital figure is calculated at the end of the year. So the balance

	(£)	(£)
Fixed assets		
Land and buildings		80 000
Machinery		13 200
Motor vehicles		8 700
		101 900
Current assets		
Stocks	9 700	
Debtors	3 750	
Bank	2 100	
Cash	970	
	16 520	
Less **Current liabilities**		
Creditors	9 000	
WORKING CAPITAL		7 520
		109 420
Less **Long-term liabilities**		
Bank loan	9 000	
Mortgage	30 000	
		39 000
		70 420
Financed by:		
Capital		70 000
Add net profit		5 286
		75 286
Less drawings		4 866
		70 420

Figure 22.5 *Balance sheet of E. Blyton at 31 May 199–*

sheet shows how the capital has increased (or decreased) since the last balance sheet was prepared.

Using the trial balance to prepare final accounts

The **trial balance** is a list of balances extracted from the ledger. Entries to the ledger are supported by source documentation. Accountants make use of the trial balance to prepare the **final accounts**. The trial balance contains a list of all the business's accounts. Accounts will have either a debit balance or a credit balance. Debit balances will generally comprise the assets of the business, expenses and the totals of purchases and costs. Credit balances will comprise any liabilities such as capital and creditors, as well as income from sales.

Each item in the trial balance will appear once in the final accounts. It is useful to tick each item in pencil as it is entered, so that none is missed. The closing stocks figure taken at the year end is not listed in the trial balance but is shown as a note underneath the balance. The closing stocks will appear twice, once in the trading account and then again in the current assets in the balance sheet.

Task

From the following trial balance of J. O. Nory draw up her trading/profit and loss account for the year-ended 31 December 19X2, together with her balance sheet at that date. The closing stocks at 31 December 19X2 were valued at £10 300.

	(£)	(£)
Stock @ 1 Jan 19X2	12 700	
Sales		81 250
Purchases	18 325	
Electricity	1 451	
Stationery	1 526	
Business rate	1 845	
Loan interest	3 955	
Advertising	2 150	
Sundry expenses	1 205	
Land and buildings	161 000	
Machinery	4 900	
Motor vehicles	18 300	
Debtors	12 100	
Bank	4 250	
Cash	325	
Bank loan		10 000
Mortgage		20 000
Creditors		4 300
Drawings	9 350	
Capital @ 1 Jan 1992		137 832
	253 382	253 382

• FINAL ACCOUNTS OF A • LIMITED COMPANY

It will help our understanding of the accounts of a limited company if we first go over some of the essential features of this type of organisation. As we have already seen in earlier chapters, in limited companies:

● the company has a legal identity separate from that of its owners

Figure 22.6 *Documents required by a limited company for corporate status*

- the owners are known as shareholders
- shareholders have limited liability
- management is delegated to a board of directors, who may or may not be shareholders
- corporation tax must be paid on profits made.

Companies must comply with the Companies Acts, and the Companies Registration Office controls their formation. There are two types of limited companies:

- public, which have their shares traded on the Stock Exchange, and
- private, for which there are restrictions on the trading in their shares.

To set up a limited company it is necessary to go through a number of legal procedures. This mainly involves the presentation of various documents to the Registrar of Companies. All limited companies must produce a **Memorandum of Association** and **Articles of Association** to receive a Certification of Incorporation.

The Memorandum spells out the nature of the company when viewed from the outside. Someone reading the memorandum should be able to gain a general idea of what the company is and the business with which it is concerned. The Memorandum sets out:

- the name of the company
- its address
- its objectives (i.e. what types of activities it will engage in)
- its capital.

The Articles spell out the rules which govern the inside working of the company. In particular they set out the details of how accounts will be kept and recorded.

Once a private company has lodged these documents with the Registrar and had them accepted it can start to trade. The Certificate of Incorporation sets up the company as a legal body *in its own right*. The company (not the individual shareholders) enters into contracts and can sue or be sued in a court of law.

A public company, however, must take further steps before being granted a Certificate. A **Prospectus** has to be issued and shares have to be allotted.

One clause of the Memorandum of Association states the **share capital** of the company and indicates how it is to be divided into separate shares. **Authorised share capital** is the amount the shareholders have authorised the directors to issue. **Issued share capital** is the amount that has actually been issued by the directors.

There are a number of types of shares. For example, there are **ordinary shares**, for which **dividends** are normally expressed as a percentage of the nominal value of the shares or as a monetary value per share. There may be **preference shares**, which carry a preferential right to receive a dividend. Companies can also issue **debentures**, which are split into units in the same way as shares; they are in effect loans made to the company and secured by specific assets of the company.

The trading/profit and loss accounts

The **trading account** of a limited company is similar to the trading account of any other type of organisation. However, in the profit and loss account:

- directors' fees or salaries may be included, because these people are employed by the company and their fees and salaries are an expense
- debenture payments, being the same as loan interest, also appear as an expense.

The appropriation account

Beneath the profit and loss account of a company will appear the **appropriation account**. This is designed to show what happens to any profit and how it is divided.

Corporation tax is the first charge on profits and has to be paid to the Inland Revenue. For example, the tax rate was 33 per cent for the tax year 1991/92 for company profits over £1 250 000. **Shareholder dividends** are the portion of the profits paid to shareholders.

Reserves are the portion of the profit which the directors and the shareholders prefer not to distribute as dividends. This money is set aside for another purpose.

Any profit left over at the end of the year, after taxes and shareholders of all kinds have been paid, is added to the balance of profit from the previous year, to give the new retained profit.

> Balance of profit at end of year = net profit from this year PLUS retained profits from previous years LESS corporation tax LESS dividends LESS transfer to reserves

An example of an appropriation account for a company with a net profit of £250 000 is shown in Figure 22.7.

	(£)	(£)
Net profit		250 000
Less Corporation Tax		100 000
Profit after taxation		150 000
Less proposed dividends:		
Ordinary shares	70 000	
Preference shares	20 000	90 000
		60 000
Less transfer to General Reserve		40 000
		20 000
Add retained profit from previous year		30 000
Balance of retained profit		50 000

Figure 22.7 *An appropriation account*

Task

Workhard Ltd has just announced a net profit of £300 000. Prepare the appropriation account from the following details:

a The taxation rate is at 25 per cent.
b There are 500 000 ordinary shares of £1 each, fully paid. A dividend of 10 per cent is proposed.
c There are 300 000 10% preference shares of £1 each, fully paid. The 10 per cent dividend is to be paid.
d £50 000 is to be transferred to General Reserve.
e Retained profit from the previous year was £125 000.

The balance sheet

In the **balance sheet** of a company the **fixed** and **current assets** are presented in the same way as in any other balance sheet.

The **current liabilities** are the liabilities due to be paid within twelve months of the date of the balance sheet. In addition to those which normally appear in this section, limited companies also have to show the Corporation Tax which is due to be paid during the next twelve months, as well as the ordinary and preference share dividends due to be paid. Long-term liabilities may include debenture payments.

At the beginning of the 'Financed by:' section of the balance sheet, details will appear of the **authorised capital**, specifying the type, value and number of shares that the company is authorised to issue. These are in the balance sheet for interest only and their value is excluded from the totals. The item on **issued share capital** contains details of the classes and numbers of shares that *have* been issued (obviously the issued share capital cannot exceed the authorised).

Reserves are shown beneath the capital. Reserves and **retained profits** are the amounts the directors and shareholders decide to keep within the company.

Example

From the trial balance of Wargrave Ltd shown overleaf and the notes tbelow, we can prepare the trading account, the profit and loss account, the appropriation account and the balance sheet for the year-ended 31 December 19X2.

Notes:

- The closing stock is £12 250.
- Corporation Tax is charged at 25 per cent of profits.
- There will be a 6 per cent dividend on ordinary shares.
- The 10% preference share dividend is to be paid.
- £2000 is to be allocated to the General Reserve.
- Authorised share capital is 400 000 ordinary shares of £1 each and 100 000 10% preference shares of £1 each.

Trial balance

	(£)	(£)
Stock @ 1 Jan 19X3	21 300	
Sales		118 100
Purchases	35 000	
Electricity	8 000	
Stationery	5 000	
Business rate	1 300	
Loan interest paid	1 000	
Debenture interest paid	800	
Advertising	3 200	
Sundry expenses	1 350	
Directors' salaries	12 000	
Land and buildings	320 000	
Machinery	24 000	
Motor vehicles	12 000	
Debtors	7 100	
Bank	23 200	
Cash	500	
Bank loan		10 000
10% debentures		8 000
Creditors		500
General Reserve		4 000
Retained profit @ 31 Dec 19X2		35 150
Issued share capital:		
200 000 ordinary £1 shares		200 000
100 000 10% £1 preference shares		100 000
	475 750	475 750

The accounts and balance sheet based on this data are shown in Figures 22.8 and 22.9. Relate each item to its corresponding entry.

	(£)	(£)	(£)
Fixed assets			
Land and buildings			320 000
Machinery			24 000
Motor vehicles			12 000
			356 000
Current assets			
Stocks		12 250	
Debtors		7 100	
Bank		23 200	
Cash		500	
		43 050	
Less **Current liabilities**			
Creditors	500		
Proposed dividends:			
Ordinary shares	12 000		
Preference shares	10 000		
Corporation Tax	10 350	32 850	
Working capital			10 200
			366 200
Less **Long-term liabilities**			
Bank loan		10 000	
10% debentures		8 000	
			18 000
			348 200
FINANCED BY:			
Authorised share capital			
400 000 ordinary shares of £1			400 000
100 000 10% preference shares of £1			100 000
			500 000
Issued share capital			
200 000 ordinary shares of £1 fully paid			200 000
100 000 10% preference shares of £1 fully paid			100 000
			300 000
Reserves			
General Reserve		6 000	
Balance of retained profit		42 200	
			48 200
			348 200

Figure 22.8 *Balance sheet of Wargrave Ltd for the year ended 31 December 19X2*

	(£)	(£)
Sales		118 100
Less cost of sales:		
Opening stock	21 300	
Add purchases	35 000	
	56 300	
Less closing stock	12 250	
		44 050
		74 050
Gross profit		
Less expenses:		
Electricity	8 000	
Stationery	5 000	
Business rate	1 300	
Loan interest paid	1 000	
Debenture interest paid	800	
Advertising	3 200	
Sundry expenses	1 350	
Directors' salaries	12 000	
		32 650
Net profit		41 400
Less Corporation Tax		10 350
Profit after tax		31 050
Less proposed dividends:		
Ordinary shares	12 000	
Preference shares	10 000	22 000
		9 050
Less transfer to		
General Reserve		2 000
		7 050
Add retained profit		
from previous year		35 150
Balance of retained profit		42 200

Figure 22.9 *Trading, profit and loss and appropriation account of Wargrave Ltd for the year ended 31 December 19X2*

Task

From the following trial balance of Twyford Ltd and the attached notes, prepare the trading account, profit and loss account, appropriation account and balance sheet for the year-ended 31 December 19X2.

	(£)	(£)
Stock @ 1 Jan 19X2	7 300	
Sales		123 400
Purchases	12 500	
Electricity	4 100	
Advertising	3 200	
Business rate	800	
Salaries	16 000	
Director's salaries	18 000	
Loan interest paid	4 400	
Debenture interest paid	1 000	
Land and buildings	124 000	
Motor vehicles	16 000	
Debtors	7 000	
Bank	15 000	
Cash	1 000	
Bank loan		25 000
10% debentures		10 000
Creditors		4 000
General Reserve		3 000
Retained profit @ 31 Dec 19X1		4 900
Issued share capital:		
50 000 ordinary shares (£1)		50 000
10 000 pref. shares (£1)		10 000
	230 300	230 300

You have been informed that:

- The closing stock has been valued at £3400.
- Corporation Tax will be charged at 25 per cent of profits.
- The 10 % share dividends are to be paid.
- £3000 is to be allocated to the General Reserve.
- Authorised share capital is the same as issued share capital.

· STATEMENTS OF CASH FLOW ·

The profit and loss account provides information which matches sales and costs, and a balance sheet is a static statement showing a business's financial position. Neither of these shows how a business has *used* its funds and cash.

In 1975 the tenth Statement of Standard Accounting Practice (SSAP) was issued which required a business with an annual turnover of £25 000 or more to provide a statement to fill this gap, as part of its final accounts. This was called a **funds flow statement**.

Funds flow statements were prepared through a process of comparison. If a company's balance sheets for two successive years were listed alongside each other, then clearly the changes during the year could be seen. Differences between the two years were then listed and grouped together either as sources or as applications of funds.

Sources of funds included profits, new loans, share issues and profits on the sale of assets. **Applications of funds** included purchase of fixed assets, tax paid, dividends paid, and loans repaid.

	(£) 31 Dec 19X0	(£) 31 Dec 19X1	(£) Comparison
Premises	3 000	3 000	0
Stocks	8 000	10 000	+2 000
Bank	3 000	3 000	0
	14 000	16 000	
Capital	14 000	14 000	0
Creditors	−	2 000	+2 000
	14 000	16 000	

Figure 22.10 *Two balance sheets for B. Regis*

The example in Figure 22.10 shows how an increase in stocks could have been financed. Clearly this increase in stocks has been financed through the credit provided by suppliers, and this fact is shown in the form of a statement (Figure 22.11).

Sources of funds – creditors	£2000
Application of funds – increasing stocks	£2000

Figure 22.11 *Funds flow statement for B. Regis*

Another way of presenting this sort of statement was to have a section which analysed *working capital changes*. The reason for this was to enable managers to exert a firmer grip upon these changes. The change in working capital between the two balance sheets would then equal the difference between the sources and applications of funds. This is illustrated in Figure 22.12.

Balance sheets

	(£) 31 Dec 19X0	(£) 31 Dec 19X1	(£) Comparison
Fixed assets	450	550	+100
Long-term investments	500	450	−50
Current assets less current liabilities	150	200	+50
	1 100	1 200	
Capital	360	400	+40
Profits	300	500	+200
Loans	440	300	−140
	1 100	1 200	

Funds flow statement

	(£)	(£)
Sources of funds:		
Capital	40	
Profits	200	
Sale of investments	50	290
Application of funds:		
Fixed assets	100	
Loan repayments	140	240
Increase in working capital		50

Figure 22.12 *Balance sheets and funds flow statement for H. O. Gate*

The new way: cash flow statements

In 1990 the Accounting Standards Board took over from the Accounting Standards Committee and this heralded a new era in accounting standard-setting. All accounting standards (SSAPs) now come under the authority of the ASB and are to be subject to scrutiny and change.

In September 1991 the ASB set out the first **Financial Reporting Standard** (FRS1) on **cash flow statements**. The standard supersedes SSAP10 on sources and applications of funds, discussed above.

The new standard FRS1 will change the nature of the third statement in a company's accounts. The aim is for the cash-flow statement to be viewed as just as important as the balance sheet and the profit and loss account.

The problems with funds flow statements were that:

- companies drew up their statements in different ways
- they were difficult to use to compare one business with another

- they looked at funds or profit rather than at cash
- the meaning of funds was not very clear.

The new cash flow statements focus on something which all business managers can identify with – the need for a steady cash flow. Figure 22.13 shows an example. The bottom line is the change in what is called 'cash and equivalents'. The cash flow statement explains the movement by placing all cash flows into five categories. Note that in this example we have adopted the more usual convention of putting outflows of cash in parentheses, rather than using a minus sign as we have been doing. Further information is given in notes, in particular a reconciliation of operating profit to operating cash flow.

The idea is that a user can see at a glance the extent to which, for example, cash flow from operations has or has not paid for dividends, tax and new investments, or the extent to which those items had to be financed by the raising of new capital. The statement should expose more quickly than before those companies that are not generating cash – even though they may be reporting profits.

	(£m)	(£m)
Net cash inflow from operating activities		6
Returns on investment and servicing of finance		
Interest received	2	
Interest paid	(4)	
Dividends paid	(4)	
Net cash outflow from returns on investment and servicing of finance		(6)
Taxation		
UK corporation tax paid		(4)
Investing activities		
Purchases of tangible fixed assets	(4)	
Purchase of subsidiary undertakings (net of cash and cash equivalents acquired)	(18)	
Sale of plant and machinery	4	
Net cash outflow from investing activities		(18)
Net cash outflow before financing		(22)
Financing		
New secured loan repayable in 19X5	17	
Repayment of amounts borrowed	(2)	
Net cash inflow from financing		15
Decrease in cash and cash equivalents		7

Figure 22.13 *A cash-low statement for the year ended 31 March 19X2*

The statement in Figure 22.13 shows that:

- the operations provided cash inflow of only £6 million
- £6 million was used up in dividends and interest
- £4 million was used up in paying tax
- £18 million was used up in new investment
- the cash balance *decreased* by £7 million
- to make all of this possible, £15 million had to be obtained by way of new finance.

It is clear immediately from the example that the operations were not even supporting the dividends and the tax payment. The company is using up cash without even considering further investment. This is exactly the kind of thing a cash flow statement is intended to bring out. This sort of information should help to provide readers of accounts with clearer warnings of business failures.

Task

If you were an investor in a company, what sort of information would you require about your investment? Make a list.

Case Study

King cash

SSAP10 on sources and applications of funds has formed an integral part of final accounts for all but the very smallest of businesses for many years. However, today it is replaced by a cash-flow statement. The change has been:

- to improve the *quality* of information provided in published accounts
- to bring the UK accounting procedures into line with international practices.

The monitoring of cash flow is probably the most significant aspect of the successful operation of any organisation. It is one thing to have a 'theoretical' profit reported in the profit and loss account, but another matter

– and probably more important – to have the physical resources available to meet payments to short-term creditors.

This need for businesses to have short-term liquidity and long-term profitability is illustrated by today's emphasis upon cash flow. Particularly in times of recession many firms strive to report a book profit figure but ignore the need to meet short-term creditors.

Many criticisms have been levelled at funds flow statements over recent years. These concentrated upon funds as movements in working capital at the expense of examining in more detail general changes in funds. Also, their format and content varied considerably between companies and this caused difficulty with interpretation and comparison. Cash-flow statements will provide more information on the connection between liquidity and profitability. They will also actually record the cash flow generated by an organisation over its financial year. Cash-flow statements will therefore assist in emphasising to investors the risks they are undertaking.

FRS1 should now be adopted by all organisations as their standard in respect of financial statements relating to reporting periods on or after 23 March 1992. SSAP10 was withdrawn as of that date.

1 Why is it important to improve the quality of information in published accounts?
2 Why is it necessary to bring UK accounting practices into line with international practices?
3 Explain the difference between profit and cash.
4 What might happen if a business fails to pay creditors?
5 Write a short report explaining why cash flow statements will improve the quality of final accounts.

I have audited the above financial statements in accordance with Auditing Standards. In my opinion the financial statements give a true and fair view of the profit and the state of affairs of the Company at 31 December 1993 and of the source and application of funds for the year then ended, and have been properly prepared in accordance with the Companies Act 1985.

PARKER & PARKER
CHARTERED ACCOUNTANTS

Figure 22.14 *The audit report*

As well as having their accounts audited, all companies must send the accounts to the Registrar of Companies. Companies must also supply:

- details of subsidiary companies
- group accounts if there is a group of companies
- a summary of their activities in the form of a directors' report
- the audit report.

Study the annual report and accounts of a major public company. Find the accounts section, details of operations, details of subsidiaries, the directors' report and the audit report.

· AUDITING ·

All registered companies in the United Kingdom are required to have their final accounts **audited** (i.e. checked) by a registered financial accountant. The purpose of the audit report is to testify that the accounts show a 'true and fair view' of the affairs of the company. The **audit report,** placed usually at the end of the final accounts, will indicate that the accounts have been produced in accordance with the law and other rules and regulations laid down. Figure 22.14 shows a typical example.

· ACCOUNTING POLICIES ·

When you look at the accounts of any major public company you find a reference to the basis upon which the accounts have been put together. This reference is likely to be a statement of the policy on:

- inflation accounting
- stock valuation
- depreciation.

Inflation accounting

For most companies, the main statements of account are based on **historical costs**. This means that, unless a company has *revalued* any of its assets, they will appear in the balance sheet at the original cost (less depreciation), no matter when they were bought. Other transactions will also appear at their original values.

> **Accounting convention.** The accounts are prepared under the historical cost convention and in accordance with Accounting Standards.

Figure 22.15 *A statement in the accounts*

At times when prices are quickly changing, historical cost accounts can lead to distortions. For example, if a company bought a machine last year which then cost £500 000 and, because of price rises, the same machine now costs £700 000, it will still appear in the accounts as being worth under half a million pounds – say £350 000 (after depreciation is taken into account). Is this an accurate reflection of the *true* value of the asset?

Some companies produce a second set of accounting statements which show **current costs**. These statements are prepared using *replacement* costs rather than historical costs (in other words, the assets are *revalued*). In the annual report they are often referred to as 'current cost accounts', although in everyday language they are often known as 'inflation accounts'.

	Low valuation		High valuation	
	(£)	(£)	(£)	(£)
Sales		50 000		50 000
Less cost of sales:				
Opening stock	25 000		25 000	
Add purchases	40 000		40 000	
	65 000		65 000	
Less closing stock	20 000		40 000	
		45 000		25 000
		5 000		25 000

Figure 22.16 *How the stock valuation affects profit*

For example, with a high valuation of stocks the profit will be high, and with a low valuation the profit will be lower. This is illustrated in Figure 22.16.

The **prudence concept** rules out the use of selling prices in the stock valuation process, as profits should only be recognised when they are actually made – after the goods are sold. The Standard **SSAP9** indicates that stocks should be valued either at their original cost or at their **net realisable value** – whichever is the *lower*. The net realisable value of the stocks is their selling price less the cost that would be incurred in getting them ready for sale and actually selling them.

Depreciation

Fixed assets do not last for ever. Organisations have expectations about the lifetimes of all their assets. They will wish to show a true asset value in the balance sheet, and charge the cost of its declining value (its **depreciation**) to the profit and loss account.

SSAP12 defines depreciation as 'the measure of the wearing out, consumption or other reduction in the useful economic life of a fixed asset, whether arising from use, time or obsolescence through technological or market changes'.

Task

What do you think gives the best reflection of the real worth of a company – assets measured in historical or in current cost terms? Look at some reports of public companies. How do they value their assets?

Stock valuation

When an accounting statement is set out, a value has to be put on the **stocks**. This value will obviously have a direct influence upon what the company declares to be its profits.

Case Study

Comparing financial statements

The following details have been taken from end-of-year financial statements prepared by two sole traders who own similar businesses:

	Jane (£)	Alan (£)
Sales	320 000	292 500
Less cost of sales	240 000	234 000
Gross profit	80 000	58 500
Less expenses	32 000	23 400
Net profit	48 000	35 100

The average stocks held by each business during the year in question were £12 000 (Jane) and £13 000 (Alan).

1 *Work out:*
   a *the gross profit for each sole trader as a percentage of sales*
   b *the net profit percentage.*
2 *Comment on the differences between the two accounts.*
3 *Alan feels that his working capital is unusually small. Advise him upon how he could increase his working capital.*

Case Study

What about quality?

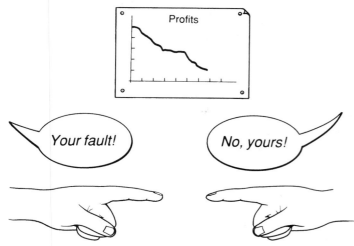

An unfortunate trait within working groups is to start blaming someone else when anything goes wrong. As long as it is not our fault, all is well! This sort of conflict often exists in an organisation, and when such disputes start to affect profits the first thing the organisation may do is resort to cutting costs. This tends to make customer/supplier relations worse, and the situation deteriorates. However, there is an increasing feeling today that improving quality across the

organisation is perhaps a better way of improving its performance.

One of the tasks of management is to find ways of involving employees in all aspects of their jobs. In this age of IT, this means giving them plenty of information and asking their opinions. Quality thus rises throughout the organisation.

Reducing waste by elevating the status of employees, consulting them more frequently and allowing them to take further responsibility for their decisions, all help to add revenues as well as reduce costs.

1 *Why do organisations seek to cut costs if profits start to fall?*
2 *How would the techniques suggested in this passage reduce the need to cut costs in the traditional way?*
3 *How does quality improve performance?*

THE FINAL ACCOUNTS OF OTHER TYPES OF ORGANISATIONS

So far in this chapter we have looked at the final accounts of two types of business organisation, the sole trade and the limited company. These are not the only types of business organisation (see Chapter 1) and each of the other different types will also be required to produce a series of financial statements.

Partnership statements

In seeking to develop their businesses further, many sole traders take in partners. An ordinary partnership can have between two and twenty partners.

Normally a **partnership agreement** will be established which will contain the following guidelines:

- details of profit sharing (for example, 75 per cent to one partner and 25 per cent to the other)
- whether interest is to be paid on the capital each partner has invested in the partnership and the rate at which it is to be paid (for example, the partnership might pay partners 10 per cent upon the amount of capital which each partner has invested)
- whether interest is to be charged on the drawings and the rate at which it is to be charged (for example, partners

might be charged at 5 per cent on the amount of drawings they make during the year).

Alternatively the members of the partnership may wish to cement their agreement in accordance with the Partnership Act of 1980.

This defines a partnership as:

'the relation which subsists between persons carrying on in business in common with a view of profit.'

The Partnership Act has the following rules:

- profits and losses should be shared equally between partners
- no partner should receive a salary
- partners are not entitled to receive interest on their capital
- interest is not to be charged on partners' drawings
- if a partner contributes more capital than agreed, he or she can receive interest at 5 per cent per annum on the excess.

There are **two** main differences between the financial statements of a partnership and those of sole trader. These are:

1 After the profit and loss account an appropriation section appears which divides the profit between partners.
2 In the balance sheet, the capital section shows each of the partners' capital and current account balances.

Example

	(£)	(£)
Net profit		18 000
Add interest on partners' drawings:		
Smith	1000	
Jones	2000	3000
		21 000
Appropriation of profits		
Salary: Smith		4000
Interest on partners' capitals:		
Smith	3000	
Jones	2000	5000
Share of residue:		
Smith (60%)	7200	
Jones (40%)	4800	12 000
		21 000

Figure 22.17 *Appropriation account of Smith and Jones*

In the business of Smith and Jones, interest on drawings is charged at 10 per cent. At the start of the year Smith draws £10 000 and Jones draws £20 000. Smith has a salary of £4000 per annum and 10 per cent interest is paid on partners' capitals.

Smith has a capital of £30 000 invested with the business and Jones has a capital of £20 000 invested with the business. When they come to divide profits their partnership agreement determines that 60 per cent are to go to Smith and 40 per cent to Jones. Their net profit for the current year is £18 000. Their appropriation account will therefore appear as shown in Figure 22.17.

Task

During the current year Black and White have made a net profit of £27 000. Interest on drawings is charged at 5 per cent and over the year Black has made drawings of £8500 and White has drawn £7000 from the business.

White has a salary of £9000 and 10 per cent interest is to be paid on partners' capitals. Black has a capital of £35 000 invested in the business and White has a capital of £30 000 invested in the business. Profits are divided equally. Draw up their appropriation account.

In the balance sheet, the capital account of each partner is fixed and only changes if partners increase or decrease their contributions. The current account balances fluctuate and to each:

- share of profit is added
- salary is added (if applicable)
- interest on capital is added
- drawings are deducted
- interest charged on drawings is deducted.

Example

A balance sheet extract from a partnership may appear as in Figure 22.18.

FINANCED BY:

Capital accounts	(£)	(£)	(£)
Tate		30 000	
Lyle		20 000	
			50 000

Current accounts	Tate	Lyle	
Opening balances	2 300	3 100	
Add: salary	5 000	–	
interest on			
capital	3 000	2 000	
share of profit	7 500	2 500	
	17 800	7 600	
Less: drawings	4 000	3 000	
interest on drawings	200	150	
	13 600	4 450	18 050
			68 050

Figure 22.18 *Extract from the balance sheet of Tate and Lyle as at 31/12/–3*

	(£)	(£)
Current accounts: Adam		580
Eve		140
Capital accounts: Adam		25 000
Eve		20 000
Drawings: Adam	8 000	
Eve	2 000	
Freehold premises (cost)	40 000	
Stock 1/1/–3	5 600	
Purchases and sales	15 000	52 480
Wages and salaries	6 850	
Business rate	2 400	
Advertising	3 750	
General expenses	8 200	
Fixtures and fittings		
(cost)	2 400	
Motor vehicles	3 500	
Debtors and creditors	4 500	7 100
Bank	3 100	
	105 300	105 300

Notes as 31/12/–3
* Stock is valued at £7500
* Interest on drawings is to be charged at 5%
* Interest on capitals of 10% is to be paid.

Figure 22.19 *Trial balance of Adam and Eve 31/12/–3*

Adam and Eve run a small lighting wholesaling business in which they share profits equally. The trial balance in Figure 22.19 was taken from their books as at 31/12/–3. Prepare final accounts as at the date of the trial balance.

Statements for non-profit-making organisations

A non-profit-making organisation is one which is generally made up of a group of individuals who co-operate together to provide some form of activity which is either for the benefit of themselves or others. More often than not, these accounts tend to be referred to as club accounts. There accounting statements include:

- a **receipts and payments account** which is just a simple version of the cash book. It is normally totalled at the end of the financial year and will not include any accruals or prepayments.
- an **income and expenditure account.** This is very similar to a normal profit and loss account. It includes most of the items from the receipts and payments account but will exclude any asset purchase which is not part of normal running expenses. It will also include any prepayments, subscriptions adjusted to account for those paid in advance, the contributions from fund-raising activities and profits from any activities such as a bar.
- an **accumulated fund**. Instead of having capital in a balance sheet a non-profit-making organisation will have an accumulated fund to account for the differences between the total assets and total liabilities of the organisation.

Many non-proft-making organisations still use traditional horizontal accounts and this is the form we have adopted for our example.

Example

On 1 January 19–2 the balance sheet of the Crown Green Bowls Club was as in Figure 22.20.

Fixed Assets		ACCUMULATED	
		FUND	14 800
Premises (cost)	10 000		
Equipment (cost)	4 525		
	14 525		
Current Assets			
Bank	275		
	14 800		14 800

Figure 22.20 *Crown Green Bowls Club balance sheet as at 1/1/–2*

During the year their payments into and out of their bank account were recorded by the receipts and payments account in Figure 22.21.

RECEIPTS	£	PAYMENTS	£
Bank balance			
1 Jan	275	Rent	350
Subscriptions	350	Heating	200
Bar takings	4400	Bar expenses	1750
Donations	500	Equipment	550
		Ground maintenance	190
		Bank balance	
		31 Dec	2485
	5525		5525

Figure 22.21 *Crown Green Bowls receipts and payments account for the year ended 31/12/–2*

The receipts and payments account has ignored that some subscriptions are prepaid for the following year. It has also recorded the purchase of equipment along with expenses. To gain a more accurate picture of the club's activities it is necessary to draw up an income and expenditure account. (Note: as the year-end is out of season there are no bar stocks left over.)

EXPENDITURE	£	INCOME	£
Rent	350	Subs (less 50	
		prepaid)	300
Heating	200	Profit on bar	2650
Ground maintenance	190	Donations	500
Surplus of income			
over expenditure	2710		
	3450		3450

Figure 22.22 *Crown Green Bowls Club income and expenditure account for the year ended 31/12/–2*

It is now possible to draw up the balance sheet for the end of the year. The surplus is added to the accumulated fund and represents the changes which have been made to the members' interests in the organisation.

		£		£
Fixed Assets		**ACCUMULATED**		
		FUND		14 800
Premises (cost)	10 000	Add surplus of		
		income over		
Equipment (cost)	5075	expenditure		2710
	15 075			17 510
Current Assets		**Current Liabilities**		
Bank		275	Subs paid in	
			advance	50
		17 560		17 560

Figure 22.23 *Crown Green Bowls Club balance sheet as at 31 December 19-2*

Task

You have recently taken over as Treasurer of Hudswell Gardening Club. From the information you have been handed you can see that the balance sheet at the beginning of the year was as in Figure 22.24.

	£		£
Fixed Assets		**ACCUMULATED**	
		FUND	7690
Equipment (cost)	4400		
Current Assets			
Stock of seeds	150		
Bank	3140		
	7690		7690

Figure 22.24 *Hudswell Gardening Club balance sheet as at 1 January 19-2*

During the year a receipts and payments account has recorded the amounts in Figure 22.25.

RECEIPTS	£	PAYMENTS	£
Bank bal 1 Jan	3140	Competition fees	45
Subscriptions	860	Rent of premises	150
Donations	200	Purchase of seeds	
	175		
Ticket sales	300	Equipment	1300
Raffles	150	Fertilisers	425
Sale of seeds	450	Bank bal 31 Dec	3005
	5100		5100

Figure 22.25 *Hudswell Gardening Club receipts and payments account for the year ended 331 December 19-2*

You have noticed that at the end of the year:

- £30 of subs have been paid in advance for 19–3

- the stock of seeds held at the end of the year is valued at £135.

1 Calculate how much profit has been made on the sale of seeds (show your workings).
2 Prepare an income and expenditure account for the year ended 31 December 19–2 and a balance sheet as at that date.

Local authority statements

The term **local authority** is one which is frequently used to describe the operation of local councils. Local authorities have responsibility for supplying a range of services. This includes: policing, housing, social services, libraries, fire services, recreational facilities, education and transport. Some of these responsibilities are shared with central goverment.

Whereas in urban metropolitan areas (e.g. West Midlands) only one level of council will exist to provide all local services, in county areas local authorities are more usually structured in three tiers each of which will provide different types of service. These three tiers will include:

- a county council
- borough or district councils
- parish councils.

Local authorities have to work within a strict legal framework laid down by central government. Decisions made by local or national government, which influence local authorities are made on political rather than commercial or financial grounds. As a result local authority accounting is quite different to that of the private sector because, except for a few activities, local authorities do not have a profit motive to pursue. Local authorities, therefore, have to look at the overall cost of the services they wish to provide, create a budget which takes into consideration how much they need to spend and then they have to consider how they can raise the funds to finance the budget.

For example, illustrated below are the spending demands of Richmondshire District Council, a district in North Yorkshire, for 1992/3. The expenditure demands are financed by the Government Standard Spending Grant, Business Rates and Financial Adjustments. The difference then has to be made up by local citizens.

(Note: Since 1 April 1993, local people pay a council tax. This means that local taxation is now paid by home-owners and the amount is based on the value of houses. Properties are banded at different value levels and the more expensive the house, the more tax the home-owner is expected to be able to pay).

Spending demands	1992/93 £	Amount per head of relevant population £ p
Richmondshire District Council	3 813 110	113.90
North Yorkshire County Council	25 737 117	768.80
	29 550 227	882.70
Sources of finance		
Government standard spending grant	(10 764 420)	(321.54)
Business rate distribution	(11 678 811)	(348.86)
Financial adjustments	(143 616)	(4.30)
Balance required from local citizens	6 963 380	208.00

Figure 22.26 *Financing Richmondshire spending demands*

Spending by local authorities (as with many other organisations) is usually divided into two distinct areas:

- **Capital expenditure:** for major projects such as new roads, hospitals and schools.
- **Revenue expenditure:** for every day running costs for services to the community, such as salaries, maintenance of buildings and roads.

Apart from the council tax (see previous page) the most important sources of finance are central government grants, local authority borrowing and charges for local services.

Central government grants will include any Specific Grants as well as the Revenue Support Grant. Specific Grants may be for any new requirement such as a new road or new housing. The Revenue Support Grant is based upon a calculation by central government of the amount of revenue expenditure which it estimates that a local authority will incur in providing its services. The process of calculating this grant is known as the Standard Spending Assessment and this is based upon a complex formula which takes into account many figures which are specific to each area.

Local authority borrowing is normally used to help to finance capital expenditure projects. Local authorities are empowered to issue Local Authority Stock on the Stock Exchange which can be bought and sold in the same way as company shares and Government Stock. Local authorities can also sell Local Authority Bonds to private investors and take out temporary loans from money brokers.

About 25 per cent of local authority income comes from charges for local services. This includes rent from council properties, income from elderly persons' homes, revenue from swimming pools and leisure centres, etc.

In order to prevent local authorities from spending too much (and raising too much local tax) the Government has the power to '**cap**'. The Secretary of State for the Environment will set limits on expenditure based on the Standard Spending Assessment. A capped authority must then submit revised expenditure plans which comply with the limitations imposed upon its expenditure.

The published accounts of local authorities are prepared from their day-to-day records. The Local Government

Planning and Land Act of 1980 states that all local authorities must produce an annual report and that the report must contain the relevant accounts. These will comprise an **income and expenditure account** for each main fund together with a **consolidated balance sheet** for all of the funds combined.

Each income and expenditure fund will show income and expenditure for a particular service. For example, income may include income received from cash payments and income received to provide that service. Payments will include all of the expenses incurred in providing each service such as wages and salaries. The consolidated balance sheet will be similar to the balance sheet for any other type of organisation except that the 'Financed by' section will show a list of reserve funds, capital receipts and revenue balances.

Local authority accounts will generally contain a series of performance indicators which allow the user to compare the figures with those of a previous year. The accounts will also be supported by a series of reports and statistics.

Task

Obtain a copy of local authority accounts for your council. Comment upon the similarities and differences between the accounts you have obtained and the accounts of a limited company.

INFLUENCE OF BUSINESS • OPERATIONS UPON FINANCIAL • STATEMENTS

The functions of businesses differ – some provide a personal service, others buy and sell and some manufacture. The type of activity businesses engage in will have an influence upon the type of financial statements they provide. So far, with all of the business organisations we have looked at, except for the accounts of non-profiting-making organisations, we have constructed a trading and profit and loss account. Because they have all had a trading section we have thus assumed that they have

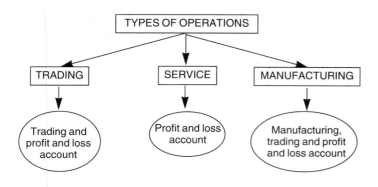

Figure 22.27 *Type of financial statement required for each type of business operation*

bought in goods and then sold them on. For example, as a business would if it were in retailing or wholesaling. Some businesses do not buy and sell but instead provide a service such as solicitors or accountants. In these situations the business would not require a trading account but would simply have a profit and loss account.

Other businesses manufacture and then trade on their products. These businesses require a manufacturing account as well as a trading and profit and loss account.

Task

Identify five local examples of trading organisations, service organisations and manufacturing organisations. Explain why their accounts will differ.

· MANUFACTURING ACCOUNTS ·

Manufacturing is the process of changing raw materials (inputs) into finished goods or part-finished goods though construction or manufacture. Companies receiving part-finished goods as their inputs and turning these into more part-finished goods or finished goods are also involved in manufacturing.

Manufacturing accounts enable an organisastion to calculate the cost of manufacturing its goods. In doing this

the manufacturing account is divided into two distinct sections. These are:

1 **Prime Cost** section. This is concerned with costs which are directly related to each product manufactured. Prime refers to the 'first' costs involved in the manufacture of any product. These costs are sometimes called **direct costs** or **variable costs** as they vary directly with output. **Raw materials** fall into this category as well as the **direct labour** attributable to each product manufactured.
2 **Cost of Manufactured Goods** section. This section is concerned with **factory overheads**. Though these costs are not directly related to each product, they do relate to the process of manufacture. For example, the rent or the factory lighting and heating. These costs are **indirect costs** or **fixed costs** because they do not vary with output.

In manufacturing an organisation could hold several different types of stocks. At the beginning of the manufacturing process there will be **stocks of raw materials**.

During the manufacturing process an organisation will hold stocks of **work-in-progress** and, at the end of the manufacturing process it will create **stocks of finished goods**.

Holding each of these stocks will ultimately influence profitability and so must be included in the accounting process. For example:

● Stocks of raw materials are accounted for in the prime cost section of the manufacturing account. The opening stock of raw materials is simply added to the purchase of raw materials and then the closing stock is deducted.
● Work-in-progress is dealt with in the cost of manufactured goods section of the manufacturing account. When looking at work-in-progress the difference in the value of work-in-progress between the beginning and the end of the year is taken into consideration. For example, if the opening stock of work-in-progress is bigger than the closing stock the result will be an increase in manufacturing costs. If the opening stock of work-in-progress is smaller than the closing stock the net result will be a decrease in manufacturing costs.
● Stocks of finished goods are accounted for in the trading account of a manufacturing company. The opening stock of finished goods is added to the cost of manufactured goods and then the closing stock is deducted.

Example

A manufacturing and trading account may appear as in Figure 22.28.

	£	£
Opening stock of raw materials		8 500
Add purchase of raw materials		85 000
		93 500
Less closing stock of raw materials		9 000
Cost of Raw Materials used		84 500
Direct labour		37 400
Prime Cost		121 900
Factory overheads:		
Factory rent	4 900	
Factory power	7 300	
Factory repairs	1 350	
Depreciation of factory machinery	7 100	
Factory salaries (indirect labour)	21 000	
		41 650
		163 550
Add opening stock of work-in-progress		4 000
		167 550
Less closing stock of work-in-progress		2 500
Cost of manufactured goods		165 050
Sales		200 000
Opening stock of finished goods	7 900	
Add cost of manufactured goods	165 050	
	172 950	
Less closing stock of finished goods	8 300	
Cost of Sales		164 650
Gross Profit		35 350

Figure 22.28 *Manufacturing and trading account of ILM Manufacturing for the year ended 31 December 19–3*

Harshaw Toys Ltd is a small manufacturing company. The following details have been extracted from its books at the end of 19–3:

	£
Stock of raw materials 1 Jan	7 350
Stock of raw materials 31 Dec	7 920
Purchases of raw materials	93 540
Stock of finished goods 1 Jan	7 100
Stock of finished goods 31 Dec	9 450
Work-in-progress 1 Jan	3 300
Work-in-progress 31 Dec	2 400
Direct labour	34 000
Factory rent	2 150
Factory power	3 750
Factory repairs	2 100
Depreciation of factory	1 300
Factory salaries	7 400
Sales	225 000

Prepare a manufacturing and trading account of Harshaw Toys for the year ended 31 December 19–3.

Local authority balance sheet

The balance sheet in Figure 22.29 (overleaf) refers to North Yorkshire County Council as at 31 March 19–2.

1 Describe how the statement differs from that of a limited liability company.

2 Calculate and then comment upon North Yorkshire's working capital at that particular point in time.

3 Explain how a long-term liability will differ from a current liability.

4 Describe what you think is meant by the following:

a a deferred debtor

b investments

c reserves

d provisions.

	19-1	19-2
Assets		
Capital Outlay	109 430	157 094
Deferred Charges	815	1 061
Deferred Debtors	4 119	4 786
Current Assets		
Stock	3 197	3 942
Debtors	43 954	27 884
Investments –		
Temporary Loans	40 350	45 950
Cash in hand	224	256
Reserves	1 035	0
	203 124	240 973
Liabilities		
Long Term Liabilities		
Loans Outstanding	88 381	104 176
Current Liabilities		
Creditors	50 944	48 263
Temporary		
Internal Loans	1 912	2 680
Cash Overdrawn	16 424	9 243
	157 661	164 362
Total Assets less		
Total Liabilities	45 463	76 611
Represented by		
Capital Fund	924	0
Capital Receipts		
Unapplied	4 270	713
Capital Discharged	0	31 357
Other Funds and Accounts	1 100	0
Revenue Account Balances	27 108	16 085
Capital Expenditure		
Reserves	11 273	7 884
Other Reserves	675	10 049
Provisions	113	1 485
Provision for Credit		
Liabilities	0	8 088
Deferred Liability	0	950
	45 463	76 611

Figure 22.29 *Consolidated balance sheet of North Yorkshire County Council*

Producing a booklet

This assignment can help you provide evidence for assessment, or claim the following Core Skills:

Communication
Present information in a vartety of visual forms
Communicate in writing

Application of number
Apply numerical skills and techniques

Personal Skills
Transfer skills gained to new and changing situations
Use information sources
Apply a range of skills and techniques to develop a variety of ideas in the creation of new/modified products, services or situations

You work in the accounts department of a limited company which employs 450 people. Over recent weeks you have been running a number of one-day seminars for senior managers called 'Understanding Financial Statements'. The directors want all employees in the company to have a basic understanding of how the business is performing in the hope that it will help to improve the quality of decisions which they have to make.

The training manager has been so pleased with your presentations that he has now asked you to create a booklet to be called 'Understanding Financial Statements' which could be handed out to all of the business's employees. You have agreed to undertake the task and have been given two weeks to complete it. The training manager has pointed out that:

- The booklet should assume that the reader has no previous accounting knowledge.
- The booklet should endeavour to acquaint the reader with the final accounts of a company.
- Simple examples should be used.
- The booklet should show the reader how to interpret financial statements.

In order to assist you with your task the training manager has provided you with trial balance and notes (Figure 22.30) for a fictitious company called Mossgrave Ltd from which you can construct a set of final accounts in your booklet.

	(£)	(£)
Stock	16 440	
Sales		125 405
Purchases	64 250	
Advertising	12 950	
Stationery	8430	
Business rate	2400	
Loan interest paid	1500	
Debenture interest paid	1000	
Sundry expenses	1450	
Directors' salaries	15 300	
Land and buildings	225 000	
Machinery	115 000	
Debtors	6900	
Bank	1400	
Cash	325	
Creditors		5440
10% debentures		10 000
General reserve		3000
Retained profit @ 31 Dec 19–2		28 500
Authorised and Issued share capital:		
200 000 ordinary £1 shares		200 000
100 000 10% £1 preference shares		100 000
	472 345	472 345

Figure 22.30 *Trial balance of Mossgrave Ltd*

Further information
- The closing stock is £12 100.
- Corporation tax is to be charged at 25 per cent of profits.
- There will be a 5 per cent dividend on ordinary shares.
- Preference share dividend is to be paid.
- A further £2000 is to be allocated to general reserve.

chapter **23** PREPARING WORK AND COLLECTING DATA FOR A BUSINESS PLAN

This chapter focuses on how work needs to be prepared and data collected to go into a business plan. The chapter starts off by looking briefly at personal planning, before going on to look at preparing a business plan. The chapter identifies a number of preparatory stages that can be employed in developing a business plan. Students should put these ideas into practice by setting up either a fictional or real business for part of the final year of their course.

The stages identified are as follows:

- Ideas for the trading of goods or a service are proposed.

- The feasibility of proposals is tested through discussion with experienced people.
- Proposals are identified and clarified.
- Objectives of trading are identified and clarified.
- Work responsibilities to achieve objectives are discussed and agreed.
- Resource requirements are identified and estimated.
- Time and resource constraints on production, sales and marketing are identified and plans are changed as necessary.
- Support for the plan from external sources is identified and marshalled.

In this book we have provided you the reader with challenges. You have been asked to communicate effectively, to work in co-operation with others, to make decisions, to investigate new areas of skill and knowledge, to interpret data, to reflect on work experience, to manage tasks and to do many other things. You have also been asked to reflect on these experiences and to set yourself realistic new targets.

In doing all this, you should have developed a better self-awareness and an increasing ability to review your own performance as well as the performances of others.

Review of performance is very important. It is important for **individuals** (e.g. how well can you do a particular task, and what improvements can you make?). It is important for particular processes (e.g. how well is a manufacturing process being carried out, and are there areas that can be improved?). Finally, it is important for **organisations** (e.g. how effectively is an organisation meeting its objectives and how can this performance be improved?).

· PLANNING AND REVIEWING · PERSONAL PERFORMANCE

We can break down a new experience or task that we need to perform into three stages, using a simple PIE model:

> P = Planning
> I = Implementation
> E = Evaluation

The stage of evaluation involves reviewing the planning and implementation in order to make improvements.

Aims and objectives

Planning an activity must start with you deciding on your aim and objectives. What are you trying to achieve?

In military terms, your aim is your main focus for concern – for example, to win a war. Your **objectives** are the main means you establish to pursue your aim: to fight a number of battles, to ensure that you have available the best possible weaponry, to strike when you have the maximum advantage, etc.

Task

1 What is your main aim in following the college course you are currently doing? What objectives have you set to pursue this main aim?

2 What is your main aim in carrying out a particular piece of work experience? What objectives have you set to pursue this aim?

It should be apparent that if you are not clear about your aim and objectives then you will not be able to define the direction in which you wish to go. If you have not yet set your aim and objectives, then try to do so now. It often helps to talk through your goals with someone else.

The next stage is to look at the 'nitty-gritty' – the means of following up your aim. What exactly do you need to do?

On a college course you may need to:

- learn new skills
- learn and be able to use new knowledge
- develop new attitudes.

The same applies to work experience.

Competency statements

Today, many of the things that you need to be able to do are expressed as **competency statements**. These show a number of CAN DO's. For example, it could be said that teaching well involves these CAN DO's:

- *can* start a lesson with interest
- *can* organise an interesting discussion
- *can* use an overhead projector with clarity
- *can* provide a range of interesting experiences for the class.

Task

Draw up lists of about ten competency statements for two of the following:

a a teacher   c a hairdresser

b a nurse   d a shop worker.

One way in which you can review your own performance in a particular activity is to make a list of competency statements for yourself. Better still, you can draw up the list after discussing the matter with colleagues. Then refer to any existing literature giving details of competency statements for a particular trade. Of course, there will be different *levels* of competency, not just 'CAN DO' or 'CAN'T DO' – you should try to find out what these particular competencies are.

One word of caution at this stage. In some areas it is quite easy to draw up competency statements (e.g. mending a bicycle tyre). However, there are other areas in which it is not so clear – for example, it is not clear-cut what makes a good teacher, or a good comedian.

Task

Think of about five activities or occupations for which it is difficult to draw up lists of competency statements.

Short-term and long-term plans

Having established your aim and objectives, you can set about developing plans to implement the objectives. Some targets that you set will be short-term while others will cover much longer periods.

- A **strategic plan** sets out long-term aims.
- A **medium-term plan** outlines the main objectives to be achieved over a period of time.
- A **short-term action plan** identifies immediate targets.

Personal action planning

You may want to set out your own action plan to cover some aspect of personal development during your GNVQ course. For example, you may want to improve your study skills, or to develop competencies at work, or to score high grades on your assignments.

Example – Action plan to develop a work-related competency

You can develop an action plan using the following headings:

- *Area for development*. Set out here the skill that you want to develop. You will then have a clearer idea of what you want to change.
- *Name of person responsible for implementing the change*. This should be you, because you are responsible for managing your own learning in this new area.
- *Task group*. Who will support you in bringing about the change? By identifying this group you will know who can help. Indeed, the task group may help you to develop the action plan. The more you communicate your needs to them, the better chance there is for them to help you.
- *Statement*. This should explain what the task group is set up to achieve. You can then communicate this mission statement to an outside group.
- *Roles*. Who should do what in the task group? What is your responsibility? What is the responsibility of your tutor or work supervisor?
- *Analysis of needs*. Carry out an analysis to identify the **strengths, weaknesses, opportunities** and **threats** in relation to the identified change. This is a SWOT analysis. The template in Figure 23.1 can be used.
- *Action steps*. List the main steps you will need to carry out your planned change. List them both in order of importance and in the order in which they will need to be carried out. The action steps will help to make it

STRENGTHS	WEAKNESSES
OPPORTUNITIES	THREATS

Figure 23.1 *Template for a SWOT analysis*

clear what you will have to do, and any resources needed to help you make the change.
- *Evaluation*. Try to identify the criteria that will be used to assess the success of your action steps. It is very important that you set these out from the start. You will need to know how to measure your success. Clearly the task group will be of great use in helping you to measure changes and improvements.

If you carry out an action plan successfully it should help you to have a greater awareness of your own ability to learn, and of your own strengths and weaknesses. It should also help you to plan new learning experiences.

Evaluation

It is important that you try to develop ways of measuring how effective you have been. You should then compare your own assessments with those of other people.

For example, imagine that as part of this GNVQ course you have to plan an effective presentation (this was one of the suggested activities in Chapter 1). Your action plan could include the evaluation sheet in Figure 23.2. You could ask other people to fill in the evaluation sheet to see how their assessments compare with your own. Who could you ask to fill in the presentation evaluation sheet? How could you discuss the sheet with them? What might you do if their evaluations of your performance were different from your own?

PRESENTATION EVALUATION SHEET

Name of presenter: Sheet filled in by

	Weak			Strong	
	1	2	3	4	5

CONTENT
Planning of presentation   – – – – – – – – – – – – – –
Language at right level   – – – – – – – – – – – – – –
Objectives clearly stated   – – – – – – – – – – – – – –
Communication of ideas   – – – – – – – – – – – – – –
Use of visual materials   – – – – – – – – – – – – – –
CONTROL OF PRESENTATION
Used time well   – – – – – – – – – – – – – –
Handled questions well   – – – – – – – – – – – – – –
Signposted different stages   – – – – – – – – – – – – – –
Used questions   – – – – – – – – – – – – – –
Paced session   – – – – – – – – – – – – – –
CONTACT WITH AUDIENCE
Involved the audience   – – – – – – – – – – – – – –
Listened to points raised   – – – – – – – – – – – – – –
Acted naturally and confidently   – – – – – – – – – – – – – –
Looked for feedback   – – – – – – – – – – – – – –
Asked for questions   – – – – – – – – – – – – – –
Tested that audience understood   – – – – – – – – – – – – – –

OVERALL ASSESSMENT   – – – – – – – – – – – – – –

Figure 23.2 *Presentation evaluation sheet*

Continuing personal awareness

The PIE model of planning, implementation and evaluation provides opportunities to develop greater self-awareness, awareness of others and awareness of important planning procedures.

This book set out to encourage you to develop suitable skills. You have found out how organisations operate, but – just as importantly – you will have found how you can fit into an organisation.

You should remember the practical experiences that you have gained from the course and be aware of your own relationships with organisations through a process of critical review.

Case Study

Your work experience

Your own work experience is the subject of this case study. Specifically, think of the work experience that has been the most important in terms of your personal and career development.

1 Give a brief job description of what was involved.
2 Who were you responsible to? What were you responsible for?
3 Comment on how you gained from this work experience in terms of:
   a increased knowledge about the work involved
   b increased skills or aptitudes
   c changed attitudes to work
   d changed plans for future career development
   e increased insights about the operation of organisations.
4 Set out a short action plan giving details of steps you may want to take to:
   a find out more about career choice, or
   b find a new appropriate work experience opportunity.

• WHAT IS A 'GOOD BUSINESS'? •

A good business has a number of distinguishing characteristics:

● It makes a profit by supplying products or services that people want to buy.
● It contributes to its own and the community's long-term prosperity by making the best use of resources.
● It minimises waste of every kind.
● It respects the environment, locally, nationally and globally.
● It sets performance standards for its suppliers, and helps in their achievement.
● It offers its employees good career prospects, professional training and job satisfaction.
● It expects the best from its employees and rewards them accordingly.

If a business is to remain a 'good business' it needs to fulfil all these criteria. For example, no business can continue to make a profit if it fails significantly to make the best possible use of available resources. It would simply be overtaken by competitors who do.

In making the best possible use of resources – whether raw materials or human potential – it automatically contributes to the general prosperity.

Of course, 'best possible use' implies more than simply 'best possible use in the short term'. Any company short-sighted enough to exploit resources simply for immediate gain, at the expense of the environment or the customer's best long-term interests, would risk failure – for example public hostility and a customer boycott. A good business should always be a good citizen.

· STARTING TO PREPARE A PLAN FOR A GOOD BUSINESS ·

1 IDEAS FOR THE TRADING OF GOODS OR A SERVICE ARE PROPOSED

In the first chapter of this book you were asked to brainstorm some good business ideas for setting up a business of your own. After working hard on your GNVQ Business course, and having had the opportunity to use the insights from your learning to become more knowledgeable about the business world, you will probably be able to come up now with some new ideas.

Task

Brainstorm a further set of ideas for a business proposal. What are you going to produce? Why is it a 'good idea'?

2 THE FEASIBILITY OF PROPOSALS IS TESTED THROUGH DISCUSSION WITH EXPERIENCED PEOPLE

When you have a good business idea, who do you turn to for advice about its feasibility? Of course, you turn to someone with business experience. For example, your local Enterprise Agency has business consultants available to give such advice. A high street bank will not only be able to give financial advice, but will provide more general guidance on other aspects of setting up a business. Most high street banks provide 'starter packs' giving guidelines on how to construct a business plan, and bookshops offer a range of slim volumes on the subject.

You may also seek advice from someone who has already experienced the problems. For example, if you were thinking of setting up as a mobile hairdresser you would want to consult someone who already operates in this field. So the first step is to consult a knowledgeable person about your overall business idea, or several 'experts' on different aspects of it.

Case Study

Chip vending

The world's first chip vending machines, the dream of the fast food business for many years, have been trialled at 15 selected test sites in California. The first man to deliver such a product was a 60-year-old inventor from Leeds, William Bartfield, who had spent ten years researching production of the machine. His Prize Frize company, backed by investors, spent £5 million on research and development.

Mr Bartfield first found a company which produced reconstituted potato for the armed forces and then began to develop a machine which would turn out hot, fresh chips within seconds of coins being deposited.

The machines cut the potato concentrate into 33 chips, then a conveyor moves them to a fryer for a 15-second fry in vegetable oil. They drop into a second cooking basket for 30 seconds and finally fall into a paper carton.

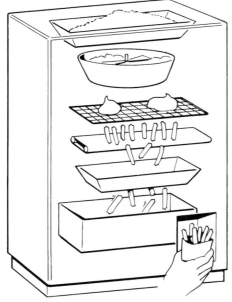

Potato concentrate
mixed with hot water

Potato partly
cut into oblongs

Conveyor moves
chips to fryer

Cooked for
15 seconds

Cooked another
30 seconds

Ketchup and salt at base of cup

Figure 23.3 *The chip vending machine*

The consumer deposits the equivalent of about 30 pence, waits for 45 seconds, and then receives a cardboard carton containing a portion of chips complete with ketchup and salt.

By late 1991 Mr Bartfield already had orders for more than 1000 machines. The cost of the machines was high, and he recognised that an important task would be to reduce his costs.

At the same time a rival company backed by Heinz was seeking to produce a chip vending machine which would deliver chips cooked from the frozen potato.

1 Why is a chip vending machine a good idea?
2 Explain how the following might be helpful in turning the idea into an effective business proposition:
   a planning
   b finance
   c organisation
   d research and development
   e teamwork
   f record-keeping
3 What else is needed to turn the idea into a business?

3 IDENTIFYING AND CLARIFYING THE PROPOSAL

By now you should be getting a clearer picture of what your proposal is. For example, you might be able to say:

My proposal is to use a desktop publishing package to produce customised stationery and business cards. I will make this service available to individuals and businesses in my locality. I have done some research and found out that there are a number of graphics artists offering a similar service, but their prices are quite high. I feel that I can undercut their prices by using a DTP system that is available to me. I have found out where it is possible to buy good-quality paper and card at a discount.

Task

Identify and clarify *your* proposal for a business idea. Use a word-processing package to outline your proposal on half a side of A4 paper. Do not go into any detail at this stage.

4 OBJECTIVES OF TRADING ARE IDENTIFIED AND AGREED

When running a business (or any form of activity) it is essential to set out a list of objectives. The objectives describe what it is you are trying to achieve. It then becomes possible to *assess the success* of the business by checking your progress towards meeting the objectives.

For example, imagine that a business has set itself the objectives of making high-quality toilet paper, becoming the market leader in selling toilet paper in the region, and selling the product at a profit. If it finds that it is making first-class toilet paper but is selling only 60 per cent in the region, and is making a loss, then clearly something is wrong and needs to be changed.

It is *essential* that you clarify your objectives so that you can check on your progress towards them.

Case Study

Checking against your original objectives

In February 1993 the chairman of the London Ambulance Board resigned as an independent enquiry criticised management for a series of failures that caused a breakdown of London' emergency services.

In October 1992, 48 hours of chaos resulted from the collapse of the £1.5 million computer-aided dispatch system of the London ambulance service. Calls disappeared while others were picked up by an answering machine. More than one ambulance arrived at the same incident, and others took several hours to turn up. A second computer failure within ten days forced operators to revert to pen and paper methods.

The enquiry report said that managers had rushed ahead with the 'high-risk' strategy of installing a system that was incomplete, had known technical problems, had not been tested and had insufficient back-up. Staff were not trained properly to use a system which was imposed by an over-zealous and misinformed management.

1 *In your opinion, had management lost sight of its key objectives in this particular instance?*
2 *Why do you think that management had opted for the new system?*
3 *Why might they have opted for a 'high-risk' strategy?*
4 *Do you think that this 'high-risk' strategy would have contradicted some of the key objectives of running an ambulance service?*

In setting out your trading objectives you will need to keep in mind a number of audiences, which can be divided into 'internal' and 'external':

● The internal audience is managers, employees and shareholders within your organisation.
● The external audience is customers, suppliers, the local authority, the media (local or national), etc.

The wider public has most confidence in enterprises with clearly set out objectives. 'Shady' businesses tend to be ones of which you will hear it said, 'I don't know exactly

what they do – they are a bit of an unknown quantity.' So set out some clear objectives for trading. Figure 23.4 shows an example.

> 1 To produce and sell gingerbread.
> 2 To trade under the name Simply Super Gingerbread
> 3 To purchase ingredients in bulk at trade prices (wherever possible).
> 4 To produce gingerbread on the morning it is sold.
> 5 To sell gingerbread from a market stall on Saturday mornings.
> 6 To sell gingerbread at prices 10 per cent below those charged by other sellers of gingerbread.
> 7 To set production and sales targets, and to monitor these targets at regular intervals.
> 8 To review trading objectives at regular intervals.

Figure 23.4 *A clear set of objectives*

Unfortunately many small businesses quickly lose sight of their initial objectives (or they fail to set any down), and then wonder why things start to go wrong.

Tasks

1 Try to discover the trading objectives of a local business. Find out from the owners (i) how and why the objectives were established, (ii) how successful the organisation is in meeting its objectives, and (iii) how and when the business reviews its objectives.
2 Set out a list of trading objectives to support your own business proposal.

5 WORK RESPONSIBILITIES TO ACHIEVE OBJECTIVES ARE DISCUSSED AND AGREED

It is vital to agree on 'who does what' when you are working jointly on a particular project. For example, a football team facing an important cup game may decide that it will try to score a goal in the early stages of a match and then defend that lead. It will start the game off by pushing players forward. Later on players will be pulled back to concentrate on defence. Before the match it is necessary to decide on a *game plan*. Work responsibilities have to be decided – i.e. who will do what and when.

The same is true in business. In our earlier gingerbread-making example (Figure 23.4), think of the tasks that need to be performed by the group. Everyone can play a part in suggesting the business name, but specialists will need to:

- arrange for the hire of the market stall
- produce the gingerbread
- sell the gingerbread
- look after the financial side
- etc.

In addition the organisation will need a **management structure** to make sure that decisions are made concerning:

- establishing the business objectives
- monitoring performance against the objectives
- making sure that tasks are carried out as and when required
- taking overall responsibility for the business

In Chapter 4 we looked at different ways of structuring an organisation. For example it can be divided into different functions – marketing, accounts, personnel, production, etc. Each function will then have specific responsibilities under the leadership of senior managers.

Task

Set out a list of work responsibilities for the business organisation you are going to set up. Show how these work responsibilities will help to achieve the objectives that you have discussed and agreed.

6 RESOURCE REQUIREMENTS TO PRODUCE THE GOODS OR SERVICE ARE IDENTIFIED AND ESTIMATED

What **resources** do you need to produce goods and services?

- **Cash resources**. The lifeblood of any business is cash. It needs to have money available to buy stock and to pay

off debts. Without cash, other vital resources that the business requires will quickly dry up.
- **Raw materials and stock**. If the business is manufacturing a product it will need ingredients. It will also usually need to have some goods available to supply to consumers immediately (unless all goods are made to special order).
- **Capital, equipment and premises**. The business will need to have somewhere to operate, and machinery to produce outputs.
- **Financial resources**. In addition to cash, the business may need to have other financial resources to set up, buy materials, and to pay off debts. For example, it may have an overdraft, loan or mortgage. Many businesses also require land.
- **Human resources**. Mental and physical labour are necessary to carry out work tasks.
- **Managerial resources.** Management experience will be needed to coordinate and control the use of other resources.
- **Information and communication resources**. An organisation today will require means of communication with its internal and external customers. It may benefit from IT systems, and other key ways of processing and communicating information.

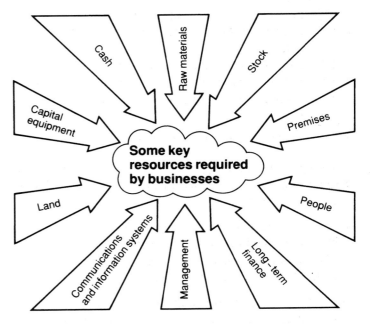

Figure 23.5 *Necessary resources for a manufacturing business*

Make a list of resources that will be required to support your business proposal to produce a good or service. Make estimates of the quantities of resources that will be required (e.g. five employees each working for 20 hours a week, £500 in cash to meet short-term liabilities and expenses, an overdraft facility of £400, one desktop computer and software, etc.).

At this stage of developing a business plan it is helpful to learn a bit more about production and the nature of **production processes**. Physical resources are important in any organisation.

The product

An organisation's **product** is the good or service it offers to consumers. A dry cleaning service is just as much a product as is a washing machine or tumble dryer.

All organisations have to analyse what their product means to their customers. Too often in the past, organisations have ignored marketing information and developed products simply because production costs appeared to be low, or because efficient use could be made of materials; they did this instead of looking at how they could develop products to meet consumer needs. Their approach was clearly **product-led** rather than market-led. In our modern competitive world where the wishes of the consumer are ever more demanding, it is rarely possible for organisations to survive without becoming market-led.

Have the Cubans become market led?

After the world's largest McDonald's opened in Moscow, Cubans probably felt a little jealous. The response from Fidel Castro, Cuba's leader, was that his regime could do anything the reforming Russians could do, but without the help of the Yankee capitalists! Over recent months a chain of hamburger restaurants has sprung up on the streets of Havana.

Known locally as McCastro's, the kiosks serve burgers and one type of soft drink, but beyond that they have little in common with McDonald's. At McCastro's, surliness and incompetence are the order of the day. Despite this, the kiosks are proving popular and Cubans now munch 80 000 hamburgers daily.

Some people remain suspicious, because meat has not been widely available in Cuba for many years. One aspiring entrepreneur was recently arrested for trying to pass off cleaning rags dipped in vinegar as beefsteak. Though the ingredients remain unknown, one official newspaper in Cuba claimed the burgers are highly nutritious and contain a minimum of 60 per cent pork. It failed to identify the other 40 per cent!

1 *How have the Cubans responded to the desire of consumers to follow Western eating habits?*
2 *Have their efforts been successful? To what extent may this move have been market-led?*
3 *What might happen to the market for burgers if a McDonald's opened up in Havana? How would the Cuban kiosks have to respond?*

Research

No matter what the source of new product ideas, it would be foolhardy for an organisation to develop a new product without first conducting **research**. Research is the systematic search for facts and information to solve problems.

Market research tries to anticipate the needs of potential and existing customers by means of a thorough understanding of their behaviour patterns. **Product research** then takes this further – it uses the knowledge of consumers' needs and wants to make changes to existing products or to develop new ones.

Distinguishing between the different characteristics of consumers to develop a product to appeal to a particular group in a particular market segment is known as **differentiation**.

Where do new ideas come from?

Product developments sometimes arise out of chance ideas. These ideas may develop from discussions with colleagues, from suggestion schemes or from brainstorming sessions.

Market gap analysis is often used. An organisation's existing range may have a number of gaps which need to be investigated and filled. Gap analysis will identify under-exploited market segments so that products can be directed at them.

Organisations will look to maximise their use of **idle resources**. Machines that are not fully used are wasteful to the organisation. By developing a new product an organisation may be able to mobilise this excess capacity.

There may be a need to spread the financial risk through **product diversification**. A narrow range may present a danger, particularly in markets such as clothes where fashions change frequently.

An organisation may have a desire to gain prestige. Producing a **flagship product** may improve the image of the whole range.

Finally, an organisation may have been asked by a customer to develop and produce a product for a specific application. The product is thus produced to **special order**.

Design

A new product should be designed to meet the needs of customers. A 'new design' is a product with details that are different from earlier products intended for much the same use.

Customers should be able to identify features of the new product that are different from and better than those of competing products. Good product design is generally agreed to relate directly to commercial success.

For most major projects a design team is established which is led by a design manager. The team then remains with the project throughout its development.

Nowadays, computer systems help designers to develop new products and solve engineering problems. Computer-aided design (CAD) involves the use of a computer, a workstation and a graphics board with a magnetic pen, which enables the operator to touch symbols and select

Figure 23.6 *The changing face of design*

operations so that a design can be made up. This technique can be used to draw two-dimensional shapes or three-dimensional views and models. CAD has completely transformed the role of the designer.

Design at Ford

The planning, design, engineering and development of a new car at Ford is an extremely complex process. With anything up to 15 000 parts, the modern car is the most complicated piece of equipment built in high volume.

Each new product starts with a series of detailed paper studies aimed at identifying the most competitive and innovative product in whichever part of the market is under review. Original research into systems and concepts is balanced against careful analysis of operating characteristics, features, performance and economy targets, projected cost of ownership and essential dimensional requirements.

Research into competitors' vehicles, market research to judge tastes in future years and possible changes in legislation are all factors that have to be taken into account by the product planners when determining the specifications of a new vehicle.

Such information is passed on to the design team. The skill and judgement of the trained and experienced

automotive designer is vital to the creation of any design concept. To assist in the design process, Ford use some of the most advanced computer-aided design equipment. For example, computer-controlled measuring bridges that automatically scan model surfaces are linked to Ford's computer centre through a highly-sophisticated satellite communication network.

The design process involves:

- designers formulating ideas as sketches and coloured drawings
- producing full-scale clay models to review the design
- development engineers testing engines in a computer-linked test cell
- wind-tunnel testing to enable designers to maximise aerodynamic efficiency
- hand-building a prototype
- using mobile laboratories to monitor test vehicles
- using prototypes for rigorous crash testing to improve safety standards
- extensive durability testing on a variety of surfaces in all conditions.

Another major responsibility of the designer is **ergonomics**. This is the consideration of human factors in the efficient layout of controls in the driver environment, and is a fundamental part of design. For example, the design of the instrument panels must take into account the driver's reach zones and field of vision. Designers also have to ensure that designs are capable of being manufactured efficiently and economically.

Five years of research, planning, design and development take place ahead of production. Today's new Ford is more than just a pleasing shape. It represents the culmination of an extensive process of development. The product's launch determines whether all of the years of work have been justified.

1 *What role does research play in the design process?*
2 *Identify areas of importance for designers when developing a new motor car.*
3 *How does technology help the designer?*

Stages of product development

A number of steps can be clearly identified in the development of a new product. As ideas and products go through

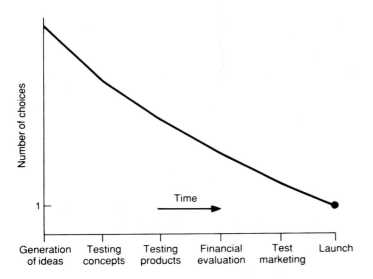

Figure 23.7 *Elimination of choices*

successive stages of research and testing, those considered less likely to succeed are eliminated (see Figure 23.7).

Testing concepts involves assessing whether or not product designs might succeed in the market-place. This means asking questions such as:

- What appeals to the consumer?
- What benefits would this product offer?
- Does the product meet the needs of the market?
- Could the idea be improved?

Testing products of the manufactured kind involves developing models or prototypes. At this stage the designer will be looking at areas such as quality, performance, safety, ergonomics and appearance. The economics of production must be taken into account, and it may be decided to build in **planned obsolescence** so that the product will need to be replaced after a certain period of time.

In some cases it may be worth while for an organisation to apply for a patent, giving it the exclusive right to produce and sell a given item.

Financial evaluation of a new product's potential is essential. Will it ultimately generate profits? Techniques of investment appraisal, and cost–volume–profit predictions using marginal costing and break-even analysis, are essential at this stage. One major difficulty, however, is the reliability of data – prediction always carries an element of risk.

Test marketing involves setting up a market situation that is as near to the real thing as possible. This is a 'dry run' and brings back information to reduce some of the risks of a full launch. Test marketing often takes place in defined television areas. For example, M&M's (the sweets) were originally test-marketed in the Tyne Tees television area – a popular choice with marketing people because the viewing public is close to the national profile, and the area does not have large areas of overlap with other TV stations.

The **launch** is the time when the product is presented to the market and is exposed to the ultimate critical test. Ideally, the launch will create an awareness of the product, followed by an interest and then a desire to purchase.

Task

Think of an item of packaged food you have recently consumed (a yoghurt perhaps, or a new soft drink). Comment on how the product would probably have been tested in its development stage.

Value analysis

The objective of **value analysis** is to satisfy consumer needs as economically as possible. All elements in the product and in its **marketing mix** are examined in order to eliminate any unnecessary or wasteful expenditure.

For example, if designers were free to operate without any cost control guidelines, they might use components or materials of a higher quality than those required to complete the task. This influences the price that has to be charged, and means that the product may not be viewed as 'value for money' by the consumer.

A value analysis team will be made up of personnel from a range of areas able to contribute to cost-cutting decisions. The team might comprise:

- a designer – for knowledge of the product
- a marketeer – for knowledge of consumer needs and the marketing mix
- a production engineer – for knowledge of processes
- an accountant – for the ability to analyse costs

- a work study expert – for experience of working procedures
- a buyer – for knowledge of sources and prices of supply.

The product life-cycle

The acceptability of a product to the market-place will determine how long it will be in demand and its overall success or failure. Designers have to base their plans upon what they expect the product's life-cycle to be. This involves working closely with marketeers to ensure that the right type of product is launched into the market at just the right time. Careful timing of the launch into the product portfolio is essential. These were matters discussed in Chapter 9.

Case Study

The products of the future

Products in the process of development for launch in 1995 include robot vacuum cleaners, microwave ovens that know what is in them, irons that sense the fabric they are pressing, and food mixers that bake cakes.

Moulinex, Europe's largest manufacturer of domestic appliances with 14 per cent of the market, recently inaugurated a £3.5 million research centre at Caen in France. Here, 35 specialists in materials, motors, robotics and computer-aided design work to raise the IQs of products to match their futuristic designs.

The pace of development and change is astronomic. With product life-cycles shortening, companies are fast making obsolete even their own inventions. A vacuum cleaner used to last twenty years and an iron seven, but now

The cake of the future?

people replace vacuums every seven years and irons every three.

Moulinex planned to spend about 2 per cent of their revenue, or £16 million, on research and development in 1991. Soon they will launch a home controller that uses electricity lines to communicate commands (such as 'on' and 'off') using specially built plugs with computer chips. These plugs can be used for appliances made by any manufacturer and the system will probably retail for about £300.

Meanwhile, in the kitchen of the Caen centre, home economists throw eggs, flour and milk into a food mixer which blends them and then bakes a cake at a touch of a button. A vacuum cleaner that looks more like R2D2 moves around a room on its own and knows where objects are. One cannot help thinking what might happen if such appliances one day decided to turn against their owners!

1 *How does this case study indicate a need to tie in marketing with research?*
2 *What does shortening product life-cycles imply for the work of the designer?*
3 *Briefly discuss the ethics of shorter product life-cycles. (Mention: care of the environment, quality of goods, consumer satisfaction, employment, standard of living.)*
4 *Identify areas in your home where you feel gadgetry could improve your quality of life.*

7 RESOURCE REQUIREMENTS TO MARKET AND SELL THE GOODS OR SERVICE ARE IDENTIFIED AND ESTIMATED

When setting up a business a key starting point is to look at the **market**. For example, if you want to set up a new take-away pizza shop there is no point in looking for a location until you are sure that people will actually want to buy your pizzas.

So it essential to know various things about the market for the product. It is necessary to allocate time and effort to finding out the answers to key market research questions, namely:

- Who will buy my product?
- Why will they want to buy it?
- How much will they buy?
- Who are my competitors?
- What are their strengths and weaknesses?
- What share of the market will I be able to win in the short-term and over a longer period?
- When will my customers buy?
- What price will they be willing to pay?
- Is the market expanding or contracting?

The most successful businesses are **market-driven**. To be successful a business must be defined in terms of what its customers want to buy. (Look at your business plan objectives – have you built in this simple rule?)

Task

What resources will you need to put into marketing in your particular business proposal? How much time and effort will be put into identifying consumer wishes and then meeting these at a profit? What types of market research will you carry out? Who will carry this out, and when? What questions will the research seek to answer? What resources will need to be put into marketing tools such as advertising and promotion?

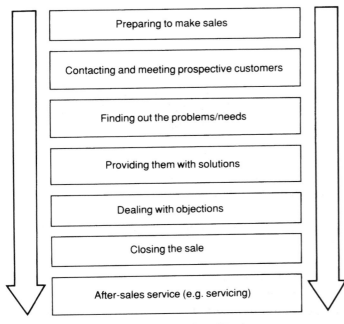

Preparing to make sales

Contacting and meeting prospective customers

Finding out the problems/needs

Providing them with solutions

Dealing with objections

Closing the sale

After-sales service (e.g. servicing)

Figure 23.9 *Meeting customer needs (selling)*

Make a list of the marketing activities that you will carry out. Then make a rough list of resources that will need to go into each of these activities.

Selling involves finding ways of meeting a customer's needs (see Figure 23.9).

Clearly a number of resources need to go into the sales operation. For example, selling electrical appliances in an electricity showroom involves training sales people, providing leaflets and brochures, spending time and effort talking to customers, spending time on concluding the sale (dealing with paperwork, etc.), and then giving after-sales service (e.g. free inspections after a period of time).

Task

Make a list of resources that will need to go into selling your particular good or service. Explain each of these resources in detail.

8 TIME AND RESOURCE CONSTRAINTS ON PRODUCTION, SALES AND MARKETING ARE IDENTIFIED

When coming up with a business proposal we tend to concentrate on the opportunities. However, it is vital that we list all the **constraints**. These are barriers that may prevent our business from being a success. Here are some of the constraints that we should think about:

Personal constraints

- Have I enough time to put into the business?
- Have I the skill or experience?
- Is my health good enough?
- Am I well organised? Can I manage time, stress, paperwork and people effectively?

Financial constraints

- Do I have enough cash/or will the business generate enough cash to meet the day-to-day needs of the business?
- Can I raise enough medium-term and long-term finance to meet the capital requirements of the business?
- Do I have an effective financial record-keeping system?

Marketing constraints

- Do I have enough resources to put into the marketing of the product?
- What is the competition like?
- What price are customers prepared to pay? Can I supply at this price?
- Where do customers want the product? Can I get it there?
- Can I supply the product that customers want?
- Can I put enough resources into promotion to make customers aware of the product?

Selling constraints

- Have I enough resources to put into selling?
- Have I the experience to deal with customers and get them to buy the product?

Legal factors

- How is the business proposal affected by employment law?
- How is the proposal affected by health and safety regulations? For example, producers of gingerbread would need to look at food safety. Setting up a market stall would involve considerations of public liability, etc.
- How is the proposal affected by consumer protection laws (e.g. the Trades Description Act).

Economic factors

- Are we in a boom or recession? How does this affect the product?
- Are interest rates high or low?
- Does the product belong to a growing or declining sector of the market?
- Can the product compete in international markets?

Task

How do the factors outlined above constrain your business proposition? Do they suggest that it would be unwise to proceed further with your idea? Do you need to do some more research and planning?

Would it be better to wait for a better time to start (e.g. when interest rates have fallen)?

9 SUPPORT FOR THE PLAN FROM EXTERNAL SOURCES IS IDENTIFIED AND MARSHALLED

It should now be clear that a lot of research needs to be carried out before you decide to put a business plan into practice. Many people with good ideas fail to translate these ideas into a good business because they fail to plan. The key to success is the planning process.

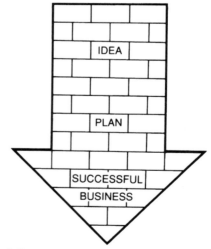

Look to the following (at least) to give you advice in organising your business proposal. You should be able to obtain a list of appropriate contacts from your local college.

- Your business studies lecturers.
- People who have set up their own business.
- Local Enterprise Agencies.
- Local banks.
- Government schemes to encourage small-business start-ups.
- The Small Firms Service.

Element assignment

Developing a business plan

This assignment can help you provide evidence for assessment, or claim the following Core Skills:

Communication
Communicate in writing

Personal Skills
Transfer skills gained to new and changing situations
Identify and solve routine and non-routine problems
Apply a range of skills and techniques to develop a variety of ideas, in the creation of new/modified products, services or situations
Use a range of thought processes

In this chapter you have been asked to carry out a series of tasks. The sum of these tasks should together make up an element assignment, as follows:

1 Propose an idea for the trading of a good or service.
2 Discuss the feasibility of your proposal with experienced advisers.
3 Identify and clarify the proposal.
4 Identify and agree your trading objectives.
5 Discuss and agree on work responsibilities.
6 Identify and estimate production resource requirements.
7 Identify and estimate selling and marketing resource requirements.
8 Identify time and resource constraints, and modify your plans if necessary.
9 Identify and use external advisers to support you in constructing and assessing the plan.

chapter **24** PRODUCING AND PRESENTING A BUSINESS PLAN

E arlier chapters have stressed the importance of the business plan. A business plan will help you to anticipate problems and to make arrangements to deal with them. It also gives vital information to those people whose support you need, particularly anyone lending money to the business. While you are working on this chapter you should produce and present a business plan of your own. This will involve a number of stages which are covered in the text:

- Explaining the purposes of a business plan.

- Identifying and explaining business objectives for a single product or service.
- Identifying a marketing plan.
- Describing a production plan.
- Identifying and explaining the resource requirements of a business and its ability to meet these requirements.
- Production of financial data and forecasts to support the plan.
- Identifying the monitoring and reviewing processes for the plan.
- Presenting the business plan to an audience.

· PURPOSES OF A BUSINESS PLAN ·

A business needs a plan so that it has a direction to follow. The business needs to know:

- where it is going
- how it is going to get there
- what resources it will need.

The plan also enables the owner(s) to check and monitor progress. Planning therefore gives structure and direction.

The business plan is needed also to show other people the direction the organisation is following. The support from people outside the organisation will almost certainly be needed. These are people who will supply the business with resources (including financial ones). If we are

looking for a loan or overdraft for the business, we need to show a bank manager how much we will need, for how long, and when we will be able to repay the loan. Lenders of money will also be interested to see cash flow projections, estimates of profits etc. Would you lend money to a business that had no clear plans?

Task

As you work through this chapter you should construct a detailed business plan. To start off your assignment, explain briefly why you are constructing a business plan. Who is your business plan for? What will they be looking for in the plan?

IDENTIFYING AND EXPLAINING · BUSINESS OBJECTIVES FOR · A GOOD OR SERVICE

In Chapter 1 we saw that businesses have a range of **objectives**. Some organisations are primarily concerned with making a profit whilst others may have charitable purposes. They may be concerned with sales *volume* so that an objective is to sell x number of products per month; or they may be interested in sales *value* (e.g. to make £x of sale per month). Other businesses may have the objective of being the market leader, whilst others may set profit targets. Some may seek just to break even.

Business objectives may also vary between the short-term and the long-term. This year your objective may be to hold on to your market share and break even, but in the longer-term you may seek to make a 20 per cent return on capital invested and become the market leader.

Task

Start off your detailed business plan by setting out the following:

- Introduction
- Details of the business
- Business organisation

Introduction
This should give a brief summary of the business idea. It will explain the objectives of the business and how it is intended they should be achieved. Perhaps you can include some personal details – brief relevant work experience, skills and education.

Details of the business
This should include the business name and address, as well as a detailed explanation of the product or service being offered. Try to show what makes your product or service different from that of competitors, and why your product will sell.

Business organisation
This should state whether the organisation will take the form of a partnership, a private limited company, etc. Also spell out the management structure of the business – be brief and concise, showing key personnel and what their functions are.

· IDENTIFYING THE MARKETING PLAN ·

Anyone with business experience who looks at a business plan will focus on a key question: *Does the person who made the plan understand their market?* In simple terms this involves looking to see whether the plan shows an understanding of why people will buy the good or service, and whether the competition has been researched.

The plan needs to show that you understand the **marketing mix** from the consumer's point of view: What product does *the customer want?* What price does *the customer want to pay?* Where does *the customer want the product?* What promotion does *the customer want?*

If you are going to be able to convince someone else that your marketing plan is well thought out, you will need to show that a sufficient quantity of customers will purchase your product. Set out to give answers to the following questions:

1 What benefits will your product or service offer to customers?
2 What price will your good or service will be offered at?
3 Will price be an important influence in the buying decision?
4 How and where are you going to sell the product or service?
5 How are you going to launch your business or service to gain maximum possible interest and take-up? What promotional and publicity methods will you employ?

In other words you will be addressing the four Ps as an essential part of your marketing plan (see Figure 24.1).

In your marketing plan you should also give an indication of how you will sell your product. Selling can be a weak

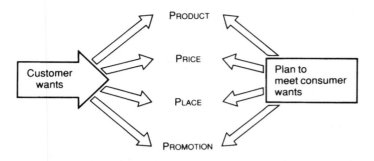

Figure 24.1 *Planning to satisfy your market*

point in business. In order to sell a product you will need to think about how you are going to **communicate** with customers, including what you are going to tell them. Selling is concerned with presenting **solutions** to meet a buyer's needs or problem. How are you going to meet your customers, explain your solutions to their problems or needs, counter any worries that they may have, and then complete the deal (as well as offering after-sales service)? An outline of these details must be built into your plan.

You should also mention the timing of your marketing and sales activities. Perhaps you could construct a flow chart showing when market research will occur, when promotion will occur, when prospective customers will be contacted, etc.

Task

Set out an outline marketing plan for your business. The plan should show details of:

- **The organisation, structure and results of market research**. This should be a brief summary only, highlighting key findings.
- **The target market**. Who are you selling to? What particular segments of a market? Why have you chosen this target market? How has your research indicated that this is the right market segment to choose?
- **Product**. What benefits does your product offer in order to meet the needs of consumers?
- **Price**. Show that your price is suitable so that an appropriate level of sales can be made.
- **Place**. Where will you be selling the product? Show that this is an appropriate place given the needs of your customers.

- **Promotion**. There is no point in getting the price, product and place right if your target market does not know that you exist. Show the various ingredients of sales promotion that you have chosen to inform your target customers of your businesses and your product.
- **Selling**. How are you going to sell your product? Remember that if you are not selling a unique product then the quality of your selling will be crucial.
- **The competition**. What are you up against? Show that you have considered and researched the competition and that your plan will put you ahead of the competition.

· DESCRIBING THE PRODUCTION PLAN ·

We saw in Chapter 1 that **production** involves converting inputs into outputs using a production **system.** This is as true of the manufacture of products as it is of the provision of services. For example, a steel works requires buildings, machinery such as a blast furnace, raw materials such as iron ore, as well as labour. A large insurance company needs an office, machinery such as computer terminals, raw materials (e.g. policies and documents) and labour.

Production planning involves combining the components involved in the production process to best effect. In setting out a production plan a business must consider the following:

1 **Premises.** What is the ideal size and location of premises? What facilities are needed (e.g. toilets, wash basins etc.)? Are the premises safe (electric wiring, ventilation, heating, etc.)? Will you need planning permission to alter the premises? Is there room for expansion if required at a later date? Do you need permission from the local council to use the premises for a particular purpose (e.g. fast food)?

2 **Machinery and equipment.** What equipment is required? What can the business afford? You might want to purchase all the latest computer equipment, but unless your business generates enough sales and work for the equipment it could prove to be a waste of cash resources.

3 **Raw materials.** What are your raw materials requirements? When will you need raw materials? How can you organise the delivery of raw materials so that you always have enough to meet your production requirements but not so much that you have idle stock around?

4 Labour. What type of, and how much, labour do you require – skilled/unskilled, full-time/part-time?

You need to show that you have planned to *combine* premises, machinery, raw materials and labour in an organised and productive way. Clearly you must think carefully about the design and layout of your plant and equipment.

Design and layout of plant and equipment

The working environment should enable people and machines to function efficiently. Though designing the layout is normally an 'organisation and methods' (O&M) responsibility, it will be carried out after extensive consultation with administrative staff and specialist engineers who might be concerned with features such as power availability and maintenance requirements.

Factors influencing the layout of plant include:

- flow of work
- type of work
- cost
- legal requirements
- safety
- ergonomics.

The flow of work has to be analysed to establish links between people, materials, paperwork and resources. The aim is to reduce unproductive movements to a minimum. Where frequent movements take place, people and resources need to be located close to each other. In a product layout, products, paperwork and materials flow constantly from one stage to another. Control is simplified because the paperwork, material handling and inspection procedures are reduced (see Figure 24.2).

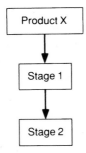

Figure 24.2 *A product layout*

In a **function** or **process layout,** all operations of the same type are performed in the same area (e.g. in the typing pool or print unit). Although this system is flexible, consid-

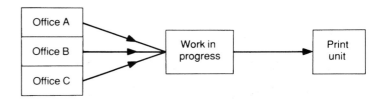

Figure 24.3 *A process layout*

erable planning is necessary to ensure that people and resources are not either over- or under-burdened (see Figure 24.3).

In a **fixed-position layout**, operations are performed and then the materials or paperwork are returned to a fixed location after each process (see Figure 24.4).

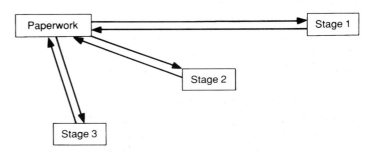

Figure 24.4 *A fixed-position layout*

The **type of work** will influence the layout of plant. Some functions may need to be in certain areas. For example, a typing pool has to be accessible to many users, a reception area has to be at the main entrance, and certain manufacturing processes need to be near specialist services.

Whenever redesigning a layout is considered, cost must be borne in mind. A budget is normally set and layout modifications have to be catered for within prescribed limits.

Legal requirements must also be met, as we saw in Chapter 10. The layout has to take into account health and safety – physical conditions such as space, ventilation, noise, cleanliness, cloakroom facilities etc.

Ergonomics is important in the design of the plant. Ergonomics considers the relationship of employees to equipment and machinery, and tries to understand how these relationships can affect performance. Workplaces should be designed from the outset around the capabilities of operators.

Hence, in planning a layout it is necessary to:

- analyse links between people, work and departments
- plan departmental locations
- take into account legal requirements, health and safety, facilities and cost
- draw a scale plan
- liaise with staff throughout the process.

Whatever techniques are used in setting up a layout, the aim must be to maximise flexibility and the ease of coordination so that process time and costs will be minimised.

The programme

All organisations have to plan their operations. Developing a programme involves looking at:

- what needs to be done
- when it needs to be implemented
- the resources necessary to fulfil the task.

The role of the planning process depends upon the type of production. With flow production, considerable thought has to be given to designing and setting up the operation. With job production, the timing of the availability of skilled workers and resources is vital. In all these situations the programmer will aim to get the most from materials, labour and plant, timetable them for use at the most appropriate times, and aim to achieve the objectives of the organisation.

Production planning and control also need to be carefully coordinated with marketing information. One aspect of this is the **product life-cycle**. The operations management needs to be aware of the changing circumstances during a product's life. For example, the initial volume requirements may be low and production may be by the batch process. As growth is achieved flow production may be more appropriate, and a smaller volume may be required in a product's maturity, as demand drops away.

Scheduling (or timetabling) is concerned with determining what should be done and when. Scheduling therefore develops detailed programmes out of initial broad plans.

Critical path analysis

A further technique in the programming process is that of **critical path analysis** (CPA). CPA is used to schedule related tasks in a way that minimises time and costs. A series of lines is drawn in the form of a **network** to find the 'critical path' of a project. Activities are thus linked diagramatically. For example, when building a house, walls have to be built before putting the roof on (see Figure 24.5).

Figure 24.5   *A simple network*

Other activities are, of course, carried out simultaneously, so that at the time the roof is put on joinery work may be completed (Figure 24.6). Network analysis can be used to programme these events in such a way as to create the most effective plan.

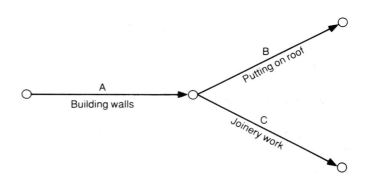

Figure 24.6   *A network with simultaneous jobs*

A further ingredient in constructing a network is the element of time. If time is incorporated into the diagrams it becomes possible to calculate the minimum amount of time to carry out a particular project. Those activities which take the longest time to complete in moving from one stage to the next are described as **critical activities.** The 'critical path' of a project is therefore the line along which these activities flow. If these activities are delayed the whole project will be delayed.

Today, CPA is applied with the aid of computer software. Packages are available to determine the best way of scheduling a complex series of tasks.

Task

Produce an outline production plan for your business product. Describe the premises, machinery, raw materials, and labour requirements. Show how you have planned to combine production resources effectively. Show the main considerations involved in designing and implementing the production of your product. You may want to use a flow chart to illustrate production processes.

IDENTIFYING AND EXPLAINING RESOURCE REQUIREMENTS

The next stage in your business plan should be to outline the physical, human and financial resources that will be required. You must show that you have researched:

- major fixed assets, looking at quality, reliability, price and suitability
- the alternatives of borrowing, buying second-hand, renting and leasing equipment
- working capital requirements.

In looking at human resources you will need to have researched the *availability* of staff. What will be the costs of recruiting, employing and training staff if required? What will be the costs of *insuring* staff at work? You will need to show that you have researched the legal aspects of employing labour.

In exploring financial resource requirements you must show that you have calculated all the likely costs and revenues of running the business. How much will you need to run the business, and what will you use the finance for? What types of finance will you require, and when? Draw up a table like Figure 24.7 to summarise the facts.

Amount and purpose of finance		Method of raising finance
Short-term finance To buy stock, raw materials	£500	Overdraft, credit from suppliers
...	£...	
Long-term finance To buy capital equipment	£2500	Bank loan, hire-purchase
...	£...	

Figure 24.7 *Summary of sources of finance*

Task

Make a list of your human, physical and financial resource requirements. Wherever possible you should try to *quantify* these.

Explain each of these resource requirements and how you will meet them. For example, you may report that you need to employ a part-time bookkeeper for one hour a week, at a total cost of £15 an hour, and that you have someone in mind.

Lenders of money want to be sure that their money is safe. You must therefore reveal what guarantees you can give. For example, a business person may put up his or her house or other possessions as *collateral* against a loan, although caution is needed because the home will be lost if the business fails.

PRODUCTION OF FINANCIAL DATA AND FORECASTS TO SUPPORT THE PLAN

You may need to review the parts of this book dealing with **cash-flow forecasting,** start-up **balance sheets**, and **profit-and-loss** accounts before tackling this section – see Chapters 19–22.

The financial data you produce should reflect different time periods. What will be the financial position *when the business is set up*? What are the cash-flow forecasts for the first year of trading (at least)? What are the projected profit-and-loss and balance sheets *after the first year (and perhaps subsequent year) of trading*?

In order to show the ability of the business to generate a profit, it is necessary to give details of expected costs and sales and the timing of these. The cash-flow forecast will indicate to prospective lenders when you will require to borrow money and how quickly you will be able to repay borrowings. It will also show when the business is expected to break even and when it should be earning profits. The expected return on capital employed (ROCE) is an important **ratio** to show the viability of a business proposal.

You will need to show how the capital that you (and others) are putting into the business will be used.

Tasks

1 Set out a projected cash-flow forecast for the first year of trading of your proposed business. Give an indication of when the business will break even and the expected profitability.
2 Set out a balance sheet for the business *at the start of trading*.

Lenders will want to look at how much of the capital of the business is to be supplied by you and how much is to be borrowed. (They may be reluctant to lend you money if you are putting up less than 50 per cent of the total capital.)

3 Present a projected profit and loss account and a balance sheet to show the state of the business and its generation of profit *at the end of the first year*.

IDENTIFYING THE MONITORING AND REVIEW PROCEDURES FOR THE PLAN

Having constructed nearly all of the essential ingredients of your plan, finally you need to show that you are going to keep a check on performance. An obvious way of doing this is to state that you will keep a monthly profit and loss account and a monthly balance sheet in order to quantify performance. These measures provide you with a **control mechanism**, so that alterations can be made to your business systems as and when required. You can, for example, check your actual cash flow against your budgeted cash flow, and you can check actual output against production targets.

Task

Identify the monitoring and review procedures that you will use to check on the performance of your business. Build this section into your business plan.

Element assignment

Presentation of a plan to an audience

This assignment can help you provide evidence for assessment, or claim the following Core Skills:

Communication
Present information in a variety of visual forms
Communicate in writing
Participate in oral and non-verbal communication

Personal skills
Transfer skills gained to new and changing situations
Identify and solve routine and non-routine problems
Apply a range of skills and techniques to develop a variety of ideas in the creation of new/modified products, services and situations
Use a range of thought processes

At each stage of the production of your business plan you should have been seeking advice. If you have followed through the tasks outlined in this chapter in a logical sequence you should by now have:

- explained the purpose of your business plan
- identified your business objectives

- identified your marketing plan
- described your production plan
- identified and explained resource requirements and your ability to meet them
- produced financial data and forecasts to support the plan
- identified ways of monitoring and reviewing procedures.

Your business plan should now be word-processed using a clear typeface. Your report should be double-spaced with wide margins, so that the person reading it can add comments. The business plan should not be too long (up to about four sides of A4 paper). *You can get an outline template for a business plan from most high street banks.* Use diagrams and graphs if you feel they would help (but not too many!). Prepare your plan in **numbered sections** with short and clear **headings.**

When you have completed your business plan you will need to present it to a small audience, including people who have advised you along the way. Aim to give a 20-minute presentation, using overheads (OHPs). You should use one OHP for each of the following:

- Objectives
- Outline of marketing plan
- Outline of production plan
- Resource requirements
- Financial support data (perhaps two or three OHPs will be needed for this last item – use large letters).

If an overhead projector is not available, use a whiteboard or a flip-chart.

chapter **25** PRODUCING PLANS FOR MARKETING AND SELLING

oday more than ever before, there is an appreciation in business circles of the importance of marketing and selling. Marketing, in particular, should be seen as a strategic weapon that enables an organisation to be in tune with its many publics. This chapter has therefore been designed to support students in producing plans for marketing and selling. It is divided into a number of key sections.

· THE PURPOSES OF A ·
MARKETING PLAN

A key part of your GNVQ course has been the study of marketing and of its importance to business organisations and to the wider economy.

People with business experience today recognise the importance of marketing and selling. This is why it is essential that in any business plan that you produce you are able to show that you understand the importance of marketing. If you ask someone for finance they will want to see that you understand your market-place.

Case Study

Bicycle repairs

Rob Jones is seeking financial support from his bank to finance a bicycle repair workshop. He has supplied his bank with the following information:

'I have decided to produce a bicycle repair service because I have always been interested in bikes. I have

been able to repair some bikes for friends and they have always been satisfied. I have decided to charge £10 an hour for my labour, and will charge for parts as well. I expect to be able to take the market by storm and within a year should have over half of the market. I expect the market to grow as more and more people use bicycles because of the recession and the high cost of petrol.'

It would appear that Rob Jones does not know a lot about marketing. Look through the information he has supplied and identify the strengths and weaknesses of his presentation. Which parts of his research and planning do you feel he needs to improve? What questions should he be seeking the answers to and spelling them out in his marketing plan?

As well as providing information for outsiders, the marketing plan sets the targets for a business. Performance can then be monitored against these targets. Progress should always be checked against initial plans.

Rob Jones' marketing plan failed to answer a number of key questions:

- **Why will people buy his product?** Some market research would have answered this crucial question. He might have found, for example, that younger and older riders prefer not to have to carry out the laborious and dirty tasks of mending, servicing and repairing their machines. This might be particularly true in the spring when people bring their cycles out of storage for the first time. Market research would have indicated the benefits that different groups of consumers were looking for. He would then have been in a better position to provide these benefits.
- **Who will buy his product?** Market research would have indicated the main groups wanting his product. he might then have been able to target benefits at specific groups.
- **How much will his customers buy?** Finding out how often customers would purchase cycle repairs would give him a clearer idea of the quantity of sales he could expect to make. This information would be vital in planning targets and in seeking financial support for his business.
- **Who are his competitors?** Research into the competition would enable Rob to find out what benefits they were offering and whether he would be able to compete with them. He would need to find out the strengths and weaknesses of his competitors. He could then concentrate on the benefits that his customers required that the competition was weak at supplying, and make sure that he was also effective in supplying the benefits that competitors were strong at.
- **What will his market share be?** Calculations of market share are important in any business plan. For example, if the total market value for bicycle repairs in

a small town was £20 000 a year and Rob expected to take 10 per cent of the market, then he would have a turnover of only £2000 a year. However, if he expected to take 60 per cent then he would take £12 000 a year.

- **When will his customers buy?** Rob needs to identify the peak periods of the year (e.g. spring and summer, school holidays, etc.). He also needs to find out on what days of the week people seek cycle repairs (e.g. weekends). He can then tailor his business activities to meet customer requirements.
- **What price will consumers be prepared to pay?** Market research might indicate that £10 an hour is too high a price. It will also indicate quantities that can be sold at different prices. Rob can then work out ways of maximising revenues.
- **Is the market growing or contracting?** Rob indicated that more people would require cycle repairs in a recession. Does he have any evidence to support this? Perhaps he should look at published sources of consumer trends. If he can show that his market is growing by 10 per cent a year, then he can start to quantify his likely sales figures in future years.

· A QUANTITATIVE APPROACH ·

It should now be obvious that marketing provides a business with valuable evidence for a business plan. It can tell us details of:

MARKET SIZE
MARKET SHARE
MARKET GROWTH
ACCEPTABLE PRICES
QUANTITIES (DEMAND)

When providing quantitative information you may want to present different **scenarios** – an *optimistic* scenario (if things go really well), a likely scenario (if things do not change a lot), and a *pessimistic* scenario (if things go badly).

Of course, a bank will tend to steer on the cautious side of the middle path when weighing up figures from a marketing plan.

Tasks

1 Jill runs a business supplying sandwiches to business premises. In 1994 she calculated that the value of the delivered sandwich market in her home town was worth £50 000. She expected to be able to win 40 per cent of this market. The market is expected to grow at 10 per cent a year. Calculate Jill's expected sales revenue for 1995.

2 Kevin is a freelance graphics artist producing business stationery and posters. The market in which he operates is currently worth £400 000. Kevin estimates that the market will increase in value by £50 000 next year. However, economic forecasts suggest that the value of the market is likely to fall by between 10 and 20 per cent next year. Kevin is likely to win 10 per cent of the total market. He is seeking a bank loan, but because of recent experience the bank is taking a pessimistic view. What value would the bank place on Kevin's likely sales next year?

• CARRYING OUT YOUR MARKET RESEARCH •

The case of Rob Jones shows the importance of basing a marketing plan on careful research. Once you have clarified a business proposal you should start to look at existing businesses that are similar. There may be an estate agent in your town who deals with business and commercial properties and who might be able to provide you with leads to similar businesses. You may also be able to interview people who run similar businesses, but it could make sense to do this in a neighbouring town in which businesses are not in direct competition with your own. People will be reluctant to talk and provide assistance to potential competitors!

Look at **published statistics** that refer to the relevant business sector. A library should be able to provide you with copies of government-produced *Business Monitors*. These look at different business sectors, so find the one that is relevant to you. Look at information about costs, sales and profits of different sizes and types of businesses.

As well as using these secondary sources, you will probably need to do primary market research. In order to carry this out effectively you should review the material in Chapter 7.

Your market research should aim to answer all the questions outlined earlier for Rob Jones' business proposal.

· PLANNING SELLING ACTIVITIES ·

Pricing

Pricing is a crucial element in the marketing mix. A low price might make you competitive but it may lead consumers to question the quality of your product. In your plan you need to explain and justify the price you have chosen, by showing how it is related to market research. You also need to bear in mind that the price needs to be pitched at an appropriate level to generate profits.

Promotion

When you start a new business you need to tell customers of your existence through advertising and promotion. You then need to get people to try out your product, possibly by giving away free samples or by sending out special offers or invitations to view. The next step will be to get people to buy, and you want customers to come back for more.

Your **promotion plan** should therefore show:

- why you need to promote your product
- what aspects of the product you are promoting
- what the promotions are and why they are likely to be successful
- how much the promotions will cost, and when
- how much profits the promotions will generate
- ways of evaluating the effectiveness of the promotions.

Sales targets

We have already seen that projected sales figures are very important in providing quantitive information. Your **sales plan** will need to set out:

- the expected volumes of sales
- the expected value of sales
- how, where and when goods will be sold
- the cost of making sales
- the likely profits generated from sales
- ways of evaluating the effectiveness of the selling operation.

Distribution

How will your goods reach the consumers? Market research will have revealed important information about consumers' preferences for distribution. The **distribution plan** additionally needs to indicate plans for getting goods to consumers in the right place, and the costs stemming from such operations.

After-sales service

Once a sale has been made it is necessary to maintain customer support for the product. Your sales plan (or your marketing plan) therefore needs to indicate that you have researched consumer preferences for after-sales service, and how and when you will provide the required service.

· ESTIMATING THE MARKETING BUDGET ·

Effective marketing costs money, but in return it should generate substantial revenues. The costs of marketing should be far smaller than the rewards.

Interested consumers will buy goods and services, and satisfied consumers will return to make repeat purchases and pass the message on about a product.

Budgeting involves deciding what marketing activities to spend money on, when to spend, and how much.

You need to have a clear idea of when you are going to carry out particular marketing and sales activities. You also need to understand why you are carrying out a specific activity at a particular time.

Tasks

1 How much time and money are you planning to make available for the marketing budget of your business proposal in Chapter 24? Produce a detailed breakdown of the timing and costs of different marketing activities. You will need to research various activities in order to find out the costs of different ones. For example, how long does it take to construct a market research questionnaire? How much does it cost to send out a mail shot? How much does it cost to prepare an advertisement and to buy advertising space in a newspaper?

2 Set out a flow chart and explanatory notes showing a time schedule for your chosen marketing and selling activities.

Remember that each section of the plan should consider the important elements of:

- Objectives
- Timing
- Resource requirements
- Ways of monitoring and evaluating progress.

Element assignment

Business planning

This assignment can help you to provide evidence for assessment, or claim the following Core Skills:

Communication
Communicate in writing

Personal skills
Identify and solve routine and non-routine problems
Use a range of thought processes

You should now be in a position to collect the various activities that you have carried out while working on this chapter into a marketing and sales plan for the business proposal you put forward in Chapter 24.

The plan should consist of the following elements:

1 market research plan
2 product plan (identification of benefits)
3 pricing plan
4 place plan (distribution)
5 promotional plan
6 sales plan

The questions which follow will give you practice in answering the type of questions you may meet in your end of unit tests.

Working through these questions will also help you to revise the range of material covered in each GNVQ unit.

There follows short answer questions, multiple choice tests and mini-case studies or activities covering each section of *Business Level 3*.

SECTION 1:
BUSINESS IN THE ECONOMY

1.1 Explain the terms: *a* wants *b* needs

1.2 What is a product?

1.3 What are the three main industrial sectors? Give two examples of industries in each sector.

1.4 Define the terms: *a* consumer *b* producer

1.5 If someone is saving to buy a new car. Why would this not represent 'demand' for a product?

1.6 What is the difference between a good and a service?

1.7 What is a charity?

1.8 Describe three essential differences between command and free enterprise economies?

1.9 Describe three weaknesses of central planning?

1.10 Explain how prices can act as signals in the market place.

1.11 What is the difference between the public and the private sector of the economy?

1.12 What is profit maximisation?

1.13 What other purposes might businesses have rather than profit maximisation? Describe three other purposes.

1.14 Explain three important factors which influence the location of a particular type of business.

1.15 Explain three reasons why Japanese car manufacturers have chosen to set up in Britain.

1.16 List four ways of identifying business opportunities.

1.17 What is *a* a closed system *b* an open system?

1.18 Define the relative market share of a business.

1.19 What is a mission statement?

1.20 What is a trade union?

1.21 What are the three fundamental questions that need to be addressed in the organisation of a national economic system?

1.22 Describe one business situation that involves conflict.

1.23 What do you understand by the term 'satisficing'?

1.24 List five major environmental factors that encourage or constrain business activity.

1.25 Explain the following terms used in systems theory:
a element *b* filter *c* controller *d* input

1.26 What is meant by the term value added?

1.27 Why is cash flow important to a business?

1.28 What is a QUANGO?

1.29 What is effective demand?

1.30 What is the largest industrial sector in the economy? List five industries contained in this sector.

1.31 What is a free market?

1.32 Explain one measure that a government can take which might reduce inequality of income.

1.33 How might a rise in interest rates affect a small business?

1.34 Briefly describe three main objectives of government policy.

1.35 What is the retail price index? What does it measure?

1.36 List the members of the European Community?

1.37 Explain how one EC regulation limits the activities of British businesses.

1.38 What are the main components of aggregate demand?

1.39 How can the UK government use fiscal policy to increase aggregate demand?

1.40 What is Value Added Tax? Who pays it?

1.41 What is meant by *laissez-faire* economic policy?

1.42 What is the difference between capital goods and consumer goods industries?

1.43 Why does the government raise taxes?

1.44 What are the main items of government expenditure?

1.45 What is a pressure group? Give two examples.

1.46 What is the difference between common and statute law?

1.47 Define monetary policy.

1.48 Which are the main bodies responsible for making EC policy?

1.49 What is a tariff?

1.50 How can a subsidy lead to increased production of a good?

1.51 Explain the EC principle of subsidiarity.

1.52 What is the Social Chapter of the Maastricht Treaty?

1.53 What is meant by having a single currency?

1.54 What is a mixed economy?

1.55 How can governments reduce inflationary pressures in an economy?

1.56 Define the term stagflation.

1.57 Explain the multiplier effect.

1.58 Explain the accelerator effect.

1.59 How can the government use monetary policy to encourage consumers to spend more?

1.60 How has the creation of a Single Market increased competition in the EC?

1.61 What is the difference between the public and private sectors of the economy?

1.62 Define the term 'price elasticity of demand'. Show how it can be measured.

1.63 What are complementary goods?

1.64 What is supply? How can it be illustrated?

1.65 Show how market prices can be determined by the interaction of demand and supply.

1.66 Describe two main costs faced by businesses.

1.67 What is a nationalised industry.

1.68 List three industries that have recently been privatised.

1.69 How does total revenue give an indication of elasticity of demand?

1.70 Why do people set up in business? Give three reasons.

1.71 What is limited liability? How does it protect shareholders in a business?

1.72 What is market leadership? How can you measure market share?

1.73 What is aggregate demand and aggregate supply?

1.74 How can supply side economics be used to create full employment?

1.75 How would you measure income elasticity of demand?

1.76 What factors influence the price elasticity of demand of a product?

1.77 Why might falling costs lead to increasing output. Explain.

1.78 List the rewards to the four factors of production.

1.79 What is an organisation? Why do organisations need to have objectives?

1.80 List three leakages from and three injections into the circular flow of income.

1.81 What types of business organisations operate in the private sector of the economy?

1.82 Who owns the following business organisations:

a partnerships *b* companies *c* municipal enterprises?

1.83 What factors would encourage: *a* the supply of a particular product to increase *b* the supply of products generally to increase?

1.84 Explain with a diagram how increased demand may encourage increased supply.

1.85 What factors might lead the price of a product to fall?

1.86 What is the main difference between wealth and welfare?

1.87 How can the supply of products be improved in qualitative terms?

1.88 Give an example of two goods that are substitutes for each other. What happens to the price and supply of one good when the demand for the other falls?

1.89 How are markets for different goods interdependent?

1.90 What is opportunity cost? Give an example.

1.91 The following shows the relative importance of different industries in a country.

Share of industries in total production.

Manufacturing...25%
Public services 16%
Distribution 13%
Other services 17%
Construction 10%
Finance 13%
Agriculture 3%
Mining 3%

The total share of production for tertiary industry is:

a *17%*
b *30%*
c *38%*
d *59%*
e *89%*

1.92 Production of goods is complete only when they have:
a *left the factory for a wholesaler*
b *left the wholesaler for the retailer*
c *been offered for sale by the retailer*
d *been sold by the retailer to the consumer*
e *been consumed.*

1.93 The United Kingdom has a mixed economy because it:

a *provides goods and services*
b *has a variety of different industries*
c *has public and private sector firms*
d *imports and exports goods*
e *has industrial and commercial firms.*

1.94 In which one of the following forms of business organisation might a member become liable for all debts:

a *co-operative society*
b *private limited company*
c *an ordinary partnership*
d *a public corporation*
e *a public limited company?*

1.95 Nationalisation involves the government:

a *selling off state industries to the private sector*
b *placing everyday control of an industry under Parliament*
c *assuming ownership of existing private enterprises*
d *establishing control of an industry by the workers*
e *setting up new enterprises to be run by the state.*

1.96 Which of the following defines a franchise:

a *it is a method of renting an expensive item of equipment*
b *it is a means of paying by instalments*
c *it gives shareholders the right to vote at company meetings*
d *it is the creation of a monopoly*
e *it involves the issue of licences to sell goods or services using someone else's name.*

1.97 A limited company is owned by the:

a *chairman*
b *board of directors*
c *public*
d *shareholders*
e *the debenture holders*

1.98 Which of the following is a 'free' good:

a *pollution in rivers*
b *sea water in the oceans*
c *crops on a farmer's land*
d *coal in a coal mine*
e *cocoa used in chocolate manufacture?*

1.99 Which of the following measures is most likely to reduce inequality of income:

a *value added tax at 20% on all consumer goods*
b *fixed television licence fee*
c *progressive income tax*
d *poll tax*
e *regressive expenditure tax?*

1.100 Which of the following is in the public sector of the economy:

a *Shell UK*
b *British Telecom*

c *The BBC*
d *British Gas*
e *Marks and Spencer?*

1.101 Which of the following methods of raising finance would not be used by an ordinary partnership:

a *bank overdraft*
b *trade credit*
c *savings*
d *loans*
e *sale of shares?*

1.102 The chairperson of a nationalised industry is appointed by:

a *the government*
b *the board of directors*
c *the public*
d *the shareholders*
e *the consumers.*

1.103 Which of the following is an injection into the circular flow of income:

a *consumption*
b *imports*
c *savings*
d *investment*
e *taxes?*

1.104 Which of the following is an example of a capital good:

a *machinery*
b *money*
c *butter*
d *insurance*
e *investment?*

1.105 Which of the following measures could be used to encourage the supply side of the economy:

a *an increase in expenditure taxes*
b *policies to give trade unions greater bargaining power*
c *increasing benefits to those out of work*
d *reducing taxes on profits made by business*
e *reducing the number and range of monopoly and restrictive practice laws?*

1.106 Penrose Pens
Penrose is a company that manufactures ballpoint pens which it then advertises in catalogues sent out free to stationery wholesalers. Market research has indicated that there is a demand for reliable low price ballpoints. Demand

has increased steadily over the last five years. Demand tends to follow changes in the business cycle in the wider economy.

The Penrose company was set up by J. Arthur Penrose in the early 1970s. In the early days the company set out to be the market leader in the south west of the country. It was initially very successful taking 40% of all sales (the nearest rival having only 18% of the market). However, because the product is so easy to produce and there are a number of very large manufacturers, market share in the south west has fallen to 10%. Penrose has 2% of the national share.

The company is now run by a board of directors and sells mainly to business customers wanting customised pens for conferences, in-house stationery etc. The company now sets out to make a healthy return on capital investment (a figure that cannot be disclosed). Pricing policies are geared towards maintaining this return. The business is very successful. It is well known amongst business customers but not amongst the general buying public.

1   *What is the main business purpose of Penrose today?*

2   *Explain how Penrose's main marketing objective has changed over time?*

3   *What has been the main cause of this change?*

4   *In which industrial sector does Penrose operate?*

5   *Give examples of four factors of production that Penrose would employ in its production processes?*

6   *How is Penrose likely to be affected by a period of national economic recession?*

1.107 Ethics in shopping habits
Two thirds of shoppers say ethical issues influence their buying habits, and the biggest ethical issue is irresponsible marketing a MINTEL survey reported in December 1990.

Percentage of sample whose buying habits are influenced by ethical issues

Source: BARB/Mintel the Green and Ethical shopper 1991

Irresponsible marketing was the main issue for four out of ten consumers, with a fifth concerned about contributions to political parties and dealings with oppressive regimes and 14 per cent saying the social policy of the firm and any involvement in armaments or weapons would deter them from buying. The ethical customer is most likely to be 35+, in the ABCI socio-economic group and to shop at J. Sainsbury or Marks and Spencer. But how do consumers actually find out about ethical issues?

TV programmes and documentaries are the main source of knowledge for seven out of ten ethical consumers; newspapers/magazines/books follow closely at 63 per cent. Just under a fifth learn from radio programmes whilst 13 per cent hear about issues chatting to friends and relatives. Sainsbury shoppers are more likely to read about ethical issues than learn about them from TV while ASDA and Co-op shoppers learn more from the radio.

1   *What are 'buying habits'?*

2   *Explain four factors influencing 'buying habits'.*

3   *Give an example of how a particular ethical issue may influence a consumer's 'buying habits' for a specific good or service.*

4   *You work for the public relations department at Sainsbury's. Suggest three ways of encouraging ethical customers to shop with you. What actions might you take to use the media to support your efforts?*

1.108 Clog Mills expansion stamped out by council
A Yorkshire clog manufacturer has called on the Department of the Environment to help fight local planners. Walkley Clogs has been producing its distinctive footwear in Hebden Bridge for 120 years. Recently the clog works has become a hugely successful tourist attraction. Tourists come to watch the clogs being made and many purchase footwear from the adjacent craft workshop. However, this has caused severe road congestion in the area. A number of residents have complained that they can barely move at weekends. The local Calderdale Council has argued that the retail side of Walkley's business is not covered by existing planning permission. The council has told the owner of Walkley's that he should pay for a road network to ease congestion at the factory site.

The owner of Walkley's has appealed to the Department of the Environment saying that the site adjacent to the factory should be a retail unit. Unless this happens, he says, people will stop visiting the site. The council is adamant that the land is available for industrial use only.

1   *In what industrial sectors is Walkley Clogs involved? Explain your answer.*

2 *What is the difference between industrial and retail use?*

3 *What main benefits are likely to accrue to people in the Hebden Bridge area from Walkley Clogs?*

4 *What are the main costs to people in the Hebden Bridge area from the existence of Walkley Clogs?*

5 *How and why is Calderdale Council involved in this particular issue?*

6 *How and why is the Department of the Environment involved in this issue?*

7 *Why might the Department of the Environment have a different view on how this issue should be resolved (compared with the view of Calderdale Council)?*

8 *You are the public relations officer for Walkley Clogs. What key points would you make to the Department of the Environment (in your submission) supporting Walkley Clogs continued retail development.*

1.109 Roachford City Council *vs* F. Willars

One year ago Roachford City Council introduced a new skip scheme into the Sparkhill residential area of the city. Every month a skip is placed in a set location so that residents can get rid of large items of rubbish. Since the introduction of the scheme Mr Frank Willars, a local resident has deducted 5 per cent from his council tax payments in protest. The council served a court summons on Mr Willars for non payment of taxes. The following statements were taken in court:

Mrs A. Gildroy Sparkhill Residents' Association (prosecution witness). 'Since the scheme started a large number of residents in the area have stated how useful they find the skip. We in the Residents' Association would be very unhappy if the scheme were to stop. Mr Willars is just being difficult'

Ms J. Tanner Roachford City Council (prosecution witness). 'The skip scheme has been in operation for up to three years in different areas of the city. In general we have had a very positive response to the scheme. Before introduction into Sparkhill a survey of ten per cent of the residents was carried out and, based on the results, the scheme was introduced. One person cannot be allowed to deduct tax money just because he or she doesn't want what the majority of other people do want.'

Mr F. Willars (defendant). 'I am 71 years old. My only income is a state pension. I have lived in Sparkhill for over 35 years. In all that time I have never needed a skip and I don't want one now. On average the city tax is 15 per cent higher than surrounding areas, due to schemes like this. Nobody asked what I want. I need money for food and heating not skips and I'll go to prison to prove it.'

1 *What did the council do to find out if the skip scheme was wanted in Sparkhill?*

2 *Imagine that you are Mr Willars. Explain two reasons why you would not be prepared to pay for the scheme.*

3 *Explain three services that are commonly provided by a local council.*

4 *Imagine that you work for Roachford City Council. Explain why you introduced the scheme.*

5 *Using the evidence provided make a judgement in this case. Is the council right to expect everyone to contribute to this scheme? What should happen to Mr Willars? Should he be made to contribute? Should he be given an additional penalty?*

1.110 Awareness of the public and private sectors

The results of a survey published in the Cabinet Office in February 1993 revealed that:

- more than half the population of Britain believes that the National Westminster Bank, British Airways and ITV are, or may be public services and utilities.
- twenty per cent think the Abbey National 'definitely is'
- only thirty per cent are sure about the status of English Heritage as a government agency.

These findings showed that even after ten years of wholesale privatisation, many people have difficulty in distinguishing between the public and private sector. Equally worrying was the finding that a large swathe of the population are ignorant of the purpose of the Citizen's Charter.

1 *You have been asked by the government to produce a short leaflet (300 words maximum) using plain English which will make the public aware of the following:*
   a *The difference between the public and private sector.*
   b *what is meant by the term privatisation.*
   c *the nature and purpose of the Citizen's Charter.*

2 *Identify the organisations represented by the five logos at the beginning of this activity. Which of the organisations are in: **a** the public sector **b** the private sector?*

1.111 The supply of Sony TVs

The supply curve in Figure 1.111 shows how many TVs Sony will be prepared to supply at various prices. The supply curve reflects the cost of making and distributing TV sets. At aprice of P_1 the market will be cleared, i.e demand will take

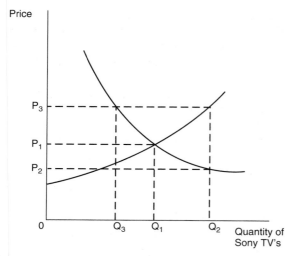

Price

P_3

P_1

P_2

0   Q_3 Q_1 Q_2 Quantity of Sony TV's

up the amount supplied to the market. We call this the equilibrium price. Consumers wanting a Sony TV at this price will get one and Sony will be left with no surplus stocks.

If the price was above P_1, e.g. P_3 then Sony would be prepared to supply a lot more TVs to the market (total supply of Sony TV's = Q_2). However at this price consumers would only by allowed to buy Q_3 sets. Sony would be left holding a lot of stock and would therefore reduce price until it reached the market clearing price of P_1.

1   *Explain why P_2 is not the market clearing price?*

2   *How would the equilibrium price be re-established from an initial price of P_2?*

3   *How does the supply curve reflect the cost of producing TV sets?*

4   *Why are some firms able to produce at lower costs than other firms?*

5   *In the long term, how might Sony be able to increase its supply of TV sets to the market and lower prices as well?*

SECTION 2: BUSINESS SYSTEMS

2.1   Identify two skills which a manager should possess.

2.2   What were the first large-scale organisations?

2.3   Explain what is meant by the term 'division of labour'.

2.4   Who wrote *The Wealth of Nations?*

2.5   Describe how the theory of comparative advantage relates to the specialisation of labour.

2.6   Identify two advantages of specialisation.

2.7   Identify two disadvantages of specialisation.

2.8   What is an entrepreneur?

2.9   Fayol identifies five functions of management. Describe two.

2.10   What is an organisation chart?

2.11   If an organisation is said to be divided by function, what does this mean?

2.12   Name four functional areas common to most organisations.

2.13   List three duties of a company secretary.

2.14   Explain the difference between financial accounting and managerial accounting.

2.15   Define what is meant by marketing.

2.16   What are the prime areas of responsibility for personnel?

2.17   Explain what is meant by the term 'matrix structure'.

2.18   What is meant by span of control?

2.19   Use an example to show the importance of unity of command.

2.20   Describe the difference between delegation and decentralisation.

2.21   Explain how a flat organisational structure differs from a tall organisational structure.

2.22   What is a line relationship?

2.23   Identify two health and safety requirements.

2.24   Explain how a staff relationship would differ from a line relationship.

2.25   Provide an example of an informal working relationship.

2.26   Draw an organisation chart for the organisation in which you work or the organisation you attend.

2.27   Identify three functions of an administration department.

2.28   What is meant by centralisation?

2.29   Outline the main responsibilities of a sales department.

2.30   Why do some organisations have a department which deals with community and public affairs?

2.31   Explain why organisations require effective communication systems.

2.32   Describe the difference between a transmitter and a receiver.

2.33   Identify two barriers to communication which may cause noise.

2.34   Name three basic communication skills.

2.35   What communication technique can be used to clarify a message and improve understanding?

2.36   What does it mean if a written message is ambiguous?

2.37   Provide two examples of body language.

2.38   How would a message from an authoritarian manager differ from a message from a democratic manager?

2.39   Identify two objectives for creating a system of effective communication within an organisation.

2.40   Name two qualities of an effective speaker.

2.41   What is a memorandum and how might it be used?

2.42   Name two uses for a report.

2.43   What structure would an informal report have?

2.44 When would minutes be taken?

2.45 Why is an agenda sent out before a meeting?

2.46 Describe the sort of information an organisation would put into a house magazine.

2.47 Why are external communications important for organisations?

2.48 Name two circumstances which might require the sending of a business letter.

2.49 Identify four features of a business letter.

2.50 When addressing a recipient in a letter with the salutation 'Dear Sir/Madam', which complimentary close should it be paired with?

2.51 Explain how a facsimile machine might improve external communications.

2.52 What is electronic mail?

2.53 Explain what advantages electronic mail has over ordinary mail.

2.54 List three potential uses a large company might have for a corporate video.

2.55 Why do many organisations frequently develop display materials and attend exhibitions?

2.56 What is point of sale material?

2.57 Explain how videoconferencing works.

2.58 List three benefits of using videoconferencing.

2.59 Name three ways in which information technology might improve both internal and external communications.

2.60 Identify two items used by your lecturers or teachers to communicate in the classroom.

2.61 What is an electronic office?

2.62 Identify three functions of an electronic organiser.

2.63 Explain the difference between general IT skills and specialist IT skills.

2.64 What is a computer network?

2.65 Describe how the use of IT helps to create a transformed business.

2.66 List three benefits of using IT.

2.67 List three dangers of depending too heavily on IT.

2.68 What does GUI stand for?

2.69 Describe how windows programmes work.

2.70 What are the benefits of using a mouse?

2.71 What is an icon?

2.72 Explain how a word processor works.

2.73 List the advantages of using a word processor.

2.74 Provide an example of how the use of a database might be linked to that of a word processor.

2.75 What is a desktop publisher (DTP) and how does it work?

2.76 Identify two provisions of the Data Protection Act which affect the use of a database.

2.77 Explain how a spreadsheet works.

2.78 Identify three uses for a spreadsheet.

2.79 What is a remote database and what uses might it have?

2.80 How might a computer help with project planning?

2.81 Describe what an expert system is and explain briefly how one could be used.

2.82 How might frequent use of a computer affect the health of an operator?

2.83 What measures could be taken to avoid the harmful affects of computer use?

2.84 What is a book computer?

2.85 Explain the difference between hardware and software.

2.86 What is a PC?

2.87 Describe briefly how the PC you use works and the options it provides.

2.88 Why do the use of PCs and networks encourage decentralisation of business functions?

2.89 What is electronic marketing?

2.90 Make a short list of your own IT skills.

2.91 One of the following is not an advantage of specialisation:

a *specialisation allows a larger output to be produced at a lower cost.*

b *concentrations of specialists can lead to a sharing of skills and experience.*

c *specialisation means that one job can be done well rather than a number of jobs badly.*

d *specialisation improves the development of technical skills.*

e *resources can be concentrated where they are most productive.*

2.92 Which of the following categories would divide an organisation into departments such as administration, accounts, personnel and marketing:

a *type of customer*

b *process*

c *function*

d *product*

e *none of the above.*

2.93 The personnel department would not be involved with:

a *recruitment*

b *terms and conditions for staff*

c *payroll*

d *training*

e *employee relations.*

2.94 An example of a conglomerate is:

a *Hanson PLC*

b *Barclays Bank PLC*

c *British Airways PLC*

d *The Body Shop*
e *British Rail.*

2.95 A matrix organisational structure:

a *divides by process*
b *creates a rigid hierarchy*
c *combines line and staff relationships*
d *will appear in a tall structure*
e *will combine different methods of grouping*

2.96 Which of the following describes what is meant by decentralisation?

a *the passing down of authority*
b *provision of services for employees' use*
c *determining what authority to pass down*
d *delegation authority*
e *implementation of controls.*

2.97 A line relationship exists:

a *between similar department heads*
b *where there is a functional relationship*
c *between a member of staff and an assistant*
d *where there are direct links between superiors and subordinates*
e *where specialist advice is given.*

2.98 Noise can take the form of any barrier acting as an impediment to the smooth flow of information. Which of the following would not be classified as noise:

a *language differences*
b *cultural differences*
c *a message relayed too quickly*
d *competing environment*
e *another more important message?*

2.99 Which of the following is not used for internal communication?

a *telephone*
b *letter*
c *report*
d *memo*
e *face-to-face exchange?*

2.100 The use of the following means of communication has expanded greatly in recent years:

a *facsimile*
b *letters*
c *reports*
d *memos*
e *house magazines.*

2.101 Videoconferencing allows:

a *people to meet in mutually acceptable surroundings with good facilities*
b *organisations to hold one meeting at two or more locations*
c *meetings to be held in specific towns*
d *organisations to communicate regularly with their competitors*
e *individuals to communicate with colleagues on a daily basis.*

2.102 In an electronic office all but one of the following would appear:

a *word processor*
b *photocopier*
c *electronic mail*
d *personal organisers*
e *adlister.*

2.103 In a transformed business:

a *IT makes most of the decisions*
b *IT provides instant information which helps with decision making*
c *IT shares business processes*
d *IT simplifies the working process*
e *staff become demoralised as IT replaces much of their job.*

2.104 A computer can deal with all but one of the following processes:

a *sorting*
b *checking*
c *retrieving*
d *reproducing*
e *thinking.*

2.105 The following computer application can organise and manipulate numbers:

a *database*
b *spreadsheet*
c *desktop publisher*
d *word processor*
e *windows.*

2.106 Educational Supplies Ltd

Educational Supplies Ltd (ESL) is a well-established company from Oldham which has, until recently, specialised in manufacturing and distributing a range of educational supplies to schools and colleges. The company has considerable experience in educational markets and currently specialises in:

- manufacturing a range of goods for schools and colleges
- acting as an intermediary between other manufacturers of educational goods and educational institutions - the company receives commission on these sales.

Recently the educational market has not been quite as profitable as ESL would have liked and so the company has been diversifying its business. In doing so it has developed the 'space system' of inter-connectable classroom and office furniture which is designed to meet specific educational and business needs. The idea is developed from fitted kitchens and uses similar principles for the fitting of furniture into classrooms and offices. To develop this idea further, given limited space at the Oldham site, ESL has found new premises in York.

At the York factory it is estimated that 50 people will be employed but, at least 15 of these, including an office manager, will be transferred from Oldham. The 35 recruited locally will be mainly joiners.

1 *Make a list of the office services and functions which you feel ought to be provided on the new site.*

2 *Using the list suggest a possible hierarchical structure for positions at the new location. Draw an organisation chart to support your answer. NB All marketing services are to continue out of Oldham.*

2.107 J. Sainsbury's

Sainsbury's now employs nearly 100000 people in the UK. During 1991 3700 new jobs were created and 8500 people promoted including over 900 into their first managerial position. At the same time more than £30 million was invested in training to help staff at all levels. This included the sponsoring of a degree in retail marketing. Sainsbury's also became a founding member of Opportunity 2000, a Business in the Community initiative which encourages companies to increase the quality and quantity of women's participation at all levels of employment.

1 *The personnel department at Sainsbury's dealt with all these initiatives and projects. Identify three other areas with which this department would have been involved.*

2 *Sainsbury's is clearly a very large business with stores across the country. Suggest how an organisation as large as Sainsbury's could divide its business activities. If necessary, draw an organisation chart to support your answer.*

3 *Being large enables Sainsbury's to specialise many of its functions. List four advantages of such specialisation.*

4 *Sainsbury's is well known for the quality and variety of the produce it supplies. What should be the overall aim of its marketing department?*

2.108 Ryton Motors PLC

At Ryton Motors PLC senior managers have been aware of the need to tell employees about matters which will be of interest to them. This includes details relating to performance, objectives, future plans and expansion programmes, employment policies and the special achievements of employees.

In order to improve internal staff communications Ryton Motors is to hold a series of one-day seminars in order to consult staff at its garages and other associated businesses across the UK to find out what the staff want. As a senior showroom supervisor you have been invited to one of these seminars.

1 *You have your own ideas about how your company should run its internal communication systems. Make a list of suggestions which you hope to make at the seminar.*

2 *Explain how the use of technology would help to execute some of the suggestions you make above.*

3 *Speaking at a seminar with large numbers of staff present is not easy, particularly for someone who rarely has to stand up and speak to large groups of people. What guidelines should you adopt in order to ensure that you speak effectively?*

2.109 Parkside Products Ltd

As distribution manager at Parkside Products Ltd your prime responsibility is to ensure that your company's products reach customers on time. This has never been a problem and you have always been proud of the ways in which the distribution systems which you initially set up have worked. Unfortunately, last weekend the main distribution depot in Romford was severely damaged by fire. The police suspect the work of vandals. Though the damage is serious and means that you will have to vacate the existing premises immediately, you predict that if you are able to lease premises straightaway you should be able to make deliveries to customers again within the next seven days.

1 *Prepare a circular letter for customers which will explain what has happened and what you are doing to restore deliveries. (Write this as a business letter and wherever necessary make-up details such as addresses, references etc.)*

2 *As you are moving to new premises you hope to use this as an opportunity to improve the use of information technology in your communication systems. How might you approach this and what systems might you install?*

2.110 Cannon Properties

Cannon Properties is a company responsible for running fifteen hotels in the Northern Region as well as another five in the Borders. Most of the hotels are in tourist locations, are profitable and particularly heavily booked during the summer months.

Thirty five administrative staff work in Carlisle. The main responsibility of the Carlisle office is to service and supervise the running of the hotels. The use of technology has, up until now, been minimal but, with the appointment of a new MD who is keen to introduce new technology, things look set to change.

1 *You are currently employed by a software consultancy business in Carlisle. You have been engaged by Cannon Properties to advise them on the introduction of technology to their head office and hotels. You have been asked to emphasise the benefits which such technology will bring . Word process your report, making suitable recommendations.*

2 *Whilst undertaking the above you have decided to devise a specimen spreadsheet for forecasting. If necessary you intend to use a chart within the report. What will you show on the spreadsheet? What will you calculate? If possible put this spreadsheet onto a computer, making up figures as it is only an example of what can be done, and print out copies.*

2.111 Harrison, Smith and Cooper

You work in the office of Harrison, Smith and Cooper (HSC), a small mail-order business. Until now your catalogues and direct mail have been sent to addresses on mailing lists which have been purchased from mailing houses. However, after much discussion, it seems likely that HSC will set up its own database and marketing facilities.

1 *You have been given the responsibility to introduce this measure and have been called into Mr Harrison's office to describe the progress so far. Explain the benefits of using a database to access, search for and sort information. Describe how this could improve the targeting of prospective customers.*

2 *Mr Harrison is concerned about the provision of the Data Protection Act. Broadly outline its provisions.*

SECTION 3: MARKETING

3.1 What is a customer?

3.2 Why do customer needs and requirements constantly change?

3.3 Define marketing.

3.4 Explain how an organisation would benefit from using market research.

3.5 What internal information might an organisation have which could be used for market research purposes.

3.6 Describe how computers and the use of IT could help market research.

3.7 How might an organisation make use of socio-economic data?

3.8 What is Mintel and why might it be useful to buy information from this organisation?

3.9 How does a retail audit work?

3.10 Why might an organisation contact consumers to set up a consumer panel?

3.11 When might Benn's *Media Directory* be used?

3.12 What is primary research and how does it differ from secondary research?

3.13 Explain the difference between a census and a sample.

3.14 What is meant by the term 'statistical reliability'?

3.15 How does a simple random sample differ from a stratified random sample?

3.16 Explain how you would divide your town into clusters for sampling purposes. Identify what you would consider to be a representative cluster.

3.17 What is a questionnaire?

3.18 Why must questionnaire design try to avoid bias?

3.19 Name three qualities of a good questionnaire.

3.20 What sort of questions should questionnaires not ask?

3.21 Describe the difference between an open question and a closed question.

3.22 What is a prompt card?

3.23 List three advantages of using a face-to-face interviewing technique.

3.24 In what circumstance would telephone interviewing be **a** appropriate and **b** inappropriate?

3.25 Name two advantages and two disadvantages of sending questionnaires through the post.

3.26 What are opinion polls and how might they be used?

3.27 Explain how IT would help with the processing of market research data.

3.28 What is EDP?

3.29 Identify three ways in which market research data could be presented.

3.30 How would the use of statistics help market researchers with data interpretation. Provide an example to support your answer.

3.31 Describe the difference between a customer who is a consumer and a customer which is an organisation.

3.32 Provide an example of an organisation which supplies a good or service to both consumer and organisational markets.

3.33 List three economic determinants of demand which clearly influence consumer behaviour.

3.34 Explain why the government might wish to influence consumer behaviour. Use an example to support your answer.

3.35 Name two goods which would be related to a consumer's physiological needs.

3.36 Name two goods which would be related a consumer's esteem needs.

3.37 Explain how the work of Maslow helps us to understand consumer behaviour and trends.

3.38 What is the self-image theory?

3.39 Identify a product which is image-orientated. what sort of consumers would purchase this product?

3.40 List three cultural factors which might influence purchasing patterns.

3.41 Explain why people in the North of England:
- tend to drink different brands of tea from those drunk by people in the south.
- drink beer which tastes different from that drunk in other parts of the country?

3.42 What is social stratification?

3.43 Explain the difference between a C1 and a C2.

3.44 Provide three examples of occupations in the A/B categories.

3.45 What sort of product would organisations target at D/E consumers?

3.46 What is meant by the term 'upwardly-mobile'?

3.47 What sort of products would be targeted at consumers who are upwardly-mobile?

3.48 Explain what is meant by the term 'yuppy'.

3.49 The demand for goods in organisational markets is derived. What does this mean?

3.50 What is a business cycle?

3.51 How will the demand for organisational goods be affected in a recession?

3.52 Identify three features of organisational markets.

3.53 How does a vertical market differ from a horizontal market?

3.54 How might the level of employment affect purchasing patterns?

3.55 Over recent years consumers have become increasingly influenced by environmental issues. Identify two goods which have responded to the changing environmental views of consumers.

3.56 Use your own experience as a consumer to identify a market which you feel is growing.

3.57 In the market for motor cars 4-wheel drive vehicles are becoming more popular and cars for the sport-minded are becoming less popular. Explain why.

3.58 Provide two examples of goods which have recently been launched. What sort of consumers are these goods designed to appeal to?

3.59 Provide one example of a market in decline and one example of a market which is expanding.

3.60 What is a sales forecast?

3.61 What is a voluntary code of practice?

3.62 Explain what is meant by the latin expression 'caveat emptor'.

3.63 Under what circumstances might disputes with consumers arise. Provide two examples.

3.64 What was the purpose of the Consumer Credit Act?

3.65 What does APR stand for?

3.66 Which Act makes it a criminal offence for a trader to falsely describe goods?

3.67 Name two sources of consumer help and advice.

3.68 What is the role of the Advertising Standards Authority?

3.69 What is a SWOT analysis?

3.70 How does direct competition differ from indirect competition?

3.71 Provide one example of two goods in direct competition and one example of two goods in indirect competition.

3.72 What is a market segment?

3.73 Why might an organisation wish to reposition a range of products. Use an example to support your answer.

3.74 Identify the four variables of the marketing mix.

3.75 How do the generic dimensions of a product differ from its sensual dimensions?

3.76 Why do product designers build-in obsolescence?

3.77 What is meant by diversification?

3.78 Name two objectives which an organisation might have when choosing a price for its range of products.

3.79 Explain how contribution pricing works.

3.80 Identify two short-term pricing policies which an organisation might have.

3.81 What is a wholesaler?

3.82 Why do advertisers use advertising agencies?

3.83 Provide one example of a strapline.

3.84 What is meant by 'coverage'?

3.85 How do sales promotions into the pipeline differ from sales promotions out of the pipeline?

3.86 What is meant by the term 'personal selling'?

3.87 Describe the purpose of public relations.

3.88 Give two examples of public relations activities.

3.89 What is the product life-cycle?

3.90 Explain how the product life-cycle can be used to help an organisation manage its product portfolio.

3.91 The marketing professional body is called:

a *The Institute of Chartered Marketing*
b *The Chartered Institute of Marketing*
c *The Certificate of Marketing*
d *The Chartered Marketing Institute*
e *The Marketing Professional Institute*

3.92 The government statistical service publishes a range of useful material for organisations. Which of the following is not published or used by the Central Statistical Office:

a *electoral register*
b *business monitors*
c *monthly analysis of statistics*
d *annual analysis of statistics*
e *Standard Industrial Classification?*

3.93 A C Nielson collects:

a *information from a panel*
b *data of retail sales*
c *information about advertising rates*
d *information about companies*
e *secondary sources.*

3.94 Stratified random sampling is a system whereby:

a *instructions are given to interviewers to interview respondents with certain characteristics*
b *a number of respondents up to a quota are interviewed*
c *random sampling takes place upon the basis of the identification of a representative area*
d *customers are weighted according to their importance in the market*
e *selected customers are chosen at regular intervals from a sampling frame.*

3.95 A good questionnaire will have all but one of the following qualities:

a *been tested*
b *information in it which relates directly to needs*
c *does not ask too many personal questions*
d *is designed in a logical sequence*
e *asks ambiguous questions.*

3.96 Which of the following organisations is not involved with market research:

a *Mintel*
b *Retail Audits*
c *UK Monitor*
d *Leatherhead Food Research Association*
e *AA?*

3.97 Factors affecting consumer demand include all but one of the following:

a *availability of resources*
b *tastes, fashions and habits*
c *size of population*
d *disposable incomes*
e *government measures.*

3.98 A postman would appear in socio-economic group:

a *A*
b *B*
c *C1/C2*
d *D*
e *E*

3.99 A number of contingency factors affect the way in which organisations behave in their markets. These include all but one of the following:

a *delaying payment for goods and services received*
b *supplier dependency*
c *consumer dominance*
d *risk of takeover*
e *credit facilities for customers.*

3.100 Direct competition exists:

a *where competitors in different market segments compete for similar customers*
b *where organisations produce similar products and appeal to the same group of consumers*
c *where organisations compete with products which are near substitutes*
d *where organisations compete with different products for different markets*
e *none of the above.*

3.101 The marketing mix includes the following:

a *price, promotion, process, place*
b *programme, place, promotion, product*
c *place, product, people, process*
d *product, place, promotion, price*
e *product, people, process, place.*

3.102 The sensual dimensions of a product would include:

a *taste*
b *colour*
c *price*
d *smell*
e *texture.*

3.103 Short term pricing policies include all but one of the following:

a *competition pricing*
b *destroyer pricing*
c *promotional pricing*
d *skim pricing*
e *penetration pricing.*

3.104 The promotional mix will include all but one of :

a *advertisements*

b *sales promotions*

c *personal selling*

d *customer selection*

e *public relations.*

3.105 Differentiated marketing involves:

a *offering a single marketing message to the whole market-place*

b *developing marketing strategies to cater for all groups of customers*

c *attacking the market-place by tailoring separate strategies to different parts of the market*

d *using similar types of strategies with all parts of the market*

e *using positioning to select a market segment to compete in.*

3.106 Sunny Travels Ltd

Over recent years Sunny Travels have experienced a decline in the number of holidaymakers visiting traditional holiday destinations in Spain, Italy and Greece. At the same time, because the markets are mature, margins in such markets have decreased. The directors recently met to discuss the increasingly difficult trading position with which they have to cope. They are all agreed that in order to stimulate demand for the packages they offer, they have to find out how consumer tastes have changed and then provide appropriate packages for which consumers can opt. In order to do this they have approached a market research agency called CosmoResearch.

You work as a market research assistant for CosmoResearch and have been asked to join the team working on the Sunny Travels account. Given the nature of their business and recent events in the economy and the market for holidays, you find their plight understandable but feel that research will reveal some interesting business possibilities.

1 *Your first action will be to ask Sunny Travels to provide you with information which they will have collected internally about their customers. What specific type of information will you to ask for?*

2 *You then intend to collect some useful secondary data which would help to provide a better picture about holiday opportunities in general. Name four sources of information which you might use.*

3 *Your next action is to prepare a questionnaire which you intend to use to collect primary data. The questionnaire should be designed to find out about the attitudes, values and beliefs of potential holidaymakers. Prepare the questionnaire. In the questionnaire refer to different holiday resorts, types of holidays and packages, prices and holiday activities and options.*

4 *Before administering the questionnaire you need to choose a sampling technique. Comment on the sampling technique you would use and explain why you would choose this particular technique.*

3.107 The Procter & Gamble Company

Procter & Gamble is a massive, multi-national company which sells more than 160 brands in nearly 140 countries. The company is a world leader in such areas as detergents, disposable nappies and health and beauty care products. In the UK, it produces numerous household brand names such as Dreft, Tide, Bold, Daz, Ariel, Fairy, Flash, Lenor, Camay, Pampers, Oil of Ulay, Head & Shoulders, Vicks and many more.

At the forefront of P & G policy is the belief that ultimately the consumer runs the business. They believe that consumer research keeps the company in touch with consumer trends and that technology creates opportunities to generate growth, and improve sales and profits. For example, Lenor is P & G's European fabric softener. Although customers appreciated its performance, many did not want to buy large plastic containers. P & G responded by producing concentrated Lenor in a pouch so consumers could refill their containers. The company's attention to detail was recently commended by the Arthritis Foundation in America when P & G developed a user-friendly snap-top lid for Tide powder detergent. The package is easy for anyone to use, but is especially helpful for people with arthritic hands and fingers.

P & G's attempts to position their company at the forefront of changes in the market-place has been based upon a more focused approach on customers and consumers alike.

1 *Explain why this short case illustrates the importance of market research.*

2 *Explain 'the consumer runs the business'*

3 *Identify four factors which might have caused the wants of P & G's customers to change over recent years.*

3.108 Database Marketing

At the Royal Mail Direct Marketing Awards for 1992, the winner in the database category was Clarks International, the company famous for its shoes.

At Clarks's shoe stores till software was redesigned to enable individuals to be recognised at the point of sale as previous customers by type. The results were analysed to discover the effect of drive times, expenditure per visit, cross purchasing, repeat purchases and seasonality. Different target groups (e.g. families, older people, single men) were given different welcome packs with their purchases.

This activity helped Clarks to adapt their activities to attract a higher level of additional purchases. For example, the scheme helped to identify customers whose behaviour was worth influencing with regular customised mailings.

Clarks feel the database created good customer information which helped them to understand customer behaviour in more detail. They could then use it to develop better customer relationships.

1 *Explain what a database is and how a database can be used to improve the understanding of customer behaviour.*

2 *List the aspects of customer behaviour which information from a till-based database might help to identify.*

3.109 Working as a solicitor

Peter Robinson is in his late twenties and qualified five years ago as a solicitor. He had always wanted to go into the legal profession and, while at university, worked hard to achieve his ambition. Since qualifying Peter has worked with two firms of solicitors and has recently achieved junior partner status in his current job which is quite an achievement for somebody of his age.

When Peter first qualified he spent a lot of his income on oil paintings which he picked up at auctions. At the same time he bought his first flat. Recently, however, he has been selling many of his paintings and has been collecting antiques. Each year Peter takes at least four holidays, three of which are normally overseas. Usually, at least one of the holidays involves him in windsurfing as he is a member of the Docklands Windsurfing Club and is on the fringe of the British team.

Peter's other hobbies include reading and eating out. He also has a small investment in a race-horse which is kept at Middleham.

1 *Explain what this short case tells you about Peter as a consumer. When answering this question refer to:*
- *economic factors*
- *social factors*
- *cultural factors*
- *socio-economic factors*
- *lifestyle*

2 If you were marketing products to Peter, given the analysis above, name three types of products which might match his consumer requirements.

3.110 The Beach Babies

For many years, the Beach Babies, with their particularly distinctive style of music, have been trying to break into the UK album market. Though successful across Europe, as well as in Japan and in the US, achieving widespread popularity in Great Britain seems to have eluded them.

Your work for Orange, The Beach Babies UK recording and distribution company, as a marketing assistant and have recently been to a series of meetings where you have discussed the UK issue. It is generally agreed that, so far, The Beach Babies albums have failed to be recognised by consumers as something different which they might like. The product seems to get lost amidst a sea of new releases. If they are to succeed it is felt that the approach to launching products has got to be completely different.

The Beach Babies are just about to release in the UK, *Sea of Sand*, their new album which has been hugely successful in the US and Japan. You are helping with this launch.

1 *Analyse each of the ingredients of the marketing mix and then comment on how you would construct the mix for the launch of 'Sea of Sand'. With each ingredient state briefly:*
- *what you would do*
- *how your approach would help to differentiate the product from that of competitors*

2 *Public relations are very important in the music business. The band is due in the UK on tour later in the year. Suggest a range of public relations activities which it could become involved with.*

3.111 Mishi

Launch date	Car type	Comment
1981	small saloon and hatchback. It competes with the Micra and Fiesta.	sales have fallen since 1991.
1984	flagship of the range. This is a large luxury vehicle.	sales are beginning to flatten out. Many consumers now have environmental considerations.
1987	4-wheel drive sporty off-road vehicle	sales are expanding rapidly. This is the the most profitable vehicle in the range.
1992	mid-range workhorse to compete with Cavalier and Mondeo	introduction was slow at depth of recession. Sales have recently shown a lot of promise

Mishi is a Japanese motor car manufacturer which has a UK manufacturing facility based in the south-west of England. The company has been building cars in the UK since 1981, during which time four models have been launched. See table.

1 *You work as a marketing assistant at Mishi and have been asked to provide a talk at a local school. You intend to make your talk visual and have a number of handouts to give to students. The title of your talk is the 'Product Life Cycle'. Using a diagram explain what the product life-cycle is and describe each stage of the cycle.*

2 *Using the table describe the Mishi product portfolio. Show all products on a single chart and then describe at which point in their life-cycle each product lies.*

3 *Using a diagram show how you inject life into products at various stages. Comment upon various types of measures which you might use.*

SECTION 4: HUMAN RESOURCES

4.1 What is internal recruitment?

4.2 Why might internal recruitment be more cost effective than external recruitment?

4.3 What is a trade union? What are the main aims of unions?

4.4 Why is multi-skilling so important?

4.5 What is a demarcation dispute?

4.6 What is a job specification?

4.7 List four details that might appear on a job description.

4.8 Who is responsible for health and safety at work?

4.9 What are vocational qualifications?

4.10 What is the difference between a craft, and an industrial trade union?

4.11 Who do general unions represent? Give an example of a general union.

4.12 Who makes up the panel on an Industrial Tribunal?

4.13 What are equal opportunities?

4.14 What is meant by the term 'redundancy'?

4.15 What details appear in a contract of employment?

4.16 How can the process of job appraisal help employees to feel more involved in decision-making in an organisation?

4.17 Give three examples of situations in which dismissal from a job would be classed as 'unfair'.

4.18 Explain three types of actions that a trade union might take to slow down the work process.

4.19 What role does ACAS play in industrial disputes?

4.20 Describe the key stages in the employment procession.

4.21 Outline the main details of the Health and Safety at Work Act.

4.22 How does civil legal action differ from criminal legal action?

4.23 Describe three actions that employers can take to reduce absenteeism at work.

4.24 How can you measure productivity?

4.25 Why is training important from the employer's point of view?

4.26 What is 'human resource management'?

4.27 How is it possible to increase motivation at work?

4.28 Describe Maslow's levels of need.

4.29 What is the difference between striking and working to rule?

4.30 What is the Trades Union Congress?

4.31 What is a sole trader? Give three examples of typical sole trader businesses.

4.32 Explain how responsibilities can be shared between the different members of a partnership.

4.33 Describe three responsibilities of managers.

4.34 Explain the main responsibilities carried out by a supervisor.

4.35 Who does a director of a company represent?

4.36 What is the difference between an executive and a non-executive director?

4.37 What is the main purpose of preparing a job description?

4.38 How can a job description be used in the appraisal process?

4.39 What is the difference between a hierarchical and a flat organisational structure?

4.40 What is the difference between a centralised and a devolved form of organisation?

4.41 What sorts of decisions can be made most effectively by hierarchical organisations?

4.42 What sorts of decisions can be made most effectively by devolved organisations?

4.43 Describe the main types of functional manager that you would find in a manufacturing company.

4.44 What types of qualities do people need to have to work effectively in teams?

4.45 What is a bureaucracy?

4.46 Why might a bureaucracy be an ineffective decision making organisation in some circumstances?

4.47 What is strategic management?

4.48 Why is it important to have effective 'operators' in an organisation?

4.49 What is meant by marginal productivity? How can it be measured?

4.50 What are the four main factors of production?

4.51 How can you measure returns to labour?

4.52 What are diminishing returns to labour?

4.53 What is the Equal Pay Act?

4.54 What is meant by *a* discrimination *b* positive discrimination?

4.55 What parties are involved in the process of collective bargaining?

4.56 What do TECs do? Who funds them?

4.57 What is the difference between 'on-the-job' and 'off-the-job' training?

4.58 What is meant by the de-layering of an organisation?

4.59 What are the benefits of de-layering an organisation?

4.60 What is performance related pay?

4.61 What is a curriculum vitae?

4.62 What details should be included in a curriculum vitae?

4.63 What legal and ethical obligations do you need to be aware of in filling in a job application form?

4.64 How should the personnel department of a company choose which applicants to interview for a post?

4.65 How can a selection panel be fair to all candidates in asking questions at an interview?

4.66 At what stage in the recruitment process does an employee receive a contract of employment to sign?

4.67 Why are references important in the recruitment process?

4.68 What sort of body language should you try to project at an interview?

4.69 Suggest three important tips to someone who is going for a job interview.

4.70 What is assertiveness? Why is it important during a job interview?

4.71 What is an equal opportunities employer?

4.72 How can you measure turnover of labour at work?

4.73 Why is turnover of labour an important measure?

4.74 What department in a company is responsible for recruitment and selection?

4.75 How does the appraisal process help to motivate employees?

4.76 What is a job role? Give examples of four different job roles in a chosen organisation.

4.77 What do you understand by the expression 'parity of esteem' in relation to vocational qualifications.

4.78 What are GNVQs? Give examples.

4.79 Why is it important for employees to be flexible in their approach to work?

4.80 What is training and professional development?

4.81 Why do many jobs ask for both qualifications and experience?

4.82 Where are management jobs likely to be advertised?

4.83 Where are jobs for operatives likely to be advertised? Give examples.

4.84 What is the function of a Job Centre?

4.85 Why is listening an important skill in the interview process?

4.86 What preparation should a candidate make before going on a job interview?

4.87 What questions should an interviewee ask at a job interview?

4.88 List three questions that a panel cannot ask at an interview. Explain why each question would not be appropriate.

4.89 What it Total Quality Management? Why is it important to organisations?

4.90 List four details that a personnel department might want to include in a person specification.

4.91 According to Maslow's hierarchy of needs the highest level of needs is that of:

a *Self-actualisation*

b *love*

c *physiological*

d *esteem*

e *safety and security .*

4.92 Which of the following need not appear in a contract of employment:

a *qualifications required to do the job*

b *the title of the job*

c *hours of work*

d *the rate of pay*

e *the period of notice that must be given.*

4.93 Which of the following is not a fair reason for the dismissal of an employee:

a *sexual or racial harassment*

b *belonging to a trade union*

c *continuous bad time keeping*

d *a negligent attitude at work*

e *wilful destruction of the organisation's property?*

4.94 Conciliation in an industrial dispute is a process whereby:

a *an independent outsider proposes the basis for settlement*

b *both parties agree to accept an outside decision*

c *both parties find it impossible to agree on principles*

d *an independent body tries to act as a channel of communication between the two sides.*

4.95 To which body can a trade union apply if an employer fails to recognise it:

a *The CBI*

b *ACAS*

c *a magistrates' court*

d *the TUC*

e *the House of Lords?*

4.96 Which of the following would be included in a job specification and not in a job description:

a *title of post*

b *the mental and physical attributes required of the post holder*

c *prime objectives of the position advertised*

d *range of decision making of the post holder*

e *supervisory/managerial responsibilities of the post?*

4.97 Which of the following organisational structures will be most suitable for quick decision-making at grass roots level:

a *bureaucracy*

b *hierarchical*

c *tall*

d *devolved*

e *centralised*

4.98 Which of the following is not a feature of multi-skilling:

a *flexibility of employees*

b *demarcation in the workplace*

c *an emphasis on training of employees*

d *responsibility of employees in own work areas*

e *flexibility of work patterns?*

4.99 Which of the following best describes strategic decision making:

a *carrying out routine tasks*

b *making on -the-spot decisions*

c *controlling the quality of organisational outputs*

d *developing longer term policies about objectives*

e *responding quickly to prevailing market conditions.*

4.100 Which form of leadership style is likely to encourage the highest level of participation in group decision making:

a *autocratic*

b *bureaucratic*

c *democratic*

d *centralised*

e *charismatic?*

4.101 Which of the following is true about the Health and Safety at Work Act:

a *it is only legally binding on registered premises*

b *employers have total responsibility for ensuring Health and Safety at work*

c *the Health and Safety Officer at a work place need only be aware of general rather than specific laws*

d *prosecutions under the Act must be done through a civil court*

e *it lays down training standards for employees in potentially hazardous occupations.*

4.102 A reason for the decline in trade union membership in recent years has been:

a *the growth of the working population*

b *the reduction in the number of trade unions through amalgamation*

c *the decline of employment in 'heavy industries'*

d *the increasing exploitation of employees in the workplace*

e *the development of Europe-wide trade union groupings.*

4.103 Which of the following union actions does not involve a withdrawal of labour:

a *working to rule*

b *striking*

c *an overtime ban*

d *a go slow*

e *blacking?*

4.104 Appraisal of people at work involves:

a *selecting candidates for an interview*

b *carrying out an interview for a job*

c *helping employees to monitor their progress and prospects*

d *dealing with individual disputes involving people at work*

e *helping new staff to fit in through an induction process.*

4.105 A disadvantage of external recruitment is that:

a *new ideas are not brought into the organisation*

b *it saves money on recruitment costs*

c *it saves on induction costs*

d *it may upset someone who already works for you*

e *there is no 'buzz of efficiency' from new ideas.*

4.106 Discrimination in the workplace
Study the three cases below and then explain why each case could be said to involve discrimination in the workplace.

Case 1: Jane Delaney v. Northshire County Council.
The following advert recently appeared in a national publication advertising a job in the primary school where Jane works.

DEPUTY HEADSHIP

Committed primary teacher wanted to take on this post of responsibility. We are looking for someone with a broad range of interests and experience. The successful applicant should be able to take charge of music, drama and boys' PE.

Jane had been working at the school for ten years. She already ran the school music department and had a keen interest in drama. She felt that she would not be given a fair opportunity at interviews for the job.

Case 2: Winston Roberts v. Household Insurance
Winston has been working for the firm for three years. Mrs Roberts had brought up their child for two years before deciding to return to work. Winston's firm has a crèche for firm's employees of two years and over. When he applied to put the child in the crèche he was told that he could not do so because the crèche was only for the children of female employees.

Case 3: Milo Kovaks v. International Sales
Milo has been working in the marketing department of the company for several years. Recently the company advertised for an international sales officer who would be in charge of departments in Brussels, Rome and Paris. The job entails a lot of travel. Milo applied for the job but was not selected for the interview, though a number of those who were had far less experience. However, Milo did notice that they were all single people.

4.107 The conduct of the employee
The action which management takes to deal with the misconduct of an employee should depend on the type of misconduct. You are the personnel manager in a small high street shoe retailer. What actions would you take

a *in the first instance* in dealing with the following examples of misconduct at work:

b *if the misconduct continues*

1 **Minor misconduct**, *this includes trivial acts such as persistent lateness by members of staff*

2 **Major misconduct**, *this includes serious acts such as fighting and swearing which affects customers and/or clients, and breach of safety regulations.*

3 **Gross misconduct**, *this would include extremely serious cases of misconduct such as theft and dishonesty.*

4.108 Misconduct outside the workplace
1 *Under what circumstances would you take disciplinary action against employees for misconduct outside the place of work. For example, consider the following two cases:*
   a *one of the employees from the shoe shop is fined in court for being drunk and disorderly on a Saturday night.*
   b *one of the employees from the shoe shop is given a suspended prison sentence for shoplifting in a supermarket.*

4.109 Working for Nissan
Nissan make it clear in their recruitment material that it is not easy working in a vehicle manufacturing plant, that it is a market environment and the work is heavy.

They stress that there are good rewards for working hard, that it is a tough and competitive working environment, but that there is mutual respect amongst employees.

The training manual at the Nissan factory in Sunderland states that:

We do not intend to mislead people about the role of manufacturing staff or the environment in which they work. All applicants should carefully consider the following points:

- the pace of work will be dictated by a moving production line and will be very demanding
- work assignments will be carefully designed and will be very repetitive
- protective clothing will be necessary for some jobs
- you may be moved onto a new operation or transferred into a different department at very short notice.

The training manual sets great store on the dignity of those who can survive in hard working conditions: 'it is important to develop an environment where an individual can fully exploit his or her talents in a climate of mutual respect, trust and confidence'.

1 *Imagine that you are applying for a production line job with Nissan. What factors would encourage you to work there? What factors would discourage you from working there?*

2 *What features would need to go into a job description for a typical production line job?*

3 *Explain three features that might appear in a person specification for a production line job in a vehicle manufacturing factory?*

4 *Why do Nissan stress the less attractive sides of working in one of their plants?*

5 *To what extent does the fact that Nissan operates in a 'market environment' influence working practices and procedures in their car plant?*

4.110 Organisation for the development of a new product
Six departments might be involved in the development of a new steam iron:

1 *design*
2 *purchasing*
3 *engineering*
4 *production*
5 *marketing*
6 *finance*

Traditionally the new product might have been developed in a linear fashion. Each department did its work and then handed the project onto the next group. (See Figure 4.110a)

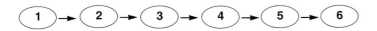

Figure 4.110a *Linear development*

Nowadays it is more common to use an integrated approach. A project team is chosen from members of all the departments involved. Senior management set an objective for the team e.g. a Honda team that designed a new sports car were told to 'develop a car that the youth segment would want to drive'. Such an approach encourages innovation, trying out new ideas, and shared views from different perspectives. Each member of the team is working from the same office and starting on their part of the project at the same time. The development sequence looks more like this:

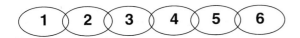

Figure 4.110b *Overlapping development*

1. *What advantages can you see from overlapping development rather than the linear approach?*

2. *Which approach will tend to be: **a** more hierarchical **b** more flexible **c** more customer oriented **d** more dynamic. Explain each answer.*

3. *What difficulties are likely to occur with overlapping development?*

4. *What qualities would you look for in individuals selected to work in an overlapping team?*

4.111 Equal opportunities and recruitment

You are the personnel manager at CZ Supermarkets. Last week you were away from work on a training course. During that time one of your assistants carried out some interviews for a shelf filling post. On returning to work you have found the following memo from the store manager awaiting your attention.

Please respond to the memo

Memo:

From Store Manager

To personnel Manager

I have received the enclosed letter of complaint from a candidate interviewed by your department last week. Please produce immediately a set of guidelines for interviewers when recruiting new staff. Guidelines to be presented on one side of A4 in clear and simple language. Please set out the guidelines under no more than 5 clear sub-headings.

3 Rothermere Drive
Rotherhampton
RT1 5HL

Dear Store Manager,

I was interviewed for a post at your store last week. I was disgusted when the interviewer asked me the following questions:

a because I have just got married would I soon be leaving to have a family
b have I ever belonged to a trade union

I certainly don't want to work for your company. You can stuff your job.

Disgusted of Rotherhampton

4.112 Douglas Sports

Douglas Sports is a national chain of 84 sports shops. This week they are hoping to advertise two appointments:

a a high quality buyer to take responsibility for purchasing stocks for all 84 of their shops
b a temporary replacement manager for one of their smaller shops in the small market town of Greyton.

1 *What media should they consider for advertising the two posts. Give reasons.*

2 *What selection procedures might they consider when choosing candidates to interview for the purchasing manager's post?*

3 *What interview techniques would you recommend to a friend who has been shortlisted for the replacement manager's job at Greyton? Explain five suggestions.*

4 *What would be **a** the advantages and **b** drawbacks to someone applying for a temporary post?*

SECTION 5: EMPLOYMENT IN THE MARKET ECONOMY

5.1 What is the largest industrial sector in the economy?
5.2 What is the difference between full-time and part-time work?
5.3 Give one example of an occupation in which technology has simplified work. Explain how work has been simplified.
5.4 What is the 'labour market'?

5.5 How important is the primary sector in the UK employment market? Give three examples of important primary sector jobs.

5.6 What do you understand by the term de-industrialisation?

5.7 Give three reason for de-industrialisation.

5.8 How does the EC Social Chapter protect employees?

5.9 Why is the UK government reluctant to adopt the Social Chapter?

5.10 Why do some employees earn more than others?

5.11 Explain which three job categories are continuing to recruit more labour.

5.12 Explain which three job categories are recruiting less labour today.

5.13 Explain how a period of recession can lead to rising unemployment.

5.14 How can technology de-skill labour?

5.15 What is a labour-intensive industry? Give three examples.

5.16 Describe the recent employment trends in one business sector.

5.17 List two published sources of national employment statistics.

5.18 How can training and education increase the supply of labour?

5.19 What is the difference between permanent and temporary work?

5.20 Explain why one particular industry is likely to recruit temporary rather than permanent workers.

5.21 How do skills shortages arise?

5.22 Who is responsible for the training of workers in this country?

5.23 What incentive is there for workers to increase their levels of skill and training?

5.24 What is meant by the accreditation of prior learning? How is this important in improving the quality of the labour force?

5.25 Mention one way in which UK employers are affected by EC employment law.

5.26 What are wage differentials?

5.27 Explain why wage differentials exist between male and female labour?

5.28 What is meant by 'structural changes' in employment patterns?

5.29 Why is manufacturing vital to the economy?

5.30 What are fringe benefits?

5.31 What factors determine the size of the working population?

5.32 What is net migration?

5.33 Explain how the interaction of supply and demand determines wage rates in the labour market?

5.34 What factors are likely to lead to an increase in the demand for labour?

5.35 How can trade unions reduce the supply of labour in a particular industry?

5.36 What is a minimum wage?

5.37 Draw a diagram to illustrate the impact of imposing a minimum wage at a level above the market rate in a particular industry.

5.38 Give two examples of capital intensive industries.

5.39 Explain how the substitution of capital for labour can increase the productivity of labour.

5.40 Why might an employer decide to invest in new technology?

5.41 Show how an increase in training can increase the demand for labour.

5.42 What is the demand for labour derived from?

5.43 Give two examples of ways in which improved technology has changed the demand for labour in specific industries.

5.44 What is the effect of increased immigration on the supply of labour? How might this affect wage rates?

5.45 Why do wage differentials occur within the same occupation?

5.46 Why do doctors earn more than roadsweepers?

5.47 Under what circumstances might a roadsweeper earn more than a doctor?

5.48 How can the development of GNVQs improve the supply of labour in the economy?

5.49 How can trade unions increase wages without there being a reduction in employment.

5.50 Why are trade unions likely to be more powerful in periods of full or near full employment?

5.51 How can firms compete for labour?

5.52 How has the development of the Single Market affected the movement of labour in the EC?

5.53 How can the use of flexitime aid employers in recruiting labour?

5.54 What actions might an employer take to reduce the level of absenteeism amongst employees? How would this reduce the employer's costs?

5.55 To what extent is full employment a thing of the past?

5.56 How can trade unions protect their members in the labour market?

5.57 Give an example of a restrictive practice in the labour market. Why would this practice be used?

5.58 What effect would the raising of the school age have on the labour market?

5.59 What actions can businesses take to increase their supply of skilled labour?

5.60 Explain three factors that would reduce the ability of a trade union to secure wage increases.

5.61 What is 'Just In Time' manufacturing?

5.62 What conditions need to exist for JIT to be most effective?

5.63 How does JIT enable businesses to develop a competitive edge?

5.64 What is 'Total Quality Manufacturing'?

5.65 How can pay be structured to encourage employees to work hard?

5.66 Describe one theory explaining motivation at work.

5.67 What factors in a particular working environment can be classed as dissatisfiers?

5.68 How can you measure work performance?

5.69 How can you monitor changes in work performance over time?

5.70 What are the key features of a 'good employer'?

5.71 List four main details of the Factories Act.

5.72 What is direct sex discrimination?

5.73 What is direct marriage discrimination?

5.74 How does the Race Relations Act affect the running of the labour market?

5.75 What is manpower planning?

5.76 How can manpower planning help a business organisation?

5.77 Why might individual companies be reluctant to train young employees?

5.78 How can the government encourage wage restraint?

5.79 How can the division of labour lead to increased output?

5.80 What are the disadvantages of specialisation for individual employees?

5.81 What actions can trade unions take to put pressures on employers for better working conditions and higher wages?

5.82 Explain three different systems of remunerating employees.

5.83 Why might an employer choose to pay wage rates which are higher than those of competitors?

5.84 How might effective Equal Opportunities policies give a business a competitive edge?

5.85 Give an example of trade union action which is:
a lawful *b* unlawful

5.86 Why does the government provide a legal framework for the employment of labour?

5.87 How can an effective health and safety record of a business enable it to increase profits?

5.88 What is the opportunity cost to a business of spending money on training?

5.89 Why are some industries able to pay higher wages than others?

5.90 What is profit-related pay? Why might a company introduce such a scheme?

5.91 Primary industries include:

a construction
b insurance
c engineering
d textiles
e farming.

5.92 At the beginning of 1993 an important change for the countries of the European Community was that:

a they started to use the same unit of currency
b barriers to trade between members were removed
c member countries adopted the same tax system
d member countries adopted minimum wage legislation
e quotas were set limiting trade with non-EC countries

5.93 The output of a country is divided between the following sectors:

Agriculture	2%
Transport and communications	20%
Manufacturing	20%
Banking, insurance and distribution	25%
Education and health	10%
Mining	1%
Other services	22%

What percentage of the output of the country is produced by the service sector:

a 22%
b 42%
c 47%
d 67%
e 77% ?

5.94 In order to combat regional decline in Britain, a government might:

a direct workers to other parts of the country
b give incentives to industry to move to areas of high unemployment
c give financial assistance to firms wishing to set up in areas of low employment
d increase unemployment benefits
e subsidise employment in all areas of the country.

5.95 Which of the following is least likely to lead to an increase in wage levels in car manufacture:

a an increase in productivity in the car industry
b the imposition of a national minimum wage
c an increased demand for cars
d an upturn in the world economy leading to higher spending
e an increase in training and skills among car workers?

5.96 Which of the following is a measure of the marginal productivity of labour in a food factory:

a the output of all employees
b the quantity of output divided by the number of people employed
c the addition to output added by an extra employee
d the cost of employing additional employees when orders increase
e the contribution to revenue resulting from the employment of labour?

5.97 Which of the following would indicate dissatisfaction of employees with their work:

a a high level of overtime worked
b a high level of labour turnover
c a willingness of employees to participate in decision making
d a high level of union membership
e variations in productivity levels?

5.98 In which of the following circumstances would employees be most likely to achieve wage increases-where there is:

a an elastic demand for the final product
b an elastic supply of labour available to make the product
c an inelastic demand for labour
d when capital can be easily substituted for labour
e when the productivity of labour is falling?

5.99 Which of the following is not a 'fringe benefit':

a company car
b pay
c luncheon vouchers
d travel allowance
e discount on company products?

5.100 Which of the following activities is the most labour intensive:

a deep sea fishing
b car manufacture
c agriculture
d hair dressing
e banking?

5.101 Which of the following might lead to a reduction in the level of unemployment in a country:

a a reduction in labour productivity
b a rise in wage rates of employees in the country's industries

c an increased use of labour saving devices in new automated factories
d an improvement in comparative advantage of the countries products on world markets.
e an increase in unemployment benefit?

5.102 A disadvantage of specialisation is:

a workers become less dependent on each other
b output levels increase only slowly
c traditional skills are passed on from one generation to the next
d training time is necessary
e employees are not able to do a range of tasks.

5.103 Which of the following can be deducted from a worker's pay at source:

a Value Added Tax
b Vehicle Excise Tax
c National Insurance contributions
d supplementary benefit
e corporation tax?

5.104 Which of the following industries accounts for the largest numbers in employment today:

a fishing
b insurance
c mining
d ship building
e forestry

5.105 Which of the following payment systems does not link pay to results:

a performance
b profit related pay
c time related pay
d piece rates
e production target bonus?

5.106 Does an economy need a manufacturing base?
In an address to British businessmen Akio Moritak, the Chairman of Sony made the following points:

'An economy which has lost its manufacturing base has lost its vital centre. Only manufacturing creates something new, which takes raw materials and fashions them into products that are of more value than the raw materials that they are made from. Services depend on manufacturing. When manufacturing prospers, all industries connected with it prosper - not only are more components, parts and salesmen needed, but also more accountants, more dentists, more petrol stations, more supermarkets and more schools.'

1 *What is :*
   a the manufacturing base
   b raw materials

2 *Is it true that only manufacturing creates something new?*

3 *What are services?*

4 *How does manufacturing depend on services?*

5 *What changes have taken place in employment in the manufacturing and service sectors during the twentieth century?*

5.107 Who deserves to earn most?

The *New Earnings Survey* which was published at the end of 1992 revealed the following differences in earnings:

Nigel Mansell, who won the Formula One World Championship, earned £7 million.

In banking an average settlements clerk earned £10 000 Pete Baring, Chairman of the merchant bank, Barings earned £511 000.

In education a new teacher earned a basic salary of £11 184. Professor David Williams vice-chancellor at Cambridge earned £85 200.

In industry a British Coal underground worker earned £10 920 (although this would be a lot more with overtime and bonuses). Neil Clarke the chairman of British Coal earned £236 211.

In football a third division player earned £305 a week. A premier division player earned £1152 a week.

The Prime Minister earned £76 234 as his annual salary.

1 *How would you explain these differences in wages:*
   a within the same occupation
   b between occupations

2 *Do you think that these differences are justified? How would you justify them?*

5.108 Labour force projections

You work in the personnel department of the head office of a major supermarket chain. The chain is carrying out a major expansion programme which will continue until the end of the century. You have been presented with the following set of statistics. See figure 5.108.

Comment on ways in which population trends are likely to affect recruitment opportunities and policies. Also comment on ways in which changes in the economic environment may combine with population changes to create or reduce recruitment problems.

5.109 Union action?

You are the shop steward in a local car plant. What action would take in each of the following situations?

1 *'Off the record' the personnel manager has told you that your members were likely to receive a 5 per cent rise. You have passed this news on to your members. However, the managing director has called you into his office to show you sales figures that indicate a fall in sales so that if you ask for a pay rise five per cent of employees will have to be made redundant.*

2 *It has come to your notice that employees are entitled to a break every two hours. They have only been getting one every two and a half hours.*

3 *Three employees have left work in a particular section because of claims of sexual harassment by a supervisor.*

5.110 Profit related pay - the way forward?

Profit-related pay (PRP) was heralded in the mid-1980s as a miracle cure for economic problems. It would cut unemployment without adding to inflation by making pay more flexible. The early over-excitement began to die down, but the scheme is still popular.

The Inland Revenue announced in April 1993 that nearly one and a quarter million people are on PR schemes. In 1991 the Chancellor of the Exchequer created tax relief on PRP

Figure 5.10.8 *Labour force projections, great britain*

	1990 (thousands)			2001 (thousands)			Percentage Change		
	Men	Women	Total	Men	Women	Total	Men	Women	Total
16-19	1 184	1 072	2.256	1 091	973	2 064	-7.9	-9.2	-8.8
20-24	1 941	1 626	3 567	1 451	1 293	2 744	-25.2	-20.5	-23.1
25-34	4 072	2 973	7 046	3 748	2 969	6 717	-8.0	0.1	-4.7
35-44	3 649	2 940	6 589	4 059	3 511	7 570	11.2	19.4	14.9
45-54	2 896	2 308	5 204	3 397	2 781	6 177	17.3	20.5	18.7
55-59(f)/64(m)	1 888	796	2 684	2 005	907	2 912	6.2	13.9	8.5
Over 60(f)/65(m)	301	507	808	204	440	644	-32.2	-13.2	-20.3
All Ages	**15 932**	**12 221**	**28 154**	**15 955**	**12 873**	**28 828**	**0.1**	**5.3**	**2.4**

Source: Employment Department

507

schemes allowing employees to receive up to £4000 or 20% of their salaries tax free.

PRP is supposed to soothe industrial conflict by giving both workers and shareholders an interest in profitability, thus boosting productivity and effort. It is also supposed to reduce job turnover, because workers' remuneration falls automatically as profits fall, reducing the need to cut costs through redundancy.

However, the case is shaky. Firms with poor industrial relations are reluctant to try PRP as it provides something else to argue about. Successful firms with contented employees are more likely to have PRP.

When profits fall, some employees demand an increase in basic pay. The best that can be said with confidence is that PRP on average hands public money to efficient companies.

1 *You work in the personnel department of a successful business with good labour relations. What arguments would you put forward to: a management b employees, in support of introducing a profit related pay scheme?*

2 *You are a trade union representative in a firm that is struggling to make sales and has a poor industrial relations record. What arguments would you put forward to: a management b your members against introducing a PRP scheme?*

5.111 The importance of training
Study the table below.

Training Received by Employees in the last four weeks by age, Great Britain, Spring 1991

Employees receiving training as % age of all employees in age group	Age					All of working age*
	16-19	20-24	25-34	35-49	50-64*	
On-the-job training only	5.1	5.0	4.8	4.2	3.1	4.3
Off-the-job training only	12.4	10.2	9.4	7.9	4.0	8.2
Both on-and off-the-job	6.5	3.7	2.4	1.7	0.7	2.3
All receiving training	24.0	118.9	16.5	13.9	7.9	14.8

*Men under 65, women under 60
Source: *Labour Force Survey.*

1 *What is the difference between on-the-job, and off-the-job training? Give examples.*

2 *What does the table show about the priority given to training in this country? What are the major trends shown in the table?*

3 *What guidelines would you establish for a manufacturing company in designing training programmes for its employees?*

SECTION 6: FINANCIAL TRANSACTIONS

6.1 What is a source document?

6.2 Explain why business documents are required.

6.3 What does MIS stand for?

6.4 Explain the difference between a debtor and a creditor.

6.5 Why might an organisation send a letter of enquiry?

6.6 Would you advise somebody to obtain a single quotation for goods or services or several quotations? Explain why in your answer.

6.7 Why might failure to quote an order number lead to delayed payment?

6.8 Explain how an advice note differs from a delivery note.

6.9 What is the purpose of an invoice?

6.10 Name three details which you would expect to appear on an invoice.

6.11 What do the letters E & O E stand for ?

6.12 Why do organisations print their VAT numbers on invoices?

6.13 Why might a seller send a pro forma invoice to a customer?

6.14 Describe what sort of information would be shown on a statement of account.

6.15 Define the word 'cheque'.

6.16 Identify five details which would appear on a cheque.

6.17 Name three advantages in using cheques rather than cash.

6.18 Explain the difference between a standing order and a direct debit.

6.19 What is BACS and how might this system help an organisation?

6.20 Name four pieces of information which you would expect to appear on a pay advice.

6.21 Why do employees pay National Insurance?

6.22 What document might an employee fill in if he had purchased a number of small stationery items for the office?

6.23 Why might someone wish to use a bank giro credit?

6.24 Explain why a cash book might periodically record a contra entry.

6.25 Why should a cash book be checked against a bank statement?

6.26 What is a bank reconciliation statement?

6.27 Identify two stages in preparing a bank reconciliation statement.

6.28 How will IT help an organisation to improve the way in which it deals with paperwork?

6.29 Explain why petty cash slips have to be authorised.

6.30 What is a sales receipt?

6.31 What would be the key objective of a purchasing department?

6.32 Why might a purchasing department receive a requisition form?

6.33 Name three details which might appear on a requisition form.

6.34 Why will a purchasing department be concerned about delivery dates?

6.35 What is a goods received note and when might it be used?

6.36 Why will a stock record have maximum and minimum numbers on?

6.37 By referring to specific types of information, explain how an invoice is checked.

6.38 Identify two functions of a credit control department.

6.39 What is a trade reference?

6.40 Who might provide a trade reference?

6.41 What is the purpose of a delivery note?

6.42 What is a credit note?

6.43 Name two situations when a credit note might be sent.

6.44 How does a debit note work?

6.45 One of the jobs of a cashier is to record incoming cheques. What details on the cheque should they make sure are correct?

6.46 How does a flat rate of pay differ from a piece rate system?

6.47 What is a clock card and why should it be used?

6.48 Name three deductions which might appear on a pay advice.

6.49 What is a tax code and why would it appear on a pay advice?

6.50 Describe how the imprest system of petty cash works.

6.51 What is meant by double-entry bookkeeping?

6.52 Name three benefits of using IT to record the details from documents.

6.53 What document would be issued after goods have been returned inwards/back from a customer?

6.54 What document would be sent monthly to a regular customer?

6.55 If goods have been sold costing £520 at a discount of 20%, work out the total invoice amount. Use the current rate of VAT.

6.56 How might the actions of the credit control department influence the cash flow of an organisation?

6.57 What is the main responsibility of a sales department?

6.58 Over what period does the tax year run?

6.59 Explain broadly how net pay is calculated.

6.60 What is a book of prime entry?

6.61 Explain the difference between qualitative and quantitative information.

6.62 Using a practical example, show how business goals and objectives help an organisation to measure performance.

6.63 What are the three basic steps in the accounting process?

6.64 Explain why managers need different financial information.

6.65 Name two other types of individuals or organisations which would be interested in the output from the accounting process.

6.66 Explain how ratios provide an indicator of performance.

6.67 What is a Statement of Standard Accounting Practice and what is it designed to ensure?

6.68 What is the purpose of a trading account?

6.69 What does a balance sheet attempt to show?

6.70 How might managerial accounting information be used?

6.71 What is meant by ROCE?

6.72 What measure of performance will ROCE provide?

6.73 Explain why organisations will usually keep a close watch upon their working capital.

6.74 How does the quick ratio differ from the working capital ratio?

6.75 Why will most organisations be concerned about their debtors collection period?

6.76 What is stock turnover and what does it show?

6.77 Why might a supplier of capital be concerned about helping to finance a highly-geared company?

6.78 List three dangers of depending too heavily upon the use of ratios.

6.79 Is management accounting used by those within an organisation or by those outside the organisation?

6.80 What is meant by responsibility accounting?

6.81 What is the purpose of budgetary control?

6.82 Explain briefly how marginal costing differs from total costing.

6.83 Identify two non-financial objectives which an organisation might have.

6.84 What is meant by environmental accounting?

6.85 Explain what is meant by the term insolvency.

6.86 What sort of information might the manager of a multiple chain store require which would help him in the running of his shop?

6.87 How would the information required by the manager from question 6.86 differ from the information required by a major shareholder of the business?

6.88 Why are tax authorities interested in the output from an accounting system?

6.89 If you were to supply a business with a number of goods on credit, what information might you require beforehand?

6.90 What is meant by the term 'interest cover'?

6.91 Management Information Systems (MIS) are designed to:

   a *record source documents and post them to the ledger*

b meet the needs of managers for planning and control

c present reports

d produce final accounts for employees

e keep track of financial records.

6.92 Which of the following could not be a response to a letter of enquiry:

a catalogue

b price list

c invoice

d quotation

e estimate?

6.93 A pro forma invoice might be sent:

a if the first invoice has not been paid

b as a copy invoice posted to the accounts sales invoice

c to reduce the amount appearing upon the first invoice

d if the seller has not transacted business with the buyer before

e to remind the supplier to pay for the goods.

6.94 BACS stands for:

a Bankers Automated Clearing Services

b Bankers Automatic Charging Service

c Borrowers Automatic Clearing Service

d Borrowers Automated Clearing System

e Bankers Automated Clearing System.

6.95 Which of the following would not appear on a pay advice:

a gross pay

b superannuation

c net pay

d coffee money

e tax due?

6.96 Upon delivery of goods a goods received note is prepared. A copy is then sent to:

a the supplier

b the accounts department

c the ledger clerk

d the personnel manager

e the credit controller.

6.97 All but one of the following should be checked when an invoice arrives:

a prices

b invoice number

c VAT calculations

d discounts

e goods received.

6.98 Which of the following does not appear on a cheque:

a cheque number

b bank branch number

c account balance

d account number

e amount in figures and words?

6.99 Petty cash is frequently recorded using the:

a Impcrest File

b Imprist System

c Imprest System

d Ipcrest File

e Impost System.

6.100 One of the following is not a book of prime entry:

a sales daybook

b cash book

c purchases daybook

d sales daybook

e daily records book.

6.101 A quantitative analysis of an organisation's performance would not include:

a a praiseworthy comment

b a record of profit

c ratio analysis

d final accounts

e managerial accounts.

6.102 For somebody to call themselves a qualified accountant they would have to become a member of a professional body. Which of the following is not an accounting professional body:

a Institute of Chartered Accountants in England and Wales

b Chartered Institute of Management Accountants

c Chartered Institute of Accountants

d Chartered Institute of Public Finance and Accountancy

e Institute of Chartered Accountants in Ireland?

6.103 SSAP stands for:

a Statement of Stewardship in the Accounting Profession

b Statement of Standard Accounting Practice

c *Statements of Systematic Auditing Process*
d *Standards of Systematic Accounting Produced*
e *Standards of Systematic Accounting Practice.*

6.104 The debtors' collection period is found using the formula:

a *sales/debtors*
b *purchases/debtors*
c *average daily purchases/debtors*
d *debtors/365*
e *debtors/average daily sales.*

6.105 Which of the following is not a non-financial objective:

a *profit*
b *market share*
c *market leadership*
d *develop image and reputation*
e *social responsibility?*

6.106 Peterson's Painters

A close friend of yours, Ron Peterson, has recently been made redundant and has decided to use his redundancy money to set up his own decorating business. Ron is well known locally and has been promised a lot of work, including some refurbishment by three local businesses. Given this workload Ron has taken on two young assistants whom he hopes to train and develop within the business.

Ron is worried about paperwork and business organisation. His wife is willing to act as bookkeeper but is unsure about the purpose and function of many of the documents with which they are being steadily inundated and which have all been placed into a large box file. You have said that you are willing to advise wherever you can.

1 *Explain the purpose and nature of the various documents which Ron and his wife will come across.*

2 *Ron knows a local printer who is willing to provide whatever business documents he requires at a discounted price. Make a list of the types of documents Ron will require. Design one of these documents so that the printer can use it as a specimen to draw up the real thing, n.b. make up details where necessary.*

6.107 Parts of an invoice

The blank invoice in figure 6.107 has numbered labels. Describe what each label refers to and explain why these details appear on an invoice.

6.108 Preparing an invoice

You work in the accounts department of Seabourn Products and have recently received the purchase order, figure 6.108 from Kwickclean Ltd.

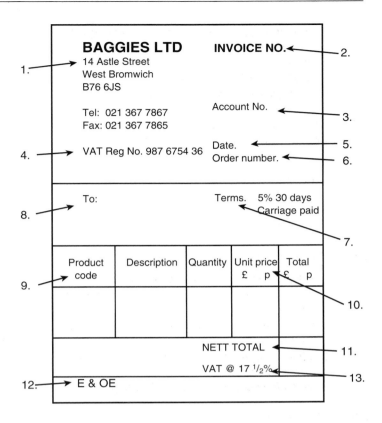

Figure 6.107 *Parts of an invoice*

Figure 6.108 *Kwickclean purchase order*

Kwickclean are entitled to a 20% trade discount. Terms are 5% 30 days. The goods have been delivered by your company on 12 July. Prepare a sales invoice dated 15 July, to send to Kwickclean. The invoice number should be 7438 and VAT should be charged at the current rate.

6.109 Dealing with customer

You work in the sales department of A1 Office Supplies Ltd. Your primary responsibility is to talk to customers and deal with any complaints and difficulties which they may have. The date is 21 August 1994 and during the course of the day you have to deal with the following:

a Mr Tree of King Kong Restaurant, 5 Southgate, Hull, North Humberside, HU5 7JK, phones. He complains that 4 of the seats which you have sent are faulty and asks for them to be collected. The unit price of each seat is £18.50.

b Mrs Gill from Safron Products phones. The office furniture which she ordered has been delivered but it is teak rather than the oak she ordered.

c Mr Thomas from Bolton & Jones has phoned to say that he is upset at your company's refusal to increase his credit limit. His business is currently up to the credit limit and two invoices have remained unpaid for five months.

State how you would deal with the above and, where necessary, issue a credit note, making up the relevant details.

6.110 Assessing company performance

Robin Nest works for a large public company at its main offices in Wokingham. He enjoys his job and has great confidence in the job opportunities being offered and his prospects for promotion. As a sign of his loyalty and commitment to the organisation he has recently invested a large proportion of his savings in company shares. Having done so, he has followed the fortunes of his investment closely in national newspapers and company bulletins. His greatest concern, however, is that though it is easy to follow share prices, how does he gain a fuller picture of the organisation? Robin's particular concerns are:

a that the business seems to be constantly cutting back particularly on stocks and stationery items. His boss keeps talking about budgets, liquidity and the need to improve credit periods

b that an internal report recently said that gearing levels were far too high

c they were recently told in a staff meeting that stocks should be turned over more quickly and that assets should be utilised more efficiently

d that he has received his first copy of the Annual Report and Accounts and does not really understand much of the information

e that there has been a considerable number of complaints about the company locally in Wokingham.

Discuss the above issues with Robin and comment upon what they mean in terms of company performance.

6.111 Twyfold Ltd

The table below shows a series of ratios which have been extracted from the books of Twyfold Ltd over a two year period:

	1993	1994
Gross profit as a percentage of sales	10%	12%
Net profit as a percentage of sales	6%	6%
Current ratio	2:1	1.5:1
Acid test ratio	1:1	0.5:1
Debtors collection period	35 days	50 days
Period of credit taken from suppliers	30 days	30 days
Stock turnover per annum	4 times	3 times
Sales per employee	£8500	£7900
Asset utilisation	6	5
Gearing	60%	90%

Comment briefly on:

a the meaning of each of the ratios

b how and why figures might have changed over a two year period and what the implications of such changes are for the business

c other information which you would like to see.

SECTION 7: FINANCIAL RESOURCES

7.1 Identify three sources of personal finance.

7.2 What is a mortgage?

7.3 Why is identifying sources of finance important when drawing up a business plan?

7.4 What is the difference between a private and public limited company?

7.5 What do the letters USM stand for?

7.6 How does a rights issue differ from a private and public limited company?

7.7 What is another name for ordinary shares?

7.8 Why do many companies have an issued capital which is different from their authorised capital?

7.9 What are deferred shares?

7.10 What preferential rights do preference shareholders have over ordinary shareholders?

7.11 What is a venture capital company?

7.12 Why do many businesses retain profits?

7.13 Explain how a debenture works.

7.14 Why might some lenders to a business require a personal guarantee from the main shareholder?

7.15 What is collateral?

7.16 How does an operating lease differ from a capital lease?

7.17 Until what time do hire-purchase goods remain the property of the lender or finance company?

7.18 Under what circumstances might an organisation approach a factoring company?

7.19 Describe the services which a factoring company might provide.

7.20 What is an overdraft and how is the interest charge on an overdraft calculated?

7.21 Why is trade credit considered to be a source of business finance?

7.22 Name one form of assistance which the government might provide for a business.

7.23 Identify the dangers of bringing a partner into a business.

7.24 What is funding?

7.25 Name one danger of funding.

7.26 When lending, a banker might use the mnemonic IPARTS. What does IPARTS stand for?

7.27 Explain how a unit trust works.

7.28 Name three different types of institution from which finance could be obtained.

7.29 What is a participating preference share?

7.30 Explain how an offer for sale by a public company works.

7.31 What are cash flows?

7.32 Identify three sources of personal income.

7.33 Identify three sources of personal expenditure.

7.34 What is a budget account?

7.35 Explain how a budget account could help with the control of personal income and expenditure.

7.36 If a person's total bills were £3600 per year, how much should he or she transfer each month to a budget account?

7.37 Explain what is meant by the term 'cash-flow forecast'.

7.38 List the advantages of preparing such a forecast.

7.39 Describe briefly what the Banking Ombudsman Scheme is.

7.40 When might an individual or an organisation wish to use this scheme?

7.41 Explain why some creditors deliberately withhold payment of their bills.

7.42 What action do you think should be taken against such creditors?

7.43 Explain how cash differs from profit.

7.44 If an organisation forecasts a negative cash-flow in six months' time, what action should it take now?

7.45 Why should cash-flow forecasts be constantly amended?

7.46 'The big question with cash flow is what happens if …' What does this statement mean?

7.47 Why are many bankers more concerned with an organisation's cash than the profit they generate?

7.48 In your opinion, should the law be changed to deal with late payers? What actions would you suggest?

7.49 A friend of yours has fallen into debt. Expenditure each month is greater than income. Produce a short action plan designed to help this person overcome their difficulties.

7.50 How would the action plan above help your friend in weeks or months when expenditure is particularly heavy?

7.51 Explain the purpose of cost accounting.

7.52 What is meant by the term 'fixed costs'?

7.53 Provide two examples of fixed costs.

7.54 What is meant by the term 'variable costs'?

7.55 Provide two examples of variable costs.

7.56 What is marginal costing?

7.57 If a selling price is £12.75 for each unit and the variable costs for each unit are £8.98, what is the contribution for each unit?

7.58 Identify three situations in which marginal costing might be useful.

7.59 Describe what is meant by the term 'break-even analysis'.

7.60 Explain how the break-even point is calculated.

7.61 Wormwood Ltd produce toy handcuffs. Their selling price is £11 per unit. Variable costs are £6.50 per unit and fixed costs are £8000. Calculate the break-even point to the nearest unit.

7.62 What is the value of sales at the break-even point from question 7.61?

7.63 If Wormwood wish to achieve a profit target of £10000, how many more handcuffs would they have to sell?

7.64 Draw a rough break-even chart to show the information provided by the example in question 7.61. Label all of the information shown.

7.65 Identify three limitations of marginal costing.

7.66 What is absorption costing?

7.67 Using a simple example, show how absorption costing differs from marginal costing.

7.68 Define the word 'overhead'.

7.69 Name two parts of an organisation where information on overheads may be stored.

7.70 What is allocation?

7.71 What is apportionment?

7.72 What does OAR stand for?

7.73 Show one method of working out the OAR.

7.74 What would it mean if over-absorption took place in one month of the year?

7.75 Explain what is meant by the term 'budgeting'.

7.76 Name two types of information a budget would require.

7.77 How does variance analysis work?

7.78 What is a master budget?

7.79 Explain how liquidation differs from receivership.

7.80 What is a white knight?

7.81 What is meant by the term 'final accounts'?

7.82 Identify two pieces of information shown by a trading account.

7.83 Explain how cost of sales is calculated.

7.84 What is a profit and loss account?

7.85 Identify three pieces of information which might appear in a profit and loss account.

7.86 What is a balance sheet?

7.87 How do assets differ from liabilities?

7.88 Provide two examples of fixed assets.

7.89 Why are current assets sometimes called circulating assets?

7.90 Name two items which would appear under 'current liabilities'.

7.91 What is working capital?

7.92 Identify one item which would appear under long-term liabilities.

7.93 What does the term 'capital' represent?

7.94 What does it mean if accounts are said to have been audited?

7.95 Using a numerical example, show how stock figures influence the profit stated.

7.96 Explain why fixed assets should be depreciated.

7.97 Some types of business have an appropriation account in their final accounts. What is an appropriation account?

7.98 Name one type of business which would use an appropriation account.

7.99 Why do non-profit-making organisations have an accumulated fund rather than a profit?

7.100 Why might some organisations not require a trading account?

7.101 What is a debtor?

7.102 Why are long-term liabilities sometimes called deferred liabilities?

7.103 What account is used to prepare final accounts?

7.104 Assets are usually set out in an inverse order of liquidity. What does this mean?

7.105 What would be a prudent working capital ratio? Explain why the figure you suggest would be prudent.

7.106 How does the title for a balance sheet differ from the title for a profit and loss account?

7.107 To whom is the capital of the business owed?

7.108 Explain how net profit is calculated from the profit and loss account.

7.109 Identify two groups who would wish to view the final accounts of a sole trader.

7.110 When buying a fixed asset does a business use capital or revenue expenditure?

7.111 Funding is a financial process which involves:

    a raising loans using security

    b raising long-term finance to pay off short term loans

    c using short-term funds to pay off long-term finance

    d borrowing short to pay long

    e selling shares against security.

7.112 Which of the following is not a form of business ownership:

    a a sole trader

    b a PLC

    c the DSS

    d a partnership

    e a private limited company?

7.113 A long-term loan obtained through the Stock Exchange is known as:

    a an equity

    b an ordinary share

    c a rights issue

    d a debenture

    e a blue chip.

7.114 Which of the following is not a cause of business collapse:

    a late payments by creditors

    b recession

    c high interest rates

    d credit control

    e fall in consumer demand?

7.115 Which of the following is not a fixed cost:

    a rent

    b business rate

    c heating bills

    d salaries

    e factory wages?

7.116 The contribution is:

    a the difference between unit selling price and unit variable cost

    b selling price less fixed costs

    c selling price less unit fixed costs

    d marginal costs less selling price

    e the difference between unit cost and unit margin.

7.117 If the selling price of a product is £10 per unit and the variable cost per unit is £5, with fixed costs of £20000, the break-even point will be:

a £8000

b £4000

c £6500

d £5000

e £4500.

7.118 If contribution is £4 per unit and fixed costs are £15000, how many units will have to be sold to reach a profit target of £30000:

a 3750

b 11250

c 22500

d 180000

e 200000?

7.119 Which of the following is not a limitation of marginal costing:

a in real situations fixed costs may vary with activity levels

b the relationship between variable costs and sales is unlikely to be linear

c break-even is dependent on the accuracy of forecasts made

d break-even charts depict short-term relationships

e break-even is only used by accountants.

7.120 Information about overheads will not be extracted from:

a the stores

b the payroll

c sales day-book

d journal entries

e cash book.

7.121 OAR stands for:

a ordinary assumption routine

b overhead absorption rate

c overhead analysis rate

d overhead absorption routine

e output absorption rate.

7.122 Which of the following is not a business expense:

a electricity

b pension contribution

c advertising

d insurances

e stationery?

7.123 The fixed assets of a business will include:

a debtors

b creditors

c capital

d stock

e fixtures and fittings.

7.124 Cost of sales is calculated by using the formula:

a opening stock plus purchases less closing stock

b closing stock plus purchases less opening stock

c sales less purchases plus opening stock

d opening stock plus sales less closing stock

e closing stock plus sales less opening stock.

7.125 Which of the following is not a current asset:

a stock of raw material

b debtors

c a bill which has been paid in advance

d money in the bank

e tax owing.

7.126 Financing a business

Over the next few months you intend to leave the organisation you work for and set up in business on your own. Before doing so you have to work out carefully how to finance your business proposition.

You intend to re-mortgage your house and together with savings plus a small investment, you expect to be able to raise £75000. This will be spent on machinery, premises and fixtures and fittings. However you still require £50000 to purchase stocks and a vehicle and also have enough to pay expenses and maintain the running of the business.

Using a table similar to the one below, compare the alternative methods of financing the business. After doing so, explain which source(s) of finance you have decided to opt for.

Option	Advantages	Disadvantages	Cost Effects	Comments
Introduce a partner				
etc				

7.127 Working for a bank

You work for the Heinemann National Bank in Oxford and have an important responsibility which involves providing advances to customers. You have just received a letter from a Mrs Shelia Whitstable who has a business account with you and who runs a sandwich business near Abingdon.

Mrs Whitstable feels that her business has come to an

important stage in its development and she has some good ideas for expansion. In developing her business she expects to approach the bank in the next few weeks and would like to know what kind of financial assistance the bank could provide. She also wishes to know, if the bank is willing to consider her propositions, what sort of information would they like her to provide and how they would assess her application.

Prepare a suitable letter which deals with Mrs Whitstable's enquiry.

7.128 Peter Atkinson

Peter Atkinson wishes to take a holiday in August. On 1 January he has £250 in his bank account and he knows that he must have at least £900 in his account in June so that he can pay for the holiday. Peter's take-home pay is £850 per month and he predicts his monthly cash-flows as follows:

- rent £290 per month payable each month
- electricity £110 per quarter payable at the end of each quarter
- car expenses £130 per month payable each month
- insurances £15 each month payable each month
- entertainment £100 per month payable each month
- food £150 per month payable each month
- holiday £900 to be paid in June

1   *Prepare Peter's cash-flow forecast for the first six months of the year.*

2   *Peter's predictions seem to be going smoothly until a major problem occurs with the car in March. Peter has to pay £1200 to get his car repaired. How will this affect his predictions and what action could he take to ensure that he can afford to pay for his holiday in June?*

7.129 Frank Chipasula

Frank Chipasula sets up in business as a book binder on 1 January by putting £27 000 into his business bank account. Frank has spent a lot of time on his business plan researching his income and expenditure. He anticipates the following:

- machinery has to be purchased in January for £17 500 and paid for by the end of the month
- purchases of raw materials and sales of finished goods are likely to be as follows:

	Purchases	Sales
	£	£
January	3400	4000
February	1400	4100
March	1300	4200
April	500	4300

May	1600	4500
June	1700	4800

- Frank has arranged two months' credit with his suppliers.
- he expects one quarter of his sales to be for cash and three quarters to be on credit. He expects two months' credit on average to be taken by credit customers
- wages are expected to be £800 per month paid for in the same month
- rent is £4800 per annum, payable in equal instalments at the end of each month
- other overheads are £500 per month, payable in the month incurred
- Frank hopes to buy a car costing £3000 in March
- Frank has been commissioned by an agency to do a special job on their behalf in May and this should bring in £400.

1   *Prepare Frank's cash-flow forecast for the first six months of the year. Use a spreadsheet to assist with your calculations.*

2   *Frank Chipasula's first three months exceeded his expectations and his actual sales were 50 per cent higher than forecast. Recalculate the forecast using the spreadsheet.*

7.130 Visiting Disney

Disneylanders Ltd is a private company that specialises in providing holidays at Disney theme parks. With the opening of EuroDisney it is finding that half of the packages it now provides are based in this one resort, while the other half are to the United States.

Disneylanders is currently reviewing its profitability for 1994. It anticipates that fixed overheads will be £500 000 for the year. For EuroDisney packages, a quarter of the variable costs go in travel costs, at an average of £40 per package. The company anticipates selling EuroDisney packages at an average of £200 each.

The American holidays are sold at an average price of £700 each. Travel costs of £200 for each holiday comprise one half of the variable costs for the holiday.

Market research has revealed that during 1994 Disneylanders will sell 4200 holidays.

1   *Work out the contribution for both the American and European holidays*

2   *Calculate the company's profit for the year before tax and interest*

3   *Market research has revealed that if Disneylanders reduced its prices by 10 per cent it could sell more holidays per year. Comment upon how this would affect profitability and advise accordingly.*

7.131 Absorption costing

You work in the small assembly department of a furniture factory. Your department has a budgeted annual output of 2400 units and your budgeted overheads are £48 000. Actual output is 1800 units.

1 *Calculate the overhead absorption rate (OAR) using the units of output method*

2 *How much of the overhead is absorbed in January?*

3 *Were overheads in January over or under-absorbed? Use figures to support your answer.*

4 *Explain how absorption costing differs from marginal costings.*

7.132 Running a bookshop

Peter Jones runs a small specialist bookshop in Leicester. Most of the books are for specialist hobbies such as cars, sports, trains etc. At the end of his first year of trading at 31 December 1993, the following figures are extracted from his books:

	DR	CR
	£	£
Capital		52 600
Premises	44 000	
Fixtures and fittings	13 300	
Motor vehicle	4 300	
Purchases	6 750	
Sales		34 700
Wages	4 400	
Vehicle expenses	925	
Telephone	450	
General expenses	125	
Business rate	600	
Electricity	150	
Stock at 1 Jan 1993	6 500	
Debtors	1 400	
Creditors		6 450
Drawings	9 500	
Bank	1 200	
Cash	150	
	93 750	93 750

Stock at 31 December is valued at £7300.

Prepare the trading and profit and loss account of P Jones for the year together with a balance sheet at 31 December 1993.

7.133 Explaining the parts of the balance sheet

You have recently started working for a firm of chartered accountants in Brighton. The firm specialises in small business work and each year contributes to talks held locally by the Brighton Enterprise Agency.

You have been asked by your senior to give one of these talks. The talk is entitled 'The Balance Sheet' and should be designed to both identify and fully explain each of the parts of this statement.

Prepare your speech together with any examples which you feel would help you to highlight the points you would like to make.

SECTION 8: BUSINESS PLANNING

8.1 What is a business plan?

8.2 What are objectives?

8.3 Give three examples of objectives that a business owner might establish for the business.

8.4 What does feasibility mean?

8.5 Describe two types of business insurance that an organisation should take out?

8.6 What are the main resource requirements of businesses? Make a short list.

8.7 Why is time an important resource for a business person?

8.8 Describe two sources of advice for people wanting to set up in business?

8.9 How does the 'economic climate' act as a constraint or an opportunity for a business?

8.10 What is the difference between marketing and sales?

8.11 What are the main physical resources required by a manufacturing business?

8.12 Why does an entrepreneur need to consider business law when setting up a new business?

8.13 Why is market research an essential starting point when developing a business proposal?

8.14 Why might a business not be able to make a profit in the first year after setting up?

8.15 What forms of business organisations are available to a new business?

8.16 A business plan may be prepared for both an internal and an external audience. Give examples of people who might be included in these two audiences.

8.17 Why is it important to estimate resources required for a business proposal before starting up?

8.18 What is the difference between primary and secondary research?

8.19 What is an Enterprise Agency? Why might this be a

useful source of advice when setting up a new business?

8.20 Explain why spending a lot of time researching a business plan will prove a valuable investment in the long term.

8.21 What are the main details a bank manager might look for in a business plan?

8.22 How can a business plan be used to monitor ongoing performance?

8.23 Why is it essential to have a cash flow forecast in a business plan?

8.24 What minimum percentage financial stake would a lender to a business expect the owner to possess in the business?

8.25 How should the marketing plan of a business relate to the 4 P's?

8.26 Why is it essential to have a sales plan as part of your business plan?

8.27 What do you need to put into your business plan to show that you will be monitoring and reviewing your performance?

8.28 What details could be put in the introduction to a business plan?

8.29 What resource requirements should be indicated in a business plan?

8.30 Why is it important for a business owner to show how these resource requirements will be met?

8.31 What is a production plan?

8.32 What are the main ingredients of a production plan?

8.33 Why is it important to show projected profit and loss accounts in a business plan?

8.34 Why might projected and actual figures vary from one to another?

8.35 How long should a business plan be? Why?

8.36 How can a business satisfy the needs of customers?

8.37 How can a business show in its business plan that it is aware of its customers needs?

8.38 Should a business plan be optimistic, pessimistic or realistic?

8.39 What is a financial forecast?

8.40 Why is business planning such a crucial activity?

8.41 Why is it important to produce a marketing budget?

8.42 What activities should be included in the marketing budget?

8.43 Why is it important to set out a schedule for sales and marketing activities?

8.44 What is a distribution plan?

8.45 What is meant by the target market? In the marketing plan how can you show that you have identified your target market?

8.46 In what ways is selling about solving other people's problems?

8.47 What are benefits?

8.48 What should be the main objectives of a promotional plan?

8.49 Why is it important to identify who makes the buying decisions in a household?

8.50 Why is marketing essential to every part of an organisation's activities?

8.51 In what circumstances is it a mistake to charge a low price for a product?

8.52 Why is it important to calculate the likely market share of a product?

8.53 What is promotion? Give three examples of promotional activities.

8.54 What is a marketing budget?

8.55 What questions do you need to seek the answers to in setting out a marketing plan?

8.56 What is the difference between selling and marketing?

8.57 How can you find out the growth potential of a particular product? What published sources of information are available?

8.58 What types of after sales service would be used to help sell: **a** electrical appliances **b** motor vehicles **c** desktop computers?

8.59 What is a market segment?

8.60 What quantitive information can be found in a marketing plan ? Why is this information helpful in assessing the viability of the plan?

8.61 To whom would you be most likely to show a business plan:

a a competitor
b a solicitor
c a trading standards officer
d a bank manager
e the Registrar of Companies?

8.62 Which of the following is least likely to be used for forward planning:

a a cash flow forecast
b a projection of market share
c an opening balance sheet
d a market research survey
e an estimate of likely profits and losses?

8.63 Secondary information for market research can be obtained by:

a interviewing people in the street
b looking up information in a publication
c using a postal questionnaire
d telephoning households directly
e asking questions of an invited panel of consumers.

8.64 Market research aims to match the product to the:

a *manufacturer*
b *importer*
c *wholesaler*
d *consumer*
e *retailer*

8.65 A business is most likely to be successful when it concentrates on producing services or goods that take account of:

a *skills of the business person*
b *the wants of the consumers*
c *strengths of competitors*
d *the size of the market*
e *the best distribution channels.*

8.66 A business person is likely to get outside finance for his or her business when able to put up at least:

a *10 per cent of the capital*
b *20 per cent of the capital*
c *30 per cent of the capital*
d *40 per cent of the capital*
e *50 per cent of the capital*

8.67 Which of the following is an example of long-term finance for a business:

a *a loan*
b *an overdraft*
c *trade credit*
d *cash*
e *factoring*

8.68 Which of the following risks is uninsurable:

a *failure of a business*
b *injury to an employee whilst at work*
c *damage to vehicles owned by the business*
d *damage to stock because of flooding*
e *injury to a member of the public on business premises.*

8.69 Which of the following is not a 'sales' activity:

a *making contact with customers*
b *market research*
c *handling customer complaints*
d *after-sales service*
e *discussing a buyer's problem or need?*

8.70 Which of the following would appear in the marketing rather than in the production plan:

a *premises*
b *competition*
c *machinery*
d *raw material*
e *labour?*

8.71 John has estimated that the size of the market will be worth £100 000 in 1994. He expects to take between 10 per cent and 20 per cent of this market. Market trends indicate that in 1995 total market sales will increase by 50 per cent. John has worked out that he will be able to maintain his market share in 1995. On the basis of these predictions what will be John's maximum sales in 1995?

a *£10 000*
b *£15 000*
c *£20 000*
d *£25 000*
e *£30 000*

8.72 A business has two costs. Equipment costs are £10 000 per annum. Raw material costs are £1 per item. The business expects to sell 20,000 goods at £2 each. How much profit will it make:

a *£40 000*
b *£30 000*
c *£20 000*
d *£10 000*
e *£0?*

8.73 All of the following are objectives of market research except:

a *assessing demand*
b *finding a target market*
c *finding an acceptable price*
d *suggesting a suitable method of production*
e *assessing the competition*

8.74 Which of the following is not a reason for drawing up a business plan:

a *to seek finance*
b *to gain finance*
c *to monitor performance*
d *to check on progress*
e *to come up with a business idea?*

8.75 Which of the following is a measure of total revenue:

a *revenue cost*
b *fixed cost + variable cost*
c *price × quantity sold*

d price × total manufactured output

e average revenue × price?

8.76   Tow-away Services

A1 Services is a petrol station and car repair garage which is situated close to the A1 at Grantham. Petrol sales have until recently been a good seller. However, in the last six months a competing service station has opened and sales have fallen considerably. A1 Services also has steady orders for car repairs. A good line used to be car exhausts and tyre replacements, but with the opening of new outlets such as Kwik Fit and Halfords offering a cheap and speedy service business has plummeted.

Fred Davis, who owns A1 Services, has therefore been faced with the bleak prospect of closing down - or coming up with a new business line that will offset the decline in demand for some of his existing lines.

Fred has hit upon the idea of setting up a tow-away business. Vehicles frequently break down on the A1   near Grantham. Vehicle owners are then prepared to pay a high price to have their vehicles towed away and repaired.

Fred needs to borrow the money to purchase a tow-away truck. He has therefore decided to put together a business plan to present to his bank manager.

1   *What information does Fred need to seek to put into his business plan? Outline and explain six crucial areas of research.*

2   *What are the main factors that will determine whether the idea is worth going ahead with or not?*

3   *Who might Fred turn to in seeking advice about constructing his business plan?*

8.77   The hot dog stall

The chart below shows some of the initial steps to be taken when planning a business venture:

1   *Identify constraints*

2   *Establish general personal and business aims*

3   *Study your business environment*

4   *Identify threats and opportunities*

5   *Set key marketing and financial objectives*

6   *Collect detailed information etc*

You have been asked by a friend to help her draw up a business plan for a hot dog stall she wants to set up outside a busy railway station.

1   *Identify three examples of constraints on the business*

2   *Give two examples of possible business aims for the stall.*

3   *What is the 'business environment'? Give examples of features of this environment and how it might influence the setting up and running of the hot dog stall.*

4   *Give an example of a financial objective that the hot dog stall might have?*

5   *What detailed information would the stall owner need to seek before starting out?*

8.78   Planning a theme night at the Happy Hotel

The Happy Hotel will be opening shortly. The manager of the Happy Hotel plans to launch the hotel by having a 'sixties dance night' in the banqueting hall. The hotel has asked its bank for an overdraft facility to get the night off the ground. The bank manager is worried that the hotel may not have thought through carefully enough the financial implications of the launch and has therefore asked the hotel manager to put together a brief business plan showing how the night will 'pay for itself'.

1   *What details should be included in the plan if the bank is to be satisfied?*

The banqueting manager has worked out that it will cost the Happy Hotel £3000 to put on a sixties night even if no one turns up! He has also worked out that it will cost the hotel an extra £10 per guest to put the dance night on.

After doing some market research the hotel has decided that they will charge £25 per ticket; they think that this is the amount people would be prepared to pay. The maximum number of people who can be catered for in the Happy Hotel's banqueting suite is 400. The manager knows that with fewer than 100 people the suite feels empty and there would be no party atmosphere.

2   *How many tickets does the hotel need to sell to break even? Plot a graph showing fixed costs, variable costs and revenue if: 100, 200, 300 and 400 people bought tickets.*

3   *How much profit will the hotel make if all 400 tickets are sold?*

8.79   The fitness studio

Judith Sealy is hoping to set up her own physical fitness studio. She needs to prepare a business plan to present to her bank. The bank has sent her an outline plan which is broken down under a number of sub-headings. Judith understands what should be included under most of the sub-headings but there are a few that puzzle her. The ones that have to be explained to her appear in bold letters below.

1   *Explain in general terms what each of the bold headings mean.*

1 Contents page
2 The owner
3 The business
4 **The market**
5 Advertising and promotion
6 **Premises and equipment**
7 Business organisation
8 **Costings**
9 Finance
10 **Cash flow**
11 **Expansion**

8.80   John's fashion clothes

John McStay has recently been made redundant. He has a good idea of how he would like to invest his redundancy money of £10 000 - he wants to open a women's fashion shop. However, he is not sure whether there is a large enough market in his home town. He has already started to look around for appropriate premises and has seen some attractive ones in the High Street.

1 What should John do to find out if there is a large enough market in his home town?

2 What factors does John need to consider when seeking premises for his clothes shop?

3 What key calculations does John need to make before he starts to look for premises?

4 Explain four major constraints which might limit John's likelihood of succeeding in his proposed business venture?

5 Why is it that so many new businesses end up failing? Would producing a detailed business plan at the start of the venture make any difference to success or failure?

8.81   The Chocolate Box franchise

Meenum Mandal is hoping to set up a small confectionery business. She has had previous experience with a confectionery wholesaler where she worked on the production and finance side of the business, but she has had little experience of marketing. Meenum has identified an opportunity to set up a high street franchise selling chocolate, toffee and small, high quality gifts under a well known name. A friend has told her that she needs to give careful attention to the 4 Ps of marketing.

1 What is a franchise?

2 What are the advantages of franchising to the franchisee?

3 What are the advantages of franchising to the franchisor?

4 What are the 4 Ps of marketing?

5 Explain how attention to each of the 4Ps will help Meenum in her chosen business.

QUICK CHECK

Answers to multiple choice questions

Section 1

1.91	d	1.96	e	1.101	e
1.92	d	1.97	d	1.102	a
1.93	c	1.98	b	1.103	d
1.94	c	1.99	c	1.104	a
1.95	c	1.100	c	1.105	d

Section 2

2.91	d	2.96	c	2.101	b
2.92	c	2.97	d	2.102	e
2.93	c	2.98	e	2.103	b
2.94	a	2.99	b	2.104	e
2.95	e	2.100	a	2.105	b

Section 3

3.91	b	3.96	c	3.101	d
3.92	a	3.97	a	3.102	c
3.93	b	3.98	d	3.103	a
3.94	d	3.99	c	3.104	d
3.95	e	3.100	b	3.105	c

Section 4

4.91	a	4.96	b	4.101	e
4.92	a	4.97	a	4.102	c
4.93	b	4.98	b	4.103	a
4.94	b	4.99	c	4.104	d
4.95	b	4.100	c	4.105	d

Section 5

5.91	e	5.96	c	5.101	d
5.92	b	5.97	b	5.102	e
5.93	e	5.98	c	5.103	c
5.94	b	5.99	b	5.104	b
5.95	b	5.100	d	5.105	c

Section 6

6.91	b	6.96	b	6.101	a
6.92	c	6.97	b	6.102	c
6.93	d	6.98	c	6.103	b
6.94	a	6.99	c	6.104	e
6.95	d	6.100	e	6.105	a

Section 7

7.111	b	7.116	a	7.121	b
7.112	c	7.117	b	7.122	b
7.113	a	7.118	b	7.123	e
7.114	d	7.119	e	7.124	a
7.115	e	7.120	c	7.125	e

Section 8

8.71	d	8.76	e	8.81	e
8.72	c	8.77	a	8.82	d
8.73	b	8.78	a	8.83	d
8.74	a	8.79	b	8.84	e
8.75	b	8.80	b	8.85	c

INDEX